THE PAPERS OF ALEXANDER HAMILTON

Alexander Hamilton
Pencil drawing by Gideon Fairman, 1804
Made from memory shortly after Hamilton's death,
and presented to Richard Harison

Courtesy of The New-York Historical Society, New York City

THE PAPERS OF

Alexander Hamilton

VOLUME XIX
JULY 1795–DECEMBER 1795

HAROLD C. SYRETT, EDITOR

Associate Editors

BRIGID ALLEN

BARBARA A. CHERNOW   PATRICIA SYRETT

 COLUMBIA UNIVERSITY PRESS

NEW YORK AND LONDON, 1973

FROM THE PUBLISHER

The preparation of this edition of the papers of Alexander Hamilton has been made possible by the support received for the work of the editorial and research staff from the generous grants of the Rockefeller Foundation, Time Inc., and the Ford Foundation, and by the far-sighted cooperation of the National Historical Publications Commission. To these organizations, the publisher expresses gratitude on behalf of all who are concerned about making available the record of the founding of the United States.

The Charles E. Merrill Trust, through a generous grant, has enabled the Press to publish this volume and three other volumes.

PREFACE

THIS EDITION of Alexander Hamilton's papers contains letters and other documents written by Hamilton, letters to Hamilton, and some documents (commissions, certificates, etc.) that directly concern Hamilton but were written neither by him nor to him. All letters and other documents have been printed in chronological order. Hamilton's legal papers are being published under the editorial direction of Julius Goebel, Jr., George Welwood Murray Professor Emeritus of Legal History of the School of Law, Columbia University. Two volumes of this distinguished work, which is entitled *The Law Practice of Alexander Hamilton*, have ben published by the Columbia University Press.

Many letters and documents have been calendared. Such calendared items include rountine letters and documents by Hamilton, routine letters to Hamilton, some of the letters or documents written by Hamilton for someone else, letters or documents which have not been found but which are known to have existed, letters or documents which have been erroneously attributed to Hamilton, and letters to or by Hamilton that deal exclusively with his legal practice.

Because all of Hamilton's significant legal opinions appear in *The Law Practice of Alexander Hamilton* they have been omitted from these volumes.

The notes in these volumes are designed to provide information concerning the nature and location of each document, to identify Hamilton's correspondents and the individuals mentioned in the text, to explain events or ideas referred to in the text, and to point out textual variations or mistakes. Occasional departures from these standards can be attributed to a variety of reasons. In many cases the desired information has been supplied in an earlier note and can be found through the use of the index. Notes have not been added when in the opinion of the editors the material in the text was either self-explanatory of common knowledge. The editors, moreover, have not thought it desirable or necessary to provide full annotation for Hamilton's legal correspondence. Finally, the editors on some occasions have been unable to find the desired information, and on other occasions the editors have been remiss.

GUIDE TO EDITORIAL APPARATUS

I. SYMBOLS USED TO DESCRIBE MANUSCRIPTS

AD	Autograph Document
ADS	Autograph Document Signed
ADf	Autograph Draft
ADfS	Autograph Draft Signed
AL	Autograph Letter
ALS	Autograph Letter Signed
D	Document
DS	Document Signed
Df	Draft
DfS	Draft Signed
LS	Letter Signed
LC	Letter Book Copy
[S]	[S] is used with other symbols (AD[S], ADf[S], AL[S], D[S], Df[S], L[S]) to indicate that the signature on the document has been cropped or clipped.

II. MONETARY SYMBOLS AND ABBREVIATIONS

bf	Banco florin
V	Ecu
f	Florin
₶	Livre Tournois
medes	Maravedis (also md and mde)
d.	Penny or denier
ps	Piece of eight

£   Pound sterling or livre
Ry   Real
rs vn   Reals de vellon
rdr   Rix daller
s   Shilling, sou or sol (also expressed as /)
sti   Stiver

III. SHORT TITLES AND ABBREVIATIONS

Annals of Congress	*The Debates and Proceedings in the Congress of the United States; with an Appendix, Containing Important State Papers and Public Documents, and all the Laws of a Public Nature* (Washington, 1834–1849).
ASP	*American State Papers, Documents, Legislative and Executive, of the Congress of the United States* (Washington 1832–1861).
Blackstone, *Commentaries*	*Commentaries on the Laws of England. In Four Books. By Sir William Blackstone, Knt. One of the Justices of His Majesty's Court of Common Pleas. The Tenth Edition, With the Last Corrections of the Author; Additions by Richard Burn, LL.D. And Continued to the Present Time, By John Williams, Esq.* (London: Printed for A. Strahan; T. Cadell, in the Strand; and D. Prince, Oxford, 1787).
Boyd, *Papers of Thomas Jefferson*	Julian P. Boyd, ed., *The Papers of Thomas Jefferson* (Princeton, 1950–).
Burnett, *Letters*	Edmund C. Burnett, ed., *Letters of Members of the Continental Congress* (Washington 1921–1938).
Bynkershoek, *Quæstionum*	Cornelius van Bynkershoek, *Quæstionum Juris Publici Libri Duo. The Translation by Tenney*

Chalmers, *Collection of Treaties*

Coke, *First Institutes*

Correspondence of the French Ministers with the United States Government

3 Dallas, *U.S. Reports*

Debrett, *A Collection of State Papers*

Frank (Oxford and London, 1930).

George Chalmers, *A Collection of Treaties Between Great Britain and Other Powers* (London: Printed for John Stockdale, Piccadilly, 1790).

The First Part of the Institutes of the Laws of England; Or, A Commentary upon Littleton: Not the Name of the Author only; but of the Law itself. Authore Edwardo Coke, Milite. The Fifteenth Edition; Revised and Corrected with further Additions of Notes, References, and Proper Tables. By Francis Hargrave and Charles Butler, Esquires, of Lincoln's Inn. Including also the Notes of Lord Chief Justice Hale and Lord Chancellor Nottingham: And an Analysis of Littleton, written by an Unknown Hand in 1658–9 (London: Printed for E. and R. Brooke, Bell-Yard, near Temple-Bar, 1794).

Correspondence of the French Ministers, Joseph Fauchet and P. Adet; with the United States Government during the Years 1794–1796 (n.p., 1797?).

A. J. Dallas, *Reports of Cases Ruled and Adjudged in the Several Courts of the United States and of Pennsylvania, Held at the Seat of the Federal Government. Vol. III, Second Edition. Edited, With Notes and References to Later Decisions, by Frederick C. Brightly* (New York and Albany, 1882).

John Debrett, *A Collection of State Papers, Relative to the War against France Now carrying on*

by *Great-Britain and the several
other European Powers, Containing Authentic Copies of
Treaties, Conventions, Proclamations, Manifestoes, Declarations,
Memorials, Remonstrances, Official Letters, Parliamentary Papers, London Gazette Accounts
of the War, &c. &c. &c. Many
of which have never before been
published in England* (London:
Printed for J. Debrett, opposite
Burlington House, Piccadilly,
1794–1797).

Executive Journal, I

*Journal of the Executive Proceed-
ings of the Senate* (Washington,
1828), I.

Freeman, *Washington*

Douglas   Southhall   Freeman,
George   Washington   (New
York, 1948–1957). Volume VII of
this series was written by John
Alexander   Carroll   and   Mary
Wells Ashworth.

A General Collection of Treatys,
I, III, IV

*A General Collection of Treatys
of Peace and Commerce, Mani-
festos, Declarations of War, and
other Publick Papers, from the
end of the Reign of Queen Anne
to   the   Year   1731* (London,
1732).

A General Collection of Treatys,
II

*A General Collection of Treatys,
Manifesto's, Contracts of Marriage, Renunciations, and other
Public Papers, from the Year
1495, to the Year 1712* (London,
1732).

Goebel, *Law Practice*

Julius Goebel, Jr., ed., *The Law
Practice of Alexander Hamilton:
Documents   and   Commentary*
(New   York   and   London,
1964–).

Grotius, *On the Law of War and
Peace*

Hugo Grotius, *De Jure Belli Ac
Pacis Libri Tres. The Translation, Book I,* by Francis W.
Kelsey (Oxford and London,
1925).

GW — John C. Fitzpatrick, ed., *The Writings of George Washington* (Washington, 1931–1944).

HCLW — Henry Cabot Lodge, ed., *The Works of Alexander Hamilton* (New York, 1904).

Isambert, *Recueil Général des Anciennes Lois Françaises* — *Recueil Général des Anciennes Lois Françaises, Depuis L'An 420 Jusqu'à La Révolution de 1789, par MM. Jourdan, Docteur en droit, Avocat à la Cour royale de Paris; Isambert, Avocat aux Conseils du Roi et à la Cour de Cassation; Decrusy, ancien Avocat à la Cour royale de Paris* (Paris, 1821–1833).

JCC — *Journals of the Continental Congress, 1774–1789* (Washington, 1904–1937).

JCHW — John C. Hamilton, ed., *The Works of Alexander Hamilton* (New York, 1851–1856).

Jenkinson, *Collection of Treaties* — Charles Jenkinson, *A Collection of All the Treaties of Peace, Alliance, and Commerce, between Great-Britain and other Powers, From the Treaty signed at Münster in 1648, to the Treaties signed at Paris in 1783* (London: J. Debrett, 1785).

Journal of the House, I, II, III, IV — *Journal of the House of Representatives of the United States* (Washington, 1826), I, II, III, IV

Martens, *Recûeil*, I — Georg Friedrich von Martens, *Recûeil de Traités d'Alliance, de Paix, de Trève, de Neutralité, de commerce, de limites, d'échange etc. et de plusieurs autres actes servant à la connaissance des relations étrangères des Puissances et etats de l'Europe tant dans leur rapport mutuel que dans celui envers les puissances et etats dans d'autres parties du globe Depuis 1761 jusqu'à pre-*

sent, 2nd edition (Göttingen, 1817–1825), I.

Martens, *Recûeil*, V, VI

Georg Friedrich von Martens, *Recûeil des principaux Traités d'Alliance, de Paix, de Trêve, de Neutralité, de Commerce, de Limites, d'Echange etc. conclus par les puissances de l'Europe tant entre elles qu'avec les puissances et etats dans d'autres parties du monde depuis 1761 jusqu'à présent*, 2nd edition (Göttingen, 1826–1829), V, VI.

Mayo, *Instructions to British Ministers*

Bernard Mayo, ed., "Instructions to the British Ministers to the United States, 1791–1812," *Annual Report of the American Historical Association for the Year 1936* (Washington, 1941), III.

Miller, *Treaties*, II

Hunter Miller, ed., *Treaties and Other International Acts of the United States of America* (Washington, 1931), II.

Monroe, *A View of the Conduct of the Executive*

James Monroe, *A View of the Conduct of the Executive, in the Foreign Affairs of the United States, Connected with the Mission to the French Republic, During the Years 1794, 5, & 6* (Philadelphia: Printed by and for Benjamin Franklin Bache, 1797).

Moore, *International Adjudications*

John Bassett Moore, ed., *International Adjudications; Ancient and Modern, History and Documents, Together with Mediatorial Reports, Advisory Opinions, and the Decisions of Domestic Commissions, on International Claims* (New York, 1929–1936).

PRO: F.O.

Transcripts or photostats from the Public Record Office of Great Britain deposited in the Library of Congress.

PRO: F.O. (Great Britain)

Public Record Office of Great Britain.

Pufendorf, *Of the Law of Nature and Nations*

Of the Law of Nature and Nations. Eight Books. Written in Latin by the Baron Pufendorf, Counsellor of State to his late Swedish Majesty, and to the late King of Prussia. Done into English by Basil Kennett, D.D. late President of Corpus Christi College in Oxford. To which are added All the large Notes of Mr. Barbeyrac, Translated from the best Edition; Together with Large Tables to the Whole. The Fourth Edition, carefully Corrected (London: Printed for J. Walthoe, R. Wilkin, J. and J. Bonwicke, S. Birt, T. Ward, and T. Osborne, 1729).

Randolph, *Vindication*

[Edmund Randolph], *A Vindication of Mr. Randolph's Resignation* (Philadelphia: Printed by Samuel H. Smith, No. 118, Chesnut Street, 1795).

1 *Stat.*

The Public Statutes at Large of the United States of America (Boston, 1845).

6 *Stat.*

The Public Statutes at Large of the United States of America [Private Statutes] (Boston, 1846).

Turner, "Correspondence of French Ministers"

Frederick J. Turner, ed., "Correspondence of the French Ministers of the United States, 1791–1797," *Annual Report of the American Historical Association for the Year 1903* (Washington, 1904), II.

Vattel, *Law of Nations*

Emeric de Vattel, *Law of Nations; or Principles of the Law of Nature: Applied to the Conduct and Affairs of Nations and Sovereigns* (London, 1759–1760).

Wharton, *Revolutionary Diplomatic Correspondence*

Francis Wharton, ed., *The Revolutionary Diplomatic Correspondence of the United States* (Washington, 1889).

IV. INDECIPHERABLE WORDS

Words or parts of words which could not be deciphered because of the illegibility of the writing or the mutilation of the manuscript have been indicated as follows:

1. ⟨-----⟩ indicates illegible words with the number of dashes indicating the estimated number of illegible words.
2. Words or letters in broken brackets indicate a guess as to what the words or letters in question may be. If the source of the words or letters within the broken brackets is known, it has been given in a note.

V. CROSSED-OUT MATERIAL IN MANUSCRIPTS

Words or sentences crossed out by a writer in a manuscript have been handled in one of the three following ways:

1. They have been ignored, and the document or letter has been printed in its final version.
2. Crossed-out words and insertions for the crossed-out words have been described in the notes.
3. When the significance of a manuscript seems to warrant it, the crossed-out words have been retained, and the document has been printed as it was written.

VI. TEXTUAL CHANGES AND INSERTIONS

The following changes or insertions have been made in the letters and documents printed in these volumes:

1. Words or letters written above the line of print (for example, 9th) have been made even with the line of print (9th).
2. Punctuation and capitalization have been changed in those instances where it seemed necessary to make clear the sense of the writer. A special effort has been made to eliminate the dash, which was such a popular eighteenth-century device.
3. When the place or date, or both, of a letter or document does not appear at the head of that letter or document, it has been inserted in the text in brackets. If either the place or date at

the head of a letter or document is incomplete, the necessary additional material has been added in the text in brackets. For all but the best known localities or places, the name of the colony, state, or territory has been added in brackets at the head of a document or letter.

4. In calendared documents, place and date have been uniformly written out in full without the use of brackets. Thus "N. York, Octr. 8, '99" becomes "New York, October 8, 1799." If, however, substantive material is added to the place or date in a calendared document, such material is placed in brackets. Thus "Oxford, Jan. 6" becomes "Oxford [Massachusetts] January 6 [1788]."

5. When a writer made an unintentional slip comparable to a typographical error, one of the four following devices has been used.
   a. It has been allowed to stand as written.
   b. It has been corrected by inserting either one or more letters in brackets.
   c. It has been corrected without indicating the change.
   d. It has been explained in a note.

6. Because the symbol for the thorn was archaic even in Hamilton's day, the editors have used the letter "y" to represent it. In doing this they are conforming to eighteenth-century manuscript usage.

THE PAPERS OF ALEXANDER HAMILTON

1795

The Defence of the Funding System [1]

[New York, July, 1795]

In speaking of the public debt hereafter, to avoid circumlocution I shall denominate the original debt of the UStates the general Debt & the separate debts of the respective States the particular Debts. As often as these terms occur they are to be understood in this sense.

ADf, Hamilton Papers, Library of Congress.

1. H prepared this essay after his resignation as Secretary of the Treasury. For several months after his resignation he wrote to some of his former associates requesting information for use in this essay. See, for example, H to Joseph Nourse, March 18, 1795; Edward Jones to H, March 21, 1795; Jeremiah Wadsworth to H, May 31, 1795; Edward Carrington to H, June 25, July 15, 1795; and Benjamin Lincoln to H, July 10, 24, 1795. That H did not always obtain the information which he needed is indicated by the numerous blank spaces throughout the essay—blank spaces which H undoubtedly expected to fill in at some later date.

The "Defence of the Funding System" was first published by Henry Cabot Lodge, who printed it as two separate, but related, essays (*HCLW*, VIII, 429–92; IX, 3–34). It seems more likely, however, that H wrote a single, coherent essay rather than two installments.

It should perhaps be noted that the "Defence of the Funding System" differs from most other articles written by H on the same or similar subjects. In the first place, it contains no tables and charts and only a few statistics. Secondly, while it is long on the kind of logic and theory frequently used by H, it is notably short on the facts with which he usually buttressed his arguments. Finally, there are few references to the past or to authorities on whom H so frequently relied in his other polemical writings.

In the course of preparing his "Defence of the Funding System," H wrote some notes and queries, which are located in the Hamilton Papers, Library of Congress, and which read:

"I What were the periods & proportions in which the pay of the army was raised

"II What is the date of the Resolution or resolutions for paying Interest on the nominal sum of certain loan Office certificates

"III What was the lowest price of Certificates at any time

"IV Proportions of the State Debt when funding system commenced

"V Date of first Resolution which took out of circulation certain emissions of Continental Money

"VI Date of the Resolution 40 to 1

"VII Write to Carrington about the nature of the provision which was made for the Virginia Debt & the causes of its low value?

The operation of these circumstances generated a variety of different sects holding different opinions. The parties in and out of Congress on the subject of a provision for the public debt may be thrown into five classes: I Those who were for providing for the general debt exclusively of the particular debts on the basis of the subsisting contracts. II Those who were for providing separately for the general debt on the principle of a discrimination between original holders and alienees. III Those who were for providing separately for the general debt without that discrimination at arbitrary rates of interest inferior to the stipulated rules. IV Those who were for providing for the general debt on the basis of the subsisting contracts and for assuming the particular debts upon an equal provision. V Those who were for providing for the general debt at arbitrary rates of interest inferior to the stipulated rates and for assuming the stat⟨e⟩ debts upon an equal provision.[2]

The classes which embraced the greatest number of real partisans [3]

"VIII Population of Rhode Island during the War

"IX Supplies of Troops of different States during the War

"X How much of their debts had Virginia Massachusettes & Connecticut absorbed.

"XI What were the descriptions & amounts of the Debts originally contracted with Congress & afterwards assumed by the States, as Depreciation &c

"XII Amount of general debt foreign & domestic—What?

"XII How much did the Western Insurrection cost?

"XIII Duration of Debts general & particular likely to be smaller on a general than on a particular provision

"XIV Examine objection against the variety & denominations of our funded Debt.

"XV Taxes before & since the funding system in Virginia.

"XVI qualified ⟨- - - - - - -⟩

"XVIII The fact of the quantity of alloy in the Debt to be discussed

"XIX Question of Discrimination to be examined.

"XX Shew how providing for Debt on contract principles was connected with the general security of property

---

"I Point—why were the later contracts respecting the debt more obligatory than the Elder?

"II Reasonableness of the prejudices against Excises."

2. See H's "Report Relative to a Provision for the Support of Public Credit," January 9, 1790, in which H presented his plan for funding the public debt. For the congressional debate on H's proposals from February 8 to August 11, 1790, see *Annals of Congress*, I, 1170–1224, 1233–39, 1247–1322; II, 1323–1463, 1466–98, 1531–71, 1576–79, 1582–99, 1638–76, 1685, 1714, 1740–55, 1757–58, 1761, 1765.

3. In MS, H wrote "sectaries" above "partisans."

were the second and fifth. The second was subdivid⟨ed⟩ apparently
at least, into those who advocated the taking the rate of interest
stipulated in the contract as the standard of provision giving to the
original holders what was witheld from the alienees—those who
were for saving to the public what was withheld from the alienees.
The last, though not in appearance, was in fact the most numerous.
Indeed it may justly be doubted whether any of those who pro-
fessed to advocate compensation to the original holders were even
sincere in the proposition. But neither of the classes in either house
of Congress was itself a majority for the general de⟨bt.⟩

Those who favoured a provision at lower than the stipulated rates
of interest were influenced respectively by different motives some
by a doubt of the ability of the Government to make a full provision, especi⟨ally⟩ with the assumption of the particular debts,
others by an opinion that from the constitution the debt and what
they called the alloy in it a rate of interest lower than that stipulated was most consistent with justice to the public, others from
a spirit of mean and fraudulent parsimony which aimed at savings
to the public *per fas* et *nefas*. These last were not distinguishable
in their principle of action from those who advocated one species
of discrimination. Collateral circumstances respecting the course
of alininations locally and otherwise gave a different direction to
their conduct.

It is easy to perceive that such a heretogenous mass of opinions
not merely speculative but actuated by different interests and passions could not fail to produce much embarrassment to the person
who was to devise the plan of a provision for the public debt—if
he had been provident enough to sound the ground and probe the
state of opinions.

It was proper for him to endeavour to unite two ingredients in
his plan, intrinsic goodness [and] a reasonable probability of success.

It may be thought that the first was his only concern—that he
ought to have devised such a plan as appeared to him absolutely
the best leaving its adoption or rejection to the chance of events
and to the responsibility of those whose province it was to decide.

But would not this have been to refine too much? If a plan had
been offered too remote from the prevailing opinions—incapable
of conciliating a sufficient number to constitute a majority—what

would have been the consequences? The Minister would have been defeated in his first experiment. Before he had established any reputation for a knowlege of the business of his department, he might be sure that the blame of his ill-success would have fallen on his want of skill not upon the ignorance or perverseness of those who had rejected his plan. Placed in a back ground he would have lost confidence and influence. A retreat or the disgrace of remaining in office without weight or credit or an adequate prospect of being useful would have been his alternative. The public interest might have been still more injured. The public deliberations left without any rallying point would have been the more apt to be distracted between jarring incoherent and indigested projects and either to conclude nothing or to conclude on something manifestly contrary to the public interests. That this is a natural inference is proved by the diversity and still more by the crudity of the opinions which have been enumerated and by the zeal with which considerable men afterwards and since have maintained opinions which would disgrace pupils not yet out of the alphabet of political science.

Had a single session passed after the subject had been once seriously entered upon without some adequate provision for the debt the most injurious consequences were to have been expected.

With but a slight dawning of previous confidence, such a delay arising from the conflict of opinions after a public display of the very unsound and heretical notions which were entertained by too many would have excited something very like despair in the Creditors and would have thrown complete discredit on the debt. The value in the market would have sunk to almost nothing to the great prejudice of those who had lately through confidence in the new Government purchased at high prices. The fluctuation would have increased the dissatisfaction with the thing itself and by its influence upon opinion would have multiplied ten-fold the obstacles to a future provision on proper principles. The contagion of the opposite opinions maintained in the Legislature would have spread through the community fixing increasing and embittering the differences of opinion there which by reaction would have strengthened and confirmed the oppositions in the legislature. No mortal could foresee the result. A total failure to provide for the debt was possible. A provision for it on terms destructive of principle & replete with injustice to the creditors was the least ill result to have been anticipated.[4]

Those who from a horrible sentiment of injustice or the maniasm of false opinions regard the public debt with detestation as a nuisance and a curse and every creditor as a criminal [5] those who would have delighted in the disgrace of a government they had resisted and vilified might have looked forward with malignant pleasure to this wreck of the public Debt. But every virtuous enlightened man would [have] foreseen in it the complicated mischief of ruined Credit—the prostration abroad and at home of the Character of the new Government—its possible subversion and with it that of the Union—and let it be added a severe blow to the general security of property.[6]

In hinting at the possible subversion of the Government, it may be proper to explain the foundation of this idea.[7] The public Creditors, who consisted of various descriptions of men, a large proportion of them very meritorious and very influential had had a considerable agency in promoting the adoption of the new Constitution for this peculiar reason among the many weighty reasons which were common to them as citizens and proprietors that it exhibited the prospect of a Government able to do justice to their claims. Their disappointment and disgust quickened by the sensibility of private interest could but have been extreme. There was another class of men and a very weighty one who had had great share in the establishment of the constitution who though not personally interested in the debt considered the maxims of public credit as of the essence of good government, as intimately connected, by the anology and sympathy of principles, with the security of property in general, and as forming an inseparable portion of the great system of political order. These men from sentiment would have regarded their labours in supporting the constitution as in a great measure

4. In MS, H wrote "apprehended" above "anticipated."

5. In MS, H wrote "culprit" above "criminal."

6. In MS this sentence reads: "But every virtuous enlightened man would must foreseen in it the complicated mischief of ruined Credit—the prostration abroad and at home of the Character of the new Government of the Union—its possible subversion, and with it that and let it be added a severe blow to the general security of property."

7. In the margin opposite this sentence H wrote: "How end any in the Governt?"

lost—they would have seen the disappointment of their hopes in the unwillingness of the government to do what they esteemed justice and to pursue what they called an honorable policy, and they would have regarded this failure as an augury ⟨of⟩ the continuance of the fatal system which had for some time prostrated the national honor interest and happiness. The disaffection of a part of these classes of men might have carried a considerable reinforcement to the enemies of the government. The lukewarmness of the residue would have left them a clearer stage to direct their assaults against it. The real failure to do right which often sinks the Governments, as well as individuals into merited contempt alienating many of its ablest friends while it would diminish its support would at the same time increase in a tenfold ratio the mass of unfavourable opinion towards it. And from the combination of these causes it would have been likely to have degenerated into a despicable impotence and after a lingering atrophy to have perished.

In pursuing too far the idea of absolute perfection in the plan to be proposed unaccommodated to circumstances the chance of an absolutely bad issue was infinitely enhanced, and of the evils connected with it.

Was this the course either of patriotism or true personal policy? It has been remarked that in the rejection of the plan which was proposed it was to be apprehended that public opinion would charge the fault upon the plan not upon the rejecters of it.

But it may be said that time and the experience of ill effects would have done justice and placed the blame at the proper door. Let it be so—would it not have been blameably selfish to have sought to secure reputation at the hazard of so great evils to the community? Was it not more fit by accommodation to circumstances within our limits to pursue a better chance of public good at the risk of an imputation that complete theoretic perfection had not been adhered to?

Would Time have pronounced a favourable sentence upon a different course? Would it not have said that goodness is often not an absolute but a relative term and that it was culpable refinement to have sacrificed the prospect of accomplishing what was substantially good to the impracticable attainment of what was deemed theoretically perfect?

I grant that the idea of accommodation was not to be carried so far as to sacrifice to it any essential principle. This is never justifiable. But with the restriction of not sacrificing principle was it not right and adviseable so to shape the course as to secure the best prospect of effecting the greatest possible good?

To me this appeared the path of policy and duty and I acted under the influence of that impression.[8]

Thus guided I resolved to give the following features to my plan.

First   To embrace in the provision, upon equal terms, the particular debts of the individual States as well as the general debt of the UStates.

2dly   To *fund* the whole by *pledging* for the payment of interest certain specified revenues adequate to the object to continue pledged until the redemption or reimbursement of the principal of the Debt.

3d   To provide in the first instance for the foreign part of the general debt in exact conformity with the contracts concerning it.[9] To endeavour to effect a new more manageable and more convenient modification of the domestic part of the general debt with consent of the Creditors upon the ground of certain equivalents to be offered to them.

Fourthly   To take as the basis of the provision for the domestic part of the general debt the contracts with the Creditors as they stood at the time of the adoption of the new Constitution according to the then *unrevoked* acts and *resolutions* of the former Government except as to such alterations as they might on *legal* principles be pronounced to have undergone by voluntary acts and acquiescences of the creditors themselves; bottoming the provision on this principle that those contracts were to be fulfilled as far and as fast as was practicable & were not to be departed from without the free consent of the Creditors.

5thly   To provide for the arrears of interest which had accumulated upon the same terms with the principal constituting them a new Capital.

Sixthly   To endeavour to carry these ideas into effect by open-

8. In MS, H wrote "sentiment" above "impassion."
9. In MS, H inserted an asterisk at the end of this sentence and wrote: "Secondly Thirdly Fifthly Sixthly." He crossed out all but "Sixthly."

ing two loans on the terms proposed, one for the domestic part of the general debt, the sums subscribed thereto to be paid in the principal and arrears of interest of the old debt, another for the particular debts of the respective States, the sums subscribed thereto to be paid in the principal and arrears of interest of those debts.[10]

Sevently. To endeavour to establish it as a rule of administration that the creation of debt should always be accompanied with a provision for its extinguishment; and to apply the rule as far as it could be applicable to a new *provision* for an *old* debt by incorporating with it a fund for sinking the debt.

Eightly. As an incident to the whole, to provide for the final settlement of Accounts between the United & Individual States charging the latter with the sums assumed for them by the subscriptions in state-debt which should be made to the proposed loan and [11]

Let us now review under each head the reasonings which led to this plan and the means and modes of execution.

I. As to the uniting in the provision upon equal terms the particular debts of the several States with the general debt of the UStates.

It appeared to me that this measure would be conducive to the greatest degree of justice and was essential to policy.

I use a qualified and comparative mode of expression in the first case because from the past course and then existing state of things perfect justice was unattainable. The object consequently was to pursue such a plan as would procure the greatest practicable quantum of Justice.

The true rule for conducting the expences of the Revolution which established independence seems to have been this. That as the benefits to be derived from it would be individually equal to the citizens of every state so the burthens ought also to be individually equal among the citizens of all the states according to individual property and ability. That for this purpose all the expences

10. In the margin opposite this paragraph H wrote: "Settlement of Accounts."

11. Space left blank in MS. In the margin opposite this blank space H wrote: "Provision for ballances—see report." This is a reference to H's "Report Relative to a Provision for the Support of Public Credit," January 9, 1790.

of the war ought to have been defrayed out of a common Treasury supplied by contributions of all the individuals of the UStates, levied under the common authority according to equal rules, by loans either direct by borrowing or indirect and implied by emissions of paper money, operated upon the *joint credit* of the Union & by bringing into common stock all auxiliary or adventitious resources as waste lands confiscated property &c.

This was the true justice of the case and the true national ground —a ground which perhaps might well have been taken by those first assemblies of the Union convened by the direct commission of the people with plenary power to take care of the Nation but which was never but partially taken & was successively abandonned in compliance with the unnational demands of state claims—the aristocracy of state pretensions.

But instead of this course that which was pursued was a compound of incoherent principles. A part of the general expenditure was defrayed on the general credit of the UStates immediately by the emissions of bills of credit and by loans of individuals mediately by the contracts of various officers and Agents who obtained services & supplies on the credit of the Union and gave certain paper evidences of them. Another part was defrayed in consequence of requisitions upon the states of men money provisions and other articles of supply according to certain estimated or conjectural quotas to be raised & furnished by the states separately. A third part was defrayed by the spontaneous exertions of the states themselves for local defence for enterprises independently undertaken to annoy * the common enemy, divest him of acquisitions ** or make acquisitions *** upon him. Each State enjoyed the exclusive

* Frigates & Carolina.[12]
** Penobscot expedition.[13]
*** Indian expeditions.[14]

12. For information on the "Frigates & Carolina," see H to Pierce Butler, February 19, 1794, note 2.

13. This is a reference to the attempt by the state of Massachusetts to dislodge the British from Castine on Penobscot Bay, District of Maine, which the British had occupied in June, 1779. The militia under General Solomon Lovell made a successful landing in July, 1779, but received no assistance from the navy under the command of Captain Dudley Saltonstall. On August 13, 1779, Commodore George Collier arrived with British naval reinforcements, and the American forces were dispersed.

14. In April, 1779, a Virginia–South Carolina force led by Colonel Evan Shelby defeated the Cherokees in the Chickamauga villages along the Tennessee

benefit of its extra resources waste lands & confiscated property.*
Geographical lines thus made a substantial difference in the condition of the citizens of one common country, engaged in a common cause.

It was impossible that such a state of things should not have led
to very disproportionate exertions and contributions—should not
have produced and left very unequal burthens on the citizens of
different states. According to the temporary energy of the councils
of each, according to their comparative degree of zeal in the
common cause—according to the pressure of circumstances, the remoteness or proximity of danger, according to the peculiar character of the citizens of each state, according to a variety of contingent impulses—were the exertions of the several states—of course
their contribution to the expences of the general defence.

Very different also was the care and accuracy of the different
states in recording and preserving the evidences of their contributions. Some states kept an account of every thing, others only of
those things which they had furnished upon regular author[iz]a-
tion of the Union. Others kept very loose & imperfect accounts of
any thing—and others lost by accidents of the war the records
and vouchers which they had taken.

Add to all this the circumstances of the valuable aids which some
states were able to derive more than others from auxiliary resources
particularly of waste land & confiscated property—two obvious consequences will result.

First that it was impossible that in the course of the War there
could have been any proportional equality between the exertions

---

River. In the fall of the same year the South Carolina force destroyed six
more Indian villages.
  * It may [15] well be disputed whether confiscation was ever the right of a
particular State certainly as it applied to the subjects of the enemy nation it
never was for here not ⟨reason⟩ but the rights of war ever in the Union⟨-⟩.[16]
  15. In MS, H wrote "was" rather than "may."
  16. On this point Grotius wrote: ". . . Who acquires the goods of the
enemy in a public and formal war; the people itself or the individuals who
are of it or within it? . . . It is not to be doubted that by agreement of the
nations either practice may be established; that is, that the ownership of captured goods may fall to the people which wages the war, or to anyone who
lays hands upon them. But we are inquiring what their will has been; and
we say that the nations have decided that the property of enemies should
stand to enemies in the same relation as ownerless property . . ." (*On the
Law of War and Peace*, Book III, Ch. VI, Sec. VIII).

contributions and burthens of the citizens of the different States.*

Secondly   that it was impossible by any after adjustment to restore the equilibrium & produce retrospective equality.

All then that could be rationally aimed at was to pursue such a course as promised *most certainly* the *greatest degree* of Justice.

The option lay between three modes of proceeding.

One—To refer the obtaining of ultimate justice to a final settlement of Accounts between the United and Individual States upon the best and most equitable principles which were practicable and to provide for the ballances which would be established in favour of certain states by that settlement.

A second: [17] to exonerate all the states from Debt by the assumption of the still existing debts and to abandon a settlement as impracticable on certain and equitable principles.

Another: To exonerate the states from debt by the assumption of their still existing debts; to charge each with the sums assumed upon its account—and to attempt an ultimate equalization by the settlement of Accounts.

The first & second plan[s] were those contrasted by official propositions & deliberations & will be considered together by way of comparison with each other: first with regard to Justice & secondly with regard to policy.

The first plan, which was that vehemently insisted upon, by those who opposed the assumption of the State Debts appeared to me liable to some conclusive objections on the score of justice.

1 It would have left certain states greatly indebted, deprived of the most easy & productive sources of revenue by the occupation of them in a provision for the general debt, to struggle for an indefinite and uncertain period with a heavier load of debt than they were able to bear depending for relief on the precarious issue, of a final settlement of Accounts and a provision for the ballances.

2 It was uncertain in the nature of the thing and so considered by all parties not only when a settlement could be effected but whether any settlement would ever be practicable. The peace took place in 1783. In 1790 very little more than the formal measures of

---

* the losses which some states sustained more than others from being the immediate or longer theatres of the War.

17. In MS, H mistakenly wrote "third."

settlement had been devised and scarcely any impression made on the business.

III It was altogether a chapter of accidents whether a settlement would bring the expected and the just relief. From the circumstances which have been mentioned a settlement must have been of necessity an artificial and arbitrary thing. It was impossible for any to be made on truly equitable or satisfactory principles. The greatest portion of human intellect & justice was unequal to it because Adequate data were wanting. Some states would have credits where others from the manner of keeping their accounts would be without the corresponding credits for similar objects. Thus bounties for engaging men were in particular States regularly brought into account & vouched, in others furnished at the expence of classes no accounts were kept. Some states from the system of management would have much larger credits for a given quantum of service and supply than others. Thus purchases at exorbitant prices procured in some stations what coertion at regulated moderate prices procured in others. Some states from the imperfect mode of keeping their accounts & from the loss of vouchers would either have too much or too little credit. Either stricter rules of evidence must be pursued which would exclude too much or looser rules must be admitted which would admit too much. These suggest sufficient and yet only a part of the causes which rendered a just settlement impracticable.

In such a posture of things consequently it might well have happened that an indebted state [18] well entitled to relief by a ballance in its favour might have been disappointed by the issue of the settlement.

Not to assume the State Debts therefore was to leave the greatly indebted states to totter under a burthen to which they were unequal in the indefinite expectation of a settlement and to involve a possibility that they might never obtain relief either from the total failure of a settlement on account of the difficulties attending it or from not receiving their just dues by the embarrassment that unavoidably rendered a settlement artificial and arbitrary.

The reference therefore to a settlement as the sole rule of justice without an assumption of the state debts was not likely to afford

18. In MS, "stated."

either such prompt or such *certain* justice as might be looked for from the immediate assumption of the State Debts.

The objection to this reasoning was that it takes it for granted that the greatly indebted States were not so through want of good management or exertion and were intitled to eventual relief but the contrary of this presumption might have been the fact.[19]

There were good grounds for the conclusion that the States most indebted were so from meritorious causes, from their exertions in the common cause, and not from extravagance in the first instance a want of effort to extricate themselves in the second.[20]

The States most involved in debt in proportion to their resources were Sh Carolina Georgia to the South Massachusettes Connecticut & Rhode Island to the North.

South Carolina and Georgia it is well known had next to New York had been the principal theatres of the War. Though the metropolis of New York was during almost the whole of the War in the hands of the enemy there were very few parts of it which at some period or other were not exposed to his ravages—yet it never was so completely overrun or so intirely a victim as were the States of South Carolina & Georgia. It is known that they were temporarily conquered.

Besides as the principal military operations in the Southern Quarter *were late* in the War when the declension of the paper money disabled Congress from affording equal succour and their remoteness from the States of the greatest pecuniary resources prevented them from deriving equal aid from their neighbours—they were of course left to sustain on their own shoulders a greater part of the weight of the War than had been borne by other states—while the seats of it.[21]

Besides exhausting all the means of Credit they were subjected a great part of the time to the military coertion of our own army

19. In the margin opposite this paragraph H wrote: "Objection—States indebted largely might have been improvident & wanting in exertion."

20. In the margin opposite this paragraph H wrote: "Examine Massachusetts, Connecticut, S Carolina, Georgia, N Carolina, R Island."

21. In the margin opposite this paragraph H wrote: "Qr. If not the time of Mr Morris administration & supply of French money." Robert Morris was Superintendent of Finance from 1781 to 1784. For a discussion of the French loans during his administration, see E. James Ferguson, *The Power of the Purse* (Chapel Hill, 1961), 126–30.

as well as to the depredations [22] of the enemy. What in other cases had been an extraordinary and momentary expedient was there an ordinary resource—the principle mean for a considerable time of carrying on the war. They were literally consumed [23] by the War. The whole moveable property of the States was taken by the enemy or thrown into the public lap. Besides this the State Governments from the same circumstance of remoteness were more ostensible in that quarter. More of the effort was in their immediate account. The consequence was that a less proportion of the supplies drawn from the Country were taken to the immediate account of the UStates by their officers & Agents and upon their acknowledgements or certificates—consequently a greater proportion of the expence assumed the shape of State Debt.

The consequence was that the particular debts of South Carolina & Georgia especially the former were comparitively speaking swelled to an enormous amount.

To face them they had but slender resources. The degree to which they had been exhausted & ravaged by the war left them in a situation to require bounties rather than to struggle with heavy Debts. The population of either of them was not great. Georgia may be considered as in its infancy. She claims a la[r]ge tract of Waste land but besides the counter claim of the UStates it had not been in her power from the situation of her frontiers with regard to the Indians to turn them to great account.[24] She had indeed

22. In MS, "deprapations."
23. In MS, H wrote "devoured" above "consumed."
24. On December 21, 1789, the Georgia legislature sold fifteen and one-half million acres in the Mississippi, Tombigbee, and Tennessee valleys to the South Carolina Yazoo Company, the Virginia Yazoo Company, and the Tennessee Yazoo Company ("An Act for disposing of certain vacant lands or territory within this state" [ASP, Indian Affairs, I, 114]). See also Henry Knox to George Washington, January 22, 1791 (ASP, Indian Affairs, I, 112–13).
Washington believed that continued settlement of the southern Mississippi valley would antagonize the Indians and the Spanish. In addition, Congress disputed Georgia's claim to the land on the basis of the Indian treaties of Hopewell, November 28, 1785, and January 3, 1786. These treaties guaranteed possession of the lands in question to the Cherokee, Choctaw, and Chickasaw tribes and established a fixed boundary for the Indian lands (J. C. Kappler, ed., Indian Affairs: Laws and Treaties [Washington, 1904], II, 8–16; ASP, Indian Affairs, I, 38–39; JCC, XXX, 187–95). The land companies were also in violation of "An Act to regulate trade and intercourse with the Indian tribes," which provided that "no person shall be permitted to carry on any trade or intercourse with the Indian tribes, without a license for that purpose" (1 Stat.

paralized a great proportion of her debt by means far from justifiable, but she was unable to provide even for the residue.

South Carolina had no auxiliary resource except what she had derived from confiscated property, which a spirit of liberality that does her honor on the return of peace prevented her turning to much account and which at best was a very inadequate resource compared with her burthens. It was manifestly impossible for her to face efficaciously the interest upon her debt much more to make any impression in the principal. In attempts to provide for the Interest Taxation had been carried in South Carolina to a length not short of any State except Massachusettes & perhaps Connecticu[t.] The inability of S C & G to provide for their debts was increased by the considerable debts which their individuals owed to foreigners.

From this sketch of various circumstances of general notoriety Sceptism itself cannot doubt that South Carolina had contracted her debt most meritoriously that her sufferings had only been equalled by her efforts that she was unable to struggle unassisted with her debt that she was chargeable with no deficiency of effort to face it since the peace and that she was equitably intitled to relief from the UStates. But her situation with regard to the regularity of her accounts & the evidence for authenticating her claims rendered it peculiarly problematical whether she would ever find relief in a general settlement of Accounts.[25]

Rhode Island had also contracted her debt meritoriously. A considerable part of her small territory had been for a great part of the war in the possession of the enemy. She kept for her population respectable forces in the field throughout the war, and had uni-

---

137 [July 22, 1790]). On March 19, 1791, Washington issued a proclamation "declaring that all persons violating the treaties and act aforesaid shall be prosecuted with the utmost rigor of the law" (*GW*, XXXI, 250). The Treaty of New York, made between the United States and the Creeks on August 7, 1790, conceded to Georgia the lands which the state had already settled, but deprived it of those south of the Altahama River. All traders had to be licensed by the United States Government, and the Creeks were authorized to expel by force any intruders on their land (*ASP, Indian Affairs*, I, 81–82). For two secret articles of the treaty, see Arthur Preston Whitaker, *The Spanish-American Frontier, 1783–1795* (Lincoln, Nebraska, 1927), 137–39; 236, note 24.

25. In the margin opposite this paragraph H wrote: "Qr. of Mr. Kean." John Kean was cashier of the Bank of the United States.

formly manifested a useful & laudable zeal. Her resources were slender. Taxes upon a population of   [26] were all she could pretend to—no waste land and none or very little confiscated property.[27]

Her debt was considerable; tis evident that if she was to provide for it the means must come from the UStates and there was every presumption that she was intitled to this aid. It is true that she had in a great measure disincumbered herself by means which will be an indelible stain in her annals.[28] But the individuals who were the

26. Space left blank in MS.

27. In the margin opposite this paragraph H wrote: "Write to Mr. Carrington about provision for Virginia Debt & causes of its low value." See Carrington to H, June 25, July 15, 1795.

28. Rhode Island's debt after the American Revolution was slightly less than $600,000 (Ferguson, *The Power of the Purse*, 280–81). To settle this debt the state embarked on a policy of monetary inflation. In May, 1786, the General Assembly of Rhode Island enacted "An Act for emitting One Hundred Thousand Pounds," which reads in part: "Whereas from a Variety of Causes, political and mercantile, the Currency of this State, now in Circulation, has become altogether insufficient in Point of Quantity for the Purposes of Trade and Commerce, and for paying the just Debts of the Inhabitants thereof. Therefore, to establish a circulating Medium, upon the firmest and most equitable Principles that may be, and for facilitating that Interchange of Property so essential to a commercial State, and a People circumstanced as are the Inhabitants of this State: *Be it Enacted by this General Assembly, and by the Authority thereof it is hereby Enacted, that One Hundred Thousand Pounds*, Lawful Money, to be forthwith emitted in Bills of Paper, and loaned on the Credit of clear landed real Estates, double the Value of the said Bills so loaned to be pledged in such real Estates. . . .

"That the said Bills when emitted shall be a good and lawful Tender, for the complete Payment and final Discharge of all Debts now due and contracted and that may hereafter become due and contracted. . . ." (*Rhode Island Laws* [May, 1786].) The Assembly subsequently enacted "An Act in Addition to and Amendment of an Act, made and passed by the General Assembly of this State, at their last May Session at Newport, for emitting the Sum of One Hundred Thousand Pounds," which provided for enforcement of the earlier act and stipulated that bills of credit should be accepted on an equal basis with silver money (*Rhode Island Laws* [June, 1786]). "An Act, in Addition to and Amendment of an Act, entituled 'An Act, in Addition to and Amendment of an Act, made and passed by this Assembly, at their Session holden at Newport, in May last, for emitting the sum of One Hundred Thousand Pounds,' in Bills of public Credit" stipulated the legal mode of procedure against persons violating the law (*Rhode Island Laws* [August, 1786]).

The validity of these acts was successfully challenged before the judges of the Supreme Court of Rhode Island in September, 1786, in the case of [John] *Trevett* v [John] *Weeden*. For this case, see John Russell Bartlett, ed., *Records of the State of Rhode Island and Providence Plantations in New England* (Providence, 1865), X, 219–20, and Irwin H. Polishook, "Trevett vs. Weeden and the Case of the Judges," *Newport History*, XXXVIII (1965), 45–69.

victims had not the less claim upon the justice of their country. The assumption has promoted this justice & has enabled & induced the State to come forward with more equitable arrangements in their favour.

The pretensions of Massachusettes & Connecticut with regard to their Debt were of the most meritorious complexion. As a general position each state may justly claim the praise of a laudable spirit of exertion in the defences of their common liberty but there were certainly marked differences in the degrees. Abstracting the impulse of being the immediate seat of the war Massachusettes & Connecticut especially Massachusettes stood preeminent for steady constant and efficient exertions immediately conducing to the great object of the war—not to collateral acquisitions & partial advantages. Massachusettes in particular might justly be denominated the Atlas of the Union uniformly zealous uniformly vigorous.[29]

The records of the Treasury & War Department witness by their results the great exertions of these States in men money and other supplies.[30]

The situation in which I myself was placed during the war gave me then an opportunity of appreciating the efforts of these different States in the results. The impression on my mind was decisive in the spirit of what I have asserted. In how many critical periods of the War were the forces of those States the sinews and and muscles of the War? Let the records beforementioned declare. Let the memories of those who charged with the chief direction of our military affairs had the best Opportunities of observing pronounce.

No well informed man then doubted the fact. Subsequent examination the evidence of official records confirm the Truth. (See appendix Page I).[31]

While the efforts of these States during the War are incontestably ascertained they are chargeable with no want of exertion since to exonerate themselves from Debt.

Taxation in connecticut embraced every object and was carried

29. In the margin opposite this paragraph H wrote: "Apply to War Dept for supplies of Troops of Different States. Enquire what Virginia Massachusettes & Connecticut had absorbed of their particular Debt from the peace to the time of assumption." See Wadsworth to H, May 31, 1795; H to Carrington, June 25, July 15, 1795; Lincoln to H, July 10, 24, 1795.

30. In the margin opposite this sentence H wrote: "My own opportunity of seeing results."

31. If H prepared an appendix, it has not been found.

as far [as] it could be done without absolutely oppressing individuals. Instead of a few scattered examples of Excise every article of consumption in Connecticut was excised.

In Massachusettes Taxation was carried still farther even to a degree too burthernsome for the comfortable condition of the Citizens. This may have been partly owing to that unskilfulness which was the common attribute of the State administration of Finance; but it was still more owing to the real weight of the Taxes. The insurrection [32] was in a great degree the offspring of this pressure.

These states had no material auxiliary resources. The moderation of fortunes had left them without much aid from confiscated property. They had claims to Waste land but that of Connecticut has issued in a very unimportant acquisition.[33] That of Massachusettes has fared better but her acquisition would have done little towards extinguishment of her debt.[34] Connecticut without any seaport of

32. That is, Shays's Rebellion.

33. In 1776 Congress was confronted by the overlapping and conflicting land claims of seven states: Massachusetts, Connecticut, North Carolina, Georgia, South Carolina, Virginia, and New York. The small states, which had no western lands, feared that the landowning states would have too much power in the government of the Confederation. Maryland, in fact, refused to ratify the Articles of Confederation without assurances that the western lands would be ceded to the national government. Congress, in return, promised that the western territory would be used to establish new states on equal terms with the original thirteen.

In ceding its western lands to the new government on May 26, 1786, Connecticut reserved a four-million-acre tract known as the Western Reserve. Connecticut, insisting on the Reserve as compensation for its small size, maintained that the sale of these lands would provide funds that could be used for compensation for losses inflicted by the raids of the British army. For the cession of Connecticut's land, and a description of the Reserve, see *JCC*, XXX, 299–300, 301. In 1792 a half million acres of the Reserve were assigned to the residents of nine Connecticut towns as compensation for Revolutionary War damages. In 1795 the remainder of the Western Reserve was sold to the Connecticut Land Company.

34. On April 18, 1785, Massachusetts ceded its lands west of New York to the national government but reserved a claim to the western portion of New York (*JCC*, XXVIII, 271–73). On November 30, 1786, delegates of Massachusetts and New York met at Hartford and decided that New York should have "sovereignty and jurisdiction" of the disputed area and that Massachusetts should have "the right of preemption of the soil from the native Indians" (*JCC*, XXXIII, 623). The agreement is printed in *JCC*, XXXIII, 617, under the date of October 8, 1787. In 1788 Massachusetts sold the tract to Oliver Phelps and Nathaniel Gorham for £300,000, but the Indians would part with only one-third of the land. The entire tract, including the Phelps-Gorham Purchase, was eventually sold to Robert Morris. See H to Morris, March 18, 1795, note 29. For information on the New York–Massachusetts land controversy, see H's "Notes on the History of North and South America," December, 1786.

Consequence not only could not derive resource from this Circumstance but had been tributary to her more fortunate neighbours.

There was therefore a priori satisfactory evidence that these overburthened States had a just claim of relief from the UStates & if we may take the settlement of Accounts as evidence, the ancipation has been fully justified by the event. For not only the sums assumed for them have been covered but they have had considerable ballances reputed in their favour.

It will strengthen the argument for the superior justice of the assumption plan, to remark that the Debts of the States represented the great mass of State effort during the War. Not much had been done by taxation. Credit had been the principal engine.

Another objection on the score of justice which was strenuously urged against the plan of assuming was that certain States by vigorous efforts had considerably reduced their particular Debts while others had made little impression on them. It was therefore unequal to assume their debt in this unequal State.

It has been already shewn that this difference as far as it may be founded in fact was owing to adventitious advantages and therefore in point of substantial justice the states which had absorbed less of their debt had not the less equitable Title to relief. I recur to the example of New York. This state by large possessions of Waste land, by a great deal of confiscated property, by not providing for payment of interest on her debt whereby its value was kept low to the great injury of the Creditors was able to absorb a considerable proportion of her debt. Connecticut without these advantages was able to do much less—though her citizens were burthened with a much more considerable effort in contributions. Was it therefore inequitable as between these states that Connecticut should find relief in an assumption? Surely it was not. Again if a settlement of accounts which was a part of the plan of Assumption was to be relied upon, any inequality created by the assumption would be rectified by the settlement. If no equitable settlement was to be relied upon then the observation returned—the indebted States however much intitled to it would then be deprived of eventual justice & relief & there was a greater probability of justice in relieving them by an assumption than in leaving them to struggle indefinitely with their actual burthens.

Supposing no settlement & that without a settlement there was a chance of injustice either way then there was another solid & pla[i]n ground of calculation & precedence.

Either an equitable settlement of accounts would take place or it would not—if it did not, the greatly indebted States without an assumption would certainly fail of justice and due relief; if it did, with an assumption, the settlement would remedy any inequality which might have been occasioned by it and restore equilibrium. An assumption and a settlement on right principles would ensure justice—no assumption & no settlement would ensure injustice. It was to be feared a settlement might not take effect. It was precarious and contingent. An assumption of course gave the greatest certainty of Justice, by an assumption or equalization of the condition of Individuals. Pursuing mature impressions this must be deemed of more consequence than any thing which regarded the states in their corporate or collective capacities.

The most simple and satisfactory notion of Justice was to secure that individuals of the same Nation who had contended in the same cause for the same object their common liberty should at the end of the contest find themselves on an equal footing as to burthens arising from the contest.

Nothing could be more revolting than that the citizens of one state should live at ease free from Taxes and the citizens of a neighbouring State be overburthened with taxes growing out of a war which had given equal political advantages to the Citizens of both States.

This condition of things previous to the assumption was remarkably exempli[fi]ed between New York & Massachusettes and between New York & Connecticut. The citizens of New York scarcely paid any taxes those of Massachusettes & Connecticut were heavily burthened. A like comparison though different in degree might be extended to other States.

The relative conditions of States depended on many artificial circumstances. These circumstances might forever have stood in the way of that equality of condition among citizens which was [35] infinitely the most important consideration and the most desireable attainmt. The measure which went most directly and certainly to this object was to be preferred. The assumption was such a measure.

35. In MS, "what."

By taking all the Debts upon the Union to be paid out of common Treasury defrayed by common contribution according to general rules the citizens of every State were on an equal footing. State provisions produced inequality from the inequality of their debts from the inequality of adventitious resources from the inequality of permanent ABILITIES.

Justice among Individuals was better promoted in another sense. The New Government had given to the US the exclusive possession of the branch of Revenue which for a considerable time to come in this country is likely to be most productive. Had the Governmt of the U S confined itself to a provision for the general Debt— the proprietors of the particular Debts would in several States have been not only in a very unequal but in a very bad situation. Thus forms would have superseded substance. Men who had contributed their services and property to the support of the common cause at the instance of a State Government would have fared worse than those who have done the same thing at the instance of the General Government. Did this comport with any rational and true scheme of justice which preferred natural to artificial consideration? (Distinction between fed one the means for equality among states others among individuals).

It would have been the more hard unjust and unnatural because a great proportion of the State Debts had been originally contracted immediately with the UStates and afterwards transferred to the particular States. Such were the depreciation of pay.[36]

A still greater part was contracted in virtue of the requisitions of Congress upon the states in which cases it was more reasonable to consider them as agents than as principals.

To resume. The superiority of the plan of a joint provision over that of a separate provision in the view of justice consists in this—

That supposing a final equitable settlement of accounts between the states either plan would produce eventual justice.[37]

But the plan of assumption was most likely to expedite justice by the immediate relief which it gave to the overburthened States.

36. In the margin opposite this paragraph H wrote: "Inquire of Mr. Wolcott." See Oliver Wolcott, Jr., to H, February 26, 1795.

37. After this paragraph H wrote and crossed out the following: "That setting aside this supposition The plan of assumption gave immediate relief to the overburthened states which there was every probability from known circumstances were intitled to relief."

That setting aside the supposition of a final equitable settlement of accounts—the plan of assumption contained the best chance of success by giving relief to the overburthened States who would otherwise have remained without it though from known circumstances there was a *moral certainty* of their being entittled to it.

That the assumption in every event better consulted justice by conducing to equalize in the first instance the burthen of citizens of the same country arising from a contest in a common cause and by securing a simultaneous and equal provision for creditors who had equal merits & who otherwise would have fared inequally.

These are the principle considerations that relate to justice—in the view of policy the argument is still more conclusive in favor of assumption.

The theory of our constitution with respect to taxation is perhaps a new example in the world—that is to say a concurrent and coordinate authority in one general head and in thirteen (now fifteen) distinct members of a confederacy united under that head to impose in detail upon all individual and upon all taxable objects.

Yet experience had demonstrated that a power in the general head to tax the states only in their collective capacities, that is by the system of requisitions was a system of imbecility and injustice—imbecility because it did not produce to the common Treasury the requisite supplies—injustice because the separate efforts of the states under such a system were and from the nature of things would ever be unequal and consequently their contributions disproportionate.

Hence all those who agreed in the necessity of a Union of the States under a common head felt and acknowleged that a change in the plan was an essential feature in a new arrangement of the constitution of general government.

But though agreed in this general principle, they were not equally agreed in the application of the rule. Some were for a general & paramount power of taxation in the National Government and either a subordinate, or a limited by being confined to particular objects, power of taxation in the State Governments. Some were for a division of the power of taxation giving certain branches of it exclusively to the general Government and other branches of it exclusively to the State Governments—others were for a general concurrent power of taxation in the Fœderal & State Governments.

The two first opinions equally presupposed a great difficulty of execution and danger of collision in a concurrent power of taxation and sought to avoid it by different means. The last seems to have considered that difficulty and danger as less formi[d]able than the embarrassments which belonged to either of the other schemes. And this opinion was adopted by the Convention except with regard to the duties of imposts and Tonnage which for cogent and obvious [reasons] was impractible and was exclusively vested in the Fœderal head.

This course was relatively to the existing state of things the wisest. The subordination of the state power of taxation to that of the general government or the confining it to particular objects would probably have been an insuperable obstacle to the adoption of the constitution. The division of the power between the Union and the States could not have been regulated upon any plan which would not either have left the General Government more restricted than was compatible with a due provision for the exigencies of the Union or would have so confined the State Governments as would have been equally an impediment to the success of the Constitution. Besides that a truly eligible division which consulted all the cases possible by the general principles of the constitution was intrinsically very difficult if not impracticable.

But though it is admitted that the course pursued by the Convention was the most expedient—yet it is not the less true that the plan involved inherent and great difficulties. It may not unaptly be styled the Gordian Knot of our political situation.

To me there appeared but one way of untying or severing it, which was in practice to leave the states under as little necessity as possible of exercising the power of taxation. The narrowness of the limits of its exercise on one side left the field more free and unembarrassed to the other and avoided essentially the interference, and collisions to be apprehended *inherent* in [38] the plan of concurrent jurisdiction.

Thus to give a clear field to the Government of the UStates was so manifestly founded in good policy that the time must come when a man of sense would blush to dispute it.

38. In MS, H wrote "from" above "in."

It was essential to give effect to the objects of the Union. As to the past the General Government was to provide for the debts which the War that accomplished our Revolution had left upon us. These were to the debts which the same events had left upon the states individually as 5 to 2 nearly. The amount of the general debt foreign and Domestic was   [39] Millions.

For the future, the general Government besides providing for the expences of its civil administration which from obvious causes would unavoidably exceed that of the State Government and for a variety of other objects tedious to enumerate or define was charged with the care of the common defence.

Reason and experience teach that the great mass of expence in every country proceeds from War. Our experience has already belied the reveries of those Dreamers or Imposters who were wont to weaken the argument arising from this source by promising to this country a perpetual exemption from war.   years out of

          [40] of the existence of our frontiers have exhibited a state of desolating and expensive hostility. How narrowly have we thus far escaped a war with a great European power? Who can say how long we shall before we may be compelled to defend our independence against some one of the great competitors still engaged in that theatre.

The violent passions which have agitated the apostles of perpetual peace and which were so near forcing our political ship upon the rock of war which at this moment still impel her [41] to the same ruinous point are the mirrors in which they may read the refutation of their silly predictions and the certainty that our nation is enough exposed to the chances of War to render a clear stage for commanding all our resources of taxation indispensable. Besides actual War & danger of still greater we have already experienced a domestic Insurrection [42] in which more than a million has been expended.

Without an assumption of the State Debts which produced this effect the first war with an European Power would have convinced

39. Space left blank in MS.
40. Spaces left blank in MS.
41. In MS, "here."
42. That is, the Whiskey Insurrection.

us of the inelig[ib]leness of our situation of the weakness and embarrassment incident to fifteen or perhaps to 50 different systems of finance.

The foundation of this observation is obvious. Different states would have and actually have different predilections and prejudices on the subject of taxation. Some incline more to Excises or taxes on articles of consumption than to taxes on real estate. Others favour the latter more than the former. In some stamp duties are not ill thought of—in others they are odious.

Suppose, what was the natural and probable effect of such a diversity of opinion, the states being left to make separate provisions for their particular debts had bottomed their provisions on different objects of Revenue—that some had occupied the most productive objects of excise—that others had had recourse to taxes on real estate—that some had preferred to either duties on stamps—that a fourth class had sought the needed Revenue from duties on the alienation of certain kinds of property—and that a fifth class had derived its provision from general assessments of real & personal estate. These with duties on imports & exposts from which they are excluded & poll taxes which are the scourge of any society comprise all the important branches of Revenue. Suppose as would have been the case if fair provisions had been made that in each case the taxes had been carried as far [as] could be done without oppression or overburthening the object or the person—what would have been the situation of the general Government in case the breaking out of a war had called for great resources?

In all but direct taxes the Constitution enjoins *uniformity*. Reason and principle enjoin it with respect to all taxes laid by the same Government upon the same Society. What was to be done? Revenue could not be had from excises because the principal objects were already burthened by certain States as much as they could conveniently bear & to lay additional burthens would be equally ruinous to industry & to persons. Indeed excessive accumulation prevents collection & defeats the end.

Similar reasons would be obstacles as to all the other great branches of Revenue because different states had previously occupied them all to the convenient extent. The hand of the General

Government would thus have been arrested [43] and the greatest part of the resources of the community would have been tied up incapable of being brought into action for the common exigencies of the Nation.

Will it be said that the General Government might still have laid the taxes on such objects as appeared to it proper leaving the states to change their ground and adopt others? Who would wish to have seen the necessity of so violent an expedient or who could calculate the consequences of it?

Is it certain that a state would have thus complaisantly changed a ground to which it had been led by the coincidence of its predilections and prejudices? If it had mortgaged the particular revenues for its debt, is it certain that it would have been able to change its ground justly & satisfactor[il]y? Is [it] not too probable that perseverance complaint controversy between the general head & its members dissatisfaction in the community & weakness of measures would have been the effects of such an experiment. [44]

No one can doubt the dangers and inconveniences of such a situation: No sound mind but must think it a great recommendation of a measure that it tended to obviate so perilous and so inauspicious a situation.

An inference has been drawn that without the assumption and with separate provisions for the State-Debts the chief part of the resources of the community would have been tied up incapable of being brought into action for the public necessities. Let this be still more particularly illustrated.

Suppose Massachusetts had provided for her particular debt by excises. It is certain from the magnitude of her debt that to make the provision adequate in this way would have required excises to be extended as far as was practicable. Suppose Connecticut to have provided for her debt by stamp duties and duties on alienation of property which carried to any extent not oppressive would not have been more than an adequate fund for her debt. Suppose South

43. The original version (which H subsequently crossed out) for the completion of this sentence reads: "as it would have acted with a violence the and the precarious resource of requisitions which experience had condemned would alone have remained as the mean—if carry on a war which might have required all the system and energy of which the subject was capable."

44. At this point H wrote and crossed out: "Far more probable is that the resource of Requisitions would be resorted to."

Carolina to have rested her debt on taxes and assessments upon real and personal estate which in any admissible extent would probably have been inadequate to her debt.

It would follow that the UStates could not touch either of those great branches of taxation which form the great trunk of taxation because they had been preoccupied in those three states as far as the subject in each case would permit and therefore additions would be insupportable to the citizens and incapable of collection & because Congress could not by the constitution or upon principle touch those branches in some states without extending it to all.

It would thence follow that computing Massachusettes Connecticut & South Carolina as   of the Union   [45] of the resources of taxation from all the great branches except duties on imports would remain unoccupied and inapplicable to the public exigencies—except as will be presently mentioned.

It may be said that the occupation of the several branches of revenue in the way which has been stated is merely suppositious. It might not have happened—a more partial & at the same time a more various distribution might have left a freer stage to the UStates.

The possibility of what has been stated in theory is a conclusive argument for prefering a plan which avoided it. But more than this it is probable and from circumstances was in a great degree unavoidable that what has been supposed should have been substantially realized in practice. The modes of thinking in particular States and the magnitude of their debts would have naturally led to it. And as far as the states in their provision had recourse to different objects though not to the full extent—so far the evil would have existed & would have been an obstacle to a due provision for the public necessities.

But besides this it would be impossible to the state Governts to command efficaciously one principal source of taxation that of *Excises*—because of the competition of industry, where they were not laid &c.

The only paliative for this paralitic state of things was requisitions upon the states to be raised in their own way. No man conversant with the effects of this system during the war of our revolution, who saw its impotent and unequal operation—who is a friend

45. Spaces left blank in MS.

to vigour in the government of his Country who has an enlighened desire to see it in a state to vindicate efficaciously its honor & interests—who wishes the reign of equal justice by equal effort among the states and their citizens—no such man but would deplore that this system should ever be again the principal reliance of the national Government.

But it might be expected to be even more impotent under the present Government than under the Confederation. There the system of requisitions had a constitutional basis. Requisitions were the mode indicated by the articles of confederation for supplying the general Treasury & it was natural that their obligation should be so much the more respected.

But under the present Government there is no authority for obtaining revenue in that way. A contrary supposition has crept in from that provision of the constitution which regulates that "*direct taxes* shall be apportioned among the States according to their respective numbers." But the true meaning of this is that when Congress are about to raise revenue by their own authority upon those objects which are contemplated as the objects of direct taxation the proportional measure of the quantum of the tax to be levied in each state must be the numbers of such State. It is a mere rule for the exercise of the general power to taxation vested in Congress as to the article of direct taxes. It does not authorise the calling upon a state to raise such a quota of money by its own authority and in its own way. This would be to change taxation by Congress into taxation by the States, *direct* taxes into taxes of any discription which it might appear adviseable to a state to substitute.

Requisitions are then unknown to our present constitution. They would amount therefore to mere recommendations, a compliance with which would be purely gratuitous and voluntary in theory as well as in fact. What could be expected from such a system?

This position alone condemns any plan which would or might have left the UStates dependent on the resource of requisitions for carrying on a War. It is against every principle of sound reasoning or constitutional or practical policy to leave the administration in a condition to depend not on legal and obligatory provisions but on such as are gratuitous & voluntary. This is to arbitrate not to govern.

Perhaps the force of these reasonings may be thought to be diminished by the reflection that the debts of the States were temporary impediments which might be expected to cease within a certain period?

But who could say when they would cease? It was certain that if fairly provided for the evil would have lasted a very considerable time. And it was uncertain how soon a war might render it embarrassing to the finances & dangerous to the safety of the country.

The certain length of duration & the greatness of the probable mischief were sufficient reasons for removing the cause when it could so well be done.

It will be argued hereafter that the duration of all the Debts both general and particular supposing a fair provision was likely to have been much greater on the plan of separate than on that of joint provision.

It was observed by way of objection to the assumption of the State Debts that this division of the business would facilitate a provision for the whole debt of the country general and particular; that the resource of imposts would alone enable Congress to provide for the general debt while the states separately could more conveniently employ other resources for the particular debts and that together they could not only better provide for the interest of the debt but for the speedy extinguishments of the principal. This was in truth the most plausible argument which was used against the assumption.

In some of its aspects it was not without foundation and in contemplating the plan to be proposed did not escape very serious reflection and examination.

It appeared to me well founded in this important view—that leaving a provision for the general debt within the compass of duties on imposts and disembarrassing Congress from the necessity of resorting to other & less agreeable modes of taxation, it avoided to expose the Government in its infancy & before it had engaged in its favour habit and opinion to the clamour and unpopularity which was to be feared from the resort to other means. To avoid this inconvenience had many charms for the person who was to propose a plan. It seemed to have much less risk for his reputation & quiet.

But on full & mature reflection I yielded without reserve to the conviction that the consideration just mentioned though not without weight was greatly outweighed by many other considerations and that in a personal view it would have been pusyllanimity & weakness to have stopped short of a provision for the aggregate debt of the Country. Some of the reasons which determined me have been anticipated.

1   The superior probability of Justice among the States and among the individuals composing them, including a greater certainty of relief to the overburthened States & their citizens and the advantage equalizing the condition of the citizens of all the states as to contribution which was incident to the plan of a joint provision.

2   The avoiding of the collisions to which fifteen different and comprehensive systems of finance connected with a separate provision for the states was subject.[46]

3   To leave the field of revenue more open to the US & thus secure to their Government for the general exigencies of the Union including defence & safety a more full & complete command of the resources of the Nation.[47]

These considerations were of themselves sufficient to outweigh that which has been stated by way of objection but I proceed to add others which concurred in determining my judgment.

1   The assumption would tend to consolidate and secure public credit.

This would happen from various causes

1   If it had not taken place there would have been a conflict of interests and feelings among the public creditors.

The Creditors of certain States from the impractica[bi]lity, admitting a disposition, of making for them a provision equal to that which was made for the Creditors of the UStates would naturally have felt jealousy and dissatisfaction. They would have considered it as unjust that their claims equally meritorious should be worse treated and the sensibility in certain cases would have been aggra-

---

46. In the margin H wrote: "heart burnings bickerings."

47. H at this point wrote and crossed out: "I shall presently add the other considerations which have been said to have outweighed the objection last noticed. But first I will be in order to remark as to the last two points & what will follow respect[ing] the policy of the measures so there are considerations included in the first point which very materially bear upon the question of policy."

In the margin opposite this part of the MS H wrote: "Forget not the argument of policies from unequal condition of Individuals."

vated by the reflection that the most productive resources before exclusively enjoyed by the state Government and applied to their benefit had been diverted to the general Governmt and applied by it to the sole benefit of the natural creditors. This jealousy and dissatisfaction would have augmented the mass of dissatisfaction from other causes which would exist against an adequate provision for the general debt. The sources of such dissatisfaction have been stated and it was certain that enmity to the Government in some & the spirit of faction in others would make them engines for agitating the public mind. Such dissatisfactions, in a popular Government, especially tend to jeopardize the security of the public creditors, and consequently of the public Credit.

The assumption by uniting the interests of public Creditors of all descriptions was calculated to produce an opposite effect. It brought into the field an auxiliary to fortify the public opinion in opposition to the efforts of faction and of the *antiproprietary* spirit, in favour of a just and reasonable provision for the debt and for the support of credit.

These considerations to a mind which has been attentive to the progress of things since will have very particular weight.

The assumption would favour public credit in another sense by promoting and enabling a more adequate provision for the intire debt of the Country. This is in direct contradiction to one of the positions which the objection that was last stated contains. These are the reasons for a contrary opi[ni]on.

Some states especially Massachusettes Rhode Island Connecticut South Carolina and Georgia could not have made adequate provision for their respective debts. There is the ground of experience to assert that some states were not disposed to do it. From the cooperation of the two causes the debts of a large majority of the states would have remained without an adequate provision and would have been in danger of being frittered away by means inconsistent with the spirit of public Credit. While the UStates by assuming the state Debts and by laying open all the resources of taxation to the command of the general Government upon a uniform plan could for reasons already detailed make a more efficacious & complete provision for every part of the debt than could possibly have been done by separate provisions.

This may seem to have been a matter of no concern to the General Government. But the cause of credit and property is one and the same throughout the states. A blow to it in whatever state or in whatever form is a blow to it in every state and in every form. The intimacy of interest & connection between the states leads to an observance in one of what passes in another. Bad precedents influence as well as good. They are greedily looked up to and cited by men of loose principles who make them instruments of instilling doctrines and feelings hostile to morals property and credit. It may be averred as a maxim without danger of material error that there cannot be a violation of public principle in any state without spreading more or less an evil contagion in all.

It is known, that the relaxed conduct of the State Governments in regard to property & credit was one of the most serious diseases under which the body politic laboured prior to the adoption of our present constitution and was a material cause of that state of public opinion which led to its adoption.

The Constitution of the U States contained guards against this evil. Its provisions inhibit to the state Governments the [48] which had been great engines of violating property destroying confidence & credit and pro[pa]gating public dishonor & private distress.

In the practice of the Fœderal Government it was wise to second the spirit of those provisions. 1   by avoiding examples of those very practices which were meant to be guarded against in the states. 2dly. by removing as far as it could be constitutionally done out of the way of the States whatever would oblige or tempt to further tampering with faith credit & property.

The assumption was calculated to do this and it is not one of its least merits. It has served to prevent the reiteration of examples from necessity or choice which could not but have a malignant aspect towards the cause of public credit.[49]

It might be added that the national character abroad has been rescued from stains by the same measure. It was not easy for foreigners to distinguish accurately between the infractions of credit by the State Governments & by the general. More or less it was natural that some confusion of ideas should prevail & that the char-

48. Space left blank in MS. H is referring to Article I, Section 10, of the Constitution of the United States.

49. Opposite this paragraph H wrote and crossed out: "Note objection that some state Debts still remain."

acter of the country at large should suffer from the *crookednesses* of parts.

Another beneficial effect of the assumption favorable to public Credit was the placing of all the public funds of the country upon the same foundation. The price and steadiness or instability of the public funds are the barometers of public credit, and with due allowance for temporary circumstances, they mark and establish the state of public credit.

It cannot be doubted by a man acquainted with the subject that the fluctuations instability and precariousness of the value of property in funds in this country would have been very much in a ratio to the variety of kinds and of the foundations on which they rested—that it would have been incomparably greater upon the plan of fifteen different provisions at different rates by different authorities upon different principles than upon that of one provision upon one principle by one authority.[50]

It is observeable in the European Markets that the principles of the different species of funds afloat influence each other though perhaps the causes that affect some ought either not to affect others or to affect them differently. Few of the many who deal habitually or occasionally in the funds are able to appreciate accurately the causes of fluctuations & what ought to have been the consequences. The knowing ones take advantage of the fact and turn it to their own advantage commonly to the disadvantage of the less knowing & to the injury of public credit.

A great mass of precarious funds in the shape of State Debts could not have failed to injure & keep down the funds of the general Government by the influence of appearances by the quick & sudden division of money from one channel to another by the manœvres of Speculation by the distractions of public opinion.

There are some who reason so much *a travers* as to regard a low state of the funds as desireable because say they, it enables the Government to sink the debt the more speedily by purchases.

But they forget that the lowness of the funds is an argument of a bad state of credit & that the Nation which loses more by the greater purchase of foreigners at low prices than the Government gains by its purchases at those prices & the Government loses infinitely more

50. In the margin opposite this paragraph H wrote: "Note objection against the variety in the Denominations of our *present funds*."

by the higher premiums and interests which it must in that case give for new loans than it can gain in purchases of the bonds given for old loans at low prices. Let it be remembered that a bond given last year is as good as a bond given to day that borrowing by the Government is in fact only sending its bonds to market and if its old bonds are low its new bonds cannot be high. What would be thought of the policy of a merchant who should wish to see his notes at ten shillings in the pound?

Much clamour has been raised against the funding system on the score of *speculation*, how justly will be examined in a proper place, but what would have been the degree of it on the plan of so many different funds or stocks depending on so many different provisions? It is evident that it would have been multiplied tenfold. The legerdemain of speculation would have had full scope for its exertion.

To give as quickly as possible elevation & stability to the funds was a most important mean of raising & fixing public credit. The assumption, by equalizing the condition of every part of the public debt & placing every part on good and on equal security was one of the most effectual expedients for that purpose.

Another consequence of the assumption, contrary to what has been supposed & favourable to public credit, is that it facilitated a speedy honorable extinguishment of the debt.

This results from the superior efficacy of unity in the Financial system the superior & better command of the national resources as well from the reason assigned as from the probab[il]ity of greater skill & order in the arrangements of the general than the state Governments.

That plan which gave a more systematic & thorough command of every branch of national resources was evidently better adapted not only to the effectual payment of interest but to the speedy discharge of principal for the very reason that greater resources could be brought into action.

Certain states would have had to have to struggle endlessly with their debts—happy to be able to face even the interest. But the general Government was able to make & has already made a joint provision which would with due dispatch absorb the whole debt.[51]

51. See "An Act making provision for the (payment of the) Debt of the United States" (1 *Stat.* 138–44 [August 4, 1790]). This act first provided for

I have annexed the epithet *honorable* to that of speedy, because certainly a more speedy extinguish[ment] could have been found in bankruptcy or fraud. There is too much cause to believe that those who favoured the intricate speckled system of State provisions secretly had an eye to this happy resource. Its evils in every sense have been delineated & no man who values his character will avow it—no sound politician will look with complacency towards it. It was of the justice & policy of the UStates to dispel so corrupting a poison from the body politic.

Besides the advantages to public safety and public credit consequences very favourable to the case and satisfaction of individuals were included in the assumption—of three kinds 1 lightening the burthens absolutely of all the Citizens of the UStates. 2 equalizing the condition as to burthens of the Citizens of one State with those of another. 3 bringing certain relief in the first instance to the over-indebted States & facilitating settlement of accounts. These are the incidents of the same superiority of faculty in the general Government to make a convenient provision for the whole debt.

It is curious fact which has not made its due impression that in every state the people have found relief from assumption while an incomparably better provision than before existed has been made for the state debts.

Let the citizens of Virginia be appealed to whether they have not in consequence of being exonerated from the necessity of providing for their debt been relieved in degree or kind from burthens which before pressed heavily upon them.[52] They must answer the affirmitave. The same inquiry will find the same answers in every state.

---

the funding of the domestic debt by means of subscriptions payable through commissioners, one of whom was to be appointed for each state. In Section 13 the act then provided "That a loan be proposed to the amount of twenty-one million and five hundred thousand dollars, and that subscriptions to the said loan be received at the same times and places, and by the same persons, as in respect to the loan herein before proposed concerning the domestic debt of the United States. And that the sums which shall be subscribed to the said loan, shall be payable in the principal and interest of the certificates or notes, which prior to the first day of January last, were issued by the respective states, as acknowledgements or evidences of debts by them respectively owing, excluding certificates issued by the commissioners of army accounts in the state of North Carolina, in the year one thousand seven hundred and eighty-six . . ." (1 *Stat.* 142).

52. In the margin opposite this sentence H wrote: "inquire Taxes before and after." See Carrington to H, June 25, July 15, 1795.

Men wonder at the lightness of their burthens and yet at the capacity of the Government to pay the interest of its debt to absorb a
portion of the principal and to find extensive resources for defence
against Indian Ravages.

The solution of the enigma is in the present Financial system of
the Country intrinsically more energetic more orderly better directed and more uniform & comprehensive than could possibly have
been the case with   [53] different systems to provide for as many
different loads of debt.

The effect of energy and system is to vulgar and feeble minds a
kind of magic which they do not comprehend and thus they make
false interpretation of the most obvious facts. The people of several
parts of the state relieved and happy by the effects of the assumption execrate the measure with its authors to which they owe the
blessing.

The equalizing the condition of the individual citizens of the
several states by the generalizing of the provision is connected with
this part of the subject. It has been already noticed in reference to
the justice of procedure. It deserves particular attention in the view
of policy.

It is impossible to imagine any thing more calculated to breed
discontent, and between the citizens of the UStates mutual jealousy
& animosity than the inequality of condition which without the
assumption would have existed.[54]

When the citizens of Massachusettes or Connecticut bordering on
New York felt themselves burthened with heavy taxes while their
neighbours of New York paid scarcely any what must have been
their sensations? How must they have been stung by the sense of so
unjust an inequality? How must their envy and dissatisfaction have
been excited? How much must this have tended to beget in them
discontent with the Government under which they lived and from
discontent to lead them to revolt?

Something of this actually took place. That spirit of dissatisfaction which produced the insurrection in Massachusettes [55] was in all
probabil[it]y promoted by a comparison which exhibited the peo-

53. Space left blank in MS.
54. Opposite this paragraph H wrote and crossed out: "pain & mischief
had it remained & no relief from settlement."
55. That is, Shays's Rebellion.

ple of that State as in a condition far worse than their neighbours.

If it be said that this effect was likely to be temporary—destined to cease upon a settlement of accounts which would bring relief to the overburthened States—

The remark before made recurs. A settlement at all was precarious and uncertain—whether it would bring relief even where it ought to do was still more precarious and uncertain. The reasons of this uncertainty have been.

Let us conceive what would have been the effect under the inequality of condition which has been stated either if a settlement had been long procrastinated [56] or if having been made it did not bring relief to the much indebted States.

What would then have been the situation of the public mind in those states? Who can calculate the mischiefs which would have attended the disappointment or dispair of relief and the prospect of continuing indefinitely under such unequal loads?

It is a great recommendation of the assumption not only that it anticipated a relief which was indispensable and which might not have come from a settlement but that it facilitated a settlement and rendered a tolerable issue far more probable.

This position is thus explained.

The circumstances which have been enumerated rendered a settlement upon strict or systematic principles impracticable. Had the state-debts remained unassumed the nature of the settlement which might be made was proportionably important and imposed on the commissioners [57] the duty of great rigour and exactness. The more this was the case the more difficult it was to come to any admissible or satisfactory result. Adherence to principle was likely on one side or on another to produce great mischiefs. Compromises and managements were essential.

The assumption of the State Debts by giving relief to the much indebted States rendered the issue & consequently the principles of the settlement less important. It allowed greater latitude to the Commissioners to deviate from rule to consult expediency to shape the

56. In MS, "procrastination."

57. This is a reference to the three commissioners who were appointed in accordance with "An Act to provide more effectually for the settlement of the Accounts between the United States and the individual States" (1 *Stat.* 178–79 [August 5, 1790]). Section 3 of this act reads: ". . . It shall be the

result by a spirit of accommodation, and concession to circumstances. Hence a settlement become more practicable in proportion
as it was less important.

I declare that I am not in the secret of the principles or maxims by
which the Commissioners were governed but from what I do know
of the State of things with a full conviction of there being as much
disposition on their part of doing as much justice as possible, I can
entertain no doubt that the settlement which they made was essentially artificial and the result of a thousand compromises of principle.
No other settlement was possible and I believe none could ever have
been made had not things been put upon a footing to unfetter the
Commissioners.

Thus then it is one of the merits of the assumption that it facilitated a settlement of Accounts which all the states were desirous
of & so has contributed to establish their harmony. And it is fortunate that it has so issued as to have produced relief to those States

---

duty of the said commissioners to receive and examine all claims which shall
be exhibited to them before the first day of July, one thousand seven hundred
and ninety-one, and to determine on all such as shall have accrued for the
general or particular defence during the war, and on the evidence thereof,
according to the principles of general equity . . . , so as to provide for the
final settlement of all accounts between the United States and the states individually; but no evidence of a claim heretofore admitted by a commissioner
of the United States for any state or district, shall be subject to such examination; nor shall the claim of any citizen be admitted as a charge against the
United States in the account of any state, unless the same was allowed by
such state before the twenty-fourth day of September, one thousand seven
hundred and eighty-eight (1 *Stat.* 179). On August 9, 1790, George Washington nominated as commissioners William Irvine of Pennsylvania, John Taylor
Gilman of New Hampshire, and John Kean of South Carolina (*Executive
Journal*, I, 59). The Senate agreed to the appointments on August 10, 1790
(*Executive Journal*, I, 60). Gilman resigned from the commission to become
treasurer of New Hampshire (H to Washington, December 2, 1790, note 6),
and on December 23, 1790, Washington chose Woodbury Langdon, also of
New Hampshire, to replace him (*Executive Journal*, I, 64). See also H to
Washington, July 2, 1792. Section 9 of "An Act to provide more effectually
for the settlement of the Accounts between the United States and the individual States" provided that the commission's powers were to expire on
July 1, 1792 (1 *Stat.* 179 [August 5, 1790]), but the commission was renewed
for one year by "An Act to extend the time limited for settling the Accounts
of the United States with the individual States" (1 *Stat.* 229 [January 23, 1792]).
The commissioners' report, dated June 29, 1793, showing each state's account
with the United States, was submitted to Congress on December 5, 1793 (*ASP,
Miscellaneous*, I, 69). See Tobias Lear to H, August 19, 1793; H to Pierce
Butler, February 19, 1794, note 4.

which notwithstanding the assumption was still left with considerable debts upon them.

This circumstances of their having remained such ballances may be urged as an objection to the reasonings in favour of the assumption. But to this two things are to be replied.

1 That my proposition to Congress embraced the intire debt of each state which would have given in the first instan⟨ce⟩ complete relief. The limitation by Congre⟨ss⟩ is not chargeable on my plan. It wa⟨s⟩ the effect of a compromise between the zealo⟨us⟩ friends of assumption & some who opposed or doub⟨ted⟩ and was dictated in some degree by a spirit of caution.[58]

But though by this limitation the relief was less complete in the first instance then was intended by my plan enough was done to obviate the principal mischiefs & to ensure th⟨at⟩ a State could not be oppressed by the peculiar burthen remaining upon it.

Another advantage incident to the assumption was the preventing the depopulation of particular States.

Had the overburthened States remained so any considerable time while the citizens of other states were lightly taxed it could not but have promoted extremely emigration from the more to the less burthened states.

This dislocation of population from any violent cause or any extraordinary pressure on parts of the Union cannot but be regarded as a serious evil. It could not but disturb in some degree the general order the due course of industry the due circulation of public benefits.

One particular inconvenience would have been to have increased the inability and distress of the overburthened states by lessening the population from the labour of which the public resources were to be derived.

Another particular inconvenience might have [been] the transferring the population of the country from more to less beneficial situations in a national sense. No one has been more uniformly nor more intirely than myself in the system of giving a free course to

58. For H's "proposition to Congress," see his "Report Relative to a Provision for the Support of Public Credit," January 9, 1790. For the action of Congress, see Section 13 of "An Act making provision for the (payment of the) Debt of the United States" (1 *Stat.* 142).

the population & settlement of our interior Country and of securing to it by the best efforts of the Government the enjoyment of those collateral advantages on which its prosperity must depend. This in my opinion is preferable as the most natural policy and as that which will best secure & cement the unity of the empire. But with this policy adopted in my most unqualified manner, I am far from regarding it as wise to give or occasion any extraordinary impulse to a transfer of people from the settled to the unsettled parts of the country. This is to retard the progress in general improvement and to impair for a greater length of time the vigour of the Nation by scattering too widely and too sparsely the elements of resource and strength. It is to weaken govern[ment] by enlarging too rapidly the sphere of its action and weak[en]ing by stretching out the links of connection between the different parts

The true politican will content himself by seeing new settlements formed by the current of a redundant population—he will submit because it is unnatural would be fruitless and unwise to oppose even a greater transfer than the mere surplus by the attractions to emigration which new countries hold out—he will seek to tie the emigrants to the friends and brethren they have by a kind and liberal conduct of the Government towards them—by efficacious protection and by sincere persevering and energetic endeavours to obtain for them the free and full enjoyment of those rights & advantage which local situation requires. But he will not accelerate the transfer by accumulating artificial disadvantages on the already settled parts of the country—he will even endeavour to avoid this by removing such disadvantages if casual causes have produced them.

Such without reserve is my sincere view of this subject and I deem it no small recommendation of the assumption that it was a mild and equitable expedient for preventing a violent dislocation of the population of particular states.

It remains to mention one consideration which naturally occurred in the reflections upon the expediency of assuming the State Debts. This is its tendency to strengthen our infant Government by increasing the number of ligaments between the Government and the interests of Individuals.

I frankly acknowlege that this tendency as far as it appeared to be founded was not excluded from the calculation for my opinion has been and is that the true danger to our prosperity is not the over-bearing strength of the Fœderal head but its weakness and imbecillity for preserving the union of the States and controuling the ex-centricities of State ambition and the explosions of factious passions. And a measure which consistently with the Constitution was likely to have the effect of strengthening the fabric would have recommended itself to me on that account.

But though this was the case, though I thought too that the assumption would have in several senses a temporary tendency of the kind alluded to and so far might serve as a prop to the Government in the infancy of its authority while there was yet a numerous party alive whose vanity and envy pledged them to opposition and before it had acquired the confirmations of habit & age—and though weight was given to the argument where it was thought most likely to have effect—Yet upon the whole it was the consideration upon which I relied least of all.[59]

It appeared to me in a considerable degree counterballanced by the suggestion of an objection which has been stated—the necessity which it imposed on the government of resorting early to unpalateable modes of taxation which jeopardized its popularity and gave a handle to its enemies to attack.[60]

It appeared to me also intitled to the less weight on the account stated because on the supposition that this Debt was to be extinguished within a moderate term of years—its influence must then be terminated and it had not pretensions to be considered as a permanent or lastly prop to the Government.

Besides that it was to be foreseen that successive transfers of considerable portions of the Debt to foreigners and accumulations at home would rapidly enough lessen the number of ligaments diminish the influence upon individuals and the taxes continuing perhaps invert the effect.

Had this then been the weightiest motive to the measure, it would never have received my patronage. The great inducements with me were those which have been previously enumerated and chiefly the giving simplicity & energy to the national finances the avoiding

59. In the margin opposite this paragraph H wrote: "Note argument that such means are not to be resorted to but the good sense & virtue of the people."
60. In MS, "attacked."

the collisions of multifarious & conflicting systems the securing to the Government for national exigencies the complete command of the national resources, the consolidation of public credit. These were the commanding motives and it is believed they were solid.

It is understood that a contrary course has been a principal cause of embarrassment in the U Netherlands. The separate debts of the different provinces have been an endless source of perplexity and financial embecil[it]y.[61]

But for the same reason that the effect of the assumption to strengthen the Government was a feeble or ambiguous motive—its importance as an objection in the view of those who fear the overbearing power of the general Government has been much exaggerated. What solid ground was there for all the declamation which has represented this measure as a premeditated plan for overthrowing the state Governments and consolidating the States into one? What room was there in a matter of so temporary & partial an operation for the dreadful alarms which were felt or affected?

The inconvenience of an early resort to modes of taxation which run counter to public prejudices has been mentioned. Its force was felt, but in addition to the reasons immediately connected with the measure which led to it, there were collateral ones which united to meet it.

The current of popularity immediately after the adoption of the Government run strongly in its favour. The immediate Chief Magistrate justly united in his person the full confidence and cordial regard of the Nation.

61. Until the spring of 1795 the Dutch Republic had had a decentralized system of government, administered locally by urban regents under the authority of the stadtholder. The government's near-bankruptcy at this time was due to the inadequacy of the system of provincial quotas, to the drain of ready money in loans to other nations such as England, and to the declining business of the East and West India companies. In January, 1795, the stadtholder William V fled to England, and the French armies overran the country. On May 16, 1795, the two powers signed a treaty according to which the Dutch agreed to pay an indemnity of one hundred million florins and to make some slight territorial concessions in exchange for centralized autonomy under the name of the Batavian Republic. This last provision was unsuccessfully opposed by a federalist movement. Under the new system the province of Holland obtained precedence over the other provinces, and because it also had to bear the heaviest share of the indemnity, the remaining provinces were threatened with taxation to equalize the burden. The federalists demanded that each province should make good its own losses.

It was not to be doubted that intrigues to unpopularise the Government would go on that the passions incident to faction the natural disease of popular Governments would grow and multiply—that the rivalships of power would increase, and it was to be feared that greater difficulties might exist at a future day to introduce the most difficult species of revenues however necessary than might be experienced in the then stage of our affairs. The delay in establishing them might even be construed into an implied condemnation of them & might be rendered an argument against their future introduction. Even negative precedents in such cases are not without force. While the advantages of present situation facilitated the introduction of these revenues at the time; the obstacles that might be afterwards created rendered it adviseable to occupy the ground and to avoid by anticipating difficulties. The Presidency of the actual chief Magistrate was a more favourable period than was likely in a short time to return to establish points favourable to just and necessary efficiency of the Government.

Besides that it would probably have been in the long run an unwise calculation even of popularity for the Government to have omitted the measure of assumption. A weak and embarrassed Government never fails to be unpopular. It attaches to itself the disrespect incident to weakness—and unable to promote the public passions its impotencies are its crimes. Without the assumption, the Government would have been for a long time at least under all the entanglements and imbecilities of a complicated clashing & disordered system of Finance.

The foregoing considerations appeared to me decisive for proposing an assumption of the State Debts. Experience has not led me to repent the measures. And I believe it will more & more recommend it even to its enemies. In the course of the remarks which have been made the considerations which combated the mode of proceeding with regard to assumption namely an intire assumption of the State Debts and a dereliction of the settlement of accounts have been anticipated. The state of public opinion was an insuperable obstacle. Almost every state flattered itself with being a Creditor & imagined a particular interest in a settlement. The renunciation of it would consequently have destroyed the confidence and disturbed the harmony of the States. Else it would undoubtedly have been the best policy & as good justice to have renounced it. There was no ground of procedure more likely to promote mutual justice & convenience than to assume as a principle that each state in the War had exerted itself to the extent of its faculties—that the subsisting debts were to be paid out of a common Treasury & that ill retrospection & reliquidation between the states was to be abandonned. But this great & liberal measure was impossible. All parties accordingly concurred in demanding a settlement.

The course of the argument has stated & replied to all the objections to the assumption except one. This is that it has tended to increase the mass of the Debt.

This observation has frequently been so managed as to infuse into the minds of many a vague confused conception that the PUBLIC Debt of the Country has been augmented in mass to the extent of the aggregate sum of State Debts assumed. But it were absurd to attempt a refutation of this idea. It is self-evident that the Assumption in this respect did nothing more than transfer the particular debts to the Union. It united fourteen sums in one and charged them upon one responsibility, that of the Union, insted of leaving them to exist separately chargeable on the separate responsibilities of the Union and the Individual states. The debt of the Union was increased but the debts of the several members of it were proportionably decreased. The MASS of PUBLIC DEBT consequently remained the same, on the infallible evidence of a mathematical axiom that a WHOLE cannot be greater than ITS PARTS.

But the objection has had a more particular signification. It has amounted to this that the debts of the States have been twice provided for once to the Individual Creditors who held evidences of State debts & once to the States in whose favour ballances were found at the settlement.

This objection like most others from the same quarter has been presented in a shape so general inexplicit and naked of explanation that it is not easy even to comprehend much less to answer it. It probably turns on a sophism or error which supposes the same item of service or supply twice represented once in the evidence or voucher given by the State to the person who served or supplied and once in the account of the State as a charge against the UStates.

But this supposition of double representation overlooks the material fact that by the plan of settlement according to the assumption the sums assumed by the US to individuals are charged to the state which incurred them and so ballance & extinguish the correlative charge for the service or supply which was the origin of the Debt.

Moreover it is manifest in point of result that the objection can have little if any foundation.

The aggregate of the sums assumed for the States was [62] Dollars.

The whole ballances found in favour of the Creditor-States & which ballances are formed by a deduction out of the mass of State charges of the sums assumed and to be paid for the States amount to no more than [63] thus distributed.[64]

But it is known & appears from official documents that after the operation of the assumption there remained Upon [65] a debt exceeding   Upon

Making together

Thus then the sum assumed being   and the sum remaining on the enumerated States being   the Total of State Debts was not less than   .

The provision made for State Debts embraces the sum assumed to Individuals.

the ballances to Creditor States

Consequently [66]

For it ought to be taken for granted in the calculation & indeed is known to be the fact that the funds in the Creditor States derive from the U States, for their ballances are applied to their remaining debts to Individuals.

Taking it for granted that the principles of settlement were right and that the ballances of debtor States which exactly ballance those of Creditor States are to be collected it seems to be impossible ⟨– –⟩ thing—either that the mass of debt can have been increased or its distribution among the Debtor⟨s⟩ improperly carried by the assumption.

62. Space left blank in MS.
63. Space left blank in MS.
64. At this point H left several lines blank in the MS.
65. H left this and the following spaces blank in the MS.
66. H presumably intended to fill in the blank space in this paragraph with information which he had received from Joseph Nourse. See H to Nourse, March 18, 1795; Nourse to H, March 30, April 1, 1795.

Tis as to [the] last particular ⟨that⟩ there may be the most question
on the supposition either of an erroneous or inadequate settlement
or the non collection of Debtor ballances.

But on the supposition of an erroneous settlement, it is impossible
to calculate what was the effect of the assumption whether to promote or produce a wrong distribution.

The original situation of the accounts was in all respects such that
it cannot be pronounced what effect any new ingredient produced.
It was much matter of chance amidst the inevitable compromises of
principle. It can only be pronounced with reasonable assurances that
the effect was not likely to have been very material in any direction.
And the effect whatever ⟨it⟩ might be was not chargeable on ⟨the⟩
intrinsic nature ⟨of⟩ the ⟨– –⟩ of assumption but on the ⟨accurate – –⟩
state of ⟨account⟩.

As to the non collection of the ballances of Debtor States, the
ultimate distribution would probably have been more inequitable
without than with the assumption. For but for the deductions made
on accot of the sums assumed there would be larger ballances both
to Creditor & Debtor States, & the non collection of the latter would
have increased the inequality ⟨– – – – – –⟩ if non collected ⟨– –⟩ situation of [67]

The second feature of the plan as stated was to *fund* the intire
debt *foreign* and *domestic original* and *assumed.*

The *funding* of the Debt has been unexpectedly the theme of
much declamation and invective. A confusion of ideas has been attempted to be produced among the ignorant. The *funding* with the
assumption have been sometimes treated as the creation of the Debt;
at others the funding has been represented as its *perpetuation,* as a
direct attempt to fasten the burthen irrevocably about the necks of
the people. A particular ingredient in the plan proposed, the rendering the debt redeemable only in certain proportions has been pressed
in to reinforce this argument & to prove the iniquitous tendency
of the plan.

The circumstance of *qualified redeemability* will be spoken of
hereafter. Remarks here will be confined to the mere *funding* of the
Debt.

67. At this point either a portion of the MS is missing or H did not complete this section.

The Revolution which gave us independence and secured us liberty left upon the country as the price of it a considerable Debt partly contracted by the UStates in their joint capacity partly by the individual states in their separate capacities.

What was to be done with the debt? Was it to be wiped off with a sponge or was it to be provided for?

The first idea[s] were the extreme of political profligacy and folly. Governments like individuals have burthens which ought to be deemed sacred, else they become mere engines of violence oppression extortion, and misery. Adieu to the security of property adieu to the security of liberty. Nothing is then safe—all our favourite notions of national & constitutional rights vanish. Every thing is brought to a question of power; right is anathematized excommunicated and banished.

In the code of moral and political obligations that of paying debts holds a prominent place. Tried by the test of utility there is perhaps none of greater force or extent. Without it, no borrowing nor lending; no selling or purchasing upon time—no credit private or public; consequently a more cramped and less prosperous agriculture, fewer and more imperfect mechanic & other industrial arts less and more embarrassed commerce, an immense contraction of national resource and strength. A most active power in the whole scheme of national happiness would be destroyed. A vast void would be created. Every thing would languish and wither.

No one will be hardy enough directly to dispute these positions or advocate the horrid doctrine of applying the sponge, but it was seen to lurk beneath some very insidious suggestions, often reiterated and urged with earnestness and exageration.

The debt has a great deal of alloy in it—a great part of it had been produced for no adequate value. To pay it therefore involved injustice and injury to the public.

The real state of the fact which is the basis of this suggestion shall be discussed in another place. Here it shall be taken for granted that it was well founded.

But what were the causes? The bad arrangements & delinquencies of Government itself, the infidelity of its own agents, the enhancements of price from the demand and scarcity incident to a long and exhausting war, the embarrassments & risks to individuals from a depreciating currency, the eventual hazard insperable from a state of Revolution. These were the essential causes of the alloy, if any, in the Debt?

Was any one or all of them a good plea to the Government not to pay? Was it just that the whole debt should be cancelled because a fifteenth or a tenth or a fifth of it had been contracted without adequate consideration? Was it equitable that those persons who had yielded their personal services—lent their money and parted with their property to the government upon fair and reasonable compensation of values, should lose their rights because others may have extorted or imposed, because the disorders in the public arrangements had prevented proper liquidations of accounts and had let in unfounded claims, because the infidelity of the governments own Agents had produced dilapidations & had emitted evidences of debt without value or for little value? Was it reasonable to object to compensations & allowances predicated upon a state of war, revolution discredit and hazard, because they were not agreeable to a standard adjusted by a state of peace established government credit & safety?

An individual may plead duress & compulsion as an objection to the performance of his engagements but this is impossible to a Government. Individuals cannot exercise over it that species of controul which may be denominated compulsive. It may oppress but it cannot be oppressed. Circumstances which according to the laws enable individuals to demand high prices for their property are never arguments of compulsion to vitiate the contract.

Where would an objection of this kind lead? War, insurrection, every great disturbance of the Social order, is apt to augment price. Is there constantly on the return of peace and order to be a revision and reliquidation or a rejection of the contracts? How long would Governments under such a system obtain any succours but by exaction & violence in similar emergencies? [68]

Another weapon indirectly used against a provision for the debt was the alienations of it at low value &c.

68. At this point in the MS H wrote and crossed out: "Tis plain that such an objection ought to be discarded as a contemptible and pernicious subterfuge. It was in the view both of justice and policy indispensable to provide fairly for the Debt. Tis afflicting that there should be a state of public opinion or feeling however limited which should encourage a man to dare to expect to give currency to a contrary insinuation to throw any degree of unpopularity upon a fair provision for the Debt."

But how could this supersede the obligation of the Government to pay or provide? The Government had received the benefit of the services, loans, or supplies which were the consideration of its contracts. These contracts were in their constitution alienable and assignable. The proprietors had a full right to part with them at any value they pleased or even to give them away. What was it to the Government how they disposed of them? By what rule of reason law or right was the government dispensed, by alienations provident or improvident of the original proprietors, from paying its debts and performing its engagements?

It is evident that the only colorable question which could be raised was not whether the debt should be provided for, but for whose benefit the provision should accrue, that of the original proprietors or of their alienees, a question which will be examined in another place.

The obligation to provide for the Debts for the benefit of those who were best intitled was indisputable. No arguments can enforce it. No man who has the least regard for his reputation will hazard a denial of it.

But anonymous publications have by insinuations attempted to raise doubts and prejudices. Not the mode merely of providing has been attacked, but by implication any provision whatever. The Debt itself has been sometimes treated by vague expressions as a nuisance as a morbid excrescence in the body politic, as the creature of a wicked combination to create a monied aristocracy & undermine the republican system. A debt created by that very Revolution which gave us this Republican system has been artfully presented in these odious colours to the dislikes of a spirit of Jealousy and Avarice, and those who were disposed to uphold the integrity and credit of the Nation have been exhibited as conspirators against Democratic principles. It is afflicting that there should be a State of public information opinion or feeling which should encourage any man to attempt to trafic for popularity by means so absurd and so base. If they could succeed we must renounce those pretensions to intelligence and light as a people which we claim hitherto on such just grounds. We must soon after renounce that Republican system of which these men affect to be so fond.

The plainest maxims of common sense and common honesty establish that our Governments had no option but to make a fair provision for the Debt. Justice, true policy, character credit interest all spoke on this head a uniform and unequivocal language. Not to have listened to it would have been to have prostrated every thing respectable among nations. It would have been an act of suicide in the Government at the very commencement of its existence.[69] It would not have strangled the serpents which threatened but it would have strangled itself.

The only possible question was about the nature of the provision. And to this point indeed were confined all the questions formally raised, though indirectly it has been endeavoured to excite prejudices in the public mind against the debt itself & consequently against all provision for it.

But among the questions raised as to the nature of the provision, I neither recollect nor can trace that among the legislative parties while the subject was under discussion there was any party against the principle of *funding* the debt as contradistinguished from other modes of providing.

Indeed but three options occurred—to pay off the principal & interest at once which was impossible, to provide annually for the interest and occasionally for reimbursing as much of the principal as the public resources permitted—to *fund* the Debt, or in other words to *pledge* specified and adequate funds for the regular payment of interest till the principal was reimbursed and as an auxiliary measure to constitute & pledge adequate funds for the reimbursement of the principal.

The last was conformable to the sense of America repeatedly and solemnly expressed. Different acts of Congress under the old Confederation embrace and enforce the propriety of this measure & frequently with una[ni]mity.[70] The states separately had all sanc-

69. In the MS, in the line above the words "at the very commencement of its existence," H wrote: "at the moment of issuing out of its cradle."

70. This is a reference to the congressional funding requisition of April 18, 1783. This resolution repeated the request, made on February 3, 1781, that the states invest Congress with the power to establish an impost (that is, to levy duties on imported goods). It also included a proposal for additional taxes to be collected by the states, but pledged to Congress. The proceeds were to be applied only to the discharge of the interest and principal of the debt of the United States. The funding requisition is printed in *JCC*, XXIV, 257-60. The requisition was before the states until 1787, and although it was never effected, all the states eventually agreed to it in some form. By 1786, Rhode Island and Virginia reversed their earlier positions and came to support

tioned it. The objectors were a few solitary individuals neither numerous nor significant enough by weight of talents or character to form a party.

In proposing therefore to fund the debt I considered myself not only as pursuing the true principles of credit & the true policy of the case, but the uniform general sense of the Union.

I had heared no lisp from any description of men in the national legislature of an objection to this idea and accordingly as before observed when the plan proposed was under discussion there appeared none in opposition to it.

The clamours therefore which have been subsequently raised on this head and patronised more or less directly by a whole party are not less strong indications of the disingenuousness of party spirit than of an immaturity of ideas on the subject of public Credit.

The substance of the argument against Funding Systems is that by facilitating Credit they encourage enterprises which produce expence by furnishing in credit a substitute for revenue; they prevent the raising as much as might be raised cotemporarily with the causes of expence to avoid the unpopularity of laying new taxes and in both ways occasion a tendency to run in debt consequently a progressive accumulation of debt and its perpetuation; at least till it is crushed beneath the load of its own enormous weight.[71]

An analysis [72] of this argument proves that it turns upon the abuses of a thing intrinsically good.

---

the idea of an impost. See, for example, Nathan Dane to Samuel Adams, February 11, 1786 (Burnett, *Letters*, VIII, 303–06); James Manning and Nathaniel Miller to John Collins, Governor of Rhode Island, September 28, 1786 (Bartlett, ed., *Records of Rhode Island*, X, 222–23). For information concerning the impost and the funding requisition, see, for example, "Continental Congress. Motion on Payment of Interest on the Domestic Debt and on Sending a Deputation to Rhode Island," December 6, 1782; "Continental Congress. Report on a Letter from the Speaker of the Rhode Island Assembly," December 16, 1782; "Continental Congress. Report on the Deputation to Rhode Island," December 17, 1782; "Notes on a Plan for Providing for the Debts of the United States," January–April, 1783; "Continental Congress. Motion and Remarks Against Limiting the Duration of the Proposed Impost," February 19, 1783; "Continental Congress. Motion that the Duties Imposed by the United States be Coexistent with the Public Debt," March 11, 1783; "Continental Congress. Motion on Establishment of Permanent Funds," March 21, 1783; and H to George Clinton, May 14, 1783.

71. In the margin opposite this paragraph H wrote the following note: "Shew how providing for the contracts were connected with the general securing of property."

72. In MS, "alalysis."

A prosperous state of agriculture commerce and manufactures nourishes and begets opulence, resource, and strength. These by inspiring a consciousness of power never fail to beget in the councils of nations under whatever form of Government a sentiment of superiority, pride ambition insolence. These dispositions lead directly to War and consequently to expences and to all the calamities which march in the train of War. Shall we therefore reprobate and reject improvements in agriculture commerce and manufactures?

Again the same causes leading to opulence, increasing the means of enjoyment naturally sharpen the appetite for it, and so promote luxury extravagance dissipation effeminacy disorders in the moral and political system convulsions revolutions the overthrow of nations and empires. Shall we therefore on this account renounce improvements in Agriculture commerce and manufactures?

Again: Science learning and knowlege promote those inventions, discoveries and improvements which accelerate the progress of labour and industry and with it the accumulation of that opulence which is the parent of so many pleasures & pains, so many blessings and calamities. Shall we therefore on this account explode Science Learning & Knowlege?

Again: True liberty by protecting the exertions of talents and industry and securing to them their justly acquired fruits, tends more powerfully than any other cause to augment the mass of national wealth and to produce the mischiefs of opulence. Shall we therefore on this account proscribe Liberty also?

What good in fine shall we retain? Tis the portion of man assigned to him by the eternal allotment of Providence that every good he enjoys, shall be alloyed with ills, that every source of his bliss shall be a source of his affliction—except Virtue alone, the only unmixed good which is permitted to his temporal Condition.

But shall we on this account forego every advantage which we are fitted to enjoy? Shall we put in practice the horrid system of the detistable Robespierre. Shall we make war upon Science & its professors? Shall we destroy the arts useful as well as pleasurable? Shall we [73] make knowlege a crime ignorance a qualification? Shall we lay in ruins our towns and deform the face of our fields. Shall we enchain the human mind & blunt all its energies under the wither-

73. In MS, "be."

ing influences of privation & the benumbing strokes of Terror? Shall we substitute the unmingled misery of a gloomy and destructive despotism to the alternate sunshine & storms of Liberty? Shall we exchange Science Civilization &c.

The very objection to funding systems makes their panygeric— *"they facilitate credit"*—they give energy solidity and extent to the Credit of a Nation—They enable it in great and dangerous emergencies to obtain readily and copiously the supplies of money of which it stands in need for its defence safety and the preservation or advancement of its interests—They enable it to do this too without crushing the people beneath the weight of intolerable taxes, without taking from industry the resources necessary for its vigorous prosecution, without emptying all the property of individuals into the public lap, without subverting the foundations of social order.

Indeed War in the modern system of it offers but two options— Credit or the devastation of private property. Tis impossible merely with that portion of the income of the community which can be spared from the wants conveniences & industrious pursuits of individuals to force the expences of a serious War during its progress. There must be anticipation by Credit, or there must be a violent usurpation of private property. The State must trench upon the Capital instead of the Revenue of the People and thus every war would involve a temporary ruin.

Tis the signal merit of a vigorous system of national credit that it enables a Government to support war without violating property destroying industry or interfering unreasonably with individual enjoyments. The citizens retain their Capital to carry on their several businesses and a due proportion of its produce for obtaining their usual comforts. Agriculture Commerce & manufactures may receive some Check but they receive no serious wound. Their stamina remain, and, on peace returning, they quickly resume their wonted elasticity. War by the use of Credit becomes less a scourge loses a great portion of its calamity.[74]

Will it be said that *equal* Credit may be established without funding systems? Then I answer, the objection made to those systems will apply to that mode whatever it is by which this equal credit is obtained. Tis Credit which giving extraordinary resources to Gov-

74. In MS, H wrote "sting" above the word "calamity."

ernment encourages to enterprises that produce expence and which furnishing a substitute for revenue relaxes the efforts of taxation and prevents the raising for the current expenditure as much as might be raised in this way. However that Credit is acquired the same consequences follow, the same evils ensue.

Will it be said that without funding systems not an *equal* but a *competent* credit might be secured? I answer by asking what is this competent Credit? Is it the power of obtaining by loans all that the State may want for extraordinary exigencies more than it can conveniently and without oppression or disorder raise on the citizens? If any thing less it is plainly not enough, and if it is this it is as much as funding systems effect. The how much in each case to be obtained in loans beyond what can be conveniently raised in taxes depends on the pressure of the occasion and the opinion of the legislature of the day. And this opinion will be affected by the temper of the times, the degree of popular favour or disfavour towards the object of expence, & the genius of the Government.[75]

Thus it appears that the great objection to funding systems resolves itself into an objection to Credit in the abstract, and if listened to drives us to the alternative of a mean surrender of our rights and interests to every enterprising invader or to the oppression of the citizens and destruction of Capital & Industry in every war in which we should be engaged and in the end, from the insupportableness of that situation, to the same surrender of our rights and interests.

Indeed as far as it is the attribute of funding systems to invigorate Credit, it is their tendency in an important particular to diminish Debt.* This relates to the lower or higher rate of interest at which money is borrowed according to the state of Credit. A Government which borrows 100 Dollars at three percent owes in fact a less debt than a Government which is obliged to borrow the same sum at five per Cent. Interest is always a part of the debt and it is self evident that the ultimate discharge of one which bears five ₩ Ct will exhaust more money or income than that of one which only bears 3 ₩ Ct.

---

* This may be supposed to contradict what is said in my report.[76]

75. In the margin opposite this paragraph H wrote: "A Credit is not good which does not extend the power of the government to borrow to the utmost limit of the power of Individuals to lend."

76. See "Report Relative to a Provision for the Support of Public Credit," January 9, 1790.

This principle runs through all the public operations in which Credit is concerned and the difference in the result of the public expenditures and consequently its debts, from a perfect or imperfect state of Credit is immense.

Every State ought to aim at rendering its credit, that is its faculty [77] to borrow, commensurate with the utmost extent of the lending faculties of the community and of all others who can have access to its loans. Tis then that it puts itself in a condition to exercise the greatest portion of strength of which it is capable and has its destiny most completely in its own hands. Tis then that the various departments of its industry are liable to the least disturbance & proceed with the most steady & vigorous motion. Tis then that it is able to supply all its wants not only in the most effectual manner but at the cheapest rate. An ignorance which benights the political world and disputes the first principles of Administration is requisite to bring this position for a moment into question. The principle, on which such a question could be founded, would equally combat every institution that promotes the perfection of the Social organisation, for this perfection in all its shapes by giving a consciousness of strength & resource & inspiring pride tends to ambitious pursuits to war expence & debt.[78]

On this question as on most others evils are traced to a wrong source. Funding systems as the engines of Credit are blamed for the Wars expences and debts of nations? Do these evils prevail less in countries where either those systems do not exist or where they exist partially and imperfectly. Great Britain is the country where they exist in most energy. Her wars have no doubt been frequent her expences great and her debts are vast. But is not this, with due allowance for difference of circumstances, the description of all the great Powers of Europe?

France Spain Austria Russia Prussia—Are they not as frequently at War as Great Britain and as often of their own choice? Have not

77. In MS, H wrote "ability" above the word "faculty."
78. At this point in the MS H wrote and crossed out the following paragraph: "The infinite importance of Credit to a State was never more signally displayed than in the example of Great Britain at this juncture. Let all that may be demanded be admitted as to the original impolicy of the war on her part or impolicy of persisting in it under the existing circumstances still it is of the utmost consequence to her that she is enabled by it to face &c."

their expences compared with their means and the state of Society been as great? Have they not all except Prussia heavy Debts?

The Debt of France brought about her Revolution. Financial embarrassments led to those steps which led to the overthrow of the Government and to all the terrible scenes which have followed.[79]

Let us then say as the truth is, not that funding systems produce wars expences & debts, but that the ambition, avarice revenge and injustice of man produce them. The seeds of war are sown thickly in the human breast. It is astonishing, after the experience of its having deluged the world with calamities for so many ages with how much precipitancy and levity nations still rush to arms against each other.[80]

Besides what we see abroad, what have we recently witnessed among ourselves? Never was a thing more manifest than that our true policy lay in cultivating peace with scrupulous care. Never had a nation a stronger interest so to do. Yet how many were there who directly and indirectly raised and joined in the cry of War. Sympathy with one nation animosity against another, made it infinitely difficult for the Government to steer a course calculated to avoid being implicated in the Vulcano which shook & overwhelmed Europe. Vague speculations about the cause of Liberty seconded by angry passions had like to have plunged this young country, just recovering from the effects of the long and desolating war which confirmed its revolution, just emerging from a state little short of anarchy, just beginning to establish system and order; to revive credit & confidence into an abyss of war confusion and distress.

After all the experience which has been had upon the point shall we still charge upon funding systems evils which are truly chargeable upon the bad and turbulent passions of the human mind?[81]

Peruse the hystory of Europe from its earliest period, were wars less frequent or pernicious before the system of credit was introduced than they have been since? They were more frequent and

79. Opposite this paragraph H wrote and then crossed out the following note: "Note Wars as frequent & more destructive before systems of Credit."
80. Opposite this paragraph H wrote: "Credit a new power of which nations have not yet learned the due use."
81. At the bottom of the MS page, which ends with this question, H wrote: "Note concerning the motives to the cry of War."

more destructive though perhaps not of as long duration at one time.[82]

But they did not equally produce debt. This is true, yet it remains to compare the evils of debt with those which resulted from the antecedent system of War—the devastations and extortions the oppressions and derangements of industry in all its branches, and it remains to consider whether expedients may not be devised which may preserve to nations the advantages of Credit & avoid essentially its evils. If this shall be practicable the argument in favour of the system of Credit has no counterpoise and becomes altogether conclusive.[83]

Credit may be called a new power in the mechanism of national affairs. It is a great and a very useful one but the art of regulating it properly, as is the case with every new and great contrivance, has been till lately imperfectly understood. The rule of making cotemporary provision for the extinguishment of principal as well as for the payment of interest in the art of contracting new debt is the desideratum—the true panacea.

But this like most others is not an absolute but a relative question. If it were even admitted that the system of anticipation by Credit is in the abstract a bad one, it will not follow that it can be renounced by any one nation, while nations in general continue to use it. It is so immense a power in the affairs of war that a nation without credit would be in great danger of falling a victim in the first war with a power possessing a vigorous and flourishing credit.

What astonishing efforts has Credit enabled Great Britain to make? What astonishing efforts does it enable her at this very moment to continue. What true Englishman, whatever may be his opinion of the merits and wisdom of the contest in which his country is engaged does not rejoice that she is able to employ so powerful instrument of Warfare. However he may wish for peace he will reflect that there must be two parties to the pacification and that it is possible the enemy may either be unwilling to make peace or only willing to make it on terms too disadvantageous & humiliating. He

82. In the margin opposite this paragraph H wrote: "State how."
83. In the margin opposite this paragraph H wrote: "Note charge against funding system in this country that it tended to prevent the war. This is the tendency of Debt."

must therefore cherish the national Credit as an engine by which war, if inevitable, can be maintained, and by which from that very possibility a better peace can be secured.

It is remarkable too that Great Britain the only power which has uniformly cultivated an enlightened and exact plan of national credit at a juncture so critical as the present continues to uphold the various branches of her commerce & industry in great energy and prosperity, and will in the end tax her adversarary in exchange for the products of her industry with a large proportion of the expences of the actual War.

The commerce and manufactures of France are so prostraited that this consequence cannot but follow. For some years to come after peace she must be customer to G Britain for vast supplies.

But let us still return too & keep in view this very material point already stated. Tis *Credit* in general, not funding systems in particular against which the objections made as far as they have foundation lie. However obtained it leads to exactly the same consequences which are charged on funding systems, which are no otherwise answerable for those consequences than as they are means of Credit.

Any provision therefore for our Revolution-Debt which from its justice and efficiency would have given satisfaction and inspired confidence would equally have conferred national credit and would have been equally liable to the evils of an abuse of Credit.

The dilemma was either to make & continue a just and adequate provision for the debt till it was discharged and thereby establish Credit and incur the chances of the evils incident to its abuse; or not to make a just and adequate provision for the debt and so commit national injustice incur national dishonor and disgrace, and it may be added shake and weaken the foundations of property and social security.

Thus we may discard from the examination of the subject the general question whether the system of Credit (and as a mean of credit the funding of Debts) is a salutary or a pernicious system. It could only with propriety arise with regard to the policy of the Government in future cases, that is how far it would or would not in future emergencies resort to anticipations by credit or find immediate resources in cotemporary contributions of the community and in the spoils of War. It could never be properly raised as to a debt previously contracted. The objections to a system of Credit could never with an honest man justify a moments hesitation about the obligation & propriety of a just and efficacious provision for a debt previously incurred either from a real necessity or from a past neglect of the Government to attend duly to the impolicy of employing credit and of contracting Debt.

A Government which does not rest on the basis of justice rests on that of force. There is no middle ground. Establish that a Government may decline a provision for its debts, though able to make it, and you overthrow all public morality, you unhinge all the principles that must preserve the limits of free constitutions—you have anarchy, despotism or, what you please, but you have no *just* or *regular* Government.

In all questions about the advantages or disadvantages of national Credit, or in similar questions, which it has been seen may be raised (and it may be added have been raised), with respect to all the sources of social happiness and national prosperity—the difference between the true politician and the political-empyric is this: The latter will either attempt to travel out of human nature and introduce institutuions and projects for which man is not fitted and which perish in the imbecility of their own conception & structure, or without proposing or attempting any substitute they content themselves with exposing and declaming against the ill sides of things and with puzzling & embrassing every practicable scheme of administration which is adopted. The last indeed is the most usual because the easiest course and it embraces in its practice all those hunters after popularity who knowing better make a traffic of the weak sides of the human understanding and passions.

The true politican on the contrary takes human nature (and human society its aggregate) as he finds it, a compound of good and ill qualities of good and ill tendencies—endued with powers and actuated by passions and propensities which blend enjoyment with suffering and make the causes of welfare the causes of misfortune.

With this view of human nature he will not attempt to warp or distort it from its natural direction—he will not attempt to promote its happiness by means to which it is not suited, he will not reject the employment of the means which constitute its bliss because they necessarily involve alloy and danger; but he will seek to promote his action according to the byass of his nature, to lead him to the developpement of his energies according to the scope of his passions, and erecting the social organisation on this basis, he will favour all those institutions and plans which tend to make men happy according to their natural bent, which multiply the sources of individual enjoyment and increase those of national resource and strength— taking care to infuse in each case all the ingredients which can be devised as preventives or correctives of the evil which is the eternal concomitant of temporal blessing.

Thus: observing the immense importance of Credit to the strength and security of nations, he will endeavour to obtain it for his own country in its highest perfection by the most efficient means; yet not overlooking the abuses to which like all other good things it is liable he will seek to guard against them, by promoting a spirit of true national œconomy, by pursuing steadily, especially in a country which has no need of external acquisition, the maxims of justice moderation and peace and by endeavouring to establish as far as human inconstancey allows certain fixed principles in the administration of the finances calculated to secure efficaciously the extinguishment of debt as fast at least as the probable exigencies of the nation is likely to occasion the contracting of it.

These, I can truly say, are the principles which have regulated every part of my conduct in my late office.

And as a first step to this great result, I proposed the *funding* of the public Debt.

The quality of funding appeared to me essential in the plan of providing for different reasons.[84]

1 First it appeared to me adviseable that the nature of the provision should be such as to give satisfaction and confidence, by inspiring an opinion of security, to the Creditors. This was important not only as it regarded their advantage but as it regarded the public interest. The material credit was intimately connected with that satisfaction & confidence. They tended besides to produce another important effect which will be noticed hereafter.

84. In the margin opposite this paragraph H wrote: "tranquility satisfaction & confidence of Creditors—to guard the Government against its own inconstancy—to give solidity & stability to the funds & prevent separ⟨ate provi-sion.⟩"

2 It was desireable to guard the Government and the Creditors against the danger of inconstancy in the public Councils. The debt being once funded it would require the concurrence of both branches of the legislature and of the President or of two thirds of both branches overruling the opposition of the President to shake the provision. Of this there was a moral impossibility, at least the highest degree of improbability. To make a provision annually would require the like concurrence in its favour, of course would be continually liable to be defeated by improper views in either of the branches or departments. Whoever has attended to the course of our public Councils and to the dispositions which have been manifested by a powerful party in them must be sensible that danger in this case was not ideal. There was good ground to apprehend that the accidental result of a single election and the accidental prevalency of ill humours in parts of the community might violate the justice and prostrate the Credit of the Nation.

It is the part of wisdom in a Government as well as in an individual to guard against its own infirmities; and having taken beforehand a comprehensive view of its duty and interest to tie itself down by every constitutional precaution to the steady pursuit of them.

3 It appeared important to give all practicable solidity & stability to the funds or Stock which constituted the debt. The funding of the Debt was essential to this end. This is but an inference from the preceding remarks. It was to result from obviating the danger of fluctuating councils concerning the debt from the satisfaction & confidence of the creditors arising from an opinion of security, from the constant estimation in which that opinion of security would cause it to be holden not only by the Creditors but by all other classes of the community & by foreigners.

One effect of this was to accelerate the period which would terminate an irregular and excessive spirit of speculation in the funds. It is evident that this must have been in proportion to the causes calculated to produce fluctuation in the public opinion with regard to the value of the funds. Insecurity, the chance of the provision being interrupted or deteriorated, occuring at every new period of making it, was a more fruitful source than any other of that fluctuation of opinion. The degree of this being always incalculable would have given the utmost scope to imagination to the arts and intrigues of Stock-jobbers and must have kept the funds constantly an object of the most gambling speculation.[85]

The moment opinion, regulated by experience, had liquidated the value of the funds, speculation would be confined within the limits necessary to give them due activity & value. The immutability of the provision by furnishing better data of calculation as well as giving security would hasten that moment & once arrived it would continue. The funds in this state would become as they ought to be an object of ordinary and temperate speculation like any other article whether of commerce manufactures or agriculture, while on the opposite plan they would be as long as they existed a mere game of chance & a subject of the most gambling speculation.

It may be remarked that it is now a considerable time since the public Stock has reached the desireable point & put an end to the excessive spirit of speculation. This has been for some time past far more active, even to intemperateness in other pursuits, in trading adventures and in lands. And it is curious to observe how little clamour there is against the spirit of speculation in its present direction; though it were not difficult to demonstrate that it is not less extravagant or pernicious in the shape of land-jobbing than in that of Stock-jobbing. But many of the noisy Patriots who were not in condition to be stock-jobbers, are land-jobbers, and have a becoming tenderness for this species of extravagance. And virtuous sensible men lamenting the partial ills of all over-driven speculation know at the same time that they are inseparable from the spirit & freedom of Commerce & that the cure must result from the disease.

Another important effect of funding the Debt was the quick appreciation of the funds from the same opinion of security. This was calculated to save immense sums to the Country. Foreigners else would have become the proprietors of the Stock at great under-values to the loss of millions to the holders and to the Country. The loss to the holders is perceived at once but the loss to the country though an obvious consequence has not been equally palpable to all.

85. In the margin opposite this paragraph H wrote and then crossed out: "Examine the question whether Debts should have been capable of being transferred to foreigners."

But a little reflection & combination must make it evident to the meanest capacity. If the sale of any article is made at an under value by one citizen to another of the same country what one loses the other gains—and [the] country containing within its own bosom the gainer as well as the loser is neither the richer nor the poorer by the operation. It possesses exactly the same property which it had before the bargain between its two citizens. But when the citizen of one country sells to the citizen of another Country residing abroad any article at an under-value a more valuable thing goes out of the Country in exchange for a less valuable thing which is brought into [it]—and the state whose citizen is the seller loses in exact proportion to the difference of value of the things exchanged whether commodity for commodity or commodity for money—that is the state loses exactly what its citizen loses by the disadvantageous sale.

It has been imagined however that if our debt had not been funded, its precariousness would have been a security against transfers to foreigners. But waving the observation, that this precariousness which it is supposed would deter foreigners would imply a depreciation and discredit of the funds and consequently a bad state of national credit, it may be replied that the effect expected from it would not have been realized.

Foreigners who possessed redundant capitals would still have devoted a part of them to play in those precarious Stocks, to buy and to sell again. And though permanent transfers of the Stock might not have taken place in the same degree; yet it is probable more property of the Country in another shape might have been extracted by the force of this gambling capital acting upon the occasional necessities & sporting with the occasional confidences of our citizens.

Another expedient has been mentioned for preventing alienations and consequently loss by alienations to foreigners. This was to forbid the alienations to foreigners in other words, to render them incapable of holding the Debt.

But this expedient was inadmissible and would have been ineffectual.

1 The original debt was alienable without restriction and foreigners had actually become the bona [fide] proprietors of a considerable sum of it which they had an indisputable title to a provi-

sion for & it was not easy in many cases to distinguish between past & future acquisition, without danger of interfering with rights already acquired.

2 The original debt being in its constitution alienable without restriction, which was an ingredient of value to the holder, it could not have been taken away without breach of contract, unless with his consent upon an equivalent, and this would have increased the embarrassment of such a modification of the Debt with consent of the creditors as would consist with the contract & with the immediate requisite accommodation of the Government.

3 It was ineligible as calculated to diminish the value of the Stock. All restraints upon alienanation by fettering the free use and circulation of an article of property naturally lessen its value. As far as foreign Capital could have been excluded from the Stock Market the effect would have been sensible upon it. It is evident that the value of an article must depend materially on the quantity of Capital employed in its negotiations; and it is known that foreign has formed & must have formed a considerable portion of that which was employed on the funds.

But in fact this exclusion would not have been taken place.[86] Foreigners under the cover of citizens would have continued to speculate in the funds; but they would have given considerably less for them on account of the additional risk from the necessity of that cover, and it might have happened that fewer of those solid & discreet capitals who meant to hold would have engaged in the business and more of those who meant a temporary profit proportioned to the risk, and in the end the probability was that the price of Stock would have been much lower & less steady and that foreigners would have had much of the property either in the shape of Stock in trust or in equivalents resulting from the traffic in it as if there was not restriction & for a less compensation to the country. This has been exemplified in the case of our waste lands in those States which do not permit foreigners to hold.[87]

The only effect then of the restriction would have been to de-

86. In the margin opposite this paragraph H wrote: "Note lowness of bonds obliges the public to give high prices for all it borrows."

87. For a discussion of alien ownership of land, see Robert Morris to H, June 7, 1795, note 37.

preciate the Stock of the Country the thermometre of its credit
without any counterballancing good.

Indeed if the exclusion of foreigners would have been effected
cui bono? What harm is there that foreigners should speculate in
our funds, if they give full value for them? Will not the money
they give for the Stock employed in extending our commerce agriculture & manufactures roads canals & other ameliorations more than
indemnify the Country for the interest which they will receive upon
the Stock till the principal is reimbursed? In a country with so much
improveable matter in a crude state as ours it cannot be doubted that
Capital employed in those ways will incomparably more than repay
the interest of the money employed.

But to overthrow this important consideration it is alleged that the
money acquired by the sales of Stock to foreigners would not be
employed on the objects which have been mentioned but would be
dissipated in the enjoyments of luxury and extravagance and sent
abroad again to pay for these objects to the loss *pro tanto* of the
Country?

This suggestion was not founded in probab[il]ity nor has been
warranted by the fact. It was true that a large increase of active
Capital and augmentation of private fortunes would beget some augmentation of expence among individuals and that a portion of this
expence would be laid out on foreign articles of luxury. But the proportion which this employment of the new Capital would bear to
the part of it which would be employed on useful and profitable objects would be and has been inconsiderable. Whoever will impartially look around will see that the great body of the new Capital
created by the Stock has been employed in extending commerce,
agriculture, manufactures, and other improvements. Our own *real*
navigation has been much increased. Our external commerce is carried on much more upon our own capitals than it was—our marine
insurances in a much greater proportion are made by ourselves. Our
manufactures are increased in number and carried on upon a larger
scale. Settlements of our waste land are progressing with more vigour than at any former period. Our Cities and Towns are increasing
rapidly by the addition of new and better houses. Canals are opening, bridges are building with more spirit & effect than was ever
known at a former period. The value of lands has risen every where.

These circumstances (though other causes may have cooperated) it cannot be doubted by a well informed or candid man are imputable in a great degree to the increase of Capital in public Debt and they prove that the predictions of its dissipation in luxurious extravagances have not been verified. If a part has gone in that way this loss has not been considerable enough to impair the force of the argument. The universal vivification of the energies of industry has laid the foundation of benefits far greater than the interest to be paid to foreigners can counterballance as a disadvantage.

Indeed it is a question whether there has not been an incidental advantage equivalent to the incidental disadvantage of an increased expence in foreign articles. It is the restoration of Stock alienated to the Country by the emigration to it of foreign settlers with Capitals. It may be said that this advantage is foreign to the operation of the plan, it arises from other causes growing out of the state of Europe. But it is to be remembered that collateral facilities, when dispositions to a certain event exist, contribute to give them an effect which they would not have without those facilities. The convenient mode of transfering property to this Country, through the medium of our Stock in the markets of Europe, has materially promoted the imigration of persons possessed of Capital. And if our Government continues to operate in a manner which will mai[n]tain the confidence of foreigners it is a question whether the possession of large sums in our funds will not bring over most of the proprietors so as to reinvest the Country with the alienated Stock, and thus procure it a double compensation on foreign alienations.

A third important effect of giving solidity & stability to the Stock, by funding the Debt, was the rendering it useful as Capital. Those who may deny that it has even this tendency in defiance of the most manifest facts, cannot dispute that it must have it, if at all, in proportion to the security of the footing upon which it stands.

The opinion of it being a safe & substantial property is essential to that ready marketable quality which will render it expedient to invest unemployed monies in it till the opportunity of employment occurs and certain that it can be brought into action when the opportunity arrives.

To be certain of its operation as active Capital it is only necessary to consider that it is *property which can almost at any moment be turned into money*. All property is Capital, that which can quickly and at all times be converted into money is active capital. It is nearly the same thing as if the possessor had an equal sum of money on hand.

The profound and ingenious HUME thus describes its effects.[88]

Who doubts that a man who has in his desk 10000 Dollars in good bank Notes has that sum of active capital? Who doubts any more, though there be two steps in the process, that a man who has in his hand 10000 Dollars of the notes of Merchants of unquestionable solidity and Credit which he can at any moment discount at the Banks has an equal sum, bating the price of discount, of active Capital? Who can doubt any more that the possession of 10000 Dollars of funded Stock which he can readily carry into the market & sell for 10000 Dollars of these merchant's or bank notes or gold & silver is equally possessor of so much of active Capital?

In this Country, where the sum of gold & silver the great organ of alienation & circulation, is comparitively more limited than in Europe, the certainty of an immediate conversion of Stock into money is not as great as in some of the great Stock markets of Europe, but the difference is not so material as to prevent the effect being substantially the same.

When the Stock is unfunded & precarious its saleableness [89] is proportionably fluctuating and uncertain, so much so that it does not

---

88. H left a blank space in the MS, which he presumably intended to fill in with the following quotation from David Hume's essay "Of Public Credit": "Public securities are with us become a kind of money, and pass as readily at the current price as gold or silver. Wherever any profitable undertaking offers itself, however expensive, there are never wanting hands enow to embrace it; nor need a trader, who has sums in the public stocks, fear to launch out into the most extensive trade; since he is possest of funds, which will answer the most sudden demand that can be made upon him. No merchant thinks it necessary to keep by him any considerable cash. . . . In short, our national debts furnish merchants with a species of money, that is continually multiplying in their hands, and produces sure gain, beside the profits of their commerce. This must enable them to trade upon less profit. The small profit of the merchant renders the commodity cheaper; causes a greater consumption; quickens the labour of the common people; and helps to spread arts and industry thro' the whole society" (Hume, *Political Discourses* [Edinburgh: Printed by R. Fleming, For A. Kincaid and A. Donaldson, 1752], 128–29).

89. In MS, H wrote "vendibleness" over "saleableness."

possess the quality of active Capital but inverts the effect by becoming a mere subject of gambling speculation. This was noticed in my first Report on the finances in these words (quote words) [90]

Some Theoretical Writers on Political œconomy have contested the effect of public funds as Capital.

Their objections and an answer to them are to be found in my Report on manufactures (recite in *here verba*) [91]

It may be useful to add some further illustrations—Trace the progress of a public Debt in a particular case.

The Government borrows of an individual 100 Dollars in specie, for which it gives its funded bonds. These hundred dollars are expended on some branch of the public service. Tis evident they are not annihilated, they only pass from the individual who lent to the individual or individuals to whom the Government has disbursed them. They continue in the hands of their new masters to perform their usual functions, as capital. But besides this the lender has the bonds of the Government for the sum lent. These from their negotiable and easily vendible nature can at any moment be applied by him to any useful or profitable undertaking which occurs; and thus the Credit of the Government produces a new & additional Capital equal to one hundred dollars the equivalent for the interest on that sum temporarily diverted from other employt. while passing into & out of the public coffers, which continues its instrumentality as a Capital while it remains not reimbursed.

When indeed the money borrowed by the Government is sent abroad to be expended the effect above described does not happen, unless the expenditure is for a purpose which brings a return. But this is a partial exception to the general rule.

90. This is a reference to the following section of H's "Report Relative to a Provision for the Support of Public Credit," January 9, 1790: "But these good effects of a public debt are only to be looked for, when, by being well funded, it has acquired an *adequate* and *stable* value. Till then, it has rather a contrary tendency. The fluctuation and insecurity incident to it in an unfunded state, render it a mere commodity, and a precarious one. As such, being only an object of occasional and particular speculation, all the money applied to it is so much diverted from the more useful channels of circulation, for which the thing itself affords no substitute: So that, in fact, one serious inconvenience of an unfunded debt is, that it contributes to the scarcity of money."

91. At this point H presumably intended to insert material from his "Report on Manufactures," December 5, 1791. For this material, see *The Papers of Alexander Hamilton*, X, 277–83.

It has been said that from the sum of the Debt acting as Capital is to be deducted the quantity of money actually employed in the negotiation of the funds. To conceive well of the immense disparity between the capital negotiated & the organ of negotiation, money, it may be useful to advert to the small quantity of specie in certain nations of immense capital in fixed & negotiable property. The specie of Great Britain for example is computed as from 15 to 20000000 Stg. How small a sum to be the organ of all the alienations of landed property, ships merchandize manufactures public funds and of insurance and other pecuniary negotiations.

The Capital value of its lands is esimated at   .[92] The public funds amount to near   . The objects of foreign and domestic commerce including manufactures and other capital objects cannot be estimated at less than   . Yet the small sum of from 16 to 20 millions of specie is directly and indirectly the instrument of all the alienations of this prodigious mass. This gives us an idea of the vast activity of the power.

A simple concise and yet comprehensive view of the effect of the funds as capital is comprised in this exhibition of it. To the mass of active capital resulting from the property and credit of all the individuals of the nation is added another mass constituted on the *joint* credit of the whole Nation and existing in the shape of the Government Stock, which continues till that Stock is extinguished by redemption or reimbursement. Is it not evident that this throwing into the common Stock of individual operations the Credit of the Nation must increase & invigorate the powers of industrious enterprise?

See what a wonderful spectacle Great Britain exhibits. Observe the mature state of her agricultural improvements under auspices of large Capitals employed to that end. Consider the extent of her navigation and external Commerce. Note the huge & varied pile of her manufactures. See her factors and agents spread over the four quarters of the Globe doing a great part of the business of other nations by force of Capital. View the great extent of her marine insurances attracting to her a considerable portion of the profits of the Commerce of most other nations. View her in fine the Creditor of the World. Consider withal that her population does not exceed   [93]

92. The spaces in this paragraph were left blank in MS.
93. Space left blank in MS.

that all the gold & silver she contains does probably fall short of
20 000000 Stg, then ask whether there be not a strong presumption
that her public funds are a principal pillar of this astonishing edifice
as her own men of business generally believe?

But another and a powerful motive to the funding of the Debt
was that it would serve as one of the equivalents to be offered to
induce the public Creditors to consent voluntarily to those modifica-
tions of their claims which the public accommodation required.

The Public Debt of this Country as I stated in my first report
upon the finances was   .[94] There was no obligation to do more
than make provision annully for the Debt. The *funding* of it was no
part of the original contract. This therefore superadded a material
advantage for the Creditors to their primitive rights. The additional
security was a reasonable ingredient of commutation to be proposed
for something to be relinquished.*

Among individuals money lent for a length of time on personal
security frequently carries a higher interest than if lent on real security. The change from one to the other would be a fair ground
for a stipulation to lower the interest as the consideration. A Government need not fear imputations on its honor or loss of Credit, by
regulating itself in its money concerns according to the rules which
prevail among fair individuals.

The third feature of my plan was to provide in the first instance
for the foreign part of the general Debt in exact conformity with
the contracts concerning it.

The propriety of this has been uncontested and speaks for itself.
It would have been highly inexpedient and would have exposed our
credit abroad to have perplexed our creditors with any new propositions concerning their debts. Even the measure of endeavouring to
transfer the foreign debt to a domestic foundation, which has been
subsequently proposed upon equivalents to be given would have
been premature till confidence had been inspired by an experience
of the efficacy of the provision.

---

* Add by way of note such part of my report on the manufactures as shews
how.[95]

94. Space left blank in MS. In his "Report Relative to a Provision for the
Support of Public Credit," January 9, 1790, H stated that "the whole debt
of the United States" was $54,124,464.

95. See note 91.

The fourth feature was "to take as the basis of the provision for the domestic part of the general debt the contracts with the Creditors as they stood at the time of the adoption of the new constitution according to the then unrevoked acts & resolutions of the former Government, except as to such alterations as they might on legal principles be pronounced to have undergone by voluntary acts, and acquiescences of the Creditors themselves; bottoming the provision on these principles, that those contracts were to be fulfilled as far and as fast as was practicable and were not to be departed from without the free consent of the Creditors." [96]

To a man who thinks justly and feels rightly for the reputation of the Country of which he is a citizen, it is a humiliating reflection that it should be at all necessary to insist on the propriety of regulating the provision for the debt by the contracts concerning it.

The obligation to fulfil contracts is so fundamental a principle of private morality and social justice so essential a basis of national Credit that nothing less than the fact itself could induce a belief that the application of the rule to our public Debt could have been controverted by leaders of parties or by any considerable portion of the community. Yet in truth it has been controverted either avowedly or virtually by a great proportion of all parties; by declarations or propositions disclaiming the application of the principle or by the rejection of propositions necessary to give it effect.

The general proposition indeed which affirms the obligation of fulfilling contracts on Governments as well as individuals was of a nature which the most profligate politican was not shameless enough to deny.

But it has been contended that the case of our public debt was an extraordinary & peculiar case, justifying principles of national Justice and Policy a departure from common rules. The quantity of alloy in its original concoction, the extensive alienations at undervalues the extreme point of depreciation for a certain period—the confused state of the debt by antecedent violations of contract & by the concession of partial advantages to particular descriptions of it— the impossibility of reinstating the primitive contracts which had been formerly violated—& the inequality of a full provision according to the new—All these were urged or espoused as reasons for an

96. This quotation appears at an earlier point in this essay.

arbitrary provision for the Debt according to certain abstract notions of Equity & right.

It has been intimated that these heretics were divided into two
principal classes one which advocated a provision for the debt on
the ground of a discrimination between original holders & alienees,
another which advocated an equal provision for all at some arbitrary
rate of interest inferior to the stipulated rates.

The first was apparently at least subdivided into three lesser sects
—one which contended for providing in favour of original holders
according to the terms of the contract and in cases of alienation by
a kind of composition or compromise between the original holders
and alienees which in the course of the debate in Congress took the
specific form of giving 10/ in the pound to one and the same to the
other, another which contended for a full provision for original
holders who had not alienated and for an inferior one to alienees
without regarding the original holders who had alienated, a third
for a reliquidation of the Debt making a full provision according to
that reliquidation for original holders and an inferior one for alienees with or without regard to the creditors who alienated.[97]

The second general sect had also a diversity of opinions, some
willing to allow a higher, some a lower rate of interest, some willing to fix the standard absolutely without compensations for the reduction others willing to give some kind of equivalent but to make

97. The congressional debate on H's "Report Relative to a Provision for
the Support of Public Credit," January 9, 1790, began on February 8, 1790.
Three days later James Madison proposed a motion in favor of discrimination
between original holders and alienees. According to Madison, there were four
classes of public creditors:
"*First*, Original creditors, who have never alienated their securities.
"*Second*, Original creditors who have alienated.
"*Third*, Present holders of alienated securities.
"*Fourth*, Intermediate holders, through whose hands securities have circulated." (*Annals of Congress*, I, 1234.) Madison observed that "The only
rival pretensions . . . are those of the original creditors, who have assigned,
and of the present holders of the assignments" (*Annals of Congress*, I, 1235).
His motion reads: "*Resolved*, That adequate funds ought to be provided for
paying the interest and principal of the domestic debt, as the same shall be
liquidated; and that in such liquidation, the present holders of public securities, which have been alienated, shall be settled with according to the
highest market rate of such securities; and that the balance of the sums due
from the public, be paid in such proportion to the original holder of such
securities" (*Annals of Congress*, I, 1237-38). Madison was supported by James
Jackson of Georgia, and Andrew Moore, Alexander White, and John Page
of Virginia. On February 16, 1790, Jackson stated to the House: "Public jus-

the provision absolute & final leaving no option to the Creditors.[98]

The latter when the subject was under debate made no direct propositions but then and since they discovered their intentions in their conversations in endeavouring to pare down the provision proposed in my report and in resisting in subsequent cases a compliance with the contracts as to those Creditors who have not accepted the terms held out to them.

The former made a formal & passionate effort to substitute their scheme to that which was contained in the plan reported from the Treasury. It failed but it has laid the foundation of the great schism which has since prevailed.[99]

There never was a doubt that if the idea of the discrimination had obtained it would have resulted in a fraud on alienees without benefit to the alienors. A large proportion of those who supported the principle of discrimination clearly manifested that they meant to leave the difference in the public pocket.

The substance of the argument for a discrimination was this: [100]

---

tice . . . had not been done; the soldiers, the original creditors, had not been paid; they had not received the equivalent; they had received but two shillings and six pence, and there was twenty shillings due them. . . .

"A gentleman (Mr. [William] Smith [of Maryland]) had observed, that this plan places those who have alienated in a better situation than the present original holder, by adding the ten shillings to what he formerly received. He [Jackson] contended, that the present original creditor would not be injured, nor would they grumble at seeing justice done their more distressed brethren; those who had parted with them had done it, in most instances, from necessity; those who hold at present, are the more wealthy." (*Annals of Congress*, I, 1268–69.)

98. On February 21, 1790, Senator William Maclay of Pennsylvania drew up the following resolutions: "*Resolved*, That funds be immediately provided sufficient to pay three per cent on the domestic debt of the United States. . . .

"*Resolved*, That a land-office be opened for the sale of the Western territory, in which certificates of the domestic debt only shall be receivable, to operate as a sinking-fund for the extinguishment of the said debt, and the arrears of interest due on the same." Maclay approached Madison with these resolutions on February 22, but Madison proved unresponsive (Charles A. Beard, ed., *The Journal of William Maclay, United States Senator from Pennsylvania, 1789–1791* [New York, 1927], 195–97).

99. Madison's motion was defeated on February 22, 1790, by a vote of thirty-six to thirteen (*Annals of Congress*, II, 1344).

100. This essay ends at this point in the middle of the MS page.

Horatius No. II

[New York, July, 1795] [1]

To The People of the U States   No. II [2]

Countrymen & Fellow Citizens

Nothing can be more false or ridiculous, candidly considered, than the assertion that great sacrifices of your interests are made in the Treaty with Great Britain. As to the controverted points between the Two Nations, the Treaty provides satisfactorily for the great and essential ones; and only foregoes objects of an inferior and disputable nature, of no real consequence to the permanent welfare of the Country. As to Trade the dilemma is this; if an article is added for granting us such privileges in the British West Indies as are satisfactory to us,[3] it will give a duration of *twelve* years to the Treaty [4] & will render it as good a one as the most sanguine could desire, and a better one than any other powers of Europe *can* make with us: For no other power of Europe can give us the advantages in the East Indies, which this Treaty confers.[5] If that article be not added, the

---

ADf, Hamilton Papers, Library of Congress.

1. This essay is incorrectly dated "May, 1795" in *JCHW*, VIII, 169, and in *HCLW*, V, 181, for the subject of the essay is the Jay Treaty, the provisions of which were not made public until June 29, 1795. See H to Oliver Wolcott, Jr., June 26, 1795, note 1.

2. "Horatius No. I" has not been found.

3. This is a reference to the manner in which the Senate consented to the Jay Treaty by suspending part of Article 12 and providing for a supplementary article to the treaty. See H to Rufus King, June 11, 1795, notes 2 and 3.

4. Article 28 of the Jay Treaty reads in part: "It is agreed that the first Ten Articles of this Treaty shall be permanent and that the subsequent Articles except the Twelfth shall be limited in their duration to Twelve years to be computed from the Day on which the Ratifications of this Treaty shall be exchanged, but subject to this Condition that whereas the said Twelfth Article will expire by the Limitation therein contained at the End of two years from the signing of the Preliminary or other Articles of Peace, which shall terminate the present War, in which his Majesty is engaged. . . ." For the full text of this article, see "Remarks on the Treaty . . . between the United States and Great Britain," July 9–11, 1795, note 78.

5. United States trade with the East Indies is covered in Article 13 of the Jay Treaty. For the text of this article, see "Remarks on the Treaty . . . between the United States and Great Britain," July 9–11, 1795, note 54.

commercial part of the Treaty will expire in *two* years; after the present war, by its own limitation.[6] It is therefore preposterous to talk of great sacrifices in a commercial sense. This observation is to be understood with the exception of the third article; which regulates the Trade between us and the neighbouring British territories, which is permanent, and which is certainly a precious article; inevitably throwing into our lap the greatest part of the furr Trade with the Trade of the two Canadas.[7] This is a full answer to the idle tale of sacrifices by the Treaty as the pretext for violating Your constitution and for sullying your faith and your honor.

It is an unquestionable truth, fellow Citizens! and one which it is essential you should understand, that the great and cardinal *sin* of the Treaty in the eyes of its adversaries is that it *puts an end to controversy* with Great Britain. We have a sect of politicians among us, who influenced by a servile and criminal subserviency to the views of France have adopted it as a fundamental tenet that there ought to subsist between us and Great Britain eternal variance and discord.

What we now see is a part of the same system which led the Ministry of Louis the 16 insidiousness to advise our Commissioners for making peace to treat with Great Britain without the acknowlegement of our Independence; wishing that the omission of this acknowlegement might perpetuate a jealousy and dread of Great Britain and occasion a greater necessity for our future dependence on France.[8]

It is a part of the same system, which during our War with Great Britain produced a resolution of our public Councils, without adequate motive or equivalent, to sacrifice the navigation of the Missisippi to Spain; and which also begat a disposition to abandon our claim to an equal participation in the Codfisheries.

It is a part of the same disgraceful system which fettered our Commissioners for making peace with the impolitic & humiliating instruction to submit all their motions to the direction of the French

6. See note 4.
7. For the text of Article 3 of the Jay Treaty, see "Remarks on the Treaty . . . between the United States and Great Britain," July 9-11, 1795, note 8.
8. For a recent discussion of the contents of this paragraph, see Richard B. Morris, *The Peacemakers: The Great Powers and American Independence* (New York, 1965), 282 ff.

Cabinet—and which attempted a censure upon them for breaking through that system, and in consequence of it effecting a peace glorious and advantageous for the Country, beyond expectation.

The present Rulers of France have proclaimed to the world the insidious and unfriendly policy of the former Government towards this Country. Their successors may hereafter unmask equally insidious and unfriendly views in the present rulers.

But if you are as discerning, as I believe you to be you will not wait for this evidence to form your opinion. You will see in the conduct of the Agents of that Government, wherever they are, that they are machinating against your independence peace and happiness; that not content with a fair competition in your trade on terms of equal privilege they are labouring to continue you at variance with Great Britain, in order that you may be dependent on France.

This conduct in the known Agents of a foreign Government is not to be wondered at. It marks the usual and immemorial policy of all the Governments of Europe.

But that any of your Countrymen, that men who have been honored with your suffrages should be the supple instruments of this crooked policy, that they should stoop to nourish and foster this exotic plant and should exchange the pure and holy love of their own Country for a meritricious foreign amour—that they should be willing to sacrifice your interests to their animosity against one foreign Nation and their devotion for another is justly matter of surprise and indignation. No terms of reprobation [9] are too severe for so faithless and so unworthy a Conduct.

Reason, Religion, Philosophy, Policy, disavow the spurious and odious doctrine that we ought to cherish and cultivate enmity with any Nation whatever. In reference to a Nation with whom we have such extensive relations of Commerce as with Great Britain—to a power, from her maritime strength, so capable of annoying us—it must be the offspring of treachery or extreme folly. If you consult your true interest Your Motto cannot fail to be "Peace and Trade with all Nations; beyond our present engagements, political connection with none" You ought to spurn from you as the box of Pandora—the fatal heresy of close alliance, or in the language of

9. In MS, "repropration."

Genet a true *family compact* with France.[10] This would at once make you a mere satellite of France, and entangle you in all the contests broils, and wars of Europe.

Tis evident that the Controversies of Europe must often grow out of causes intirely foreign to this Country. Why then should we by a close political connection with any power of Europe expose our peace & interest as a matter of course to all the shocks with which their mad rivalships and wicked ambition so frequently convulse the earth? 'Twere insanity to embrace such a system. The avowed and secret partisans of it merit our contempt for their folly or our execration for their depravity.   HORATIUS

10. On May 23, 1793, Edmond Charles Genet, who was then French Minister to the United States, wrote to Secretary of State Thomas Jefferson: "The French republic . . . has charged me to propose to your government to establish, in a true family compact, that is, in a national compact, the liberal and fraternal basis, on which she wishes to see raised the commercial and political system of two People, all whose interests are confounded" (*ASP, Foreign Relations*, I, 147).
ADf, Hamilton Papers, Library of Congress; *The* [New York] *Argus, or Greenleaf's New Daily Advertiser*, August 1, 1794.

The Defence No. IV [1]

[New York, August 1, 1795]

An accurate enumeration of the breaches of the Treaty of peace on our part would require a tedious research. It will suffice to select and quote a few of the most prominent and early instances.

One of the earliest is to be found in an Act of this state for granting a more effectual relief in cases of certain Trespasses passed the 17 of March 1783.[2]

1. For background to this document, see the introductory note to "The Defence No. I," July 22, 1795.
2. *New York Laws*, 6th Sess., Ch. XXXI. On March 5, 1792, George Hammond, British Minister to the United States, wrote to Thomas Jefferson "an abstract of such particular acts of the United States as appear to me infractions, on their part, of the definitive treaty of peace, concluded between the king, my master, and the United States." At the end of this letter there is an appendix consisting of a list of state laws that Hammond considered violations of the treaty. On May 29, 1792, Jefferson replied to Hammond's letter and discussed in considerable detail each of Hammond's allegations. The New York act of March 17, 1783, as well as all the other state statutes which H

This act takes away from any person (subjects of Great Britain of every description included) who had during the war occupied injured destroyed or received property real or personal of any inhabitant without the British lines the benefit of the plea of a military order; consequently the justification which the laws and usages of war give, and the immunity resulting from the reciprocal amnesty which expressly or virtually is an essential part of every Treaty of peace. To this it may be added, that it was considered by Great Britain as a direct infraction of the 6th article of her Treaty with us, which exempts all persons from prosecution "by reason of the part they might have taken in the War." [3]

Mr. Jefferson, not controverting the point that the provisions of this act were contrary to the Treaty, endeavours to get rid of the inference from it, by alleging three things.[4]

1st. That it passed antecedently to the Treaty, and so could not be a violation of an act of subsequent date.

2 That the Treaty was paramount [to] the laws of the particular States & operated a repeal of them.

3 That the exceptionable principle of this act was never sanctioned by the Courts of Justice and in one instance (the case of Rutgers and Waddington in the Mayors Court) [5] was overruled.

As to the first point, it is sufficient to answer that the law continued to operate, *in fact*, from the time of the Treaty till the 4th of April 1787, when there was a repeal of the exceptionable clause by an act of our legislature.[6] During this period of four years, many suits were brought and many recoveries had—extending even to persons who had been in the military service of Great Britain.

To the second point, these observations may be opposed.

---

mentions in "The Defence No. IV," is considered by both Hammond and Jefferson, whose letters on this subject are printed in *ASP, Foreign Relations*, I, 193–237.

3. For the text of Article 6 of the definitive peace treaty, see Miller, *Treaties*, II, 155.

4. See Jefferson to Hammond, May 29, 1792 (ADf, Thomas Jefferson Papers, Library of Congress). This letter is printed in *ASP, Foreign Relations*, I, 201–37.

5. For the full and authoritative treatment of this case and H's part in it, see Goebel, *Law Practice*, I, 282–419. See also H to Jefferson, April 19, May 20–27, 1792.

6. See "Remarks on the Treaty . . . between the United States and Great Britain," July 9–11, 1795, note 30.

The articles of confederation did not like our present constitution declare that Treaties were *supreme laws* of the land. The U States under that system had no courts of their own to expound and enforce their Treaties as laws. All was to depend on the comparitive authority of laws and Treaties in the judgment of the State Courts.

The question, whether Treaties were paramount to and a virtual repeal of antecedent laws was a question of theory, about which there was room for, and in this country did exist much diversity of opinion. It is notorious, that it has been strenuously maintained that however a national Treaty ought in good faith to be conclusive upon a state to induce a repeal of laws contrary to it—yet its actual laws could not be controuled [7] by Treaty without an actual repeal by its own authority. This doctrine has been emphatically that of the party distinguished by its opposition to national principles.

And it is observable that Congress not relying intirely upon the force of the Treaty to abrogate contravening laws, in their address already cited,[8] urge the states to a repeal of those laws. It is likewise observiable in respect to the very act under consideration that the Legislature of this State in April 1787 thought a positive repeal of the exceptionable clause necessary.[9]

The complaints of a power, whose treaty with us was *in fact* violated by the operation of a state law, could never be satisfactorily answered by referring to a *theoretic abstract disputed* proposition. Such a power might reply with irresistible force. Tis not for us to concern ourselves about the structure or meaning of your political constitutions, or the force of the legal maxims deducible from the forms and distributions of power which you have adopted for your Government—'tis the *fact*, in which alone we are interested. You have stipulated *this* and *that* to us. Your stipulation in practice is contravened. Tis your duty to see that there is no impediment from conflicting authorities within yourselves to the exact fulfilment of your promises. If you suffer any such impediment to exist, you are answerable for the consequences.

As to the third point it is to be observed that though there may have been no express formal decision of our Courts enforcing the

7. In the newspaper this word is "controverted."
8. See "The Defence No. III," July 29, 1795, note 6.
9. See note 6.

exceptionable principle of the Trespass act—yet there never was a decision of a superior Court against it. And it may not be amiss to remark incidentally that the decision of the Mayors Court from which Mr. Jefferson is glad to derive an exculpation of our conduct [10] was the object of severe animadversion at a popular meeting in this City as a judiciary encroachment on the legislative authority of the State.[11]

The truth on this point is that according to the general opinion of our bar a defence under a military order was desperate; and it was believed that a majority of our Supreme Court Bench would overrule the plea. Hence in numerous cases where it might have been used it was waved; and the endeavour on behalf of defendants was either to effect on collateral grounds a mitigation of damages or to accomplish the best compromises that could be obtained. Even the suit of Rutgers & Waddington after a partial success in the Mayors Court was terminated by a compromise according to the advice of the defendants counsel owing to the apprehension of an

10. See Jefferson to Hammond, May 29, 1792 (ADf, Thomas Jefferson Papers, Library of Congress; *ASP, Foreign Relations*, I, 201–37).

11. This meeting was held on September 13, 1784. On the day of the meeting, the following notice, addressed "To the CITIZENS of NEW-YORK," appeared in *The New-York Packet. And the American Advertiser:* "You are invited to meet at Mrs. Vandewater's on Monday evening, for the purpose of taking measures in consequence of the late decision in the Mayor's Court, in the cause of Rutgers and Waddington. Before you accept this invitation, let me request you to reflect on the impropriety and danger of meddling in this business. . . . Is not the Mayor's Court an inferior court of limited jurisdiction? and if that court has erred in a point of law, is there not a natural and easy remedy—an appeal to the Supreme Court by writ of error? If that Court should not reverse but confirm the sentence of the Mayor's Court, is there not still left a further and higher mode of legal and constitutional redress—an appeal to the Court ordained by the thirty-second article of the constitution, for the trial of impeachments and the correction of errors? a Court which will consist of one branch of the Legislature, to wit, the Senate, together with the Chancellor, and Judges of the Supreme Court? . . .

"If the Judges of the Mayor's Court have acted erroneously, let their error be rectified by an appeal to a higher tribunal; if they have acted corruptly, let them be impeached. This last is the proper business of the Legislature, and let us leave the Legislature to their own business." The *Packet* did not give an account of the meeting, but its issue of November 4, 1784, contained an open letter to the people of the state of New York from a committee which had been set up at the meeting. This letter is printed in Henry B. Dawson, *The Case of Elizabeth Rutgers versus Joshua Waddington, Determined in the Mayor's Court, in the City of New York, August 7, 1786. With an Historical Introduction* (Morrisania, New York, 1866), xxv–xl. See also Goebel, *Law Practice*, I, 289, note 17; 313, note 85.

unfavourable issue in the Supreme Court; and this notwithstanding the defendant was a British subject.

It is pertinent to remark, that the British Commander in Chief very early remonstrated against this act, but the remonstrance produced no effect.[12]

Under these circumstances which are faithfully represented, is it possible to doubt that the Act in question operated a breach of our Treaty with Great Britain? and this from the very commencement of its existence? Can we reasonably expect that the nations with whom we have treaties will allow us to substitute theoretic problems to performances of our engagements, and will be willing to accept them as apologies for actual violations?

Another Act of the State of New York may be cited as a violation of the Treaty on our part which must have been nearly cotemporary with that of the detention of the posts. Its date is the 12 of May 1784.[13] This act confirms in express terms all confiscations before made, nothwithstanding errors in the proceedings, and takes away the writ of error upon any judgment previously rendered.

This was in substance a new confiscation. Judgments which from error were invalid were nullities. To take away the writ of error by which their nullity might be established was to give them an efficacy which they did not before possess—and as to the operation cannot be distinguished from the rendering of new judgments. To make voidable acts of confiscation valid and conclusive is equivalent to new acts of confiscation. A fair execution of the Treaty required that every thing in this respect should be left where it was and forbade the remedying of defects in former proceedings as much as the institution of new   .[14]

Another and an unequivocal breach of the Treaty is found in an Act of South Carolina of March 26. 1784.[15] This Act suspends the

12. See "Remarks on the Treaty . . . between the United States and Great Britain," July 9–11, 1795, note 34.

In the newspaper version this paragraph is printed after the succeeding one.

13. "An Act for the speedy Sale of the Confiscated and forfeited Estates within this State, and for other Purposes therein mentioned" (*New York Laws*, 7th Sess., Ch. LXIV).

14. At this point H wrote and crossed out the word "proceedings." In the newspaper version the conclusion of this sentence reads: "as much as the institution of new judgments."

15. See "Remarks on the Treaty . . . between the United States and Great Britain," July 9–11, 1795, note 36.

recovery of British Debts for nine months, and then allows them
to be recovered only in four yearly installments cont[r]ary to the
express stipulation of the 4th article *"that Creditors on either side
shall meet with no lawful impediment to the recovery of the full
value in Sterling money of all* BONA FIDE *debts theretofore contracted"*.

It is idle to attempt to excuse infractions of this kind by the
pleas of distress and inability. This is to make the convenience of
one party the measure of its obligation to perform its promises to
another. If there was really an impossibility of payment, as has been
pretended, there was no need of legislative obstruction. The thing
would have regulated itself, and the very interest of the creditor was
a pledge that no general evil could have resulted from allowing a
free course to the laws. If such impediments could be justified, what
impediments might not be justified? What would become of the
Article—the only one in the Treaty to be performed by us of real
consequence to Great Britain?

This infraction by South Carolina was prior to that of the detention of the Posts by Great Britain.

But the case of Virginia is still stronger than that of South Carolina. There is evidence which cannot be disputed that her courts
in defiance of the Treaty have constantly remained shut to the recovery of British Debts, in virtue of laws passed during the War.

An Act of her General Assembly of the 22 of June 1784 [16] after
suggesting as breaches of the Treaty by Great Britain the carrying
off of the negroes and the detention of the posts, after instructing
her delegates in Congress to request a remonstrance to the British
Court complaining of those infractions and desiring reparation, and
after declaring that the national honor and interest of the Citizens
of that commonwealth obliged the Assembly *to* WITHOLD *their cooperation in the complete fulfilment of the said Treaty* until the
success of the aforementioned remonstrance is known, or Congress
shall signify their sentiments touching the premises—concludes with
the following resolution:

"That *so soon as* reparation is made for the foregoing infraction,

16. This was not an act but a series of resolutions made by the Virginia
House of Delegates on June 22, 1784. See "Remarks on the Treaty . . . between the United States and Great Britain," July 9-11, 1795, notes 37 and 38.

or Congress shall judge it indispensably necessary, such acts of the legislature *passed during the late war as inhibit the recovery of British Debts ought to be repealed and payment thereof made in such time and manner as shall consist with the exhausted situation of the Commonwealth.*" [17]

The plain language of these resolutions is—that there were acts, passed during the War, which then actually inhibited the recovery of British Debts and that for the removal of this inhibition a repealing Act by the Authority of Virginia was necessary.

However unsound this position may have been in theory, it is conclusive evidence that the fact in Virginia was conformable with it—that her Courts had been ever since the peace, then were, and until a repealing law was passed were likely to continue to be, shut against the recovery of British Debts. When testimony of this kind was urged by the British Minister was it possible for our envoy to make any solid reply? Who could be supposed to know better than the Legislature of Virginia the real state of the fact? When that Legislature had declared it to be as has been stated who or what could contradict it? With what truth has it been asserted that "it was at all times *perfectly understood* that TREATIES CONTROULED the laws of of the States?" [18]

Additional Proof of the contrary is found in the subsequent conduct of Virginia. On the 12th of December 1787 that state passed an act repealing all such acts or parts of acts of the state as *had prevented* or *might prevent* the recovery of Debts due to British subjects according to the true intent of the Treaty; but with this proviso that there should be a suspension of the repeal till the Governor with advice of Council had by proclamation notified that Great Britain had delivered up the Posts and was taking measures for the further fulfilment of the Treaty by delivering up the negroes or making compensation for them.[19] This denotes clearly that in the opinion of the legislature of Virginia, there were acts of that

17. See "Remarks on the Treaty . . . between the United States and Great Britain," July 9–11, 1795, note 37. See also "The Defence No. III," July 29, 1795, note 5.

18. Jefferson made this statement in his letter to Hammond of May 29, 1792 (ADf, Thomas Jefferson Papers, Library of Congress; *ASP, Foreign Relations*, I, 201–37).

19. See "Remarks on the Treaty . . . between the United States and Great Britain," July 9–11, 1795, note 38.

State which *had prevented* and *might prevent* the recovery of Debts according to the Treaty.

It is observable too that the resolutions of June 1784 do not even give the expectation of a complete repeal of the impeding laws, in the event of a reparation of the breaches of Treaty by G: Britain. They only promise such a modification of them as would permit the payment *in such time and manner as should consist with the exhausted situation of the Commonwealth;* that is, not according to the true intent of the Treaty, but according to the opinion of the legislature of Virginia of the ability of the Commonwealth.

As the infraction, which these proceedings of Virginia admit, resulted from acts passed during the war, it of course was coeval with the first existence of the Treaty of peace—and seems to preclude the possibility of any prior breach of Great Britain. It has been at least demonstrated, that the detention of the posts was not such prior breach—as there was no obligation to surrender till after the exchange of the ratifications of the definitive Treaty in England.

I pass by the serious contraventions of the Treaty, in this important article of the Debts, which are of later date, because they do not affect the question of the first breach; though they are of great weight to demonstrate the obligation of the U States to make compensation.

The argument then, upon the whole, as to the question of first breach stands thus—It is a great doubt whether the carrying away of the negroes was at all a breach. If it was one, the Trespass Act [20] of this state preceded it in date and went into operation the very moment it was possible to issue process. The detention of the posts, is subsequent to breaches of the article concerning the recovery of Debts on our part. This in the case of South Carolina is determined by the date of her act (March the 26. 1784) which is before the exchange of the ratifications of the definitive Treaty could have taken place.[21] In that of Virginia it results from her own testimony, that impediments to the recovery of British Debts created by acts passed during the war continued from the first moment of the peace till after the war 1787. Or if contrary to our own interpreta-

20. See note 2.
21. Ratifications of the definitive treaty were exchanged on May 12, 1784 (Miller, *Treaties*, II, 151).

tion, we are disposed to adhere to the provisional treaty as the act from which performance was to date we were guilty of a breach in not acting ourselves upon that Treaty—a breach at least cotemporary with any that can be imputed to G Britain.[22] From all which it follows, that take what ground we will, we must be perplexed to fix the charge of the first breach of the Treaty upon Great Britain.

Let the appeal be to the understandings and hearts of candid men, men who have force of mind sufficient to rescue themselves from the trammels of prejudice and who dare to look even unpalatable truths in the face. Let such men pronounce whether they are still satisfied that Great Britain is clearly chargeable with the first breaches of the Treaty—whether they are not on the contrary convinced that the question is one so mixed and doubtful as to have rendered a waver of it even on the score of intrinsic merits expedient on our part—and principally whether they can entertain a particle of doubt, that it was wiser to wave it than to suffer it to prove a final obstacle to the adjustment of a controversy on which the peace of the Country was suspended.

This was undoubtedly the alternative to our Envoy. In the choice he made, the final opinion of an enlightened Country cannot fail to applaude his prudence. CAMILLUS

22. Instead of the words "a breach at least cotemporary with any that can be imputed to G Britain," the concluding part of this sentence in the newspaper reads: "a breach, which, being cotemporary with the existence of the treaty, seems not to admit of any prior contravention."

From George Washington

Mount Vernon 3d Augt 1795

Dear Sir,

The enclosed was written, as you will perceive, on the 29th. Ulto;[1] & with many other letters, was sent to the Post Office in Alexandria; to proceed with the Northern Mail next morning. But the blundering Post Master[2] of that place, in putting the letters addressed *to*, put all the letters *from me*, into my own bag: of course they were returned to me. Since which the unusual (at almost any season of the year), and violent rains which have fallen, have given such interruption to the Post, as to detain my letters 'till this time: and altho' I am now sending them to the Post Office, I have little expectation of their proceeding tomorrow; the waters being yet very high, & the bridges all gone. In short, the damage of *every* sort, is very great in these parts.   Yours always   G Washington

Colo Hamilton

ALS, Hamilton Papers, Library of Congress.
    1. Washington to H, July 29, 1795.
    2. James M. McRea.

From Oliver Wolcott, Junior

[*Philadelphia, August 3, 1795.* On August 5, 1795, Hamilton wrote to Wolcott: "I have received yours of the 3d instant." *Letter not found.*]

From William Bradford

Philada. Aug. 4. 1795.

My dear Sir,

The record of the proceedings in the cause relating to the Carriage Tax is not yet returned [1]—but I expect it this week. I learn however that Taylor, who has published his speech,[2] has advised the defendant to make no further argument & to let the Supreme Court do as they please & that in consequence of this advice no counsel will appear in support of the writ of Error. I have denied that the District Attorney [3] would take measures to counteract this manœvre which is of a piece with the rest of Taylor's conduct. Having succeeded in dividing the opinions of the Circuit Court, he wishes to prevent the Effect which a decision of the Supreme Court *on full argument* would have, & perhaps by the circulation of his pamphlet in the mean time to indispose the people of Virginia to paying the next annual duty on their Carriages. If the Defendant persists in pursuing this advice, I presume your attendance will not be necessary;[4] for in such case I would think it most advisable to submit the cause to the court upon the two arguments that have been already made. That of Mr. Wickham's,[5] has arrived in manuscript: that of Taylor we expect by the next post. I will take Care however to apprize you as soon as the record arrives what is to be expected.

In consequence of the situation of things & some new occurences, it has been thought advisable to request the president to return to Philada.[6] He is expected to be here next week.

The crazy speech of Mr. Rutledge [7] joined to certain information that he is daily sinking into debility of mind & body, will probably prevent him to receiving the appointment I mentioned to you.[8] But should he come to Philada. for that purpose, as he has been invited to do—& especially if he should resign his present Office [9]— the embarrassment of the President will be extreme—but if he is disordered in mind in the manner that I am informed he is, there can be but one course of procedure. I write in great haste, & can only add that I am with great regard

　　　Your friend & hum sert.　　　　　　　　　　WB.

Alexander Hamilton Esq.

ALS, Hamilton Papers, Library of Congress.
　　1. For information on the Carriage Tax case (*Hylton* v *United States*), see 3 Dallas, *U.S. Reports*, 171–84, and the forthcoming Goebel, *Law Practice*, III. See also Tench Coxe to H, January 14, 19, 1795; H to Coxe, January 26, 1795; Bradford to H, July 2, 1795; Edmund Randolph to H, July 21, 1795; Oliver Wolcott, Jr., to H, July 28, 1795.
　　2. For the speech of John Taylor of Caroline, see Bradford to H, July 2, 1795, notes 16 and 17.
　　3. William Rawle, United States attorney for the District of Pennsylvania.
　　4. H had been engaged an auxiliary counsel to the United States Government to defend the carriage tax. See Bradford to H, July 2, 1795; Randolph to H, July 21, 1795.
　　5. John Wickham, a noted lawyer in Richmond, Virginia.
　　6. See Wolcott to H, July 30, 1795, note 1.
　　7. This is a reference to a speech against the Jay Treaty which John Rutledge made on July 16, 1795, at a meeting at St. Michael's Church in Charleston, South Carolina. See Wolcott to H, July 28, 1795, note 3.
　　8. See Bradford to H, July 2, 1795.
　　9. Chief justice of South Carolina.

From Tench Coxe [1]

[Philadelphia, August 4, 1795]

Sir

I have been prevented from answering your last letter [2] partly by a journey into the woods, which I have since risqued in person to secure justice in laying the warrants under Ball & Smith, and partly by the difficulties arising with Messrs. Wheelen, Miller & Co. they had from me certain counter Notes for the Greater part of the Notes furnished by them, which I do assure you I was not able to procure after applications once or twice a week for a quarter of year. I have however within a few Days obtained the return of two of those counter Notes of mine, & a promise to search for & send me one more, which is not yet done. At present I am e[n]gaged in another question with them, which is, whether they are bound to give notes or Bonds for the 2d. & 3d. payments. This new difficulty will evince to you, what I have to contend with, & I have not yet got them to consent to the matter.

As I learn you are coming to Philada. on the Subject of the Carriage Tax, which will be argued before the approaching supreme Court,[3] opportunity will then be given for such adjustment as is now practicable.

I am, Sir,   your very obedt. hble. servant   Tench Coxe

Philada. August
th4. 1795
Alexr. Hamilton Esqr.
Atty. of J. B. Church Esqr.

Copy, Tench Coxe Papers, Historical Society of Pennsylvania, Philadelphia.
    1. For an explanation of the contents of this letter, see the introductory note to Coxe to H, February 13, 1795. See also Coxe to H, February 17–18, 22, May 10, 1795; H to Joseph Anthony, March 11, 1795; Anthony to H, May 16, 1795.
    2. Letter not found.
    3. For information on the Carriage Tax case (*Hylton* v *United States*), see 3 Dallas, *U.S. Reports*, 171–84, and the forthcoming Goebel, *Law Practice*, III. See also Coxe to H, January 14, 19, 1795; H to Coxe, January 26, 1795; William Bradford to H, July 2, August 4, 1795; Edmund Randolph to H, July 21, 1795; Oliver Wolcott, Jr., to H, July 28, 1795.

The Defence No. V[1]

[New York, August 5, 1795]

The discussion in the two last numbers has shewn if I mistake not, that this Country by no means stands upon such good ground with regard to the inexecution of the Treaty of peace as some of our official proceedings have advanced and as many among us have too lightly creditted. The task of displaying this truth has been an unwelcome one. As long as a contrary doctrine was either a mere essay of polemical skill or a convenient ingredient of negotiation it was natural for those who thought indifferently of it to prefer silence to contradiction. But when it is made the engine of great errors of national conduct of excessive pretensions which forbid a reasonable accommodation of national differences and endanger rupture and war on grounds which reason disapproves and prudence condemns—it becomes an indispensable duty to expose its hollowness and fallacy. Reserve then would be a crime. The true Patriot who never fears to sacrifice popularity to what he believes to be the cause of ⟨public⟩ good, ⟨canno⟩t hesitate to endeavour to unmask the error, ⟨though with the certainty of incuring⟩ the displeasure and [censure of the prejudiced and unthinking.

The disposition to infract the treaty, which in *several* particulars discovered itself among us, almost as soon as it was known to have been made, was from its first appearance a source of humiliation, regret, and apprehension to those who could dispassionately estimate the consequences, and who felt a proper concern for the honour and character of the country. They perceived that besides loss of reputation, it must sooner or later lead to very serious embarrassments. They have been hitherto mistaken in no part of their

ADf, Hamilton Papers, Library of Congress; *The* [New York] *Argus, or Greenleaf's New Daily Advertiser*, August 5, 1795.
    1. For background to this document, see the introductory note to "The Defence No. I," July 22, 1795.
    Two different parts of the draft are missing. These missing sections have been taken from the newspaper and are enclosed in brackets. At other points a few words in the draft are illegible. These words have also been taken from the newspaper and are enclosed in broken brackets.

anticipations, and if their faithful warning voice, now raised to check the progress of error, is as listened to as when it was raised to prevent the commencement of it, there is too much cause to fear, that the experience of extensive evils may extort regrets which the foresight of an enlightened people ought to avert.

Citizens of United America! as you value your present enviable lot, rally round your own good sense! expel from your confidence, men who have never ceased to misadvise you! Discard intemperate and illiberal passions! Aspire to the glory of the greatest] triumph which a people can gain, a triumph over prejudice. Be just, be prudent. Listen impartially to the unadulterated language of Truth. And above all guard your peace with anxious vigilance against all the artful snares which are laid for it. Accompany me with minds open to conviction in a discussion of unspeakable importance to your welfare!

Weigh well as a preliminary to further investigation this momentous proposition—"PEACE in the particular situation of this Country is an object of such great and primary magnitude—that it ought not to be relinquished unless the relinquishment be clearly necessary to PRESERVE our HONOR in some UNEQUIVOCAL POINT, or to avoid the sacrifice of some RIGHT or INTEREST of MATERIAL and PERMANENT importance." This is the touchstone of every question which can come before us respecting our foreign Concerns.

As a general proposition scarcely any will dispute it, but in the application of the rule, there is much confusion of ideas—much false feeling and falser reasoning. ⟨The ravagings of anger and⟩ pride are mistaken for [the suggestions of honor. Thus are we told in a delirium of rage, by a gentleman of South Carolina,[2] that our envoy should have demanded an *unconditional* relinquishment of the Western Posts as a right; 'till which was granted, and until Lord Grenville had given orders to Lord Dorchester to that effect, *open to be sent to our president, to be by him forwarded*, he should not have *opened his lips about the treaty. It was prostituting the dearest rights of free men, and laying them prostrate at the feet of royalty.*[3]

2. This is a reference to a speech which John Rutledge made on July 17, 1795, in Charleston, South Carolina. For this speech, see Oliver Wolcott, Jr., to H, July 28, 1795, note 3.

3. According to a newspaper account of this speech, Rutledge said: "Mr. Jay should have demanded an unconditional relinquishment of those posts as

In a case of incontestible, *mutual* infractions of a treaty, one of the parties is to demand, peremptorily of the other, an *unconditional* performance on his part, by way of preliminary and without negociation. An envoy sent to avert war, carrying with him the clearest indications of a general solicitude of his country, that peace might be preserved, was at the very first stept of his progress to render hostility inevitable, by exacting, not only what could not have been complied with, but what must have been rejected with indignation. The government of Great Britain must have been the most abject on earth, in a case so situated, to have listened for a moment to such a demand. And because our envoy did not pursue this frantic course; did not hold the language of an IMPERIOUS BASHAW to his TREMBLING SLAVE, he is absurdly stigmatized as having *prostrated the rights of freemen, at the feet of royalty*. What are we to think of the state of the mind which could produce so extravagant a folly? Would a prudent people have been willing to have entrusted a negociation which involved their peace to the author of it? Will they be willing to take him as their guide in a critical emergency of their affairs? *

True honor is a rational thing. It is as distinguishable from Quixotism as true courage from the spirit of a bravo. It is possible for one nation to commit so undisguised and unqualified an outrage upon another, as to render a negociation of the question dishonourable. But this seldom, if ever, happens. In most cases it is consistent with honor to preceed rupture by negociation, and whenever it is, reason and humanity demand it. Honor cannot be wounded by consulting moderation. As a general rule, it is not till after it has become manifest that reasonable reparation for a clear premeditated wrong cannot be obtained by an amicable adjustmen[t], that honor demands a resort to arms. In all the questions between us and Great Britain, honor permitted the moderate course; in those which regard

---

a right; till which was granted, and until Lord Grenville [British Secretary of State for Foreign Affairs] had given orders to Lord Dorchester [Governor in Chief and Captain General of the British Provinces on North America] to that effect, open to be sent to our President, to be by him forwarded, he should not have opened his lips upon the treaty. It was prostituting the dearest rights of free men, and laying them prostrate at the feet of royalty" (*The* [New York] *Argus, or Greenleaf's New Daily Advertiser,* July 30, 1795).

* *No man in the habit of thinking well either of Mr. Rutleges head or heart, but must have felt at reading the passages of his speech, which have been published, pain, surprise, and mortification. I regret the occasion, and the necessity of animadversion.*

the inexecution of the treaty of peace, there had undoubtedly been mutual faults. It was therefore a case for negociation and mutual reparation. True honor, which can never be separated from justice, even requires reparation from us to Great Britain, as well as from her to us. The injuries we complain of in the present war were also of a negociable kind.[4] The first was bottomed on a controverted point in the laws of nations. The second left open the question, whether the principal injury was a designed act of the government or a misconstruction of its courts. To have taken, therefore, the imperious ground which is recommended, in places of that which was taken; would have been not to follow the administration of honor, but to have submitted to the impulse of passion and phrenzy.

So likewise, when it is asserted that war is preferable to the sacrifice of our rights and interests, this, to be true, to be rational, must be understood of such rights and interests as are certain, as are important, such as regard the honor, security or prosperity of our country. It is not a right disputable, or of small consequence, it is not an interest temporary, partial and inconsiderable, which will justify, in our situation, an appeal to arms.

Nations ought to calculate as well as individuals, to compare evils, and to prefer the lesser to the greater; to act otherwise, is to act unreasonably; those who counsel it are impostors or mad men.

These reflections are of a nature to lead to a right judgment of a conduct of our envoy in the plan of adjustment to which he has given his assent.

Three objects, as has appeared, were to be aimed at, on behalf of the United States, 1st, Compensation for the negroes carried away. 2d, Surrender of the Western Posts. 3d, Compensation for spoliations during the existing war.

Two of these objects, and these in every view the most important, have been provided for, how fitly will be examined hereafter.[5] One of them has been given up (to wit) compensation for the negroes.

It has been shewn, as I trust, to the conviction of dispationate men, that the claim of compensation for the negroes, is in point

4. See "The Defence No. XV," September 12 and 14, 1795.
5. See "The Defence No. VII," "The Defence No. VIII," and "The Defence No. IX," August 12, 15, and 21, 1795, for discussions of Article 2 of the Jay Treaty and "The Defence No. XV," September 12 and 14, 1795, for a discussion of the first part of Article 7 of the Jay Treaty.

of right, a very doubtful one,[6] in point of interest, it certainly falls under the description of partial and inconsiderable; affecting in no respect, the honor or security of the nation, and incapable of having a sensible influence upon its prosperity. The pecuniary value of the object is, in a national scale, trifling.

Not having before me the proper document, I can only speak from memory. But I do not fear to be materially mistaken in stating that the whole number carried away, so ascertained as to] have afforded evidence for a claim of compensation was short of 3000 persons,[7] men women and children. Computing these at an average of 200 dollars per head which is certainly a liberal price the amount would be 600 000 Dollars—and not two or three millions as has been pretended.

It is a fact which I assert on the best authority, that our envoy made every effort in his power to establish our construction of the article relating to this subject, and to obtain compensation, and that he did not relinquish it till he became convinced that to insist upon it would defeat the purpose of his mission and leave the controversy between the two Countries unsettled.

Finding at the same time, that the two other points in dispute could be reasonably adjusted—is there any one who will be rash enough to affirm that he ought to have broken off the negotiation on account of the difficulty about the negroes? Yes! there are men who are thus inconsiderate and intemperate! But will a sober reflecting people ratify their sentence?

What would such a people have said to our Envoy had he returned with this absurd tale in his mouth? "Countrymen! I could have obtained the surrender of your posts and an adequate provision for the reparation of your losses by unjust captures. I could have terminated your controversy with Great Britain and secured the continuance of your peace but for one obstacle, a refusal to compensate for the negroes carried away—on this point, the British Government maintained a construction of the Treaty different from

6. See "The Defence No. III," July 29, 1795.

7. In the newspaper the rest of this paragraph was expanded and changed to read: "of whom about 1300 were of sixteen years and upwards, men, women, and children. Computing them at an average of 150 dollars per head, which is a competent price, the amount would be 450,000 dollars, and not two or three millions as has been pretended."

ours and adhered to it with inflexibility. I confess, that there appeared to me much doubt concerning the true construction. I confess also that the object was of inconsiderable value. Yet it made a part of our claims, and I thought the hazards of War preferable to a renunciation of it."

What would his adversaries have replied to him on such an occasion? No ridicule would have been too strong, no reproach too bitter. Their triumph would have been complete. For he would have been deservedly left without advocate or apologist.

It cannot admit of a serious doubt, that the affair of the negroes was too questionable in point of right, too insignificant in point of interest, to have been suffered to be an impediment to the immense objects which were to be promoted by an accommodation of differences acceptable in other respects. There was no general principle of national right or policy.[8] No consideration of honor forbid the renunciation—every calculation of interest invited to it. The evils of War for one month would outweigh the advantage, if at the end of it there was a certainty of attainment.

But was War the alternative? Yes War, or disgrace.

The U States and Great Britain had been brought to issue. The recent spoliations of our commerce superadded to the evils of a protracted Indian War connected with the detention of the Western Posts and accompanied with indications of a design to contract our Western boundaries, obstructing the course of our settlements and the enjoyment of private rights and producing serious and growing discontent in our Western Country—rendered it indispensable, that there should be a settlement of old differences and a reparation of new wrongs, or that the sword should vindicate our rights.

This was certainly and with reason the general sense of our Country when our Envoy left it. There are many indications that it was the opinion of our Government, and it is to be inferred that our Envoy understood the alternative to be as has been stated.

Indeed what else could be contemplated? After the depredations which had been committed upon our commerce—after the strong sensibility which had been discovered upon the occasion in and out of our public councils—after an envoy extraordinary had been sent

8. In the newspaper, the words "to be renounced" are added to this sentence. In the draft, H first wrote and then crossed out these words.

to terminate differences and obtain reparation—if nothing had resulted—was there any choice but reprisals? Should we not have
rendered ourselves ridiculous and contemptible in the eyes of the
whole world by forbearing them?

It is curious to observe the inconsistency of certain men. They
reprobate the Treaty as inconsistent with our honor and yet they
affect to believe that an abortion of the negotiation would not have
led to War. If they are sincere, they must think that national honor
consists in perpetually railing, complaining, blustering and submitting. For my part, much as I deprecate War, I entertain no doubt
that it would have been our duty to meet it with decision had the
negotiation failed—that a due regard to our honor our rights and
our interests would have enjoined it upon us. Nor would a pusyl-
lanimous passiveness have saved us from it. So unsettled a state of
things would have led to fresh injuries and aggravations, and circumstances too powerful to be resisted would have dragged us into
War. We should have lost our honor without preserving our peace.
Nations in similar situations have no option but to accommodate
differences or to fight. Those which have strong motives to avoid
War should by their moderation facilitate the accommodation of
differences. This is a rule of good sense, a maxim of sound policy.

But the misfortune is that men will oppose imagination to fact.
Though we see Great Britain predominant on the ocean—though
we observe her pertinaciously resisting the idea of pacification with
France amidst the greatest discouragements—though we have employed a man whose sagacity and integrity have been hitherto undisputed and of a character far from flexible to ascertain what was
practicable though circumstances favoured his exertions, though
much time and pains were bestowed upon the subject—though
there is not only his testimony but the testimony of other men who
were immediately on the scene and in whom there is every reason
to confide—that all was attained which was attainable—Yet we still
permit ourselves to imagine that more and better could have been
done, and that by taking even now a high and menacing tone Great
Britain may be brought to our feet.

Even a stile of politeness in our Envoy has been construed to his
disadvantage. Because he did not mistake strut for dignity and rudeness for spirit, because he did not by petulance and asperity enlist

the pride of the British Court against the success of his mission—
he is represented as having humiliated himself and his nation. It is
forgotten that mildness in the *manner* and *firmness* in the *thing* are
most compatible with true dignity, and almost always go farther
than harshness and stateliness.

Suppositions that more could have been done by displaying what
is called greater spirit are not warranted by facts. It would be extremely imprudent on that basis to trust ourselves to a further
experiment—to the immense vicissitudes in the affairs of Europe
which from moment to moment may essentially vary the relative
situations of the contending parties. If there ever was a state of
things which demanded extraordinary circumspection and forbade
a spirit of adventure, it is that of the U States at the present juncture
viewed in connection with the present very singular and incalculable
posture of Europe.

But it is asked, to avoid Sylla may we not run upon Charybdis?
If the Treaty should preserve our peace with Britain, may it not
interrupt it with France? I answer, that to me there appears no room
for apprehension. It will be shewn in the course of the discussion,
that the Treaty interferes in no one particular with our engagements
to France, and will make *no alteration whatever in the state of
things between us and her* except as to the selling prizes in our
ports,[9] which not being required by Treaty, was originally permitted
merely because there was no law to forbid it,[10] and which being
confined to France was of very questionable propriety on the
principles of neutrality and has been a source of dissatisfaction to
the other belligerent powers. This being the case, no cause of umbrage is given to France by the Treaty, and it is as contrary to her
interest as to her inclination wantonly to seek a quarrel with us.
Prostrate indeed were our situation if we could not without offending France make a Treaty with another power which merely tended
to extinguish controversy and to regulate the rules of Commercial
Intercourse; and this not only without violating any duty to France

9. This is a reference to Article 24 of the Jay Treaty. For this article, see
"Remarks on the Treaty . . . between the United States and Great Britain,"
July 9-11, 1795, note 74.

10. See H to George Washington, April 27, 1793; H to Edmund Randolph,
May 10, 1793; "Treasury Department Circular to the Collectors of the Customs," May 30, 1793.

but without giving any preference to another. It is astonishing that those who assert so much nicety about national honor do not feel the extreme humiliation of such an idea. As to the denomination of ALLIANCE with G Britain which has been given to the Treaty, it is an insult to the understandings of the people to call it by such a Name. There is not a tittle of it which warrants the appellation.

Camillus

To Oliver Wolcott, Junior

New York Aug 5. 1795

Dr. Sir

I have received yours of 3d instant.[1] You make no mention of having received one from me inclosing another for the Attorney General [2] in which I tell him that I will attend the cause which involves the question respecting direct taxes [3] when notified of the time it will come on.

The silence of your letter makes me fear it may have miscarried.

I do not wonder at what you tell me of the author of a certain piece.[4] That man is too cunning to be wise. I have been so much in the habit of seeing him mistaken that I hold his opinion cheap.

Yrs. truly   A Hamilton

Oliver Wolcott Esq

ALS, Connecticut Historical Society, Hartford.
1. Letter not found.
2. H's letter to William Bradford has not been found, but see Bradford to H, August 4, 1795.
3. For information on the Carriage Tax case (*Hylton* v *United States*), see 3 Dallas, *U.S. Reports*, 171–84, and the forthcoming Goebel, *Law Practice*, III. See also Tench Coxe to H, January 14, 19, 1795; H to Coxe, January 26, 1795; Bradford to H, July 2, August 4, 1795; Edmund Randolph to H, July 21, 1795; Wolcott to H, July 28, 1795.
4. At the end of this sentence in the MS an asterisk appears. At the bottom of this letter Wolcott wrote: " * Tench Coxe author of a piece signed *Juriscola*. O W." Coxe wrote four articles which he signed "Juriola" (rather than "Juriscola"). These articles, which are entitled "An Examination of the pending Treaty with Great Britain" and are addressed "To the President of the United States of America," appeared in *The Philadelphia Gazette and Universal Daily Advertiser*, July 31, August 4, 8, 12, 1795.

Philo Camillus No. 2 [1]

[New York, August 7, 1795]

For the ARGUS.

CITIZEN GREENLEAF,[2]

A WRITER, who signs himself CINNA [3] has come forward to refute the argument which has been stated by CAMILLUS, as that of Great Britain, in support of her construction of the article respecting the Negroes.[4] If illiberal insinuation is argument, CINNA is an adept. But he mistakes the people to whom he addresses himself, if he hopes to supply the want of good reasons by invectives. If *Camillus* were known, it would be also known that no citizen of the United States has exceeded him in proofs of determined attachment to his country, and of determined opposition to the injustice of Great Britain; that no man is more incapable than he, of becoming the obsequious apologist of that country; of justifying her acts however wanton; or, of depreciating our own, and placing it improperly in the wrong, as calumniating *Cinna* has alledged. *Camillus* has no *exotic* ingredients in his creed. It is neither *Grecian* nor *Trojan;* neither *French* nor *British.* It is purely *American.* It would grieve him in the inmost recesses of his soul to see a country to which he is devoted, and to which he has made great sacrifices, destined to revolve like a satellite round either France or Great Britain. Would to heaven all his opponents could lay their hands upon their hearts and say as much! We should not then have seen the systematic efforts, which have continued from the time of our war with Great Britain to the present moment, to make the interests of our country subservient to

---

The [New York] *Argus, or Greenleaf's New Daily Advertiser,* August 7, 1795.
　1. The other "Philo Camillus" essays are dated July 27, August 12, 19, 1795.
　2. Thomas Greenleaf, the publisher of *The Argus.*
　3. "Cinna" was the pseudonym used by Brockholst Livingston in a series of articles attacking the Jay Treaty. For the authorship of the "Cinna" essays, see the introductory note to "The Defence No. I," July 22, 1795.
　4. "Cinna's" criticisms are directed against statements made in "The Defence No. III," June 29, 1795, and are contained in the first of his six essays (*The* [New York] *Argus, or Greenleaf's New Daily Advertiser,* August 1, 1795).

those of France: We should not see, at this moment, such violent exertions to keep us, as it were, insulated from all the world but France. There would be no set of men who would not see and acknowledge the wisdom of multiplying and extending pacific and commercial relations with as many other powers as we can; avoiding close alliances, and the making of common cause, with all of them.

But while *Camillus* prides himself in this truly and only American creed; he distinguishes patriotism from a blind partiality for national errors, and from the art of making these errors the foundation of still greater. In our contests with other nations, he thinks it a duty to examine with candour, how far they, or ourselves may be to blame, as the true guide to a just and reasonable result; and he despises the cowardice of not telling his fellow-citizens what he believes to be true, because it may happen not to accord with their prepossessions.

Having replied this much to the calumny of Cinna, let us proceed to what he may call his argument. I affirm, that it does not meet fairly a single point, nor obviate a single difficulty in the opposite argument.

His first observation is this. "Whenever the meaning of an instrument is doubtful, there cannot be a safer or fairer way to attain its true sense, than by considering the circumstances and views of the parties at the time of making the contract, and that they acted with good faith to each other. To apply this rule: during the late war, many Negroes had been taken by, or had voluntarily joined the armies, or gone into the garrisons of Great Britain. To reclaim them and prevent their being carried away, was an object which our commissioners had much at heart, and it is not easy to conceive how this object could have been expressed in plainer or less ambiguous terms."

Answer. The general rule here laid down is a good one; but by the very terms of it, "the circumstances and views" not of *one party* but of "the *parties*" are to be considered. Now, as on the one hand it was natural for us to wish to get back the Negroes, so on the other it was very unnatural that Great Britain should intend to violate the faith pledged to them, and after having declared them free, to abandon them to slavery. Hence the abandonment cannot be presumed to have accorded with the views of both parties, and therefore does not come within the rule.

But secondly, it is not good reasoning to draw a rule of interpretation of a promise to *do several things,* from a motive which is applicable *to only one* of the things to be done, and which is unreasonable as applied to the others. Cinna derives the reason of the stipulations from the single article of the negroes, while the stipulation itself speaks of "negroes *and other property.*" It is as true that many ships, horses, oxen, and other cattle; much furniture and various other articles of personal property, had been taken by the British forces, as that negroes had been taken by, or joined them. An intention, therefore, must be sought applicable to other property as well as to negroes. Then comes the question—Is it presumable that the United States meant to demand, or Great Britain to promise, an abandonment of all the booty of a seven years war? If the terms are in the least ambiguous, this must be answered in the negative. That they are ambiguous, no man who reads them will doubt, notwithstanding the inference from the alledged accuracy of Franklin, who, by the way, it is known, had less agency in that treaty than any other of the commissioners, and it is probable, did not pen a line of it. But the imperfection of language, and the urgency of conjunctures, frequently occasion the most accurate men to use inaccurate expressions. How much dispute has there been about the meaning of several parts of our treaty with France, in which Franklin had a predominant agency?

Cinna says it is not easy to conceive how the object could have been expressed in plainer or less ambiguous terms. I will convince him that nothing was more easy. These expressions would have been perfectly clear "without carrying away any negroes, which immediately previous to their being captured by, or to their joining the forces of his Britannic majesty, were the property of American inhabitants." This would have avoided the ambiguity as to time, and as to the effect of capture, and by standing without the words *"and other property"* would have steered clear of the difficulty incident to the idea of a general and indiscriminate abandonment of booty, which is inseparable from our sense of the stipulation as it is now worded.

The second observation of *Cinna* is in these words; "It could not be necessary to guard against new depredations—peace being made, all hostilities of every kind ceased. To confine this article, therefore, to an engagement to abstain from further plunder[5] is rendering it altogether negative and useless."

Camillus anticipated this objection to the construction opposite to ours, and has conclusively answered it. But *Cinna* found it more convenient to pass by his answer, than to attempt a refutation of it. *Camillus's* answer is founded upon this clause of the same article, *"without causing any destruction,"* which immediately precedes the provision respecting the negroes. The cessation of hostilities as much precluded the causing of further destruction, as the taking further plunder, and it was as unnecessary in strictness to provide against *further destruction* as against *further plunder:* but it is indisputable, that the first of these two unnecessary things is done by the article, and therefore, it being unnecessary with respect to the other part of the provision is no objection to understanding it in a similar sense. But the truth is, that nothing is more common in treaties than to insert, for greater caution, particular provisions, which are in strictness unnecessary, because they are comprehended in, or result from, other provisions, or from the nature of the thing.

But it may be remarked, that the article might have been intended to prevent the *carrying away* of negroes not taken in war, but who had joined the British, either previous to the invitations by proclamation, or after the cessation of hostilities.

The next observation of *Cinna* is, that "the reasoning of *Camillus* is constrained and contradictory; that in one breath he likens negroes to horses, cattle, and other moveables, and as such, liable to become booty; in the next, considers them as rational beings, and as intitled to liberty under British proclamations." But what contradiction is there in this? on the contrary, these different aspects of the subject are incident to the nature of it.

The laws of certain states which give an ownership in the service of negroes as personal property, constitute a similitude between them and other articles of personal property, and thereby subject them to the right of capture by war. But being men, by the laws of God and nature, they were capable of acquiring liberty—and when the

5. In the newspaper, "to obtain from further plunster."

captor in war, to whom by the capture the ownership was transferred, thought fit to give them liberty, the gift was not only valid,
but irrevocable.

Weakly, then, does *Cinna* put his question, "admitting that slaves
may become booty, and that their property becomes vested in the
captor, has he not a right to restore them, if he pleases, at a peace?"

I answer, yes; if he has *retained till that time* the property acquired by the capture; but most certainly not if he had previously
parted with it by infranchisement of the slave—his right had then
ceased. Liberty once gained could not be revoked. There was no
legal or moral power of doing it, and to have done it at all would
have been the extreme of treachery, perfidy, and baseness. All the
observations of Cinna, founded upon a contrary supposition, are
futile and absurd.

It is a mere sophism to say, that it was less immoral to abandon
the negroes to slavery, than not to make restitution to the owners
from whom they had been allured to be armed against their masters.
Two wrongs do not make a right—one immoral thing does not
obviate the immorality of a prior immoral thing. However censur-
able the first act was, the last would not have repaired the criminality. It would have added guilt to guilt—nor is there any comparison between the degree of turpitude of the two things. To
have withdrawn slaves from their masters as a public enemy, and
to have employed them against those masters, was an act, tho'
odious, far less odious than would have been the abandonment of
those persons to the bondage of their former masters, after they
had been so used *on the promise of liberty*. The feelings of every
real friend to liberty must be in unison with this assertion.

Considering the first act as improper, & supposing there was an
intention to make reparation, the true and the only way consistent
with justice and morality was to stipulate compensation for the
negroes in question.

But this the article does not do. If it promises any thing more
than to abstain from new acts of depredation, it promises specifically
the abandonment of the negroes to their former slavery.

This CAMILLUS has truly asserted to be odious and immoral, and
as such forming an objection to our construction of the article. And
he also truly asserts that the substitution of compensation does not
obviate the difficulty.

For no proposition in EUCLID is more clear than this, "that where a specific thing is promised, nothing but the doing *that very thing* is performance of the promise." The giving an equivalent may amount to *reparation*, but it is not *performance*. Whence it follows incontestibly, that the possibility of an equivalent, as a substitute which is not odious or immoral, cannot obviate an objection to such a meaning of a promise as would require a specific thing, which is odious and immoral.

It is a mere evasion of this argument to say with *Cinna*, that "nothing is more common than a satisfaction in *damages* for the breach of a promise to do a specific thing." This presupposes, and so in all law proceedings it is constantly charged, that the *promise has been broken*, and the damages are awarded not as performance of the promise, but as satisfaction for the breach.

But this does not touch the point of Camillus's argument, "*that you cannot suppose a thing to be promised* which is *in itself* odious or immoral, because pecuniary compensation may be made; inasmuch as compensation is not performance, but a substitute for it, which, especially as between nations, the party to whom the promise is made is not obliged to accept. Consequently if the thing itself was improper to be promised, or is improper to be performed, it is not the less objectionable, because it is possible by way of reparation to do another thing in lieu of it; that is, to make compensation." This argument, if rightly understood is, unanswerable. If *Cinna* does not comprehend it, 'tis not Camillus's fault. He was not bound to find *Cinna* argument and understanding too.

Cinna charges *Camillus* with blazoning the virtues and humanity of his Britannic Majesty, and with representing him as very scrupulous about doing an odious or immortal act. This is false and despicable rant. There is not a syllable in *Camillus* which warrants the suggestion. He speaks of *things* only, and without any allusion whatever to the character of his Britannic Majesty.

He says, indeed, that the abandonment of negroes, who had been promised freedom, to bondage and slavery, would be odious and immoral, and as such cannot be presumed to have been intended. This is a general argument without allusion to personal character, and would have been equally true whether a *Caligula* or a *Marcus Aurelius* had filled the throne of Great Britain.

Cinna recommends a perusal of Mr. Jefferson's letter as an antidote to the doctrines of Camillus,[6] and as a convincing vindication of our pretensions. That letter does not even examine the point as to the true construction of the article in question, but takes our sense of it for granted, and builds on that foundation. On the score of ingenuity and good penmanship, it does credit to its writer; but its general complexion is that of the harangue of an advocate, resolved to justify his client through thick and thin. Camillus has truly observed that it's the first public act which attempts to vindicate or excuse in the gross the conduct of this country in regard to the treaty of peace. It may be added, that it has the merit of attaching to the general government, by the justification of them, the disrepute of measures which was before confined to particular states, and which it had been the policy of the union to repel from itself, on the ground of its inability to prevent. And, in general, it is a piece which speaks loudly the prejudice of its writer, and more than any state paper of this country tends to do mischief, by misleading the public opinion. Camillus has shewn that its reasonings about the first breach of the treaty are inconclusive, and in doing this has pointed out two great errors; one, that it dates the obligation to performance on the part of Great Britain from the provisional articles, while it virtually considers the United States as not bound till after the definitive treaty; the other, that it asserts it to have been "perfectly understood, that treaties controuled the laws of the States," when documents which itself quotes, prove, that the State of Virginia by solemn acts of its general assembly expressed and acted upon a different understanding.[7] Errors like these overthrow the whole fabric.

The last observation of Cinna is by way of question. He asks "if Camillus is right, how happened it that a majority of the Senate

6. "Cinna" had written: "It is proper to subjoin, that the construction of the article by Camillus is opposed to the interpretation which our government have uniformly put upon it, is contrary to the explanation of it, by Mr. Jefferson, the perusal of whose correspondence witih Mr. Hammond is recommended, as the best antidote against the mischievous and humiliating doctrines, so warmly inculcated by this writer" (*The* [New York] *Argus, or Greenleaf's New Daily Advertiser,* August 1, 1795). "Cinna" is referring to Thomas Jefferson's letter of May 29, 1792, to George Hammond, the British Minister to the United States (ADf, Thomas Jefferson Papers, Library of Congress; *ASP, Foreign Relations,* I, 201–37).

7. See "Remarks on the Treaty . . . between the United States and Great Britain," July 9–11, 1795, notes 37 and 38.

at their late session agreed to invite the President to renew negociations for a compensation for the negroes?"[8] By the way, while
Camillus has stated the arguments which support the British construction, he has given no opinion of his own, except that it is a
very doubtful point. But the measure of the Senate which *Cinna*
cites is very easily explained. The claim of compensation for the
negroes was near the heart of a respectable portion of the people
of the United States. A right to it had become extensively a part
of the public creed. It was desireable by every possible effort to give
satisfaction. It is no proof that a Senator thought the merits of the
question with us, because he was willing by one more experiment
to mask his attention to the opinions and interests of a number,
not inconsiderable of his fellow-citizens.   PHILO-CAMILLUS.

8. The motion was made by Senator James Gunn of Georgia on June 24,
1795, and with the deletion of one paragraph it was passed on June 25 (*Annals
of Congress*, IV, 863-64).

The Defence No. VI[1]

[New York, August 8, 1795]

There is one more objection to the Treaty for what it does not
do, which requires to be noticed. This is an omission to provide
against the empressment of our seamen.[2]

It is certain that our Trade has suffered embarrassments in this
respect, and that there have been abuses which have operated very
oppressively upon our seamen; and all will join in the wish that they
could have been guarded against in future by the Treaty.

But it is easier to desire this than to see how it could have been
done. A general stipulation against the impressment of our seamen
would have been nugatory if not derogatory. Our right to an ex-

ADf, Hamilton Papers, Library of Congress; *The* [New York] *Argus, or
Greenleaf's New Daily Advertiser*, August 8, 1795.
    1. For background to this document, see the introductory note to "The
Defence No. I," July 22, 1795.
    2. For an example of this criticism of the Jay Treaty, see "Cinna No. 2" by
Brockholst Livingston (*The* [New York] *Argus, or Greenleaf's New Daily
Advertiser*, July 17, 1795). For the authorship of the "Cinna" essays, see the
introductory note to "The Defence No. I," July 22, 1795.

emption is perfect by the laws of nations,[3] and a contrary right is not even pretended by Great Britain. The difficulty has been and is to fix a rule of evidence by which to discriminate our seamen from theirs and by the discrimination to give ours protection, without covering theirs in our service.[4] It happens that the two nations speak the same language and in every other exterior circumstance closely resemble each other—that many of the natives of Great Britain and Ireland are among our citizens and that others without being properly our citizens are employed in our vessels.

Every body knows that the safety of Great Britain depends on her Marine. This was never more emphatically the case, than in the war in which she is now engaged. Her very existence as an independent power seems to rest on a maritime superiority.

In this situation can we be surprised that there are difficulties in bringing her to consent to any arrangement which would enable us by receiving her seamen into our employment to detach them from her service? Unfortunately there can be devised no method of protecting our seamen which does not involve that danger to her. Language & appearance instead of being a guide, as between other nations, are between us and Great-Britain sources of mistake and deception. The most familiar experience in the ordinary affairs of society proves that the oaths of parties interested can not be fully relied upon. Certificates of citizenship by officers of one party would be too open to the possibility of collusion and imposition to expect that the other would admit them to be conclusive. If inconclusive, there must be a discretion to the other party which would destroy their efficacy.

In whatever light it may be viewed there will be found an intrinsic difficulty in devising a rule of evidence safe for both parties and consequently in establishing one by Treaty. No nation would readily admit a rule which would make it depend upon the good

3. No statement by any writer on the laws of nations regarding the impressment of seamen has been found. Vattel, however, wrote: "Mercenary soldiers engage themselves, and enlist voluntarily. The sovereign has no right to compel foreigners; he is not even to make use of artifice or surprize, for inducing them to engage in a contract, which, like all others, should be founded on candor and probity" (*Law of Nations*, Book III, Chap. II, Sec. 14).

4. See Thomas Jefferson to George Washington, February 7, 1792 (LC, George Washington Papers, Library of Congress; *ASP, Foreign Relations*, I, 131).

faith of another and the integrity of its agents whether her seamen in time of War might not be withdrawn from her service and transferred to that of a neutral power. Such a rule as between Great Britain and us would be peculiarly dangerous on account of the circumstances which facilitate a transfer of seamen from one to the other. Great Britain has accordingly perseveringly declined any definitive arrangement on the subject—notwithstanding earnest & reiterated efforts of our Government.

When we consider candidly the peculiar difficulties which various circumstances of similitude between the people of the two countries oppose to a satisfactory arrangement, and that to the belligerent party it is a question of *national safety*, to the neutral party a question of commercial convenience & individual security, we shall not be the less disposed to think the want of such a provision as our wishes would dictate, a blemish in the Treaty.

The truth seems to be that from the nature of the thing it is matter of necessity to leave it to occasional and temporary expedients—to the effect of special interpositions from time to time to procure the correction of abuses and if the abuse becomes intolerable to the *ultima ratio*. The good faith of the parties and the motives which they have to respect the rights of each other and avoid causes of offence, and vigilance in noting and remonstrating against the irregularities which are committed are probably the only peaceable securities of which the case is susceptible. Circumstances appear to forbid any thing more; and it was not to be expected of our envoy that he would accomplish impossibilities. Those who are in the habit of seeing that there is always more than one side to a question will be most ready to acknowlege the justice of this conclusion.[5]

Our Minister Plenapotentiary, Mr. Pinkney, it is well known has long had this matter in charge and has strenuously exerted himself to have it placed upon some acceptable footing. But his endeavours have been unsuccessful further than to mitigate the evil by some additional checks and by drawing the attention of the British Government to the observance of greater caution.[6] A more sensible

5. The last two sentences of this paragraph are omitted in the newspaper.
6. See Lord Grenville to Thomas Pinckney, December 26, 1794, January 8, 14, March 13, 14, 20, 1795 (copies, RG 59, Despatches from United States

effect of our representations has been latterly experienced; and with attention and vigilance that effect may be continued and perhaps increased. But there is reason to conclude that it will be constantly found impracticable to establish a conventional and efficacious guard.

I proceed now to the examination of the several articles of the Treaty in the order in which they stand.

The first contains merely a general declaration that there shall be peace and friendship between the contracting parties the countries and people of each, without exception of persons or places.[7]

One would have imagined that this article at least would have escaped a formal objection, however it might have been secretly viewed as the most sinful of all, by those who pant after war and enmity between the two Countries. Nothing but the fact could have led to a surmise, that it was possible for it to have been deemed exceptionable; and nothing can better display the rage for objection which actuates the adversaries of the Treaty than their having invented one against so innocent a provision.

But the Comittee appointed by a Meeting at Charlestown South Carolina have sagaciously discovered that this article permits "the unconditional return to our Country of all persons who were proscribed during the late war." [8]

Ministers to Great Britain, 1791–1906, Vol. 3, November 29, 1791–May 4, 1797, National Archives); Pinckney to Edmund Randolph, October 21, 1794, February 2, March 17, 1795 (ALS, RG 59, Despatches from United States Ministers to Great Britain, 1781–1906, Vol. 3, November 29, 1791–May 4, 1797, National Archives). On February 2, 1795, Pinckney wrote to Randolph: "Mr. Jay and I continue to be treated with great Attention by the Members of the Administration and I have lately been more successful than heretofore in obtaining the Liberation of our impressed Mariners. The Decisions in the Court of Admiralty appear also to be more favorable to our Citizens than they were some time past" (ALS, RG 59, Despatches from United States Ministers to Great Britain, 1791–1906, Vol. 3, November 29, 1791–May 4, 1797, National Archives). Again on March 17, 1795, he wrote: ". . . my Applications through the Department of State to the Admiralty in behalf of impressed Mariners are much more expeditiously decided on and Answers given than heretofore, and . . . in general this Government seems disposed to give the friendly System a fair Trial" (ALS, RG 59, Despatches from United States Ministers to Great Britain, 1791–1906, Vol. 3, November 29, 1791–May 4, 1797, National Archives).

7. For the text of Article 1 of the Jay Treaty, see "Remarks on the Treaty . . . between the United States and Great Britain," July 9–11, 1795, note 2.

8. A committee of fifteen, elected by ballot on July 17, 1795, after a meeting of citizens the previous day in Charleston, presented its findings on the Jay Treaty at a public meeting on July 22. The committee's statement on Article 1 of the treaty reads: "The first article, though usual in treaties, would be par-

With all but men determined to be dissatisfied it would be a sufficient answer to such an objection to say that this article is a formula in almost every treaty on record and that the consequence attributed to it was never before dreamt of, though other nations besides ourselves have had their proscriptions and their banishments.

But this is not all. Our Treaty of Peace with Great Britain in 1783 has an equivalent stipulation in these words (Article 6) "There shall be a firm and perpetual peace between his Britannic Majesty and the said States and between the subjects of the one and the Citizens of the other." [9] In calling this an equivalent stipulation I speak with reference to the objection which is made. The argument to support that objection would be to this effect. "Exiles and criminals are not regarded as within the peace of a country: but the people of each are by this article placed within the peace of the other: therefore proscribed persons are restored to the peace of the U States and so lose their character of exiles and criminals."

Hence the argument will turn upon the word "peace" the word friendship will have no influence upon the question. In other respects there is no difference in substance between the two articles. For the terms "people" "subjects" "citizens" as used in the two treaties are synonimous. If therefore the last Treaty stipulates that there shall be peace between the Governments countries and *people* of the two Nations—the first stipulates what is equivalent that there shall be peace between the two Governments and the *subjects* & *citizens* of each. The additional words, without exception of persons or places can make no difference—being mere surplussage. If A says to B "I give you all the money in this purse"; the gift, is as complete as if he had said, "I give you all the money in this purse, *without exception of a single dollar.*"

But the object of the stipulation and the subject of the objection

---

ticularly mischievous in this, inasmuch as it permits the unconditional return to our country, of all persons who were proscribed during the late war, though their return is repugnant to our laws, and to the feelings of our injured fellow citizens, and though the state legislatures have already proceeded as far in readmitting such persons, as they judged consistent with good faith or sound policy" (*REPORT OF THE SELECT COMMITTEE, Chosen by Ballot of the Citizens of the United States, in Charleston, South-Carolina, in pursuance of a Resolution of a general Meeting of the Citizens, in St. Michael's Church, on Thursday, the sixteenth of July, 1795* [Charleston: Printed by W. P. Young, Broad-Street, n.d. (George Washington Papers, Library of Congress)]).

9. H was mistaken, for the quotation is from Article 7 rather than Article 6 of the definitive treaty of peace of 1783. See Miller, *Treaties,* II, 155.

have no relation whatever to each other. National stipulations are to be considered in the sense of the laws of nations. Peace in the sense of those laws defines a state which is opposite to that of *War*. Peace in the sense of the municipal law defines a state which is opposite to that of criminality. They are consequently different things and a subject of Great Britain by committing a crime may put himself out of the peace of our Government in the sense of our municipal laws while there might be perfect peace with him in the sense of the laws of Nations & vice versa there might be war with him in the sense of the laws of Nations & peace in that of the municipal law.

The punishment of a subject of Great Britain as a felon would certainly not constitute a state of war between the parties nor interfere with the peace which is stipulated by this article—though it is declared that it shall be *inviolable* and might as well be affirmed to prevent the punishment of future as of former criminals.

But who in the contemplation of the laws of the respective States are the proscribed persons? They must be understood to have been subjects or citizens of the states which proscribed them—Consequently can not be presumed to be comprehended in an article which stipulates peace between the nations and their respective Citizens. This is not a stipulation of peace between a nation and its own criminal citizens—nor can the idea of expatriation be admitted to go so far as to destroy the relation of citizen as it regards amenability for a crime. To this purpose at least the offender must remain a citizen.

There can hardly have been a time when a Treaty was formed between two Nations, when one or the other had not exiled criminals or fugitives from justice which it would have been unwilling to reinstate. Yet this was never deemed an obstacle to the article nor has an immunity from punishment ever been claimed under it, nor is there the least ground to assert that it might be claimed under it.

It follows that the objection which has been taken to this article is wholly without foundation. It is humiliating to the human understanding or disreputable to the human heart that similar objections should come from sensible men. It is disgustful to have to refute them. The regard I feel for some of those who have brought it for-

ward makes it a painful task. How great is the triumph of passion
over judgment on this occasion!   CAMILLUS

From a note of the *Editor* of this paper it is to be inferred that ☞
a piece has been sent to him charging the Writer of Camillus with
having liberated some person from jail to insult or fight those who
are called respectable Whigs.[10] The suggestion is a total falsehood.
The Writer of Camillus has not recently liberated any person from
Jail—though if he had it would not be the first instance that laudable
actions have been misconstrued and imputed to him as crimes. This
is a specimen of the detestable arts which are employed to excite
resentment against the supposed Author of *Camillus*. What does all
this mean?

10. On August 5, 1795, the following notice appeared in *The* [New York]
Argus, or Greenleaf's New Daily Advertiser: "*The address to* CAMILLUS PACIFI-
CUS, *Esq. we have thought proper to postpone publishing, its being, in our
opinion, rather premature. The gentleman to whom it is addressed seems to be
doing his own business as fast as he can—let him have rope enough. If he has
(tho' poor) liberated a* JAIL BIRD, *for the purpose of employing him to insult or
*FIGHT *any of our respectable whigs, the time is fast approaching when we shall
know who and who are together in firm determination to oppose treachery.*"
    In the newspaper version of this document an asterisk appears after "whigs"
and the following paragraph appears in brackets at the end of H's note: "[* It
will be observed, that this note is written by *Camillus*. For ought Camillus
knows, a *disbelief* of the *'suggestion'* induced the Editor of the Argus to *reject*
the piece, as he generally does all observations of a personal nature.]"

To Oliver Wolcott, Junior

New York Aug 10. 1795

Dr Sir

I have received your letter by Saturday's Post.[1] The one you
inquire about was received.

I incline very much to the opinion that this will be the proper
course of conduct in reference to the order to seize our vessels with
provisions (viz) [2] to send to our Agent [3] the Treaty ratified as
advised by the Senate with this instruction—that if the order for
seizing provisions is in force when he receives it he is to inform
the British Ministry that he has the Treaty ratified but that he is
instructed not to exchange the ratifications till that order is re-

scinded [4]—since the UStates cannot ever give an implied sanction to the principle. At the same time a remonstrance ought to go from this Country well considered and well digested *even to a word* to be delivered against the principle of the order.

My reasons for this opinion are summarily these—1 that in fact we are too much interested in the exemption of provisions from seizure to give even an implied sanction to the contrary pretension. 2 that the exchange of ratifications pending such an order would give colour to an abusive construction of the XVIII th article of the Treaty [5] as though it admitted of the seizure of provisions. 3 That this would give *cause* of umbrage to France because it would be more than merely to refrain from resisting by force an innovation injurious to her but it would be to give a sanction to it in the midst of a war. 4 It would be thus construed in our country & would destroy confidence in the Government. 5 It would scarcely be respectable to a nation to conclude a Treaty with a power to heal past controversies at the very *moment* of a new & existing violation of its rights.

Yrs. truly   A Hamilton

P.S. Deliver the inclosed as soon as it gets to hand.

If an order has existed & has been rescinded the remonstrance ought still to be presented after the exchange of ratification as a protest against the principle &c

Oliver Wolcott Esq

ALS, Connecticut Historical Society, Hartford; copy, Hamilton Papers, Library of Congress.
  1. Letter not found.
  2. This is a reference to a British order in council, dated April 25, 1795, calling for the British seizure of cargoes of grain on American ships bound for France. For the text of the British order in council, see Washington to H, July 7, 1795, note 3.
  3. Because Thomas Pinckney, the United States Minister Plenipotentiary to Great Britain, had left London to negotiate a treaty with Spain, William A. Deas, secretary of the legation, was made United States chargé d'affaires and temporarily became the ranking United States diplomat in London. Because George Washington decided that the task of exchanging ratifications of the Jay Treaty with the British should be entrusted to a higher ranking diplomat

than Deas, John Quincy Adams, United States Minister Resident at The Hague, was selected. On August 14, 1795, Edmund Randolph wrote to Adams directing him "to repair without any delay to London" (LC, RG 59, Diplomatic and Consular Instructions of the Department of State, 1791–1801, Vol. 3, June 2, 1795–January 21, 1797, National Archives), and on August 25, 1795, Secretary of War Timothy Pickering, who had taken over the responsibilities of the office of the Secretary of State following Randolph's resignation, sent Adams instructions for the exchange of ratifications (LC, RG 58, Diplomatic and Consular Instructions of the Department of State, 1791–1801, Vol. 3, June 2, 1795–January 21, 1797, National Archives). In addition, Deas was instructed to exchange ratifications with the British if the treaty reached London before Adams's arrival (Pickering to Deas, August 25, 1795 [LC, RG 59, Diplomatic and Consular Instructions of the Department of State, 1791–1801, Vol. 3, June 2, 1795–January 21, 1797, National Archives]).

4. At one time Washington and Secretary of State Randolph seriously considered making the ratification of the Jay Treaty contingent on the repeal of the British order in council of April 25, 1795; but when Washington did ratify the Jay Treaty on August 14, 1795, he did so without stipulating that the British rescind the order in council. See Wolcott to H, July 30, 1795, note 2.

5. For the text of Article 18 of the Jay Treaty, see "Remarks on the Treaty . . . between the United States and Great Britain," July 9–11, 1795, note 63.

To the Editor of the Minerva [1]

New York August 11.[2] [1795]

The Editor of the Minerva having received information, through an authentic channel, that Mr. Pinckney, our Minister at London, had written to this Country in a manner, which indicated that he had been consulted by Mr. Jay on the subject of the Treaty lately negotiated with Great Britain, and that it had met with his approbation; felt himself warranted in stating these ideas to the public. Having been called upon, in the Argus of Saturday last,[3] in a manner not very decent, for evidence of the fact; & knowing that Mr. Jay must be able to give a confirmation of it; and thinking it probable that he might not be unwilling to do so—The Editor took the liberty through a friend to make the Inquiry of him. Mr. Jay has obligingly furnished the following extract of a letter from himself to the Secretary of State: which fully establishes the truth of what has been alleged. (viz)

Extract of a Letter from Mr Jay to the Honb. Edm. Randolph Esqr Secy of State. dated at London the 19 Novr 1794.[4]

"I ought not to omit mentioning the acknowledgments due from me to mr. Pinckney: with whom I have every Reason to be satisfied, and from whose advice and opinions I have derived Light and advantage in the course of the negociation. His approbation of the Treaty gives me pleasure; not merely because his opinion corresponds with my own, but also from the Sentiments I entertain of his Judgment and Candour." [5]

ADf, MS Division, New York Public Library; [New York] *American Minerva; an Evening Advertiser*, August 11, 1795.

1. Noah Webster, Jr., was the editor of the [New York] *American Minerva; an Evening Advertiser*.

2. The date is not in H's handwriting.

3. On August 8, 1795, the following letter appeared in *The* [New York] *Argus, or Greenleaf's New Daily Advertiser:*
"CITIZEN GREENLEAF,
"THE Editor of the Minerva asserts, that Mr. Pinckney, our minister in London, knew of and approved the treaty. This is so high a charge upon the character of that gentleman, that it ought not to be credited upon the bare ipse dixit of a printer, not remarkable for a scrupulous adherence to facts. A friend of Mr. Pinckney calls upon the Editor of the Minerva to produce proof of this assertion, otherwise the public will regard it as a most infamous aspersion, calculated to lessen the popularity of a minister who has hitherto deserved well of his country.   Z."
The words "Saturday last" are not in H's handwriting.

4. The extract, which is attached to H's draft, is in the handwriting of John Jay.

5. H's letter and the extract of Jay's letter were reprinted in *The* [New York] *Argus, or Greenleaf's New Daily Advertiser*, August 13, 1795. Immediately below them the following "Remarks" appeared: "It may be observed on the above—
"First, That the letter is from Mr. Jay—not from Mr. Pi[n]ckney.
"Secondly, That Mr. Jay is giving testimony in his own cause.
"Thirdly, That it does not appear whether Mr. Jay shewed him the whole treaty, or only mentioned some of the articles to him.
"Fourthly, That it would have been extremely rude in Mr. Pinckney, to have told Mr. Jay, that he disapproved of the treaty.
"Fifthly, That if Mr. Pi[n]ckney really approved of the treaty, it must be easy to produce some letter from him to that effect—And
"Lastly, That the public ought to suspend their opinion, rather than condemn Mr. Pinckney on the evidence of a person so much interested in the question as Mr. Jay is. Time will discover the truth.   Z."

The Defence No. VII[1]

[New York, August 12, 1795]

The *Second Article* of the Treaty[2] stipulates that his Britannic Majesty will withdraw all his troops and garrisons from *all posts* and *places* within the boundary lines assigned by the Treaty of Peace to the U States; and that this evacuation shall take place on or before the first day of June 1796—the United States in the mean time *at their discretion* extending their settlements to any part within the said boundary line *except within the Precints or Jurisdictions* of any of the said posts—that all settlers and traders within the precincts or jurisdiction of the said posts shall continue to enjoy unmolested all their property of every kind and shall be protected therein—that they shall be at liberty to remain there or to remove with all or any part of their effects also to sell their lands houses or effects or to retain the property thereof at their discretion, that such of them as shall continue to reside within the said boundary lines shall not be compelled to be come citizens of the U States, but shall be at liberty to do so if they think proper, making and declaring their election within a year after the evacuation, and that those who should continue after the expiration of a year without having declared their intention of remaining subjects of His Britannic Majesty shall be considered as having elected to become citizens of the U States.

This article, which accomplishes a primary object of our Envoy's mission, and one of primary importance to the U States, has been as much clamoured against as if it had made a formal cession of the Posts to Great Britain—on this point an uncommon degree of art has been exerted and with no small success. The value of the principal thing obtained has been put out of sight by misrepresentations of incidental circumstances.

ADf, Hamilton Papers, Library of Congress; *The* [New York] *Argus, or Greenleaf's New Daily Advertiser*, August 12, 1795.

1. For background to this document, see the introductory note to "The Defence No. I," July 22, 1795.

Because the MS of this document is incomplete, the last part of the essay has been taken from the newspaper and is enclosed in brackets.

2. For the text of Article 2 of the Jay Treaty, see "Remarks on the Treaty .. between the United States and Great Britain," July 9-11, 1795, note 3.

But the fact is nevertheless that an object has been accomplished of vast consequence to our Country. The most important *desiderata* in our concerns with foreign powers are the possession of the Western posts and a participation in the navigation of the River Mississippia. More or fewer of Commercial privileges are of vastly inferior moment. The force of circumstances will do all we can reasonably wish in this respect, and in a short time without any steps that may convulse our trade or endanger our tranquillity will carry us to our goal.

The recovery of the Western Posts will have many important sides. It will extinguish a source of controversy with Great Britain which at a period not distant must have inevitably involved the two countries in War—and the thing was becoming every day more and more urgent. It will enable us effectually to controul the hostilities of the Northern and Western Indians and in so doing will have a material influence on the Southern Tribes. It will therefore tend to rescue the Country from what is at present its greatest scourge, Indian Wars. When we consider that these wars have for four years past taken an extra million annually from our Revenue, we cannot be insensible of the importance of terminating that source of expence. This million turned to the redemption of our debt would complete its extinguishment in less than   .[3] The benefits of tranquillity to our frontier, exempting its inhabitants from the complicated horrors of Savage warfare, speak too loudly to our humanity as well as to our policy to need a commentary.

The advantages of the recovery of the posts do not stop here. An extension of Trade is to be added to the catalogue.[4] This however need only be mentioned at this time as it will come again into view in considering the third article.[5]

But two consequences not commonly adverted to require a particular notice in this place.

There is just ground of suspicion, corroborated by various concurring circumstances, that Great Britain has entertained the project

3. Space left blank in MS. The newspaper reads: "its extinguishment in about twenty years," followed by a note at the bottom of the page reading: "*This is a rough calculation, but it cannot materially err.*"

4. In MS, "catalouge."

5. See "The Defence No. X," August 26, 1795; "The Defence No. XI," August 28, 1795; and "The Defence No. XII," September 2–3, 1795.

of contracting our boundaries to the Ohio.[6] This has appeared in Canada, at the British garrisons, at the Indian towns, at Philadelphia and at London. The surrender of the posts for ever cuts up by the roots this pernicious project. The whole of our Western interests are immediately and deeply concerned in the question.

The harmonious and permanent connection of our Western with our Atlantic count[r]y materially depends on our possession of the Western posts. Already had great discontent been engendered in that Country by their detention. That discontent was increasing and rankling dayly. It was actually one of the ailments [7] of the insurrection in the Western parts of Pensylvania. While the posts remained in the hands of Great Britain dangerous tamperings with the inhabitants of that Country were to be apprehended. A community of views between Britain and Spain might have taken place and by force and seduction events formidable to our general Union might have been hazarded. The dissolution or prevention of that community of views is a point of the greatest moment in our system of

6. One aim of British diplomacy from 1791 to 1795 was the creation of an Indian buffer state between the United States and Canada, which was to be carved entirely out of the recognized territory of the United States. This nominally neutral zone would have contracted the northern boundary of the United States to the Ohio River. British policy was clearly set forth in the following instructions from Lord Grenville to George Hammond, dated March 17, 1792: ". . . you are authorized to make to the American Government, in such Manner and Form as you shall judge most expedient, a Ministerial offer of the good Offices of this Country in restoring Peace between them and the Indians. The general Grounds on which it is intended that You should endeavour to negotiate such an accomodation are to be, the securing to the different Indian Nations, along the British and American Frontiers, their Lands and hunting Grounds, as an independent Country, with respect to which, both His Majesty and the United States shall withdraw all Claims or Possessions whatever, shall agree never to establish any Forts within the Boundaries to be expressed in such Agreement, and shall bind themselves to each other not to acquire or to suffer their Subjects to acquire, by purchase, or otherwise, from the Indians, any Lands or Settlements within the said Boundaries. . . .
". . . And you will understand yourself to be distinctly authorized, . . . to offer, that His Majesty will abandon the Posts still occupied by His Troops to the Southward and Westward of the Lakes supposing that the Americans should consent, on their Part, to renounce all claims of theirs to those Posts, and to leave them, in common with the rest of that Country, in the undisturbed and independent Possession of the Indians. . . ." (Mayo, *Instructions to British Ministers*, 25–26.)
For a map of the proposed buffer state and for additional information on the project, see Samuel Flagg Bemis, *Jay's Treaty: A Study in Commercial Diplomacy* (Reprinted: New Haven, 1962), 147–82.
7. In MS, "aliments."

national policy. It presses us to terminate differences, to extinguish misunderstandings with Great Britain. It urges us to improve the favourable moment and stamps with the charge of madness the efforts to let go the hold which the Treaty if mutually ratified would give us.

Whoever will cast his eye upon the map of the U States will survey the position of the Western posts their relations to our Western Waters and their general bearings upon our Western Country—and is at the same time capable of making the reflections which an accurate view of the subject suggests—will discover multiplied confirmations of the position that the possession of those posts by us has an intimate connection with the preservation of union between our Western and Atlantic territories—and whoever can appreciate the immense mischiefs of a disunion will feel the prodigious value of the acquisition. To such a man the question may be confidently put. Is there any thing in the Treaty conceded by us to Great Britain to be placed in competition with this single acquisition? The answer could not fail to be in the negative.

But it is said by way of objection that admitting the posts will be surrendered at the time stipulated—it is no acquisition by this Treaty—it is only the enjoyment of a right which was secured by the Treaty of Peace.[8]

With as much good sense might it be said that the stipulation of reparation for the spoliations of our property, or even immediate actual reparation if it had been obtained was nothing gained—because the laws of nations gave us a right to such reparation? [9] And it might in this way be proved to have been impossible for our envoy to have effected any thing useful or meritorious.

Let us see what is the real state of the case. Great Britain had

8. For the text of Article 7 of the definitive treaty of peace between the United States and Great Britain of September 3, 1783, to which H is referring, see "Remarks on the Treaty . . . between the United States and Great Britain," July 9–11, 1795, note 19.

9. Vattel, for example, wrote: "He who does an injury is bound to repair the damage, or to make a just satisfaction, if the evil be not irrepairable, and even to penalty, if penalty be necessary, by way of example, for the safety of the party offended, and also for that of human society. This is the case of a prince who is the author of an unjust war. He is to restore whatever he has taken, send back the prisoners at his own expence; he is to make compensation to the enemy for the injuries and losses he brought upon him . . ." (*Law of Nations*, Book III, Ch. XI, Sec. 185). See also Grotius, *On the Law of War and Peace*, Book III, Ch. X, Sec. 4.

engaged by the Treaty of Peace to surrender the Western posts *with all convenient speed,* but without fixing a precise time. For the cause, or on the pretext of our not having complied with that Treaty, on our part, especially in not removing the impediments which the antecedent laws of particular states opposed to the recovery of British Debts,[10] she delayed & afterwards refused to make the surrender; and when our envoy left this country there was too much appearance of an intention on her part to detain them indefinitely and this, after having actually kept them ten years. The Treaty of peace was consequently in this particular suspended if not superseded. It was either to be reinstated by a new agreement or enforced by arms. The first our envoy has effected. He has brought Great Britain to abandon the dispute, and to fix a precise determinate time when at furthest the posts are to be delivered up. It is therefore to this new agreement that we shall owe the enjoyment of them, and it is of course intitled to the merit of having obtained them. It is a positive ingredient in its value which cannot be taken from it; and it may be added that this is the first time that the merit of procuring by negotiation *restitution* of a *right witheld* was ever denied to the instrument which procured it.

But it is objected, that as much has not been done as might have been done, that restitution of the posts has not been procured but only a promise to restore them at a remote period in exchange for a former promise which had been violated—that there is no good ground of reliance upon the fulfilment of this new promise for the performance of which there ought to have been some surety or guarantee—that the restitution of the posts ought to have been accompanied with indemnification for the detention & for the expences of the Indian Wars which have been occasioned by that detention and by the instigation of British intrigue—that it was better to go to war than to reli[n]quish our claim to such indemnification, or if our present circumstances did not recommend this, it was better to wait till it was more convenient to us to enforce our claim than to give it up. These are the declamations by which this part of the Treaty is arraigned. Let us see if they are the random effusions of enthusiasm or the rational dictates of sound policy.

10. For example, see "Remarks on the Treaty . . . between the United States and Great Britain," July 9–11, 1795, notes 36, 37, 38.

As to the suggestion that more might have been done than was done, it must of necessity be mere conjecture and imagination. If the picture given of the situation of Great Britain was better justified by facts than it is, it would not follow that the suggestion is true. For the thing would depend not on the real situation of that Country, but on the opinion entertained of it by its own administration— on the personal character of the Prince and of his Council—on the degree in which they were influenced by pride and passion or by reason. The hypothesis that the dispositions of a Government are conformable with its situation is as fallacious a one as can be entertained. It is to suppose contrary to every days experience that [cabinets are always wise. It is, on the part of those who draw the inference, to suppose, that a cabinet, the most violent, rash, and foolish, of Europe, is at the same time moderate and prudent enough to act according to the true situation of the country. Who of our enthusiasts, reasoning from his view of the abased condition of Great Britain, has not long since imagined, that she ought to be on her knees to France suing for mercy and forgiveness? yet how different hitherto is the fact. If we carefully peruse the speeches of the leading members of the Convention, we shall observe the menaces against Great Britain frequently intersperced with invitations to peace. While the British government maintains a proud and distant reserve, repels every idea of peace, and inflexibly pursues the path of war. If the situation of Europe in general, and of Great Britain in particular, as is pretended, authorized us to expect, to exact whatever we chose, how happens it, that France, with all her victories, has not yet been able, even to extort peace?

But the picture given us of the situation of Great Britain, to warrant the inferrences which are drawn, is exaggerated and false. It cannot be denied, that she is triumphant on the ocean; that the acquisitions which she has made upon France, are hitherto greater than those which France has made upon her. If, on the one hand, she owes an immense debt, on the other, she possesses an immense credit, which there is no symptom of being impaired. British credit has become in a British mind, an *article of faith,* and is no longer an object of reason. How long it may last, how far it may go, is incalculable. But it is evident, that it still affords prodigious resources, and that it is likely for some time to come, to continue to afford them. In addition to this, it is a well ascertained fact, that her government possesses, internally, as much vigour, and has as much national support as it perhaps ever had at any former period of her history. Alarmed by the unfortunate excesses in France, most men of property cling to the government, and carry with them the great bulk of the nation almost the whole of the farming interest, and much the greatest proportion of other industrious classes. Her manufactures, though probably wounded by the war, are still in a comparitively flourishing condition. They suffice not only for her own supply, but for the full extent of foreign demand, and the markets for them have not been materially contracted by the war. Her foreign commerce continues to be immense; as a specimen of it, it may be mentioned, that the ships from India this year, announced to have been seen upon or near the British coast, amounted to 35 in number, computed to be worth between four and five millions sterling. It is no light circumstance in the estimate of her resources, that a vast preponderancy in that quarter of the globe continues to nourish her wealth and power.

If from a view of Great Britain singly we pass to a view of her in her foreign connections, we shall still find no cause to consider her as a prostrate nation. Among her allies, are the two greatest powers of Europe (France excepted) namely, Russia and Austria, or the Emperor—Spain and Sardinia continue to make common cause with her. There is no power of Europe which has displayed a more uniform character of perseverance than Austria; for which she has very strong motives on the present occasion. Russia too, is remarkable for her steadiness to her purpose, whatever it may be. It is true, that heretofore she has not discovered much zeal in the coalition, but there are symptoms of her becoming more closely and cordially engaged. If she does, she is a great weight in the scale.

Against this will be set the astonishing victories, heroic exploits, and vast armies of France, her rapid conquests to the Rhine, the total reduction of Holland, the progress of her arms in Spain and Italy the detaching of the king of Prussia from the coalition, and the prospect of detaching some others of the German Princes; and it will be added, that the continental enemies of France appear exhausted, despairing and unable to continue the war.

This, if offered only to shew that there is no probability that the enemies of France can succeed in the original object of the war against her, or can divest her of her acquisitions on the continent, has all the force that may be desired to be given to it, but when it is used to prove that the situation of Great Britain is so desperate and humbled as to oblige her to receive from France, or the United States, any conditions which either of them may think fit to impose; the argument is carried infinitely too far. It is one thing for a country to be in a posture not to receive the law from others, and a very different thing for her to be in a situation which obliges others to receive the law from her, and what is still stranger, from all her friends. France evidently cannot annoy Russia—she can, with great difficulty, from their geographical position, make any further acquisitions upon the territories of Austria. Britain and her possessions are essentially safe, while she maintains a decided maritime superiority. As long as this is the case, even supposing her abandoned by all her allies, she never can be in the situation which is pretended by the opposers of the treaty.

But in describing the situation of France, only one side of the medal is presented. There is another side far less flattering, and which, in order to a just conclusion, must be impartially viewed.

If the allies of Great Britain are fatigued and exhausted, France cannot be in a better condition. The efforts of the latter, in proportion to intrinsic resources, have no doubt been much greater than those of the former. It is a consequence from this, physically certain, that France must be still more fatigued and exhausted even than her adversaries. Her acquisitions cannot materially vary this conclusion; the low countries, long the theatre of the war, must have been pretty well emptied before they fell into her hands. Holland is an artificial power—her life and strength were in her credit—this perished with her reduction. Accordingly the succours extracted from her, compared with the scale of the war, have been insignificant.

As to the true position of France, we are not left to mere inference. All the official reports, all the private accounts from thence acknowledge a state of extreme embarrassment and distress: an alarming derangement of the finances, and a scarcity not distant from famine. To this are to be added, a continuance of violent and destructive conflicts of parties, and the unextinguished embers of insurrection.

This fair comparison of the relative situation of the contending parties will, I know, be stigmatized as blazoning the strength and resources of Great Britain, and depreciating the advantages of France. But the cant phrases of party cannot alter the nature of truth —nor will they prevent the people of the United States from listening impartially to it, or from discerning that it is a mark of fidelity to their interests to counteract misrepresentation, by placing facts fairly before them, and a duty which they owe to themselves, and which they cannot omit to perform without betraying their own interests, to receive them candidly, and weigh them maturely.

The conclusion is, that all those highly charged declamations which describe Great Britain to us as vanquished and humbled; as ready to pass under the yoke at our command, and to submit to any conditions which we may think fit to prescribe, are either the chimeras of over-heated imaginations, or the fabrications of impostume; and if listened to, can have no other effect than to inspire a delusive presumption, and a dangerous temerity.

But to judge the better of the extravagance of these declamations, it will be useful to go back to the periods when the negociation began and ended. Our envoy arrived in England and entered upon the business of his mission, at the moment when there was a general elation on account of the naval victory gained by Lord Howe,[11] and previous to those important successes which have terminated in the conquest of Holland; [12] and the treaty was concluded by the 19th of November last, prior to the defection of the king of Prussia.[13] The posture of things at the time it was in negocia-

11. This is a reference to the naval battle known as the "Glorious First of June." It was fought in 1794 in the North Atlantic between the fleets of Lord Howe and Admiral Villaret-Joyeuse.
12. H is referring to a series of French victories in northeastern France in the early summer of 1794, including the battles of Turcoing on May 18 and Fleurus on June 25 and the surrender of Charleroi on June 24. Pursued by the French, the English army under the Duke of York fled eastward, became separated from the Austrians, and passed through Holland into Germany. The English army eventually sailed home, much depleted, from Bremen, in March, 1795.
13. On April 19, 1794, Great Britain and the United Provinces signed a convention and treaty of subsidies witih Prussia at The Hague. Frederick William of Prussia agreed to furnish an army of 62,400 men to fight the French beginning on May 24, 1794, in exchange for a monthly subsidy from the maritime

tion, and not at this time, is the standard by which to try its merits; and it may be observed, that is is probable the negociation received its first impression, and even its general outline anterior to the principal part of the disasters sustained by the coalesced powers in the course of the last campaign.

It may not be improper to add, that if we credit the representations of our envoy Great Britain manifested similar dispositions with regard to the treaty at the commencement as at the close of the negociation: whence it will follow, that too much has been attributed, in this country to the victories of France.

The subject of the second article will be resumed and concluded in the next number.[14]   CAMILLUS.]

---

powers of £50,000 until the end of the year (Martens, Recûeil, V, 610–14). Distracted by the recent Polish rising, Frederick William delayed the supply of troops to Flanders indefinitely. By October the British cabinet had resolved to suspend the subsidy if Prussia continued to fail in fulfilling the conditions of the treaty, and by early November the treaty was effectively recognized as void by both sides.

14. See "The Defence No. VIII," August 15, 1795.

Philo Camillus No. 3 [1]

[New York, August 12, 1795]

For the Argus

CINNA pursues his animadversions upon CAMILLUS but he gives new proofs that he depends more on the prejudices than on the reason of his auditory. To represent CAMILLUS as the abject apologist of Great Britain and the defamer of his own Country—to render him odious because he does not flatter and nourish public errors, but honestly and boldly tells his countrymen salutary though un-

---

ADf, Hamilton Papers, Library of Congress; The [New York] Argus, or Greenleaf's New Daily Advertiser, August 12, 1795.
1. This essay was written in reply to the second article by "Cinna" (Brockholst Livingston), which appeared in The [New York] Argus, or Greenleaf's New Daily Advertiser on August 4, 5, 1795, and was devoted to an attack of "The Defence No. IV," August 1, 1795. For the authorship of the "Cinna" articles, see the introductory note to "The Defence No. I," July 22, 1795.
"Philo Camillus No. 3" is one of four essays. The other essays in this series are dated July 27, August 7, 19, 1795.

pleasant truths—are evidently with *Cinna* the chief hope of his cause. Nor is he very wrong in the course he takes. Such props are necessary to him. But he ought to be more cautious in the employment of them, lest by the too free use he impair their efficacy. Does he not fear that these very obvious reflections may occur to a sensible people? Why is it that the opposers of the Treaty so constantly appeal to our passions, and to convince us they are in the right endeavour first to make us angry? Do they imagine that we can only feel, that we can not reason? Do they suppose that a man is best-fitted to judge in proportion as he is agitated and incensed? Or is it that they really dare not trust their cause to the sober result of fair discussion and calm reasoning? Is it that they desire to shut our ears to the wholesome advice of tried and faithful friends, by raising unmerited prejudices and resentments against them? Do they mean to lead us captive by our passions and thus to make us instruments of designs repugnant to our interests and subversive of our present happy condition?

Can CINNA seriously imagine, that he will be able to dupe a discerning people into a distrust of men, whose public and private conduct have been a uniform series of evidence of public and private integrity? Is he so weak as to suppose that his fellow Citizens will give credit to the gross suggestion that such men who have also been among the most steady and persevering [2] defenders of their country against Great Britain have now become her partizans or advocates? Is it any proof of this, that this endeavour to shew that in particular questions arising subsequent to the peace there is reasonable ground of doubt whether the delinquency imputed to Great Britain has been as great as has been alleged and that there have been mutual faults? Are sincerity and plain dealing marks of want of friendship? Are they not rather proofs of the truest friendship of one that dares offer honest advice even at the hazard of displeasing?

In Courts, sycophants flatter the errors & prejudices of the Prince —in Republics sycophants flatter the errors and prejudices of the people. In both, honest and independent men are frequently obliged to tell unpalatable truths, which are well or ill received according

2. In MS, "perserving."

to the virtue & good sense of those to whom they are addressed. *Cinna* knows that they are not always well received. He hopes this will be the case in the present instance, but he will probably be disappointed.

In an altercation between two individuals in which there were mutual faults who would deserve to be called the true friend? He who should tell one of the disputants of the faults on his part and advise him to moderation and amicable adjustment—or he who should assure him that his antagonist was intirely in the wrong that he had nothing to blame himself for & that his honor was concerned in pursuing the quarrel without relaxation at the peril of life & fortune?

CINNA, if he knows CAMILLUS, knows that this is not the first time he has stemmed the current of prejudice and has been traduced and vilified for it. But experience on former occasions has taught him to believe that he may safely rely on the ultimate good sense of his fellow Citizens for a justification of his motives.

It is curious to observe an expedient, which has lately been adopted by the party to which CINNA belongs. They affect to brand their opponents with the charge of *Toryism.* Men, who in this state have for a long time upheld their power and by means of it amassed wealth, with the aid and support of a long list of tories—who even now count among their most zealous adherents men of this description * & some of them of the most profligate character have the audacity to bring the charge of Toryism against a majority of the most conspicuous most tried and most determined Whigs of the Country. Can the Spirit of Whigghism hear this obloquy without indignation? Can these whom that generous spirit truly actuates endure an attempt to blast the characters of its most faithful votaries?

It cannot be: the people of America know the men who have acted a part in their public affairs and they know how to appreciate them. Their esteem will be an impenetrable shield against malice and detraction.

CAMILLUS did not take the course which he has pursued of choice. It no doubt would have been more agreeable to him to have been silent on such topics. But the antagonists of the Treaty made it

---

* Not only the standard bearers of public meetings but some of their Champions in print are notoriously of this class.

necessary to place the real state of the question before the people to enable them to judge of the justice of the virulent attack which has been made on our envoy for not attempting to extort from great Britain an acknowlegement of delinquency, though at the price of our national peace and though they who make the attack know in their consciences that such an attempt would not have been made with the least prospect of success.[3]

But while Camillus has shewn that there have been breaches of the Treaty of peace on our part and that it is difficult to pronounce where the first breach lay [4]—he has done nothing that warrants the imputations of having held up this country as "a faithless and treacherous nation" of having justified "a perfidious Prince for his breaches of faith and violences towards America." [5] From an imperfect social organization like ours under the consideration and from the strong impulse of particular circumstances and passions there may have been infractions of a particular Treaty by parts of the Community without amounting to what would fix on a nation the stigma of "*faithless* and *treacherous*." The King of Great Britain may not have been as culpable in particular things as he has been charged to be and yet his conduct towards us in other respects may have been unjust and violent. Camillus evidently admits the latter to have been the case and asserts that we had suffered wrongs of such a nature as ought either to have been adjusted by reparation or avenged by reprisals. Enough has been replied to Cinna's railing. It is time to come to his reasoning.

He in vain endeavours to derive a vindication of the Trespass act [6] from a display of the aggravating circumstances of our war with Great Britain, another auxiliary pressed into the service to

3. At this point H wrote and crossed out: "In yielding to this necessity he has been cautious too not to pronounce a definitive opinion of his own—he has confined himself to these conclusions, that the question with regard to the right of compensation for the negroes & to the first breach of the Treaty of peace were very mixed difficult and doubtful such as."
4. See "The Defence No. IV," August 1, 1795.
5. These quotations are from "Cinna No. 2" (*The* [New York] *Argus, or Greenleaf's New Daily Advertiser*, August 4, 1795).
6. "An Act for granting a more effectual Relief in Cases of certain Trespasses," passed March 17, 1783 (*New York Laws*, 6th Sess., Ch. XXXI). See "The Defence No. IV," August 1, 1795. For "Cinna's" criticism of this essay, see *The* [New York] *Argus, or Greenleaf's New Daily Advertiser*, August 5, 1795.

inflame the passions. Whatever may be the effect of these to excuse the act in *foro conscientiæ*, or in reference to the frailties of the human passions, it does nothing to prove that it was conformable with the principles of PUBLIC RIGHT as received among nations, or that its operation did not infract the Treaty of peace. Nothing could be a clearer violation of the laws of War than to say that no military order of a public enemy should be pleaded in bar of a civil action of Trespass. Nothing could be a more certain contravention of a Treaty of Peace than to allow actions of Trespass to be maintained against the subjects of a public enemy for acts done during the war under his military authority and in exclusion of the plea of a military order. No matter what may have been the manner in which the war was carried on. Tis the essence of a Treaty of Peace to extinguish all questions on that head and to secure to each party amnesty and indemnity. Without this the state of war would continue and would be inextinguishable. Reason and writers agree that this amnesty & indemnity are always implied though in some treaties there are for greater caution express clauses; an example pertinent in reference to the article respecting the negroes [7] to shew that there are sometimes express stipulations of what would be understood without them.

It is true as alleged that the plea of a military order might have been used to cover great abuses but what war does not produce multiplied abuses? The peace of nations requires nevertheless that these abuses should be submitted to rather than controvert the efficacy of military authority—because to do it is to subvert all the rights of War—and to deny all the effects of acquisition and capture in war.

But it is unlucky for the apology which is made for this act that it passed only *seven days* before the news of the provisional articles arrived in this Country and when it was known that negotiations for peace were going on and expected that the event would speedily take place [8]—and also that the act could only have its effect when

7. H is referring to Article 7 of the definitive treaty between Great Britain and the United States, September 3, 1783. For the text of this article, see "Remarks on the Treaty . . . between the United States and Great Britain," July 9–11, 1795, note 19. For an earlier discussion of this article, see "The Defence No. III," July 29, 1795.

8. In the newspaper the remainder of this sentence has been replaced by the following words: "It is also too evident that it must have passed in contempla-

in consequence of that event and by an evacuation of the Southern District process could be issued upon it. It is certain that good men concurred in this act but this is only one proof among a myriad that the passions of a revolution are apt to hurry even good men into excesses.

CINNA recurring to the subterfuge which Camillus has noticed and refuted says "A mind not warped by prejudice nor disposed to deceive itself is at some difficulty to imagine how an act passed six months before the definitive Treaty was signed can be tortured into an infraction of that very Treaty." [9] But let me ask Cinna how on the principle of this argument the carrying away of the negroes which happened four months before the same signing could be any more a breach of the Treaty? The answer in each case must be that though positive *restitutions* by either party may have been postponed to the definitive Treaty, yet the provisional Treaty ought to have arrested the progress of all acts on either side contrary to its provisions—a principle however which bears hard upon our omission to act upon the fifth article till after the Definitive Treaty. [10]

Mr. Jefferson has taken better ground than CINNA, by saying that the Trespass Act was not an infraction of the Treaty because it dated prior to the provisional articles. [11] But if Camillus is right in the fact his answer to this is conclusive—namely that the Trespass Act continued to *operate* not only after the provisional but after the definitive Treaty down to [April 1787]. [12]

The plainest understanding however must perceive that there can

---

tion of this event, since it could only have its effect when, by means of peace and an evacuation of the southern district, process could be issued upon it."

9. This is a quotation from "Cinna No. 2" (*The* [New York] *Argus, or Greenleaf's New Daily Advertiser,* August 4, 1795).

10. The provisional treaty of peace between the United States and Great Britain was signed on November 30, 1782, and ratifications were exchanged on August 6, 1783. The definitive treaty was signed on September 3, 1783. Ratifications were exchanged on May 12, 1784 (Miller, *Treaties,* II, 96–107, 151–57). Article 5 of both treaties declared that Congress should recommend to the states the restitution of all Loyalist property.

11. The reference in this sentence is to Thomas Jefferson's letter to George Hammond of May 29, 1792, in which Jefferson defended the alleged breaches of the treaty by the United States (ADf, Thomas Jefferson Papers, Library of Congress; *ASP, Foreign Relations,* I, 201–37). For an earlier discussion of this subject, see "Remarks on the Treaty . . . between the United States and Great Britain," July 9–11, 1795.

12. Space left blank in MS. The material within brackets has been taken from the newspaper.

be no difference whether an act passed before or after the Treaty if *in fact* it had an operation contrary to the Treaty. Tis the *operation*, the *effect*, not the date of the law, which is the material thing.

But Cinna following Mr. Jefferson labours to prove that it is a clear position that the Treaty did controul the laws of States which were contrary to it—and in the course of his remarks makes these assertions—1 that the proposition is so self evident to an American Lawyer, that without any proof it forces the same conviction upon his mind as the plainest axioms of Euclid—and 2d. that the Supreme Court of this State in the case of another act decided in conformity with this position.[13]

Camillus has justly observed upon this position [14] that it is a question of theory, and that whether true or not if there were laws of any States the operation of which did in fact contravene the Treaty, it was no justification to the Power whose Treaty with us was contravened that in the theory of our constitution Treaties were paramount to laws. That Power might reply—your theories are nothing to us—tis the fact alone which concerns us and tis enough that we know that laws of certain States do in fact contravene our Treaty.

Cinna replies—that he does not comprehend "what is meant by a law being a question of theory." [15] Camillus said, not that a law was a question of theory for this would be senseless, but that [it] is a question of theory whether a Treaty of the U States under the consideration did *ipso facto* controul a state law contrary thereto, or whether it only operated to lay an obligation on the state to repeal such law. This proposition is surely one not difficult to be comprehended, and it is manifestly true.

Camillus would probably not dispute with Cinna that the better opinion is that a Treaty *ought* to controul a state law, but still it is a question about which there was room for and did exist a diversity of opinion, and it may be added of practice.

Self evident as Cinna may affect to consider the proposition, he will find it is one on the principle of which theoretic Writers are

13. For the points made in this paragraph, see "Cinna No. 2" (*The* [New York] *Argus, or Greenleaf's New Daily Advertiser*, August 4, 5, 1795).

14. See "The Defence No. IV," August 5, 1795.

15. This quotation is from "Cinna No. 2" (*The* [New York] *Argus, or Greenleaf's New Daily Advertiser*, August 4, 1795).

not agreed. Rutherford in his Institutes of Natural Law (B II Chap III Page 61) [16] speaking of the Legislative Power has this sentiment "In ALLIANCES LEAGUES or CONVENTIONS, if they bind any members (of the society) to give up their private claims or to do any thing which is inconsistent with *the civil laws then in being* its authority (The Legislative authority) makes *them* void of course *unless it interposes to establish them.*" This passage denies the power of Treaty to abrogate the antecedent civil laws as to the claims and acts of Individuals.

But not only was there room for difference of opinion, but it actually existed in a very great degree in many of the States. If Cinna be a lawyer and was at the bar of this State when the question on the Trespass Act was pending, he must know in his heart that the prevailing opinion of our professional men was against the position which he considers as self evident and that the contrary Doctrine was strenuously and seriously maintained in argument by some of our most respectable practicers.[17]

16. Thomas Rutherforth, *Institutes of Natural Law: Being the substance of a Course of Lectures on Grotius de Jure Belli et Pacis* (Cambridge, 1754-1756), II, 59. The correct page reference is given in the newspaper version.

17. At this point H wrote in the margin: "1782
11 April 1783
9 Aug 1786."
H was apparently referring to statements made by "Philo Cinna" in an article entitled "Camillus refuted by A. Hamilton," which appeared in *The* [New York] *Argus, or Greenleaf's New Daily Advertiser*, August 10, 1795. This article began by contrasting H's statement in "The Defence No. III," July 29, 1795—that the United States had not uniformly charged the British with the carrying away of Negroes and the detention of the western posts as the first infractions of the treaty of peace until May 29, 1792, when Jefferson wrote to Hammond (see note 10)—with a resolution which H had put forward in the Continental Congress on May 26, 1783, that the United States should remonstrate with the British government (see "Continental Congress. Motion of Protest against British Practice of Carrying off American Negroes," May 26, 1783). "Philo Cinna" continued: "If then, Congress, as early as May 1783, complained of this infraction, they must have regarded it as the *first* breach, for Great Britain had not yet had time to hear of what was passing in this country on the subject of the treaty, much less to complain of any violation on our part. It will be recollected that the treaty had been received by Congress early in the preceding month.

"By this resolve, it also appears, that Colonel Hamilton thought the treaty binding from the signature of the provisional articles, but Camillus contends, that it was not so until the exchange of the ratification of the definitive articles which took place more than one year later.

"Nor is this the only instance in which our government *formally* and explicitly took the ground, although one would be led to conclude from Camillus, that to Mr. Jefferson alone belonged the credit of discovering it."

He has thought fit to quote Mr. Hamilton as having in the case of Rutgers and Waddington relied on the Treaty against the law.[18] He is right in this, but he might have added that for some time Mr. Hamilton was almost the only practicer who maintained the doctrine, and that by doing it he rendered himself not a little unpopular among that description of men with whom if I mistake not Cinna is connected in politics, and who reprobated it as a very heretical and unpatriotic opinion.

Camillus has also observed that it was understood that a Majority of our Supreme Court Bench would have maintained the principle of the Trespass act against the Treaty. Cinna asks how this was understood? Did the judges give Camillus an extrajudicial opinion?

Is it then a very uncommon thing for the opinions of Judges to be sounded by the bar in private conversations or on collateral questions in Court? Are judges always so much upon their guard that their leanings are not discerned by attentive observers before they are expressed by judicial determinations? Are there never clues to their opinions before they have pronounced them on the Bench?

An experienced professional man will be at no loss how to answer these questions—and will know that the opinions of Judges are often understood before hand with moral certainty—and one who was at our bar at the period referred to will also know that there was little doubt what would have been the determination of our Supreme Court on the point in question, and that it would have supported the objectionable clause of the act.

"On the 11th April 1783, Congress agreed to a proclamation, declaring a cessation of hostilities and only four days after

"Resolved, That the commander in chief be instructed to make the proper arrangements with the commander in chief of the British forces for receiving possession of the posts in the United States occupied by the troops of his Britannic Majesty, and *for obtaining the delivery of all negroes and other property of the inhabitants of the United States in possession of the British forces, or any subject of, or adherent to his Britannic Majesty.*

"Again, on the 9th August 1786, Congress resolved, that the Secretary for foreign affairs cause to be made out separate lists of the number, name, and owners of the negroes belonging to the citizens of each State, and carried away by the British in *contravention of the treaty,* and that he transmit said lists to the executives of the States to which they respectively belong."

18. The case of *Rutgers* v *Waddington,* in which H represented the defendant, was heard in the New York Mayor's Court in 1784. For details of the case, see Goebel, *Law Practice,* I, 282–419. See also H to Jefferson, April 19, 1792.

If we were to review how many suits were brought under this act in the Supreme Court & how many recoveries had—without any example of an obstacle from the Treaty, we should find a strong negative confirmation of the supposed disposition of the Bench and of the opinion of the Bar.

Nor is this any impeachment of the Court as *Cinna* would have it. It was a fair question whether a Treaty did or did not controul a legislative act—or whether it only operated to render it the duty of the Legislature to repeal it. And in the particular case, the provision of the Act was so special & peremptory, that it left no room for restraining constructions.

But CINNA asserts further that the Supreme Court did in another case admit the principle of the controuling influence of the Treaty —and he quotes a letter from our District Attorney in proof of it.[19] Mr. Harrison it is true states that with regard to British Creditors the Superior Courts soon *restrained the operation* of the Act relative to debts due to persons within the enemies lines.[20] But he does not affirm, and I am much mistaken if he would affirm, that the rest[r]aint in this particular was on the principle of the effect of the Treaty to controul the law.

There is good reason to believe that the Treaty was a *collateral motive* with the Court for giving a restrictive interpretation to the law but it is believed that they never admitted *Cinna's* position as the ground of determination.

19. "Cinna" quoted the following extract from a letter written on December 4, 1790, to Jefferson by Richard Harison, a New York lawyer and Federalist, who became United States attorney for the District of New York: " 'The operation of the act,' says he, speaking of the act relative to debts due to persons within the enemies lines, 'became soon after the peace a subject of much complaint, grounded upon that article of the treaty, which forbids any impediment to the recovery of the full value in sterling money of all bona fide debts, and that which declares that no person shall suffer any future loss in his person, liberty or property. With regard to British creditors who were supposed to be the proper objects of the 4th article of the treaty, the *superior courts of the state soon restrained the operation of the act, and I do not know a single instance* where they have been held to be affected by it' " (*The* [New York] *Argus, or Greenleaf's New Daily Advertiser,* August 5, 1795). Harison's draft of this letter is in the New-York Historical Society, New York City. The extract of the letter is printed in *ASP, Foreign Relations,* I, 231–32. See also Goebel, *Law Practice,* I, 271–74.

20. "An Act Relative to Debts due to Persons within the Enemies lines" was passed by the New York legislature on July 12, 1782 (*New York Laws,* 6th Sess., Ch. I).

There were expressions in the law itself which countenanced a restrictive interpretation. The Title is "An Act relative to Debts due to persons *within the enemy's lines.*" The Preamble relates, as objects of the act, to *inhabitants of this state* who had not *remained* within the enemy's power who were indebted to *others* who did *so remain.* The creditors described in the body of the act are persons who *remained* with the enemy or went into or were sent within *the enemy's lines.* It is evident that this act gives locality to the situation of the Creditors who were to be affected by it and could not fairly have been extended to British Creditors who were resident in the British dominions. It was natural too to understand the word *inhabitants* as equivalent to *citizens* and the mode of expression seems to look to *inhabitant* or *citizen* creditors as well as to inhabitant or Citizen Debtors; so that it was easy without resorting to the effect of the Treaty to consider British subjects as not within the act— by which construction an interference with the Treaty was avoided without admitting its controuling influence. The Courts shewed a uniform and a laudable disposition to narrow the operation of this act on account of its infraction of private contracts, and they were no doubt glad to find in the act itself the means of escaping from a violation of the Treaty.

This from the best sources of information is believed to be a faithful account of the transaction. It is at the same time one that does not confirm the representation of Cinna. The further observation will be pursued in a subsequent paper.[21]   Philo Camillus

21. "Philo Camillus No. 4," August 19, 1795.

The Defence No. VIII [1]

[New York, August 15, 1795]

One of the particulars in which our Envoy is alleged to have fallen short of what might and ought to have been done respects the time for the surrender of the Western posts. It is alleged, that there

ADf, Hamilton Papers, Library of Congress; *The* [New York] *Argus, or Greenleaf's New Daily Advertiser,* August 15, 1795.

1. For background to this document, see the introductory note to "The Defence No. I," July 22, 1795.

ought either to have been an immediate surrender or some guarantee or surety for the performance of the new promise. Both parts of the alternative presuppose that Great Britain was to have no will upon the subject—that no circumstances of security or convenience to her were to be consulted, that our Envoy was not to negotiate but to command.[2] How unsubstantial the foundation on which this course of proceeding is recommended has been already developped.[3]

The fact was, that our Envoy urged a prompt surrender. The British Minister answered that this could not be—that representations against it had been received from the companies concerned in the Western Trade upon considerations which that Government could not refuse to respect—that the arrangements of those companies were made without expectation of the event which was then contemplated—that it required not less than Eighteen months to wind up pending enterprises and make new dispositions corresponding with the proposed change—that among other inconveniences to be anticipated from a sudden change they might be exposed to the resentment of the Indians—to prepare whose minds for the event time was requisite—that shortly after the Treaty of Peace, Agents of the U States had held a language to the Indians importing that they had been abandonned and sacrificed by Great Britain,[4] an intimation from which much embarrassment had been experienced— that this circumstance was a motive to caution—as what had happened once might happen again and much mischief might ensue.[5]

2. The allegations in the preceding sentences were made by several opponents of the treaty, but in this particular instance H is apparently paraphrasing the arguments advanced in the first "Cato" essay by Robert R. Livingston (The [New York] Argus, or Greenleaf's New Daily Advertiser, July 15, 1795). For the authorship of these essays, see the introductory note to "The Defence No. I," July 22, 1795. See also "Remarks on the Treaty . . . between the United States and Great Britain," July 9–11, 1795; "The Defence No. III," July 29, 1795; "The Defence No. IV," August 12, 1795.
3. See "The Defence Nos. II, III, IV, V," July 25, 29, August 1, 5, 1795.
4. H is referring to a speech delivered by the United States Indian commissioners on October 12, 1784, during the negotiations for the Treaty of Fort Stanwix (Neville Craig, ed., The Olden Time [Cincinnati, 1876], II, 414).
5. This paragraph is a paraphrase of a portion of one of John Jay's dispatches to Secretary of State Edmund Randolph, November 19, 1794. See "Remarks on the Treaty . . . between the United States and Great Britain," July 9–11, 1795, note 4.
It should also be noted that the paragraph in question from the MS does not appear in the newspaper. In its place are two paragraphs which read: "The fact was that our envoy pressed an early evacuation of the Posts; but there was

What [6] was to be done in this case? Was the negotiation to break off or was the delay to be admitted? The last was preferred by our envoy and the preference was rightly judged.

The consequence of breaking off the Negotiation has been stated. No reasonable man will doubt that delay was preferable to War, if there be good ground of reliance that the stipulation will be fulfilled at the appointed time. Let us calmly examine this point.

The argument against it is drawn from the breach of the former promise. To be authorised to press this argument we ought to be sure that all was right on our part. After what has been offered on this subject, are we still convinced that this was the case? Are we able to say that there was nothing in our conduct which furnished a ground for that of Great Britain? Has it not been shewn to be a fact that from the arrival of the provisional articles in this country till after the ratification here of the definitive Treaty acts of States

---

an inflexible adherence on the other side to the term limited in the treaty. The reasons understood to have been assigned for it, were to this effect: (viz.) That according to the course of the Indian trade, it was customary to spread through the nations, goods to a large amount, the returns for which could not be drawn into Canada, in a shorter period than was proposed to be fixed for the evacuation; that the impression which the surrender of all the Posts to American garrisons might make on the minds of the Indians, could not be foreseen; that there was the greater reason for caution, as on a former occasion it had been intimated to them by public agents of the United States, that they had been *forsaken* and *given up* by the British government: that the protection promised on our part, however sincere and however competent in other respects, might not be sufficient in the first instance to prevent the embarrassment which might ensue; that for these reasons the traders ought to have time to conclude their adventures, which were predicated upon the existing state of things; that they would in future calculate upon the new state of things but that in the mean time the care of government ought not to be withdrawn from them.

"There is ground to believe that there were representations on behalf of the Canada traders, alledging a longer term than that which was adopted in the treaty, to be necessary to wind up and adopt their arrangements to the next state of things; and that the term suggested by them was abridged several months. And it may not be useless to observe, as explanatory of the reasons given, that in fact it is the course of the trade to give long credits to the Indians, and that the returns for goods furnished in one year only, come in the next year."

6. In the draft H started this paragraph with the following sentences, which he crossed out: "These were the reasons principally assigned by the British negotiator. Though they were not without weight, answers could be and were given to them. The answers which were given to them did not satisfy. The first of June 1796 was insisted upon as the shortest practicable term."

interdicting the recovery of British Debts [7] and other acts militating against the Treaty continued in operation? Can we doubt that subjects of Great Britain affected by these acts carried their complaints to the ears of their Government? Can we wonder if they made serious impressions there, if they produced dissatisfaction and distrust? Is it very extraordinary, if they excited the idea of detaining the posts as a pledge till there were better indications on our part? Is it surprising, if the continuance of those acts and the addition of others which were new & positive breaches of the Treaty prolonged the detention of the posts?

In fine—was the delay in surrendering so intirely destitute of cause, so unequivocal a proof of a perfidious character as to justify the conclusion that no future dependence can be made on the promises of the British Government? Discerning men will not hastily subscribe to this conclusion.

Mutual charges of breach of faith are not uncommon between nations. Yet this does not prevent their making new stipulations with each other and relying upon their performance. The argument from the breach of one promise, if real, to the breach of every other is not supported by experience—and if adopted as a general rule would multiply infinitely the impediments to accord and agreement among nations.

The truth is, that though nations will too often evade their promises on colorable pretexts, yet few are so profligate as to do it without such pretexts. In clear cases, self interest dictates a regard to the obligations of good faith. Nor is there any thing in the history of Great Britain which warrants the opinion that she is more unmindful than other nations of her character for good faith.

7. At this point in the draft H wrote and crossed out the following: "continued unrepealed that when the ratification was received in England it was unaccompanied by an account of their repeal? Can we doubt that these laws were represented by the British Merchants to the British Government as subsisting obstacles to the recovery of their debts for the removal of which they had a right to some pledge? Is it not a fact that our general Government had manifested symptoms of impotency which gave just cause to doubt its power to enforce the fulfilment of its engagements? that among other causes of inability it was even destitute of Indians of its own? Did not these circumstances afford real occasion of doubt to the British Government whether the article respecting the debts would be complied with by us? Did this furnish no excuse for delay in surrendering the posts? Did not a continuance of the same circumstances continue the excuse for further delay?"

Yet she must be so, and in an extreme degree, if she be capable of breaking without real cause, a second promise on the same point, after the termination by a new Treaty of an old dispute concerning it and this too on the basis of mutual reparation. It would indicate a destitution of principle, a contempt of character much beyond the usual measure; & to an extent which it may be affirmed is intirely improbable.

It is a circumstance of some moment in the question that the second promise is free from the vagueness of the first as to the time of execution. It is not to be performed *with all convenient speed*,[8] but by a day certain, which cannot be exceeded.[9] This would give point to violation, and render it unequivocal.

Another argument against the probability of performance has been deduced from the supposed deficiency of good reasons for the delay, which is represented as evidence of want of sincerity in the promise.

Besides the reasons which were assigned for that delay there are others that may be conjectured to have operated which it would not have been equally convenient to avow but which serve to explain the delay different from the supposition of its having been calculated for ultimate evasion. If, as we have with too much cause suspected, Great Britain or her Representative in Canada, whether with or without orders, has really countenanced the hostilities of the Western Indians, it was to be expected that she would think it incumbent upon her to give them sufficient time to make peace before an evacuation of the posts should put them intirely in our power. She might otherwise have provoked them to hostilities against her own settlements; and have kindled in their minds inextinguishable resentments. It was not certain how soon a peace could be brought about, and it might be supposed that the disposition to it on our part might be weakened or strengthened by the proximity or remoteness of the period of the surrender. Moreover some considerable time might be requisite to prepare those estab-

8. The words in italics are from Article 7 of the definitive treaty of peace of 1783 (Miller, *Treaties*, II, 155).

9. Article 2 of the Jay Treaty reads in part: "This Evacuation shall take place on or before the first Day of June One thousand seven hundred and ninety six . . ." (Miller, *Treaties*, II, 246). For the text of Article 2, see "Remarks on the Treaty . . . between the United States and Great Britain," July 9–11, 1795, note 3.

lishments for the security of Canada which the relinquishment of the posts on our side would be deemed to render necessary.

The latter motive is one not justly objectionable. The former implies an embarrassment resulting from a culpable policy, which was intitled to no indulgence from us, but which nevertheless must have had a pretty imperious influence on the conduct of the other party and must have created an obstacle to a speedy surrender not easy to be surmounted. Taken together, we find in the reasons assigned and in those which may be presumed to have operated a solution of the pertinacity of Great Britain on the subject of time, without impeaching on that account the sincerity of the promise to surrender.

But we have very strong holds for the performance of this promise upon the interest of Great Britain—1 the interest which every nation has in not intirely forfeiting its reputation for honor and fidelity 2 the interest which results from the correlative stipulation with regard to the indemnification for the British Debts,[10] a point upon which there will be no inconsiderable mercantile sensibility 3 the interest of preserving peace with this country, the interruption of which after all that has passed could not fail to attend the non-surrender of the posts at the stipulated time.

It is morally certain, that circumstances will every day add strength to this last motive. Time has already done much for us and will do more. Every hour's continuance of the war in Europe must necessarily add to the inconvenience of a rupture with this country and to the motives which Great Britain must feel to avoid an increase of the number of her enemies, to desire peace, and if obtained to preserve it.

The enemies of the Treaty upon their own calculations can hardly dispute, that if the War continues another year after the present, the probable situation of Great Britain will be a complete security for her compliance with her promise to surrender the posts. But let us suppose that a general peace takes place in Europe this Winter—what may then be the disposition of Great Britain in June next as to War or peace with this Country?

I answer that the situation will be of all others that which is most

10. This is a reference to Article 6 of the Jay Treaty. For the text of this article, see "Remarks on the Treaty . . . between the United States and Great Britain," July 9–11, 1795, note 13.

likely to indispose her to a War with us. There is no juncture at which War is more unwelcome to a Nation than immediately after the experience of another War which has required great exertions and has been expensive bloody & calamitous. The minds of all men then dread the renewal of so great an evil, and are disposed rather to make sacrifices to peace than to plunge afresh into hostilities. The situation of Great Britain at the end of the war in which she is now engaged is likely to be the most discouraging that can be imagined to the provocation of new wars. Here we may discover a powerful security for the performance of her stipulations.[11]

As to the idea of a Gu[a]rantee or Surety for the fulfilment of the promise, it cannot be seriously believed that it was obtainable. It would have been an admission of the party that there was a well founded distrust of its faith. To consent to it therefore would have been to subscribe to its own humiliation and disgrace, the expectation of which has been shewn too ridiculous.

But why was there not equally good reason that we should give a guarantee or surety for the performance of our new promise with regard to the Debts? And if there was to have been reciprocity, where should we have conveniently found that guarantee or surity? Should we have thought it very reputable to ourselves to have been obliged to furnish it?

The arguments of the opposers of the Treaty are extremely at variance with each other. On the one hand they represent it as fraught with advantages to Great Britain without equivalents to the U States—as a premeditated scheme to sacrifice our Trade and Navigation to hers as a plan dictated by her for drawing the two countries into close connection and alliance and for making our interests subservient to hers; on the other hand, they tell us that there is no security for the surrender of the posts according to stipulation. How is the one thing to be reconciled with the other? If the Treaty is such an immense boon to Great Britain, if it be such a master piece of political craft on her side—can there by any danger that she will destroy her favourite work by not performing the conditions on which its efficacy & duration must depend? There is no better

11. At this point in the draft H wrote and crossed out: "But it may be asked did not consideration of similar import ensure us better terms from Great Britain in the formation of the Treaty."

settled position than that the breach of any article of a Treaty by one party gives the other an option to consider the whole Treaty as annulled. Would Great Britain give us this option in a case in which she had so much to lose by doing it?

This glaring collision of arguments proves how superficially the adversaries of the Treaty have considered the subject, and how little reliance can be placed on the views they give of it.

In estimating the plan which the Treaty adopts for the settlement of the old controversy, it is an important reflection, that from the course of things, there will be nothing to be performed by us before the period for the restitution of the posts will have elapsed, and that if this restitution should be evaded we shall be free to put an end to the whole Treaty, about which there could not be a moments hesitation. We should then be where we were before the Treaty, with the advantage of having strengthened the justice of our cause by removing every occasion of reproach which the infractions of the Treaty of peace may have furnished against us.

Two other particulars, in which this part of the Treaty is supposed to be defective, regard the want of indemnification for the detention of the posts and for the expences of Indian Wars.

Those who make the objection may be safely challenged to produce precedents of similar indemnifications, unless imposed by *conquering* powers on the vanquished, or by powers of overbearing strength upon those which were too weak to dispute the logic of superior force. If this were the relative situation of the U States and Great Britain then is the Treaty inexcusably faulty—but if the parties were to treat and agree as equal powers, then is the pretension extravagant and impracticable. The restitution of the specific thing detained is all that was to be expected, and it may be added, it is all that was ever really expected on the part of this country so far as we may reason either from official acts or informal expressions of the public opinion.[12]

12. In the margin opposite this sentence H wrote "Qr." In addition, at this point in the draft H wrote and crossed out: "A demand of the surrender of the posts has been repeatedly made but unaccompanied in any instance to my recollection with a demand of compensation for the detention. As to indemnification for the expence of Indian Wars, the mention of it till the present moment would have been considered as little less than insanity.

"What British Minister would have been hardy enough to have gone to the House of Commons to ask provision for such a stipulation?"

In cases where clear injuries are done affecting objects of known or easily ascertainable values, pecuniary compensation may be expected to be obtained by negotiation; but it is believed that it will be impossible to cite an example of such compensation so obtained, in a case in which territory has been held on a dispute of Title or as a hostage for some other claim, (as in the present instance for securing the performance of the [4th] [13] article of the Treaty of Peace.) The recovery of the territory witheld is the usual satisfaction.

The want of a rule to adjust consequential damages is in such cases a very great difficulty. In the instance under discussion, this difficulty would be peculiarly great. The posts are for the most part in a wilderness. There are but two of them which have any adjacent settlements—Point au fer or Dutchmans point to one of which a part of a tract of land called Caldwells Manor has been claimed as appurtenant.[14] Lake Champlain with very few inhabitants is appurtenant.[15] Detroit which has a settlement in the town & neighbourhood of between two & three thousand souls. In the vicinity of the other posts there is scarcely an inhabitant. It follows that very little damage could be predicated either upon the loss of revenue from or of the profits of Trade with the settlements in the vicinity of the posts. The trade with the Indians within our limits would consequently be the basis of the claim of compensation. But here the ignorance or spirit of exaggeration of the opponents of the Treaty has been particularly exemplified. The annual loss from this source has been stated by a very zealous Writer against the Treaty who signs himself CATO at 800 000 Dollars.[16]

Now it is a fact well ascertained that the mean value of the whole

---

In the margin opposite this crossed-out material H wrote and crossed out: "Qr. as to Mr Jays instructions."

13. Space left blank in MS. The bracketed material has been taken from the newspaper. For the text of Article 4 of the definitive peace treaty of 1783, see "Remarks on the Treaty . . . between the United States and Great Britain," July 9-11, 1794, note 14.

14. Point au Fer and Dutchman's Point were British posts at the northern end of Lake Champlain. Point au Fer is on the western shore of the lake about seven miles from the Canadian border. Dutchman's Point, on the island of North Hero, included in its jurisdiction Caldwell's Manor, which occupied part of a spit of the mainland in the neighborhood of Alburg, Vermont. See "Conversation with George Beckwith," June 15, 1791.

15. This sentence is omitted in the newspaper.

16. This statement is from the first article by "Cato" (Robert R. Livingston) in The [New York] Argus, or Greenleaf's New Daily Advertiser, July 15, 1795.

exports from Canada in peltries (which constitute the returns of
Indian Trade) in the years 1786 & 1787 was something short of
800 000 Dollars. It is also a fact in which all men informed on the
subject agree that the Trade with the Indians within our limits [17]
is only about one eighth of that which furnishes the peltry exported
from Canada. Hence the total *product* of our Indian Trade could
not be computed at more than 100 000 Dollars. What proportion of
this may be profit is not easy to be determined but it is certain that
the profits of that Trade from the diminution of wild animals and
the inferiority of their kinds are not considerable. Many assert that
it is scarcely any longer worth following. Twenty ⅌ Cent therefore would probably be a large allowance, which would bring the
loss on our Indian Trade by the detention of the posts to about
20 000 instead of 800 000 Dollars per annum as has been asserted.

But might not a claim even of this sum by way of indemnification
be encountered with some force by the observation that there is the
highest probability that the capital and labour which would have
been employed producing 20 000 Dollars profit on the Trade with
the Indians have been quite as productively employed in other channels and consequently that there may have been no loss at all?

Thus we see how erroneous the data which serve to magnify
claims in themselves insignificant, and which from the great uncertainty of their quantum, are exposed to serious objections. Are
claims like these proper subjects on which to stake the peace of the
U States?

The reasonableness of indemnification for the expences of Indian
Wars, independent of the unusual nature of the claim might have
been matter of endless debate. We might have been told that the
Indians ascribe those wars to pretensions upon their lands by virtue
of Treaties with the former Government of the U States imposed
by violence or contracted with partial and inadequate representations of their Nation—that our own public records witness that the
proceedings of our Agents at some of those Treaties were far from
unexceptionable—that the wars complained of are to be attributed
to errors in our former policy or mismanagements of our public
Agents not to the detention of the posts—that it must be problematical how much of the duration or expences of those wars are

17. At this point in the newspaper there is an asterisk referring the reader
to the table printed at the end of this essay.

chargeable upon that detention and that the posts having been detained by way of security for the performance of the article respecting debts there was no responsibility for collateral and casual damages. Had we resorted to the charge of their having instigated or prompted those wars, they would have denied the charge as they have repeatedly done before, and though we might have been able to adduce circumstances of suspicion against them they would have contested their validity and force, and would have thought their honor concerned in avoiding the most distant concession of having participated in so improper a business.

In every view therefore the claim for indemnification was a hopeless one, and to insist upon it could have answered no other purpose than to render an amicable adjustment impossible. No British Minister would have dared to go to a British Parliament to ask provision for such an expenditure. What then was to be done? Were we now or hereafter to go to War to enforce the claim? Suppose this done and fifty or a hundred millions of Dollars [18] expended in the contest—what certainty is there that we should at last accomplish the object? Moreover the principle of such a war would require that we should seek indemnification for the expences of the war itself in addition to our former claim. What prospect is there that this would be effected? Yet if it was not effected it is evident that we should have made a most wretched bargain.

Why did we not insist on indemnification for the expences of our Revolution War? Surely not because it was less reasonable but Because it was evident that it could not have been obtained and because peace was necessary to us as well as to our enemy.

This likewise would be the end of a war undertaken to enforce the claim of indemnification for the detention of the posts. We should at length be glad to make peace either without the indemnification sought or at best at an expence to carry on the war without a chance of reimbursement witih which the thing gained would bear no comparison.

The idea which has been thrown out of leaving the posts in the hands of the British till we might be better able than at present to go to war for indemnification is a notable political expedient. This would be to postpone of choice the possession of an object which has been shewn to be demanded by very urgent and important gen-

18. In the newspaper these figures are "fifty or a hundred dollars."

eral considerations—to submit to certain and great inconveniences from that privation including probably the continuance or renewal of Indian hostilities and to run the risk from the growth of the British settlements in the neighbourhood of the posts and various unforeseen casualties of their ultimate acquisition becoming difficult and precarious—for what? Why to take at last the chances of War, the issue of which is ever doubtful, for obtaining an object which if obtained will certainly cost more than it is worth. The expences of war apart, pecuniary indemnification upon any possible scale would ill compensate for the evils of the future detention till the more convenient time for going to War should arrive. What should we think of this policy if it should turn out that the posts and the indemnification too were to be finally abandonned? [19]

CAMILLUS [20]

19. On the same day on which this issue of "The Defence" appeared in *The* [New York] *Argus, or Greenleaf's New Daily Advertiser,* the following letter, written by "A Loyalist of '75" and addressed to H, was printed in the same newspaper: "As wounds heal far better before, than after they have festered, I beseech you to use your influence with *Camillus,* to discontinue his *laborious work* of defending the Treaty, for a few days, and take up the justification of Capt. Home, of the Africa, for his *trifling curiosity,* at Rhode-Island; and also, of the little *Faux pas* made by another British Captain, in getting *a peep* at Mr. Munroe's dispatches from France. *A defence* of these two occurrences, will be found much easier, than the tedious defence he is now engaged in; besides he can continue the old thread of occurrences after he has quieted the minds of the *Swinish Multitude* upon the two events aforementioned."

For Captain Rodham Home of H.M.S. *Africa,* see George Washington to H, August 31, 1795, note 3.

On May 21, 1795, Secretary of State Edmund Randolph wrote to George Hammond to remonstrate ". . . that on board of the Pomona, which was lately carried as a prize into Halifax, were three letters addressed to me, as Secretary of State, by Mr. Monroe, our minister at Paris: That they were *opened* in the Admiralty there by the Attorney General: . . . that in all probability copies have been taken of them, and that the officers in possession of them refused to deliver them up.

". . . it must have been manifest from the address, the signature, and the ·purport of the first sentence, that the letters were *official:* and that the violation of them was perpetrated in the face of a Court, and in the sight and hearing of numbers." (LC, RG 59, Domestic Letters of the Department of State, Vol. 8, December 6, 1794–October 12, 1795, National Archives.)

20. On the back of this document H wrote:
"lower Town of Niagara ⎫
Stedmans Carrying place ⎬
14 miles in length
20 or 40 houses in town ⎬
2 or 3000 souls." ⎭
Philip Stedman was a contractor for the transport of goods over the Niagara portage.

[ENCLOSURE][21]

Account of Peltries exported from Canada in 1786 & 1787:

	1786	1787
Beaverskins	116,509	139,509
Martinskins	58,132	68,132
Otters Do	26,330	26,330.
Minks Do	9,951	17,951
Fishers Do	5,813	5,813
Foxes Do	6,213	8,913
Bears Do	22,108	17,108
Deers Do	126,000	102,656
Racoons Do	108,346	140,346
Cats cased Do	3,026	5,426
Do. open Do	2,925	1,825.
Elks do Do	7,515	9,815.
Wolves Do	12,987	9,687
Carcajoux Do	503	653
Tygers Do	77	27
Seals Do	157	125
Muskrats Do	202,456	240,456
Drest deerskins	5,488 lbs.	1,788 lbs.
Castorum	1,454 lbs.	1,454 lbs.

21. This enclosure is not in H's handwriting. In addition, the MS has a third column of figures which has no date and which was added at some later time. This third column does not appear in the newspaper.

Hamilton-Oneida Academy Mortgage [1]

[*August 15, 1795.*] "Be it remembered that on the fifteenth day of August in the Year one thousand seven hundred and ninety five, The Trustees of Hamilton Oneida Academy, to wit Alexander Hamilton, Eli Bristoll, Erastus Clark, James Dean, Moses Foot, Sewall Hopkins, Thomas R. Gold, Michael Myers, Jonas Platt,

Jedediah Sanger, John Sergeant, Timothy Tuttle, Samuel Wells, Asahel S. Norton and Joel Bradley . . . for securing The Payment of seven hundred Dollars within two Years from the twenty ninth day of July 1795, with lawful Interest annually, Have mortgaged unto Erastus Clark . . . and Jonas Platt and Thomas R. Gold . . . two certain Pieces, Parcels or Tracts of Land lying in . . . Town of Paris [2] on a large Tract of Land granted to the Rev. Samuel Kirkland. . . ."

Copy, Oneida County Clerk's Office, Utica, New York.
1. The Hamilton-Oneida Academy was the forerunner of the present-day Hamilton College in Clinton, New York. In 1793 the state of New York granted Samuel Kirkland, an Indian missionary, a charter for the Hamilton-Oneida Academy. In January of the same year Kirkland had taken "the stage to Philadelphia, in order to confer with the Honbl Mr Hamilton, Secretary of the United States, and others, upon the subject of the School." On January 8, 1793, Kirkland wrote in his journal: "Mr Hamilton chearfully consents to be a Trustee of the said Seminary, and will afford it all the aid in his power; which was requested by Good Peter and several other Indian Chiefs when at Philadelphia the last spring" (Joseph D. Ibbotson and S. N. D. North, eds., *Documentary History of Hamilton College* [Clinton, N.Y., 1922], 57-58).
2. Paris is in Oneida County, New York.

From Thomas and Richard Lee and Son [1]

Leeds [England] August 15, 1795. Announces that the firm's name has been changed to Richard Lee and Son.

LS, Hamilton Papers, Library of Congress.
1. The Lees were a firm of merchants in Leeds. H had served as their agent in the United States in the seventeen-eighties. See H's Cash Book, March 1, 1782-1791, note 115.

From Marquis de Rouvray [1]

New York, August 15, 1795. States that in March, 1790, he gave Henri Jacques Guillaume Clarke,[2] an agent of the Duke of Orleans, two "billets d'honneur" in the amount of twelve thousand livres to cover the cost of a debt incurred by his son [3] for a commission as captain in the Hussars. Complains that Clarke's suit, commenced in the United States to recover the amount of the notes, is not valid, for the sale of commissions was illegal, that "billets d'honneur" were not negotiable, that Clarke had not demanded payment when the notes were due, and that French rather than United States courts should have jurisdiction over such matters.[4]

ALS, Hamilton Papers, Library of Congress.
   1. This letter is written in French. Laurent-François Le Noir, Marquis de Rouvray, a member of a Norman family, served in Canada and in the American Revolution, in which he became a field marshal. After the Revolution he moved to Santo Domingo, where he bought sugar and coffee plantations. In 1789 he became a deputy for the northern province of Santo Domingo in the Constituent Assembly at Versailles. In June, 1790, he returned to Santo Domingo and commanded a corps in the eastern part of the colony against the slave insurrectionists. In October, 1792, he fled to New York (Malcolm E. McIntosh and Bernerd C. Weber, eds. *Une Correspondance Familiale au temps des troubles de Saint-Domingue: Lettres du Marquis et de la Marquise de Rouvray a leur Fille, Saint-Domingue-Etats-Unis, 1791-1796* [Paris, 1959], 5-10).
   2. Clarke was a captain of dragoons in the Duke of Orleans's regiment at the outbreak of the French Revolution. He subsequently became a staff officer (*Une Correspondance Familiale,* 67).
   3. Probably Gaston, Vicomte de Rouvray, the younger son of the Marquis (*Une Correspondance Familiale,* 89).
   4. Also in the Hamilton Papers, Library of Congress, is a memorandum written by Rouvray entitled "Idees Sur la juridiction du Tribunal des Marechaux de france Et Sur Les billets d'honneur" and dated August 12, 1795.

From Oliver Wolcott, Junior

Phila. Aug 15. 1795

Dear Sir

The President has decided that the Treaty shall be ratified & transmitted for exchange immediately and in my opinion he has decided right.[1] I regret that this was not done long since, as I presume much of the party spirit which has been excited would have been prevented.

A government like ours can rarely take a middle course on any point which interests the public feelings—delay for whatever reason would be construed into a dislike of the Treaty itself, and this opinion diffusing among the people would generate the most inveterate factions. Circumstances have happened tending to incite a distrust of the sincerity of this Govt, in the British Cabinet, which can be no otherwise explained than by a ratification.

I am with sincerity yours   Oliv. Wolcott, Jr.

Alexr. Hamilton Esqr.

ALS, Hamilton Papers, Library of Congress; copy, Connecticut Historical Society, Hartford.
1. Washington ratified the Jay Treaty on August 14, 1795. See Wolcott to H, July 30, 1795, note 2.

From Edmund Randolph

Philadelphia August 16. 1795

Dear sir

I expected to have the pleasure of seeing you here at the supreme court;[1] when I meant to Enter into, a full conversation with you. But being disappointed, I shall only beg you to read a letter, which I have this day written to Mr. Jay; and requested him to shew to you. If I do not mistake, your ideas and mine were not very different as to the *provision-order*[2]

I am dear sir with real esteem and regard yr. mo. ob. serv.
Edm: Randolph.

ALS, Hamilton Papers, Library of Congress.
1. This is a reference to H's intention to participate in arguments before the Supreme Court over the constitutionality of the carriage tax. See William Bradford to H, July 2, August 4, 1795; Oliver Wolcott, Jr., to H, July 28, 1795; and H to Wolcott, August 5, 1795.
2. This is a reference to a British order in council of April 25, 1795, calling for the British seizure of cargoes of grain on American ships bound for France. For the text of the order in council, see Washington to H, July 7, 1795, note 3. At issue was whether or not Washington should make his ratification of the Jay Treaty conditional on British rescinding of the order. Randolph thought that he should (Wolcott to H, July 30, 1795, note 2), and H agreed with Randolph (Wolcott to H, August 10, 1795). Washington disagreed, for on August 14, 1795, he ratified the treaty without the condition proposed by Randolph and H. See Wolcott to H, July 30, 1795, note 2.

[ENCLOSURE]

Edmund Randolph to John Jay [3]

Private

Philadelphia August 16. 1795.

Sir

I have forwarded, agreeably to your Excellency's request, the letter, which you inclosed to me for General Lee.[4]

It was always my intention to inform you of the President's final act on the treaty. This being now taken by an assurance in writing to Mr. Hammond that it would be immediately ratified;[5] and the necessary forms being on the point of completion, little need be added on that head. But candor induces me to explain to you some opinions, produced by a recent occurrence, relative to an immediate exchange of ratifications.

You know, sir, the sentiments, which I have always entertained, and still entertain, upon the treaty. To dictate the terms we could not expect; and therefore the single question with me was, whether *under all circumstances,* the pleasant things did not outweigh the unpleasant. My mind told me, that in this view we ought to ratify. So that *upon the treaty itself,* I have been constantly prepared to give my affirmative. But the late order for seizing our provision-vessels goes beyond the treaty; and required, that for the sake of national dignity, and of silencing the complaint of the French, one effort ought to be made for removing that order out of the way. To exchange ratifications, and afterwards object, was a feeble and unavailing expedient. The means of rendering the effort effectual seemed to consist in not consummating the treaty, until the minister who was to exchange, should urge the rescinding of the order, and,

3. ALS, Hamilton Papers, Library of Congress. For an explanation of the contents of this letter, see Wolcott to H, July 30, 1795, note 2.
4. On August 12, 1795, Jay had written a note to Randolph, asking him "to add to the superscription of the enclosed letter the name of the place where General [Henry] Lee lives, and to be so obliging as to send it to the post office" (AL, Columbia University Libraries).
5. Randolph to George Hammond, August 14, 1795 (LC, RG 59, Domestic Letters of the Department of State, Vol. 8, December 6, 1794–October 12, 1795, National Archives).

upon being refused, should receive further instructions. I saw no danger of losing the treaty by this measure; because the President might as well have the ratifications exchanged a few months hence, as now; and the difference of time between an immediate exchange and a future one would have been but a few weeks—the space sufficient for the passage of the papers from London, if the British king should assent to the exchange being made in the United States. I had a hope too, that even if the order was not withdrawn, by that time the present campaign, which is probably the last, would be so far advanced, and the French harvest would have banished famine to such a degree, that we should have avoided the suspicion of a desire to cooperate in the attempt to starve France. I was persuaded also, that the treaty will for the most part be postponed for its effect, until congress shall pass auxiliary laws. I doubted too, whether the surrender of the posts would be much quickened by concluding the treaty immediately; since I feared, that the unexpected waste of this summer, without its completion, might prompt the British government to take a further time.

The President was occupied until the 13th. of July in considering, what was to be done; and then decided on a course, somewhat analogous to these ideas. He left Philadelphia on the 15th.; and about a week afterwards I sent down to him at Mount Vernon the draught of a memorial to Mr. Hammond upon the subject of the treaty.[6] From the blunder of the postmaster in Alexandria;[7] And the great floods of rain; his instructions and the memorial were not returned to me, until the 6th. of August. Alth⟨o⟩ I was at perfect liberty to announce publickly the President's decision, and was rather urged to do so; yet I held it best to keep him at liberty to mature the business farther; and accordingly he on thursday last thought proper to take A course, very different from that which he first projected. In that course I acquiesed, and shall certainly support it to the best of my faculties.

I make these last observations; because from something which I have seen, I am confident, that it has been supposed, that unnecessary

6. Randolph to Washington, July 24, 1795 (ALS, RG 59, Miscellaneous Letters, 1790–1799, National Archives).

7. See Washington to H, August 3, 1795. See also Washington to Randolph, July 31, 1795 (ALS, George Washington Papers, Library of Congress).

delay has occurred and for a purpose, not reconcileable with a friendship to the treaty. In this view, I will go into the following statement of the papers, which I had drawn, upon the plan, which the President at first preferred.

These were a memorial and instructions.[8]

The memorial declared, that the President would ratify, upon the provision order being laid aside: that If this was not done, the President would take the subject into farther consideration: that the doing of this should be the *only* obstacle to the pursuing of the advice of the Senate: that in order however to produce perfect cordiality, the king was *invited* 1. to provide by some clear distinction against the impressment of our citizens: 2. to reconsider the compensation of the negroes: 3. to cause the execution of the 7th. article [9] to be expedited and the expence thereof lessened: 4. to give instructions against the vexations of privateers, and the rigours of some of the American admiralties. The reason, why I again brought up the negroes was, that, as the amount would to the British nation be small; so the King might, upon reconsideration, be desirous of giving the best chance for conciliation by removing one of the chief irritations.

You perceive, sir, that there was no ultimatum in all this; nor yet the semblance of one, except as to the provision-order, which could be an obstruction for only a few months more.

The instructions went upon a broader scale; but as the negotiation under them was *subsequent* to the ratification, it was referred to the discretion of the minister to endeavour to procure a greater latitude of advantages, than we enjoy. This being so familiar a practice, that I need not detail the particulars of that instrument.

I ought to add, that the reason, why a memorial was at all thought of, was, that the President at first believed (as I confess I did) that he could not ratify, until the new suspending article was agreed to by the British king. It thereby became necessary to assure him in writing, that we affected no delays; and meant to ratify, if the provision order was abolished.

8. Washington to Randolph, July 29, 1795 (ALS, RG 59, Miscellaneous Letters, 1790–1799, National Archives). See also Washington to Randolph, July 31, 1795 (ALS, George Washington Papers, Library of Congress).
9. For Article 7 of the Jay Treaty, see "Remarks on the Treaty . . . between the United States and Great Britain," July 9–11, 1795, note 39.

I will thank you to permit Mr. King [10] and Colo. Hamilton to see this letter; and I beg you to receive the tender of that respect and esteem, with which I have the honor to be sir

Yr. Excellency's mo. ob. serv.   Edm: Randolph

10. Rufus King, United States Senator from New York.

Philo Camillus No. 4 [1]

[New York, August 19, 1795]

FOR THE ARGUS

Camillus has stated several infractions of the Treaty of peace by us, besides that of the Trespass act,[2] which according to the solution given by our own conduct to the question whether performance was to date from the provisional or definitive Treaty must have been prior to the British infraction by the detention of the posts [3]—(viz)

1 An Act of South Carolina of March 26th 1784 suspending the recovering of British Debts for nine months and allowing them then to be recovered only in four yearly installments.[4] 2 An act of this state of the 12 of May 1784 confirming all confiscations before made notwithstanding errors in the proceedings and taking away the writ of error.[5] 3 Acts of Virginia passed during the war which prohibitted the recovery of British debts [6] and which according to the

ADf, Hamilton Papers, Library of Congress; *The* [New York] *Argus, or Greenleaf's New Daily Advertiser*, August 19, 1795.
1. The other "Philo Camillus" essays are dated July 27, August 7, 12, 1795. *The Argus* mistakenly numbered this essay "No. 5."
2. See "The Defence No. IV," August 1, 1795. H is referring to "An Act for granting a more effectual Relief in Cases of certain Trespasses," passed March 17, 1783 (*New York Laws*, 6th Sess., Ch. XXXI).
3. See "Philo Camillus No. 3," August 12, 1795.
4. "An Ordinance Respecting Suits for the Recovery of Debts" (*South Carolina Laws*, 1784 Sess. [March 26, 1784]).
5. "An Act for the speedy Sale of the Confiscated and forfeited Estates within this State, and for other purposes therein mentioned" (*New York Laws*, 7th Sess., Ch. LXIV).
6. For these acts of the Virginia legislature, see enclosure No. 6 in Thomas Jefferson to George Hammond, May 29, 1792 (ADf, Thomas Jefferson Papers, Library of Congress; *ASP, Foreign Relations*, I, 201–37).

testimony of the General Assembly of Virginia contained in two several acts [7] continued to operate till after the year 1787.

To all these acts CINNA gives one general answer in substance this "that it was a *clear principle* of Constitutional Law, that the Treaty controuled all laws of the States inconsistent with it." [8] The absurdity of opposing this theoretic dogma, this speculative rule, to actual operating contraventions has been more than once pointed out. It may be likened to the conduct of the Physician who when he was assured that his patient was dead attempted to prove that according to the principles of an infallible theory it was impossible he should die after the remedies which had been administered. Let inquiry be made if the act of South Carolina did not go into full operation from the time it was passed. Let it be examined if a single writ of error has been brought and maintained since the act of this state of May 1784. If there be an instance of a single judgment rendered in a superior court of Virginia in favour of a British Creditor where the question between the law and the Treaty has fairly arisen, during the period referred to, let it be produced. The result of inquiry in each of the cases will confirm the fact that the laws cited did operate in contravention of the Treaty.

As to Virginia, no man who understands the English language will dispute that the acts quoted *attest,* as far as the *knowlege* and *opinion* of the Legislature of Virginia went, this *fact*—that the acts of that State prohibitting the recovery of British Debts did continue to operate notwithstanding the Treaty. This I affirm is such high evidence of the fact that nothing short of solemn decisions of the Superior Courts to the contrary can overthrow it.

It is in vain that Cinna endeavours to get rid of the force of this

7. See "Remarks on the Treaty . . . between the United States and Great Britain," July 9–11, 1795, notes 37 and 38.
8. See the second essay by "Cinna" (Brockholst Livingston) (*The* [New York] *Argus, or Greenleaf's New Daily Advertiser,* August 4, 5, 1795). For background to this essay, see "Philo Camillus No. 3," August 12, 1795. H's reference is not a direct quotation from the essay, but a paraphrase of several statements in it. It is closest in wording to the following: "Treaties, then, from the very nature of our union, being the supreme laws of the land, it results necessarily, that its provisions [i.e., those of the treaty of peace of 1783] could not be controuled by the laws of any state, and that no one could reasonably complain of the existence of such acts, which, by the treaty, were rendered nugatory, until obedience to them was enforced by the courts to whom the exposition of such acts and treaties was delegated" (*The* [New York] *Argus, or Greenleaf's New Daily Advertiser,* August 5, 1795).

testimony by arguing that it is not of the legislative province to pronounce what is the effect of a law and that consequently the opinion of the legislature of Virginia as to the operation of its laws is not evidence of the truth. Cinna by this observation confounds two things, the *legal* effect and the *actual* effect. The opinion of a legislature may not always be valid evidence of the first but it is very high and authoritative evidence of the last. It is one thing to consider them as judges of a principle of law—another to consider them as witnesses of a matter of fact. In the last character who can have better pretensions? Who can be presumed better to know the state of a fact in which the feelings and interests of a community are much concerned than the legislative representatives of that community? It is in this sense Camillus quotes and relies upon the two acts of Virginia; the first of which by necessary implication and the last of which in express terms informs that its acts *had prevented* the recovery of Debts due to British subjects according to the true intent and meaning of the Treaty of Peace.[9] The words are these "Be it enacted by the General Assembly that such of *the* acts or parts of acts of the legislature of this Commonwealth as *have prevented* or *may prevent the recovery* of debts due to British subjects according to the true intent and meaning of the Treaty of Peace be and are hereby repealed" [10]—to which however a proviso is added suspending the repeal till the British infractions respecting the Negroes & the posts were repaired.[11] This provision is a confirmation that the General Assembly considered the fact to be that its laws

9. H is referring to resolutions of the Virginia House of Delegates on June 22, 1784 (see "Remarks on the Treaty . . . between the United States and Great Britain," July 9–11, 1795, notes 37 and 38), and "An act to repeal so much of all and every act or acts of assembly as prohibits the recovery of British debts," passed December 12, 1787 (*Virginia Laws*, 12th Sess., Ch. XXXIV).

10. In MS, "respealed."

11. Article 2 of "An act to repeal so much of all and every act or acts of assembly as prohibits the recovery of British debts" states: "That this act shall be suspended until the governor with the advice of council shall by his proclamation, notify to this state, that Great Britain hath delivered up to the United States the posts therein now occupied by British troops, which posts were stipulated by treaty to be given up to congress immediately after the conclusion of peace; and is also taking measures for the further fulfilment of the said treaty by delivering up the negroes belonging to the citizens of this state taken away contrary to the seventh article of the treaty, or by making such compensation for them as shall be satisfactory to congress" (*Virginia Laws*, 12th Sess., Ch. XXXIV [December 12, 1787]).

did obstruct the recovery of debts. The testimony of the legislature of Virginia *to the matter of fact* is therefore complete and peremptory; and it is [in] this light as before observed that their acts are quoted. Can it be believed that they could be mistaken about a fact, which if it existed at all had existed four years? Or can we suppose that they meant to practice a deception upon Congress upon Great Britain and upon their own Citizens?

It may not be useless to observe that Mr. Jefferson himself understood the meaning of the Legislature of Virginia, in their act of June 1784 in the same sense with Camillus.[12] He states it as "resolving, *that the Courts shall be opened* to British suits as soon as reparation shall be made &c." The direct inference is that the courts *were not then open* to British suits.

One would have imagined that Mr. Jefferson when he undertook to contradict this solemn and reiterated testimony of the Legislature of Virginia would have drawn the proofs of his contradiction from no sources inferior to the records of the courts of Virginia. Nothing less than this could be satisfactory. The non production of such proofs is an argument that they did not exist, and if they did not exist, it is a strong negative confirmation of the declaration of the Virginia Legislature.

What does Mr. Jefferson oppose to it? Two letters, in answer to inquiries made by him upon the spur of the occasion, one from Mr. Monroe, a senator, the other from Mr. Giles a representative.[13]

Mr. Monroe speaks of a case in April 1791 in the District Court of Fredericksburgh where the law of the state was pleaded in bar of the Debt and the plea overruled.[14]

12. This is a reference to Thomas Jefferson's letter of May 29, 1792, to George Hammond, the British Minister, respecting alleged violations of the treaty of peace by the United States (ADf, Thomas Jefferson Papers, Library of Congress; *ASP, Foreign Relations*, I, 201–37).

13. The letter from James Monroe to Jefferson is dated May 1, 1792; that from William B. Giles, May 6, 1792. They are printed as enclosures to Jefferson's letter to Hammond of May 29, 1792 (*ASP, Foreign Relations*, I, 234–35).

14. Monroe describes the case as follows: "In April, 1791, in the district court of Fredericksburg, the case Mitchell against Wallis, in which the law of the State was plead, in bar of the debt, the following were the circumstances:

"Mitchell, a native of Great Britain, residing and trading in Virginia, having debts due him, to great amount, conveyed them, with other property, just before the war, to the use of his creditors in Great Britain, and of one creditor in Virginia. In this situation the debts remained through the war, and the action

The case was that one Mitchel a *native* of Great Britain *residing* and trading in Virginia, conveyed his debts and other property *before the War* to the use of his Creditors in Great Britain and *one Creditor* in Virginia. It was argued for the Defendant that this was a case provided for by the Treaty & prohibited by the law, but judgment was given for the plaintiffs and other jugments were entered in favour of the same parties in that and a subsequent term.

But we are not told on what principle judgment was given for the plaintiffs. It does not appear in what situation Mitchell was during the War. Though a native of Great Britain his situation & conduct might have rendered him a citizen of the U States which is a very common case. If this was not the case, the judgment might have proceeded on the ground that among the creditors for whose benefit the assignment was made there was *one citizen* and that this interest of a citizen took the case out of the prohibitory acts. In fine nothing precise being said we are left to conjecture what we please.

It is to be observed likewise, that the case cited was subsequent to the present constitution of the U States, which *expressly declares* that Treaties shall be supreme *laws* of the land and which was ratified by the People of the several States, long posterior to the impeding Acts. The Court may have considered this express subsequent provision as a repeal of preexisting contrary laws. It in fact did settle the theoretic question by an express constitutional declaration. And it is to be observed that this provision is new & peculiar to that constitution & has been made an objection to it.

Mr. Monroe relates further that it was always the opinion of the ablest counsel at the bar that British Debts were recoverable, that no law prohibited it and if it were otherwise, that the Treaty would control it. And he adds that since the establishment of the present Constitution of the U States he has heared several judges say that they had entertained the same opinion.

But amidst these vague assertions of the opinions of lawyers and judges, Mr Monroe confesses one fact which infinitely outweighs

---

was brought in favor of the British creditors, in 1788, or '89, and judgment rendered for the plaintiffs. Several other judgments were entered in favor of the same parties, in that and the subsequent term. This must be deemed such a debt as was supposed to be prohibited and provided for by the treaty. It was so argued on the part of the defendant, whose counsel I was, and yet judgment was given against him." (*ASP, Foreign Relations*, I, 234.)

all that he has put in the opposite scale. It is this—*That the British Merchants declined generally bringing suits prior to the establishment of the present National Government.* What does this prove? Demonstrably that they were advised that it would be useless to bring them—that no recovery could be had. Can we believe that individual interest did not lead them to take the best opinions to be had, and can we doubt from their passiveness that these opinions were against the probability of success?

The neglect of the British Merchants to bring suits for the long term of six or seven years is a decisive corroboration that the opinion of the bar of Virginia coincided with that of the Legislature and that the effect of the prohibitory laws of that State was to obstruct the recovery of British Debts.

As to Mr. Giles' letter it conveys no real information.[15] It totally omits dates, and leaves us to conjecture whether the incidents stated happened prior or subsequent to the present constitution of the U States and were or were not an effect of that constitution. To reconcile him with Mr. Monroe we must understand him as speaking of things subsequent.

Surely we must be convinced that these are feeble authorities against the declarations of two solemn acts of the legislature of Virginia; and considering the industry displayed by Mr. Jefferson on the occasion we must regard the weakness of his evidence on this point as a clear indication of his embarrassment.

I pass by all the testimonies produced from the other states.[16]

15. Giles's letter reads in part: "Previously to my election to Congress, I had been engaged for several years in the practice of law in the State of Virginia. In the prosecution of that business, I was often applied to upon the subject of debts due to British subjects, and had an opportunity of observing the proceedings of several of the courts, in suits brought for the recovery of such debts.

"The rules of several of the county courts were not entirely uniform. In some of the counties, suits of that description were generally continued upon the dockets without trial; but they were such as were not much pressed by the plaintiff's counsel. In other counties they were brought to trial, and in all the cases within my recollection, in which the debts were established by competent testimony, judgments were rendered for the plaintiffs; except in one instance, in the court for the county of Chesterfield, where, upon an *issue* of *fact* upon the plea of a *British debt*, the jury found the plaintiffs to be British subjects, which finding caused some delay; but judgment was afterwards rendered in the same court for the same debt, and the money since paid under the judgment." (*ASP, Foreign Relations*, I, 234–35.)

16. See Jefferson to Hammond, May 29, 1792 (ADf, Thomas Jefferson Papers, Library of Congress; *ASP, Foreign Relations*, I, 210–37).

They only prove that in *several* of the states, the theoretic position that Treaties controuled the local laws was reduced to practice. But they do not prove that this was the case in all of them. From several of the States there is no such testimony.

Discarding what relates to Virginia—the two acts which have been mentioned of South Carolina and New York of the 26 March & 12 May 1784 are conclusive as to the point of there having been contraventions on our part prior to that of the detention of the posts, if performance was to date from the definitive Treaty; because the ratification by us did not arrive in England till the 28 of May of that year and the exchange of ratifications was about the beginning of June.

The reason given by Camillus why performance ought to date from the definitive Treaty is unanswerable.[17] It is this that *by our own conduct in not acting upon* the provisional Treaty especially the fifth article [18] we practically determined that performance was not to date from that Treaty—consequently that it was to date from the definitive Treaty. This too is the best ground to be taken for us; since upon a different principle there would come home to *Congress itself* an infraction of the Treaty from the first moment of its Ratification.

A Writer signed PHILO-CINNA has endeavoured to put Camillus at variance with himself, for notwithstanding his conclusion 'tis evident that he means to have it understood that Mr. Hamilton & Camillus are the same person.[19] For argument sake be it so—and let us see if he has made out the contradiction.

CAMILLUS says, "that our Government has *constantly charged* as *breaches* of the Treaty the two particulars of carrying away the Negroes and detaining the posts but that it is believed to be not true that it has uniformly charged them *as first breaches* of the Treaty— that as far as is recollected this ground was never *formally* or *explicitly* taken by our Government till in the letter quoted from Mr. Jefferson to Mr. Hammond." [20]

17. See "The Defence No. III," July 29, 1795.
18. Article 5 of the definitive treaty of peace of 1783 declared that Congress should recommend to the states the restitution of all Loyalist property (Miller, *Treaties*, II, 154).
19. See "Philo Camillus No. 3," August 12, 1795, note 17.
20. This and the following paragraph are paraphrases of statements made by "Philo Cinna" (*The* [New York] *Argus, or Greenleaf's New Daily Advertiser*, August 10, 1794). See "Philo Camillus No. 3," August 12, 1795, note 17.

May 26, 1783, a Resolution was moved by Mr. Hamilton in Congress which recites that "a considerable number of negroes belonging to Citizens of these States *had been carried off by the British contrary to the true intent and meaning of the provisional articles*" and instructs the Ministers of the US for negotiating peace in Europe to remonstrate thereon to the Court of G Britain and to take proper measures for obtaining reparation.

Upon which PHILO CINNA makes this sage comment. "If then Congress as early as May 1783 complained of this infraction they must have regarded it as the first breach; *for Great Britain had not yet had time to hear of what was passing in this Country on the subject of the Treaty, much less to complain of any violation of our part.*"

Since Camillus affirms that our Government has *constantly charged* the carrying away the negroes as *a Breach* of the Treaty when he adds that it did not *uniformly charge* it as a *first breach*, and that this ground was for the first time *formally* and *explicitly* taken by Mr. Jefferson—to reconcile him with himself in the same paragraph, he must necessarily be translated thus—"Though from the beginning our Government charged the carrying away of the negroes as a breach of Treaty, yet till it was done by Mr. Jefferson, it never *formally* and *explicitly* raised the question whether this was or was not the first breach of the Treaty. It is one thing to charge a matter as a breach of Treaty by one party, another to affirm formally and explicitly there it was the first breach committed by either party." [21]

Mr. Hamilton's motion only does the first; it only charges the act in question as a breach of the Treaty—it is intirely silent on the point whether it was or not the first breach.

But PHILO-CINNA resorts to an inference to make it speak this last language. He says this must have been the intent, because Great Britain had not yet had time to complain of a violation on our part. Thus he substitutes an *implication*, founded upon a reason good or bad of his own, for a *formal* and *explicit allegation* of a thing. This is a sample of the logic of the party.

But his reason for his *implication* is not a good one. Mr. Hamilton and Congress knew that the Trespass act existed of a prior date, and, if my memory serves me as to dates, that it had been remonstrated

21. In MS this word is "part."

against the British Commander in Chief as inconsistent with the Treaty. This was sufficient reason for silence as to the first breach.

But the argument that Great Britain had not had time to plan [22] turns against its object. For the question who had committed the first breach of the Treaty was a relative one, which could not have been raised till mutual infractions had been charged and consequently till Great Britain had had time to complain. A solution of that question could therefore not be implied in Mr. Hamilton's motion or the resolution of Congress upon it.

The same observations apply to the other acts quoted by PHILO CINNA. They all of them charge the carrying away of the negroes as *a breach*, but they are all of them equally silent on the point whether it was *a first breach* of the Treaty.

PHILO-CINNA endeavours to fix another inconsistency upon the supposed *Camillus*. He represents the having charged the carrying away the negroes as a Breach of the Treaty to be inconsistent with the doctrine that performance as to the restitution of the posts, was to date from the definitive Treaty. In a former paper, I have noticed an important distinction.[23] The Provisional Treaty was to arrest the doing of any acts contrary to the spirit of its several provisions, but acts of restitution were to wait for the definitive Treaty.

But I will tell PHILO-CINNA something which he may not know. I have understood that it was in fact Mr. Hamilton's policy to establish the construction that execution was to date from the Provisional Treaty; for besides that he thought this most agreeable to just & liberal procedure, he foresaw that the contrary conduct on our part would authorise the other party to delay the surrender of the posts, to the prejudice of our interests. Accordingly he made a formal motion to engage Congress to act upon the   [24] article of the Treaty, but his motion was negatived almost unanimously.[25] Thus it appears that Congress differed from Mr. Hamilton and thereby sanctionned what has been the construction of Great Britain.

This is only one of the instances, in which if Mr. Hamilton's

22. In the newspaper this word is "complain."
23. See "The Defence No. III," July 29, 1795.
24. Space left blank in both MS and newspaper.
25. See "Continental Congress. Report on Measures to be Taken for Carrying into Effect the Peace Treaty," May 30, 1783. The report called on the states to abide by Articles 4, 5, and 6 of the definitive peace treaty.

opinions had prevailed, we might be much less embarrassed than we now are as to the question who committed the first breach of the Treaty.

Another instance of incongruity between Camillus and Mr. Hamilton has been insinuated. It is said that the allegations contained in the motion which has been cited is inconsistent with the doctrine maintained by Camillus with regard to the meaning of the article concerning negroes.[26] But to this different answers may be given each of which is satisfactory.

First CAMILLUS has not given a direct opinion of his own as to the meaning of that article, he has only stated the arguments which support the British Construction, and has drawn this conclusion, that it is a *very doubtful point* whether that be right or wrong.

Secondly—Mr. Hamilton's motion in Congress is no evidence that he did not then consider it in the same light with CAMILLUS—that is, as a very doubtful point. In a case where an article admitted of two constructions, one in which the interest in some degree and the feelings in a greater degree of a large part of our Country was concerned—a member of Congress, though he might think it doubtful, which of the two constructions was right would naturally assert that which was advantageous to ourselves, in order to endeavour to obtain reparation for what upon our construction was an infraction. And In proportion as it might be his policy to engage Congress to carry the Treaty on their part into execution, would be his zeal to assert a construction favourable to our pretensions.

But thirdly, if the motion in question was dictated by an opinion at the time produced by the contagion of a general current of opinion, that ours was the better construction—it would not follow that a candid man, upon more mature reflection and after hearing and weighing the arguments of the other side, might not be convinced and ready to acknowledge, that the question was very doubtful, and that it was very possible his first opinion might be erroneous. It is the prerogative only of the Democratic Society and their allies to be *infallible*.   PHILO CAMILLUS

26. See "The Defence No. III," July 29, 1795.

The Defence No. IX [1]

[New York, August 21, 1795]

It was my intention to have comprised in two numbers the examination of the second article; [2] but on experiment it was found expedient to add a third. I resume for a moment the subject of indemnification for the detention of the Posts.

As an inducement to persist in this claim, we are assured that the magnimity of France would have procured for us its establishment. In the first place this supposes that we were to have become a party in the war for otherwise it would be silly to imagine that France would on our account embarrass herself with a difficulty of this sort. In this case, and supposing the object accomplished, still the injuries losses and expences of war would have greatly overballanced the advantage gained. But what certainty have we that France will be able to dictate terms even for herself? Could we expect or rely, after the terrible and wasting war, in which she has been engaged, that she would be willing to encumber the making of peace with additional obstacles to secure so trifling a point for us? Would it be even humane or friendly in us to ask her to risk the prolonging of her calamities for so trivial an object? [3]

A conduct like this with reference either to France or to ourselves would resemble that of the Gamester who should play *millions* against *farthings*. It is so preposterous in every sense that the recommendation of it, if sincere, admits of but one construction, namely, that those who recommend it wish our envoy to have acted not as if he had been sent *to make peace* but as if he had been sent to

ADf, Hamilton Papers, Library of Congress; *The* [New York] *Argus, or Greenleaf's New Daily Advertiser*, August 21, 1795.

1. For background to this document, see the introductory note to "The Defence No. I," July 22, 1795.

2. See "The Defence No. VII," August 12, 1795, and "The Defence No. VIII," August 15, 1795. For the text of Article 2 of the Jay Treaty, see "Remarks on the Treaty . . . between the United States and Great Britain," July 9–11, 1795, note 3.

3. At this point in the draft H wrote and crossed out the following sentence: "And have we so entirely reconciled our minds to becoming a dependency of France as to be ready to augment her pretensions upon us, by multiplying our obligations to her, even when no essential interest impels us."

make war, to blow and spread the desolating flames of discord and contention.[4]

There is a marked disingenuousness running through the observations which are made to the prejudice of the Treaty—they endeavour constantly to have it understood that our envoy abandonned without effort the claims which have not been established? Whence is this inferred? Is it from the silence of the Treaty? Surely we can only expect to find there what was *agreed upon,* not what was *discussed* and *rejected.* The truth is, that as well on this point of indemnification for the detention of the posts; as on that of compensation for the negroes our envoy urged our pretensions as far and as long as he could do it without making them final obstacles to the progress of the Negotiation.

I shall now enumerate and answer the remaining objections which have appeared against this article. They are these 1   That the posts to be surrendered instead of being described in general terms should for greater certainty have been specifically enumerated—that now the uncertainty of a part of the boundary line may furnish a pretext for detaining some of them.[5] 2   that the expressions "precints and jurisdictions" which are excepted from our right of settlement previous to the surrender are so vague and indeterminate as to be capable of being made to countenance encroachments. 3   that it was improper to have stipulated for the inhabitants the option of residing & continuing British subjects, or of becoming American Citizens; that the first was to establish by Treaty a British colony within our limits, the last to admit, without the power of exception, bitter enemies of the Country to the privileges of citizens.[6] 4   that the

4. At this point in the draft H wrote and crossed out: "Alas poor suffering humanity! hast thou not already bled at every pore? hast thou not already agonised in every limb and feeble joint? Art thou to have no peaceable asylum no consecrated spot where thou might safely repose? What is it that thy persecutors would have? Will nothing satisfy their fanatical rage for slaughter and devastation? Will they not be content 'till the world has become a desert inhabited only by beasts of prey and erratic hordes of savage men?"

5. For this "objection" to the Jay Treaty, see the first essay by "Decius" (Brockholst Livingston), which appeared in *The* [New York] *Argus, or Greenleaf's New Daily Advertiser,* July 10, 1795. The relevant section of this essay is quoted below in "Notes of Objections to the British Treaty," August, 1795, note 3. For the authorship of the "Decius" essays, see the introductory note to "The Defence No. I," July 22, 1795.

6. For this "objection" to the Jay Treaty, see *REPORT OF THE SELECT COMMITTEE, Chosen by Ballot of the Citizens of the United States, in*

securing to those inhabitants the enjoyment of their property is exceptionable, as being a "cession without equivalent of an *indefinite extent of territory*." This is the character given to it by the Meeting at Philadelphia.[7]

The answer to the first objection is that the enumeration proposed might have included the very danger which is objected to the provision as it stands and which is completely avoided by it. The principal posts occupied by the British are known and might easily have been enumerated—but there is a possibility of there being others not known which might have escaped. Last year there started up a post which had not been before heard of,[8] on the pretence of an old trading establishment. Who knows with absolute certainty how many similar cases may exist in the vast extent of wilderness as far as the Lake of the Woods which for several years past have been inaccessible to us? If our Envoys information could have been perfect at the time of his last advices from America, between that period and the signing of the Treaty changes might have taken place that is trading houses might have grown into military

----

Charleston, South-Carolina, in pursuance of a Resolution of a general Meeting of the Citizens, in St. Michael's Church, on Thursday, the sixteenth of July, 1795 (Charleston: Printed by W. P. Young, Broad-Street, n.d. [George Washington Papers, Library of Congress]). It is quoted below in "Notes of Objections to the British Treaty," August, 1795, note 9.

7. This "objection" is taken from "The Memorial of the Citizens of Philadelphia, the Northern Liberties and District of Southwark, in the State of Pennsylvania," July 25, 1795 (DS, George Washington Papers, Library of Congress). The first clause reads: "Because it [the Jay Treaty] does not provide for a fair and effectual settlement of the differences, that previously subsisted, between the United States and Great Britain, inasmuch as it postpones the surrender, and affords no compensation for the detention, of the Western Posts; inasmuch as it cedes, without affording any equivalent, an indefinite extent of territory to the settlers under British titles, within the precincts, and jurisdiction of those Posts; inasmuch as it waves a just claim for the value of the Negroes, who were carried off at the close of the war, in violation of positive compact; and inasmuch as it refers all the hopes of indemnity, for the recent spoliations, committed on the commerce of the United States, to an equivocal, expensive, tedious, and uncertain process."

8. On February 17, 1794, Guy Carleton, Lord Dorchester, Governor in Chief and Captain General of the British Provinces in North America, ordered John Graves Simcoe, Lieutenant Governor of Upper Canada, to build Fort Miami on the Maumee River to protect Detroit from a possible attack by Major General Anthony Wayne (E. A. Cruikshank, ed., *The Correspondence of Lieut. Governor John Graves Simcoe, with Allied Documents Relating to His Administration of the Government of Upper Canada* [Toronto, 1923–31], II, 154).

posts as they did in the case referred to, a case which in fact happened after the departure of our envoy from the U States. Was it not far better than to hazard an imperfect specification to use terms so general and comprehensive as could not fail in any circumstances, to embrace every case? Certainly it was—and the terms *"all posts and places"* which are those used in the article are thus comprehensive. Nothing can escape them.

Neither is there the least danger that the uncertainty [9] of a part of the boundary line can be made a pretext for detaining any post which it was possible to enumerate. This will appear from an inspection of the Map. The only uncertain part of the boundary line (except that depending on the River St Croix which is on a side unconnected with the position of the posts) is that which is to run from the Lake of the Woods to the Mississippi. The most Western of our known Posts is at Misshilimacnac [10] at or near the junction of the Lakes HURON and MICHIGAN, Eastward, near eleven degrees of longitude of the Lake of the Woods, and about ten degrees of longitude of that point on the Mississippi below the falls of St. Anthony [11] where a survey in order to a settlement of the line is to begin. Moreoever Our line by the Treaty of peace is to pass through the middle of Lake Huron and the water communicated between that lake and lake Superior and through the Middle of Lake Superior and thence Westward through other Waters to the Lake of the woods—that is about half a degree of latitude more Northward and about Eight degrees of longitude more Westward than any part of Lake Michigan. Whence it is manifest that any closing line to be drawn from the Lake of the Woods to the Mississippi must pass at a distance of several hundred Miles from Misshilimacnac. If the British therefore should be disposed to evade the surrender, they will seek for it some pretext more plausible than one which involves a palpable Geographical absurdity. Nor can we desire a better proof of the

9. At this point in the newspaper is the following note: "This uncertainty, it is to be observed, results not from the late treaty, but from the treaty of peace. It is occasioned by its being unknown, whether any part of the Mississippi extends far enough north to be intersected by a due west line from the lake of the Woods."

10. H is referring to a post held by the British on Michilimackinac (Mackinac) Island.

11. The Falls of St. Anthony, the upper limit of the navigable Mississippi, are now within the city of Minneapolis.

ignorance or disingenuousness of the objectors to the Treaty than their having contrived one of this nature.

The general terms were to be preferred for the very reason that there was a doubt about the course of a part of the boundary line; for if there should chance to exist any post now unknown so near that line as to render it questionable in the first instance on which side it may fall, the moment the line is settled the obligation to surrender will be settled with it.

The second objection loses all force when it is considered that the exception can only operate till the first of June next, the period for the surrender of the posts; and that in the mean time, there is ample space for settlement without coming near them.[12] There was besides real difficulty in an accurate definition. What the precincts and jurisdiction of the posts are is a question of fact. In some instances, where from there being no settlement over which an actual jurisdiction had been exercised, a good rule might have been the distance of gun shot from the fortifications which might have been settled at a certain extent in miles, say three or four. But in some cases, an actual jurisdiction had been exercised under circumstances which created obstacles to a precise definition. The case of Caldwell's Manor, in the vicinity of Dutchman's point is an example.[13] There a mixed jurisdiction has been exercised by the British for military purposes, by the state of Vermont for some civil purposes. It was not easy to fix any convenient rule in this case.[14] Detroit and its vicinity would also have occasionned embarrassment. From the situation of the settlements and of a number of dispersed trading establishments, a latitude was likely to have been required, to which it might have been inexpedient to give a sanction. In such situations, where a thing is to last but a short time, it is commonly the most eligible course to avoid definitions. It is obvious that no ill can result from the want of a

12. In the newspaper the concluding part of this sentence reads: "without coming to disputable ground."

13. See "The Defence No. VIII," August 15, 1795, note 14.

14. In the newspaper these two sentences have been changed to read: "There a mixed jurisdiction has been sometimes exercised by the British, and by the state of Vermont, connected with a disputed title to that manor; one party claiming under an ancient French grant, the other under the state of Vermont." H is referring to the appointment by the United States of a collector of customs at Alburg, Vermont. See "Conversation with George Beckwith," June 15, 1791, notes 9 and 11.

definition if the posts are surrendered at the time agreed; if not, it is equally plain that it can be of no consequence, because the whole article will be void.

The third objection becomes insignificant the moment the real state of things is adverted to. This has been described in a former number for another purpose,[15] but will now be recapitulated with one or two additional facts. The first posts beginning Eastward are Point au fer and Dutchmans point on Lake Champlain.[16] The whole number of persons in their vicinity, over whom jurisdiction has been claimed by the British, may amount to a hundred families. But the claim of jurisdiction here has been only occasionally and feebly urged; and it is asserted in addition by well informed persons that the abovementioned families have been for some time regularly represented in the legislature of Vermont the ordinary civil jurisdiction of which state has with little interruption extended over them. At neither of the other posts (to wit) Oswego, Niagara, The Miami, Detroit, Michillimacnac, is there any settlement, except at Detroit where and in the vicinity of which there may be between two and three thousand persons chiefly French canadians and their descendants. It will be understood that I do not consider as a settlement two or three log houses for Traders.

It follows, that the number of persons who can be embraced by the privileges stipulated is too inconsiderable to admit of attaching any political consequence whatever to the stipulation. Of what importance can it possibly be to the U States, whether two or three thousand persons, men women and Children, are permitted to reside within their limits either as British or American subjects at their option? If the thing was an object of desire to Great Britain for the accommodation of the Individuals concerned, could it have merited a moment's hesitation on our part? As to residence, it is of the ordinary curtesy of nations at peace to permit the mutual residence of the citizens of each other within their respective territories. British subjects are now free by our laws to reside in all parts of the U States.

As to the permission to become Citizens, it has been the general policy & practice of our Country to facilitate the naturalization of

15. See "The Defence No. VIII," August 15, 1795.
16. See "The Defence No. VIII," August 15, 1795, note 14.

foreigners. And we may safely count on the interest of the Individuals & on that desire to enjoy equal rights which is so deeply planted in the human breast, that all who resolve to make their permanent residence with us will become Citizens.

It is true that there may be a few obnoxious characters (though I do not recollect to have heared of more than two or three) among the number of those who have acquired by the stipulation a right to become citizens of the U States—but would it ever have been worthy of the dignity of the national wrath to have launched its thunders against the heads of two or three or half a dozen despicable individuals? Can we suppose that without a stipulation it would have been thought worth the while to make a special exception of their cases out of the operation of our general laws of naturalization? and if this had not been done would they not have found means, if they desired it, after the lapse of a short period to acquire the rights of citizens? It is to be observed that citizens of our own, who may have committed crimes against our laws, not remitted by the Treaty of Peace, would find no protection under this article.

Suppose the stipulation had not been made what would have been the probable policy of the U States? Would it not have been to leave the handful of settlers undisturbed in quiet enjoyment of their property, and at liberty if British subjects to continue such or to become American Citizens on the usual conditions? A system of depopulation or of coertion to one allegiance or another would have been little congenial with our modes of thinking and would not, I am persuaded, have been attempted.

If then the Treaty only stipulates in this respect what would have been the course of things without it what cause for serious objection can there be on this account?

The matter of the fourth objection can only derive a moment's importance from misapprehension. It seems to have been imagined that there are large tracts of land held under British grants made since the peace, which are confirmed by the part of the article that gives the Inhabitants the right of removing with, selling, or *retaining* their property.

In the first place, it is to be observed that if such grants had been made the stipulation could not be deemed to confirm them; because our laws must determine the question what is the property of the

Inhabitants, and they would rightfully decide that the British Government since the treaty of peace could make no valid grants of lands within our limits. Upon the ground even of its own pretensions, it could not have made such grants. Nothing more was claimed than a right to detain the posts as a hostage. The right to grant lands presupposes much more, a full right of sovereignty and territory.

But in the second place it has always been understood and upon recent and careful inquiry is confirmed—*That the British Government has never since the peace made a grant of lands within our limits.* It appears indeed to have been its policy to prevent settlements in the vicinity of the posts.

Hence the stipulation as it affects lands does nothing more than confirm the property of those which were holden at the Treaty of peace.[17] Neither is the quantity considerable; and it chiefly if not altogether depends on titles acquired under the French Government while Canada was a province of France.

In giving this confirmation it only pursues what is a constant rule among civilized nations. When territory is ceded or yielded up by one Nation to another it is a common practice, if not a special condition, to leave the inhabitants in the enjoyment of their property. A contrary conduct would be disgraceful to a nation; nor is it very reputable to the objectors to the Treaty, that they have levelled their battery against this part of it. It is a reflection upon them too, that they employ for the purpose terms which import more than is true even on their own supposition, and are therefore calculated to deceive; for the confirmation of property to Individuals could be at most a cession only of the right of soil, & not of *territory*, which term has a technical sense & includes jurisdiction.

Let it be added that the Treaty of Peace in the article which provides "that there should be no future confiscations nor prosecutions against any person or persons by reason of the part which he or they might have taken in the war and that no person should on that account suffer any future loss or damage either in his person liberty or property" [18] did substantially what is made an objection to the

17. At this point in the draft H wrote and crossed out: "as to this it may be affirmed that not to have protected it would have been to violate a rule which is common among civilized nations."

18. H's quotation differs slightly from the actual wording of Article 6 of the definitive treaty of peace (Miller, *Treaties,* II, 155).

Treaty under consideration.[19] It will not I believe be disputed that it gave protection to all property antecedently enjoyed and not confiscated. Indeed it is a question whether the stipulations cited would not have effected with regard to other rights than those of property a great part of what is regulated by the last Treaty. Its provisions were perhaps in the main unnecessary, further than to obviate a doubt which might have arisen from the suspension of the Treaty by the witholding of the Posts.[20]

Thus have I gone through every objection to the second article which is in any degree colorable and I flatter myself have shewn not only that the acquisition made by it is of great and real value but that it stands as well as circumstances permitted, and is defensible in its details. I have been the more particular in the examination, because the assailants of the Treaty have exerted all their ingenuity to discredit this article from a consciousness no doubt that it is a very valuable item of the Treaty—and that it was important to their cause to envelope it in as thick a cloud of objections as they were able to contrive. As an expedient of party, there is merit in the artifice. Tis a false calculation that the people of this country can ever be ultimately deceived.   CAMILLUS

19. At this point in the draft H wrote and crossed out the following sentence and footnote: "For the boundary line was assigned * on the principle of ancient limits not on that cession, whence it follows that no inhabitant who fell within our limits could be divested of what was before his property without a violation of the abovementioned stipulation.

"* This expression 'assigned' has been matter of Cavil though it is merely equivalent to 'settled fixed or delineated.' "

20. At this point in the draft H wrote and then crossed out: "Moreover it may be observed, in the last place, that similar provisions frequently accompany settlements of boundaries and cessions on relinquishments of territory between Nations. A recent example may be cited from the Treaty of Peace and friendship between France & England dated the 3 of September 1783. The VII article of that Treaty which restores St Lucie & cedes Tobago to the French stipulates that the British inhabitants shall retain their possessions upon the same titles and conditions upon which they acquired them; and that for the better securing them the French King should issue letters Patent containing an *abolition* of the 'droit d'aubaine' in other words removing the disability of alienage. The 8th article contains a correspondent stipulation by G Britain with regard to their Islands."

For the text of the definitive Treaty of Peace and Friendship between Great Britain and France, September 3, 1783, see Chalmers, *Collection of Treaties*, I, 495–517. The seventh article of this treaty stipulated that the king of France should abolish the *droit d'aubain* in Tobago. By the eighth article, France restored to Great Britain the islands of Grenada and the Grenadines, St. Vincent, Dominica, St. Christopher, Nevis, and Montserrat.

The Defence No. X[1]

[New York, August 26, 1795]

The object of the third article[2] is connected with that of the second.[3] The surrender of the posts naturally drew with it an arrangement with regard to inland Trade and navigation. Such an arrangement convenient in several respects appears to be in some respects necessary. To restrain the Indians on either side of the line from trading with the one party or the other at discretion, besides the questionableness of the right, could not be attempted without rendering them disgusted and hostile. The truth of this seems to have influenced the conduct of Great Britain and France while the latter was in possession of Canada. The 15th article of the Treaty of Peace of Utrecht in the year 1713 allows free liberty to the Indians on each side to resort for Trade to the British and French Colonies.[4] It is to be observed too that the Indians not only insist on a right of going to Trade with whom they please but of permitting whom

ADf, Hamilton Papers, Library of Congress; *The* [New York] *Argus, or Greenleaf's New Daily Advertiser*, August 26, 1795.

1. For background to this document, see the introductory note to "The Defence No. I," July 22, 1795.

2. For the text of Article 3 of the Jay Treaty, see "Remarks on the Treaty . . . between the United States and Great Britain," July 9–11, 1795, note 8.

3. For H's discussion of Article 2 of the Jay Treaty, see "The Defence Nos. VII, VIII, IX," August 12, 15, 21, 1795.

4. H is referring to "A Treaty of Peace and Friendship between the most serene and most potent Princess Anne, by the grace of God, Queen of Great Britain, France and Ireland, and the most serene and most potent Prince Lewis XIV, the most Christian King, concluded at Utrecht the 31/11 day of March/April 1713." Article 15 of this treaty reads: "The subjects of France inhabiting Canada, and others, shall hereafter give no hindrance or molestation to the five nations or cantons of Indians, subject to the domination of Great Britain, nor to the other natives of America, who are friends to the same. In like manner, the subjects of Great Britain shall behave themselves peaceably towards the Americans who are subjects or friends to France; and on both sides they shall enjoy full liberty of going and coming on account of trade. As also the natives of those countries shall, with the same liberty, resort, as they please, to the British and French colonies, for promoting trade on one side, and the other, without any molestation or hindrance, either on the part of the British subjects, or of the French. But it is to be exactly and distinctly settled by commissaries, who are, and who ought to be accounted the subjects and friends of Britain or of France" (Jenkinson, *Collection of Treaties*, II, 36–37).

they please to come to Trade with them and also to reside among them for that purpose. Thus the Southern and South Western Indians within our limits maintain a constant intercourse with Spain established on the basis of Treaty [5]—nor has their right to do it been hitherto contested by the U States. Indeed on what clear principle of justice, could this natural right to Trade of a people not subject to our ordinary jurisdiction be disputed? This claim on their part gives a corresponding claim to neighbouring nations to Trade with them. Spain would think the pretension to exclude her inadmissible. And Great Britain would have thought the same, if she had found it her interest to assert the right of intercourse; views which would always be seconded by the Indians from regard to their own interest and independence. It was a point therefore, which it much concerned the preservation of good understanding between the parties and with the Indians, to regulate on some equitable plan, and the more liberal the plan, the more agreeable to a natural course of things, and to the free participation of mutual advantages, the more likely was it to promote and prolong that important benefit.

In the second place, the expediency of some arrangement was indicated by the circumstance of the boundary line between the parties running for an extent of sixteen hundred Miles through the middle of the same Rivers lakes and Waters. It may be deemed impossible from the varying course of winds and currents for the ships of one party to keep themselves constantly within their own limits without passing or trangressing those of the other. How indeed was the precise middle line of those great lakes to be always known?

It appears evident, that to render the navigation of these waters useful to and safe for both parties, it was requisite that they should be common. Without this frequent forfeitures to enforce interdictions of intercourse might be incurred, and there would be constant danger of interference and controversy. It is probable too that when

5. In June, 1784, the Spaniards met first with the Creeks at Pensacola and then with the Chickasaws, Choctaws, and Alibamons at Mobile. At both meetings they extracted a promise from the Indians to acknowledge Spanish protection in their territories. The treaties also stipulated that the tribes should exclude all traders without a Spanish license. On July 6, 1792, the Spaniards made a second treaty with the Creeks and Talapoosas at New Orleans confirming the grants of land made to the Indians at Pensacola and allowing them arms and ammunition with which to defend themselves against the Americans.

those waters are better explored in their whole extent it will be found that the best navigation of the Lakes is sometimes on one side sometimes on the other, and that common convenience will in this respect also be promoted by community of right.

Again. It is almost always mutually beneficial for bordering territories to have free and friendly intercourse with each other. This relates not only to the advantages of an interchange of commodities, for the supply of mutual wants and to those of the reciprocal reaction of industry connected with that interest but also to those of avoiding jealousy collision and contest of preserving friendship and harmony. Proximity of territory invites to Trade—the bordering inhabitants in spite of every prohibition, will endeavour to carry it on—if not allowed, illicit adventures take place of the regular operations of legalised commerce—individual interest leads to collusions to evade restraining regulations—habits of infracting the laws are produced—morals are perverted. Severities necessarily great in proportion as they counteract the natural course of things lay the foundation of discontents and quarrels. Perhaps it may be safely affirmed that freedom of intercourse or violent hatred and enmity are the alternative in every case of contiguity of territory.

The maxims of the U States have hitherto favoured a free intercourse with all the world. They have conceived that they had nothing to fear from the unrestrained competition of commercial enterprise, and have only desired to be admitted to it upon equal terms. Hence not only the communication by sea has been open with the adjacent territories on our Continent as well as with more distant quarters of the globe, but two ports have been erected on Lake Champlain for the convenience of an interior commerce with Canada; and there is no restriction upon any nation to come by the Mississippi to the only port which has been established for that side of the Union.[6] These arrangements have excited neither c[r]iticism nor censure.

6. The two ports on Lake Champlain were Alburg, Vermont, and Cumberland Head, New York. See "Conversation with George Beckwith," June 15, 1791, notes 9 and 11; H to George Washington, June 11, 1793. For the "only port" for those who "come by the Mississippi," see Section 1 of "An Act to provide more effectually for the collection of the duties imposed by law on goods, wares and merchandise imported into the United States, and on the tonnage of ships or vessels," which reads in part: "For the district of Louisville a collector shall be appointed, to reside thereat, whose Authority

Our Envoy therefore in agreeing to a liberal plan of intercourse with the British Territories in our neighbourhood has conformed to the general spirit of our Country and to the general policy of our laws. Great Britain in acceding to such a plan departed from her system of Colonial monopoly and exclusion—a departure which ought to be one recommendation of the plan to us; for every relaxation of that system paves the way for other and further relaxations. It might have been expected also that a spirit of jealousy might have proved an obstacle on the part of Great Britain; since especially if we consider the composition of those who inhabit and are likely to inhabit Canada, it is morally certain that there must be as the result of a free intercourse a far greater momentum of influence of the U States upon Canada than of Canada upon the U States. It would not have been surprising, if this jealousy had sought to keep us at a distance, and had counteracted the wiser policy of limiting our desires by giving us possession of what is alone to us truly desireable, the advantages of commerce—rather than of suffering our wishes to be stimulated and extended by privation and restraint.

New ideas seem of late to have made their way among us. The extremes of commercial jealousy are inculcated. Regulation, restriction exclusion are now with many the favourite topics. Instead of feeling pleasure, that new avenues of Trade are opened a thousand dangers and mischiefs are pourtrayed when the occasion occurs. Free Trade with all the world seems to have dwindled into Trade with France and her Dominions. That Country, in the eyes of a certain party, appears to be an epitome of the Universe.[7]

These new doctrines of commercial jealousy have been remarkably exemplified [8] with respect to the article immediately under consideration. Truly estimated it is a valuable ingredient in the Treaty; and yet there is perhaps no part of it which has been more severely reprobated. It will be easy to shew that it has been ex-

---

shall extend over all the waters, shores and inlets included between the rapids and the mouth of the Ohio river on the south side thereof" (1 *Stat.* 150 [August 4, 1790]).

7. In the newspaper this sentence was omitted and the following sentence was substituted: "The love-sick partizans of that country appear to regard her as the epitome of the universe, and to have adopted for their motto, 'All for love, and the world well lost.'"

8. This word has been taken from the newspaper. In MS it reads "explified."

tremely misrepresented—and that what have been deemed very exceptionable features do not exist at all.

We will first examine what the article really does contain and afterwards what are the comparitive advantages likely to result to the two countries.

The main stipulation is that "it shall at all times be free to his Majesty's subjects and to the Citizens of the United States and also to the Indians dwelling on either side of the boundary line freely to pass and repass, *by land and inland navigation*, into the respective territories and countries of the two parties on the Continent of America (the country within the limits of the Hudson's Bay company only excepted) and to navigate all the Lakes Rivers and Waters thereof and freely to carry on Trade and commerce with each other."

The subject matter of this stipulation is plainly *inland trade and commerce* to be carried on *by land passage and inland navigation* between the subjects and citizens of the U States and the Indians dwelling on each side of the boundary line. This appears first from the terms of the article. The subjects and citizens of the two parties and also the Indians dwelling on each side of the boundary line are freely to pass and repass—what? The boundary line in what manner? by *land* and *inland navigation*—to what places? into the respective territories and countries of the two parties on the Continent of America (the Country of the Hudsons bay company only excepted). They are also to navigate all the Lakes Rivers and *Waters thereof* and freely to carry on trade and commerce with each other. This right to navigate lakes Rivers and Waters must be understood with reference to inland navigation, because this gives it a sense conformable with the antecedent clause with which it is immediately connected as part of a sentence; the right to *pass* and *repass* being expressly restricted to land and inland navigation it would not be natural to extend it by implication, on the strength of an ambiguous term, to passage by sea or by any thing more than inland navigation; because the words Lakes and Rivers have direct reference to inland navigation shewing that to be the object in view and the word "waters" from the order in which it stands will most consistently with propriety of composition be understood as something less than lakes and rivers, as ponds canals and those amphibious waters to which it is scarcely possible to give a name—and because the waters mentioned are "waters thereof" that is waters of the territories and countries of the two parties on the Continent of America—a decription which can not aptly be applied to the sea or be supposed to include navigation by sea to the U States or from them to the British territories.[9]

This conclusion is confirmed by the general complexion of the Treaty. It is the manifest province of the Eighteen articles which succeed the first ten to regulate external commerce and navigation. The regulations they contain are introduced thus by the 11th article "It is agreed between his Majesty and the U States of America that there shall be a reciprocal and intirely perfect liberty of Navigation and Commerce between their respective people in the manner under the limitations and on the conditions specified in the following articles" Then follow articles which provide fully and distinctly for Trade and Navigation between the U States and the British West Indies, between the Asiatic Dominions of GB and the U States, and lastly between the European dominions of G Britain and the U States. These Eighteen articles properly constitute the Treaty of commerce and navigation between the two Countries. Their general scope and some special provisions which they contain prove that the object of the third article is local and partial, that it contemplates exclusively an interior commerce by land and inland navigation (except as to the Mississippi) and particularly that it does not reach at all our Atlantic sea ports. An instance of one of the special provisions alluded to will be cited in the further examination of this article.[10]

In opposition to this construction, much [11] stress is laid upon the

9. At this point in the newspaper the following material was added: "It is true that nations, for various purposes, claim and exercise jurisdiction over the seas, immediately adjacent to their coasts; yet this is subject to the common right of nations, to the innocent use of those seas for navigation and it is not *prima facie* presumable, that two nations, speaking of the waters of each other, would mean to give this appropriate denomination to waters, in which both claimed some common right. The usual description of such waters in treaties is, '*the seas near* the countries, &c.' But were it otherwise, still the navigating from the *open* sea into those waters, could not be within the permission to navigate those waters, and might be prohibited."

10. See "The Defence No. XI," August 28, 1795, and "The Defence No. XII," September 2–3, 1795.

11. In MS this word is "must."

provisions which immediately succeed the clauses that have been quoted. They are in these words "But it is understood that this article does not extend to the admission of Vessels of the U States into the sea ports harbours bays or Creeks of his Majestys said territories, nor into such parts of the rivers in his said Territories as are between the mouth thereof and the highest port of entry from the sea except in small vessels trading bona fide between Montreal and Quebec; nor to the admission of British Vessels from the sea into the Rivers of the U States beyond the highest ports of entry for foreign vessels from the sea." The last it is said contains an implication that under this article British vessels have a right to come to our highest ports of entry for foreign vessels from the sea, while we are excluded from the sea ports of the British territories on this Continent.

But this is altogether an erroneous inference. The clauses last cited are inserted for greater caution, to guard expressly against any construction of the article, by implications more or less remote, contrary to the actual regulations of the parties with regard to external commerce and navigation. Great Britain does not now permit a Trade by sea to Nova Scotia and Canada.[12] She therefore declares that the article shall not be deemed to contravene this regulation. The U States now permit foreign Vessels to come to certain ports of Entry from the sea but exclude them from other more interior ports of entry to which our own vessels may come.* [13] It is therefore

* An example of this is found in the State of New York. Foreign vessels can only enter & unlade at the City of New York. Vessels of the U States may enter at the City of Hudson & unlade there & at NYork [14]

12. See "Remarks on the Treaty . . . between the United States and Great Britain," July 9–11, 1795, note 80.

13. See "An Act to provide more effectually for the collection of the duties imposed by law on goods, wares and merchandise imported into the United States, and on the tonnage of ships or vessels" (1 Stat. 145–78 [August 4, 1790]). Section 1, which set up ports of entry and of delivery in all the states on the eastern seaboard, provided that ". . . In the state of New York shall be two districts—to wit: Sag Harbor on Nassau or Long Island, and the city of New York, each of which shall be a port of entry. . . . The district of the city of New York shall include such part of the coasts, rivers, bays and harbors of the said state, not included in the district of Sag Harbor; and moreover the several towns or landing places of New Windsor, Newburgh, Pough-keepsie, Esopus, city of Hudson, Kinderhook, and Albany, as ports of delivery only. . . ." Section 2 provided: "That it shall not be lawful to make entry of any ship or vessel which shall arrive from any foreign port or place within the United States, or of the cargo on board such ship or vessel, elsewhere

declared on their part that the article shall not be construed to con-travene this regulation. This was the more proper as the right of inland navigation might have given some colour to the claim of going from an outer to an inner port of entry.[15]

But this negative of an implication, which might have found some colour in the principal provision, can never be construed into an affirmative grant of a very important privilege, foreign to that prin-cipal provision. The main object of the article it has been seen, is Trade by land and inland navigation. Trade and navigation by sea

---

than at one of the ports of entry herein before established, nor to unlade the said cargo, or any part thereof, elsewhere than at one of the ports of de-livery herein established: *Provided always*, That every port of entry shall be also a port of delivery: *And provided further*, That none but ships or vessels of the United States shall be admitted to unlade at any other than the ports following—to wit: . . . New York, in the state of New York . . . or to make entry in any other district than in one in which they shall be so admitted to unlade. . . ."

14. In the newspaper "Albany" is substituted for "New York."

Section 4 of "An Act supplementary to the act, intituled 'An act to pro-vide more effectually for the collection of the Duties on goods, wares and merchandise imported into the United States, and on the tonnage of ships or vessels'" reads in part: "*And be it further enacted,* That from and after the last day of May next, there shall be established the following new districts and ports of delivery, to wit: In the state of New York, a district to be called the district of Hudson; which shall include the city of Hudson, and all the waters and shores northward of the said city on Hudson river, and the town of Catskill below the said city; and the said city of Hudson shall be the sole port of entry for the said district; to which shall be annexed the towns or landing-places of Catskill, Kinderhook and Albany, as ports of delivery only; and the collector for the said district shall reside at Hudson, and a surveyor to reside at Hudson, and another, at Albany, as is now by law established . . ." (1 *Stat.* 421 [February 26, 1795]).

Section 5 of the same act reads in part: "*And be it further enacted,* That the master or commander of any ship or vessel, bound from a foreign port or place, to the district of Hudson, or to the district of Bermuda Hundred and City Point, shall, if bound to the former, first come to, with his ship or vessel, at the city of New York, and if to the latter, after the last day of September next, at Hampton Road or Sewell's Point, and there make report to the col-lector of New York, or of Norfolk and Portsmouth, or to the collector of the port of Hampton, as the case may be, and take on board an inspector of the customs, before he shall proceed to the district of Hudson, or to the district of Bermuda Hundred and City Point . . ." (1 *Stat.* 421-22).

15. At this point in the draft H wrote and crossed out the following para-graph: "It is said negatively that the article shall not be understood to admit British vessels from the sea, *beyond* the highest ports of entry for foreign vessels from the sea—but it is not said that it shall be understood to admit British vessels from the sea to those highest ports of entry for foreign vessels. This is left to the operation of the existing laws and of those parts of the Treaty which regulate external commerce and navigation."

with our sea ports is an intirely different thing. To infer a positive grant of this privilege from a clause which says that the right of inland navigation shall not be construed to permit vessels coming from the sea to go from the ports of entry to which our laws now restrict them to more interior ports would be contrary to reason and to every rule of sound construction. Such a privilege could never be permitted to be founded upon any thing less than a positive and explicit grant of it. It could never be supported by an implication drawn from an article relative to a local and partial object—much less by an implication drawn from the negative of another implication. The pretension, that all our ports were laid open to Great Britain by a covert and side-wind provision and this without reciprocity [16] would be too monstrous to be tolerated for an instant.[17] It would be the more inadmissible, because the object is embraced and regulated by other parts of the Treaty on terms of reciprocity.

The different mode of expression, in the clauses last cited, when speaking of the British territories and when speaking of the UStates, has furnished an argument for the inference which has been stated. But this difference is accounted for by the difference in the actual regulations of the parties as described above. The object was on each side to *oust* an implication interfering with these regulations. The expressions to effect it were commensurate with the state of the fact on each side; and consequently do not warrant any collateral or special inference.

The only positive effect of these clauses is to confine the right of inland navigation from Montreal to Quebec to what are called "small vessels trading bona fide between Montreal and Quebec." [18] Those

16. At this point in the newspaper the following words were added: "without a right of access to a single sea-port of the other party in any part of the world."

17. At this point in the newspaper the following sentence was added: "The principles of equity between nations, and the established rules of interpretation would unite to condemn so great an inequality, if any other sense could possibly be found for the terms from which it might be pretended to be deduced."

18. At this point in the newspaper the following two sentences were added: "In determining their sense, it merits some observation, that they do not profess to *except from* the operation of the general provisions of the article, the *sea ports*, &c. of the British territories; but declare, that it is understood that those provisions *do not extend to* them. This is more a declaration that the antecedent provisions were not so broad as to comprehend the cases, than an exception of the cases from the operation of those provisions."

who are not familiar with laws and Treaties may feel some difficulty about the position that particular clauses are introduced only for greater caution without producing any new effect, but those who are familiar with such subjects know that there is scarcely a law or a Treaty which does not offer examples of the use of similar clauses, and it not unfrequently happens that a clear meaning of the principal provision is rendered obscure by the excess of explanatory precaution.

The next clause of this article is an exception to the general design of it confirming the construction I have given to it: "The River Mississippi shall *however*, according to the Treaty of Peace be entirely open to both parties; and it is further agreed that all the ports and places on its Eastern side to which soever of the parties belonging may freely be resorted to and used by both parties in as ample a manner as any of the Atlantic Ports or places of the U States or any of the ports or places of his Majesty in Great Britain."

If the general provision gives access to all our ports, which must be the doctrine if it gives access to our Atlantic ports, then it would equally have this effect with regard to the Mississippi. But this clause clearly implies the contrary not only by introducing a special provision for the ports of the Mississippi but by introducing it expressly as a further or additional agreement—the words are "it is *further* agreed &c" and these ports are to be enjoyed by each party *in as ample a manner as any of the Atlantic ports or places of the U States, or any of the ports or places of his Majesty in Great Britain*. This reference to our Atlantic Ports coupling them with the ports of Great Britain shews that the Mississi[ppi] Ports are to be regulated by a rule or standard different from the ports for that inland navigation which is the general object of the article; else why that special reference? why not have stopped at the words "used by both parties"? If it be said, that the reference to our Atlantic Ports implies that they are within the purview of the article, let it be observed that the same argument would prove that the ports of Great Briain are also within its purview, which is plainly erroneous, for the main provisions are expressly confined to the territories of the parties on this continent. The conclusion is that the reference is to a standard out of the article and depending on other parts of the Treaty.

It may be useful to observe here, that the Mississippi Ports being to be used only in as ample, and not in a more ample, manner than our Atlantic Ports and the ports of Great Britain will be liable at all times to all the regulations privileges & restrictions of the ports with which they are assorted.

The next clause is a still further refutation of the construction which I oppose—"All goods and merchandize, *whose importation into his Majestys said territories in America shall not be intirely prohibited*, may freely for the purposes of commerce be carried into the same *in the manner aforesaid* by the Citizens of the U States, and such goods and merchandize shall be subject to no *higher or other duties than would be payable by his Majestys subjects on the importation of the same from Europe into the said territories:* And in like manner all goods and merchandize *whose importation into the U States shall not be wholly prohibitted*, may freely for the purposes of commerce be carried into the same *in the manner aforesaid subject to no higher or other duties* than would be *payable by the Citizens of the U States* on the importation of the same in *American Vessels into the Atlantic Ports of the said States:* and all goods not prohibitted to be exported from the said territories respectively may *in like manner* be carried out of the same by the two parties respectively paying duty as aforesaid".

The words "*in the manner aforesaid*" occur twice in these clauses and their equivalent "*in like manner*" once? What is the meaning of this so often repeated phrase? It cannot be presumed that it would have been inserted so frequently without having to perform some office of consequence. I answer that it is evidently the substitute for these other words of the main provision, "*by land and inland navigation.*" This is "*the manner aforesaid.*" This is the channel through which goods and merchandizes passing would be subject to no other or higher duties than would be payable in the British territories by British subjects, if imported from Europe—in the territories of the U States, by citizens of the U States, if brought by American Vessels into our Atlantic ports. No other reasonable use can be found for the terms. If they are denied this sense, they had much better been omitted, as being not only useless but as giving cause to suppose a restriction of what it is pretended was designed to be general—a right of importing in every way and into all parts of the U States goods and merchandize, if not intirely prohibited, on the same duties as are payable by our own citizens when brought in our own vessels.

These words "whose importation into the UStates *shall* not be *intirely* prohibitted" is a further key to the true sense of the article. They are equivalent to these other words—"whose importation *into all parts* of the U States shall not be prohibitted." The design of this clause is to prevent importation through the particular channels contemplated by the article being obstructed by a partial, or by any other than a general prohibition. As long as certain goods may be introduced into the U States through the Atlantic ports they may also be brought into them through the channels designated by this article, that is by land and inland navigation. The making a prohibition in the given case to depend on a general prohibition is conclusive to prove, that the article contemplates only *particular channels*. On any other supposition the clause is nonsense. The true reading then of this part of the article must be as follows—"Goods and merchandize whose importation into *all parts* of the U States shall not be prohibitted may freely for the purposes of commerce be carried into the same *in manner aforesaid*, that is by *land and inland navigation*, from the territories of His Majesty on the Continent of America."

There are still other expressions in the article which are likewise an index to its meaning. They are these *"would be payable* by the Citizens of the UStates on the *importation of the same* in American vessels *into the Atlantic Ports of the said States."* This reference to a rate of duties which would be payable on importation into the Atlantic ports, as a rule or guide for the rate of duties which is to prevail in the case meant to be comprehended in the article is full evidence that importation in the Atlantic ports is not included in that case. The mention of importation in American vessels confirms this conclusion as it shews that the article itself contemplates that the discrimination made by our existing laws may continue.

But the matter is put out of all doubt by those parts of the fifteenth article [19] which reserve to the British Government "the right of imposing such duty as may be adequate to *countervail the difference* of duty *now payable* on the importation of European and Asiatic goods when imported into the UStates in British and in American Vessels"—and which stipulate that "the United States

19. For the text of Article 15 of the Jay Treaty, see "Remarks on the Treaty . . . between the United States and Great Britain," July 9–11, 1795, note 57.

will not *increase the now subsisting difference* between the duties payable on the importation of any articles in British or in American Vessels."

This is demonstration, that the Treaty contemplates, as consistent with it, a continuance of the present difference of duties on importations in American and British Vessels, and consequently that the third article, which stipulates equal duties, as to the cases within it, does not extend to importations into our Atlantic ports, but is confined to importations by land and inland navigation.[20]

If it were necessary to multiply illustration of this position, it might be asked whether tis probable G B could have meant by this article to give us free admission to any ports she may ever have on the Pacific Ocean within the American Continent? The jealousy with which she guards her ports in Canada & Nova Scotia is a negative answer to this question. And yet on the doctrine, opposite to mine, as there is no special exception but of the last mentioned ports, the right of access to Ports on the Pacific would be granted. It is also known that Great Britain has extensive views in that quarter, as appeared in the question of Nootka sound.[21] There is a large district of Country denominated *New Albion*.[22]

These different views of the Article establish beyond the possi-

20. At this point in the newspaper the following sentence was added: "Though this article be of temporary duration, yet as an evidence of the sense of parties, it will always serve as a rule of construction for every part of the instrument."

21. The Nootka Sound controversy was the outcome of rival British and Spanish claims to the use of trading facilities at Nootka on Vancouver Island. In 1789 the Spanish, who claimed the area by the Treaty of Tordesillas of 1494, seized two British trading ships at Nootka and imprisoned their seamen on the ground that Britain was violating Spanish rights. After negotiation, by the Nootka Convention of October 28, 1790, Spain conceded to Britain rights of commerce, navigation, and settlement on the Pacific coast north of San Francisco. In return, Britain agreed not to trade illicitly with Spanish subjects in that area. Spain thus obtained confirmation of her existing settlements but lost her claim to the sovereignty of the Pacific coast. See George Washington to H, August 27, 1790; H to Washington, September 21, 29, 1790; and "Conversation with George Beckwith," September 26-30, 1790.

22. This entire paragraph was omitted in the newspaper.

New Albion was the name given by Sir Francis Drake to a part of the Pacific coast, which he reached in the summer of 1579. It now seems certain that after a short voyage to the northward and back, Drake landed at 38° of latitude just north of San Francisco and gave the name of New Albion to a nearby stretch of the California coast. It is possible, however, that H may have shared the once prevailing belief that Drake reached 48°, and that New Albion extended from northern California as far as Vancouver Island.

bility of Doubt that except with regard to the Mississippi, inland trade and navigation are its sole objects—that it grants no right or privilege whatever in our Atlantic ports—and that with regard to the ports of the Mississippi it only establishes this principle that Great Britain shall always enjoy there the same privileges which by Treaty or Law she is allowed to have in our Atlantic Ports.

I remark incidentally, for a purpose which will appear hereafter, that as far as this article is concerned we are free to prohibit the importation into the U States at large of any British article whatever, though we cannot prohibit its importation *partially*, that is merely from her territories in our neighbourhood by land or inland navigation, but we may prohibit the importation by sea from those territories; *nor is there any other part of the Treaty by which this is prevented.*

The remaining clauses of this article establish the following points "that no duty of entry shall be levied by either party on pelt[r]ies brought by land or inland navigation into the respective territories" that Indians passing and repassing with their own goods shall pay no impost or duty upon them but goods in bales or other large packages unusual among Indians shall not be considered as their goods, that tolls and rates of ferriage shall be the same on both sides as are paid by natives, that no duties shall be paid by either party on the mere transit of goods across portages and carrying places from one part to another of the territory of the same party, that the respective Governments will promote friendship good neighbourhood and amicable intercourse by causing speedy and impartial justice to be done and necessary protection to be extended to all who may be concerned therein.

I shall conclude this paper with an observation or two on the meaning of the terms inland navigation. These terms have no technical meaning defined in the laws of either country, nor have they any precise meaning assigned by the laws of Nations. They however *ex vi termini* exclude navigation from the sea. And as a general rule I should say that inland navigation begins there, where sea navigation ends. Where is this? I answer at the ports of entry from the sea. By the laws of Great Britain and of the U States all Rivers are arms of the sea as far as the ordinary tides flow. It would be a consequence of this principle that sea navigation would reach to the head of tide water. But as some more obvious and notorious rule ought to govern the interpretation of national compacts the ports of entry from the sea are conceived to be the proper rule.[23]

In the case under consideration the general spirit of the article will require that all the waters which divide the territories of the parties should be in their whole extent common to both. As to other communicating waters accessible under the article the reciprocal limit of the right will be the ports of entry from the sea. This is with the exception of the Mississippi to the ports of which access from the sea is granted under the qualification which has been pointed out.   CAMILLUS

23. See "Remarks on the Treaty . . . between the United States and Great Britain," July 9–11, 1795, note 9.

To Philip Schuyler

[*New York, August 27, 1795.* On August 31, 1795, Schuyler wrote to Hamilton: "I thank for you[r] favor of the 27th Instant." *Letter not found.*]

The Defence No. XI[1]

[New York, August 28, 1795]

The foregoing analysis of the third article,[2] by fixing its true meaning, enables us to detect some gross errors which have been principal sources of prejudice against it.

ADf, Hamilton Papers, Library of Congress; *The* [New York] *Argus, or Greenleaf's New Daily Advertiser*, August 28, 1795.

1. For background to this document, see the introductory note to "The Defence No. I," July 22, 1795.

Throughout most of this essay, H is attempting to refute the first essay by "Decius" (*The* [New York] *Argus, or Greenleaf's New Daily Advertiser*, July 10, 1795) and the fourth essay by "Cato" (*The* [New York] *Argus, or Greenleaf's New Daily Advertiser*, July 25, 1795). "Decius" was the pseudonym used by Brockholst Livingston and "Cato" was that used by Robert R. Livingston. For the authorship of these essays, see the introductory note to "The Defence No. I," July 22, 1795.

The relevant part of the first "Decius" essay reads:

"Article III

"The advantages conceded to Great Britain by the third article are much greater than which we derive in return. Considering the extent of the United States, it is evident that the mutual liberty here granted, to pass by land or inland navigation into each other's respective territories upon this continent, is a much greater acquisition to Great Britain than to us; not only the territory of the former is small when compared with our own, but the whole fur trade, which we might have secured to ourselves, will now not only be participated by, but probably fall altogether into the hands of British traders, notwithstanding our country is much more extensive, and our rivers and lakes more numerous than those of Great Britain, into all of which she has free admission; the latter has taken care, very unjustly, to exclude our vessels from the 'sea ports, harbours, bays and creeks of his Majesty's said territories,' and also from 'such parts of the rivers as are between the mouths thereof, and the highest port of entry from the sea, except in small vessels trading between Montreal and Quebec.' Where is the consideration for this manifest inequality? A British trader may set out from Canada, traverse our lakes, and pass with his merchandize down the Hudson or Delaware to New York or Philadelphia, with his own vessel. Why ought we not, in return, to have the free navigation of the Saint Lawrence and other British rivers? Instead of this, we are stopped, in our passage down at the highest port of entry, and must there hire British vessels to pursue our voyage, or sell our cargoes for the best price we can get.

"There is a curious proviso in this article, which deserves notice. Upon a cursory reading, it appears to lay Great Britain under a similar restraint, but the least attention will discover this not to be the case. It is this, *British vessels from the sea* are not to be admitted into our rivers beyond the highest port of entry for foreign vessels from the sea.' What can Great Britain wish for more? *would her sea vessels* ever attempt, if permitted, to go further than the highest port of entry.

"That part of this article, which interdicts the laying of duties, on peltries brought by land or inland navigation, is also highly unequal and disadvantageous to America. The peltry which we shall carry through the British dominions, considering the construction of this article, must be inconsiderable indeed —while we may expect that very great quantities will annually be brought through the United States by his Majesty's subjects, all of which must pass free of duty. Nay, under this article, Great Britain may import into any part of the United States, European, East and West India goods, upon which we can impose no other or higher duties than are payable by our own citizens."

The relevant part of the fourth essay by "Cato" reads: "In considering the commercial article, I shall begin with the Indian Trade, after having submitted a few rules, to the force of which, every communicative man will readily acknowledge.

"1st. That all things else being equal; that trader who has the greatest capital, most knowledge of trade, an established set of customers, and the most extensive acquaintance with the dealers in the commodities he buys and sells, will be able to maintain himself against any rival merchant that does not enjoy these advantages.

"2d. That if in addition to this he has advantages in the transportation of his goods; in the sale of the commodities he purchases; and in the establishment of factories he must ruin all competitors. By the treaty of peace our boundaries are fixed and the British are to evacuate our territory without any stipulation whatever, in favour of British merchants or British traders; by this treaty therefore, so much of the fur and peltry trade, at least as lay within our own territory was necessarily and exclusively ours, as we possessed all

the posts at which the trade had been carried on for a century past, and
most of the portages. As our communication from the sea was much easier
than that by the St. Lawrence, we could furnish Indian goods cheaper, and
of course would have still continued the Indian trade in its usual channel, even
from the British sides of the lakes, nor could they by any means have prevented it without giving such disgust to the Indians as would have made them
dangerous neighbours. Lord Grenville's treaty with Mr. Jay stipulates, that
the British traders may continue to live at our posts; and to hold the property
they possess; to trade in every part of our territory as freely as our own
citizens; to navigate our rivers *from the sea* as high as our own citizens may,
that is, to the highest port of entry, and from thence to navigate our inland
waters. It must follow then, that under these circumstances, they stand exactly
upon the same footing with our own citizens. It will also be admitted, that
having been for twelve years in the exclusive possession of the Indian trade,
having in general much larger capitals; having an extensive acquaintance
amongst the Indian nations, and with the Canadians who are the general
carriers in that country, American traders will not be able to maintain a
competition with them, even if they had no other advantages than those I
have enumerated. But this unhappily is far from being the case, First, They
have of course a right to settle factories in every part of their own territory;
their factors being always upon the spot, and cultivating an acquaintance with
the natives, will certainly be able to command the trade of their country, and
thus render absolutely useless the stipulation which admits American traders
to travel into that territory; for it is observable that the navigation Act, 12
Chap. 2d, 18, which is preserved in full force, by the 14th Art. of the treaty,
prevents our establishing any factory or trading house, or residing as merchant-
factor within the British territories, *out of Europe;* while the treaty permits
the British to *reside* in any part of the United States; to hire and possess
houses and warehouses for the purpose of commerce, &c. so that while by
this means they have an exclusive trade in their own territory, notwithstanding
the apparent grant of a right to us, they have all the advantages our citizens
enjoy in ours, with those they have acquired from large capitals, knowledge
of the trade, &c. Our trader may indeed travel like a pedler, through their
country with his shop upon his back, but cannot have any fixed residence
at which to open a store. Were not Mr. Jay a chief justice, I should be
tempted to believe that he did not know of the provision of the Act of 12th
Ch. 2d. Ch. 18. which he has kept in full force by the 14th Art. of the treaty.
This exclusive trade in their own country by means of the factories they
may establish, gives them another considerable advantage; it is well known
to merchants that the more extensive any branch of commerce is, the less
liable to interruptions, the more profitable it must be, and of course the better
it enables the trader to undersell his competitors. If then our merchants can
only trade in our own territories, and there with no advantage over the
British, and if the British merchant can trade with equal advantage in our
territory, and superior in the British territory, the last can employ a greater
capital in his commerce; and as the Indian trade is liable to frequent interruptions by wars and bad seasons, which may prevail in our country, while
that of the British is unmolested, the whole capital of our trader remains
inactive, while a considerable part of that of the British trader is employed.
This again must render the competition very unequal. A writer who has
shewn much more anxiety to maintain, than candour in defence of the treaty,
has overlooked all these circumstances which will effectually prevent our
traders from contending with the British, and which in fact, amounts to an
absolute surrender of this important branch of commerce, and consoles us
with the hope of being able to find a market for East India goods, through

the intervention of this treaty. I must confess that I have yet to learn, that any East India articles are consumed by the Indians; it is possible however that a few coarse calicoes may now and then be worn by the squaws; but I will venture to assert, that the whole amount of East India articles sold to the Indians on the north of the Lakes, will not exceed one hundred dollars a year; or hope the writer means that the inhabitants of Canada will receive them through this channel; if we should even admit this, which however we shall be able to shew is highly improbable, yet it would appear a very insignificant advantage, when we reflect that the whole number of inhabitants in Canada and Labrador, as appears by a census taken by General Haldiman, only amounted in 1784, including Upper Canada, 123,082 souls, but few of these are in the habit of drinking any tea, and all are too poor to consume any but the coarsest articles; so shall the whole consumption of Canada, in India goods, if we had the monopoly of that trade, would fall far short of what is consumed in one half of the little state of New Jersey; and we should certainly make a miserable exchange if for this we sacrifice a branch of commerce of such immense importance as the Indian trade. But what can be more absurd than to suppose that articles which come duty free from Britain (a draw back being allowed on exportation) and are carried into the heart of the settled parts of Canada in the same vessels that bring them from Europe, cannot be sold cheaper than the same articles subject to a heavy duty, and carried an immense distance by land, and an expensive inland navigation; this indeed may not apply to the upper posts, but who are the consumers of East-India articles in those cold, poor, and barren regions?

"In short, the more any one considers this article, the more fully he will be convinced that it contains a compleat and absolute surrender of the fur trade, the greater part of which we might have exclusively possessed under the treaty of peace, had not Lord Grenville prevailed on Mr. Jay, to introduce a rival who will always be too powerful for us. And what renders this circumstance the more peculiarly oppressive, is that this article is to be permanent; Lord Grenville was too sensible of its importance to permit any time or circumstances to unloose these galling fetters.

"In a political, this article is not less exceptionable than in a commercial view. We know from sad experience, the cost and danger of Indian wars; we know too from the same experience, that they can be and have been fomented by Britain, whenever her interest or her malevolence prompted her to distress us. By permitting the British traders to remain amongst the Indians, and to extend themselves to every village, we add to their influence, and by the terms of the XXVI articles are prohibited from expelling them, *even in case of war with Britain* herself, unless their conduct should render them suspected, and not even then in less than twelve months from the publication of the order. What but the blindest infatuation could induce our minister to stipulate thus a secret, nay even an open enemy to remain without restraint among savages, that the slightest circumstance stimulates to war? Did we not know what we formerly should suffer from the residence of a few Canadian priests and traders residing among the Indians, and how many endeavours were used by the government to get the Six Nations to expel them? It will be said, this article is reciprocal, and that if their agents remain within our lines, ours remain also within theirs: this however is, not the fact, for if at any time, a war should break out, our traders (if we should have any which I much doubt) will for their own safety retire from places so remote as the British territories; besides that they not having any right as I have before shewn, to reside within the British territories *out of Europe,* which is expressly prohibited by the navigation act, and no such right being given by the treaty, it must follow, that no American merchant or trader,

One of these is that the article gives to the other party a right of access to all our ports, while it excludes us from the ports of Nova Scotia and Canada.[3] It has been clearly shewn that it gives no right of access to any one of our Atlantic Ports, and that it gives only a qualified and conditional access to the ports which we may have on the Mississippi to be regulated by the privileges at any time allowed by law or compact in our Atlantic Ports and liable to cease with the interruption of access to the last mentioned ports. The charge therefore of want of reciprocity in this particular vanishes, and with it all the exceptionable consequences which have been the fruit of the error. Such is the assertion of DECIUS, that a British Trader may set out from Canada traverse our lakes rivers and waters to New York and thence to Philadelphia, while we are precluded from the navigation of St Laurance and other British Rivers lower than the highest ports of Entry from the sea.[4] It would be an indulgent construction of the article not to stop the British Trader at Hudson, as the highest port of entry from the sea and the boundary of inland navigation;[5] but he could certainly have no claim of right under it to go from New York to Philadelphia, because he must necessarily go by sea to arrive at the last[6] place and no such permission is stipulated by the article. Such also is the assertion of Cato that G Britain is admitted to all the advantages of which our Atlantic Rivers are susceptible.[7] The Rivers

not settled in Europe, can have the least benefit by this provision, while hundreds of British emissaries may, under the pretence of trade, maintain the most dangerous stations in the heart of our country."

2. See "The Defence No. X," August 26, 1795. For Article 3 of the Jay Treaty, see "Remarks on the Treaty . . . between the United States and Great Britain," July 9–11, 1795, note 8.

3. In the newspaper this sentence ends with the following words: "from the ports of the British territories in our neighbourhood."

For H's discussion of the question raised in this sentence, see "The Defence No. X," August 26, 1795.

4. This is a reference to the discussion in the first essay by "Decius." See note 1.

5. For the establishment of Hudson, New York, as a port of entry, see Section 4 of "An Act supplementary to the act, intituled 'An act to provide more effectually for the collection of the Duties on goods, wares and merchandise imported into the United States, and on the tonnage of ships or vessels'" (1 *Stat.* 421 [February 26, 1795]). For this section, see "The Defence No. X," August 26, 1795, note 14.

6. In the newspaper, "first."

7. This is a reference to an assertion in the fourth essay by "Cato." See note 1.

upon which no part of their territory borders and which their vessels can only approach by sea are certainly excepted.

Another of the errors referred to is this—That goods and merchandize may under this article be imported into any part of the U States upon the same duties as are now payable when imported by citizens of the UStates in vessels of the U States. It has been clearly proved that there is no pretence for this position, and that equality of duties only applies to importations from the British territories in our neighbourhood by land and inland navigation.[8]

CATO DECIUS and other writers against the Treaty have fallen into this strange error and have founded upon it much angry declamation.[9] The first, however, embarrassed in his construction by the provision which reserves to Great Britain the right of laying countervailing duties, endeavours to escape from it by distinguishing between goods imported for Indian Trade and those imported for other uses. Whatever may be the case with regard to the latter, the former, he is convinced, are certainly intitled to admission into our Atlantic Ports on the privileged rates of duty; though he is very naturally perplexed to see how the discrimination could be maintained in practice. But Where does he find room for this distinction? Not in the provision respecting countervailing duties, for that is general—not in the clause of the third article to which he gives the interpretation for that is directly against his disti[n]ction. The goods and merchandize for the privileged importation of which it provides are restricted to no particular object have no special reference to Indian more than to other Trade. On the contrary they are expressly to be imported for "the purposes of Commerce" at large; so that in the cases in which they are privileged they are equally so whether it be for a Trade with our Citizens or with Indians. The distinction therefore only proves the embarrassment of its inventor without solving the difficulty. A curious assertion has been made on this article of duties. It has been said that while we are obliged to admit British goods on the same duties with those paid by our own Citizens on importation in our own vessels— Great Britain under the right to lay countervailing duties may encumber us with an additional ten per Cent. Can any thing be more

8. See "The Defence No. X," August 26, 1795.
9. See note 1.

absurd than the position that the right to lay *countervailing* duties exists in a case where there is no difference of duty to *countervail?* The term is manifestly a relative one & can only operate where there is something on our side to be countervailed or counterballanced and in an exact ratio to it. If it be true that a very high law chara[c]ter is the Writer of *Cato* we cannot but be surprised at such extreme inaccuracy.

Other errors no less considerable will appear in the progress of the examination; but it will facilitate the detection of these and tend to a more thorough understanding of the article to state in this place some general facts which are material in a comparison of the advantages and disadvantages of the article to the respective parties.

1   The furr trade within our limits is to the furr Trade within the British limits as one to seven nearly, that is, the Trade with the Indian[s] on the British side of the Boundary line is about seven times greater than the same Trade on our side of that line. This fact is stated as the result of repeated inquiry from well informed persons for several years past. It will not appear extraordinary to those who recollect how much the Indians on our side are circumscribed in their hunting grounds and to what a degree they are reduced in numbers by the frequent wars in which they have been engaged with us—while the tribes on the British side of the line, are not only far more numerous, but have an immense undisturbed range of wilderness. The more rapid progress of settlement on our side than on the other will fast increase the existing disparity.

2   Our communication with the sea is more easy safe and expeditious than that of Canada by the St. Laurance. Accordingly while our vessels ordinarily make two voyages in a year to and from Europe the British Vessels in the Canada Trade are from the course of the seasons and the nature of the Navigation confined to one voyage a year. Though hitherto from temporary circumstances this difference has not made any sensible difference in the price of transportation—yet in its permanent operation it is hardly possible that it should not give us a material advantage in the competition for the supply of European goods to a large part of Canada especially that which is denominated upper Canada. The city of Hudson [124] [10] Miles from the City of New York is as near to the junction

10. Space left blank in MS. The figure has been taken from the newspaper.

of the River [Cataraquy] [11] and Lake Ontario as Montreal which last is near four hundred miles distant from the mouth of the St. Laurance. When the Canals now in rapid execution are completed there will be water communication the whole way from the City of Hudson to Ontario.

3 The supply of East India Goods to Canada must always be easier and cheaper, through us, than in any other way. According to the present British system Canada is supplied through Great Britain. It is obvious how much the charges of this double voyage must enhance the prices of the articles when delivered in Canada. But if a direct Trade between the East Indies and Canada should hereafter be opened, a thing which supposes a change in the British system to which there are many obstacles, still from the nature of the voyage and other circumstances, the supply through us must continue most easy and cheap. It is a fact which serves to illustrate our advantages that East India articles are commonly upon an average   per Cent [12] cheaper in the U States than in England.

These facts demonstrate that a Trade between us and the British territories in our neighbourhood upon equal terms as to privilege must afford a ballance of advantages on our side. As to the furr Trade, for a participation in one eighth of the whole which we concede we gain a participation in seven Eig[h]ths which is conceded to us. As to the European and East India Trade we acquire the right of competition on equal terms of privilege with real and considerable advantages of situation. In regard to the East India Trade it is presumed that they are such as to be decisive.[13]

The stipulation with regard to equal duties was essential to the preservation of our superiority of advantages in this Trade—while it could not interfere with the general policy of our regulation concerning the difference of duties on goods imported in our own and in foreign bottoms; because the supplies which can come to us through Canada for the reasons already given must be inconsiderable —because also distance would soon countervail in expences of trans-

11. Space left blank in MS. This word has been taken from the newspaper. The Cataraquy (Cataraqui) flows southwest from Rideau Lake to the eastern end of Lake Ontario. It formed part of the boundary between the United States and British North America as established by the treaty of peace in 1783 (Miller, *Treaties*, II, 152).

12. Space left blank in MS. In the newspaper, "per Cent" is omitted.

13. This sentence is omitted in the newspaper.

portation the effect of the difference of duties in our market and because in the last place this difference is not very sensible, owing to the large proportion of goods which are imported in the names of our own citizens. I say nothing here of the practicability on general grounds of long maintaining with effect this regulation.

Is it not wonderful considering the real state of the Trade as depending on locality that the Treaty should be charged with sacrificing the furr Trade to the British? If there be any sacrifice, is it not on their side—when the fact is that the quantity of Trade in which they admit us to equal privileges is seven times greater than that in which we admit them to equal privileges?

The arguments against the Treaty on this point are not only full of fallacy but they are in contradiction with each other.

On the one hand, it is argued that our communication from the sea with the Indian Country being much easier than by the St Laurance we could furnish English goods cheaper and of course could have continued the Indian Trade in its usual channel, even from the British side of the Lakes nor could they have prevented it without giving such disgust to the Indians as would have made them dangerous neighbours—on the other hand it is argued that from superiority of Capital, better knowlege of the Trade, a better established connection of customers—The British will be able to supplant us even in our own territories and so acquire a monopoly of the whole furr Trade.*

Propositions so opposite cannot all be true. Either the supposed faculty of supplying English goods cheaper, which it is said would give us a command of the Indian Trade even on the British side of the Lakes, not in the power of the British to prevent, overballances the advantages which are specified on the other side or it does not. If it does not, then is it not true that it could draw to us the Trade from the British side of the Lakes. If it does, then is it not true that the British can supplant us in the Trade on either side the lakes; much less that they can obtain a monopoly of it on both sides.

Besides, if it be true that the British could not prevent our trading with the Indians on their side without giving them such disgust as

* Decius No.
Cato No.[14]
14. See note 1.

to make them dangerous neighbours—why is it not equally true that we could not prevent their trading with the Indians on our side without producing a similar effect? And if they have really a superiority of advantages, why would they not, on the principle of this argument, attract and divert the Trade from us, though a mutual right to trade with the Indians in each others territories had not been stipulated.

The difficulty of restraining the Indians from trading at pleasure is an idea well founded—as has been admitted in another place.[15] But there results from it strong arguments in favour of a reciprocation of privileges in the Indian Trade by Treaty. One of them, its tendency to preserve peace and good understanding, has been already noticed [16]—another arises from the consideration that it will probably be the policy of the British to maintain larger military establishments on their frontier than we shall think eligible on ours, which will render it proportionably more easy to them to restrain their Indians than it will be to us to restrain ours. This greater difficulty of executing restraints on our side is a powerful reason for us to agree mutually to throw open the door. It will not be surprising if upon some other occasion, the adversaries of the Treaty should abandon their own ground & instead of saying the Treaty is faulty for what it stipulates on this point should affirm merely that it has no merit on this account, since it only does what the disposition of the Indians would have brought about without it. But, it is always a merit to divest an advantageous thing of cause of dispute, and to fix by amicable agreement a benefit which otherwise would be liable to litigation opposition and interruption.

As to relative advantages for carrying on the Trade the comparison ought to be made with caution. That which has been stated on our side, namely greater facility in conveying the materials of the Trade from Europe to the scene where it is to be carried on is a real one, and in process of time may be expected to make itself to be felt; yet hitherto as before observed it has had no sensible effect.

Of the advantages, which have been stated as belonging to the other side there is but one which has substance, and this is previous possession of the ground. But even this from the very nature of it

15. See "The Defence No. X," August 26, 1795.
16. See "The Defence No. X," August 26, 1795.

is temporary. With our usual enterprise and industry it will be astonishing if we do not speedily share the ground to the full extent of our relative advantages.

As to superiority of Capital it amounts to nothing. It has been seen that the Capital requisite for the whole Trade is small.[17] From a hundred to a hundred and fifty thousand pounds Sterling would be a high statement. The whole of this, if we were able to monopolise the intire trade, could not create a moments embarrassment to find it, in the opinion of any man who attends to the great pecuniary operations which are dayly going on in our Country. But that very Capital which is represented as our rival could be brought into action for our benefit in this very Trade. The solution is simple. Our Credit would command it in obtaining the goods necessary for the Trade upon as good terms as the British Merchants who now carry it on. The same objection of superiority of Capital may with as much reason be applied to any other branch of Trade between us and G Britain. Why does it not give her a monopoly of the direct Trade between her European Dominions and the U States? The argument if valid would prove that we ought to have no commerce, not only with G Britain, but with any Nation which has more commercial Capital than ourselves.

As to superior knowlege of the particular branch of business there is still less force in that argument. Tis not a case of abstruse science or complicated combination—And we are in no want of persons among us who are experimentally acquainted with the subject.

As to customers for the proceeds of the Trade we should stand upon as good a footing as the British Merchants. What we did not want for our own consumption might be sent upon equal terms to the very markets to which they send theirs—and to others which might be found preferable because less well supplied with the kind of articles.

As to whatever may depend on enterprise we need not fear to be out done by any people on Earth. It may almost be said that enterprise is our element.[18]

17. See "The Defence No. X," August 26, 1795.
18. At this point in the draft H wrote and crossed out: "The conclusion is that we have made in this particular a good bargain. We have staked upon equal privileges one against seven. And it will be extraordinary if we should

It has been alleged that our Trade with the Indians would be interrupted by bad[19] seasons and occasional wars while that of G Britain would be steady and uniform.[20] As to the casualties of seasons 'tis evident they must fall upon Great Britain as much as upon us unless we suppose the elements in conspiracy against us—and as to wars the possession of the posts would essentially change our situation & render it peculiarly advantageous for preventing or repressing hostilities so that with equally good management our territories would not be more exposed than the British.[21]

But the intrigues of the British Traders residing among our Indians would excite them to hostility against us. It could not be in the private interest of the Traders to do this, because, besides being amenable to punishment if discovered, besides that both the traders and the Indians within our limits, by the possession of the posts would be under our controul—wars interrupt of course the hunting of the Indians and so destroy their means of trading.

As to Great Britain she never could have had but one interest to prompt Indian hostilities, that was to induce the U States to relinquish a part of their present boundary. The restitution of the posts will put an end to this object. In regard to Trade, she and her Traders will have a common interest with us and our Traders to keep all the Indians at peace for the reason assigned above. This interest will be the stronger, because the best communication even with her own Indians will be partly through our territory, and it would be impossible that it should not be impeded and interrupted by the operations of War between us and the Indians. In fact under the circumstances of common privileges, there is every possible link of common interest between us and G Britain in the preservation of peace with the Indians.

In this question of danger to our peace, by the British participation in the Trade with our Indians—the difficulty of restraining the Indians from trading with whom they please, (which is admitted

---

lose the game with such great odds in our favour. Tis at least just a hazard as it must be every way prudent to run."

19. In MS, "said."

20. These allegations were made in the first essay by "Decius" and the fourth essay by "Cato." See note 1.

21. In the margin opposite this paragraph H wrote: "Note source of quarrels"; "danger if factories to carry on trade through us"; "drawbacks"; "smuggling"; and "equal duties necessary."

by the argument of both sides) is a very material consideration. Would there not be greater hazard to our peace, from the attempts of the British to participate in a Trade from which we endeavoured to exclude them seconded by the discontents of the Indians, than from any dispositions to supplant us when allowed a free competition—when no cause of dissatisfaction was given to the Indians and when it was certain that war must interfere with their means of carrying on the Trade? The security for our peace appears to be much greater in the latter than in the former state of things.

A suspicion is also suggested that Great Britain without exciting war will indirectly trammel and obstruct our Trade.[22] To objections which suppose a want of fair-dealing in the other party it is very difficult to answer. All that a Treaty can do is to establish principles which are likely to operate well if well executed. It is no objection to its merits that the benefits aimed at may be frustrated by ill faith. The utility of any compact between nations must presume a sincere execution. The reverse may disappoint the best conceived plan. And the security against it must be the mutual interest to perform and the power of retaliation. If Great Britain acts with infidelity or chicanery towards us we must retract the privileges granted on our side.

Another objection which is made is that while the British would have a right to reside among us to hire houses and warehouses and to enjoy every convenience for prosecuting the Trade systematically we should not be intitled to similar privileges with them having only a right to pass "like Pedlars with our shops upon our backs." These are the expressions of *Cato*.[23]

The position is founded on that clause of the British Act of Navigation which forbids any but a natural born or naturalized subject to exercise the occupation of a merchant or factor in any of the British Dominions in Asia Africa and America.[24]

In the first place it is to be observed that as far as the article under discussion is concerned there is no pretence to say that one party has greater rights as to residence than the other. If therefore Great Britain can prevent our citizens residing in their territories in our

22. This "suspicion" is suggested by "Cato" in his fourth essay. See note 1.
23. See the quotation from the fourth essay by "Cato" in note 1.
24. See "Remarks on the Treaty . . . between the United States and Great Britain," July 9-11, 1795, note 80.

neighbourhood we are free by this article to apply to them a similar exclusion. And any right of residence which may be claimed under any other part of the Treaty will be temporary.

In the second place, the prohibition of residence in the Act of navigation proceeds on the ground of excluding foreigners from carrying on Trade in the territories to which it extends. But the third article expressly gives us a right freely to carry on trade and commerce with the British territories on this continent—a right which, necessarily includes the privilege of residing as Merchants and factors. For wherever an *end* is granted the *usual* and *proper means* of enjoying it are implied in the grant. Residence is a usual and necessary mean of freely carrying on trade without it the right to trade becomes essentially nugatory. This reasoning has peculiar force in relation to inland Trade. And it agrees with decisions at common Law and with the opinion of Lord Coke—who tells us that "of an house for *habitation* an alien Merchant may take *a lease for years, as incident to Commerce, for without habitation he cannot merchandize or trade.*" [25] This, among other things, he informs us was resolved by all the Judges assembled for that purpose in a case of Sir James Croft in the Reign of Queen Elizabeth; and we learn from it that the right to hire houses and warehouses is derived from the right to Trade as its incident. The same principle in *toto* has been recognised in other cases.

The whole of the article is an innovation upon the British Act of Navigation. Being abrogated as to the principal thing, there is no difficulty in supposing it so as to incidents—on the other hand to pretend to exclude us from the right of residence could not be deemed a fair execution of the article. Hence we find that the charge of want of reciprocity in this particular also fails and with it the supposed disadvantage on our side, in the competition for the Trade.

25. Coke, *First Institutes*, Book I, Ch. I, Sec. 1, page 2b.

From Philip Schuyler

[Albany, August 31, 1795]

Introductory Note

The opening paragraph of this letter contains the first reference in Hamilton's extant correspondence to a series of business transactions in which he was to be involved for several years as the representative of Schuyler and certain other New Yorkers. When Schuyler wrote this letter, he believed that he, Barent Bleecker, Edward Goold, and William Greene [1] had a claim to a portion of Cosby Manor in upstate New York.[2] But as Schuyler's letter to Hamilton indicates, he was not altogether certain of the validity of his claim and was willing to settle for a "compromise." In addition, if a compromise proved impossible, he wished Hamilton to purchase at least some of the land in question. Schuyler and his associates based their claim to "the lands . . . within the patent commonly called Cosby's manor" on the fact that they had purchased them "at a sherif's sale, in the year 1772"; and in a statement dated April 21, 1795, they "advise[d] all persons who may have been inclined to purchase such . . . [lands] that every such purchaser will purchase at his peril." [3]

Schuyler's ambivalence—or at least his willingness either to compromise or to purchase—arose from the fact that a part of Cosby Manor had been sold to the American Iron Company, a British concern which before the Americn Revolution had bought the assets of the Ringwood Company, an important iron producer in northern New Jersey.[4] In 1765 and 1766 Peter Hasenclever,[5] in his capacity as agent for the American

ALS, Hamilton Papers, Library of Congress.

1. Bleecker was an Albany merchant and land speculator. Goold and Greene were New York City merchants.

For the claim by Schuyler and his associates, see their statement in the [New York] *Daily Advertiser*, April 24, September 7, 1795. See also Peter Goelet to Robert Morris, April 20, 1795 (copy, Miscellaneous Chancery Papers, American Iron Company, Clerk of the Court of Appeals, Albany, on deposit at Queens College, New York City).

2. Cosby (or Cosby's) Manor, or the Cosby Patent, comprised two tracts on either side of the Mohawk River. One tract consisted of "20,000 acres of land, on both sides of the Mohawk river, (Schuyler, and Frankfort, Herkimer Co.,)" and the other of "22,000 acres of land, on both sides of the Mohawk river, (Deerfield, Marcy, Utica and New Hartford, Oneida Co.,)" (*Calendar of N.Y. Colonial Manuscripts: Indorsed Land Papers; in the Office of the Secretary of State of New York. 1643–1803* [Albany, 1864], 1003).

3. [New York] *Daily Advertiser*, April 24, 1795.

4. For information on the American Iron Company, see Charles S. Boyer, *Early Forges & Furnaces in New Jersey* (Philadelphia, 1931), 12–22.

5. For information on Hasenclever, a native of Westphalia, and his management of the American Iron Company, see Irene D. Neu, "The Iron Plantations of Colonial New York," *New York History*, XXXIII (January, 1952),

Iron Company, purchased 6,755 acres in Cosby Manor. This tract was subsequently seized and sold for non-payment of the quit rent due the Crown. The company protested the seizure, and the land in question was apparently returned to the British concern, although Schuyler continued to maintain that there was some validity to his claim.[6] When Schuyler wrote to Hamilton, the American Iron Company had been bankrupt for more than two decades, and its assets were in the hands of three trustees—Peter Goelet, Judge Robert Morris of New Jersey, and William Popham.[7] To satisfy the creditors of the American Iron Company, the trustees had announced their plans to sell various pieces of property—including the land in Cosby Manor—owned by the company.[8]

The English stockholders of the American Iron Company were not prepared, however, to stand by and permit the trustees to dispose of the company's assets. They accordingly appointed Phineas Bond to represent them as their attorney in the United States.[9] The trustees, in turn, hired Richard Harison and Robert Troup, two of Hamilton's closest friends and fellow New York attorneys, to represent them in any legal proceedings that might develop.[10] When Hamilton first became involved

11–19; Gerhard Spieler, "Peter Hasenclever, Industrialist," *Proceedings of the New Jersey Historical Society*, LIX (October, 1941), 231–54; and Peter Hasenclever, *The Remarkable Case of Peter Hasenclever . . .* (London, 1773).

6. Lawrence Reade and Richard Yates to the American Iron Company, February 3, 1773 (ALS, Miscellaneous Chancery Papers, American Iron Company, Clerk of the Court of Appeals, Albany, on deposit at Queens College, New York City); undated statement describing "the Manor of Cosby" (D, Miscellaneous Chancery Papers, American Iron Company, Clerk of the Court of Appeals, Albany, on deposit at Queens College, New York City); [New York] *Daily Advertiser*, September 7, 1795.

7. [New York] *Daily Advertiser*, September 7, 1795; *The* [New York] *Herald, A Gazette for the Country*, November 24, 1794, July 15, 1795.

Goelet was a New York City merchant. Robert Morris, who should not be confused with the "financier" of the same name, was a United States judge of the District of New Jersey and the former chief justice of the Supreme Court of New Jersey. Popham, a resident of Scarsdale in Westchester County, New York, was clerk of the New York Court of Exchequer from its founding in 1786 until its abolition in 1828. This court, which was a division of the state Supreme Court, had jurisdiction over all matters "concerning Fines, Forfeitures, Issues, Amerciaments, and Debts due to the People of this State" (*New York Laws*, 9th Sess., Ch. IX [February 9, 1786]).

8. [New York] *Daily Advertiser*, September 7, 1795; *The* [New York] *Herald, A Gazette for the Country*, November 24, 1794, July 15, 1795.

9. Boyer, *Early Forges & Furnaces in New Jersey*, 22.

Bond had served in the United States as a representative of the British government since 1786. His first appointment was as British consul for the states of New York, New Jersey, Pennsylvania, Delaware, and Maryland. In addition, he was commissary for commercial affairs of all the states. The Continental Congress, however, recognized him only as British consul for Philadelphia. From February, 1793, until 1812 or 1813, Bond was British consul general for the middle and southern states, and from August, 1795, until March, 1796, he served as Britain's chargé d'affaires.

10. H to Bond, September 1, 1795; Morris to Goelet and Popham, May 31, 1794 (ALS, Miscellaneous Chancery Papers, American Iron Company, Clerk

in the negotiations, in September, 1795, he hoped that ". . . the Trustees and Mr. Bond [would] agree to make a joint sale or release for a consideration to be settled—leaving the right to this, as between themselves to be settled by a judicial determination." [11] No such settlement, however, was made, and in the future Hamilton dealt directly with Goelet, Popham, and Morris.

Although specific evidence is lacking, subsequent events make it clear that Schuyler and his associates eventually reached the conclusion that the American Iron Company had a clear title to the lands which its trustees wished to sell. In any event, they decided to bid for these lands, and Hamilton was entrusted with the negotiations for the purchase from Goelet, Popham, and Morris.[12] On December 17, 1795, Hamilton, acting on behalf of Schuyler and his associates, purchased from the trustees of the American Iron Company 6,755 [13] acres "situate lying and being at a place called and Known by the name of the Manor of Cosby on the north side of the Mohawks River formerly in the County of Albany." [14] The price was £2,422.13.10, which was due in four equal installments of £605.13.5 each, plus "Lawfull Intrest." [15] The first installment was paid on the date of the sale, and the remaining three installments were due on April 6 and October 7, 1796, and on April 4, 1797. Schuyler, Bleecker, Goold, and Greene each assumed one-fourth of the purchase price.

It was Hamilton's responsibility to collect the money for each installment from Schuyler and his three associates [16] and to transfer what they

---

of the Court of Appeals, Albany, on deposit at Queens College, New York City).

11. H to Morris, September 1, 1795.

12. For the trustees' advertisements for the land sales, see *The* [New York] *Herald, A Gazette for the Country*, July 15, November 11, 1795; [New York] *Daily Advertiser*, September 7, 1795.

13. This figure has been taken from the undated statement describing "the Manor of Cosby" (D, Miscellaneous Chancery Papers, American Iron Company, Clerk of the Court of Appeals, Albany, on deposit at Queens College, New York City). In H to Bleecker, March 20, 1796, H puts the number of acres at 6,761.

14. The quotation is from the undated statement describing "the Manor of Cosby" (D, Miscellaneous Chancery Papers, American Iron Company, Clerk of the Court of Appeals, Albany, on deposit at Queens College, New York City). All other information in this and the following paragraph, unless otherwise indicated, has been taken from H to Bleecker, March 20, 1796, April 5, 1797; Goelet to H, June 25, 27, 1796, May 30, August 21, September 21, 1799, May 16, 1800; "Receipt from Peter Goelet," October 4, 1796; Goelet, Morris, and Popham to H, December 18, 1798; and the undated "Acct. of Money Received on Sales of Land of American Iron Company both principal & interest," enclosed in Goelet to H, May 16–18, 1800.

15. This is the figure given in the enclosure to Goelet to H, May 16–18, 1800. In Goelet to H, June 27, 1796, the figure is £605.13.4, and the equivalent in dollars is put at $1,514.18.

16. For these collections, see entries in H's Cash Book, 1795–1804 (AD, Hamilton Papers, Library of Congress; also in forthcoming Goebel, *Law Practice*, III), under the following dates: December 16, 17, 19, 1795; January 8, March 23, April 6, September 14, October 11, November 5, 1796; April 14,

paid him to Goelet as the representative of the trustees of the American Iron Company. Hamilton paid the first three installments on the dates on which they were due; but the final installment, which was due on April 4, 1797, was not paid until November 2, 1799.[17] Some interest, however, remained to be paid, and on November 16, 1800, Goelet placed the interest still owed by Schuyler and his associates at £52.14.6.[18] It is unlikely that this interest was ever paid, for Hamilton maintained that he had already overpaid the trustees,[19] and in 1802 he threatened to "file a Bill in Chancery against the Trustees for the money over paid them." [20] If Hamilton did file such a suit, no record of it has been found.

Albany Monday August 31st: 1795

My Dear Sir

I thank for you[r] favor of the 27th Instant.[21] Inclose you a line to Mr Nicholas Low [22] who will pay you what money you may want to discharge my proportion of the purchase money,[23] in case a compromise or purchase should be made of the Cosby manor lands.

May 17, 1797. H never did receive all the money which was owed by Greene. In a document which he drew up shortly before his duel with Aaron Burr and which he entitled "Statement of my property and Debts July 1. 1804," H made the following entry under the heading of "Good Debts": "Due me from W Greene on account of a Purchase of Trustees of Ringwood Company on the Guaranty of P. Schuyler & others say principal & interest abt . . . [$]500."

17. These payments are listed in Goelet to H, May 16–18, 1800.

18. Goelet to H, May 16–18, 1800.

19. Peter P. Goelet to Robert Morris, May 15, 1800 (ALS, Miscellaneous Chancery Papers, American Iron Company, Clerk of the Court of Appeals, Albany, on deposit at Queens College, New York City). Subsequently Peter Goelet stated that the amount still owed on December 24, 1799, was $126.94. See Goelet's note written on Morris to Goelet, January 6, 1801 (AL, Miscellaneous Chancery Papers, American Iron Company, Clerk of the Court of Appeals, Albany, on deposit at Queens College, New York City).

20. Goelet to Morris, April 20, 1802 (ALS, Miscellaneous Chancery Papers, American Iron Company, Clerk of the Court of Appeals, Albany, on deposit at Queens College, New York City).

Shortly before his duel with Burr, H estimated in the "Statement of my property and Debts July 1. 1804" that the "sum still unpaid to the Trustees [was] ab. [$]250."

21. Letter not found.

22. Nicholas Low was a New York City merchant and a director of the Society for Establishing Useful Manufactures.

23. For Low's payment, see the entry under December 19, 1795, in H's Cash Book, 1795–1804 (AD, Hamilton Papers, Library of Congress; also in forthcoming Goebel, Law Practice, III).

Caty and her Niece [24] arrived here this morning at five O'Clock. I most sincerely wish that My Eliza and the Children had Accompanied them. I dread the Sickly months of September, especially Its baneful effects on Children at New York. Pray intreat my Eliza to send them up Whether you & she can Accompany them or not.

I continue so exceedingly weak that I can but barely walk across my room once or twice in a day, It is to be imputed to a profuse and constant perspiration, which has hitherto yielded little to medicine.

The Negro boy & woman are engaged for you. I understand Mr. Witbeck [25] has written you on the Subject and that he waits Your Answer finally to conclude the bargain.

We all Join in love, adieu Yours most Affectionately &c

Ph: Schuyler

Alexander Hamilton Esqr.

24. Schuyler is referring to his wife, Catharine Van Rensselaer Schuyler, and to one of Robert Van Rensselaer's daughters.
25. Thomas L. Witbeck was an estate manager for Stephen Van Rensselaer.

From George Washington

Philadelphia 31st. Augt. 1795

(Private)

My dear Sir,

Since my return to this city, I have recd: a letter from you dated August —[1]

We know officially, as well as from the effects, that an order for siezing all provision vessels going to France has been issued by the British government: but so secretly, that as late as the 27th. of June it had not been published in London: It was communicated to the cruisers only, and not known until the captures brought it to light.[2] By these high handed measures of that government, and the outrageous, & insulting conduct of its officers, it would seem next to impossible to keep peace between the United States & G. Britain.

To this moment we have received no explanation of Homes' conduct [3] from their charge des affaires here; [4] altho' application was made for it before the departure of Mr. Hammond: [5] on the statement of Govr. Fenner,[6] and complaint of the French Minister.[7] Conduct like this, disarm the friends of Peace and order, while they are the very things which those of a contrary description are wishing to see practiced.

I meant no more than barely to touch upon these subjects, in this letter; the object of it being, to request the favor of you to give me the points on which, in your opinion, Our *new* Negociator [8] is to dwell; when we come into the field of negociation again; agreeably to the recommendation of the Senate; [9] agreeably to what appears to have been contemplated by Mr. Jay & Lord Grenville, at the close of the treaty subscribed by them; and agreeably also to what you conceive *ought* to be brought forward, and *insisted* upon on this occasion.

I am sorry I have been so late in applying for this opinion; but a coincidence of unexpected events have involved me in more than usual business; and some of it not of a very pleasant nature.[10] This has occasioned the delay: but the pro's & con's relative to the Treaty that *is*, and the treaty that *ought* to be, in the judgment of the opponents; are so much in your view, that if you wanted a remembrancer, you would be at no loss from these discussions to advert to them; and you will require but little time to furnish me with what I have here asked. This I press with more earnestness, inasmuch as circumstances will render it very inconvenient for me to remain here longer than the present week (before I return to Mount Vernon for my family) but which I must do, until the Instructions for the new Negociator is compleated.

Altho' you are not in the Administration—a thing I sincerely regret—I must, nevertheless, (knowing how intimately acquainted you are with all the concerns of this country) request the favor of you to note down such occurrences as, in your opinion are proper subjects for communication to Congress at their next Session; and particularly as to the manner in which this treaty should be brought forward to that body: as it will, in any aspect it is susceptible of receiving, be the sourse of much declamation; & will, I have no doubt, produce a hot Session.

With sincere regard   I am My dear Sir   Your Affecte & Obedt.

Go: Washington

Colo. Hamilton

ALS, Hamilton Papers, Library of Congress.

1. Letter not found.

2. For the British order in council of April 25, 1795, to which Washington is referring, see Washington to H, July 7, 1795, note 3. For the effect of this order in council on Washington's decision to ratify the Jay Treaty, see Oliver Wolcott, Jr., to H, July 30, 1795, note 2.

3. Captain Rodham Home of H.M.S. *Africa* had impressed several seamen from American vessels in the harbor of Newport, Rhode Island. In addition, on August 1, 1795, he stopped the packet boat *Peggy* in American territorial waters. Jean Antoine Joseph Fauchet, who had been succeeded by Pierre Auguste Adet as French Minister to the United States, had boarded the *Peggy* at New York and was en route to Newport to embark on the *Medusa* for France. But Fauchet was not on board the *Peggy* when it was stopped, for having been warned of Home's intentions, he had left the *Peggy* at Stonington, Connecticut, and proceeded overland to Newport. Home, however, thoroughly searched Fauchet's baggage on the *Peggy*. For the relevant documents concerning this incident, see *Correspondence of the French Ministers with the United States Government*, part I, 79–97; *ASP, Foreign Relations*, I, 662–67.

4. Phineas Bond, who had been British consul general at Philadelphia, was named chargé d'affaires on August 14, 1795. As such, he was the ranking British officer in the United States in the interval between George Hammond's return to England and the arrival in the United States of his successor. Edmund Randolph wrote to Bond concerning Home's action on August 15, 1795 (LC, RG 59, Domestic Letters of the Department of State, Vol. 8, December 6, 1794–October 12, 1795, National Archives), and Timothy Pickering wrote to him on the same subject on August 21, 1795 (LC, RG 59, Domestic Letters of the Department of State, Vol. 8, December 6, 1794–October 12, 1795, National Archives).

5. On August 10, 1795, Randolph wrote to Hammond: ". . . within the landlock of the United States, at no greater a distance from the shore of the United States than two miles, a Sloop, belonging to a citizen of the United States and accustomed to carry for hire passengers from New York to Rhode Island, was, with the colours of the United States flying, by force of arms brought to by the British ship of war Africa, commanded by Capt. Rodham Home, and boarded by five officers and several of the crew of the said ship, that all the trunks and boxes in the cabin of the said Sloop were opened and searched, and particularly those of the late Secretary of the French Legation in the united States: and that the object was to seize the papers or person, or both, of the late minister of the French Republic, who, being on his return to France, is intitled from the united States to the same immunities as tho' he continued in office. It is added in a letter from the abovementioned Secretary, which the present French minister has transmitted to me, that Mr. [Thomas William] Moore, the British Consul at Newport has been active in this attempt upon the late minister" (LC, RG 59, Domestic Letters of the Department of State, Vol. 8, December 6, 1794–October 12, 1795, National Archives).

6. The letter of Governor Arthur Fenner of Rhode Island to Randolph, which was dated August 11, 1795, has not been found, but see Timothy Pickering to Fenner, August 21, 1795 (LC, RG 59, Domestic Letters of the De-

partment of State, Vol. 8, December 6, 1794–October 12, 1795, National Archives; copy, Massachusetts Historical Society, Boston).

7. Pierre Auguste Adet to Randolph, August 10, 1795 (*Correspondence of the French Ministers with the United States Government*, part I, 79–81).

8. John Quincy Adams. See H to Oliver Wolcott, Jr., August 10, 1795, note 3.

9. For the recommendation of the Senate concerning the Jay Treaty, see H to Rufus King, July 11, 1795, notes 2 and 3.

10. This is a reference to the events leading up to Randolph's resignation as Secretary of State. See Wolcott to H, July 30, 1795, note 1.

Notes of Objections to the British Treaty [1]

[New York, August, 1795]

Article II [2]

Decius [3]	Cato [4]
I Posts imperfectly described should be enumerated	1 reparation for loss of Trade by the detention

ADf, Hamilton Papers, Library of Congress.

1. H used these notes to assist him in the preparation of "The Defence Nos. VIII, IX, XI, and XII," August 15, 21, 28, and September 2–3, 1795. As H's headings in this document indicate, he was replying to essays written by "Decius" (Brockholst Livingston) and "Cato" (Robert R. Livingston). For the authorship of these essays, see the introductory note to "The Defence No. I," July 22, 1795.

2. For the text of Article 2 of the Jay Treaty, see "Remarks on the Treaty . . . between the United States and Great Britain," July 9–11, 1795, note 3.

3. "Decius" discusses Article 2 of the Jay Treaty in his first essay (*The* [New York] *Argus, or Greenleaf's New Daily Advertiser,* July 10, 1795). The relevant part of this essay reads: "The second article would have been better and less liable to future difficulty and construction, if it had defined particularly from what places his Majesty was to withdraw his troops, instead of saying generally from within the boundary 'lines assigned by the treaty of peace;' for it appears that those very lines are a matter in dispute, and hereafter to be settled. As this boundary will certainly not be adjusted by next June, it will furnish a pretext for holding those forts a few years longer, and put us to the expence of a second embassy. Why not declare, that Mickillimackinac, Detroit, Niagara, Oswego, Oswegatche, Point-au-fer, Dutchman's Point, &c. should be delivered up? This would have been explicit; but as we progress, we shall find, that precision and perspicuity are not very striking features in this ministerial lucubration. The time limited for their evacuation is another objection to this article; it is too remote to hope for its performance. If peace takes place this summer, none will be surprised if Great Britain continues her garrisons where they now are! Nor is it very pleasing, that the inhabitants within this territory may remain in it, and continue *British subjects.*

"That clause of this article which permits us to extend our settlements within

II Boundary *assigned* by the   2 compensation for expences
    Treaty of Peace   of the Indian War
    part in dispute may furnish
    pretext for detaining post

---

the said boundary, is also by far too indefinite. The exception to it may be so explained as to defeat the permission altogether. It is in these words, 'except within the precincts or *jurisdiction* of any of the said posts:' who is to determine how far this jurisdiction may extend? Lastly, as the treaty of peace gave us these posts, what great benefit is obtained by this article? Who would regard the second promise of a man who had already, without any excuse, violated the first."

4. The first ten "notes" under the heading of "Cato" refer to arguments advanced by "Cato" in his first essay (*The* [New York] *Argus, or Greenleaf's New Daily Advertiser,* July 15, 1795). This essay reads in part: "By the 2d article of the treaty, the British promise to evacuate the Western Posts by the 1st of June, 1796. By the treaty of Paris, in 1782, they promised to evacuate with all convenient speed, which, if we may judge by the speed with which they have found it convenient to evacuate all their posts in France, Flanders, Germany, Holland, and Brabant, one would have supposed must have meant a much shorter time than eighteen months, so that all that the treaty acquires with respect to the posts, is less than we were entitled to. By the treaty of Paris, surely we might expect better security than a mere promise from a nation which has already shewn, in their violation of the past, the little reliance that can be placed on their future engagements. By June 1796, it is not improbable that our situation or that of Britain may be changed; what security shall we then have for the performance of the treaty? If it is said, as has been already said (by those shameless apologists, who are determined to find every ministerial measure right) that every treaty is a promise, and that if we are not to rely upon a promise, there can be no treaties. I answer, that it is the practice of negociators, where the character of the nation, or other circumstances give reason to suspect a violation of their engagements, *not to rely* upon a naked promise, but to expect some guarantee or surety for the performance; that in the present case, as the promise was evidently extorted by the pressure of existing circumstances, we should see to the performance while those circumstances continue to exist. It is evident, before Mr. Jay left this country, that the British were so far from intending to evacuate the posts, that they had determined to extend their limits; this may not only be inferred from all the encouragement they gave to the depredations of the Indians, but undeniably proved by Lord Dorchester's speech, which, though disavowed by Dundas, is now admitted to have been made in consequence of express instructions. The promise, then to evacuate, has been extorted by French victories, by the humiliation of the British nation, and by their apprehension that we might at last be provoked to do ourselves justice while they were embarrassed with France. Surely then the evacuation should have been insisted upon, while these circumstances operated with full force; what was there to impede an immediate evacuation of Oswego, which is only occupied by a lieutenant's command? what was to prevent our troops being put in immediate possession of Niagara and the upper posts, under an engagement to protect, for a limited time, the British property that remained there? in one week this might have been effected, considering the situation of the posts, upon navigable waters, as well as in one year. May we not reasonably suppose, that the British still entertain a hope, that peace

III   Time limited too remote to   3   public punishment of the
      hope for performan[ce]   British subjects who appeard
                                           in arms with them

between them and France, dissentions between the United States and that
Republic, the seeds of which are so plentifully sown by the treaty itself, may
enable them to violate their second, with the same impunity that they have
their first engagement. If the supposed non-performance of the treaty of Paris
(which, however, has been so ably refuted by Mr. Jefferson in his correspondence with Mr. Hammond on that subject) has hitherto served as a
pretext for retaining the posts; how many such pretences must the complexity
and obscurity of the present treaty afford? But suppose the war with France
to continue, suppose they have the magnanimity to forgive our predilection
for their enemy, suppose the spirit of our own nation to get the better of that
disgraceful stupor into which a venal system has lulled it—suppose the increasing imbecility of Britain shall forbid her to hope for impunity in a
further breach of faith, will it still be a matter of little moment whether or
not she retains garrisons in the midst of our territory for twelve months
longer or not?—are we not at this moment at war with the savages? is not
this war attended with much expence to the nation, much private distress;
is not the blood of our citizens daily shed? these evils must continue as long
as the posts are in the hands of the British, or a peace, if practicable, must be
purchased by the United States at very considerable expence; were we to estimate the difference in this point of view, between an immediate evacuation,
and one that is to take place in June, 1796, it would certainly not fall short of
one million of dollars, independent of the destruction of our fellow-citizens,
whose lives are beyond all price. If to this we add the annual profits of the
Indian trade, amounting to 800,000, it will appear that the United States loose
near two millions of dollars, by the retention of the posts. Supposing (which
is at least problematical) that they shall be surrendered at the period proposed.
Those who think with me, that decision on the part of our government, and
firmness in our minister could not have failed to effect an immediate restitution of our territory, will know of what account to charge this heavy loss of
blood and treasure.

"But was the evacuation of the posts all we had a right to ask on that subject; if the retention of them occasioned those expensive Indian wars which
have so often drained our treasury, and thinned our ranks. If for twelve years
we have lost thereby a lucrative branch of commerce, are we entitled to no
compensation for these losses? If the honor of the nation has been insulted,
both by Lord Dorchester and the subjects of Great-Britain under his command, are we to expect no reparation for these insults? Have we reason,
from what we have seen of Mr. Jay's correspondence with Lord Grenville
to presume that any has been asked? are we not assured that none has been
obtained? What then is this boasted article about, which so much has already
been said, which was the only one communicated to the public as the only
one that was imagined would bear the light; what is it but a declaration on
the part of Britain, that though she has already stripped us of millions,
though she has occasioned the death of thousands of our fellow-citizens, yet
she now *promises* that if we will let her pocket another million, and pay as
much more out of our own treasury for a peace with her Indian allies, she
will consent, in case the war with France should continue, and she should be
too weak to contend with us, to let us possess *our own territory*. And what is
our submission to these terms, and the unrequited insults we have received,
but the lowest political degradation? If it is said that these were the best

IV Not pleasing that the inhabitants may remain & continue British subjects

V "precin[c]ts or jurisdiction" indefinite

V A Treaty of peace gave us the posts what benefit by this article [5]

4 Removal of Lord Dorchester

5 No reliance on their promise

6 should have had a gurantee or surety for the performance & should have seen that it took place during the pressure of circumstances

Article III [6]

I Disadvantageous from the relative extent

II The whole furr Trade which we might have secured to ourselves will be participated with G Britain if not fall into their hands.

III Our vessels excluded from sea ports &c & such parts of Rivers—while they are admitted into all our ports

A British Trader may set

7 promise to evacuate was produced by fear of French victories—every thing ascribed to France—glad to debase our own government charged constantly by that party with meaness & perfidy

8 Is it a matter of little moment that she detains garrisons a twelve month longer

9 a million of dollars in In-

---

that could be obtained, I boldly deny the assertion; the state of Europe, the state of England itself, their submission to Denmark and Sweden, even to the little state of Genoa, warrant the denial. But should it even have been otherwise, it would have been infinitely better, both in point of honor and interest, to have waited, after having spoken with dignity of our rights, till circumstances should have enabled us to enforce them, than to have relinquished our well founded claim to a compensation of at least ten millions; to have relinquished that satisfaction which our national honor demanded; can we doubt that if we were ourselves too weak, which I am far from supposing, that the magnanimity of France would have permitted her to conclude a peace with England, without procuring us the satisfaction which her guarantee of our territories entitled us to ask. I am warranted in asserting, from the best authority, that she would not."

5. H replied to these five arguments in "The Defence No. IX," August 21, 1795.

6. For the discussion of Article 3 of the Jay Treaty by "Decius," see "The Defence No. XI," August 28, 1795, note 1. For the text of Article 3, see "Remarks on the Treaty . . . between the United States and Great Britain," July 9–11, 1795, note 8.

out from Canada—traverse our lakes &c to N York or Philad

Why ought we not to have free navigation of St Laurance and other British Rivers?

Instead of this are stopped in our passage down at the highest port of Entry from the sea

I Curious provision not to admit beyond the highest ports of Entry.

What would G B desire more than such an admission?

Inderdiction of duties on peltries.

Under this article G Britain may import into any part of the U States European East & W India goods upon

dian Wars & loss of Indian Trade 800 000 Dollars

---

10 4000,000 of Dollars Capital magnaminity of France would have procured us reparation

State of Europe state of England submission to Denmark & Sweden even to Genoa [7]

---

11 rights to Traders a *cession* of Territory [8]

Charles Town
1 establishes a British Colony within our limits & gives privileges of citizens to our bitterest enemy [9]

---

7. Of the preceding ten arguments by "Cato," H replied to the first, second, fifth, sixth, and ninth in "The Defence No. VIII," August 15, 1795. He commented on the tenth point in "The Defence No. IX," August 21, 1795.

In the MS, H drew a line through all the points except the third, fourth, and ninth.

8. This is a reference to an argument advanced in the fourth essay by "Cato." See "The Defence No. XI," August 28, 1795, note 1.

9. This refers to the objection to Article 2 of the Jay Treaty presented to the public by a select committee of the citizens of Charleston, South Carolina, on July 22, 1795. See "The Defence No. VI," August 8, 1795, note 8. The committee's statement reads: "The second article sanctions the continuance of an injury, which, in violation of the treaty of peace, has already existed eleven years: it either establishes a British colony within our limits, with peculiar privileges, or, in case the inhabitants of such colony choose to become citizens of the United States, it gives the privileges of citizens of these States to a number of men, who have been their most bitter and irreconcileable enemies . . ." (*REPORT OF THE SELECT COMMITTEE, Chosen by Ballot of the Citizens of the United States, in Charleston, South-Carolina, in pursuance of a Resolution of a general Meeting of the Citizens, in St. Michael's Church, on Thursday, the sixteenth of July, 1795* [Charleston: Printed by W. P. Young, Broad-Street, n.d. (George Washington Papers, Library of Congress)]).

which we can impose no
other or higher duties than
are paid by our Citizens [10]

3d Article

1   This gives to G B what with her Capital ⎫
     will be a monopoly & opens a door for ⎬   S Carolina
     smuggling [11] ⎭

2   admits G B to share in our interior traffic on equal terms with our own citizens through our whole territorial dominions while the advantages ostibly reciprocated to our citizens are limited both in their nature and extent [12]

3   gives access to our ports on Mississippi? What ports has G Britain [13]

10. H replied to most of the preceding arguments by "Decius" concerning Article 3 of the Jay Treaty in "The Defence No. XI," August 28, 1795. In addition, he replied to the point on the "Inderdiction of duties on peltries" made by "Decius" in "The Defence No. XII," September 2–3, 1795.

11. This is a paraphrase of the argument against Article 3 of the Jay Treaty in the report of the select committee of the citizens of Charleston, July 22, 1795. See note 9. This report reads in part: "The third article gives to the British, what to them, with their capital, will be nearly equivalent to a monopoly of the trade with the Indians, and with our Western Territories, and opens a door for smuggling on an extensive scale, to the great injury of our revenue." H replied to this and the following three points in "The Defence No. XII," September 2–3, 1795.

12. See the fourth essay by "Cato," which is quoted in "The Defence No. XI," August 28, 1795, note 1.

13. This is a reference to an argument advanced in the tenth essay by "Cato" (*The* [New York] *Argus, or Greenleaf's New Daily Advertiser*, August 26, 1795). The relevant section of this essay reads: "The Indian trade in the southern part of our territories, is principally in peltries, which are too bulky to be transported in any other way than upon large rivers; the Mississippi will be the outlet for a very great proportion of them. This commerce must have been exclusively ours, for though, by the treaty of Paris, the British might navigate the Mississippi, yet as they did not own a foot of land upon either of its banks, it became impossible for them to avail themselves of this advantage; whereas the United States, possessing all the Indian country in the vicinity of that river, and the east bank for many hundred miles, could, when they pleased, establish factories, and monopolize that commerce; and, in addition to this, carry on a very important (though illicit) trade with the Spaniards, who own the opposite bank. This our minister extraordinary was too munificent to allow us to avail ourselves of. He, therefore, provides, in the third article, 'that all the ports and places, on its *eastern side, to whichsoever of the parties belonging*, be freely restored to and used by both parties in as ample a manner as any of the Atlantic ports or places, &c:' then comes a clause declaring, 'that all goods and merchandizes, whose importation into the United States is not wholly prohibited, may freely, for the purposes of commerce, be carried into the same, in the

4 we are excluded from B sea Ports & limits of Hudsons bay
   Company [14]

5 GB is admitted to all the advantages of which our Atlantic Rivers
   are susceptible [15]

Cato No. 5 [16]

I   Superiority of Capital
II better knowlege of Trade
II established Customers

"As our communication from the sea was much easier than by
the St Laurance we could furnish English goods cheaper & of
course would have continued the Indian Trade in its usual channel, even from the British side of the lakes, nor could they have
prevented it without giving such disgust to the Indians as would
have made them dangerous neighbours."

---

gives a right to navigate up to our ports of Entry—& thence by
inland N— 12 years in possession of Indian Trade

I   They permitted to reside here houses ware house &c by British
    Navigation A[ct] kept in full force by the 14 article of the
    Treaty

---

manner aforesaid, by his Majesty's subjects; and such goods and merchandizes
shall be subject to, *no other or higher duties* than would be payable by the
citizens of the United States on the importation of the same in *American
vessels* in the Atlantic ports of the said States.' I have already shewn, that
the effect of this last provision is to give British ships a *bounty* proportioned
to the amount of the equalizing duty on the out and home voyage, taken
together, to the prejudice of American vessels; which, with the perfect
equality of rights, that they hold in common with our own citizens, and an
addition of 46 cents extra tonnage, and light money, with which, as I have
before shewn, our vessels will be charged, must put this important commerce
into the hands of the British. This, I presume, must have been the intention
of our minister, when he speaks of the ports on the *eastern* bank of the
Mississippi, *to which soever of the parties belonging;* for, as the British have
no ports on the eastern side, Mr. Jay must have looked forward to a time
when these extraordinary bounties to their commerce and perfect security
for their establishment, should have enabled them to possess themselves of
that country: And that, though the article is not reciprocal *at present*, by
the prudence and good management of our envoy, it may, in time, be
rendered so. . . ."

14. This is a reference to an argument advanced in the fourth essay by
"Cato." For the text of this essay, see "The Defence No. XI," August 28,
1795, note 1.

15. See "The Defence No. XI," August 28, 1795, note 7.

16. This is a mistake, for H is referring to the fourth essay by "Cato." See
"The Defence No. XI," August 28, 1795, note 1.

II   We only to travel

III Our Trade interrupted by wars & bad seasons
     that of G B remains unchanged

IV   Small population of Canda [17] renders consumption of Indian
     Goods &c insignificant in comparison with sacrifice of Indian
     Trade

V   But articles coming duty free from Britain
     why not sold cheaper than same articles subject to heavy duty
     & carried immense distance by land and inland Navigation

VI   Stimulation of Indian Wars by Traders residing among us
     whom we cannot expel without cause of suspicion & that in
     not less than twelve months.
     not reciprocal because our Traders would retire when there
     was war & cannot reside.

VI   gives a right to import into our Sea ports upon equal terms of
     duties with our Citizens.[18]
          at least goods for Indian Trade.

17. In the margin H wrote: "census 1784 123082 souls." See "The Defence
No. XII," September 2–3, 1795, note 7.
18. This and the following point have been taken from the fifth essay by
"Cato" (*The* [New York] *Argus, or Greenleaf's New Daily Advertiser,* July
31, 1795). The relevant part of this essay reads: "I am at some loss to understand what is intended by the following words in the 3d article—'And in like
manner, all goods and merchandize, whose importation *into the United States*
shall not be wholly prohibited; may freely, for the purposes of commerce,
be carried *into the same, in manner aforesaid, by his majesty's subjects;* and
the same shall be subject to no *higher, or other duties* than would be payable
by the citizens of the United States on the importation of the same in
American vessels into the atlantic ports of the said states.' The *manner
aforesaid,* alludes to the former part of the article, which gives the British a
right to navigate our rivers from the sea to the highest ports of entry for
foreigners, and from thence by land into the Indian country, the only natural
construction of these words, is, that the British shall have a right to import
into the United States upon the same terms as Americans, and yet I can
hardly conceive that Mr. Jay could intend, in the face of a law of the
United States (act making further provision for the payment of the debts
of the United States, chap. 39, sec. 2.) which imposes an additional duty of
ten per cent on articles imported in vessels not of the United States; I say I
should hardly conceive that he should presume to enter into such stipulation
directly in the face of a law of the United States, and that too in favour of
a nation whose navigation act is at war with our commerce; did it not
breathe the same spirit with the 12th, 14th, and 15th articles, all of which
strike directly at the navigation of these states. Nor do I know any other
construction that can possibly be put on the words which I have stated at
large, that every reader may judge for himself. It is however, possible, that
Mr. Jay may have *intended* (for never was a public instrument drawn with
less precision than the one before us) that this provision should only extend

VI   10 ℔ Ct. disadvantage in the competition because England may
      lay countervailing duties to that extent

---

to goods brought in for the purposes of the Indian trade, yet how the words
can be made to bear this construction I am at a loss to conceive. But should
even this be admitted to be the true meaning, it will again prove the extreme solicitude of the framers of the treaty to secure to the British the whole
benefit of the Indian trade; without this article, goods, might be purchased of
our merchants for the purpose of this commerce, which would, on account
of the ten per cent difference, have been imported in American vessels; but
this slight advantage it seems was deemed too much for the sacrifice of the
whole profits of the Indian trade. It is therefore stipulated, that the British
shall navigate our rivers to the highest port of entry for foreign vessels, and
that upon this construction they shall pay *no foreign duty* for the articles
they import, so that all that the British merchants will have to do, will be to
establish factories at the ports of entry, and under pretence of the Indian
trade (if it should be thought that the words should be confined to that)
import in British bottoms upon the same terms as we do in our own ships:
and as by the 15th article our vessels are to pay a duty, which is to countervail the duty paid here by the British, that is, ten per cent every article imported this way, as Indian goods, will yield ten per cent more profit to the
British merchant, taking the outward and homeward voyage into consideration, than it will to the American, and the navigation and revenue law be
eluded—But supposing it possible to prevent these goods so imported into
New-York for instance, and there put on board river vessels, & from thence
carried by land and by inland navigation for a considerable distance, from
being sold before they get into the western territory; yet even then this provision must operate as a bounty on British vessels, in preference to all other
foreigners, and as an encouragement of ten per cent in favour of the British
merchant who carries on the Indian trade, to the prejudice of our own commerce and our own revenue. Thus, to make myself more fully understood, a
British merchant sends in his *own* ship articles intended for the Indian trade,
or indeed any other under that pretence, he has a right to enter them without paying any other duty than the American does, his return cargo pays
no duties in England. The American merchant ships in his own vessel the
same articles, on the same terms, but by the general operation of the 15th
article, Britain has a right to lay on the return cargo, a duty of ten per cent.
The words of the article are, 'but the British government reserves to herself
the right of imposing on American vessels entering into the British ports in
Europe, a tonnage duty equal to that which shall be payable by British vessels
in the ports of America, and also such duty as may be adequate to countervail
the difference of *duty now* payable on the importation of European and
Asiatic goods when imported into the United States in British or in American
vessels.' If, then, against all obstacles, the American merchant should carry
on the Indian trade, will he not by this circumstance, be compelled to import and export in British vessels? By the 12th article, British vessels may
import into the United States from their islands, without paying greater
duties than the Americans; this again is direct opposition to a law of the
United States above recited. . . ."

To Phineas Bond [1]

New York Sep. 1. 1795

Dr. Sir

Inclosed is a letter to Judge Morris which speaks for itself.[2] I shall be glad to hear from you on the subject of it & that at any rate if you do not come, you will authorise some discreet person to cooperate with me on your behalf. If you should turn your attention to a law character, it may be well you should know that Messrs. R: Harrison & R Troupe are concerned for the trustees.[3]

With esteem I am   Sir   Yr. Obed ser   A Hamilton

P. Bond Esq

ALS, Historical Society of Pennsylvania, Philadelphia.
   1. For an explanation of the contents of this letter, see the introductory note to Philip Schuyler to H, August 31, 1795.
   2. H to Robert Morris, September 1, 1795.
   3. This letter is endorsed: "answered 2d. Sept." Bond's reply has not been found.

To Robert Morris [1]

New York. Septr. 1. 1795

Dear Sir

General Schuyler and other persons concerned with him have empowered me to act for them in the case of certain lands in Cosby's Manor which you and others as Trustees of the Ringwood Iron Company have advertised for sale on the fifth instant. Though from what I learn of the matter, I am led to conclude that my friends have a valid legal title to the premises yet there are considerations which incline me on their behalf to make some moderate concession to the claimants under the original title. I understand that the regularity of the proceedings which have constituted you a Trustee is questionable and that an opposite claim is interposed by Mr. Bond of Philadelphia. In this case could not the Trustees and Mr. Bond agree to make a joint sale or release for a consideration to be settled —leaving the right to this, as between themselves, to be settled by a judicial determination? This seems to be clearly their mutual interest since it would certainly turn the land to better account.

I shall make this suggestion to Mr. Bond also. But it were well that both you and he were either present in this City before the appointed day of sale or were represented by discreet Persons with competent authority to make a united arrangment.

With esteem I am Dr sr.   Your Obedt. sr.   A Hamilton

Copy, Historical Society of Pennsylvania, Philadelphia.
    1. For an explanation of the contents of this letter, see the introductory note to Philip Schuyler to H, August 31, 1795. See also H to Phineas Bond, September 1, 1795.
    This letter was enclosed in H to Bond, September 1, 1795.

From Phineas Bond

[*Philadelphia, September 2, 1795.* A letter which Hamilton wrote to Bond on September 1, 1795, is endorsed: "answered 2d. Sept." *Letter not found.*]

The Defence No. XII [1]

[New York, September 2–3, 1795]

The remaining allegations in disparagement of the 3 article [2] are to this effect   1   That the exception of the country of the Hudsons Bay Company owing to its undefined limits renders the stipulations in our favour in a great measure nugatory.[3] [2. That the privileges granted to Great Britain in our Missisippi ports, are impolitic,

ADf, Hamilton Papers, Library of Congress; *The* [New York] *Argus, or Greenleaf's New Daily Advertiser,* September 2 and 3, 1795.
    1. For background to this document, see the introductory note to "The Defence No. I," July 22, 1795.
    2. This issue of "The Defence" is a continuation of "The Defence No. XI," in which H defended Article 3 of the Jay Treaty. For the text of Article 3, see "Remarks on the Treaty . . . between the United States and Great Britain," July 9–11, 1795, note 8.
    3. This "allegation" was made in the fourth essay by "Cato" (Robert R. Livingston). For "Cato No. 4," see "The Defence No. XI," August 28, 1795, note 1.

because without reciprocity.] [4] [3] that the agreement to forbid to lay duties of entry on peltries is the surrender without equivalent of a valuable item of Revenue and will give to the British the facility of carrying on their furr trade through us with the use of our advantages.[5] [4] that the articles which will be brought from Europe into Canada coming duty free can be afforded cheaper than the same articles going thither from us charged with a heavy duty on their importation into the U States and with the expence of a long transportation by land and inland navigation.[6] [5] that the population of canada, which by a census in 1784 amounted to only 123082 souls [7] is too small to render the supply of European and Asiatic commodities through us of so much importance as to bear any comparison with the loss by the sacrifice of the furr Trade. [6] that the intercourse to be permitted with the British territories, will facilitate smuggling, to the injury of our Revenue.[8] [7] that the much greater extent of the U States than of the British territories destroys real reciprocity in the privileges granted by the article giving in fact far greater advantages than are received.[9] These suggestions will be discussed in the order in which they are here stated.

1   It is true that the Country of the Hudsons Bay company is not well defined. Their Charter granted in 1670 gives them "the sole

4. This is a reference to "Cato No. 10," which is quoted in "Notes of Objections to the British Treaty," August, 1795, note 13. This "allegation" appears in the newspaper but not in the MS. In the newspaper it is numbered "2," and the subsequent numbers have been changed accordingly to make the total number of "allegations" seven. Brackets have been used throughout this essay to indicate material which appeared in the newspaper but not in the MS.

5. This "allegation" was made in the first essay by "Decius" (Brockholst Livingston). See "The Defence No. XI," August 28, 1795, note 1.

6. This and the following "allegation" were made in "Cato No. 4." See "The Defence No. XI," August 28, 1795, note 1.

7. See "Notes of Objections to the British Treaty," August, 1795, note 17.

8. This "allegation" was made in the REPORT OF THE SELECT COMMITTEE, Chosen by Ballot of the Citizens of the United States, in Charleston, South-Carolina, in pursuance of a Resolution of a general Meeting of the Citizens, in St. Michael's Church, on Thursday, the sixteenth of July, 1795 (Charleston: Printed by W. P. Young, Broad-Street, n.d. [George Washington Papers, Library of Congress]). See "Notes of Objections to the British Treaty," August, 1795, note 11. See also the first article by "Decius" (The [New York] Argus, or Greenleaf's New Daily Advertiser, July 10, 1795), which is quoted in "The Defence No. XI," August 28, 1795, note 1.

9. The "allegation" was made in the first "Decius" essay. See "The Defence No. XI," August 28, 1795, note 1.

trade and commerce of and to all the seas bays streights Creeks lakes Rivers and sounds in whatsoever latitude they shall be that lie within the entrance of the streight commonly called Hudsons Streights together with all the lands countries and territories upon the coasts and confines of the said seas streights bays &c *which are [not] now actually possessed by any of our subjects or by the subjects of any other Christian Prince or State.*" [10]

To ascertain their territorial limits according to Charter, it would be necessary to know what portion of country at the time of the grant was *actually possessed* by subjects of G Britain or of some other Christian Prince or state; but though this be not known, the general history of the Country as to settlement will demonstrate that it could not have extended far Westward, certainly not to that region which is the scene of trade in furrs commonly called the North West Trade carried on by the Canada Company,[11] the possession of which, as far as possession exists, is recent.

We learn from a Traveller who has lately visited that region that one of this Company's establishments is in latitude $56°9''$ North, Longitude $117°43''$ West,[12] that is about 20 degrees of longitude Westward of the Lake of the Woods; and it is generally understood that the intire scene of the Trade of this Company is Westward of the limits of the Hudsons Bay Company.

Canada on the North is bounded by the territories of the Hudsons Bay Company. This is admitted by the Treaty of Utretcht and established by the act of Parliamt passed in 1774 commonly called the Quebec Act.[13] The treaty of Utrecht provides for the settle-

10. For the text of the company's charter of 1670, see E. E. Rich, ed., *Minutes of the Hudson's Bay Company, 1671–1674* (Toronto, 1942), 131–48. H omitted the bracketed word in his quotation of the company's charter.

11. This is presumably a reference to the North West Company, which was originally formed in 1779 and re-established in 1783. The company consisted of a number of Canadian trading houses which had formerly been rivals.

12. H received this information from Alexander Mackenzie, an explorer and employee of the North West Company. See Mackenzie to H, November 9, 1794, note 6.

13. "An Act making more effectual Provision for the Government of the Province of Quebec in North America." This act stated that the boundary of the English possessions in North America ran "northward to the southern boundary of the territory granted to the Merchants Adventurers of England, trading to Hudson's Bay" (14 Geo. III, C. 83).

ment of the boundary by commissaries.[14] I have not been able to trace whether the line was ever actually settled but several maps lay down a line as the one settled by the Treaty of Utrecht which runs north of the Lake of the Woods. In a case thus situated the UStates will justly claim under the article access to all that Country, the trade of which is now carried on through Canada. This will result both from the certainty that there were no actual possessions at the date of the Charter so far interior, and from the fact of the trade being carried on through a different channel by a different Company under the superintendence and protection of a different Government, that of Canada.

It may be asked why was the article embarrassed by the exception of the Country of the Hudsons bay Company. The answer is this—that the Charter of this Company gives to it a monopoly within its limits and therefore a right to trade there could not with propriety have been granted to a foreign power by Treaty. It is true that it has been questioned whether this monopoly was valid against British subjects, seeing that the Charter had not been confirmed by act of parliament. But besides that this doubt has been confined to British subjects, it would appear that in fact the Company has enjoyed the monopoly granted by its Charter even against them, and with at least the implied approbation of Parliament. In the year 1749 petitions were referred to the House of Commons by different trading towns in England for rescinding the monopoly and opening the Trade. An inquiry was instituted by the House. The report of its Committee was favourable to the conduct and pretensions of the Company and against the expediency of opening the Trade, and the business terminated there.[15]

14. The tenth article of the Treaty of Utrecht, concluded between England and France on March 31 (O.S.), 1713, stipulated that "The . . . most Christian King shall restore to the kingdom and Queen of Great Britain, to be possessed in full right forever, the bay and streights of Hudson, together with all lands, seas, sea-coasts, rivers, and places situate in the said bay, and streights, and which belong thereunto, no tracts of land or of sea being expected, which are at present possessed by the subjects of France . . ." and that ". . . it is agreed on both sides, to determine within a year, by commissaries to be forthwith named by each party, the limits which are to be fixed between the said Bay of Hudson and the places appertaining to the French; which limits both the British and French subjects shall be wholly forbid to pass over, or thereby go to each other by sea or by land" (Jenkinson, *Collection of Treaties*, II, 34).

15. See David Macpherson, *Annals of Commerce, Manufactures, Fisheries, and Navigation* (London, 1805), III, 270--71.

This circumstance of there being a monopoly confirms the argument drawn from the fact that North West Trade, is carried on through Canada by the Canada Company, a [decisive] presumption that the scene of that Trade is not within the country of the Hudsons Bay Company and is consequently within the operation of the privilege granted to us.

I cannot forbear in this place (though it will be partly a digression) to notice some observations of CATO in his Xth number.[16] After stating that in 1784 the peltry from Canada sold in London for £230000 Sterling he proceeds to observe, that excluding the territories of the Hudsons Bay Company Nine tenths of this trade is within the limits of the UStates, although with studied ambiguity of expression endeavours to have it understood that Nine tenths of the Trade which yielded the peltry that sold in London for 230000 £ Sterling in 1784 was within our territories.

It is natural to ask how he has ascertained with so much exactness the limits of the Hudson's Bay Company (which at other times is asserted, by way of objection to the article to be altogether indefinite) as to be able to pronounce what proportion if any of the Trade carried on through Canada may have come from that Country, towards the calculation which has led to the conclusion that nine tenths of the whole lies within our limits? The truth is indubitably and notoriously that whether any or whatever part of the peltry exported from Canada may come from the Country of the Hudsons bay company seven eights * of the whole trade which furnishes that peltry has its source on the British side of the boundary line. It follows, that if it were even true that only $\frac{1}{10}$ of the whole lay in

* Some accounts place it between 6 & 7 eighths but none lower than 6.[17]

16. The section of "Cato No. 10" to which H is referring reads: "It may not be improper now to review our commerce, as it would stand, were the treaty carried into effect. The Indian trade from Canada alone, produced at public sales in London, 1784, £230,000 Sterl. The duties thereon were in round numbers £17,000. The tonnage of furs and peltry, about 1000 tons. The export from Canada in furs, exceeded in 1785, that of the preceding year, about 70,000 sterling, and has I believe, continued to increase; so that this branch of trade may be fairly estimated at near 100,000 of dolls. yearly. As nine tenths of the Indian nations, who carry on this trade (if the territories of the Hudson bay company are excepted) live within the boundaries of the United States, as we enjoyed every advantage in the right to the posts and postages, the greatest part of this valuable trade must have been ours, had not Mr. Jay thought proper to *cede it*, in effect to the British, as I have before stated" (*The* [New York] *Argus, or Greenleaf's New Daily Advertiser*, August 26, 1795).

17. In the newspaper "but none lower than 6" has been omitted.

that part of the British Territory which is not of the H Bay company inasmuch as only $\frac{1}{7}$ of it lies within our limits,[18] the result would be that the Trade in which we granted an equal privilege was to that in which a like privilege was granted to us was as $\frac{1}{7}$ to $\frac{1}{10}$, and not according to Cato as nine to one. This legerdemain in argument and calculation is really too frivolous for so serious a subject or to speak more properly it is too shocking, by the spirit of Deception which it betrays. Cato has a further observation with regard to the trade with the Indians in the vicinity of the Mississippi and from that River into the Spanish territories.[19] The product of all this trade, he says, must go down the Missippi and but for the stipulation of the third article would have been exclusively ours—because "by the Treaty of Paris though the British might navigate the Mississippi yet they did not own a foot of land upon either of its banks [20] whereas the UStates possessing all the Indian Country in the vicinity of that river and the East bank for many hundred Miles could when they pleased establish factories and monopolise that commerce."

This assertion with regard to the Treaty of Paris is in every sense incorrect; for the 7 article of that Treaty establishes as a boundary between the dominions of France and His Britannic Majesty "a line drawn along the middle of the River Mississippi from *its source* to the River Iberville and from thence by a line drawn along the middle of this River and the Lakes Maurepas & Pont Chartrain to the sea" and cedes to His BRITANNIC MAJESTY all the Country on the East side of Mississippi except the town & Island of New Orleans.[21]

18. See "The Defence No. XI," August 28, 1795.

19. This "observation" is from "Cato's" tenth essay. See "Notes of Objections to the British Treaty," August, 1795, note 13.

20. "Cato" actually wrote: "yet as they did not own a foot of land upon either of its banks, it became impossible for them to avail themselves to this advantage, whereas. . . ." See "Notes of Objections to the British Treaty," August, 1795, note 13.

21. The seventh article of the Treaty of Paris, concluded between France, England, and Spain on February 10, 1763, reads: "In order to re-establish peace on solid and durable foundations, and to remove for ever all subject of dispute with regard to the limits of the British and French territories on the continent of America; it is agreed, that, for the future, the confines between the dominions of his Britannick Majesty and those of his Most Christian Majesty, in that part of the world, shall be fixed irrevocably by a line drawn along the middle of the River Mississippi, from its source to the river Iber-

By the Treaty of Paris then His Britannic Majesty owned all the territory on the East side of the Mississippi instead of not having a foot of land there. Whether a part of this territory does not still belong to him is a point not yet settled. The Treaty of Peace between the U States and Great Britain supposes that part will remain to G Britain, for one line of boundary between us and her is a line due west from the Lake of the Woods to the Mississippi.[22] If in fact this River runs far enough North to be intersected by such a line, according to the supposition of the last mentioned Treaty then so much of that River and The land upon it as shall be North of the line of Intersection will continue to be of the dominion of Great Britain. The Treaty lately made not abandonning the possibility of this being the case provides for a survey in order to ascertain the fact; and in every event the intent of the Treaty of peace will require that some closing line directly or otherwise shall be drawn from the Lake of the woods to the Mississippi. The position therefore that Great Britain has no land or ports on the Mississippi takes for granted what is not ascertained and of which the contrary is presumed by the Treaty of Peace.

The trade with the Indian Country on our side of the Mississippi from the Ohio to the Lake of the Woods (if that River extends so far North) some fragments excepted, has its present direction through Detroit and Michillimacnac, and is included in my calculation heretofore stated of the proportion which the Indian Trade within our limits bears to that within the British limits. Its estimated amount is even understood to embrace the proceeds of a clandestine traffic with the Spanish territories; so that the new scene suddenly

---

ville, and from thence, by a line drawn along the middle of this river, and the lakes Maurepas and Potchartrain to the sea; and for this purpose, the Most Christian King cedes in full right, and guaranties to his Britannick Majesty the river and port of the Mobile, and every thing which he possesses, or ought to possess, on the left side of the river Mississippi, except the town of New Orleans and the island in which it is situated, which shall remain to France, provided that the navigation of the river Mississippi shall be equally free, as well to the subjects of Great Britain as to those of France, in its whole breadth and length, from its source to the sea, and expressly that part which is between the said island of New Orleans and the right bank of that river, as well as the passage both in and out of its mouth . . ." (Jenkinson, *Collection of Treaties*, III, 182–83).

22. See Article 2 of the definitive treaty of peace between the United States and Great Britain, September 3, 1783 (Miller, *Treaties*, II, 153).

explored by Cato is old and trodden ground, the special reference to which cannot vary the results that have been stated. It is unquestionably true that the furr Trade within our limits bears no proportion to that within the British limits. As to the contingent traffic with the territories of Spain, each party will be free to pursue it according to right and opportunity. Each would have independent of the Treaty the facility of bordering territories. The geography of [the] best regions of the furr trade in the Spanish territories is too little known to be much reasonned upon and if the Spaniards according to their usual policy incline to exclude their neighbours [23] their precautions along the banks of the Mississippi will render the access to it circuitous—a circumstance which makes it problematical whether the possession of the opposite Bank is as to that object an advantage and whether we may not find it convenient to be able under the Treaty to take a circuit through the British territories.

[2. It is upon the suggestion of Great Britain having no ports on the Missisippi, that the charge of want of reciprocity in the privileges granted, with regard to the use of that river, is founded. The suggestion has been shewn to be more peremptory than is justified by facts. Yet it is still true, that the ports on our side bear no proportion to any that can exist on the part of the British, according to the present state of territory. It will be examined in a subsequent place,[24] how far this disproportion is a proper rule in the estimate of reciprocity. But let it be observed in the mean time, that in judging of the reciprocity of an article, it is to be taken collectively. If upon the whole, the privileges obtained are as valuable as those granted, there is a substantial reciprocity; and to this test, upon full and fair examination of the article, I freely refer the decision. Besides, if the situation of Great Britain did not permit in this particular, a precise equivalent, it will not follow that the grant on our part was improper, unless it can be shewn, that it was attended with some inconvenience, injury or loss to us; a thing which has not been, and

23. On December 26, 1793, Josef de Jaudenes and Josef de Viar, Spanish commissioners to the United States, wrote to Thomas Jefferson: "The opposition which . . . [Spain] has hitherto made, and intends to make, to the passage along the Mississippi, by the citizens of the United States, above the 31st degree of latitude, is neither unjust nor extraordinary, since you well know that we have been, are, and will remain, in possession of it, until, by agreement or force, we yield our right" (*ASP, Foreign Relations*, I, 308).
24. See H's arguments below against the seventh "allegation."

I believe cannot be shewn. Perhaps there is a very importantly beneficial side to this question. The treaty of peace established between
us and Great Britain, a common interest in the Missisippi; the present
treaty strengthens that common interest. Every body knows that
the use of the river is denied so by Spain, and that it is an indispensi-
ble outlet to our western country. Is it an inconvenient thing to
us, that the interest of Great Britain has in this particular been more
completely separated from that of Spain, and more closely connected
with ours?]

[3] The agreement to forbear to lay duties of entry on peltries,
is completely defensible on the following grounds (viz)—It is the
general policy of Commercial Nations, to exempt raw materials
from duties. This has likewise been the uniform policy of the
UStates, and it has particularly embraced the article of *peltries*,
which by our existing laws may be imported into any part of the
UStates *free from duty*. The object of this regulation is the encouragement of manufactures by facilitating a cheap supply of raw
materials. A duty of entry therefore, as to such part of the article
as might be worked up at home would be prejudicial to our manu-
facturing interest, as to such part as might be exported, if the duty
was not drawn back would injure our Commercial interest. But it
is the general policy of our laws, in conformity with the practice
of other commercial countries to draw back and return the duties
which are charged upon the importation of foreign commodities.
This has reference to the advancement of the export Trade of the
Country so that with regard to such peltries as should be reexported,
there would be no advantage to our Revenue from having laid a
duty of Entry. Such a duty then being contrary to our established
system and to true principles, there can be no just objection to a
stipulation against it. As to its having the effect of making our country the channel of the British Trade in peltries, this if true and it is
indeed probable could not but promote our interest. A large proportion of the profits would necessarily remain with us to compensate for transportation and agencies. It is likely too, that to secure the fidelity of Agents, as is usual, copartnerships, would be
formed, of which British Capital would be the principal instrument
and which would throw a still greater proportion of the profits into
our hands. The more we can make our country the *entrepot* the

emporium of the Trade of foreigners the more we shall profit. There is no commercial principle more obvious than this, more universally agreed, or more generally practiced upon in Countries where Commerce is well understood.

[4] The [fourth] of the above enumerated suggestions is in its principal point answered by the practice just stated of drawing back the duties on importation, when articles are reexported. This would place the articles, which we should send into the British territories, exactly upon the same footing as to duties with the same articles imported there from Europe. With regard to the additional expence of transportation, this is another instance of the contradiction of an argument which has been relied upon by both sides, which is that taking the voyage from Europe in conjunction with the interior transportation the advantage upon the whole is likely to be in our favour. And it is upon this aggregate transportation that the calculation ought to be made. With respect to India or Asiatic articles, there is the circumstance of a double voyage.

[5] As to the small population of Canada which is urged to depreciate the advantage of the Trade with the white inhabitants of those countries it is to be observed that this population is not stationary. If the date of the Census be rightly quoted, it was taken eleven years ago when there were already 123,082 souls. It is presumeable that this number will soon be doubled, for it is notorious, that settlement has proceeded for some years with considerable rapidity [25] in Upper Canada and there is no reason to believe that the future progress will be slow. In time to come the Trade may grow into real magnitude—but be it more or less, if beneficial, it is so much gained by the article; and so much clear gain, since it has been shewn not to be true that it is counterballanced by a sacrifice in the furr Trade.[26]

[6] With regard to the supposed danger of smuggling, in the intercourse permitted by this article, it is very probable it will be found less than if it were prohibitted. Intirely to prevent trade between bordering territories is a very arduous perhaps an impracticable task. If not authorised, so much as is carried on must be illicit. And it may reasonably be presumed that the extent of illicit trade

25. In MS, "rapiditity."
26. See "The Defence Nos. X and XI," August 26, 28, 1795.

will be much greater in that case than where an intercourse is permitted under the usual regulations and guards. In the last case, the
inducement to it is less, and such as will only influence persons of
little character or principle while every fair Trader is from private
interest a sentinel to the laws; in the other case, all are interested
to break through the barriers of a rigorous and apparently unkind
prohibition. This consideration has probably had the weight with
our Government in opening a communication through Lake Champlain with Canada—of the principle of which regulation the Treaty
is only an extension.

[7] The pretended inequality of the article, as arising from the
greater extent of the UStates than of the British Territories is one
of those fanciful positions which are so apt to haunt the brains of
visionary politicians. Traced through all its consequences, it would
terminate in this that a great empire could never form a treaty of
commerce with a small one, for to equalize advantages, according to
the scale of territory, the small state must compensate for its deficiency in extent by a greater *quantum* of positive privilege in
proportion to the difference of extent, which would give the larger
state the monopoly of its trade. According to this principle, what
wretched treaties have we made with France Sweden Prussia and
Holland? [27] For our territories exceed in extent those of either of
these powers. How immense the sacrifice in the case of Holland,
for the United States are [one hundred] [28] times larger than the
U Provinces?

But how are we sure that the extent of the U States is greater than
the territories of Great Britain on our Continent? We know that
she has pretensions to extend to the Pacific Ocean and to embrace
a vast wilderness incomparably larger than the United States, and
we are told as already mentioned that her trading establishments
now actually extend beyond the 56th degree of North Latitude
and the 117 degree of West Longitude.

Shall we be told that not extent of territory, but extent of population is the measure? Then how great is the advantage which we
gain in this particular by the Treaty at large? The population of

27. See "Remarks on the Treaty . . . between the United States and Great
Britain," July 9–11, 1795, note 70.
28. Space left blank in MS.

Great Britain is to that of the U States about two and a half to one, and the comparitive concession by her in the trade between her European dominions and the U States must be in the same ratio. When we add to this the great population of her East India possessions in which privileges are granted to us without any return,[29] how prodigiously will the value of the Treaty be enhanced, according to this new and extraordinary rule!

But the rule is in fact an absurd one, and only merits the notice which has been taken of it, to exhibit the weak grounds of the opposition to the Treaty. The great standard of reciprocity is equal privilege. The adventititious circumstances which may render it more beneficial to one party than to the other can seldom be taken into the account, because they can seldom be estimated with certainty. The relative extent of country or population is of all others a fallacious guide. The comparitive resources and faci[li]ties for mutual supply regulate the relative utility of a commercial privilege; and as far as population is concerned, it may be laid down as a general rule that the smallest population graduates the scale of the Trade on both sides, since it is at once the principal measure of what the smaller state can furnish to the greater, and of what it can take from the greater or in other words of what the greater state can find a demand for in the smaller state. But this rule too like most general ones admits of numerous exceptions.

In the case of a Trade by land and inland navigation the sphere of the operation of any privilege can only extend a certain distance. When the distance to a given point through a particular channel is such that the expence of transportation would render an article dearer than it could be brought through another channel to the same point, the privilege to carry the article through that particular channel to such point becomes of no avail. Thus the privilege of trading by land or inland navigation from the British territories on this Continent can procure to that Country no advantage of Trade with Princeton in New Jersey, because supplies can come to it on better terms from other quarters. Whence we perceive that the absolute extent of territory or population of the U States is no

29. This is a reference to Article 13 of the Jay Treaty. For the text of this article, see "Remarks on the Treaty . . . between the United States and Great Britain," July 9–11, 1795, note 54.

measure of the relative value of the privileges reciprocally granted by the article under consideration, and consequently no criterion of the real reciprocity of the article.[30]

The objectors to the Treaty have marshalled against this article a quaint figure, of which from the use of it in different quarters, it is presumeable they are not a little enamoured. It is this, that the article enables Great Britain to draw A LINE OF CIRCUMVALLATION [31] round the UStates. They hope to excite prejudice by presenting to the mind the image of a siege or investment of the Country. If Trade is War, they have chosen a most apt figure; and we cannot but wonder how the unfortunate Island of Great Britain has been able so long to maintain her Independence amidst the beleaguering efforts of the number of Nations with whom she has been imprudent enough to form treaties of Commerce, and who from her insular situation have it in their power to beset and hem her in on all sides. How lucky is it for the U States that at least one side is covered by Spain and that this formidable line of Circumvallation cannot be completely perfected! Or rather how hard driven must those be who are obliged to call to their aid auxiliaries so preposterous!

Can any good reason be given why one side of a Country should not be accessible to foreigners for purposes of Trade equally with another? Might not the Cultivators on the side from which they

30. At this point in the draft H wrote and crossed out the following paragraph: "The result of all that has been said is, that we have made by this article a good bargain—that in respect to the furr Trade with equality of privilege and at least equal advantage of situation, we have staked one against seven as to the value of the prize to be won."

31. In "Features of Jay's Treaty" Alexander J. Dallas wrote: "The first striking effect of the treaty *to endanger the interests and disturb the happiness* of the United States may be detected by a geographical sketch of the *cordon, or line of circumvallation, with which it enables Great Britain to fetter and enclose us*" (*Dunlap and Claypoole's* [Philadelphia] *American Daily Advertiser*, July 25, 1795). See also "The Memorial of the Citizens of Philadelphia, the Northern Liberties and District of Southwark, in the State of Pennsylvania," which was addressed to George Washington on July 25, 1795. The citizens' third objection to the Jay Treaty reads: "Because the Treaty is destructive to the domestic Independence and prosperity of the United States; inasmuch as it admits Aliens, professing a foreign allegiance, to the permanent and transmissible rights of property, peculiarly belonging to a Citizen; and inasmuch as it enables Great Britain to draw an invidious and dangerous line of circumvallation round the territory of the Union, by her fleets on the Atlantic, and by her settlements from Nova Scotia to the mouth of the Mississippi" (DS, George Washington Papers, Library of Congress).

were excluded have cause to complain that the carriage of their productions was subject to an increased charge by a monopoly of the national Navigation, while the Cultivators in other quarters enjoyed the benefit of a competition between that and foreign Navigation? And might not all the inhabitants have a right to demand a reason why their Commerce should be less open and free than that of other parts of the Country?

Let us remember too that privileges of Trade do not extend the line of Territorial Circumvallation. The extent of contiguous British Territory will remain the same whether the communications of Trade are open or shut. By opening them, we may be rather said to make so many breaches in the wall or intrenchment of this newly invented Circumvallation; if indeed it be not enchanted. Alass! Alass!

The argument, upon this article, has hitherto turned as to the Trade with the whole Inhabitants of the B Territories on European and East India Goods. But there can be no doubt that a mutually beneficial commerce in native commodities ought to be included in the catalogue of advantages. Already there is a useful interchange of certain commodities; which time and the progress of settlement and resources cannot fail to extend. It is most probable too that a considerable part of the productions of the British territories will find the most convenient channel to foreign markets through us; which as far as it regards the interest of external commerce will yield little less advantage than if they proceeded from our own soil or industry. It is evident, in particular, that as far as this shall be the case, it will prevent a great part of the competition with our commodities which would exist, if those productions took other routes to foreign markets. In considering the subject on the side of a Trade in home commodities, it is an important reflection that the UStates are much more advanced in industrious improvement than the British Territories. This will give us a material and a growing advantage while their articles of exchanging with us will essentially consist in the products of agriculture and of mines, we shall add to these manufactures of various and multiplying kinds, serving to increase the ballance in our favour.

In proportion as the article is viewed on an enlarged and permanent scale, its importance to us magnifies. Who can say how far

British colonization may spread Southward and down the west side of the Mississippi—Northward & Westward into the vast interior Regions towards the Pacific Ocean. Can we view it as a matter of indifference that this new world is laid open to our Enterprize— to an enterprise seconded by the immense advantage already mentioned of a more improved state of industry? Can we be insensible that the precedent furnishes us with a cogent and persuasive argument to bring Spain to a similar arrangement? And can we be blind to the great interest we have in obtaining a free communication with all the territories that environ our Country from the St. Mary's to the St Croix?

In this large view of the subject the furr trade which has made a very prominent figure in the discussion becomes a point scarcely visible. Objects of great variety and magnitude start up in perspective eclipsing the little atoms of the day and growing and maturing with time.

The result of the whole is that the U States make by the third article of the Treaty a good bargain, that with regard to the furr trade, with equality of privileges and superior advantages of situation, we stake one against seven or at most one against six, that as to the Trade in European and East Indian goods and in home productions we make an equal stake, with some advantages of situation, that we open an immense field of future enterprize, that we avoid the embarrassments and dangers ever attendant on an artificial and prohibitory policy, which in reference to the Indian Nations was particularly difficult and hazardous, and that we secure those of a natural and liberal policy and give the fairest chances for good neighbourhood between the U States and the bordering British territories and consequently of good understanding with Great Britain conducing to the security of our peace. Experience no doubt will demonstrate that the horrid spectres which have been conjured up are fictions, and if it should even be slow to realise the predicted benefits (for time will be requisite to give permanent causes their due effect in controuling temporary circumstances), it will at least prove that the predicted evils are chimeras and cheats.

CAMILLUS.

From Nicholas Olive [1]

[*New York, September 3, 1795.* On September 4, 1795, Hamilton wrote to Olive and referred to "your letter of yesterday." *Letter not found.*]

1. Olive was a New York City merchant who had migrated from France to the United States in 1793. He became interested in the Castorland project, which planned to establish a French colony on land formerly owned by Alexander Macomb on the Black River in northern New York. The prospectus for this project was published in Paris in 1792.

To Nicholas Olive

New York, September 4, 1795. Acknowledges receipt of Olive's "letter of yesterday." [1] States that Olive's dispute with his "late partners" has been referred to arbitrators, who will either transfer "the management . . . of your late partnership" or "constitute an indifferent person as Receiver and Agent for it." [2]

ALS, Mr. Hugh Fosburgh, New York City; copy, Hamilton Papers, Library of Congress.
1. Letter not found.
2. An entry in H's Cash Book, 1795–1804, for August 28, 1795, reads: "Nicholas Olive Dr. to Account of Fees & Costs for this sum due for advice &c in the case of Daniel Cotton   20" (AD, Hamilton Papers, Library of Congress; also in forthcoming Goebel, *Law Practice*, III).
    Cotton was a New York City merchant.

To George Washington

New York   Sepr. 4. 1795

Sir

I had the pleasure of receiving two days since your letter of the 31 Ulto. A great press of business and an indifferent state of health have put it out of my power sooner to attend to it.

The incidents which have lately occurred have been every way

ALS, George Washington Papers, Library of Congress.

vexatious and untoward. They render indispensable a very serious though calm and measured remonstrance from this Government, carrying among others this idea that it is not sufficient that the British Government entertain towards our nation no hostile dispositions—tis essential that they take adequate measures to prevent those oppressions of our Citizens and of our Commerce by their Officers & Courts of which there are two frequent examples and by which we are exposed to suffer inconveniences too nearly approaching to those of a state of war. A strong expectation should be signified of the punishment of Capt Holmes [1] for the attemp⟨t⟩ to violate an ambassador passing through our territory and for the hostile and offensive menaces which he has thrown out.[2] The dignity of our country and the preservation of the confidence of the people in the Government require both solemnity and seriousness in these representations.

As to the negotiation for alterations in and additions to the Treaty I think it ought to embrace the following objects.

A new modification of the 12th article [3] so as to extend the Tonnage and restrain the prohibition to export from this country to articles of the growth or production of the British Islands. The more the tonnage is extended the better; but I think ninety tons would work advantageously if nothing better can be done. I had even rather have the article with *seventy* as it stood than not at all, if the restriction on exportation is placed on the proper footing. Some of our merchants however think its value would be questionable at so low a tonnage as seventy. It would be also desireable that the article should enumerate the commodities which may be carried to and brought from the British Islands. This would render it more precise and more intellig[ib]le to all.

Great Britain may have substantial security for the execution of the restriction if it be stipulated on our side "That a law shall be passed and continued in force during the continuance of the article, prohibiting the exportation in vessels of the U States of any of the articles in question if brought from British Islands, on pain of forfieture of the Vessel for wilful breach of the law—and that the

1. Rodham Home.
2. See Washington to H, August 31, 1795, note 3.
3. For the text of Article 12 of the Jay Treaty, see H to Rufus King, June 11, 1795, note 2.

same law shall provide that the regulations contained in our laws respecting drawbacks shall be applied to all exportations in our vessels of the articles in question, to ascertain that they were imported into the UStates from other than British Islands, & this whether a drawback of the duty is required or not by the exporter —and shall also provide that all such articles exported in our vessels from the UStates shall be expressed in the clearance with a certificate of the Collector indorsed specifying that he has carefully examined according to the Treaty & to the law the identity of the articles exported and that it did *bona fide* appear to him that they had not been imported from any British Island or Islands." This security is the greatest difficulty in the case and would in my opinion be given by a provision similar to the foregoing.

It would be a very valuable alteration in the XIII article [4] if a *right could be stipulated* for the U States to go with articles taken in the British territories in India to other parts of Asia. The object of the present restriction upon us to bring them to America was I believe to prevent our interference with the British East India Company in the European Trade in India Goods. If so, there could be no objection to our having a right to carry commodities from the British territories to other parts of Asia. But if all this latitude cannot be obtained, it would be a great point gained to have a right to carry them thence to China. It is a usual & beneficial course of the Trade to go from the U States to *Bombay* & take in there a freight for *Canton,* purchasing at the last place a cargo of Teas &c.

It would be well if that part of the XV article which speaks of *countervailing* duties [5] could be so explained as to fix its sense. I am of opinion that its only practicable construction is and ought to be that they may lay on the *exportation* from their *European dominions,* in Vessels of the U States, the *same additional* duties on articles which we lay on the *importation* of the *same articles* into the U States *in British Vessels.* But the terms of the clause are vague & general and may give occasion to set up constructions injurious and contentious.

As to the more exact equalization of duties of which this article

4. For the text of Article 13, see "Remarks on the Treaty . . . between the United States and Great Britain," July 9–11, 1795, note 54.

5. For the text of Article 15, see "Remarks on the Treaty . . . between the United States and Great Britain," July 9–11, 1795, note 57.

speaks it is a ticklish subject and had better I think be left alone. It would be right that it should be expressly agreed that wherever our vessels pay in the ports of GBritain higher charges than their own vessels a proportional deduction shall be made out of any duty of Tonnage which may be laid on our vessels to countervail the difference of Tonnage on theirs in our ports.

The XVIII article [6] is really an unpleasant one and though there is I fear little chance of altering it for the better, it may be necessary for the justification of the President to attempt it. The standard to be approached by us as nearly as possible is that in our Treaty with France.[7] As to the point of free Ships making free goods though it be desireable to us to establish it if practicable—and ought to be aimed at—Yet I neither expect that it will be done at present nor that the *great maritime powers* will be permanently disposed to suffer it to become an established rule & I verily believe that it will be very liable though stipulated to be disregarded as it has been by France through the greatest part of the present war. But naval stores and provisions ought if possible to be expressly excluded from the list of contraband—except when going to a blockaded or beseiged port town or fortress or to a fleet or army engaged in a military operation—for I can imagine no other cases in which there is a just pretence to make *provisions* contraband.

Some provision for the protection of our seamen is infinitely desireable. At least G Britain ought to agree that no seamen shall be impressed out of any of our vessels at sea, and that none shall be taken out of such vessel in any of her colonies, which were in the

6. For the text of Article 18, see "Remarks on the Treaty . . . between the United States and Great Britain," July 9–11, 1795, note 63.

7. The Treaty of Amity and Commerce with France, February 6, 1778, unlike Article 18 of the Jay Treaty, did not define contraband. H is presumably referring to the following passages from the 1778 treaty with France: "The merchant Ships of either of the Parties, which shall be making into a Port belonging to the Enemy of the other Ally and concerning whose Voyage & the Species of Goods on board her there shall be just Grounds of Suspicion shall be obliged to exhibit as well upon the high Seas as in the Ports and Havens not only her Passports, but likewise Certificates expressly shewing that her Goods are not of the Number of those, which have been prohibited as contraband.

". . . it shall not be lawful to break up the Hatches of such Ship, or to open any Chest, Coffers, Packs, Casks, or any other Vessels found therein, or to remove the smallest Parcels of her Goods . . . unless the lading be brought on Shore in the presence of the Officers of the Court of Admiralty and an Inventory thereof made. . . ." (Miller, *Treaties*, II, 12, 13.)

vessel *at the time of her arrival at such colony.* This provision ought to be pressed with energy as one unexceptionably just & at the same time safe for G Britain.

The affair of the negroes to give satisfaction may be retouched but with caution & delicacy. The resolution proposed in the Senate will afford a good standard for this.[8]

As to the croud of loose suggestions respecting the Treaty which have no reasonable foundation, it would not consist with the reputation of the Government to move concerning them. Only reasonable things merit or can with propriety have attention.

I beg Sir that you will at no time have any scruple about commanding me. I shall always with pleasure comply with your commands. I wish my health or the time for it would permit me now to be more correct. The other part of your letter shall be carefully attended to in time.

With the truest respect & the most affectionate attachment   I have the honor to be Sir   Your obedient & humble servant

A Hamilton

The President of the U States

8. This is a reference to a resolution which was presented to the Senate in the special session called to consider the Jay Treaty. The resolution was introduced on June 24, 1795 (*Annals of Congress,* IV, 863), and was defeated in an amended version by a vote of 15 to 14 on June 25 (*Annals of Congress,* IV, 865). In its final form the resolution reads: "*Resolved.* That the Senate recommend to the President of the United States to renew by friendly negotiation with his said Majesty, the claims of the American citizens to compensation for the negroes and other property so alleged to have been carried away; and in case the disagreement, that has hitherto existed relative to the construction in this behalf of the said article, cannot be removed by candid and amicable discussions, that it be proposed, as a measure calculated to cherish and confirm the good understanding and friendship which it is desired may prevail between the two countries, that Commissioners be appointed in the manner directed by the 6th article of the Treaty of Amity, Commerce, and Navigation, lately concluded between the United States and his said Majesty, with authority to ascertain and decide, as well the interpretation of the said 7th article, in this respect, as likewise the amount of the losses sustained by the alleged violation of the same" (*Annals of Congress,* IV, 865).

The Defence No. XIII [1]

[New York, September 5, 1795]

The 4th and 5th articles of the Treaty from similarity of object will naturally be considered together.[2] The fourth, reciting a doubt "whether the River Mississippi extends so far Northward as to be intersected by a line to be drawn due West from the Lake of the Woods in the manner mentioned in the Treaty of Peace" agrees, that measures shall be taken in concert between the two Governments to make a joint survey of that River from one degree of latitude below the falls of St Anthony to the principal source or sources thereof and of the parts adjacent thereto, and that if in the result it should appear that the said River would not be intersected by such a a line as above mentioned, the two parties will proceed by amicable negotiation to regulate the boundary line in that quarter as well as all other points to be adjusted between them according to justice and mutual convenience and the intent of the Treaty of Peace. The fifth, reciting that doubts have arisen what River was truly intended under the name of the River St Croix mentioned in the Treaty of Peace, and forming a part of the boundary therein described, provides that the ascertainment of the point shall be referred to three Commissioners, to be appointed thus—one to be named by his Britannic Majesty, another by the President of the USstates with the advice & consent of the Senate, the third by these two, if they can agree in the choice; but if they cannot agree, then each of them to name a person and out of the two persons named one drawn by lot in their presence to be the third Commissioner. These Commissioners are to meet at Halifax with power to adjourn to any place or places they may think proper—are to be sworn to examine and decide the question according to the evidence

ADf, Hamilton Papers, Library of Congress; The [New York] Argus, or Greenleaf's New Daily Advertiser, September 5, 1795.

1. For background to this document, see the introductory note to "The Defence No. I," July 22, 1795.

2. For the text of Articles 4 and 5 of the Jay Treaty, see "Remarks on the Treaty . . . between the United States and Great Britain," July 9-11, 1795, notes 10 and 12.

which shall be laid before them by both parties and are to pronounce their decision, which is to be conclusive, by a written declaration under their hands and seals containing a description of the
River and particularising the latitude and longitude of its mouth
and of its source.

These articles, though they have been adjusted with critical propriety, have not escaped censure. They have even in one instance
been severely reprobated as bringing into question things about
which there was no room for any and which a bare inspection of
the map [3] was sufficient to settle.[4]

With regard to the Mississippi there is no satisfactory evidence
that it ever has been explored to its source. It is even asserted, that
it has never been ascended beyond the 45 degree of North latitude,
about a degree above the falls of St. Anthony. FADEN's Map of
1793 [5] will serve as a specimen of the great uncertainty which attends the matter. It notes, that the River had not been ascended
beyond the degree of latitude just mentioned, and exhibits three
streams, one connected with the *Marshy Lake* in that latitude, an-

3. This is a reference to John Mitchel's "Map of the British & French
Dominions in North America," 1775, printed in Moore, *International Adjudications*, I, facing page 1. For a discussion of the St. Croix River boundary
dispute, see A. L. Burt, *The United States, Great Britain, and British North
America. From the Revolution to the Establishment of Peace After the War
of 1812* (New Haven, 1940), 71–81. See also "Conversation with George
Beckwith," October 15–20, 1790, note 6; "Conversation with George Ham-
mond," January 1–8, 1792, note 7. For the confusion in the spelling of
Mitchel's name, see Moore, *International Adjudications*, I, 6–7, and Burt,
The United States, 71–73.

4. This may be a reference to the following statement by "Caius" in his
"Address to the President of the United States," July 21, 1795: "The 4th
article contains a fruitful source for future war, because it puts the uncertainty it states upon a worse ground than it stood before; it being a well
known historical fact, that by a similar omission in the treaty of Utrecht,
in not providing a mode for ascertaining definitively the boundary line between the French and British possessions in America, the famous seven years
war was produced between those two nations, which terminated in the Peace
of Paris, and a total relinquishment of all the possessions of France in America
to the English" (Mathew Carey, ed., *The American Remembrancer; or An
Impartial Collection of Essays, Resolves, Speeches, &c., Relative or Having
Affinity to the Treaty with Great Britain*, 3 Vols. [Philadelphia: Printed by
Henry Tuckniss, for Mathew Carey, No. 118 Market-Street, 1795–1796], I,
109).

5. This map is entitled "The United States of North America with the
British Territories and Those of Spain, according to the Treaty of 1784. En-
graved by Wm. Faden. 1793" (copy, New York Public Library). Faden was
an English geographer.

other with the *White bear Lake* near the 46th degree, and a third with the *Red Lake* in the 47th degree [6]—denominating each of the two first "The Mississippi by conjecture" and the last "Red Lake River or Lahontans Mississippi" [7]—all of them falling considerably short in their Northern extent of the Lake of the Woods, which is placed as high as the [fiftieth] [8] degree of North Latitude. Thus stands this very clear and certain point, which we are told it was disgraceful on the part of our Envoy to have suffered to be brought into question.

There is however a specific topic of blame of the article which has greater plausibility. It is this, that it does not finally settle the question, but refers the adjustment of the closing line to future negotiation, in case it should turn out that the River does not stretch far enough North to be intersected by an East & West line from the Lake of the Woods.

I answer, that the arrangement is precisely such as it ought to have been. It would have been premature to provide a substitute 'till it was ascertained that one was necessary. This could only be done by an actual survey. A survey is therefore provided for and will be made at the joint expence of the two Countries.

That survey will not only determine whether a substitute be requisite or not; but it will furnish data for judging what substitute is proper and is most conformable with the true intent of the Treaty. Without the data which it will afford any thing that could have been done would have been too much a leap in the dark. National acts, especially on the important subject of boundary ought to be

6. "Marshy Lake" is perhaps Marsh Lake, a small widening of the Minnesota River between Big Stone Lake and Lac Qui Parle, near the 45th parallel. The Minnesota is a tributary of the Mississippi. White Bear Lake, to the northeast of Minneapolis at 45.06° of latitude, is near the St. Croix River, which joins the Mississippi below St. Anthony's Falls. Red Lake is in northern Minnesota and is roughly bisected by the 48th parallel. This lake has no connection by water with the Mississippi. It is, however, connected by Red Lake River with Red River, which flows northward from a source which was at one time believed also to be the source of the Mississippi.

7. Several western tributaries of the Mississippi, including the Minnesota, have been identified with the apparently fictitious "Long River" which Louis-Armand de Lom de l'Arce, Baron de Lahontan, claimed to have ascended in 1688. For Lahontan's account of his journey, see *New Voyages to North-America*, 2 Vols. (London: Printed for H. Bonwicke, 1703).

8. Space left blank in MS. The bracketed word has been taken from the newspaper.

bottomed on a competent knowlege of circumstances. It ought to be clearly understood how much is retained—how much relinquished. Had our envoy proceeded on a different principle, if what he had agreed to had turned out well, it would have been regarded as the lucky result of an act of supererogation. If it had proved disadvantageous, it would have been stigmatised as an act of improvidence and imprudence.

The strong argument for having settled an alternative is the avoiding of future dispute. But what alternative could have been agreed upon, which might not have bred controversy? The closing line must go directly or indirectly to the Missi[ssi]ppi. Which of the streams reputed or conjectured to be such above the falls of St Anthony is best entitled to be so considered. To what known point was the line to be directed? How was that point to be indentified with adequate certainty? The difficulty of answering these questions will evince that the danger of controversy might have been increased by an impatience to avoid it and by anticipating without the necessary lights an adjustment which they ought to direct.

The facts with regard to the River St Croix are these. The question is which of two Rivers is the true St Croix. The dispute concerning it is as old as the French possession of Nova Scotia. France set up one River Great Britain another. The point was undecided, when the surrender of Nova Scotia by the former to the latter put an end to the question as between those parties. It was afterwards renewed between the Colonies of Nova Scotia & Massachusettes Bay, which last in the year 1762 appointed Commissioners to ascertain, in conjunction with Commissioners which might be appointed by the province of Nova Scotia, the true River; but no final settlement of the matter ensued.

The Treaty of Peace gives us for one boundary the River St Croix but without defining it.[9] Hence it has happened, that not long after the peace was concluded, the question which had before been

9. Article 2 of the definitive treaty of peace between the United States and Great Britain stated that the northern boundary of the United States began its western course "From the North West Angle of Nova Scotia, viz. That Angle which is formed by a Line drawn due North from the Source of Saint Croix River to the Highlands. . . ." It defined the eastern boundary of the United States ". . . by a Line to be drawn along the Middle of the River St Croix, from its Mouth in the Bay of Fundy to its Source; and from its Source directly North . . ." (Miller, *Treaties*, II, 152–53).

agitated between France and Great Britain and between the provinces of Massachusettes & Nova Scotia was revived between the State of Massachusettes & that province and it has ever since continued a subject of debate.

A mode of settling the dispute was under the consideration of Congress in the year 178[5] [10] and powers were given to our then Minister at the Court of London [11] to adjust the affair, but nothing was concluded.[12] And We learn from a letter of Mr. Jefferson to Mr. Hammond dated the 15 of December 1791 [13] that it then engaged the attention of our Government, that the ascertaining of the point in dispute was deemed a matter of "present urgency" and that it had been before the subject of application from the U States to the Government of Great Britain.

It is natural to suppose that a dispute of such antiquity between such different parties is not without colourable foundation on either side: at any rate it was essential to the preservation of peace that it should be adjusted.

If one party could not convince the other by argument of the superior solidity of its pretensions, I know of no alternative, but ARBITRATION or WAR. Will any one pretend that honor required us in such a case to go to war, or that the object was of a nature to make it our interest to refer it to that solemn calamitous and precarious issue?

No rational man will answer this question in the affirmative. It follows, that an arbitration was the proper course—and that our Envoy acted rightly in acceding to this expedient. It is one too not without precedents among nations, though it were to be wished for the credit of human moderation that they were more frequent.

Is there any good objection to the mode of the arbitration? It seems impossible that any one more fair or convenient could have been devised, and it is recommended by its analogy to what is common among individuals.[14]

10. H wrote "1784" and then crossed out the last digit. In the newspaper the figure reads "1785."
11. John Adams. See *JCC*, XXIX, 753–54.
12. See "Report of the Secretary for Foreign Affairs, respecting the Eastern Boundary," April 21, 1785 (*ASP, Foreign Relations*, I, 94).
13. This letter is printed in *ASP, Foreign Relations*, I, 190.
14. At this point in the draft H wrote and crossed out: "The U States choose one Referree Great Britain another and these two choose a third if

What the mode is has been already detailed and need not be repeated here. It is objected, that two much has been left to chance;
but no substitute has been offered which would have been attended
with less casualty. The fact is that none such can be offered. Con-
scious of this, those who make the objection have not thought fit
to give an opportunity of comparison by proposing a substitute.

What is left to chance? Not that there shall be a final decision,
for this is most effectually provided for. It is not only positively
stipulated that commissioners with full and definitive power shall be
appointed, but an ultimate choice is secured by referring in the last
resort to a decision *by lot* what it might not be found practicable
to decide by agreement. This is the *ne plus ultra* of precaution. Is
it that this reference to lot leaves it too uncertain of what character
or disposition the third Commissioner may be? If this be not rather
a recommendation of the fairness of the plan, how was it to be
remedied? Could it have been expected of either of the parties to
leave the nomination to the other? Certainly not. Would it have
been adviseable to have referred the ultimate choice to some other
state or Government? Where would one have been found in the
opinion of both parties sufficiently impartial? On which side would
there have been the greatest danger of successful employment of
undue influence? Is it not evident that this expedient would have
added to equal uncertainty as to character and disposition, other
casualties and more delay? Should it have been left to the two
Commissioners appointed by the parties to agree at all events? It
might have been impossible for them ever to come to an agreement
and then the whole plan of settlement might have been frustrated.

Would the sword have been a more certain Arbiter? Of all uncertain things the issues of War are the most uncertain. What do
objections of this kind prove but that there are persons resolved
to object at all events?

The submission of this question to arbitration has been represented as an eventual dismemberment of empire, which it has been
said cannot rightfully be agreed to but in a case of extreme necessity. This rule of extreme necessity is manifestly only applicable

---

they can agree upon a person—if they cannot agree, each is to name one
and it is to be determined by lot, which of the two named shall be the third
Referree."

to a cession or relinquishment of a part of a Country held by a clear and acknowledged title—not to a case of disputed boundary. It would be a horrid and destructive principle that nations could not terminate a dispute about the title to a particular parcel of territory, by amicable agreement or by a submission to arbitration as its substitute; but would be under an indispensable obligation to prosecute the dispute by arms till real danger to the existence of one of the parties should justify by the plea of extreme necessity surrender of its pretensions.

Besides, the terms in which writers lay down the rule and the reason of it will instruct us that where it does apply, it relates not to territory as such but to those who inhabit it, on the principle, that the social compact intitles all the members of the society to be protected and maintained by the common strength in their rights and relations as members. It is understood that the territory between the two Rivers in dispute is either uninhabited or inhabited only by settlers under the British. If this be so, it obviates all shadow of difficulty on our side—but be it as it may, it would be an abuse of the rule to oppose it to the amicable adjustment of an ancient controversy about the title to a particular tract of country depending on the question of fact whether this or that river be the one truly intended by former treaties between the parties. The question is not in this case, shall we cede a tract of our country to another power? It is this—to whom does this tract of country truly belong? Should the weight of evidence be on the British side, our faith pledged by Treaty demands an acquiescence in their claim. If the parties are not able to agree in opinion concerning the point it is most equitable & most consident with good faith to submit it to the decision of impartial judges.

It has been asked among other things whether the U States were competent to the adjustment of the matter, without the special consent of the State of Massachusettes. Reserving a more particular solution of this question to a separate discussion of the constitutionality of the Treaty [15]—I shall content myself with remarking here that our Treaty of peace with Great Britain by settling the boundaries of the U States without the special consent or authority of any state, assumes the principle that the Government of the U States

15. See "The Defence No. XXXVII," January 6, 1796.

was of itself competent to the regulation of boundaries with foreign powers, that the actual Government of the Union has even more plenary authority with regard to Treaties than was possessed, under the confederation, and that acts both of the former and of the present Government presuppose the competency of the National Authority to decide the question in the very instance under consideration. I am informed also that the State of Massachusettes has by repeated acts manifested a corresponding sense on the subject.[16]

A reflection not unimportant occurs here. It was perhaps, in another sense than has been hitherto noticed, a point of prudence in both Governments to refer the matter in dispute to arbitration. If one has yielded to the pretensions of the other it could hardly have failed to draw upon itself complaints and censures more or less extensive, from quarters immediately interested or affected.[17]

CAMILLUS

16. For the documents relating to this subject, see *ASP, Foreign Relations,* I, 90–100.

17. H wrote and crossed out the following concluding paragraph: "A practical consideration on each side for referring the point to arbitration was to prevent the complaints more or less extensive which could hardly have failed to be produced against the Government of whichever party had acceded to the pretensions of the other."

From Elie Williams [1]

Philadelphia, September 7, 1795. "At the time of my appointment as Agent for Militia supplies of provision, no allowance was fixed or mentioned for my subsistance. . . . I find . . . that without your interference I shall very probably be left without relief or remedy on that score. . . . I beg leave to request you will be good enough to say something about it either in a letter to myself or Mr. Wolcott. . . ." [2]

ALS, Hamilton Papers, Library of Congress.

1. Elie Williams and his late partner, Robert Elliot, had been contractors for the supply of the militia army ordered to march against the insurgents during the Whiskey Insurrection. For the appointment of Elliot and Williams, see H to Williams, September 12, 1794.

2. William's account was unsettled as late as May 4, 1799, when the Government maintained that he owed the United States $33,683.80 (RG 217, Miscellaneous Treasury Accounts, 1790–1894, Account No. 9550, National Archives).

The Defence No. XIV [1]

[New York, September 9, 1795]

The sixth article [2] stipulates compensation to British Creditors for losses and damages which may have been sustained by them, in consequence of certain legal impediments, which since the Treaty of Peace with Great Britain,[3] are alleged to have obstructed the recovery of debts *bona fide* contracted with them before the peace.

To a man who has a due sense of the sacred obligation of a just debt, a proper conception of the pernicious influence of laws, which infringe the rights of creditors, upon morals upon the general security of property, upon public as well as private credit, upon the spirit and principles of good government—who has an adequate idea of the sanctity of the national faith explicitly pledged, of the ignominy attendant upon a violation of it in so delicate a particular as that of private pecuniary contracts—of the evil tendency of a precedent of this kind to the political and commercial interests of the Nation generally—every law which has existed in this Country interfering with the recovery of the debts in question must have afforded matter of serious regret and real affliction. To such a man, it must be among the most welcome features of the present Treaty, that it stipulates reparation for the injuries which laws of that description may have occasionned to individuals, and that as far as is now practicable, it wipes away from the national Reputation the stain which they have cast upon it. He will regard it as a precious tribute to Justice, and as a valuable pledge for the more strict future observance of our public engagements: and he

ADf, Hamilton Papers, Library of Congress; *The* [New York] *Argus, or Greenleaf's New Daily Advertiser,* September 9, 1795.

1. For background to this document, see the introductory note to "The Defence No. I," July 22, 1795.

2. For the text of Article 6 of the Jay Treaty, see "Remarks on the Treaty . . . between the United States and Great Britain," July 9–11, 1795, note 13.

3. Article 4 of the definitive treaty of peace between the United States and Great Britain, September 3, 1783, reads: "It is agreed that Creditors on either Side shall meet with no lawful Impediment to the Recovery of the full Value in Sterling Money of all bona fide Debts heretofore contracted" (Miller, *Treaties,* II, 154).

would deplore as an ill omened symptom of the depravation of public opinion the success of the attempts which are making to render the article unacceptable to the People of the U States. But of this there can be no danger. The spontaneous sentiments of Equity of a moral and intelligent people, will not fail to sanction with their approbation a measure which could not have been resisted without inflicting a new wound upon the honor and character of the Country.

Let those men who have manifested by their actions a willing disregard of their own obligations as Debtors—those who secretly hoard or openly and unblushingly riot on the spoils of plundered creditors—let such men enjoy the exclusive and undivided satisfaction of arraigning and condemning an act of National Justice, in which they may read the severest reproach of their iniquitous principles and guilty acquisitions. But let not the People of America tarnish their honor by participating in that condemnation or by shielding with their favourable opinion the meretricious apologies which are offered for the measures that produced the necessity of reparation.

The recapitulation of some facts will contribute to a right judgment of this part of the Treaty.

It is an established principle of the laws of nations that on the return of peace between Nations which have been at War, a free and undisturbed course shall be given to the recovery of private debts on both sides.[4] In conformity with this principle, the 4th article of the Treaty of Peace between the US and G Britain expressly stipulates "that Creditors on either side shall meet with no lawful impediment to the recovery of the *full value* in *Sterling money* of all *bonafide* Debts theretofore contracted."

Two instances of the violation of this article have been already noticed with a view to another point one relating to certain laws of the State of Virginia passed prior to the peace which for several years after it appear to have operated to prevent the legal pursuit of

4. In the newspaper the following footnote was supplied for this sentence: "Grotius, b. iii, c. xx, s. xvi." The reference is to the following statement by Grotius: "It is well established that things which have been captured after the conclusion of a treaty of peace must be restored. The right of war had, in fact, already expired" (*On the Law of War and Peace*).

their claims by British Creditors[5]—another relating to a law of the state of South Carolina which suspended the recovery of their debts for Nine months, and after that period permitted the recovery only in four yearly installments.[6]

But these were not all the instances. There were other laws of South Carolina prolonging the installments and obliging the Creditors to receive in payment the property of debtors at appraised values; and there were laws of Rhode Island, New Jersey, North Carolina and Georgia making paper money a legal tender for the debts of those Creditors;[7] which it is known sustained a very great depreciation in every one of those States. These very serious and compulsory interferences with the rights of the Creditors have received from DECIUS the soft appellation of a modification of the recovery of British Debts.[8] Does he expect to make us believe by this smooth phraze that the right to recover the *full value* of a debt *in sterling money*, is satisfied by the obligation to take, as a substitute, one half one third or one fourth of the real value in paper?

It must necessarily have happened that British Creditors have sustained from the operation of the different acts alluded to, losses more or less extensive, which the mere removal of the legal impediments that occasionned them could not repair. In many instances, the losses must have actually accrued and taken their full effect. In others, where no proceedings may have been had, the lapse of so many years must have created inabities to pay in debtors, who were originally competent and who might have been compelled to pay, had there been a free course to justice.

5. For the acts of the Virginia legislature, see Enclosure No. 6 in Thomas Jefferson to George Hammond, May 29, 1792 (ADf, Thomas Jefferson Papers, Library of Congress; *ASP, Foreign Relations*, I, 201–37).

6. See "Remarks on the Treaty . . . between the United States and Great Britain," July 9–11, 1795, note 36.

7. See Jefferson to Hammond, May 29, 1792, sections 32–34 (ADf, Thomas Jefferson Papers, Library of Congress; *ASP, Foreign Relations*, I, 201–37).

8. This is a reference to an article by "Decius" (Brockholst Livingston) in *The* [New York] *Argus, or Greenleaf's New Daily Advertiser*, July 10, 1795. In this article "Decius," referring to Jefferson's letter to Hammond, May 29, 1792, wrote that Jefferson in this letter demonstrated that ". . . Great Britain having broken the treaty by a refusal to evacuate the upper posts, and carrying away more than three thousand negroes, some of the States, urged by dire necessity, and the calamities of a long war only modified the recovery of debts." For the authorship of the "Decius" articles, see the introductory note to "The Defence No. I," July 22, 1795.

The removal of the impediments therefore, by opening of the Courts of Justice, was not an adequate satisfaction. It could not supersede the obligation of compensating for losses which had irretrievably accrued by the operation of the legal impediments, while they continued in force. The claim for this was still open on the part of Great Britain, and still to be adjusted between the two Nations.

The excuse that these laws were retaliations for prior infractions of Treaty by Great Britain was in no view an answer to the claim.*

In the first place, as has already been proved,[9] the fact of such prior infractions was too doubtful to be finally insisted upon, and was, after a fruitless effort to obtain the acquiescence of the other party, properly and necessarily waved, so that it not serve as a plea against reparation.

In the second place, if that fact had been indubitable, the species of retaliation was unwarrantable. It will be shewn when we come to discuss the tenth article [10] that the debts of private individuals are in no case a proper object of reprisals, that independent of Treaty the meddling with them was a violation of the public faith and integrity, and that consequently it was due as much to our own public faith and integrity as to the individuals who had suffered to make reparation. It was an act demanded by the justice probity and magnanimity of the Nation.

In the third place, it was essential to reciprocity in the adjustment of the disputes which had existed concerning the Treaty of Peace. When we claimed the reinstatement and execution of the article with regard to the Posts,[11] it was just that we should consent to the re-

Note   * It may not be improper to observe that this excuse implies a palpable violation of the then constitution of the UStates. The Confederation vested the powers of War and of Treaty in the Union. It therefore lay exclusively with Congress to pronounce whether the Treaty was or was not violated by Great Britain & what should be the satisfaction. No state individually had the least right to meddle with the question and the having done it was a usurpation on the constitutional authority of the U States. It might be shewn on a similar principle, that all confiscations or sequestrations of *British Debts* by particular States during the War were also unconstitutional.

9. See "The Defence Nos. III, IV, V," July 29, August 1, 5, 1795.

10. See "The Defence Nos. XVIII, XIX, XX, XXI, XXII," October 6, 14, 23-24, 30, November 1, 1795.

11. This is a reference to Article 7 of the definitive treaty of peace. See Miller, *Treaties*, II, 155.

instatement and execution of the article with regard to Debts.[12] If the obstruction of the Recovery of Debts was the equivalent by way of retaliation for the detention of the posts, we could not expect to have restitution of the thing withheld and to retain the equivalent for it likewise. The dilemma was to be content with the equivalent and abandon the thing, or to recover the thing and abandon the equivalent. To have both was more than we could rightly pretend. The reinstatement of the article with regard to the debts necessarily included two things, the removal of legal impediments as to future recovery, compensation for past losses by reason of those impediments. The first had been effected by the new constitution of the U States, the last is promised by the Treaty.

Did our Envoy reply that the reinstatement of the article with regard to the posts included likewise compensation for their detention? Was it an answer to this destitute of reason, that our loss by the detention of the posts which resolved itself essentially into the uncertain profits of a Trade that might have been carried on admitted of no satisfactory rule of computation, while the principal and interest of private debts afforded a standard for the computation of losses upon them, that nevertheless while this was the usual and must be the admitted standard it is an inadequate one in cases where payment is protracted beyond the allowed term of credit; since the mere interest of money does not countervail among merchants the profits of its employment in Trade and still less the derangements of credit and fortune which frequently result to Creditors from procrastinations of payment: and that the final damage to Great Britain in these two particulars, for which no provision could be made, might well exceed any losses to us by the detention of the posts?

In the last place, the compensation stipulated was a *sine qua non* with Great Britain of the surrender of the posts and the adjustment of the controversy which had subsisted between the two Countries. The making it such may be conceived to have been dictated more by the importance of the precedent than by the quantum of the sum in question. We shall easily understand this, if we consider how

12. This is a reference to Article 6 of the Jay Treaty. For the text of this article, see "Remarks on the Treaty . . . between the United States and Great Britain," July 9–11, 1795, note 13.

much the Commercial Capital of Great Britain is spread over the world. The vast credits she is in the habit of extending to foreign Countries render it to her an essential point to protect those Credits by all the sanctions in her power. She cannot forbear to contend at every hazard against precedents of the invasion of the rights of her Merchants, and for retribution where any happen. Hence, it is always to be expected that she will be peculiarly inflexible on this point, and that nothing short of extreme necessity can bring her to relax in an article of policy which perhaps not less than any other is a necessary prop of the whole system of her political Oeconomy.

It was therefore to have been foreseen that whenever our controversy with Great Britain was adjusted compensation for obstructions to the Recovery of Debts would make a part of the adjustment. The option lay between compensation, relinquishment of the Posts or war. Our Envoy is intitled to the applause of all good men for preferring the first. The extent of the compensation can on no possible scale, compare with the immense permanent value of the posts, or with the expences of War. The sphere of the interferences has been too partial to make the sum of the compensation in any event a very serious object; and as to War a conscientious or virtuous mind could never endure the thought of seeing the country involved in its calamities to get rid of an Act of Justice to individuals, whose rights in contempt of public faith, had been violated.

Having reviewed the general considerations which justify the stipulation of compensation, it will be proper to examine if the plan upon which it is to be made is unexceptionable.

This plan contains the following features. 1 The cases provided for are those "where losses and damages occasionned by the operation of lawful impediments (which since the peace have delayed the full recovery of British Debts *bona fide contracted before the peace and still owing to the Creditors* and have impaired and lessenned the value and security thereof) *cannot now for whatever reason be actually obtained in the ordinary course of Justice."* 2 There is an express exception out of this provision *of all the cases* in which losses and damages have been occasionned *by such insolvency of the Debtors, or other causes, as would equally have operated to produce them, if no legal impediments had existed, or by the mani-*

fest delay or negligence or wilful omission of the claimants. 3 The amount of the losses and damages for which compensation is to be made is to be ascertained by five Commissioners to be appointed as follows—two by his Britannic Majesty two by the President with the advice & consent of the Senate—the fifth by the unanimous voice of these four, if they can agree—if they cannot agree, then to be taken by lot out of two persons one of whom to be named by the two British Commissioners, the other by the two American Commissioners. 4 The five Commissioners thus appointed are before they proceed to the execution of their trust to take an oath for its faithful discharge. Three of them to constitute a Board but there must be present one of the two Commissioners named on each side and the fifth Commissioner. Decisions to be made by majority of voices of those present. They are first to meet at Philadelphia but may adjourn from place to place as they see cause. 5 Eighteen months after the Commissioners make a Board are assigned for receiving applications, but the Commissioners in particular cases may extend the term for any further term not exceeding six months. 6 The Commissioners are empowered to take into consideration all claims, whether of principal or interest or ballances of principal and interest, and to determine them according to the merits and circumstances thereof and as justice and Equity shall appear to them to require; to examine persons on oath or affirmation and to receive in evidence depositions books papers or copies or extracts thereof either according to the legal forms existing in the two countries, or according to a mode to be devised by them. 7 Their award is to be conclusive and the U States are to cause the sum awarded in each case to be paid in specie to the Creditor without deduction and at such time and place as shall have been awarded; but no payment to be required sooner than twelve months from the day of the exchange of the Ratifications of the Treaty.

This provision for ascertaining the compensation to be made, while it is ample, is also well guarded.[13]

It is confined to debts contracted before the peace, and still owing to the creditors. It embraces only the cases of loss or damage in consequence of legal impediments to the recovery of those debts

13. The draft ends at this point. The remainder of this essay has been taken from the newspaper.

which will exclude all cases of voluntary compromise, and can include none where the laws have allowed a free course to justice.
It can operate in no instance where, at present, the *ordinary course
of justice* is competent to full relief, and the debtor is solvent, nor
in any, where insolvency or other cause would have operated to
produce the loss or damage, if no legal impediment had existed,
or where it has been occasioned by the wilfull delay, negligence
or omission of the creditor.

If it be said that the Commissioners have nevertheless much latitude of discretion, and that in the exercise of it they may transgress
the limits intended, the answer is, that the United States, though
bound to perform what they have stipulated with good faith, would
not be bound to submit to a manifest abuse of authority by the
Commissioners. Should they palpably exceed their commission, or
abuse their trust, the United States may justifiably, though at their
peril, refuse compliance. For example, if they should undertake to
award upon a debt contracted since the peace, there could be no
doubt that their award would be a nullity. So likewise there may
be other plain cases of misconduct, which in honor and conscience
would exonerate the United States from performance. It is only
incumbent upon them to act *bona fide,* and as they act at their
peril to examine well the soundness of the ground on which they
proceed.

With regard to the reference to Commissioners to settle the
quantum of the compensation to be made, this course was dictated
by the nature of the case. The tribunals of neither country were
competent to a retrospective adjustment of losses and damages, in
many cases which might require it. It is for this very reason of
the incompetency of the ordinary tribunals to do complete justice,
that a special stipulation of compensation, and a special mode of
obtaining it became necessary. In constituting a tribunal to liquidate
the quantum of reparation in the case of a breach of treaty, it was
natural and just to devise one likely to be more certainly impartial
than the established Courts of either party. Without impeaching
the integrity of those Courts, it was morally impossible that they
should not feel a byas towards the nation to which they belonged,
and for that very reason they were unfit arbitrations. In the case
of the spoliations of our property, we should undoubtedly have

been unwilling to leave the adjustment in the last resort to the British Courts; and by parity of reason, they could not be expected to refer the liquidation of compensation in the case of the debts to our Courts. To have pressed this would have been to weaken our argument for a different course in regard to the spoliations. We should have been puzzled to find a substantial principle of discrimination.

If a special and extraordinary tribunal was to be constituted, it was impracticable to contrive a more fair and equitable plan for it, than that which has been adopted. The remarks on the mode of determining the question respecting the river St. Croix,[14] apply in full force here, and would render a particular comment superfluous.

To the objection of the Charleston committee, that the article erects a tribunal unknown to our constitution, and transfers to commissioners the cognizance of matters appertaining to American courts and juries,[15] the answer is simple and conclusive. The tribunals established by the constitution do not contemplate a case between nation and nation arising upon a breach of treaty, and are inadequate to the cognizance of it. Could either of them hold plea of a suit of Great Britain plaintiff against the United States defendant? The case therefore required the erection or constitution of a new tribunal, and it was most likely to promote equity to pass by the Courts of both the parties.

The same principle contradicts the position that there has been any transfer of jurisdiction from American courts and juries to commissioners. It is a question not between individual and individual, or between our government and individuals, but between our government and the British government. Of course, one in which our courts and juries have no jurisdiction. There was a necessity for an extraordinary tribunal to supply the defect of ordinary jurisdiction,

14. See "The Defence No. XIII," September 5, 1795.
15. This is a reference to the *REPORT OF THE SELECT COMMIT-TEE, Chosen by Ballot of the Citizens of the United States, in Charleston, South-Carolina, in pursuance of a Resolution of a general Meeting of the Citizens, in St. Michael's Church, on Thursday, the sixteenth of July, 1795* (Charleston: Printed by W. P. Young, Broad-Street, n.d. [George Washington Papers, Library of Congress]). The report stated: "This [the sixth] article, moreover, erects a tribunal, new and unknown to our constitution, inasmuch as it transfers the right of deciding on the claims of British creditors, from the courts and juries of America, to commissioners; a majority of whom may be British subjects, and by their decisions, tax the revenue of these states at pleasure."

and so far is the article from making the transfer imputed to it, that it expressly excepts the cases in which effectual relief can be obtained in the ordinary course of justice.

Nations acknowledging no common judge on earth, when they are willing to submit the questions between them to a judicial decision, must of necessity constitute a special tribunal for the purpose. The mode by Commissioners, as being the most unexceptionable, has been repeatedly adopted.

I proceed to reply to some other objections which have been made against the provision contained in this article.

It is charged with fixing a stigma on the national character, by providing reparation for an infraction, which, if it ever did exist, has been done away, there being now a free course to the recovery of British debts in the courts of the United States.[16]

An answer to this objection has been anticipated by some observations heretofore made. The giving a free course to justice in favour of British creditors, which has been effected by the new constitution of the United States, though it obviates the future operation of legal impediments does not retrospectively repair the losses and damages which may have resulted from their past operation. In this respect the effects continued and reparation was due. To promise it, could fix no stigma on our national character. That was done by the acts which created the cause to reparation. To make it, was as far as possible to remove the stigma.

It has been said, that the promise of compensation produces injustice to those states which interposed no legal impediments to the recovery of debts, by saddling them with a part of the burden arising from the delinquencies of the transgressing States.[17] But the burden was before assumed by the treaty of peace. The article of

16. This is a reference to a statement by "Decius," who wrote: "that . . . it was at all times perfectly understood, that *treaties controuled the laws of the State.* That the federal and state judiciaries have so decided, that upon this principle the courts are every where open to British creditors, who have been for some time in the habit of recovering their debts at law" (*The* [New York] *Argus, or Greenleaf's New Daily Advertiser,* July 10, 1795).

17. This is a reference to a statement by "Decius," who wrote: "The mode of adjusting the sum due to British creditors, agreeably to the sixth article, will be unjust towards those States which have interposed no lawful impediments in the way of recovering such debts, as they must also bear part of the burden, and thus suffer for the delinquency of others" (*The* [New York] *Argus, or Greenleaf's New Daily Advertiser,* July 10, 1795).

that treaty which engaged that there should be no lawful impediments to the recovery of debts, was a *guarantee* by the United
States of justice to the British creditors. It charged them with
the duty of taking care that there was no legal obstacle to the recovery of the debts of those creditors, and consequently with a
responsibility for any such obstacle which should happen, and
with the obligation of making reparation for it. We must therefore
refer to the treaty of peace, not to the last treaty, the common
charge which has been incurred by interference in the recovery of
British debts. The latter only carries into execution the promise
made by the former. It may be added that it is a condition of the
social compact that the nation at large shall make retribution to
foreign nations for injuries done to them by its members.

It has been observed, that Mr. Jefferson has clearly shewn, that
interest in cases like that of the British debts, is liable, during the
period of the war, to equitable abatements and deductions; and
that, therefore, the discretion given to the commissioners on this
head, ought not to have been as large as it appears in the article.[18]

Mr. Jefferson has, no doubt, offered arguments of real weight
to establish the position that judges and juries have, and exercise
a degree of discretion in an article of interest, and that the circumstances of our war with Britain, afford strong reasons for abatements of interest. But it was foreign to his purpose, and accordingly
he has not attempted to particularise the rules which ought to gov-

18. This is a reference to a statement by "Decius," who wrote: "Mr. Jefferson has shewn in a letter already alluded to, that interest being no part of the
debt, may be disallowed in many cases, and has cited a great variety of instances from English law-books, in which it is not given; some of which
apply with too much force to the situation of the parties in question, not to
be mentioned. He observes, that a great national calamity has been adjudged
a sufficient cause to suspend the payment of interest. That in the present
case, the law of the party creditor, had cut off the personal access of his
debtor; that the transportation of his produce or money to the country of his
creditor was interdicted; that where the creditor prevents payment of both
principle and interest, the latter at least is justly extinguished; that the departure of the creditor, leaving no agent in the country, would have stopped
interest of itself—that debtor not being obliged to go abroad to seek for him.
"That the declarations of congress and our plenipotentiaries, previous to
the definitive treaty, and the silence of that instrument, afford proof, that
interest was not intended on our part, nor insisted upon by the other. And
that upon the whole, it was the proper province of the judiciary to determine
in what cases interest ought or ought not to be allowed." (*The* [New
York] *Argus, or Greenleaf's New Daily Advertiser*, July 10, 1795.)

ern in the application of this principle to the variety of cases in which the question may arise—and he has himself, noted that the practice in different states and in different courts, has been attended with great diversity. Indeed, admitting the right to abate interest under special circumstances, in cases in which it is the general rule to allow it, the circumstances of each case, are, perhaps, the only true criterion of the propriety of an exception. The particular nature of the contract, the circumstances under which it was entered into, the relative situation of parties, the possibility or not of mutual access; these and other things would guide and vary the exercise of the discretion to abate. It was, therefore, right to leave the commissioners, as they are left, in the same situation with judges and juries; to act according to the true equity of the several cases, or of the several classes of cases.

Let it be remembered, that the government of Great Britain has to consult the interests and opinions of its citizens, as well as the government of the United States those of their citizens. The only satisfactory course which the former could pursue, in reference to its merchants, was to turn over the whole question of interest as well as principal, to the commissioners. And as this was truly equitable, the government of the United States could make no well founded opposition to it.   CAMILLUS

The Defence No. XV [1]

[New York, September 12 and 14, 1795]

[IT is the business of the seventh article [2] of the treaty, to provide for two objects: one, compensation to our citizens for injuries to their property, by irregular or illegal captures or condemnations; the other, compensation to British citizens for captures of their

ADf, Hamilton Papers, Library of Congress; The [New York] Argus, or Greenleaf's New Daily Advertiser, September 12 and 14, 1795.
    1. The first part of the draft of this document has not been found. The material within brackets has been taken from the newspaper.
    For background to this document, see the introductory note to "The Defence No. I," July 22, 1795.
    2. For the text of Article 7 of the Jay Treaty, see "Remarks on the Treaty . . . between the United States and Great Britain," July 9–11, 1795, note 39.

property within the limits and jurisdiction of the United States, or elsewhere, by vessels originally armed in our ports, *in the cases in which the captured property having come within our posts and power, there was a neglect to make restitution.*

The first object is thus provided for: 1. It is agreed, that in all cases of irregular or illegal captures or condemnations of the vessels and other property of citizens of the United States, under colour of authority or commissions from his Britannic majesty, in which adequate compensation for the losses and damages sustained, cannot, for whatever reason, be actually obtained in the ordinary course of justice, full and complete compensation for the same will be made by the British government to the claimants; except where the loss or damage may have been occasioned by the manifest delay, or negligence, or wilful omission of those claimants. 2. The amount of the losses and damages to be compensated is to be ascertained by five commissioners, who are to be appointed in exactly the same manner as those for liquidating the compensation to British creditors.[3] 3. These commissioners are to take a similar oath, and to exercise similar powers for the investigation of claims with those other commissioners, and they are to decide according to the merits of the several cases and to justice, equity, and the laws of nations. 4. The same term of eighteen months is allowed for the reception of claims, with a like discretion to extend the term as in the case of British debts. 5. The award of these commissioners or of three of them, under the like guards as in that case, is to be final and conclusive, both as to the justice of the claim and the amount of the compensation. And, lastly, His Britannic majesty is to cause the compensation awarded to be paid to the claimants in specie, without deduction, at such times and places, and upon the condition of such releases or assignments, as the commissioners shall prescribe.

Mutually and dispassionately examined, it is impossible not to be convinced, that this provision is ample and ought to be satisfactory. The course of the discussion will exhibit various proofs of the disingenuousness of the clamours against it, but it will be pertinent to introduce here, one or two samples of it.

It has been alledged, that while the article preceding and this

3. This is a reference to Article 6 of the Jay Treaty. For H's discussion of this article, see "The Defence No. XIV," September 9, 1795.

article provide effectually for every demand of Great Britain against the United States, the provision for this important and urgent claim of ours is neither explicit, nor efficient, nor co-extensive with the object, nor bears any proportion to the *summary method*, adopted for the satisfying of British claims.[4]

This suggestion is every way unfortunate. The plan for satisfying our claim, except as to the description of the subject which varies with it, is an exact copy of that for making compensation to British creditors. Whoever will take the pains to compare, will find, that in the leading points, literal conformity is studied, and that in others, the provisions are assimilated by direct references; and will discover also, this important distinction in favour of the efficiency and summariness of the provision for our claim—that while the commissioners are expressly restricted from awarding payment to British creditors, to be made sooner than one year after the exchange of ratifications of the treaty, they are free to award it, to be made the very day of their decision, for the spoliations of our property. As to compensation for British property, captured within our limits, or by vessels originally armed in our ports and not restored, which is the only other British claim that has been provided for, it happens that this, forming a part of the very article we are considering, is submitted to the identical mode of relief, which is instituted for making satisfaction to us.

So far then is it from being true, that a comparison of the modes of redress provided by the treaty, for the complaints of the respective parties, turns to our disadvantage, that the real state of the case exhibits a substantial similitude with only one material difference, and that in our favor; and, that a strong argument for the equity of the provisions on each side, is to be drawn from their close resemblance of each other.

The other suggestion alluded to, and which has been shamelessly

4. This charge was made by several opponents of the Jay Treaty, but H is presumably referring to a statement made by Alexander J. Dallas in his "Features of Jay's Treaty": "The 6th and 7th articles provide for satisfying every demand which Great Britain has been able, at any time, to make against the United States (the payment of the British debts due before the war, and the indemnification for vessels captured within our territorial jurisdiction) but the provision made for the American claims upon Great Britain, is not equally explicit or efficient in its terms, nor is it co extensive with the object" (*Dunlap and Claypoole's* [Philadelphia] *American Daily Advertiser,* July 18, 1795).

reiterated, is, that Denmark and Sweden, by pursuing a more spirited conduct, had obtained better terms than the United States.[5] It is even pretended, that one or both of them had actually received from Great Britain a gross sum on account—in anticipation of an ultimate liquidation. In my second number,[6] the erroneousness of the supposition, that those powers had obtained more than the United States was intented, but the subsequent repetition of the idea, more covertly in point, and very openly and confidently in conversation, renders expedient an explicit and peremptory denial of the fact. There never has appeared a particle of evidence to support it, and after challenging the asserters of it to produce their proof, I aver, that careful enquiry at sources of information, at least as direct and authentic as their's, has satisfied me, that the suggestion is wholly unfounded, and that at the time of the conclusion of our treaty with Great Britain, both Denmark and Sweden were behind as in the effect of their measures for obtaining reparation.

What are we think of attempts like these, to dupe and irritate the public mind? Will any prudent citizen still consent to follow such blind or such treacherous guides?

Let us now, under the influence of calm and candid temper, without which truth eludes our researches, by a close scrutiny of the provision, satisfy ourselves whether it be not really a reasonable and proper one. But previous to this it is requisite to advert to a collateral measure which was also a fruit of the mission to Great Britain, and which ought to be taken in conjunction with the stipulations of this article. I refer to the order of the British king in council, of the 6th of August, 1794, by which order, the door before shut by lapse of time, is opened to appeals from the British West India courts of Admiralty, to be brought at any time which shall be judged reasonable by the lords commissioners of appeals in prize causes.[7] This of itself was no inconsiderable step towards the redress of our grievances, and it may be hoped, that with the aid which the government of the United States has given to facilitate appeals, much relief may ensue from this measure. It will not be

5. For examples of such assertions by opponents of the Jay Treaty, see "The Defence No. II," July 25, 1795, note 4.

6. "The Defence No. II," July 25, 1795.

7. For the order in council of August 6, 1794, see Edmund Randolph to H, January 5, 1795, note 1.

wonderful if it should comport with the pride and policy of the British government by promoting justice in their courts, to leave as little as possible to be done by the commissioners.

I proceed now to examine the characteristics of the supplementary provision made by the article, in connection with the objection to it.

It admits fully and explicitly the principle, that compensation is to be made for the losses and damages sustained by our citizens, by irregular or illegal captures, or condemnations of their vessels and other property] under *colour* of *authority* (which includes Governmental orders and instructions) or of commissions from his Britannic Majesty. It is to be observed that the causes of the losses and damages are mentioned in the disjunctive, "captures *or* condemnations" so that damages by captures which were not followed by condemnations are provided for as well as those where condemnations did follow.

A cavil has been raised on the meaning of the word *colour*, which it is pretended would not reach the cases designed to be enbraced [8] because the spoliations complained of were made not merely by *colour* but actually by *virtue* of instructions from the British Government.[9]

For the very reason that this subtil and artificial meaning ascribed to the term would tend to defeat the manifest general intent of the main provision of the Article, which is plainly to give reparation

8. In the newspaper this word is "entraced."

9. This is a reference to a statement by "Cato" (Robert R. Livingston), who wrote: "They [the commissioners appointed under the seventh article of the Jay Treaty] are not to relieve against captures under the order of April, November or January, 1st because neither of these are complained of, and the preamble of the article expressly relates to the injuries 'divers merchants and others' complain of having sustained by *irregular* captures or condemnations of their vessels and other property under colour *of authority and commission, &c.* Now it would be absurd to suppose that this can have any reference to what is done by the *express order* of the sovereign, or to any act but such as is an abuse of that order and authority; but these abuses make but a small part of our cause of complaint (which goes to the order itself) and are besides necessarily relievable in a court of appeals without the intervention of a minister extraordinary; and were so before the treaty. The great cause of complaint, the *instructions*, which are the laws of the court of admiralty not being complained of, all condemnations fairly made under them, must be confirmed by the treaty" (*The* [New York] *Argus, or Greenleaf's New Daily Advertiser*, July 22, 1795). For the authorship of the "Cato" essays, see the introductory note to "The Defence No. I," July 22, 1795.

for irregular or illegal captures or condemnations of American property contrary to the laws of nations—that meaning must be deemed inadmissible.

But in fact, the expression is the most accurate that could have been used to signify the real intent of the article. When we say a thing was done by colour of an authority or commission, we mean one of three things—that it was done on the pretence of a sufficient authority or commission not validly imparted or on the pretence of such an authority or commission validly imparted, but abused or misapplied—or on the pretence of an insufficient authority or Commission regularly as to form imparted and exercised. It denotes a defect of rightful and just authority, whether emanating from a wrong source or improperly from a right source; whereas the phrase "by virtue of" is most properly applicable to the valid exercise of a valid authority. But the two phrases are not infrequently used as synonimous. Thus in a Proclamation of the British King of the 25 of May 1792, he among other things forbids all his subjects, *by virtue or under colour of* any foreign commission or Letters of Reprisals to disturb infest or damage the subjects of France.[10]

In whose mouths does the article put the expression? In those of citizens of the U States? What must they be presumed to have meant? Clearly this—that by colour of instructions or commissions of his Britannic Majesty either exercised erroneously, or issued erroneously as being contrary to the laws of Nations,[11] the Citizens of the U States had suffered loss and damage by irregular or illegal captures or condemnations of their property. What is the standard appealed to to decide the irregularity or illegality to be redressed? Expressly the laws of Nations. The Commissioners are to decide "according to the merits of the several cases, to justice equity and the *laws of Nations.*" Wherever these laws as received and practiced among Nations pronounce a capture or condemnation of neutral property

10. The section of the proclamation of George III to which H is referring reads: ". . . his Majesty doth hereby strictly forbid all his subjects to receive any commission for arming and acting at sea as privateers, or letters of reprisals, from any enemy of the Most Christian King; or, by virtue or under colour of such commissions or reprisals, to disturb, infest, or anywise damage his subjects . . ." (*The Annual Register, or a View of the History, Politics, and Literature for the Year 1792* [London, 1821], 177).

11. See "Remarks on the Treaty . . . between the United States and Great Britain," July 9–11, 1795, note 64.

to have been irregular or illegal, though by color of an authority or commission of his Britannic Majesty, it will be the duty of the Commissioners to award compensation.

The criticism however fails on its own principle when tested by the fact. The great source of grievance intended to be redressed by the article proceeded from the instruction of the 6th of November 1793.[12] That instruction directs the Commanders of Ships of War and Privateers to stop and detain all ships laden with goods the produce of any colony belonging to France or carrying provisions and other supplies for the use of such colony and to bring the same with their cargoes to *legal adjudication* in the British Courts of Admiralty. These terms *"legal adjudication"* were certainly not equivalent to any rational construction to condemnation. Adjudication means simply a *judicial decision,* which might be either to acquit or condemn. Yet the British West India Courts of Admiralty appear to have generally acted upon the term as synonimous with condemnation. In doing this they may be truly said, even in the sense of the objection, to have acted by colour, only of the instruction.

The British Cabinet have disavowed this construction of the West India Courts and have, as we have seen, by a special act of interference [13] opened a door which was before shut to a reversal of their sentences by appeal to his Courts in England. We find also that the term adjudication is used in the XVIIth. article of our late Treaty as synonimous only with judicial decision, according to its true import.[14] This, if any thing were wanting, would render it impossible for the Commissioners to refuse redress on the grounds of the condemnations, if otherwise illegal, being warranted by the pretended sense of the words legal adjudication. But in reality as before observed their commission will be to award compensation in all cases in which they are of opinion that according to the established laws of Nations captures or comdemnations were irregular or illegal, however otherwise authorised; and this in contempt of the quibbling criticism which has been so cunningly devised.

12. H is referring to the "Additional instructions to the commanders of all our ships of war and privateers that have, or may have, letters of marque against France" (*ASP, Foreign Relations,* I, 430). See "The Defence No. II," July 25, 1795, note 8.

13. This is a reference to the order in council of August 6, 1794. See note 7.

14. For the text of Article 17 of the Jay Treaty, see "Remarks on the Treaty . . . between the United States and Great Britain," July 9-11, 1795, note 59.

2dly   The provision under consideration obliges the British Government, in all the cases of illegal captures or condemnations in which adequate compensation cannot for whatever reason be actually had in the ordinary course of Justice to make full and complete compensation to the Claimants which is to be paid in Specie to themselves without deduction at such times and places as shall be awarded.

They are not sent for redress to the Captors or obliged to take any circuitous course for their payment, when decreed, but are to receive it immediately from the Treasury of Great Britain.

3   The amount of the Compensation in each case is to be fixed by five Commissioners two appointed by the U States two by G Britain—the fifth by these four or in case of disagreement by lot. These Commissioners to meet and act in London.

It seems impossible, as has been observed and shewn in the analogous cases to imagine a plan for organising a Tribunal more completely equitable and impartial than this; [15] while it is the exact counterpart of the one which is to decide on the claims of British Creditors. Could it have been believed, that so palpable an error could have been imposed on a Town Meeting in the face of so plain a provision as to induce it to charge against this article that in a national concern of the U States, redress was left to British Courts of Admiralty? Yet strange as it may appear, this did happen even in the truly enlightened Town of Boston.[16]

The truth is that according to the common usage of Nations, the Courts of Admiralty of the belligerent parties are the channels through which the redress of injuries to neutrals is sought. But Great Britain has been brought to agree to refer all the cases in which justice cannot be obtained through those channels to an ex-

15. See "The Defence No. XIII and XIV," September 5, 9, 1795.
16. This is a reference to a statement in support of a resolution condemning the ratification of the Jay Treaty adopted "At a meeting of the Inhabitants of the Town of Boston, duly & legally warned & convened, by adjournment at Faneuil Hall on Monday the thirteenth day of July, One thousand Seven hundred and ninety five" (copy, George Washington Papers, Library of Congress). This statement reads: "Because the capture of Vessells, & property of Citizens of the United States, during the present war, made under the authority of the Government of Great Britain, is a National Concern, and claims arising from such captures, ought not to have been submitted to the decision of their Admiralty Courts, as the United States are thereby precluded from having a voice in the final determination of such cases. . . ."

traordinary Tribunal; in other words to Arbitrators mutually appointed.

It is here that we find the reparation of the national wrong which we had suffered. In admitting the principle of compensation by the Government itself, in agreeing to an extraordinary Tribunal in the constitution of which both parties have an equal voice to liquidate that compensation—Great Britain has virtually and effectually acknowleged the injury which had been done to our neutral rights and has consented to make satisfaction for it. This was an apology in fact, however it may be in form.

As it regards our honor, this is an adequate atonement and the only species usual in similar cases between nations. Pecuniary compensation is the true reparation in such cases. Governments are not apt to go upon their knees to ask pardon of other governments. Great Britain in the recent instance of the dispute with Spain about Nootka sound was glad to accept a like reparation.[17] It merits an incidental remark that the instrument which settles this dispute expressly waves like our Treaty reference to the merits of the complaints & pretensions of the respective parties. Is our situation such as to authorise us to pretend to impose humiliating conditions on other Nations?

It is necessary to distinguish between injuries and insults which we are too apt to confound. The seizures and Spoliations of our property fall most truly under the former head. The acts which produced them embraced all the neutral powers—were not levelled particularly at us—bore no mark of an intention to humiliate us by any peculiar indignity or outrage.

These acts were of June [8th] [18] and of November 6th 1793.[19] The seizure of our vessels going with provisions to the dominions of France under the first was put on the double ground of a war

17. For the Nootka Sound dispute, see George Washington to H, August 27, 1790; H to Washington, September 21, 29, 1790; "Conversation with George Beckwith," September 26–30, 1790; and "The Defence No. X," August 26, 1795, note 21.
18. Space left blank in MS. The date within brackets has been taken from the newspaper.
For the principal provision of the British order in council of June 8, 1793, see "Remarks on the Treaty . . . between the United States and Great Britain," July 9–11, 1795, note 66.
19. See note 12.

extraordinary in its principle * and of a construction of the laws of Nations which it was said permitted it—a construction not destitute of colour, and apparently supported by the authority of Vatel,[20] though in my opinion ill founded. It was accompanied also by compensation for what was taken and other circumstances that evinced a desire to smooth the act. The indiscriminate confiscation of our property upon the order of the 6th of November which was the truly flagrant injury was certainly unwarranted by that order (and no secret one has appeared)—and the matter has been so explained by the British Government. It is clear that the evils suffered under acts thus circumstanced are injuries rather than insults, and are so much the more manageable as to the species and measure of redress. It would be quixotism to assert that we might not honorably accept in such a case the pecuniary reparation which has been stipulated.

But it is alleged that in point of interest it is unsatisfactory—tedious in the process—uncertain in the event—that there ought to have been actual and immediate indemnifaction or at least a payment upon account.[21]

A little calm reflection will convince us that neither of the two last things was to be expected. There was absolutely no criterion either for a full indemnification or for an advance upon account. The value of the property seized and condemned (laying out of the case damages upon captures where condemnations had not ensued)

Note * Though this country has viewed the principle of the War favourably—it is certain that Europe generally, the neutral powers not wholly excepted, has viewed it in a different light so that this was not a mere pretence.

20. Vattel wrote: "On the other hand, whenever I am at war with a nation, both my safety and welfare prompt me to deprive it, as far as possible, of every thing which may enable it to resist or hurt me. Here the law of necessity shews its force. If this law warrants me on occasion, to seize what belongs to another, shall it not likewise warrant me to stop every thing relative to war, which neutral nations are carrying to my enemy. Even if I should by taking such measure render all these neutral nations my enemies, I had better run the hazard than suffer him who is actually at war with me, to be thus freely supplied to the great increase of his power. It is therefore very proper and very suitable to the law of nations, which disapproves of multiplying the causes of war, not to consider those seizures of the goods of neutral nations as acts of hostility" (Vattel, Law of Nations, Book III, Ch. VII, Sec. iii).

21. See "Cato No. 3" (The [New York] Argus, or Greenleaf's New Daily Advertiser, July 22, 1795).

was not ascertained even to our own government with any tolerable accuracy. Every well informed man will think it probable that of this a proportion not inconsiderable was covered French property. There were therefore no adequate data upon which our government could demand or the British Government pay a determinate sum. Both governments must have acted essentially by guess. Ours could not in honor or conscience have made even an estimate but upon evidence. It might have happened that a sum which appeared upon the evidence that had been collected sufficient might have proved on further evidence insufficient. Too little as well as too much might have been demanded & paid. But it will perhaps be said that some gross estimate might have been formed, and that of this such part might have been advanced upon account as was within the narrowest probable limit liable to eventual adjustment. Let us for a moment suppose this done. What good end would it have answered? How could the U States have distributed this money among the sufferers till it was ascertained which of them were truly intitled and to how much? Is it not evident that if they had made any distribution before the final and perfect investigation of the right of each claimant it would be at the risk of making mispayments and of being obliged to replace the sums mispaid, perhaps at a loss to the U States, for the benefit of those who should be found to be better intitled? Would it have been expedient for our Government to have incurred this risk to its constituents? And if the money was to be held undistributed till an investigation of claims was completed to what purpose the haste about an advance?

On the other hand—Is it in this loose gross way, that nations transact affairs with each other? Do even individuals make indemnifications to each other in so lumping a manner? Could it be expected of Great Britain that she would pay till it was fairly ascertained what was to be paid—especially when she had too much cause to suspect that a material proportion of the property claimed might turn out to be French? Would it have been justifiable on our part to make her compliance with such a demand the *sine qua non* of accommodation and peace? Whoever will believe that she would have complied with so humiliating a requisition must be persuaded that we were in a condition to dictate and she in a condition to be obliged to receive any terms that we might think fit to prescribe? The person who can believe this must be in my opinion under the influence of a delirium, for which there is no cure in the resources of reason and argument. Unhappy the Country that should take him as a guide!

If it must be admitted that it was matter of necessity that investigation should precede payment, then I see not what more summary mode could have been devised. Who more capable of proceeding with dispatch than Arbitrators untrammelled with legal forms—vested with powers to examine parties and others on oath and to command and receive all evidence in their own way? Here are all the means of expedition, divested of every clog.

Eighteen months are allowed for preferring claims, but the Commissioners are at liberty to adjust them as fast as they are preferred. In every case in which it appears to them *bona fide* that the ordinary course of Justice is inadequate to relief, they may forthwith proceed to examine and decide. There is no impediment, no necessary cause of delay whatever, more than the nature of a due investigation always requires.

The meeting of the Commissioners at London was recommended by the circumstance that the Admiralty Courts were likely to concenter there a considerable part of the evidence on which they were to proceed—which upon the whole might favour dispatch as well as more complete justice. In many cases the decisions of those Courts may come under their review.

As to uncertainty of the event, this, as far as it may be true, was inseperable from any plan bottommed on the idea of a previous investigation of claims. And it has been shewn that some such plan was reasonable and inevitable.

It may be also added that the plan affords a moral certainty of substantial justice, which is all that can rationally be expected in similar affairs. Compensation where due is explicitly stipulated. A fair and adequate mode of deciding and liquidating it has been settled. All the arguments which were adduced to prove the probability of good faith in regard to the posts [22] apply equally to this subject. The interest which every nation has in the preservation of character and which the most profligate nations dare not intirely disregard—the consideration of defeating the fulfilment of the stipulations on our part—the size of the object, certainly not of great magnitude—the

22. See "The Defence No. VIII," August 15, 1795.

very discouraging situation for replunging suddenly into a new war in which the present war will in every event leave Great Britain—These are reasons which afford solid ground of assurance that there will be no evasion of performance.

As to the Commissioners, two of the five will certainly be of our choice, a third may be so likewise, but should it prove otherwise it will be surprising if one of the other three all acting under oath and having character at stake shall not be disposed to do us reasonable justice.

3dly.   While their power is coextensive with *all* losses and damages from irregular or illegal captures *or* condemnations, their sentence in each case is to be conclusive, and the rules which are to govern it as prescribed by the article are the merits of each case, justice equity and the laws of Nations. What greater latitude could have been desired to be given? What greater latitude could have been given? What else in the case was there to have been provided for? What is meant by the assertion that the provision is not commensurate with the object?

The general and unqualified reference to the laws of Nations dismisses all pretence to substitute arbitrary regulations of Great Britain as rules of decision. Her instructions or orders, if incompatible with those laws are nullities. Thus The Treaty unfetters the questions between us and her from the commencement of the War, and with her own consent commits them at large to a Tribunal to be constituted by mutual choice.

Will any man of candour and Equity say that a better provision ought to have been expected than has been accomplished?

The alternative was Immediate Indemnification by actual payment in whole or in part without examination of the extent or justice of the claims—or future indemnification after a due investigation of both in some equitable and effectual mode. The first was attended with difficulties on our side and with solid objections on the other side. The last was therefore the truly reasonable course, and it has been pursued on a very proper plan. The causes of loss and damage are fully embraced—they are referred to the decision of an unexceptionable Tribunal to be guided by unexceptional rules and the indemnification which may be awarded is to be paid fully immediately and without detour by the British Government itself. Say Ye impartial and enlightened if all this be not as it ought to have been!   Camillus

The Defence No. XVI[1]

[New York, September 18, 1795]

The second object of the seventh article,[2] as stated in my last number, is "compensation to British Citizens, for captures of their property within the limits and jurisdiction of the U States, or elsewhere by vessels originally armed in our ports, *in the cases in which the captured property having come within our power, there was a neglect to make restitution.*"

This precise view of the thing stipulated is calculated to place the whole subject at once before the mind in its true shape—to evince the reasonableness of it—and to dismiss the objections which have been made, as being foreign to the real state of the fact. These objections are in substance, that the compensation promised is of great and indefinite extent and amount—that an enormous expence is likely to be incurred,[3] and that it is difficult to prove that a neutral Nation is under an obligation to go the lengths of this stipulation.[4]

ADf, Hamilton Papers, Library of Congress; *The* [New York] *Argus, or Greenleaf's New Daily Advertiser*, September 18, 1795.

1. For background to this document, see the introductory note to "The Defence No. I," July 22, 1795.

2. For the text of Article 7 of the Jay Treaty, see "Remarks on the Treaty . . . between the United States and Great Britain," July 9–11, 1795, note 39.

3. At this point in the draft H wrote and crossed out: "(Mr Hammond the British Minister having estimated the captures described at 1800000 £ Sterling)."

4. These objections to Article 7 of the Jay Treaty were made by "Decius" (Brockholst Livingston), who wrote: ". . . If . . . [the United States] are to be charged with all the prizes therein referred to, no one can foresee what will be the amount. It is said, that, long since, Mr. Hammond stated the demand at eighteen hundred thousand pounds sterling. It is no excuse in those who defend the treaty, to say, that the president had already pledged the government to this measure; he had no right to do so; and we are now enquiring, not what the president has done, but what is proper and incumbent on the United States. It will be difficult to show that a neutral nation is obliged to go to the lengths which the present treaty imposes upon us"

These remarks obviously turn upon the supposition—erroneously entertained or disingenuously affected—that compensation is to be made for *all captures* within our limits or jurisdiction, or elsewhere by vessels originally armed in our ports, where restitution has not in fact been made. Did the stipulation stand on this broad basis it would be justly liable to the criticism which has been applied to it. But the truth is that its basis is far more narrow, that instead of extending to all those captures, it is confined to the *particular cases* of them only in which the captured property came or was after the capture within our power so as to have admitted of restitution by us, but restitution was not made through the *omission* or *neglect* of our government. It does not extend to a single case where the property if taken within our jurisdiction was immediately carried out of our reach—or where if taken without our jurisdiction it was never brought within our reach—or where if at any time within our reach due means were employed without success to effect restitution.

It will follow from this that the cases within the purview of the article must be very few—for except with regard to three prizes made in the first instance,[5] where special considerations restrained the government from interposing, there has been a regular and constant effort of the Executive, in which our courts have efficaciously

(*The* [New York] *Argus, or Greenleaf's New Daily Advertiser*, July 11, 1795). For the authorship of the "Decius" essays, see the introductory note to "The Defence No. I," July 22, 1795.

5. On August 7, 1793, Thomas Jefferson wrote to George Hammond: "A constant expectation of carrying into full effect the declaration of the President, against permitting the armament of vessels within the ports of the United States, to cruize on nations with which they are at Peace, has hitherto prevented my giving you a final answer on the subject of such vessels and their prizes. Measures to this effect are still taking, and particularly for excluding from all further asylum in our ports, the vessels so armed, and for the restoration of the Prizes, the Lovely Lass, the Prince William Henry and the Jane of Dublin, taken by them: and I am authorized, in the mean time to assure you, that should the measures for restoration fail in their effect, the President considers it incumbent on the United States to make compensation for the Vessels" (ALS, letterpress copy, Thomas Jefferson Papers, Library of Congress; Miller, *Treaties*, II, 270).

For information concerning the *Lovely Lass, Prince William Henry,* and *Jane of Dublin,* see "Cabinet Meeting. Opinion Respecting Certain French Vessels and Their Prizes," August 5, 1793; "Cabinet Meeting. Opinions Concerning the Relations of the United States with Certain European Countries," November 1-22, 1793; H to Jefferson, December 18, 1793; "Treasury Department Circular to the Collectors of the Customs," December 19, 1793.

cooperated, to restore prizes made within our jurisdiction or by vessels armed in our ports. The extent or amount therefore of the compensation to be made can by no possible means be considerable.

Let us however examine if the construction I give to the clause be the true one.

It is in these words—"It is agreed that in all such cases where *restitution* shall not have been made *agreeably to* the tenor of the letter from Mr. Jefferson to Mr. Hammond dated September 5th 1793,[6] a copy of which is annexed to this Treaty, the complaints of the parties shall be and hereby are referred to the Commissioners to be appointed by virtue of this article, who are hereby authorised and required to proceed in the like manner relative to these as to the other cases committed to them: and the United States undertake to pay to the complainants in specie without deduction the amount of such sums as shall be awarded to them respectively &c."

The letter of Mr. Jefferson by this reference to it and its annexation to the Treaty is made virtually a part of the Treaty. The cases in which compensation is promised are expressly those in which restitution has not been made agreeably to the tenor of that letter.

An analisis of the letter will of course unfold the cases intended.

I   It recapitulates an assu[r]ance before given by a letter of the 7 of August to the British Minister [7] that measures were taken for [8] excluding from *further asylum* in our ports vessels armed in them to cruise on nations with which we were at peace, and for the restoration of the prizes the Lovely Lass, Prince William Henry, and the Jane of Dublin, and *that should the measures of restitution fail in their effect, The President considered it as incumbent on the U States to make compensation for the Vessels.*[9] These Vessels had been captured by French Privateers originally armed in our ports and had been afterwards brought within our ports.

II   It states that we are bound by our treaties with three of the

---

6. ADf, Thomas Jefferson Papers, Library of Congress; Miller, *Treaties,* II, 265–66. This letter is also printed in *ASP, Foreign Relations,* I, 174–75.

7. See note 5.

8. In MS, "from."

9. At this point in the MS H wrote and crossed out the following sentences: "These vessels captured by the privateers fitted out of Charleston & brought into our ports. This is one of the cases of restitution contemplated compensation intended by the article applys specifically to these vessels."

belligerent nations * by all the means in our power to protect and defend their vessels and effects in our ports or waters or on the seas near our shores, and to recover and restore the same to the right owners when taken from them—adding that *if all the means in our power are used* and fail in their effect we are not bound by our treaties to make compensation.

It further states that though we have no similar Treaty with Great Britain, it was the opinion of the President that we should use towards that Nation the same rule which was to govern us with those other nations, and even to extend it to captures made on the high seas and *brought into our ports* if done by vessels which had been armed within them.[11]

III It then draws this conclusion—that *having for particular reasons forebore to use all the means in our power* for the restitution of the three vessels mentioned in the letter of the 7th of August, The President *thought it incumbent upon the U States to make compensation for them:* And though nothing was said in that letter of other vessels *taken under like circumstances* and *brought in* after the 5th of June and before the date of that letter, yet *when the same forbearance* had taken place it was his opinion that *compensation would be equally due.* The cases then here described are those in which illegal prizes had been made & *brought into our ports* prior to the 7 of August 1793 and in which *we had foreborne to use all the means in our power* for restitution. Two characters are made essential to the cases in which the compensation is to be made, one that the prizes *were brought within our ports* the other that we *forebore to use all the means in our power* to restore them.

IV The letter proceeds to observe that, as to prizes *made under the same circumstance* and *brought in* after the date of that letter, The President had determined that *all the means in our power should*

* France Holland and Prussia—and our Treaty with Sweden includes a like provision.[10]

10. Treaty of Amity and Commerce with France, February 6, 1778 (Miller, *Treaties,* II, 3–34); Treaty of Amity and Commerce with the Netherlands, October 8, 1782 (Miller, *Treaties,* II, 59–90); Treaty of Amity and Commerce with Prussia, September 10, 1785 (Miller, *Treaties,* II, 162–84); Treaty of Amity and Commerce with Sweden, April 3, 1783 (Miller, *Treaties,* II, 123–50). See also "Remarks on the Treaty . . . between the United States and Great Britain," July 9–11, 1795, note 75.

11. In MS, H mistakenly numbered this paragraph "III." In the newspaper it appears correctly as part of "II."

be used for their restitution—that if *these failed,* as we should *not be bound to make compensation to the other powers* in the analogous case, he did *not mean to give an opinion that it ought to be done* to Great Britain. But still if any cases shall arise subsequent to that date, *the circumstances of which shall place them on a similar ground with those before it,* The President would think *compensation equally incumbent on the U States.* The addition of cases of which an expectation of compensation is given in this part of the letter must stand *on similar ground* with those before described—that is they must be characterised by the two circumstances of a *bringing within our ports* and a *neglect to use all the means in our power* for their restitution. Every where the idea of compensation is negatived where the prizes have not come within our power or where we have not foreborne to use the proper means to restore them.

The residue of the letter merely contains suggestions for giving effect to the foregoing assurances.

The analysis leaves no doubt that the true construction is such as I have stated. Can there be any greater doubt that the expectations given by the President in the first instance and which have been only ratified by the Treaty were in themselves proper and have been properly ratified?

The laws of nations as dictated by reason as received and practiced upon among nations, as recognised by writers establish these principles for regulating the conduct of neutral powers.

A neutral nation (except as to points to which it is clearly obliged by antecedent treaties) whatever may be its opinion of the justice or injustice of the war on either side cannot without departing from its neutrality, *favour* one of two belligerent parties more than the other—benefit one to the prejudice of the other—furnish or permit the furnishing to either the instruments of acts of hostility or any warlike succour or aid whatever, especially without extending the same advantage to the other—cannot suffer any force to be exerted or warlike enterprise to be carried on from its territory by one party against the other or the preparation or organisation there, of the means of annoyance—has a right and is bound to prevent acts of hostility within its jurisdiction—and if they happen against its will to restore any property which may have been taken in exercising them. These positions will all be found supported by the letter or

spirit of the following Authorities—BARBEYRAC's note on PUFFEN-
DORF B VIII C VI § 7 [12] GROTIUS B III C: XVII § III [13] BYNKERSHOEK
B I C VIII Page 61. 65 C: IX Page 69.70.[14] VATEL B III C VII [15]—
BYNKERSHOECK cites examples of restitution in the case mentioned.

Every Treaty we have made with foreign powers promises protection within our jurisdiction and the restoration of property taken
there. A similar stipulation is indeed a general formula in Treaties
giving an express sanction to the rule of the laws of Nations in this
particular.

An Act of Congress of the 5 of June 1794 [16] which is expressly a
declaratory act recognizes at large the foregoing principles of the
laws of Nations—providing among other things for the punishment
of any person who within the UStates fits out & arms or attempts
to fit out and arm or procures to be fitted out and armed or is knowingly concerning in furnishing fitting out or arming of any ship or
vessel with intent to be employed in the service of a foreign State
to cruise or commit hostilities upon the subjects or citizens of another foreign State with which the U States are at peace or issues or
delivers a commission for any such Ship or Vessel or increases or aug-
ments or procures to be increased or augmented or is knowingly concerned in increasing or augmenting the force of any ship of War
cruiser or other armed vessel in the service of a foreign state at war
with another foreign state with which the U States are at peace or
within the territory of the U States begins or sets on foot or provides or prepares the means of any military expedition or enterprise
to be carried on from thence against the dominions of any foreign
State with which the U States are at peace.

Our Courts have also adopted in its fullest latitude as conformable
in their opinion with those laws the principle of restitution of property when either captured within our jurisdiction or elsewhere by
vessels armed in our ports. The Supreme Court of the U States has
given to this doctrine by solemn decisions the most complete and
comprehensive sanction.[17]

12. Pufendorf, *Of the Law of Nature and Nations.*
13. Grotius, *On the Law of War and Peace.*
14. Bynkershoek, *Quæstionum.*
15. Vattel, *Law of Nations.*
16. "An Act in addition to the act for the punishment of certain crimes against the United States" (1 *Stat.* 381–84).
17. This is a reference to the decision in the case of *Talbot* v *Jansen*, which was heard on August 22, 1795 (3 Dallas, *U.S. Reports,* 131–69).

It is therefore undoubtedly the law of the land, determined by the proper constitutional Tribunal in the last resort, that restitution is due in the abovementioned cases.

And It is a direct & necessary consequence from this that where it is not made by reason of the neglect of the Government to use the means in its power for the purpose—there results an obligation to make reparation. For between Nations as between Individuals, wherever there exists a perfect obligation to do a thing, there is a concomitant obligation to make reparation for omissions and neglects.

The President was therefore most strictly justifiable upon principle in the opinion which he communicated, that in the cases of such omissions or neglects compensation ought to be made. And in point of policy nothing could be wiser, for had he not done it there is the highest probability that war would have ensued.

Our Treaty with France forbids us expressly to permit the privateers of her enemy to arm in our ports or to bring or sell there the prizes which they have made upon her.[18] We could not for that reason have made the privilege of arming in our ports, if it had been allowed to France, reciprocal. The allowance of it to her would consequently have been a clear violation of neutrality, in the double sense of permitting a military aid, and of permitting it to one and refusing it to the other. Had we suffered France to equip privateers in our ports to cruise thence upon her enemies and to bring [19] back and vend there the spoils or prizes taken, we should have become by this the most mischievous foe they could have. For While all our naval resources might have augmented the force of France our neutrality if tolerated would in a great degree have sheltered and protected her cruisers. Such a state of things no nation at war could have acquiesced in. And as well to the efficacy of our endeavours to prevent equippments in our ports, as to the proof of the sincerity of those endeavours, it was essential that we should restore the prizes which came within our reach made by vessels armed in our ports. It is known that notwithstanding the utmost efforts of the government to prevent it French privateers have been clandestinely equipped in some of our ports subsequent to the assurances which

18. This is a reference to Article 22 (originally 24) of the Treaty of Amity and Commerce between the United States and France, February 6, 1778 (Miller, *Treaties*, II, 19–20).
19. In MS, "brink."

were given that the practice would be discountenanced.[20] If prizes made by such vessels were suffered to be brought into our ports and sold there, this would be not only a very great encouragement to the practice, but it would be impossible that it should be regarded in any other light than as a connivance.

In such a circumstance can we blame our Chief Magistrate—can we even deny him praise for having diverted an imminent danger to our peace, by incurring the responsibility of giving an expectation of compensation? The conjuncture we may remember was critical and urgent. Congress were at the time in recess. A due notice to convene them in so extensive a country can hardly be rated at less than three months.

In this situation our envoy found the business. It is not true in the sense in which it has been advanced that he was to be governed by the fitness of the thing unmindful of the opinion of the President. An opinion of the Chief Magistrate of the Union was to a diplomatic Agent an authority and a guide which he could not justifiably have disregarded. The claim of compensation on the other side was greatly *fortified* by that opinion. Nor was it a matter of indifference to our national delicacy and respectability [21] that the expectation given by it should be fulfilled. It would have been indecent in our envoy to have resisted it. It was proper in him by acceding to it to refer the matter to the ultimate decision of that authority which by our constitution is charged with the power of making Treaties. It was the more proper because the thing was intrinsically right. Every candid man, every good citizen will rejoice that the President acted as he did in the first instance, that our Envoy acted as he did in the second, and that the conduct of both has received the final constitutional Sanction.[22]

The opinions of Mr. Jefferson when they can be turned to the discredit of the Treaty are with its adversaries oracular truths. When they are to support it they lose all their weight. The presumption that the letter referred to had the concurrence of the judgment of

20. See "Cabinet Meeting. Opinion Respecting Certain French Vessels and Their Prizes," August 5, 1793, note 4.

21. In the newspaper this word is "dignity."

22. In the margin opposite this paragraph H wrote and crossed out: "This is an instance that all that G Britain might have ever claimed was not provided for."

that officer results from a fact generally understood and believed namely that the proceedings of the President at the period when it was written in relation to the War were conformable with the unanimous advice of the heads of the Executive Departments.

This case of British property captured by Privateers originally armed in our ports falsifies the assertion of the adversaries of the Treaty that all the pretensions of Great Britain have been fully provided for.[23] She had a colorable ground to claim compensation for *all captures* made by vessels armed in our ports whithersoever carried or howsoever disposed of—especially where the equipment had been tolerated by our Government. This toleration was to be inferred as well from a forbearance to suppress those vessels when they came within our power as from an original permission. Had compensation been stipulated on this scale it is not certain that it would not have amounted to as much more than that which has been promised —as would counterballance our claims for negroes carried away and for the detention of the posts. But instead of this, it is narrowed down by the Treaty to such prizes of those vessels as were brought within our ports and in respect to which we forbore to use all the means in our power for restitution. Here then is a sett off against doubtful and questionable claims relinquished on our side. Here also is another proof how much the antagonists of the Treaty are in the habit of making random assertions. But can we wonder at it when we reflect that they have undertaken to become the instructors of their fellow citizens on a subject, on the examination of which they unite a very superficial knowlege with the most perverse dispositions?   CAMILLUS

23. At this point in the draft H wrote and crossed out: "It has been represented on the other side that Mr Hammond the British Minister had estimated the loss by such captures at one Million Eight hundred thousand pounds Sterling."

From Ezekiel Gilbert [1]

Hudson [New York] September 18, 1795. "The appointment of a new Sheriff for Columbia will take place at the meeting of the Council next week.[2] As I consider the Office of Sheriff, decidedly, the most influential of any other in the County, and feel the Importance of placing it in proper hands . . . permit me to suggest my Sentiment. . . . Among the Competitors for the Office I do most Sincerely hope Capt Peter B Ten Broeck [3] may have it. . . . If you consider this Appointment, civilly, and politically, of as much Consequence as I do . . . you will not fail bringing into the View of the President of the Council [4] my Judgt. upon this point. . . ."

ALS, Hamilton Papers, Library of Congress.
1. Gilbert, a lawyer in Hudson, was a member of the House of Representatives from 1793 to 1797.
2. Appointments to state office in New York were made by the Council of Appointment. The power of nomination was exercised by the governor, who served as presiding officer of the Council.
3. Ten Broeck, an officer in the American Revolution, had served as deputy sheriff of Albany County before Columbia County was separated from Albany County in 1786.
4. Governor John Jay.

To Oliver Wolcott, Junior

[New York] Sepr. 20. 1795

My Dear Sir

A slight indisposition prevented my meeting you at E Town [1] which I should otherwise have done with great pleasure.

It is wished for a particular purpose to know who are the Writers of *Valerius Hancock Bellisarius Atticus*.[2] If any thing about them is known in a manner that can be depended upon I will thank you for it in confidence.

The fever in this Town has become serious.[3] The alarm however exceeds the quantum of disease & danger. It is not ascertained that the fever is contagious. It is clearly traced to local causes—but it is sufficiently mortal. Bleeding is found fatal. Most of our physicians purge more or less some with Calomel—I fear more than does good Bark Wine &c plentifully used and with good effect. They however all behave well and shrink not from their duty.

Adieu   Yrs.   A Hamilton

Oliver Wolcott Esq

Shew the last paragraph of this letter to Doctor Stevens [4] from whom though I have written to him [5] I have not received a line since I came to NYork.[6]

ALS, Connecticut Historical Society, Hartford.

1. Wolcott had left Philadelphia on September 18, 1795, to meet his wife in Elizabeth, New Jersey. He returned to Philadelphia on September 22 (Timothy Pickering to George Washington, September 23, 1795 [ALS, RG 59, Miscellaneous Letters, 1790–1799, National Archives]).

2. These articles, which opposed the Jay Treaty, were printed in Benjamin Franklin Bache's [Philadelphia] *Aurora. General Advertiser.* "Valerius" wrote eleven articles from August 22 to December 1; five articles by "Hancock" appeared in August and September; five articles by "Belisarius" appeared in September and October; and "Atticus" wrote at least nine articles for the [Philadelphia] *Independent Gazeteer* between July and October, of which seven were reprinted in the *Aurora.*

3. There was a yellow fever epidemic in New York City from mid-July until the onset of cold weather in November, 1795.

4. Edward Stevens was H's boyhood friend and a physician in Philadelphia. Stevens had been H's doctor when H had contracted yellow fever in 1793. See George Washington to H, September 6, 1793; H to the College of Physicians, September 11, 1793.

5. Letter not found.

6. Wolcott endorsed this letter: "ansd. 25." Actually Wolcott's reply is dated September 26, 1795.

The Defence No. XVII[1]

[New York, September 22, 1795]

The VIII article[2] provides merely that the Commissioners to be appointed in the three preceding articles shall be paid in such manner

ADf, Hamilton Papers, Library of Congress; *The* [New York] *Argus, or Greenleaf's New Daily Advertiser,* September 22, 1795.

1. For background to this document, see the introductory note to "The Defence No. I," July 22, 1795.

The material within brackets in this document has been taken from the newspaper.

Part of this essay is based on notes supplied by Rufus King. See "Remarks on the Treaty . . . between the United States and Great Britain," July 9–11, 1795, note 44. King wrote: "The Stipulation is in favor of the american, & its reciprocity in favor of the Frenchman, to ascertain the limits of the reciprocity, we must first Know the Extent of the Stipulation. The first clause in the article is in these words—'The Subjects and Inhabitants of the said U.S. or any one of them, shall not be reputed aubains (that is aliens) in France.'

"'There are,' says M. Argou in his celebrated Institutes of the French Law, 'two sorts of Strangers in France, one those who are naturalized, & who enjoy the Privileges, Franchises, liberties, immunities & Rights, and are on the Footing in every Respect, of Natives; the Other, those who are not naturalised, and who denominated aubains, are subject to various alien Disabilities, among which are incapacities in acquiring, conveying, & succeeding to real Estates.'

"If the americans shall not be reputed aliens in France, the incapacities in Question must be abolished, and in respect to that subject they must stand on the Footing of Natives. So on the other Hand, as Frenchmen shall not be reputed aliens in the U.S. of consequence their alien Disabilities are in like

as shall be agreed between the parties at the time of the exchange of
the Ratification of the Treaty, and that all other expences attending

---

manner abolished, and in respect to the tenure of Lands they also must stand
on the footing of Natives.

"It is not proposed to enquire what other Laws of the two Nations are
affected by this abolition of alienism—our object being confined to an elucida-
tion of its Effect upon the Laws relative to lands.

"Should any one doubt the interpretation, let him pursue the article a
little further. After declaring that the american Citizens shall not be reputed
aliens in France it proceeds to affirm as *a consequence* thereof their exemption from alien Forfeitures, and asserts, that they 'pourront disposer par
Testament Donation, ou autrement, *de leurs Biens meubles & immeubles* en
faveur de telles personnes que bon leur semblera, & leur Heritiérs subjets de
dits E.U, residans soit in France soit ailleurs pourront leur succéder ab in-
testat, sans qu'ils aient besoin d'obtenir des Lettres de Naturalité &c. &c.' The
exposition of this clause must be sought for not in our law books but in those
of France. It is from their inattention to this Circumstance that any misconception has existed in the interpretation of the article. The words 'Biens
meubles & immeubles' have been translated 'Goods moveable & immoveable';
from our use of the word '*Goods*' to signify personal as distinguished from
real Estate, we have been led to give to the words 'Goods moveable &
immoveable,' A sense equivalent to Chattels real & personal thereby excluding
real Estate or Lands. But let us consult the French authorities.

"Biens—C'est en général tout ce qui compose nos richisses. Il y a deux
Sortes de Biens, les meubles & les immeubles. Meuble, tout ce qui peust être
transporté d'un lieu a un autre. Immeubles—Biens en Fonds, ou qui sont
présumé avoir la nature de fonds. On distingue deux sorts d'immeubles, les
réels & les fictifs—les immeuble reel sont non seulment la substance meme de
la Terre, qui est ce qu'on appelle le Fonds, mais tout ce qui est adhérent a
la surface, soit par la nature comme les arbres, soit par la main des Hommes
comme les maisons, & autres bâtiments. On a appellé l'autre espece d'immeubles, immeuble fictifs, parce qu'ils ne sont tels que par Fiction; de ce
nombre sont les Office venaux casuels & les rentés constitué &c &c—M. au
Droit francois Lib 1 &c a Argou.

"Thus it appears that 'goods moveable & immoveable' comprehend the
Estates real as well as personal; immoveable Goods being say the french
authorities not only the very substance of the Earth, but also all that which
is attached to its surface, whether by nature as the Trees, or by the agency
of Man as Houses and other Buildings.

"And as by this interpretation the article confers upon the American
Citizens a Right to take & hold by purchase or Descent to alienate by Will
or otherwise, lands in France and as it stipulates an entire & perfect reciprocity in favor of Frenchmen within the US. the inference results that the
alienism of French men in respect to the tenure of lands within the U.S. is
by this article abolished, so that they may take, hold & convey lands in like
manner as natives.

"A question on this article arose in the year 1786 when Mr. Jefferson was
our Minister in France. The Marquis Bellgarde & the Chevr. de Meziere, who
were sons of the two sisters of Gen. Oglethorp, claimed the Lands that had
belonged to the General in Georgia and having represented to the Count
Vergennes that they met with impediments in the prosecution of their
Claim, on account as they supposed of the Laws in Georgia prohibiting aliens
to hold lands. The Count Vergennes stated to Mr. Jefferson the complaint,

the Commissions shall be defrayed jointly by the two parties the same being previously ascertained and allowed by a Majority of the Commissioners, and that in case of death sickness or necessary absence of a Commissioner, his place shall be supplied in the same manner as he was first appointed, the new Commissioner to take the same oath or affirmation and to perform the same duties as his predecessor.

Could it have been imagined that even this simple & equitable provision was destined not to escape uncensured? As if it was predetermined that not a single line of the Treaty should pass as guiltless—nothing less than an infraction of the constitution of the U States has been charged upon this article. It attempts we are told a disposition of public money unwarranted by and contrary [to] the Constitution. The examination of this wonderfully sagacious objection with others of a similar complexion must be reserved for the separate discussion which has been promised of the constitutionality of the Treaty.[3]

Let us proceed for the present to the IXth. article.[4]

---

and further that by the article in question the alien Disability of the Marq. Bellgarde & the Chev. Mezieres having in common with that of all French men been removed by our treaty—they ought not to experience any impediment on that account in succeeding to the Estate in Georgia of their Uncle Genl. Oglethorpe and that the Georgia laws ought to be repealed so as to agree with the treaty.

"Mr. Jefferson in reply to the C. Vergennes states the Case of the Nephews of Gen. Oglethorp, & proves that they were precluded from the Succession [to] their Uncles Estate for reasons altogether distinct from that of their alienism—respecting which are as well as their complaints of the existence of a State law in opposition to the treaty Mr. Jefferson says, 'the Treaty with France has placed the subjects of France on a Footing with Natives, as to conveyances & *Descent* of Property—there is no necessity for the Assemblies to pass laws on the subject, the Treaty being a law, as I conceive, superior to those of particular assemblies, & repealing them when they stand in the way of its Operation.'

"Extract of Mr. Jefferson letter to the Secy. of For. Affairs dated Jan 2. 1786.

"The case of the Chevalier Meziere and the Marquis Bellgarde.

"P.S. Argou's institutes is a work of authority and is with french lawyers what the Commentaries of Blackstone is with us." (AD, Hamilton Papers, Library of Congress.)

2. For the text of Article 8 of the Jay Treaty, see "Remarks on the Treaty . . . between the United States and Great Britain," July 9–11, 1795, note 42.

3. See "The Defence Nos. XXXVI, XXXVII, XXXVIII," January 2, 6, 9, 1796.

4. For the text of Article 9 of the Jay Treaty, see "Remarks on the Treaty . . . between the United States and Great Britain," July 9–11, 1795, note 43.

This article agrees that British subjects who *now hold* lands in the territories of the UStates and American Citizens who now *hold* lands in the dominions of his Britannic Majesty shall continue to hold them *according to the nature and tenure of their respective estates and titles therein;* and may grant sell or devise the same to whom they please in like manner as if they were natives; and that neither they nor their heirs or assigns *so far as may respect the said lands* and the legal remedies incident thereto *be regarded as aliens.*

The misapprehension of this article which was first ushered into public view in a very incorrect and insidious shape and was conceived to amount to the grant of an indefinite and permanent right to British subjects to hold lands in the U States [5] did more, it is believed, to excite prejudices against the Treaty, than any thing that is really contained in it. And yet when rightly understood it is found to be nothing more than a confirmation of those rights to lands, which prior to the Treaty the laws of the several states allowed British subjects to hold; with this inconsiderable addition perhaps, that the heirs and assigns of those persons, *though aliens*, may hold the same lands: But no right whatever is given to any lands of which our laws did not permit and legalise the acquisition.

These propositions will now be elucidated.

The term *hold* in the legal code of Great Britain & of these states has the same and that a precise technical sense. It imports a *capacity legally* and *rightfully* to *have* and *enjoy* real estate and is contradistinguished from the mere capacity of *taking* or *purchasing*, which is sometimes applicable to the acquisition of a thing that is forfieted by the very act of acquisition. Thus an alien may *take* real estate by *purchase* but he cannot *hold* it. *Holding* is synonymous with *tenure* which in the feudal system implies *fealty* of which an alien is in-incapable. Land therefore is forfieted to The Government the instant it passes to an alien. The Roman law nullifies the contract intirely, so that nothing passes by the grant of land to an alien but our law derived from that of England permits the land to pass for the purpose of forfieture to the State. This is not the case with regard to

5. This is apparently a reference to the analysis of Article 9 of the Jay Treaty by "Decius" (Brockholst Livingston) in *The* [New York] *Argus, or Greenleaf's New Daily Advertiser*, July 11, 1795. For the authorship of the "Decius" articles, see the introductory note to "The Defence No. I," July 22, 1795.

descent, because the succession or transmission there being an act of law, and the alien being disqualified to hold, the law consistent with itself casts no estate upon him.

The following legal authorities selected from an infinite number of similar import establish the above positions.

COKE on LYTTLETON Page 2. 3. "Some men have *capacity* to *purchase* but not *ability* to *hold.* Some *capacity* to *purchase* and ability to *hold* or *not* to *hold,* at the election of themselves and others. Some capacity to *take* and to *hold.* Some *neither capacity* to *take nor* to *hold.* And some specially disabled to *take* some *particular thing.* If an *alien* Christian or Infidel *purchase houses lands tenements or hereditaments* to him and his heirs, albeit he can have no heirs, yet he is of capacity to *take* a fee simple but not to *hold.*" [6] The same, Page 8 "If a man seized of lands in fee hath issue an *alien* he cannot be heir *propter defectum subjectionis.*" [7] Blackstones Commentaries Book II Ch: 18 § 2 No. 2 "Alienation to *an alien* is a cause of forfieture to the crown of the lands so alienated, not only on account of his *incapacity to hold* them [8] but likewise on account of his presumption in attempting by an act of his own to acquire real property." Idem Ch 19 § 1 "The case of an alien born is also peculiar. For he may *purchase* a thing but after purchase he can *hold* nothing except a lease for years of a house for the convenience of merchandize."

Thus it is evident, that by the laws of England which it will not be denied agree in principle with ours, an *alien* may *take* but cannot *hold* lands.

It is equally clear, that the laws of both countries agreeing in this particular the word *hold* used in the article under consideration must be understood according to those laws and therefore can only apply to those cases in which there was a *legal* capacity *to hold,* those in which our laws permitted the subjects and citizens of the two parties to *hold* lands in the territories of each other.[9]

6. Coke, *First Institutes,* Book I, Ch. I, Sec. 1, page 2b. See also "The Defence No. XI," August 28, 1795, note 25.

7. Book I, Ch. I, Sec. 1, page 8a.

8. Blackstone wrote: " . . . his incapacity to hold them which occasions him to be passed by in descents of land. . . ."

9. At this point in the draft H wrote and crossed out the following paragraphs: "It has constantly been admitted that the   article of the treaty of peace cooperating with the maxims of the common law protected all the

Whatever lands therefore may have been purchased by any British subject since the Treaty of Peace which the laws of the State wherein they were purchased did not permit him to acquire and hold are intirely out of the protection of the article under consideration. The purchase will not avail him. The forfieture which was incurred by it is still in full force. As to those lands which the laws of a State allowed him to purchase & hold he owes his title to them not to the Treaty.

Let us recur to the words of the article. "British subjects who *now hold* lands shall *continue* to *hold* them *according to the nature and tenure of their respective estates and titles therein.*" But it has been seen that to *hold* lands is to own them in a legal and competent capacity and that an alien has no such capacity. The lands therefore which by reason of the alienage of a British subject he could not prior to the Treaty legally purchase and hold, he cannot under the Treaty continue to hold.

As if it was designed to render this conclusion palpable the provision goes on to say "according to the nature and tenure of their respective estates and titles therein." This is equivalent to saying, they shall continue to hold as they before held. If they had no valid estate or title before they will of course continue to have none. The expressions neither give any new nor enlarge any old estate.

The succeeding clauses relate only to descents or alienations of the land originally legally holden. Here the disability of alienage is taken away from the heirs and assigns of the primitive proprietors.

While this will conduce to private justice by enabling the families and friends of the individuals to enjoy their property by descent or devise, which it is presumeable was the main object of the provision, there is no consideration of national policy that weighs against it. If we admit the whole force of the argument which opposes the expediency of permitting aliens to hold lands, (& concerning which I shall barely remark here that it is contrary to the practice of several

---

property of those British subjects who previous to the peace held land in the U States. The only difficulty in the case was the descent or conveyance of those rights to others. This difficulty is obviated by the last Treaty which protects the transmission of those lands to the heirs and assigns though aliens of the persons who were proprietors at the time of the peace—and this is the only alteration which is made by the article.

"I speak with respect to those States where the law concerning aliens has not been altered by particular statutes, as in the State of New York. In this."

of the states [10] and to a practice from which some of them have hitherto derived material advantages) the extent to which the principle is affected by the present Treaty is too limitted to be felt: and in the rapid mutations of property it will every day dimish. Every alienation of a parcel of the privileged land to a citizen of the U States will as to that land put an end to the future operation of the privilege, and the lapse of no great number of years may be expected to make an intire revolution in the property, so as to divest the whole of the privilege.

To manifest the unreasonableness of the loud and virulent clamour which was raised against this article, it has been observed by the friends of the Instrument that Our Treaty with France [11] not only grants a much larger privilege to the citizens of France but goes the full length of removing universally and perpetually from them the disability of alienism as to the ownership of lands. This position has been flatly denied by some of the writers on the other side. Decius [12] in particular after taking pains to shew that it is erroneous, that the terms "goods moveable and immoveable" in the [13] article of our Treaty with France mean only Chattels real and personal in the sense of our law, and exclude a right to the freehold or inheritance of lands, triumphantly plumes himself on the detection of a fallacy of the Writer of certain "Candid Remarks on the Treaty" [14] who gives the interpre[t]ation above stated to that article.

The error of Decius's interpretation proceeds from a misunderstanding of the term *goods* in the English translation of the article, to which he annexes the meaning assigned to that term in our law, instead of resorting as he ought to have done to the French laws for the true meaning of the correspondent term *"biens"* which is that used in the French original. Goods in our law no doubt mean chattel

10. For a discussion of alien ownership of land, see Robert Morris to H, June 7, 1795, note 37.
11. This is a reference to the Treaty of Amity and Commerce between the United States and France, February 6, 1778. See Miller, *Treaties,* II, 3–27.
12. See note 5.
13. Space left blank in MS, but H is referring to Article 11 (originally 13) of the Treaty of Amity and Commerce between the United States and France. For this article, see "Remarks on the Treaty . . . between the United States and Great Britain," July 9–11, 1795, note 47.
14. "Candid Remarks on the Treaty of Amity and Commerce between Great Britain and the United States" appeared in *The* [New York] *Daily Advertiser,* July 4, 1795.

—interests—but goods or "biens" in the French law mean all kinds of property *real* as well as *personal*. It is equivalent to and derived from the term BONA in the Roman law answering most nearly to "estates" in our law & embracing inheritances in land, corporeal and incorporeal hereditaments as well as property in moveable things. When it is necessary to distinguish one species from another it is done by the adjective "*biens meubles et immeubles*" answering to *bona* or *res mobilia et immobilia,* things moveable and immoveable, estates real and personal. The authorities at foot * will shew the analogy of these different terms in the three languages. But for fixing the precise sense of those used in the Treaty, I have selected and shall quote two authorities from French books which are clear and conclusive on the point. One will be found in the work of a French Lawyer intitled COLLECTIONS DE DECISIONS NOUVELLES ET DE NO-TIONS RELATIVES A LA JURISPRUDENCE ACTUELLE [16] under the Article BIENS [17]—and is in these words (viz) "The word *bien* has a general signification and comprehends *all sorts of possessions,* as *moveables, immoveables, purchases, acquisitions by marriage inheritances* &c. It is distinguished into these particulars, *moveables* and *immoveables purchases* and *inheritances,* subdividing inheritances *into paternal and maternal* old and new. Moveable *biens* are those which may be moved and transported from one place to another as wares merchandizes and current mony, plate, beasts household utensils &c. Immoveable *biens* are those which cannot be moved from one place to another as inheritances houses &c. *Biens* are distinguished again

* JUSTINIANS INSTITUTES Lib III Tit: X. XI. XII. XIII Lib IV Tit: II Domats' Civil & Public Law Prel: [15] Book   Tit: III Sect: I. II Book IV Sect I

15. Jean Domat, *Les Loix Civiles Dans Leur Ordre Naturel, le Droit Public, et Legum Delectus* (2nd edition, Paris, 1695). An English translation of this by William Strahan was published in London in 1722.

16. J. B. Denisart, *Collection de Décisions Nouvelles et de Notions Relatives à la Jurisprudence Actuelle* (7th edition, Paris, 1771).

17. In the newspaper a footnote was inserted at this point which does not appear in the draft. The note reads: "*Biens.* Le mot *bien* a une signification generale, & comprend toutes sorts de possessions, comme meubles, immeubles, acquéts, conquéts, propres, &c.

"On distingue dans les *biens* des particuliers, les meubles & les immeubles, les acquéts & les propres, & entre les propres, les paternels & les maternels, les anciens & les naissans. Les *biens* meubles sont ceux qui peuvent se mouvoir & se transporter d'un lieu en un autre, comme des denrees, des marchandises, de deniers comptans, de la vaisselle d'argent, des bestraux, des utensiles d'hotel. Les *biens* immeubles sont ceux qui ne peuvent se mouvoir ou se transporter d'un lieu dans un autre, comme des heritages, des maisons, &c."

into corporeal and incorporeal" Another [18] is drawn from the celebrated institutes of the French law by Mr. Argou [19] & is in these words "*Biens*—This is in general whatever composes our riches. There are two sorts of *biens*, moveable and immoveable—Moveable, all that may be transported from one place to another—Immoveable, lands or what are presumed to have the nature of lands. They are distinguished into two kinds real and fictitious. Real are not only the *substance of the earth*, which is called *Fonds*, but all that adheres to its surface, whether from nature, as Trees, or from the hand of man, as houses and other buildings. The others are called fictitious, because they are only *real* by fiction, as offices which are vendible & subject to fiscal reversions rent charges &c." The signification of *bona* in the Roman law corresponds as was observed above with that of *biens* in the French. "Bonorum appellatio universitatem quandam et non singulas res demonstrat" which may be thus rendered "The appellation BONA designates the totality of property or estate, and not particular things" and hence it is that the *cessio bonorum* of a debtor is the surrender of his whole fortune.

Both these terms "*bona*" and "*biens*" are indiscriminately translated "*goods*", *estates effects property.** In our treaty with France they are translated "goods." But it is evidently a great mistake to understand the expression in the limitted sense of our law. Being a mere word of translation, it must be understood according to the meaning of the French text. For it is declared in the conclusion of

* See authorities before cited.

See also Puffendorf Book VIII Ch V § VIII. Grotius Book III Chap V § XI. XII   Vatel Book I Chap XX § 245 246. 247.[20]

18. In the newspaper version of this essay a footnote was inserted at this point which does not appear in the draft. The note reads: "*Biens*—C'est en generale tout ce qui compose nos richesses; il y a deux sorts de *biens*, les meubles & les immeubles; meubles, tout ce qui peut etre transporte d'un lieu a un autre, immeubles—*Biens* en fonds, ou qui sont presume avoir la nature de fonds—On distingue deux sorts d'immeubles, les reels & les fictifs; les immeubles reel sont non seulment la substance meme de la terre qui est ce qu'on appelle le fond, mais tout ce qui est adherent a sa surface, soit par la nature comme les arbres, soit par la main des hommes, comme les maisons, & autre batiments—On a appelle l'autre espece d'immeubles, immeubles fictifs, parcequ'ils ne sont tels que par fiction: de ce nombre sont les offices venaux, casuels & les rentes constitutes." This quotation also appears in King's notes. See note 1.

19. H is referring to Gabriel Argou, *Institution au droit françois* . . . *Histoire du droit françois*, 2 Vols. (Paris, 1692).

20. For the titles of the books to which H is referring, see "The Defence No. XVI," September 18, 1795, notes 12, 13, and 15.

the Treaty, that it was originally composed and concluded in the French tongue. Moreover the term *goods,* when used in our language as the equivalent of the term *bona* or *biens* is always understood in the large sense of the original terms; in other words as comprehending real and personal estate, inheritances as well as chattel interests.

Having now established the true meaning of the terms "goods moveable and immoveable" let us proceed with this guide to a review of the article.[21]

Its first and principal feature is "that the subjects and inhabitants of the United States or of any of them shall not be reputed AUBAINS in France."

This is the same as if it had been said "they shall not be reputed aliens"—For the definition of AUBAINS as given in the work before first cited [22] is this "AUBAINS are persons who are not born under the dominion of the King"—the exact equivalent of the definition of ALIEN in the English law. If our citizens are not to be reputed aliens in France, it follows that they must be exempt from alien disabilities and must have the same rights with natives as to acquiring conveying and succeeding to real and other estate.

Accordingly the Article having pronounced that our citizens shall not be reputed *aliens* in France proceeds to draw certain consequences. The first is that they shall not be subject to the *droit d'aubaine.* The *droit d'aubaine* was under the monarchy one of the regalia—it was the right of the Prince to succeed to all estates or property, situate in the kingdom, belonging to foreigners who died without legitimate children born in the Kingdom.

It is to be observed that the laws of France permitted foreigners to acquire and hold even real estate, subject to this right of the sovereign in case of demise without issue born under his allegiance. But this right of the sovereign as to American Citizens is abrogated by the Treaty, so that their legal representatives wherever born, may succeed to all the property real or personal, which they may have acquired in France.

And in conformity with this, it is further declared that they may

21. See note 13.
22. See note 16.

by testament donation or otherwise dispose of their goods move-able and immoveable (that is as we have seen their estates real and personal) in favour of such persons as to them shall seem good and that their heirs, subjects of the U States, whether residing in France or elsewhere may succeed to them *ab intestato* without be-ing obliged to obtain letters of naturalization &c.

These are the stipulations on the part of France, and they amount to a removal from the citizens of the U States of alien disabilities as to property. I say as to property, because as to civil and ecclesi-astical employments it seems to have been a principle of the French law that the incapacity of foreigners could only be removed by special dispensations directed to the particular object.[23]

What are the correlative stipulations on the part of the U States. They are in these terms. "The subjects of the most Christian King shall enjoy on their part in all the dominions of the said States an *entire* and *perfect reciprocity* relative to the stipulations con-tained in this article, but it is at the same time agreed that its con-tents shall not affect the laws made or that may be made hereafter in France against emigrations, which shall remain in all their force and vigour, and the U States on their part or any of them shall be at liberty to enact such laws relative to that matter as to them shall seem proper."

Since then the article removes from our citizens the disabilities

23. The article "Etranger" in Pierre Jean Jacques Guillaume Guyot's *Réper-toire Universel et Raisonné de Jurisprudence Civile, Criminelle, Canonique et Beneficiale* . . . (Paris, 1784), VII, 114–17, states: ". . . Les Etrangers qui ne sont pas naturalisés par lettres du prince dûment enregistrées, ne peuvent posséder ni office, ni bénéfice, ni faire aucune fonction publique dans le royaume. Par arrêt du 24 juillet 1615, rendu entre les nobles de Bresse, Bugey, Gex & Valromey, & les officiers du présidial de Bourg, le conseil ordonna que les justices de ces seigneurs seroient excercées par les sujets du roi. . . .

"Dans les lettres de naturalité accordées à l'effet de pouvoir tenir des bénéfices dans le royaume, on a soin d'inférer, 1º que l'impétrant residéra en France & y finira ses jours; 2º qu'il ne pourra être pourvu de bénéfices qui conformément aux saints décrets, concordats, libertés & franchises de l'église gallicane. . . .

"Suivant l'article 4 de l'ordonnance de Blois, les Etrangers, quelques lettres de naturalité ou de dispense qu'ils aient obtenues, ne peuvent être pourvus d'archevêchés, d'évêchés, ni abbayes chefs d'ordre. Mais . . . le roi les relève de leur incapacité par une clause particulière. . . .

". . . Les Etrangers ne peuvent point être reçus au serment d'advocat, ni être principaux ou régens dans les universités. . . ."

of aliens as to property in France, and stipulates for her citizens an intire and perfect reciprocity in the UStates, it follows that Frenchmen are equally exempt in the U States from the like disabilities. They may therefore hold, succeed to, and dispose of real estates.

It appears that the sense both of the French and of the American Government has corresponded with this construction.

In the year 1786, the Marquis Bellegarde & The Chevalier Meziere sons of the two sisters of General Oglethorpe,[24] who claimed the lands of the General in Georgia, represented to the Count De Vergennes, the French Minister for foreign affairs, that they met with impediments to their claims from the laws of Georgia prohibiting aliens to hold lands.[25] Mr. Vergennes communicated their complaint to Mr. Jefferson our then Minister in France, observing that the alien disabilities of the complainants having in common with those of all Frenchmen been removed by the Treaty between the two Countries, they ought to experience no impediment on that account—in the succession to the estate of their uncle, and that the interfering laws of Georgia ought to be repealed so as to agree with the Treaty.

Mr. Jefferson in reply states the case of the complainants, proving that they are precluded from the succession for other reasons than that of alienism; and then adds, that as the Treaty with France has placed the subjects of France in the U States on a footing with natives as to conveyances and *descents* of property, there is no necessity for the assemblies to pass laws on the subject, the Treaty

24. The Chevalier de Mézières was the son of the oldest sister of General James Oglethorpe, the colonizer of Georgia. The Marquis de Bellegarde was the grandson, not the son, of one of Oglethorpe's sisters.

25. "An ACT for ascertaining the Rights of Aliens, and pointing out a Mode for the Admission of Citizens," passed in Georgia on February 7, 1785, states: "That all free white persons, being aliens, or subjects of any foreign state or kingdom at peace with the United States of America, who shall register or enrol their names in the office of the Clerk of the Superior Court of the county where such aliens purpose to reside, may be, and they are hereby vested with the rights and privileges of acquiring, possessing, or holding, and selling, devising, or otherwise disposing, of all kinds of personal property, and renting houses or lands from year to year, and shall have the right of suing for all such debts, demands, or damages, other than for real estate, as may arise, or have arisen since the twelfth July, one thousand seven hundred and eighty-two" (copy, Microfilm Collection of Early State Records, Library of Congress).

being a law, as he conceives, superior to those of particular assemblies and repealing them when they stand in the way of its operation.[26]

26. This information was given to H by Rufus King. See note 1.

The case of the Chevalier de Mézières is described by Thomas Jefferson in an enclosure to a letter to John Jay on January 2, 1786. The enclosure is Jefferson's account of a conversation which he had with Charles Gravier, Count de Vergennes, French Minister for Foreign Affairs. In his account, Jefferson included an "Amplification of Subjects Discussed with Vergennes" which he had written on or about December 20, 1785, and subsequently had handed to Joseph-Matthias Gerard de Rayneval, principal secretary to the Count de Vergennes. The "Amplification" described the Mézières case (and incidentally that of the Marquis de Bellegarde) as follows: "The Case of the Chevr. de Mezieres was supposed to furnish an instance of our Disregard to Treaties; and the Event of that Case was inferred from Opinions supposed to have been given by Mr. Adams and myself. This is ascribing a Weight to our Opinions to which they are not entitled. They will have no Influence on the Decision of the Case. The Judges in our courts would not suffer them to be read. Their Guide is the Law of the Land, of which Law its Treaties make a Part. Indeed I know not what Opinion Mr. Adams may have given on this Case. And if any be imputed to him derogatory of our Regard to the Treaty with France, I think his Opinion has been misunderstood. With Respect to myself, the Doubts which I expressed to the Chevr. de Mezieres as to the Success of his Claims, were not founded on any Question whether the Treaty between France and the United States would be observed. On the contrary I venture to pronounce that it will be religiously observed, if his Case comes under it. But I doubted whether it would come under the Treaty. The Case, as I understand it is this. Genl. Oglethorpe, a British subject, had Lands in Georgia. He died since the Peace, having devised these Lands to his Wife. His heirs are the Chevr. de Mezieres, Son of his eldest Sister, and the Marquis de Bellegarde, Son of his younger Sister. This Case gives Rise to legal Questions, some of which have not yet been decided, either in England or America, the Laws of which Countries are nearly the same. . . .

"Seeing no Event, in which, according to the Facts stated to me, the Treaty could be applied to this Case, or could give any Right whatever to Heirs of Genl. Oglethorpe, I advised the Chevr. de Mezieres not to urge his Pretensions on the Footing of Right, or under the Treaty, but to petition the Assembly of Georgia for a Grant of these Lands. If in the Question between the State and the Widow of Genl. Oglethorpe, it should be decided that they were the Property of the State, I counted on their Generosity and the friendly Dispositions in America towards the Subjects of France, that they would be favorable to the Chevr. de Mezieres. There is nothing in the preceding Observations which would not have applied against the Heir of Genl. Oglethorpe had he been a native Citizen of Georgia, as it now applies against him being a Subject of France. The Treaty has placed the Subjects of France on a footing with Natives as to Conveiances and Descent of Property. There was no Occasion for the Assemblies to pass Laws on this Subject, the Treaty being a Law, as I conceive, superior to those of particular Assemblies, and repealing them where they stand in the Way of its Operation." (Boyd, *Papers of Thomas Jefferson,* IX, 107-10, 136-46.)

Where now DECIUS is thy mighty Triumph? Where the trophies of thy fancied Victory? Learn that in political as in other science

"Shallow draughts intoxicate the brain—
And drinking largely sobers us again." [27]

The fixing the true sense of the article in the Treaty with Great Britain is alone a refutation of most of the objections which have been made to it by shewing that they apply not to what really exists but to a quite different thing. It may be useful however to pass them briefly in review with some cursory remarks.

The article, it is said, infringes the rights of the states & impairs the obligation of private contracts, permits aliens to hold real estates against the fundamental policy of our laws, and at the hazard of introducing a dangerous foreign influence—is unequal, because no American has been hardy enough since the peace to purchase land in England, while millions of acres have been purchased by British subjects in our country with knowlege of the risk—is not warranted by the example of any other Treaty we have made, for if even that of France should contain a similar provision (which is denied) still the difference of circumstances would make it an inapposite precedent, since this was a Treaty made *flagrante bello,* in a situation which justified sacrifices.

These objections have been formally and explicitly urged. One writer afraid of risking a direct assertion but insidiously endeavouring to insinuate misconception, contents himself with putting a question. What (says he) will be the effect of this article as to the revival of the claims of British subjects, traitors or exiles? [28]

As to the infraction of the rights of the states, this it is presumed must relate to the depriving them of forfietures of alien property. But as the article gives no right to a British subject to hold any lands, which the laws of a state did not previously authorise him to hold, it prevents no forfieture to which he was subject by them, and consequently deprives no state of the benefit of any such forfieture. With regard to escheats, for want of qualified heirs, it depended on every proprietor to avoid them by alienation to citizens.

27. This is a quotation from Alexander Pope, *Essay on Criticism.*
28. This point was made by Alexander J. Dallas in "Features of Jay's Treaty" (*Dunlap and Claypoole's* [Philadelphia] *American Daily Advertiser,* July 18, 1795).

As to impairing the obligation of private contracts it is difficult to understand what is meant. Since land purchased by an alien passes from the former proprietor & becomes forfieted to the State can it be afterwards the subject of a valid private contract? If the effect of the article was to confirm a defective title derived from the alien how could this impair the obligation of any other private contract concerning it? But whatever may be intended, it is enough to say that the article does not confirm the title to any land which was not before good, so that the ground of the objection fails.

As to permitting aliens to hold land contrary to the policy of our laws; it has been shewn that on a true construction it only applies to the very limitted case of the alien heirs and assigns of persons who before rightfully held lands, and is confined to the identical lands so previously holden, that its greatest effect must be insignificant, and that this effect will continually decrease.

As to the millions of acres said to have been purchased by British subjects, since the peace; it has been shewn that if by the laws of the States in which the purchases were made, they were illegally acquired, they still remain in the situation in which they were before the Treaty.

As to there being no precedent of a similar stipulation with any other country; it has been proved that with France we have one much broader. The idea that this was a sacrifice to the necessity of our situation *flagrante bello*, is new. Are we then to understand that we in this instance gave to France as the price of her assistance a privilege in our Country which leads to the introduction of a foreign influence dangerous to our independence and prosperity? For to this result, tends the argument concerning the policy of the exclusion of aliens. Or is it that no privilege granted to France can be dangerous?

Those who are not orthodox enough to adopt this last position may nevertheless tranquillise themselves about the consequences. This is not the channel through which a dangerous foreign influence can assail *us*. Notwithstanding all that has been said, it may perhaps bear a serious argument whether the permission to foreigners to hold lands in our country might not by the operation of private interest give us more influence upon foreign countries than they will ever acquire upon us from the holding of those lands. Be this as it may, could we not appeal to some *good patriots,* as they stile themselves by way of eminence for the truth of the observation that foreign Governments have more direct and powerful means of influence than can ever result from the right in question?

Moreover there was a peculiar reason for the provision which has been made in our last treaty not applicable to any Treaty with another Country. The former relative situation of the U States and Great Britain led to the possession of lands by the citizens of each in the respective territories. It was natural & just to secure by Treaty their free transmission to the heirs & assigns of the parties.

As to the revival of the claims of traitors or exiles; if property *confiscated* and *taken away,* is property *holden* by those who have been deprived of it, then may there be ground for alarm on this score. How painful is it to behold such gross attempts to deceive a whole people on so momentous a question! How afflicting that imposture and fraud should be so often able to assume with success the garb of Patriotism! And that this sublime virtue should be so frequently discredited by the usurpation & abuse of its name.

CAMILLUS

From Oliver Wolcott, Junior

Private   Phila. Sepr. 26. 1795

My dear Sir

I have recd. you Letter of the 20th. and regret the cause which deprived me of the pleasure of seeing you.

Nothing is *known* of the authors to which you allude. The "Features of the Treaty" were doubtless painted by Dallas.[1] Doctrs. Logan[2] & Leib,[3] Bache,[4] Beckley,[5] T. L. Shippen,[6] are much *suspected*—S. *Sayre*[7] of New Jersey is I understand very violent—perhaps the avowed intemperance of these men against the government is the only evidence against them. I can furnish no direct proof.

Mr. Randolph has published a *preface* which you have seen,[8] this is the opening of a new & very extraordinary campaign—perhaps you know something of the cause of his hostility. I consider

Mr. R. as perfectly desperate & malignant. He will do all the mischief in his power. His long acquaintance with our affairs—the predominating influence which he has possessed in those which concerned his own Department & his skill in misrepresentation furnish him with important advantages. Dallas is Councillor in all his Councils, and will of course prune away many indiscretions & render a bad cause as plausible as the nature of it will admit. I rely however upon the sense & virtue of the public, & trust that the truth will prevail.

The public affairs are certainly in a critical state. I do not clearly see how those of the Treasury are to be managed. Our foreign resources are dried up—our domestic are deeply anticipated at least as respects the Bank. Banks are multiplying like mushrooms—the prices of all our Exports are enhanced by paper negociations, and unfounded projects so that, no foreign market will indemnify the Shippers—our Commerce is harrased by the war & our internal resources unproductive of the expected sums, owing to prejudice, combination, & the want of competent officers. Usury absorbs much of that Capital, which might be calculated upon as a resource if visionary speculations could be destroyed.

You know however that I shall do the best in my power, & that intimations from you will always be thankfully recd.

I am assuredly yrs.   Oliv Wolcott Jr.

Colo. Hamilton

ALS, Hamilton Papers, Library of Congress; copy, Connecticut Historical Society, Hartford.

1. Alexander J. Dallas was secretary of the Commonwealth of Pennsylvania and one of the state's leading Republicans. Wolcott was correct in assuming that Dallas was the author of these articles, which were entitled "Features of Jay's Treaty" and were published in *Dunlap and Claypoole's* [Philadelphia] *American Daily Advertiser*, July 18, 22, 25, 31, August 7, 1795.

2. George Logan, a graduate in medicine from the University of Edinburgh, served in the Pennsylvania Assembly from 1785 to 1788. He became a Republican and as such was elected to the legislature in 1795, 1796, and 1799. He was a close friend of Thomas Jefferson.

3. Michael Leib, a prominent Philadelphia physician, was active in the Philadelphia Democratic Society and a Republican spokesman in the Pennsylvania legislature.

4. Benjamin Franklin Bache was editor of the [Philadelphia] *Aurora. General Advertiser*.

5. John Beckley of Virginia was clerk of the House of Representatives.

6. Thomas Lee Shippen was a Philadelphia Republican.

7. Stephen Sayre had been a London banker before the American Revolution. Arthur Lee appointed him secretary of his mission to Berlin in May, 1777. Subsequently he was a self-appointed agent for the United States to Copenhagen and Stockholm. After the war he returned to the United States and became a supporter of Francisco de Miranda. He repeatedly petitioned Congress for payment for his European activities during the Revolution. On March 3, 1807, Congress passed "An Act for the relief of Stephen Sayre" for services in Berlin (6 *Stat.* 65).

8. This is a reference to a letter which Edmund Randolph had written to George Washington on September 15, 1795, and which Randolph had released to the press for publication. This letter was part of Randolph's effort to clear himself of the charges which had arisen from the interception of Fauchet's Dispatch No. 10 and which had led to his resignation as Secretary of State. See Wolcott to H, July 30, 1795, note 1.

Randolph's letter to Washington reads: "In my letter of the 19th Ultimo, I informed you of my purpose to over take Mr. Fauchet, if possible. I accordingly went to Newport in Rhode Island; where I had an interview with him. The abrupt and unexpected sailing of the French Frigate, La Meduse, on the morning of the day, after I arrived there, had nearly deprived me of the object of my journey. But I trust, that I am in possession of such materials, not only from Mr. Fauchet, but also from other sources, as will convince every unprejudiced mind, that my resignation was dictated by considerations, which ought not to have been resisted for a moment, and that every thing, connected with it, stands upon a footing perfectly honorable to myself.

"Having passed thro' New-York on my return, I am under the necessity of remaining at the distance of five miles from Philadelphia until saturday next. This circumstance prevents me from consulting my private and other papers upon the matters in question. But I shall lose no time in digesting them into proper form, and on transmitting the result to you. Nor will my solicitude on this head be doubted, when I state to you, that malicious whispers have been more than commonly active and absurd upon this occasion." (ALS, RG 59, Miscellaneous Letters, 1790–1799, National Archives.) This letter is printed in *The* [New York] *Argus, or Greenleaf's New Daily Advertiser,* September 23, 1795.

To Oliver Wolcott, Junior

New York October 3. 1795

Dear Sir

I have received your letter of the [1] and thank you for the information. As to Randolph, I shall be surprised at nothing—but if the facts come out, his personal influence is at all events damned. No colouring will remove unfavourable impressions. To do mischief he must work in the Dark.

What you say respecting your own department disquiets me; for I think we shall for the present weather all storms but those from real deficiencies in our public arrangements. Not knowing details I can attempt to suggest nothing except this general observation—that if the means heretofore provided are seriously likely to prove inadequate—Congress ought to be explicitly told so in order to a further provision. It was a maxim in my mind that Executive arrangements should not fail for want of full disclosure to the Legislature. Then if adequate provision be not made the responsibility is theirs. The worst evil we can struggle with is *inefficiency* in the measures of Government.

If I remember right, it never appeared that Fauchet[2] had any power to make a Commercial Treaty with us and the late Attorney General (Bradford)[3] informed me that *Adet*[4] had power only *to treat* none to *conclude.* How are these things? I ask for special reasons.[5]

What is the object of the Dispatch boat from France?[6] Nothing menacing I hope.

Mrs. Hamilton joins me in affect Compliments to Mrs. Wolcott. Adieu.

Yrs. with great   A Hamilton

O Wolcott Esq

ALS, Connecticut Historical Society, Hartford; extract, in the handwriting of H, Hamilton Papers, Library of Congress; copy, Hamilton Papers, Library of Congress.

1. Although H omitted the date, he is referring to Wolcott's letter of September 26, 1795.
2. Jean Antoine Joseph Fauchet, who succeeded Edmond Charles Genet as French Minister to the United States, arrived in the United States in February, 1794.
3. William Bradford had died on August 23, 1795. George Washington asked Charles Lee of Virginia to accept the position on November 19, 1795 (ALS, George Washington Papers, Library of Congress; LC, George Washington Papers, Library of Congress). Lee, who had served as collector of customs at Alexandria from 1789 to 1793 and as a member of the General Assembly of Virginia for Fairfax County from 1793 to 1795, accepted Washington's offer on November 30, 1795 (ALS, George Washington Papers, Library of Congress).
On December 9, 1795, Washington sent Lee's nomination to the Senate, and the appointment was confirmed the following day (*Executive Journal,* I, 193).
4. Pierre Auguste Adet succeeded Fauchet as French Minister in June, 1795. For Adet's authority to negotiate a commercial treaty, see Adet to Edmund Randolph, June 20, 1795, and "Extract from the instructions given to P. A. Adet Minister Plenipotentiary of the French Republic, near the United States of America by the Committee of Public Safety of the National

Convention charged by the law of 7 Fructidor 2d year, with the direction of foreign affairs" (*Correspondence of the French Ministers with the United States Government*, Nos. 110 and 111).

5. The "special reasons" refer to H's preparation of the "Camillus" essays. In "The Defence No. XXIV," November 14, 1795, which was drafted by Rufus King, H added a paragraph in which he discussed the inability of Adet and Fauchet to conclude a commercial treaty.

6. On October 2, 1795, *The* [New York] *Argus, or Greenleaf's New Daily Advertiser* printed the following item: "Yesterday the sloop of war the Ranger, belonging to the Republic of France, arrived at this port with DISPATCHES for the minister of the Republic in America, and our government. She sailed from Brest on the 11th of August, and confirms the account of Peace with Spain." The Treaty of Basel between France and Spain had been concluded on July 22, 1795.

From Samuel Ogden[1]

Newark [*New Jersey*] *October 5, 1795.* "Being informed that Mr Dessasure[2] has lately resigned his Office as director of the Mint; and that several Characters of the very first respectability of this State, have recommended to the President of the United States, David Ford,[3] as a proper person to succeed him; I take up my pen to inform you, that I think him very well Quallified to fill that Office, and that I believe, as a Man, of Business, and strict integrity, none will be found to exceed him, or give more general satisfaction. . . ."[4]

ALS, Hamilton Papers, Library of Congress.

1. Ogden, the brother-in-law of Gouverneur Morris and the founder of Ogdensburg, New York, was a New Jersey iron manufacturer and land speculator.

2. David Rittenhouse had resigned as Director of the Mint in June, 1795, and was succeeded by Henry William De Saussure on July 9. For De Saussure's temporary commission, see Edmund Randolph to De Saussure, July 9, 1795 (LC, RG 59, Domestic Letters of the Department of State, Vol. 8, December 6, 1794–October 12, 1795, National Archives). Although De Saussure wished to resign at the end of September, 1795 (De Saussure to George Washington, September 7, 1795 [ALS, RG 59, Miscellaneous Letters, 1790–1799, National Archives]), he remained in office until October 28, 1795 (RG 217, Miscellaneous Treasury Accounts, 1790–1894, Account Nos. 7228, 7302, National Archives). See also Washington to De Saussure, November 1, 1795 (ALS, George Washington Papers, Library of Congress; LC, George Washington Papers, Library of Congress), and De Saussure to Washington, November 1, 1795 (ALS, George Washington Papers, Library of Congress).

3. Captain David Ford of the New Jersey militia applied to Washington for the position of Director of the Mint on September 5, 1795 (ALS, George Washington Papers, Library of Congress). His application was supported by letters of recommendation from Richard Forrest to Washington, August 29,

1795, from J. J. Feasch to Washington, August 27, 1795, and from Theodore Frelinghuysen to Oliver Wolcott, Jr., August 28, 1795 (ALS, George Washington Papers, Library of Congress).

4. Ford did not receive the appointment. On September 10, 1795, Acting Secretary of State Timothy Pickering offered the position to Elias Boudinot, a New Jersey lawyer and businessman who had been a member of the House of Representatives from March 4, 1789, to March 3, 1795 (ALS, George Washington Papers, Library of Congress). Boudinot accepted the offer on September 16 (ALS, George Washington Papers, Library of Congress). As Congress was not in session, Boudinot received a temporary commission on October 28, 1795 (Pickering to Boudinot [LS, RG 59, Domestic Letters of the Department of State, Vol. 9, October 12, 1795–February 28, 1797, National Archives]). Washington nominated Boudinot on December 10, 1795, and the Senate agreed to his appointment on the following day (*Executive Journal*, I, 194, 195).

The Defence No. XVIII [1]

[New York, October 6, 1795]

It is provided by The tenth article of the Treaty that "Neither Debts due from individuals of the one Nation to Individuals of the other, nor shares nor monies, which they may have in the public funds, or in the public or private banks, shall ever in any event of War or national differences be sequestered or confiscated, it being unjust and impolitic that debts and engagements contracted and made by individuals having confidence in each other and in their respective Governments should ever be destroyed or impaired by national authority on account of National Differences and Discontents."

The virulence with which this article has been attacked [2] cannot fail to excite very painful sensations in every mind duly impressed with the sanctity of public faith and with the importance of national credit and character; at the same time that it furnishes the most cogent reasons to desire that the preservation of peace may

ADf, Hamilton Papers, Library of Congress; *The* [New York] *Argus, or Greenleaf's New Daily Advertiser*, October 6, 1795.

1. For background to this document, see the introductory note to "The Defence No. I," July 22, 1795.

2. For examples of criticism of Article 10 of the Jay Treaty, see Alexander J. Dallas's "Features of Jay's Treaty" (*Dunlap and Claypoole's* [Philadelphia] *American Daily Advertiser*, July 18, 1795) and the article by "Decius" (Brockholst Livingston) in *The* [New York] *Argus, or Greenleaf's New Daily Advertiser*, July 13, 1795. For the authorship of these articles, see the introductory note to "The Defence No. I," July 22, 1795.

obviate the pretext and the temptation to sully the honor and wound the interests of the country by a measure which the truly enlightened of every nation would condemn.

I acknowlege without reserve that in proportion to the vehemence of the opposition against this part of the Treaty is the satisfaction,[3] I derive from its existence; as an obstacle the more to the perpretation, of a thing which in my opinion besides deeply injuring our real and permanent interest would cover us with ignominy. No powers of language at my command can express the abhorrence I feel at the idea of violating the property of individuals which in an authorised intercourse in time of peace has been confided to the faith of our Government and Laws, on account of controversies between Nation and Nation. In my view Every moral and every political sentiment unite to consign it to execration.

Neither will I dissemble that the dread of the effects of the spirit which patronises that idea has ever been with me one of the most persuasive arguments for a pacific policy on the part of the UStates. Serious as the evil of War has appeared at the present stage of our affairs the manner in which it was to be apprehended it might be carried on was still more formidable than the thing itself. It was to be feared that in the fermentation of certain wild opinions, those wise just & temperate maxims which will for ever constitute the true security & felicity of a state would be overruled & that a war upon credit, eventually upon property and upon the general principles of public order might aggravate and embitter the ordinary calamities of foreign war. The confiscation of debts due to the enemy might have been the first step of this destructive process. From one violation of justice to another the passage is easy. Invasions of right still more fatal to credit might have followed, & this by extinguishing the resources which that could have affarded might have paved the way to more comprehensive & more enormous depredations for a substitute. Terrible examples were before us and there were too many not sufficiently remote from a disposition to admire and imitate them.

The earnest and extensive clamours against the part of the Treaty

3. At this point in the draft H wrote and then crossed out the following: "... is my satisfaction (which gives greater cause than I had imagined to suppose it possible that a conduct contrary to the principle it contains might be obtruded in our public Councils)."

under consideration confirm that anticipation, and while they enhance the merit of the provision, they also inspire a wish that some more effectual barrier had been erected against the possibility of a contrary practice ever being at any ill fated moment obtruded upon our public Councils. It would have been an inestimable gem in our national constitution had it contained a positive prohibition against such a practice; [4] except *perhaps* by way of reprisal for the identical injury on the part of another Nation.

Analagous to this is that liberal and excellent provision in the [5] British *Magna Charta* which declares that * "if the Merchants of a Country at war with England are found there in the beginning of the War, they shall be attached without harm of body or *effects*, till it is known in what manner English Merchants are treated in the enemy Country; and if they are safe that the foreign Merchants shall also be safe." The learned Coke pronounces this to be the *jus belli* or law of War: [6] And the elegant and enlightened Montesquieu

Note * Si Mercatores sint de terra contra nos guerrina et tales inveniantur in terra nostra in principio guerrae attachientur sine damno corporum suorum vel *rerum* donec sciatur a nobis vel a Capitali Justiciario nostro quo modo Mercatores terrae nostrae tractantur qui tunc inveniantur in terra illa contra nos guerrina; Et si nostri salvi sint ibi alii salvi sint in terra Nostra. *Magna Charta Cap* XXX.

4. H originally wrote this sentence as follows: ". . . prohibition against the forfeiture or seizure of any property which strangers in an authorised intercourse in time of peace had committed to the faith of our Government and laws."

5. At this point in the draft H wrote and crossed out the following; "The cause, which is given by the clamours against the prohibition in the Treaty, to suspect it possible that a practice contrary to the principle of it might at some inauspicious moment be obtruded on our public Councils is of a nature not only to reconcile us the more to that provision but to inspire a strong wish that our Constitution had opposed a perpetual bar to a practice inconsistent with it—except perhaps towards us on the part of another Nation. In this sense Montesquieu understands that the clause of the British MAGNA CHARTA. . . ."

6. This is taken from Coke's commentary on Chapter 30 of the Magna Charta, which reads: "Now touching Merchant Strangers, whose Sovereign is in War with the King of England.

"There is an exception, and provision for such, as be found in the Realm at the beginning of the War, they shall be attached with a priviledge and limitation, Viz. without harm of body, or goods, with this limitation, until it be known to us, or our Chief Justice (that is our Gardian, or keeper of the Realm in our absence) how our Merchants there in the Land in War with us shall be intreated, and if our Merchants be well intreated there, theirs shall be likewise with us, and this is *jus belli*. *Et in republica maxime conservanda sunt jura belli*.

"But for such Merchant strangers as come into the Realm after the War

speaking of the same provision breaks out into this exclamation[b]—
"It is noble that the English Nation have made this one of the articles
of its Liberty." How much is it to be regretted that our *Magna
Charta* is not unequivocally decorated with a like feature; and that
in this instance we who have given so many splendid examples to
mankind are excelled in constitutional precaution for the mainte-
nance of Justice.

There is indeed ground to assert that the contrary principle
would be repugnant to that article of our constitution which provides that "No state shall pass any law impairing the obligation of
Contracts." The spirit of this clause though the letter of it be restricted to the States individually must on fair construction be
considered as a rule for the UStates and if so could not easily
be reconciled with the confiscation or sequestration of private debts
in time of war. But it is a pity that so important a principle should
have been left to inference & implication and should not have received an express and direct sanction.

This position must appear a frightful heresy in the eyes of those
who represent the confiscation or sequestration of Debts as our
best means of retaliation and coertion, as our most powerful, sometimes as our only weapon of defence.

But so degrading an idea will be rejected with disdain by every
man who feels a true and well informed national pride, by every
man who recollects and glories that in a state of still greater immaturity we atchieved independence without the aid of this dis-

---

beginn, they may be dealt withall as open enemies: and yet of ancient time
three men had priviledge granted them in time of War. *Clericus, Agricola, &
mercator, tempori belli. Ut oretq; colat, commutet, pace fruuntur.*" (Sir Edward Coke, *The Second Part of the Institutes of the Laws of England: Containing The Exposition of many ancient, and other Statutes, Whereof you
may see the particulars in a Table following* [London: Printed by W. Raw-
lins, for Thomas Basset at the George near St. Dunstan's Church in Fleet-
street, 1681], 57–58.)

   b Spirit of Laws Book XX Ch XIV.[7]

   7. Charles Louis de Secondat, Baron de La Brède et de Montesquieu, *De
l'esprit des loix, ou Du rapport que les loix doivent avoir avec la constitution
de chaque gouvernement, les moeurs, le climat, la religion, le commerce, &c,
à quoi l'auteur a ajouté des recherches nouvelles, sur les loix romaines tou-
chant les successions, sur les loix françoises, et sur les loix feodales* (Geneva:
Barrillot & Fils, 1748).

honorable expedient; * [8] that even in a revolutionary War a war of Liberty against usurpation our national Councils were never provoked or tempted to depart so widely from the path of rectitude by every man who though careful not to exaggerate for rash and extravagant projects can nevertheless fairly estimate the real resources of the Country for meeting dangers which prudence cannot avert.

Such a man will never endure the base doctrine that our security is to depend on the tricks of a Swindler. He will look for it in the courage and constancy of a free brave and virtuous people—in the riches of a fertile soil—an extended and progressive industry—in the wisdom and energy of a well constituted & well administered Government—in the resources of a solid, if well supported, national Credit—in the armies which if requisite could be raised—in the means of maritime annoyance which if necessary we could be organised and with which we could inflict deep wounds on the commerce of a hostile nation. He will indulge an animating consciousness, that while our situation is not such as to justify our courting imprudent enterprises, neither is it such as to oblige us in any event to stoop to dishonorable means of security or to substitute a crooked and piratical policy for the manly energies of fair and open war.

What is the consequence of the favourite doctrine that The confiscation or sequestration of private Debts is our most powerful if not our only weapon of defence? Great Britain is the only Power against whom we could wield it; since tis to her citizens alone that ours are largely indebted. What are we to do then against any

---

* The Fœderal Government never resorted to it, and a few only of the State Governments stained themselves with it.[9] It may perhaps be said that the Fœderal Government had no power on the subject; but the reverse is truly the case. The Fœderal Government alone had power. The State Governments had not though some of them undertook to exercise it. This position is founded on the solid ground that the confiscation or sequestration of the debts of an enemy is a high act of reprisal and War necessarily & exclusively incident to the power of making war which was always in the Fœd Govt.

8. At this point H wrote and then crossed out the following insertion: "while with one breath they march us to war with Great Britain on the ground that we can meet her on terms not only of equal but of superior advantage in another."

9. See "Remarks on the Treaty . . . between the United States and Great Britain," July 9-11, 1795, note 50.

other Nation which might think fit to menace us? Are we for want of adequate means of defence to crouch beneath the uplifted rod and sue for mercy? Or has providence guaranteed us specially against the malice or ambition of every power on earth but Great Britain?

Tis at once curious & instructive to mark the inconsistencies of the disorganising sect. Is the question to discard a spirit of accommodation and seek war with Great Britain? Columns are filled with the most absurd exaggerations to prove that we are able to meet her not only on equal but upon superior terms. Is the question—Whether a stipulation against the confiscation or sequestration of private debts ought to have been admitted into the Treaty? Then are we a people destitute of the means of war—with neither armies fleets nor magazines—then is our best if not our only weapon of defence—the power of confiscating or sequestrating the debts which are due to the subjects of Great Britain—in other words the power of committing fraud of violating public faith of sacrificing the principles of commerce of prostrating Credit.

Is the question—whether free ships shall make free goods, whether naval stores shall or shall not be deemed contraband? Then the appeal is to what is called the *modern* law of Nations then is the cry that recent usage has changed and mitigated the rigor of ancient maxims. But is the question whether private debts can be rightfully confiscated or sequestered? Then the utmost rigour of the ancient doctrine is to govern and modern usage and opinion are to be discarded. The old rule or the new is to be adopted or rejected just as may suit our convenience.

An inconsistency of another kind but no less curious is observable in a position, repeatedly heared from the same quarter, namely that the sequestration of Debts is the only *peaceable* mean of doing ourselves justice and avoiding war. If we trace the origin of the pretended right to confiscate or sequester Debts—We find it & that in the very authority principally relied upon to prove it to be this—(Bynkershoek Questiones Juris Publici [10] L I C II) "Since it is the *condition* of WAR that ENEMIES may be deprived of all their rights, it is reasonable that every thing of an ENEMY's found among his ENEMIES should change its owner and go to the Treasury." Hence

10. Bynkershoek, *Quæstionum.* The reference is to Chapter VII (not Chapter II), Sec. 52.

it is manifest that the right itself, if it exists, presupposes as the condition of its exercise an actual state of War and the relation of enemy to enemy. Yet we are fastidiously told that this high and explicit act of war, is a *peaceable* mean of doing ourselves justice and avoiding war. Why are we thus told—Why is this strange paradox attempted to be imposed upon us—Why but that it is the policy of the conspirators against our peace to endeavour to disguise the hostilities into which they wish to plunge us with a specious outside and to precipitate us down the precipice of War while we imagine we are quietly and securely walking along its summit.

Away with these absurd and degrading sophisms. Blush ye Apostles of temerity of meaness & Deception. Cease to beckon us to war and at the same to freeze our courage by the cowardly declaration that we have no resource but in fraud. Cease to attempt to persuade us that peace may be maintained by means which constitute War. Cease to tell us that War is preferable to dishonor; and yet as our first step urge us into irretrievable dishonor. A magnanimous a sensible people cannot listen to your crude lessons. Why will ye persevere in accumulating ridicule and contempt upon your own heads?

In the further observations which I shall offer on this article [11] I hope to satisfy not ye but all discerning men and good citizens that instead of being a blemish, it is an ornament to the instrument in which it is contained; that it is as consistent with true policy as with substantial justice [12] & that the objections to it are futile.[13]

11. See "The Defence Nos. XIX and XX," October 14, 23 and 24, 1795.
12. In the newspaper this sentence ends with the following: "that it is in substance, not without precedent in our other treaties, and that the objections to it are futile."
13. In the margin opposite the end of the paragraph H wrote and crossed out: "note zeal for confiscation one of the greatest objections to War."

To Robert Morris

[*New York, October 6, 1795.* On October 8, 1795, Morris wrote to Hamilton: "I have received your letter of the 6th." *Letter not found.*]

From Oliver Wolcott, Junior

Phila. Oct. 6. 1795

Dear Sir (Private)

I will in a few days inform you of the facts upon which my former Letter [1] was predicated.

The inclosed case of the Betsey [2] Capt. Furlong [3] excites much alarm here & I think with reason: the same principles will extirpate nine tenths of our claims for spoliations & lead to new assaults upon our Commerce.

I wish to know your opinion of the *mode of proceeding* under the 7th. Article of our Treaty with England.[4] Must *all cases* go

ALS, Hamilton Papers, Library of Congress; copy, Connecticut Historical Society, Hartford.

1. Wolcott to H, September 26, 1795.

2. On October 3, 1795, Timothy Pickering, Acting Secretary of State, received a "packet" describing the outcome of the case of the *Betsey* from Samuel Bayard, who was the United States agent representing the claims of United States citizens before the prize courts in England (Pickering to George Washington, October 5, 1795 [LC, RG 59, Domestic Letters of the Department of State, Vol. 8, December 6, 1794–October 12, 1795, National Archives]).

John Bassett Moore has summarized the facts in this case as follows: "The claimants in this case were William and George Patterson, citizens of the United States and partners in trade, resident and carrying on business at Baltimore, in the State of Maryland. The Brigantine *Betsey*, an American vessel and the sole property of George Patterson, sailed on December 19, 1793, from Baltimore to the French island of Guadaloupe, in the West Indies, with a cargo belonging jointly to the two partners and consisting chiefly of provisions. George Patterson was aboard as supercargo. The *Betsey* arrived at Guadaloupe on January 8, 1794, and soon afterwards the administration of the island took the provisions by force, but with a promise to pay for them. George Patterson then loaded the vessel with a return cargo of produce of the island, but remained at Guadaloupe for the purpose of obtaining payment for the first cargo. The vessel was captured two days out from Guadaloupe by a British privateer, and was taken to Bermuda and condemned" (Moore, *International Adjudications*, IV, 179). In the summer of 1795 the High Court of Admiralty in London upheld the condemnation of the *Betsey* by the Vice Admiralty Court in Bermuda (Moore, *International Adjudications*, IV, 182).

For an extensive discussion of the issues which were raised by this case and which are discussed by Wolcott in the above letter, see H to Washington, April 25, 1794; Pickering to William Lewis and William Rawle, October 6, 1795; and Pickering to John Jay, October 10, 1795 (LC, RG 59, Domestic Letters of the Department of State, Vol. 8, December 6, 1794–October 12, 1795, National Archives).

3. William Furlong.

4. For the text of Article 7 of the Jay Treaty, see "Remarks on the Treaty . . . between the United States and Great Britain," July 9–11, 1795, note 39.

through a process of litigation before the English *Courts*, before they are submitted to Commissioners? If so, for what purpose? Is the *"legality* or *illegality* the *regularity* or *irregularity"* [5] of a capture to be determined solely in those Courts? Or will the Commissioners take up claims de novo. This is an interesting question for there is now little doubt, but that the Commissioners of Appeals, will *affirm* most of the judgments of condemnation.

My doubt on this subject principally arises, from finding, that the 6th. article [6] provides for the British debts in the same manner as the 7th. provides for the spoliation cases & moreover defines the cases to be those where relief cannot be had in the *ordinary course of judicial proceedings.* Now it appears to me that it would be a very dilatory expensive & unnecessary process to compel an Englishman to travel through our Courts merely to ascertain that they could not do him justice, & to prepare his case for the Commissioners. The same objections exist against a similar operation in the British Courts of Admiralty. Is it not therefore the meaning of the Treaty, that *Commissioners* shall *settle* both descriptions of claims & award compensation according to principles of *equity?* And if this is the case, why is Mr. Bayard trying questions which are decided against him, at an expence which he estimates may amount to 75.000 £ Sterling.

I must own I do not *see through this business*, & though you may think it strange, I beg you to remember that I knew *nothing* concerning the Treaty 'till *lately*, & cannot devote much time to it without sacrificing objects more immediately in the line of my duty.

The fact is, that the old doctrines of *inalienable allegiance*,[7] & that Neutrals may not in *time of War* carry on a Commerce *inhibited in time of Peace*,* [8] are to be advanced against the United States, & from present appearances, they will govern the Courts of Admiralty.

* also the *new* doctrine that places can be *blockaded* by *proclamation.*[9]

5. The first sentence of Article 7 refers to "irregular or illegal Captures or Condemnations of . . . vessels."

6. For the text of Article 6, see "Remarks on the Treaty . . . between the United States and Great Britain," July 9–11, 1795, note 13.

7. See William Bradford and H to Edmund Randolph, November 4–December 9, 1794, note 4.

8. This is a reference to the British Rule of 1756, or the Rule of the War of 1756, which was applied for the first time in the Seven Years' War by British prize courts.

9. For example, see the British order in council of June 8, 1793 (*ASP, Foreign Relations*, I, 240). A slightly different version of this document is printed in Moore, *International Adjudications*, IV, 14–15. See "Remarks on

The effects which these principles will have, I need not state to you —if all this subject cannot be taken up by Commissioners & compromised equitably, the discussion of the Claims, will work infinite mischief. I wish therefore to see some way in which Mr. Bayards agency at the British *Courts* might be arrested.

Mr. Fauchet made no overtures relative to a Treaty of any kind. Mr. Adet says he is authorised to *digest* a new Treaty of Commerce & a new Consular Convention but not to *conclude*. Mr. Randolph agreed to meet him on this ground, but nothing has been done that I know of.[10]

I know nothing of dispatches;[11] the French Minister is reserved; he thinks more than he expresses, & his expressions breath something of disatisfaction. We are I think in no very good way, but must make the best of circumstances. What you say of *efficiency* is true,[12] but there are no *materials* to be efficient with. Colonel Pickering & myself are perfectly agreed & he is as firm industrious & intelligent as any body could wish—there is however a mass of business, & few of that class of men in the public service who understand details & endeavour to keep things in order. Even our able Clerks cannot be retained—several have actually gone.

Be pleased to present my respects to Mrs. Hamilton & believe me ever yours

Oliv. Wolcott.

Col A. Hamilton

N B. I have found your *Ordinnance de la Marine*, but have no way to send it.[13]

---

the Treaty . . . between the United States and Great Britain," July 9–11, 1795, note 66.

10. The statements in this paragraph consist of answers to questions which H asked Wolcott in his letter of October 3, 1795. On October 6, 1795, Pickering wrote to Wolcott: "Mr. [George] Taylor informs me that Mr. [Jean Antoine Joseph] Fauchet never, to his knowledge, made even any *overtures* relative to a treaty of any kind. I have cast my eye over those of Mr. [Pierre Auguste] Adet, by which it appears that he is authorized to 'digest' with the American Government a new treaty of commerce & a new consular convention; but not to *conclude* any thing. Mr. Randolph agreed to meet him on this ground. If the articles digested should meet the approbation of the respective governments, they might give full powers to constitute of those articles the proposed new treaties" (ALS, Connecticut Historical Society, Hartford). See H to Wolcott, October 3, 1795, note 4.

11. H to Wolcott, October 3, 1795.

12. H to Wolcott, October 3, 1795.

13. See Wolcott to H, July 10, 1795. This is presumably a reference to the famous "Ordonnance de la Marine" issued by Louis XIV in August,

1681. According to Andreas Lange, an edition of the "Ordonnance" was published in Paris in 1687 (*Brevis Introductio in Notitiam Legum Nauticarum et Scriptorum Juris Reique Maritimae* [Lübeck, 1713], 73–74). It is also included in Isambert, *Recueil Général des Anciennes Lois Françaises*, XIX, 282–366.

From Robert Morris

Alexander Hamilton Esqre   Phila 8 Octo. 1795
New York

Dear Sir

I have received your letter of the 6th [1] at a moment when I am extreamly hurried in preparing letters Papers &ca. &ca. for the Dispatch of my Son in Law James Marshall [2] Esqr for Europe. My Daughter [3] goes with him and they expect to Sail on Sunday. I must therefore pray your Excuse untill they are gone when I will take up the Subject [4] of your letter I expect to your satisfaction notwithstanding the pressure of the times.

Yrs.   RM

LC, Robert Morris Papers, Library of Congress.
    1. Letter not found.
    2. James Marshall was about to leave for Europe as the representative of both Morris and the North American Land Company. See the introductory note to Morris to H, June 7, 1795.
    3. Hetty Morris Marshall was James Marshall's wife.
    4. The "Subject" was either Morris's debt to H or his debt to John B. Church. See the introductory note to H to Morris, March 18, 1795, and the introductory note to Morris to H, June 7, 1795.

To James Greenleaf [1]

New York October 9. 1795

Sir

You request my opinion [2] of your title to the lands lately purchased by you of James Gunn and his Associates called the Georgia Company.[3] I wish it was more in my power than it is to give you one embracing the whole subject, but never having had an opportunity of examining the title of the state of Georgia, I can pronounce nothing on that head. I can only say that from all that came under my observation, in the course of the transaction between you and

Messrs. Prime and Ward,[4] acting as their counsel—I have drawn
this conclusion, that if Georgia at the time of the grant to Messieurs
Gun & Company; was in capacity to make a valid title to them,
your title to the lands you have purchased from them is then also
valid. In saying this, I take for granted the execution of the measures,
which I was informed were in train for completing the payment of
the consideration money to Georgia and cancelling the mortgage;[5]
and I must be understood as only speaking of *the right of preemption*, with regard to all such lands as may not have been regularly
acquired from the Indians, of which alone Georgia could have power
to dispose

　　With esteem I am Sir　Your Obed servant

James Greenleaf Esq

ADf, Hamilton Papers, Library of Congress.
　　1. Greenleaf, a native of Massachusetts and a partner with James Watson
in the former New York City mercantile firm of Watson and Greenleaf,
speculated extensively in land and securities. In March, 1793, he was appointed United States consul at Amsterdam (*Executive Journal*, I, 136). In
1793, Greenleaf, Robert Morris, and John Nicholson made vast purchases of
land in the Federal City. See H to Morris, March 18, 1795, note 21; Morris to
H, June 7, 1795, note 7.
　　2. H's opinion, dated October 10, 1795, reads: "Having acted as Counsel
for Messrs. Prime and Ward, in a purchase made by them of James Greenleaf, of certain lands granted by the State of Georgia to Messrs. Gunn and
his associates—I certify that Mr. Greenleaf had deposited with me a deed of
conveyance for the same and that Messrs. Prime and Ward have given their
bond for the performance of the Stipulations on their part" (ADS, Dickinson
College Library, Carlisle, Pennsylvania; also in forthcoming Goebel, *Law
Practice*, III).
　　An entry in H's Cash Book, 1795–1804, under the date of October 12,
1795, reads: "James Greenleaf Dr. . . . on question concerning a certain
contract & retainer as Counsel 10—" (AD, Hamilton Papers, Library of
Congress, also in forthcoming Goebel, *Law Practice*, III).
　　3. Gunn, a Federalist member of the United States Senate from Georgia,
was the most important member of the Georgia Yazoo Company. See H to
Rufus King, June 20, 1795, note 2.
　　The first Yazoo land companies had collapsed by the middle of 1791. See
"The Defence of the Funding System," July, 1795, note 24. On January 7,
1795, however, the Georgia legislature enacted "An Act supplementary to an
Act, entitled, 'an Act for appropriating a part of the unlocated territory of
this state, for the payment of the late state troops, and for other purposes
therein mentioned,' declaring the right of this state to the unappropriated
territory thereof, for the protection and support of the frontiers of this
state, and for other purposes" (Microfilm Collection of Early State Records,
Library of Congress). By this act Georgia sold thirty-five million acres of
land to the Georgia, Georgia Mississippi, Tennessee, and Upper Mississippi
companies for five hundred thousand dollars in specie. The new Yazoo

companies were backed by politically prominent men, including two United States Senators (James Gunn of Georgia and Robert Morris of Pennsylvania), two Congressmen (Thomas P. Carnes of Georgia and Robert Goodloe Harper of South Carolina), three judges (James Wilson, associate justice of the Supreme Court of the United States, Nathaniel Pendleton, United States judge for the District of Georgia, and William Stith of the Superior Court of Georgia), and one territorial governor (William Blount of Tennessee).

The charge of fraud in connection with these land sales arose because of evidence that all but one of the legislators who had voted for the law had been bribed by land speculators. A new legislature on February 13, 1796, rescinded the act of 1795 by enacting "An Act Declaring null and void a certain usurped act passed by the last legislature of this state, at Augusta, on the seventh day of January, one thousand seven hundred and ninety-five, under the pretended title of 'An act supplementary to an act entitled, an act for appropriating a part of the unlocated territory of this state, for the payment of the late state troops, and for other purposes therein mentioned; declaring the right of this state to the unappropriated territory thereof, for the protection of the frontiers, and for other purposes:' And for expunging from the face of the public records the said usurped act, and for declaring the right of this state to sell all lands laying within the boundaries therein mentioned" (Microfilm Collection of Early State Records, Library of Congress). The Georgia Company, however, had already sold its tract to the New England Mississippi Company, which in turn sold to investors in New England and the middle states. These purchasers organized and sought to validate their claims. In 1810 the Supreme Court in *Fletcher* v *Peck* decided in favor of the claimants. For H's role in the Yazoo land cases, see the forthcoming Goebel, *Law Practice*, III.

4. Nathaniel Prime and Samuel Ward were New York City merchants. Under the date of October 6, 1795, the following entry appears in H's Cash Book, 1795–1804:
"Samuel Ward & Associates   Dr.
for this sum which he informed me he was to pay on account of advice & sundry writing relating to purchase of Georgia lands   200—"
(AD, Hamilton Papers, Library of Congress; also in forthcoming Goebel, *Law Practice*, III).

Under the date of December 1–5, 1795, H recorded in his Cash Book, 1795–1804: "Dr. to Sundries
To Samuel Ward for this sum received of him for services concerning their purchase of Georgia Lands   200—"
(AD, Hamilton Papers, Library of Congress; also in forthcoming Goebel, *Law Practice*, III).

5. The Georgia Company was required to pay one-fifth of the purchase money down and the remainder before November 1, 1795. Payment was secured by a mortgage on the land (Microfilm Collection of Early State Records, Library of Congress).

From Philip Schuyler

Albany Monday Octr: 12th 1795

I thank you my Dear Sir for informing me [1] that you and all the family are in health; may you continue so is my anxious wish, but I am Still not without my fears.[2] If you should remain, I hope the heavy rain of Yesterday has reached NYork.

I have written to Mr. Church and my daughter [3] recommending that she should bring out with her all the articles relative to which she has requested information from my Eliza & me as they will come cheaper and be of better quality.

I have also informed Mr. Church, that If It was not possible to Obtain a house by lease that I would recommend to you to purchase either Mr. Lynchs [4] or Mr. Mortons [5] house both of which I understand are for sale. If they could be obtained at such a price, that in case he should incline hereafter to sell again, he might sell without much loss, or If he did not chuse to sell, that he might rent at 5 per Cent clear of deductions on the principal which he should pay, but that hiring a house would be most Eligable If one can be Obtained sufficiently commodious, Even If an Extra rent was given.

Perhaps Mr Nicholas Lows [6] house in hanover square; or the house now Occupied by Mrs: Living.[7] of which Mr. John Watts [8] has the disposition, or the house in which Mr. Izard Lived,[9] which belongs to Mr. Ellison [10] who lives in the broadway or the house belonging to Mrs. Robert Watts in which Mr. Siexas [11] the Jew lives, may be obtained in lease for three or four Years, and either of these would probably suffice.

Mrs. Church wishes that whatever house may be hired a plan thereof should be sent her as soon as may be and duplicates of the plans that she may make her Arrangements Accordingly. Should you not be able to hire a house and deem It Elegible to purchase, It would be proper to send a plan thereof. Mrs. Schuylers apprehensions are so great that she will not consent to my going to NYork, which I would otherwise do to relieve you from the trouble which these negociations will impose on you, knowing how very much You are engaged.

Embrace my Eliza & the Children, we are all well here and Join in Love

Yours Ever most affectionately   Ph: Schuyler

Alexander Hamilton Esqr

Mrs. Church mentioned one of Mr. Watsons new houses in the battery,[12] or the house in which Mr Macomb [13] lives, as most agreable to her wish. I have written Mr Church that I believed neither could be obtained, perhaps I may be mistaken.

ALS, Lloyd W. Smith Collection, Morristown National Historical Park, Morristown, New Jersey.

1. Letter not found.

2. Schuyler's "fears" arose because of the yellow fever epidemic in New York City. See H to Oliver Wolcott, Jr., September 20, 1795.

3. John B. and Angelica Church lived in England. H was Church's agent or business representative in the United States.

4. Dominick Lynch, a merchant, lived at 35 Broadway.

5. Jacob Morton, a lawyer, lived at 57 Broadway.

6. Nicholas Low, a merchant, lived at 24 Broadway.

7. Mrs. Robert C. Livingston, a widow, lived at 24 Cortlandt Street.

8. John Watts lived at 3 Broadway.

9. During the period in which the United States Congress met in New York City, Ralph Izard, a Senator from South Carolina, lived at 99 Broadway.

10. Thomas Ellison, a merchant, lived at 13 Broadway.

11. Benjamin Seixas, a New York City merchant and broker, lived at 76 Broad Street.

12. James Watson, a merchant, lived on State Street.

13. Alexander Macomb, one of New York City's wealthiest merchants, lived at 39 Broadway.

To Peter Smith [1]

[*New York, October 12, 1795.* Concerns the case of *Leonard Gansevoort* v *Gerrit Boon.*[2] *Letter not found.*[3]]

1. Smith was sheriff of Herkimer County, New York.

2. Gansevoort, a resident of Albany, was a member of the New York Assembly in 1778, 1779, and 1788. He served in the Continental Congress in 1787 and 1788 and was a member of the New York Senate from 1791 to 1793. He was judge of Albany County from 1794 to 1797.

Boon, a native of the Netherlands, was one of the agents of the six Dutch banking firms which formed the Holland Land Company on February 13, 1796.

For the case of *Gansevoort* v *Boon*, see the MS minutes of the New York Supreme Court, January 22, April 19, July 29, 1796 (Hall of Records, New York City), and H's Law Register, 1795–1804, 4 (D, partially in H's handwriting, New York Law Institute, New York City; also in forthcoming Goebel, *Law Practice*, III).

3. Letter listed in "List of Papers of S. W. Mitchell," sold at auction May 19, 1941 (Papers of Silas Weir Mitchell, Library of Congress).

To Oliver Wolcott, Junior [1]

New York October 13. 1795.

Dr. Sir

I have received your letter of the 6 instant.

I am of opinion that the Commissioners to be appointed under the 7th article [2] are competent to grant relief, in all cases of captures or condemnations of our property, during the present war and antecedent to the Treaty, which were *contrary to the laws of Nations* and in which there is *adequate evidence* (of which they are to judge *bona fide*) that compensation could not at the time of the Treaty *for whatever reason* be actually obtained. I think their power competent to relief *after* a decision *in the last resort*, that is by the Lords Commissioners of Appeals, and, *if* the proper steps have been taken to ascertain that justice cannot be had in the ordinary course of justice, *before* and *without* such decision.

This opinion is founded upon the following reasons—1 The subject of complaint to be redressed is *irregular* or *illegal* captures or *condemnations.* The word "condemnations" is general—it is not restricted to condemnations in the inferior courts or in the final court of appeals. It may then apply to either—condemnations *in the last resort* may have been had prior to the Treaty. There being no restriction they like those in inferior tribunals were equally within the terms of complaint. But could they be *illegal?* Yes in controversies between Nations, respecting the application of the rules of the laws of Nations, decisions of the highest court of one of the parties, if contrary to those rules are illegal—in other words they are contrary to that law which is the standard of legality and illegality between Nations and if manifestly so are a cause of War. Moreover, this rule of legality or illegality is recognised by the article itself, in that part which authorises the Commissioners to decide according

ALS, Connecticut Historical Society, Hartford; copy, Hamilton Papers, Library of Congress.

1. This letter contains H's answers to the questions which Wolcott had asked in Wolcott to H, October 6, 1795.

2. For the text of Article 7 of the Jay Treaty, see "Remarks on the Treaty . . . between the United States and Great Britain," July 9–11, 1795, note 39.

to the merits of the several cases, to justice equity and *the laws of Nations*. 2   The article contemplates that *"various* circumstances" may obstruct compensation in the ordinary course of Justice. These terms would not be fully satisfied by tying the article down, as has been attempted, to cases of insolvency and absconding. 3   The article expressly declares that when compensation cannot, *"for whatever reason"* be had in the ordinary course of justice it shall be made by the British Government upon the award of the commissions. It is inadmissible to narrow down these very comprehensive terms to the two cases of *insolvency* or *absconding*—they are commensurate with every cause of irregularity or illegality pronounced such by the laws of Nations. The exceptions of manifest delay or negligence or wilful omission confirm the extensive interpretation. 4th   The Commissioners are not restricted in the description of the cases they are to take up and they are to decide them according to their *merits* to *justice equity* and the *laws of Nations*. These terms are as latitudinary as they could be made. They seem framed on purpose to overrule any technical difficulties with regard to local tribunals or positive rules of decision in those tribunals. 5   The nature of the circumstances which led to the article and which involved a controversy between two nations respecting the rules of the laws of Nations as well as the application of those rules—The natural presumption is that it was meant to refer this controversy, in all its latitude to the extraordinary tribunal created—to transfer the right of judgment of each nation, which being exercised differently might have ended in war, to that tribunal. Any thing less than this would be inadequate to the origin of the business, to the solemnity of the provision, or to the views which from the facts must be conceived to have governed the parties.

All this appears so clear to me that I confess I am confounded at an opinion which I have seen of Messieurs Louis and Rawle.[3] They

3. On October 6, 1795, Timothy Pickering, Acting Secretary of State, had written to William Lewis, a distinguished lawyer in Philadelphia, and William Rawle, United States attorney for the District of Pennsylvania, asking them for an opinion on the same questions which Wolcott had submitted to H on October 6, 1795 (LC, RG 59, Domestic Letters of the Department of State, Vol. 8, December 6, 1794–October 12, 1795, National Archives; copy, Massachusetts Historical Society, Boston). On October 10, 1795, Pickering wrote to John Jay, enclosing copies of his letter to Lewis and Rawle and of their replies. These copies have not been found, but Pickering

seem to pare away the object of the articles to the two cases mentioned above, founding their opinion upon the maxim that the Courts of the belligerent power are the competent tribunals to decide similar questions between that power & a neutral Nation.

This maxim is true, but how can be deemed to apply to the instance of a controversy between two nations about the interpretation of the laws of Nations—and about decisions of Courts founded upon an interpretation concerning which they disagreed—and this when an extraordinary Tribunal has been constituted by the joint acts of the two parties to decide their differences plainly as a substitute for a controversy by arms. Is not the constitution of such a tribunal by the two parties a manifest abandonment of the pretension of one to administer justice definitively through its tribunals? How can it be presumed after such a proceeding that the neutral power meant to be concluded by the decisions of those tribunals? Is not the reverse the obvious presumption? Why else was it not left to the British Courts of Admiralty to liquidate the damages in the admitted cases of insolvency & absconding to be paid by the Government. These circumstances could call for a substitute only in *the person to pay*—not in the person or tribunal *which was to liquidate*. There was no need on the principle set up for an extraordinary Tribunal to liquidate & award damages.

I confess that the opinion referred to appears to me destitute of colour—contrary to the antecedent course of the transaction contrary to the positive expressions of the article and to what can reasonably be presumed to be the intention of the parties. It fritters

---

wrote: "Their answer . . . does not, I confess, correspond with my ideas of the meaning of the seventh article of the treaty which you negociated with Lord Grenville. I always conceived that the principal ground of our complaints of spoliations was the capture of our vessels under the orders of the Privy Council of Great Britain, especially the order of the sixth of November 1793, as being repugnant to the laws of nations: but one opinion expressed by those Gentlemen amounts to an abandonment of this ground, and an admission of consequences beyond even the present claims of the British Admiralty Courts: it would put an end to our commerce with the French West India Islands, by subjecting all our vessels, in the present course of that trade, to *legal* captures, by the British on one hand and by the French on the other" (LC, RG 59, Domestic Letters of the Department of State, Vol. 8, December 6, 1794–October 12, 1795, National Archives; LC, Massachusetts Historical Society, Boston; LC, Columbia University Libraries). See also H to Rufus King, June 15, 1793.

away to nothing a very solemn & important act between two contending Nations.

The exception of the cases in which justice might be obtained in
the ordinary course appears to me to decide nothing. It might be
unobtainable in that court, as well from the obstructions of positive
regulations of the belligerent parties controuling the courts—& from
false principles adopted by the Courts as from the inability or default of the Captors. The Commissioners, who are the *Court of the
two nations* are to pronounce whether justice is unobtainable in the
ordinary court for any of these reasons. As the Tribunal of both parties they are necessarily superior to the Tribunals of either. And they
are the Judges in their own way & upon their own grounds of the
question whether & when justice can or cannot be obtained in the
ordinary course.

But they ought to exercise their discretion reasonably not to abuse
otherwise they may release the party injured from the obligation to
perform.

Hence though it is not necessary that every *individual case* of
capture should be prosecuted to a decision *in the last resort*—it appears to me proper that by such prosecution of some *one case* of the
several classes of cases, it may be ascertained by a final decision on
the principle of each class, that redress cannot be obtained: Else the
Commissioners may object that there has been a neglect to procure
for them satisfactory evidence that justice could not be had in the
ordinary course.

I would advise then that our Agent[4] be instructed to lay all the
cases, with the evidence, before our Counsel;[5] and to desire them to
make a selection of one of each class, in which a defence can be
made with probability of success, on some difference of principle—
to have these cases prosecuted to an ultimate decision and to leave
all the rest pending if possible undecided in a course of Appeal. This
will give reasonable evidence to the Commissioners strengthened, in
the view of those appointed by the other party, by the character of
our Counsel, who I learn are every way men of respectability.

4. Samuel Bayard. See H to Wolcott, October 6, 1795, note 2.
5. Sir William Scott and Dr. John Nicholl. See Moore, *International
Adjudications*, IV, 30–34.

The other points in your letter I shall pursue hereafter.

Yrs. with esteem & regard   A Hamilton

Oliver Wolcott Esq

In a consultation on insurance case between our district attorney [6] Mr Burr [7] B: Livingston [8] & myself the above points incidentally occurred—and I understood all these Gentlemen as agreeing the opinion I have stated.[9] You are at liberty to communicate this to Mr. Pickering.

6. Richard Harison.
7. Aaron Burr.
8. Brockholst Livingston.
9. This may be a reference to *Le Guen* v *Gouverneur and Kemble*. At some date before November, 1795, Louis Le Guen had retained H, Richard Harison, and Aaron Burr. Martin S. Wilkins, Brockholst Livingston, and John Cozine were the attorneys for Isaac Gouverneur and Peter Kemble. For this case and related cases involving Le Guen, see Goebel, *Law Practice*, II, 48–164.

The Defence No. XIX [1]

[New York, October 14, 1795]

The objects protected by the 10th. article [2] are classed under four heads, 1 debts of *individuals* to *individuals* 2 property of individuals in the public funds 3 property of individuals in public banks 4 property of individuals in private banks. These, if analised, resolve themselves, in principle, into two discriminations—(viz) private debts & private property in public funds. The character of private property prevails throughout. No property of either Government is protected from confiscation or sequestration by the other. This last circumstance merits attention, because it marks the true boundary.

The propriety of the stipulation will be examined under these several aspects—the right to confiscate or sequester private debts or

ADf, Hamilton Papers, Library of Congress; *The* [New York] *Argus, or Greenleaf's New Daily Advertiser*, October 14, 1795.

1. For background to this document, see the introductory note to "The Defence No. I," July 22, 1795.

2. For the text of Article 10 of the Jay Treaty, see "Remarks on the Treaty . . . between the United States and Great Britain," July 9–11, 1795, note 48. See also "The Defence No. XVIII," October 6, 1795.

private property in public funds on the ground of reason and principle—the right, as depending on the opinions of jurists and on usage—the policy and expediency of the practice—the analogy of the stipulation with stipulations in our other treaties—and in treaties between other Nations.

First, as to the right on the ground of reason and principle.

The general proposition on which it is supported is this—"That every individual of a nation with whom we are at war wheresoever he may be is our enemy and his property of every kind and in every place liable to capture by right of War."

The only exception admitted to this rule respects property within the jurisdiction of a Neutral State; but the exemption is referred to the right of the neutral nation not to any privilege which the situation gives to the enemy Proprietor.

Reason, if consulted, will dictate another exception. This regards all *such property as the laws of a country permit foreigners to acquire within it, or to bring into it*.[3] The right of holding or having property in a country always implies a duty on the part of its Government to protect that property and to secure to the owner the full enjoyment of it. Whenever therefore a Government grants permission to foreigners to acquire property within its territories or to bring & deposit it there, it tacitly promises protection and security. It must be understood to engage, that the foreign proprietor, as to what he shall have acquired or deposited, shall enjoy the rights privileges and immunities of a native proprietor—without any other exceptions than those which the established laws may have previously declared. How can any thing else be understood? Every state, when it has entered into no contrary engagement, is free to permit or not to permit foreigners to acquire or bring property within its jurisdiction, but if it grant the right, what is there to make the tenure of the foreigner different from that of the native, if antecedent laws have not pronounced a difference? Property as it exists in civilized Society, if not a creature of, is at least regulated and defined by, the laws. They prescribe the manner in which it shall be used, alienated, or transmitted—the conditions upon which it may be held preserved or forfieted. Tis to them we are to look for its

3. See "Remarks on the Treaty . . . between the United States and Great Britain," July 9-11, 1795, note 49.

rights limitations and conditions. No condition of enjoyment, no cause of forfieture, which they have not specified can be presumed to exist. An extraordinary discretion to resume or take away the thing, without any personal fault of the proprietor is inconsistent with the notion of property. This seems always to imply a contract between the Society and the individual, that he shall retain and be protected in the possession and use of his property so long as he shall observe and perform the condition, which the laws have annexed to the tenure. It is neither natural nor equitable to consider him as subject to be deprived of it for a cause foreign to himself especially for one which may depend on the volition or pleasure even of the very government to whose protection it has been confided: For the proposition, which affirms the right to confiscate or sequester, does not distinguish between offensive or defensive war, between a war of ambition on the part of the power which exercises the right or a war of self preservation against the assaults of another.

The property of a foreigner placed in another country by permission of its laws may justly be regarded as a *deposit*, of which the Society is the Trustee. How can it be reconciled with the idea of a trust to take the property from him when he has personally given no cause for the deprivation?

Suppose two families in a state of nature, and that a member of one of them had by permission of the head of the other placed in his custody some article belonging to himself—and suppose a quarrel to ensue between the two heads of famil⟨ies⟩ in which the member had not participated by his immediate counsel or consent. Would not natural Equity declare the seizure and confiscation of the deposited property to be an act of perfidious rapacity?

Again—Suppose two neighbouring nations, which had not had intercourse with each other, and that one of them opens its ports and territories for the purpose of commerce to the Citizens of the other, proclaiming free and safe ingress and egress—suppose afterwards a war to break out between the two nations and the one, which had granted that permission to seize and convert to its own use the goods and credits of the Merchants of the other within its dominion. What sentence would Natural Reason, unwarped by particular dogmas, pronounce on such conduct? If we abstract ourselves from extraneous impressions, and consult a genuine moral feeling, we shall not doubt that the sentence would inflict all the opprobrium and infamy of violated faith?

Nor can we distinguish either case in principle from that which constantly takes place between nations that permit a commercial intercourse with each other whether with or without national compact. They equally grant a right to bring into and carry out of their territories the property which is the subject of the intercourse, a right of free and secure ingress and egress, and in doing this they make their territories a sanctuary or asylum which ought to be inviolable, and which the spirit of plunder only could have ever violated.

There is no parity between the case of the persons and goods of enemies found in our own country, and that of the persons and goods of enemies found elsewhere. In the former, there is a reliance upon our hospitality and justice, there is an express or an implied safe conduct, the individuals and their property are in the custody of our faith, they have no power to resist our will—they can lawfully make no defence against our violence—they are deemed to owe a temporary allegiance, and for endeavouring resistance would be punished as criminals; ⟨a cha⟩racter inconsistent with that of [an] enemy. To make them a prey is therefore to infringe every rule of generosity and equity—it is to add cowardice to treachery. In the latter case, there is no confidence whatever reposed in us—no claim upon our hospitality, justice, or good faith—there is the simple character of enemy, with intire liberty to oppose force to force. The right of war consequently to attack and seize whether to obtain indemnification for an injury received—to disable our enemy from doing us further harm—to force him to reasonable terms of accommodation—or to repress an overbearing ambition—exists in full vigour—unrestrained and unqualfieid by any trust or duty on our part. In pursuing it though we may inflict hardships, we do not commit injustice.

Moreover: the property of the foreigner within our country may be regarded as having paid a valuable consideration for its protection and exemption from forfieture. That which is brought in commonly enriches the Revenue by a duty of entry. All that is within our territory, whether acquired there or brought there, is liable to contributions to the Treasury in common with other similar property.

Does there not result an obligation to protect that which contributes to the expence of its protection? Will Justice sanction, upon the breaking out of a War, the confiscation of a property, which during peace serves to augment the resources and nourish the prosperity of a State?

The principle of the proposition gives an equal right to subject the person as the property of the foreigner to the rigours of War. But What would be thought of a Government which should seize all the subjects of its enemy found within its territory and commit them to durance as prisoners of War? Would not all agree that it had violated an asylum which ought to have been sacred, that it had trampled upon the laws of hospitality and civilization that it had disgraced itself by an act of cruelty and barbarism? * Why would it not be equally reprehensible to violate the asylum which had been given to the property of those foreigners?

Reason left to its own lights would answer all these questions in one way, and would severely condemn the molestation on account of a national Contest as well of the property as person of a foreigner found in our country, under the permission and guarantee of the laws of previous amity.

The case of property in the public funds is still stronger than that of private debts.[4] To all the sanctions which apply to the latter it adds that of an express pledge of the public faith to the foreign holder of Stock. The constituting of a public debt or fund, transferrable without limitation or distinction, amounts to a promise to all the world, that whoever, foreigner or citizen, may acquire a title to it, shall enjoy the benefit of what is stipulated. Every transferree becomes by the act of transfer the immediate proprietor of the promise. It enures directly to his use, and the foreign promisee no more than the native can be deprived of that benefit, except in consequence of some act of his own, without the infraction of a positive engagement.

Public debt has been truly defined "*A property subsisting in the faith of Government.*" Its essence is promise.[5] To confiscate or se-

* Note All that [can] rightfully be done is to oblige the foreigners who are subjects of our enemy to quit our country.

4. For H's views on this subject, see "Report on a Plan for the Further Support of Public Credit," January 16, 1795.

5. H took these two sentences from the concluding section of "Report on a Plan for the Further Support of Public Credit," January 16, 1795.

quester it is emphatically to rescind the promise given, to revoke the faith plighted. It is impossible to separate the two ideas of a breach of faith, and the confiscation or sequestration of a property subsisting only in the faith of the Government by which it is made.

When it is considered that the promise made to the foreigner is not made to him in the capacity of member of another Society, but in that of citizen of the world, or of an individual in a state of nature—the infraction of it towards him, on account of the fault real or pretended of the Society to which he belongs, is the more obviously destitute of colour. There is no real affinity between the motive and the consequence. There is a confounding of relations. The obligation of a contract can only be avoided by the breach of a condition express or implied, which appears or can be presumed to have been within the contemplation of both parties or by the personal fault or crime of him to whom it is to be performed. Can it be supposed that a citizen of one Country would lend his money to the Government of another, in the expectation that a war between the two countries, which without or against his will might break out the next day, could be deemed a sufficient cause of forfieture?

The principle may be tested in another way. Suppose one Government indebted to another in a certain sum of money and Suppose the creditor Government to borrow of a citizen of the other a less sum of money. When he came to demand payment, would justice, would good faith permit the opposing to his claim by way of set off the debt due from his Government? Who would not revolt at such an attempt? Could not the individual Creditor answer with conclusive force that in *a matter of contract* he was not responsible for the Society of which he was a member and that the debts of the Society were not a proper set off against his private claim?

With what greater reason could his claim be refused on account of an injury which was a cause of War received from his sovereign, and which had created on the part of the sovereign a *debt* of reparation? It were certainly more natural and just to set off a debt due *by contract* to the citizen of a foreign Country against a debt due *by contract* from the sovereign of that country—than to set it off against a claim of indemnification for an injury or aggression of which we complain, and of which the *reality* or justice is seldom undisputed on the other side.

The true Rule which results from what has been said, and which reason sanctions, with regard to the right of capture is this "It may be exercised every where except within a neutral jurisdiction * or where the property is under the protection of our own laws" [7] and it may perhaps be added that it always supposes the possibility of rightful combat—of attack and defence—These exceptions involve [8] [no refinement—they depend on obvious considerations, and are agreeable to common sense and to nature—the spontaneous feelings of equity accord with them. It is indeed astonishing that a contrary rule should have been countenanced by the opinion of any jurist, or by the practice of any civilized nation.

We shall see in the next number how far either has been the case, and what influence it ought to have upon the question.   CAMILLUS.]

* There are exceptions to this exception; but they depend on special circumstances which admit the principal exception, and need not be particularized.[6]

6. This footnote, which is not in the extant portion of the MS, has been taken from the newspaper.

7. See "Remarks on the Treaty . . . between the United States and Great Britain," July 9–11, 1795, note 49.

8. The last page of the draft has not been found. The remaining material within brackets has been taken from the newspaper.

To George Washington

New York October 16. 1795

Sir

About a fortnight since arrived here Mr. Fristel with G W. Fayette son of the Marquis.[1] The former, who is in capacity of Tutor

ALS, George Washington Papers, Library of Congress; copy, Hamilton Papers, Library of Congress.

1. This is a reference to George Washington Motier Lafayette, son of the Marquis de Lafayette, and his tutor Felix Frestel. Before going to New York, they had been in Boston, where they had arrived from France. On August 31, 1795, George W. M. Lafayette had written to the President from Boston: "Après bien des peines et des traverses, c'est en Amerique, c'est auprès de vous, que je viens chercher un azyle, et mon pere. j'avois aspiré depuis long-temps après cet heureux moment, qui toujours avoit fui devant moi.

"je commence à espérer maintenant davantage.

"comme c'est à votre nom, que je dois le bonheur de me trouver enfin dans ma seconde Patrie; ce sera sûrement encore à vous, que je devrai celui d'y voir aussi mon pere, heureux et libre, ainsi que tout ce qui m'est cher.

to the latter, requested me to mention their arrival to you, and that
they meant to retire to some place in the neighbouring country 'till

---

"Voudrez-vous bien permettre au fils infortune d'un homme, que vous avez
honoré de quelque amitié, et qui de bonne-he(ure) apprit de lui à vous re-
garder comme son père, de venir vous offrir l'expression de sa reconnoissance,
et l'hommage d'un respect aussi profond que tendre . . . oserai-je dire filial?"
(ALS, George Washington Papers, Library of Congress.)

Frestel also wrote to Washington on August 31, 1795, requesting an interview with the President as well as advice concerning young Lafayette's
future in the United States (ALS, George Washington Papers, Library of
Congress).

On September 2, 1795, Henry Knox, who was also in Boston, wrote to
Washington: "The son of Monsieur La Fayette is here—accompanied by
an amiable french man as a Tutor—young Fayette goes by the name of
Motier, concealing his real name, lest some injury should arise, to his mother.
. . . Your namesake is a lovely young man, of excellent morals and con-
duct . . ." (ALS, George Washington Papers, Library of Congress).

On September 7, 1795, in a letter to George Cabot, United States Senator
from Massachusetts, Washington enclosed young Lafayette's and Frestel's
letters and wrote: ". . . Let me in a few words, declare that I *will be his
friend*, but the manner of becomg. so considering the obnoxious light in
which his father is viewed by the French government, and my own situation, as the Executive of the U States, requires more time to consider in all
its relations, than I can bestow on it at present. . . .

"The mode which, at the first view strikes me as the most eligable to
answer his purposes; & to save appears. is, 1 to administer all the consolation
to young Gentleman that he can derive from the most unequivocal assurances
of my standing in the place of and becoming to him, a *Father—friend—pro-
tector*—and *supporter*. but 2dly. for prudential motives, as they may relate to
himself; his mother and friends, whom he has left behind; and to my *official*
character it would be best not to make these sentiments public; of course, it
would be ineligable, that he should come to the Seat of the genl. government
where all the foreign characters (particularly that of his own nation) are
residents, until it is seen what opinions will be excited by his arrival; especially too as I shall be necessarily absent five or Six weeks from it, on business, in several places. 3. considering how important it is to avoid idleness &
dissipation; to improve his mind; and to give him all the advantages which
education can bestow; my opinion, and my advice to him is, (if he is qualified
for admission) that he should enter as a student at the University in Cambridge altho' it shd. be for a short time *only*. The expence of which, as also
of every other mean for his support, I will pay; and now do authorize you,
my dear Sir, to draw upon me accordingly; and if it is in any degree
necessary, or *desireable*, that Mr. Frestel his Tutor should accompany him to
the University, in that character, any arrangements which you shall make
for the purpose and any expence thereby incurred for the same, shall be
borne by me in like manner." (ADfS, George Washington Papers, Library of
Congress.)

On September 16, 1795, Cabot replied to Washington: "The letter which
you did me the honor to write on the 7th was received last evening, when I
immediately waited on the Gentlemen who are the subject of it. They were
in a state of anxiety respecting a new place of residence where they might
live unnoticed—considerations of the kind which you have mentioned &
some other render this eligible for the present, but it is found impracticable
here. Already Mr Motier is known to too many persons. . . .

they should receive some direction from you. Thus at least I understood him—and accordingly they are gone to a house between Hackensack & Ramapough in the Jerseys to which may be conveyed any letter you may confide to me for them. They are *incog*.

Having been informed you were speedily expected from Philadelphia [2] & being oppressed with occupation I delayed writing till this time.

Mr. Fristel, who appears a very sedate discreet man, informs me that they left France with permission, though not in their real characters, but in fact with the privity of some members of the Committee of safety who were disposed to shut their eyes and facilitate their departure.

The young Fayette also appears to me very advantageously, modest, of very good manners, and expressing himself with intelligence and propriety.

Shall I trespass on your indulgence in hazarding a sentiment upon the subject of this young Gentleman? If I do let it be ascribed to the double interest I take in a son of the Marquis and in whatever interests the good fame and satisfaction of him to whom I write.

On mature reflecti⟨on⟩ and on sounding opinions, as far as opportunity & the nature of the case have permitted, I fully believe that the President need be under no embarrassment as to any good offices his heart may lead him to perform towards this young man. It will not, I am persuaded, displease those in possession of the power of the Country from which he comes, and in ours it will be singularly and generally grateful. I am even convinced that the personal

---

"In addition to the motives already explained for removing further than Cambridge it was urged that the studies now actually pursuing by Mr Motier are entirely different from those prescribed in any of our universities, & that your desires will therefore be best accomplished by a continuance in his present course under Mr. Frestel; it was admitted however that other aids wou'd be requisite in those branches of education which Mr Frestel does not profess—with a view to these & to combine with them abstinence from society it is thought best to seek a position near some principal town where all the *desiderata* can be found . . . to day on their visiting me I found they had concluded it wou'd be best to go to New York. . . .

". . . I shall give them letters to Colonel [Jeremiah] Wadsworth & to Coll Hamilton the latter of whom will probably know where they may be found after they shall be established. . . ." (ALS, George Washington Papers, Library of Congress.)

2. Washington had left Mount Vernon on October 12, 1795, and arrived at Philadelphia on October 20.

and political enemies of the President would be gratified should his ideas of the policy of the case restrain him from that conduct which his friendship to the Marquis and his feelings otherwise would dictate. The Youth of this person joined to the standing of his father make the way easy.

I even venture to think it possible that the time is not very remote when the Marquis will again recover the confidence and esteem of his Country when perhaps the men in power may be glad to fortify themselves and their cause with his alliance.[3] This however is supposition merely to be indulged as a reflection not to be counted upon as a fact.

There is another subject upon which I will hazard a few words. It is that of Mr. Randolph. I have seen the intercepted letter, which I presume led to his resignation.[4] I read it with regret, but without much surprise for I never had confidence in Mr. Randolph, and I thought there were very suspicious appearances about him on the occasion to which the letter particularly refers.

I perceive that rendered desperate himself he meditates as much mischief as he can. The letter he calls for I presume is that above alluded to.[5] His object is, if he obtains it, to prejudice others—if any

3. See H to William Bradford, June 13, 1795.

4. This is a reference to Fauchet's Dispatch No. 10, which had been intercepted by the British and turned over to the Washington Administration. For the way in which the contents of this dispatch led to Edmund Randolph's resignation as Secretary of State, see Oliver Wolcott, Jr., to H, July 30, 1795, note 1.

It is not possible to ascertain how H obtained a copy of Fauchet's Dispatch No. 10, for H's correspondence indicates that Wolcott did not send him a copy of it until November 13 or 14, 1795. See H to Wolcott, October 30–November 12, 1795, note 15, and Wolcott to H, November 16, 1795, note 2. Moreover, in a letter which H wrote to Wolcott on October 30 and mailed on November 12, 1795, he stated: "I am very anxious that *Fauchet's* whole letter should appear just as it is. . . . Is it to come out? Can't you send me a copy?"

5. H's assumption was incorrect, for Randolph was not requesting Dispatch No. 10. Instead on October 8, 1795, Randolph wrote to Washington: "Until monday last I did not obtain from the office those of my own letters, which I deem proper to be introduced into my vindication. But I still want the inspection of a letter from you, dated July 22. 1795, and received by me. I applied personally at the office on saturday last for the sight of your letters to me. The Chief Clerk went into the room, in which Mr. Pickering sits, to consult him, at my desire, upon my application. He afterwards carried to Mr Pickering a brown paper, and on his return placed it before me. It contained *many* of your letters; and was indorsed to this purport 'The President's letters.' I presumed that they were *all* there; as no mention was made

part is kept back, to derive advantage to his cause from the idea, that there may be something reserved which would tend to his exculpation and to produce suspicion that there is something which you are interested to keep from the light.

Though from this state of public prejudices I shall probably for one be a sufferer by the publication; yet upon the whole I incline to the opinion that it is most adviseable the whole should come before the public. I acknowlege that I do not express this opinion without hesitation and therefore it will deserve as it will no doubt engage your mature reflection but such is the present byass of my judgment. I am the more inclined to the opinion as I presume that the subject being in part before the public, the whole letter will finally come out through the quarter by which it was written, and then it would have additional weight to produce ill impressions.

With great respect & Affectionate attachment   I have the honor to be   Sir   Yr. very obed ser   A Hamilton

The President of The UStates

---

to me of any, that were missing. But not finding that of July 22. 1795, I asked for it; and the chief clerk replied, that Mr. Pickering had just taken it out; and that upon his saying, that I might wish to see it, Mr. Pickering had observed, that, if I did, I would ask for it. I accordingly asked for it again; but was answered, that it was necessary to consult Mr. Wolcott. Not hearing any thing late on Monday from the Chief Clerk, I reminded by a note, and on tuesday received thro' him the rancorous and insolent answer of Mr. Pickering, which amounts to a positive refusal, and of which due notice will be taken in its proper place. I affirm to you, that I hold that letter to be important to me of the views, which the question will bear. As I aim at accuracy in my statements; I am anxious to prevent a mistake in my recollection of that letter, and therefore request the inspection of it . . ." (ALS, George Washington Papers, Library of Congress).

On October 21, 1795, Washington, in reply to Randolph's letter, wrote in part: ". . . It is not difficult, from the tenor of that letter, to perceive what your objects are, but that you may have no cause to complain of the withholding any paper (however private & confidential) which you shall think necessary in a case of so serious a nature, I have directed that you should have the inspection of my letter of the 22d. of July agreeably to your request; and you are at full liberty, to publish, without reserve, *any*, and *every* private & confidential letter I ever wrote you—nay more—every word I ever uttered to, or in your hearing, from whence you can derive any advantage in your vindication.

"I grant this permission, inasmuch as the extract alluded to manifestly tends to impress on the public mind an opinion that something has passed between us which you should disclose with reluctance; from motives of delicacy which respect me." (ADf, with interlineations in Timothy Pickering's handwriting, George Washington Papers, Library of Congress.)

To Abraham Van Vechten [1]

New York, October 22, 1795. "In a letter by the last Post [2] I mentioned that I should take the liberty to send you the papers for levying a fine [3] Leonard *Ganseevort* against Gerrit Boon.[4] They are now herewith sent. . . ."

AL, Hamilton Papers, Library of Congress.
1. Van Vechten was an Albany lawyer.
2. Letter not found.
3. See Sections I, III, and V of "An Act concerning Fines and Recoveries of Lands and Tenements" (*New York Laws*, 10th Sess., Ch. XLIII [February 26, 1787]).
4. See H to Peter Smith, October 12, 1795.

To Defence No. XX [1]

[New York, October 23 and 24, 1795]

The point next to be examined is the right of confiscation or sequestration, as depending on the opinions of Jurists and on usage.

To understand how far these ought to weigh, it is requisite to consider what are the elements, or ingredients, which compose what is called the laws of Nations.

The constituent parts of this system are, 1 The *necessary* or *internal* law, which is the *law of Nature* applied to Nations; or that system of rules for regulating the conduct of Nation to Nation which reason deduces from the principles of natural right as relative to political societies or States. 2 The *voluntary* law, which is a system of rules resulting from the equality and independence of nations, and which, in the administration of their affairs and the pursuit of their pretensions, proceeding on the principle of their having no common judge upon earth, attributes equal validity, as to external

ADf, Hamilton Papers, Library of Congress; *The* [New York] *Argus, or Greenleaf's New Daily Advertiser*, October 23 and 24, 1795.
1. For background to this document, see the introductory note to "The Defence No. I," July 22, 1795. This essay is a continuation of H's discussion of Article 10 of the Jay Treaty, a subject to which he also devoted "The Defence Nos. XVIII and XIX," October 6, 14, 1795.

effects, to the measures or conduct of one as of another without regard to the intrinsic justice of those measures or that conduct. Thus captures in war are as valid when made by the party in the wrong as by the party in the right. 3   The *Pactitious* or *Conventional* law, or that law which results from a Treaty between two or more nations. This is evidently a particular not a general law; since a treaty or pact can only bind the contracting parties: Yet when we find a provision universally pervading the Treaties between nations for a length of time, as a kind of formula, it is high evidence of the general law of Nations. 4   The *customary law*, which consists of those rules of conduct that in practice are respected and observed among Nations. Its authority depends on usage implying a tacit consent and agreement. This also is a particular not a general law, obligatory only on those nations whose acquiescence has appeared or from circumstances may fairly be presumed. Thus the customary law of Europe may not be that of a different quarter of the Globe. The three last branches are sometimes aggregately denominated the *positive law* of Nations.

The two first are discoverable by reason; the two last depend on proof as matters of fact. Hence the opinions of Jurists though weighing, as the sentiments of judicious or learned men who have made the subject a particular study—are not conclusive as authorities. In regard to the *necessary* and *voluntary* law, especially, they may be freely disregarded, unless they are found to be adopted and sanctioned by the practice of Nations: For where REASON is the guide, it cannot properly be renounced for mere OPINION, however respectable. As Witnesses of the customary law, their testimony, the result of careful researches, is more particularly intitled to attention.

If then it has been satisfactorily proved, as the dictate of sound reason, that private debts and private property in public funds, are not justly liable to confiscation or sequestration, an opposite opinion of one or more jurists, could not controul the conclusion in point of principle. So far as it may attest a practice of nations which may have introduced a positive law on the subject, the consideration may be different. It will then remain to examine upon their own and other testimony whether that practice be so general as to be capable of varying a rule of reason by the force of usage, and whether it still continues to bear the same character, or has been weakened or done away by more recent or more modern usage.

I will not avail myself of a position advanced by Writers, that usage if derogating from the principles of natural Justice is null, further than to draw this inference, that a rule of right deducible from them cannot be deemed to be altered by usage, partially contradicted, and fluctuating.

With these guides, our further inquiries will serve to confirm us in the negative of the pretended right to confiscate or sequester in the cases supposed.[2]

The Notion of this right is evidently derived from the Roman Law. It is seen there in this peculiar form—"Those things of an enemy which are among us belong not to the State but to the first

2. At this point in the draft H wrote and crossed out the following paragraphs: "Among the antients, as far as my leisure has permitted examination, little that is pertinent or instructive occurs. The Roman Law adopts this general position—'Those things, which we take from our enemies, by the law of Nations immediately become ours, so that even freemen may be brought into a state of servitude by capture' (Just: Insts: L II T I § XVII). But this is too general to touch the particular question whether those things of our enemy's which we find in our Country may be taken by right of War.

"Neither are the examples which have been cited with indirect reference to this question at all apposite. Such is the instance of Alexander who when he had become Master of Thebes by conquest remitted to the Thessaliens a hundred talents which they owed to the Thebans. This was the debt of one people to another not of an individual to an individual—neither was it a debt due to a foreign country or the Citizens, by the conquered territory or its Citizens—but the reverse. Moreover, it is settled on good ground that when one Prince or State conquers another all the public property accrues to the Conqueror. The debt due to the Thebans was public property and consequently belonged to Alexander by right of Conquest and in remitting it to the Thessalians he only disposed of a thing which he had acquired by arms. Other examples cited by Grotius are of a similar description—indeed they appear to be quoted merely to prove that *incorporeal* rights may be the subject of capture, but without a particular view to the question under discussion.

"The Roman Lawyer TRYPHONIUS indeed lays it down that 'those who go into a foreign Country in time of peace, if war is suddenly kindled, are made the slaves of those among whom, now become enemies, they are apprehended.' * [* "in pace qui pervenernunt ad alteros, si bellum subito exarcissit eorum servi efficiuntur apud quos iam hostes suo facto deprehenduntur. D 1 xlix t 15 1 xii] But the practice of civilized nations for centuries past, rejecting the idea of making slaves captives in war, wherever taken, will permit this opinion to be regarded in no other light than as a symptom of the ferocity of the times in which it was expressed. It prostrates the rights of humanity before the prerogatives of war.

"Among the modern authorities whom I have had an opportunity of consulting, I find but one who affirms absolutely the right to confiscate private

occupant" * which seems to mean that the things of an enemy at the commencement of a War found in our country may be seized by any citizen and will belong to him who first gets possession. It is known that the maxims of the Roman law, are extensively incorporated into the different codes of Europe; and particularly that the Writers on the law of Nations have borrowed liberally from them.

This source of the Notion does not stamp it with much authority. The history of Rome proves that War and Conquest were the great business of that People & that for the most part Commerce was little cultivated. Hence it was natural that the rights of War should be carried to an extreme, unmitigated by the softening and humanizing influence of Commerce. Indeed the world was yet too young—moral science too much in its cradle—to render the Roman jurisprudence a proper model for implicit imitation. Accordingly in this very particular of the rights of War, it seems to have been equally a rule of the Roman law, "that those who go into a foreign Country in time of peace, if war is suddenly kindled, are made the slaves of those among whom, now become enemies, by ill fortune, they are apprehended." † This right of capturing the property and of making slaves of the persons of enemies is referred, as we learn from CICERO, to the right of killing them, which was re-

---

debts and not one who specifically asserts that of confiscating private property in public funds. The one alluded to as affirming the right to confiscate private debts is Bynkershoek who bestows a chapter upon the subject and who in support of the conclusion which was quoted in a former number (to wit)."

H's first reference is to *Institutiones tutionum civilium libri quatuor . . .* (Paris, 1550), 198–99. For his second reference, see note 3.

* Digest: L XLI Tit I Et qua res hostiles apud nos &c.[3]

† In pace qui pervenerunt ad alteros, si bellum subito exarcisset, eorum servi efficiuntur, apud quos iam hostes suo facto deprehenduntur. DIGEST L XLIX T XV 1 xii [4]

3. *Digestorum seu Pandectarum iuris civilis tomus tertius, quod vulgo Digestum novum appelant: ex emendationibus Antonii Augustini restitutus, scholiisque illustratus* (Paris, 1550), Vol. III, Book XLI, Ch. I, Sec. LI. The quotation reads in full:

"Celsus

"Transfugam iure belli recepimus, & que res hostiles apud nos sunt: non publice, sed occupantium fiunt."

The *Digest* was a collection of extracts on Roman law from thirty-nine authors, compiled for the emperor Justinian and enforced by him as a statute in December, A.D. 533. It formed part of the *Corpus Iuris Civilis,* which became the authoritative compilation of Roman law.

4. See note 3.

garded as absolute and unqualified extending even to Women and Children.[5] Thus it would seem that on the principle of the Roman Law, we might rightfully kill a foreigner who had come into our Country during peace and was there at the breaking out of a War with his Country. Can there be a position more horrible, more detestable?

The improvement of moral science in modern times restrains the right of killing an enemy to the time of battle or resistance, except by way of punishment for some enormous breach of the laws of nations, or for self preservation in a case of immediate and urgent danger, and rejects altogether the right of imposing slavery on captives.[6]

Why should there have been a hesitation to reject other odious consequences of so exceptionable a principle? What respect is due to maxims which have so inhuman a foundation?

And yet a deference for those maxims has misled writers who have professedly undertaken to teach the principles of National Ethics; and the spirit of Rapine has continued to a late period to consecrate the relics of ancient barbarism with too many precedents of imitation. Else it would not now be a question with any, whether the person or property of a foreigner, being in our country with permission of the laws of peace, could be liable to molestation or injury by the laws of War, merely on account of the War.

Turning from the ancients to the moderns we find that the learned Grotius quotes and adopts as the basis of his opinions the rules of the Roman law; though he in several particulars qualifies them by the humane innovations of later times.[7]

5. This is a reference to *De Officiis*, III, vi, which reads: "Nulla enim nobis societas cum tyrannis, sed potius summa distractio est; neque est contra naturam, spoliare eum, si possis, quem honestum est necare; atque hoc omne genus pestiferum atque impium ex hominum communitate exterminandum est" (M. Tullius Cicero, *Opera* [Oxford, 1783], III, 264–65).

6. At this point in the draft H wrote and crossed out the following paragraph: "What respect is due to laws or maxims which have so odious a basis? Had not the spirit of rapine checked the progress of reason and humanity the universal suffrage of nations would long ago have discarded the pretension to violate or injure either the property or person of a foreigner."

7. For example, Grotius wrote: ". . . foreigners who have gone to a country in a period prior to the war, after the lapse of a moderate time, in which they could have departed, are apparently to be regarded as enemies according to the law of nations" (*On the Law of War and Peace*, Book III, Ch. IV, Sec. 7). Grotius then cites Cicero's defense (in the oration for Q.

On the very question of the right to confiscate or sequester private debts, his opinion as far as it appears seems to be at variance with his premises [8] steering a kind of middle course. His expressions (L III C: XX § XVI) [9] are these "Those debts which are due to private persons at the beginning of the War are not to be accounted forgiven, (that is when peace is made) for these are *not acquired* by the right of War, but only *forbidden to be demanded* in time of War, therefore the *impediment* being removed, that is the War ended, they retain their full force." His idea appears from this passage to be that the right of war is limited to the arresting of the payment of private debts during its continuance and not to the confiscation or annihilation of the debt. Nor is it clear whether he means that this arrestation is to be produced by a special act of prohibition, or by the operation of some rule of law which denies to an alien enemy a right of action. This feeble and heterogeneous opinion may be conceived to have proceeded from a conflict between a respect for ancient maxims and the impression of more enlightened views inculcated by the principles of Commerce and civilization.

Bynkershoeck is more consistent. Adopting with GROTIUS the rule of the Roman Law in its full rigor, he is not frightened at the consequences, but follows them throughout. Hence he bestows a chapter upon the defence of the proposition quoted in a former number [10] (to wit) that * "Since it is the condition of War that enemies may with full right be deposited and proscribed, it is reasonable that whatsoever things of an enemy are found among his enemies should change their Owner and go to the Treasury" and in several places he expressly applies the rule to *things in action*, or debts & credits as well as to things in possession.

In confirmation of his doctrine he adduces a variety of examples which embrace a period of something more than a century beginning in the year 1556 and ending in the year 1667 and which comprehend

---

Ligarius) of an individual staying in an enemy country in case of need or duty. See Cicero, *Opera*, VI, 252.

* QUÆSTIONUM JURIS PUBLIC Liber I Caput VII. "Cum ea sit belli conditio ut hostes sint omni jure spoliati proscriptique rationis est quascunque res hostium apud hostes inventas, dominum matare et Fisco cedere." [11]

8. In MS, "permisses."
9. *On the Law of War and Peace.*
10. See "The Defence No. XVIII," October 6, 1795.
11. Bynkershoek, *Quæstionum*, Book I, Ch. VII, 49.

as actors on the principle he espouses, France Spain The States General Denmark the Bishops of Cologne and Munster. But he acknowleges that the right has been questioned, and notes particularly that when the King of France and the Bishops of Munster and Cologne in the year 1673 confiscated the debts which their subjects owed to the Confederated Belgians, the States General by an Edict of the 6th of July of that year censured the proceeding and decreed that those debts could not be paid but to the true Creditors and that the exaction of them whether by force or with consent was not to be esteemed valid.

If, from the great pains which appear to have been taken by this learned writer to collect examples in proof of his doctrine we are to conclude that the collection is tolerably complete—we are warranted in drawing this inference, that he has not cured any defect which reason may discern in his principle, by any thing like the evidence of such a general uniform and continued usage as is requisite to introduce a *rule* of the positive law of Nations in derogation from the natural.

A minority only of the powers of Europe are shewn to have been implicated in the practice, and among the majority not included are several of the most considerable and respectable. One of these, Great Britain, is represented as having acquiesced in it in the Treaties of peace, between her and some of the powers who went into the practice to her detriment by relinquishing the claim of restitution.[12] But War must at length end in peace, and the sacrifices a nation makes to the latter is a slight argument of her consent to the principle of the injuries which she may have sustained. I have not been able to trace a single instance in which Great Britain has herself set the example of such a practice; nor could she do it, as has elsewhere appeared [13] without contravening an article of MAGNA CHARTA, unless by way of reprisal for the same thing done towards her. The suggestion of an instance in the present war with France will be hereafter examined. In such a question the practice of a Nation which has for ages figured so preeminently in the Commercial Wor[l]d is intitled to particular notice.

It is not unworthy of remark that the Common law of England

12. The treaties which Bynkershoek cites are those of July, 1667, between England and Denmark, and of September, 1667, between England and Spain (*Quæstionum*, Book I, Ch. VII, 58).
13. See "The Defence No. XVIII," October 6, 1795.

from its earliest dawnings contradicted the rule of the Roman Law. It exempted from seizure, by a subject of England, the property of a foreigner brought there before a war, but gave to the first seizer or occupant the property which came there after the breaking out of war.[14] The noble principles of the Common law cannot cease to engage our respect while we have before our eyes so many monuments of the excellence, in our own jurisprudence.

It also merits to be dwelt upon, that the United Netherlands for some time the first and long only the second in Commercial consequence formally disputed the right and condemned the practice of confiscating private debts, though themselves in some instances guilty of it.

And it is likewise a material circumstance that Bynkershoeck who seems to have written in the year 1737 does not adduce any precedent later than the year 1667 seventy years before his publication.

The subsequent period will it is believed be found upon strict inquiry equally barren of similar precedents. The exceptions are so few,* that we may fairly assert that there is the negative usage of near a century and a half against the pretended right. This negative usage of a period the most enlightened as well as the most commercial in the annals of the world is of the highest authority. The former usage, as being partial and with numerous exceptions, was insufficient to establish a rule. The contrary usage, or the renunciation of the former usage, as being general, as attended with few or no exceptions, is sufficient even to work a change in the

note * The case of Prussia & the Silesia loan is the only one I have found.[15]

14. Blackstone, for example, wrote: "Thus, in the first place, it hath been said, that any body may seise to his own use such goods as belong to an alien enemy. For such enemies, not being looked upon as members of our society, are not entitled during their state of enmity to the benefit or protection of the laws; and therefore every man that had opportunity is permitted to seise upon their chattels, without being compelled as in other cases to make restitution or satisfaction to the owner. But this, however generally laid down by some of our writers, must in reason and justice be restrained to such captors as are authorized by the public authority of the state, residing in the crown; and to such goods as are brought into this country by an alien enemy, after a declaration of war, without a safe-conduct or passport. And therefore it hath been holden, that where a foreigner is resident in England, and afterwards a war breaks out between his country and ours, his goods are not liable to be seised . . ." (Commentaries, II, 401).

15. H discusses this matter in some detail at a later point in this essay. See note 30.

rigour of an ancient rule, if it could be supposed to have been established. Much more is it sufficient to confirm and enforce the lesson of reason, and to dissipate the clouds which error and some scattered instances of violence and rapine may have produced.

Of the theoretical Writers whom I have had an opportunity of consulting, VATEL [16] is the only remaining one, who directly treats the point. His opinion has been said to favour the right to confiscate and sequester. But when carefully analized it will add to the proofs of the levity with which the opposers of the Treaty make assertions.

After stating among other things that "War gives the same right over any sum of money due by a neutral nation to our enemy as it can give over his other goods" he proceeds thus * "When Alexander by conquest became absolute Master of Thebes he remitted to the Thessalians a hundred talents which they owed to the Thebans. The sovereign has *naturally* the same right over *what his subjects may be indebted to his enemies.* Therefore he may *confiscate debts* of this nature, *if the term of payment happen in the time of War, or at least* he may *prohibit his subjects from paying while the War last[s]. But at present* in regard to the *advantage* and *safety* of *Commerce,* ALL THE SOVEREIGNS *of Europe have departed from this Rigour.* And as this CUSTOM has been *generally received,* he who should act contrary to it would *injure the public faith;* for strangers trusted his subjects only from a *firm persuasion* that the GENERAL CUSTOM would be observed. The State *does not so much as touch* the sums which it owes to the enemy. *Every where,* in case of a War *funds creditted to the public* are exempt from *confiscation* and *seizure.*" [17]

The first proposition of the above passage amounts to this, that "A sovereign *naturally* that is, *according to the law of Nature* may confiscate debts, which his subjects owe to his enemies, if the term of payment happen in the time of War, or *at least* he may prohibit his subjects from paying while the War lasts."

So far as this goes, it agrees with the principle, which I combat, that there is a *natural* right to confiscate *or* to sequester private debts in time of War: So far, Vatel accords with the Roman Law and with Bynkershoek.

* Book III Chap V § 77
16. Vattel, *Law of Nations.*
17. See "Report on a Plan for the Further Support of Public Credit," January 16, 1795.

But he annexes a whimsical limitation—"*if the term of payment happens in the time of war*"—and there is a marked uncertainty and hesitation—The sovereign may confiscate "or *at least* he may prohibit his subjects from paying while the War lasts." 'Tis evident that the circumstance of the time of payment can have no influence upon the right. If it reaches to confiscation which takes away the substance of the thing, the mere incident of the happening of payment must be immaterial. If it is confined to the arresting of payment during the war, the reason of the rule the object being to prevent supplies going to the enemy will apply it as well to debts which had become payable before the war as to those which became payable in the War. Whence this inaccuracy in so accurate a thinker? Whence the hesitation about so important a point, as whether the pretended right extends to confiscation or simply to sequestration? They must be accounted for as in another case by the conflict between respect for antient maxims and the impressions of juster views seconded by the more enlightened policy of modern times.

But while VATEL thus contenances in the first part of the passage the opinion that the *natural* law of Nations authorises the confiscation or sequestration of private debts, in what immediately follows he most explicitly and unequivocally informs us that the rule of that law in this respect has been abrogated by modern usage or custom—in other words that the modern *customary* law has changed in this particular the antient *natural* law. Let his own words be consulted.

"At present (says he) in regard to the *advantage* and *safety* of COMMERCE ALL THE SOVEREIGNS of europe have departed from this Rigor. And as this CUSTOM has been *generally received* he who should act contrary to it would *injure the public faith;* for strangers trusted his subjects only from the firm persuasion that the GENERAL CUSTOM would be observed."

This testimony is full, that there is a GENERAL CUSTOM received & adopted by ALL THE SOVEREIGNS of Europe, which obviates the rigor of the antient rule, that is, alters the rule; the non observance of which Custom would violate the public faith of a Nation; as being a breach of an implied Contract by virtue of the Custom upon the strength of which foreigners trust his subjects.

Language cannot describe more clearly a rule of the customary law of Nations, the essence of which we have seen is general usage implying a *tacit* agreement to conform to the rule. The one alleged is denominated a *custom generally received* a *general custom; all the sovereigns* of Europe are stated to be parties to it, and it is represented as obligatory on the public faith, since this would be injured by a departure from it. The consequence is that if the right pretended did exist by the natural law it has given way to the customary law; for tis a contradiction to call that a right which cannot be exercised without breach of faith. The result is that by the present customary law of Nations, within the sphere of its action, there is no right to confiscate or sequester private Debts in time of War. The reason or motive of which law is the advantage and safety of commerce.

As to private property in public funds, the right to meddle with them is still more emphatically negatived—"The State does not *so much as touch* the sums it owes to the enemy. *Every where* in case of a War funds creditted to the Public are exempt from confiscation and *seizure*." These terms manifestly exclude sequestration as well as confiscation.

In another place the Author gives the reason of this position—Book II Chapt XVIII [18] "In reprisals, the goods of a subject are seized in the same manner as those of the State or the Sovereign. Every thing that belongs to the nation is liable to reprisals as soon as it can be seized *provided it be not a deposit trusted to the public faith*. This DEPOSIT [19] is found in our hands only in consequence of the *confidence* which the proprietor has put in our good faith, and it ought to be respected even in case of open War. Thus it is usual to behave in France England and elsewhere with respect to the money which foreigners have placed in the public funds." The same principle if he had reflected without byas, would have taught him that reprisals could rightfully extend to nothing that had been committed with their permission to the custody and guardianship of our laws during a state of peace; and consequently that no property of our enemy which was in our Country before the breaking

18. Vattel, *Law of Nations*, Book II, Ch. XVIII, Sec. 344. The first quoted sentence reads: ". . . in reprisals they [the citizen body] seize the goods of the subject in the same manner. . . ."

19. "Depositum" in Vattel, *Law of Nations*, Book II, Ch. XVIII, Sec. 344.

out of war is justly liable to them. For is not all such property equally a deposit trusted to the public faith? What foreigner would acquire property in our country or bring and lodge it there but in the confidence that in case of war it would not become an object of reprisals? Why then resort to Custom for a denial of the right to confiscate or sequester private debts? Why not trace it to the natural injustice and perfidy of taking away in war what a foreigner is permitted to own and have among us in peace? Why ever have considered that as a natural right which was contrary to good faith tacitly pledged? Tis evidently the effect of too much deference to ferocious maxims of antiquity, of undue complaisance to some precedents of modern rapacity.

He had avoided the error by weighing maturely the consequences of his own principle in another case. "He who declares war (says he) does not confiscate the *immoveable* goods possessed in his Country by his enemy's subjects. *In permitting them to purchase and possess those goods* he has in this respect admitted them into the number of his subjects." [20] That is, he has admitted them to a like privilege with his subjects as to the real property they were permitted to acquire & hold. But Why should a less privilege attend the license to purchase possess or have other kinds of property in his Country? The reason, which is the permission of the sovereign, must extend to the protection of one kind of property as well as another, if the permission extends to both.

Vatel advances in this and in the passage quoted immediately before it the true principles which ought to govern the question, though he does not pursue them into their consequences; else he would not have deduced the exemption of private debts from confiscation or sequestration from the customary law of Nations but would have traced it to the natural or necessary law; as founded upon the obligations of good faith; upon the tacit promise of security connected with the permission to acquire property within or bring property into our Country; upon the protection which every government owes to a property of which it legalizes the acquisition or the deposit within its jursidiction—and in the case of *immoveable* goods, or real estate, of which he admits a right to sequester the *income* to prevent its being remitted to the enemy,

20. Vattel, *Law of Nations*, Book III, Ch. V, Sec. 76.

he would have perceived the necessity of leaving this effect to be produced by the obstructions intrinsically incident to a State of War; since there is no reason why the Income should be less privileged than the substance of the thing.

It appears then that the doctrine of VATEL collectively taken amounts to this, that there is a natural right of War in certain cases to confiscate or sequester enemy's property found within our Country; but that on motives relative to Commerce and Public Credit, the Customary Law of Europe has restrained that right as to *private debts* and *private property* in public funds. His opinion therefore favours the principle of the article of the Treaty under examination, as consonant with the present European Law of Nations. And it is an opinion of greater weight than any that can be cited; as well on account of the capacity diligence information and the precision of ideas which characterise the work in which it is contained as on account of the recency of that work.*

A question may be raised. Does this customary law of Nations as established in Europe bind the UStates? An affirmative answer to this is warranted by conclusive reasons.

I The U States when a member of the British Empire were in this capacity a party to that law, and not having dissented from it when they became independent they are to be considered as having continued a party to it. II The common law of England which was & is in force in each of these states adopts the law of Nations, the positive equally with the natural, as a part of itself. III Ever since we have been an Independent nation we have appealed to and acted upon the modern law of Nations as understood in Europe. Various resolutions of Congress during our revolution [22]—the correspondencies of Executive officers [23]—the decisions of our Courts of Admiralty,[24] all recognised this standard. IV Executive and legislative Acts and the proceedings of our Courts under the present government speak a similar language. The President's Proclamation

note * It appears to have been written about the year 1760.[21]
21. The date is actually 1758.
22. See, for example, *JCC*, XXI, 1136-37.
23. See the President of Congress to the Several States, November 31, 1781 (Burnett, *Letters,* VI, 271). The letter is incorrectly dated. See Burnett, *Letters,* VI, 271, note 2.
24. See *JCC*, XVI, 62; 1 *Stat.* 73-93; Goebel, *Law Practice,* II, 779-918.

of Neutrality [25] refers expressly to the *modern* law of Nations, which must necessarily be understood of that prevailing in Europe and acceded to by this Country. And the general voice of our Nation, together with the very arguments used against the Treaty accord in the same point. 'Tis indubitable that the customary law of European Nations is as a part of the common law and by adoption that of the U States.

But let it not be forgotten, that I derive the vindication of the article from a higher source; from the natural or necessary law of nations, from the eternal principles of morality & good faith.

There is one more authority which I shall cite in reference to a part of the question—property in the public funds. It is a Report to the British King in the year 1753, from Sir George Lee Judge of the Prerogative Court Doctor Paul [26] Advocate General in the Courts of Civil Law Sir Dudley Ryder [27] and Mr. Murray [28] Attorney & Solicitor General * on the subject of the Silesia loan sequestered by the King of Prussia by way of reprisal for the capture and condemnation of some Prussian Vessels.[30] This Report merits

* Sir George Lee was afterwards the very celebrated Chief Justice [29] & Mr. Murray was the late Lord Mansfield.

25. George Washington's neutrality proclamation is dated April 22, 1793. For the text, see John Jay to H, April 11, 1793, note 1.

26. George Paul, who died in 1763.

27. Ryder was attorney general from 1734 until 1754. He then became lord chief justice of the King's Bench. In 1756 he was created first baron Harrowby.

28. William Murray, who subsequently became first earl of Mansfield, was solicitor general from 1742 until 1754. He succeeded Sir Dudley Ryder, first as attorney general and then as lord chief justice.

29. Lee was dean of arches and judge of the Prerogative Court of Canterbury from 1751 until his death in 1758. His brother, Sir William Lee, was the "very celebrated Chief Justice" from 1737 until 1754.

30. In 1735, the emperor Charles VI had borrowed one million crowns from British creditors, to be repaid ten years later from the mortgaged Silesian revenues. In 1740, Frederick II of Prussia overran Silesia, and in his first treaty of annexation (at Breslau in 1742) he assumed responsibility for the debt to the British. Later, as the ruler of a neutral power during the war between Great Britain and France and Spain, which had broken out in 1744, he protested the capture by British ships of Prussian vessels which were alleged to be carrying contraband supplies to France. In reprisal, Frederick suspended repayment of the loan, which according to the original agreement should already have been repaid, and he issued a formal justification for his actions. The answer of the British court was the "Report of the Committee Nominated by his Britannic Majesty to Reply to the Statement of Reasons Formulated by the Court of Berlin," January 18, 1753 (Thomas Baty, ed., *Prize Law and Continuous Voyage* [London, 1915], 116–34). This report, in

all the respect which can be derived from consummate knowlege and ability in the Reporters, but it would lose much of its weight from the want of impartiality which might fairly be imputed to the Officers of one of the Governments interested in the Contest— had it not since received the eulogies and concurrence of impartial and celebrated foreign Writers. Among these, VATEL calls it an *excellent piece* on the law of Nations.[31]

The following is an extract—"The King of Prussia has pleged his Royal word to pay the Silesia Debt to *private men*. It is negotiable and many parts of it have been assigned to the subjects of other powers. It will not be easy to *find an instance*, where a Prince has thought fit to make reprisals upon *a debt due from himself to private men*. There is a *confidence that this will not be done*. A private man *lends money to a Prince upon an engagement of honor, because a prince cannot be compelled like other men in an adversary way by a Court of Justice*. So scrupulously did England and France adhere to this *public faith*, that even during the War, they suffered no inquiry to be made whether any part of the public Debt was due to the subjects of *the enemy*, though it is certain many English had money in the French Funds and many French had money in our's." [32]

The universal obligation of good faith is thus reenforced on a special ground by the *point of honor;* to confirm the position that money which a sovereign or State owes to private men is not a proper object of Reprisals.

---

addition to summarizing the facts of the case, contained a statement of the law of nations on the rights of powers at war to make prizes of neutral ships. On September 10, 1794, Sir William Scott, King's advocate-general, and John (later Sir John) Nicholl, in a letter replying to John Jay's request for a "Statement of the general Principles of Proceeding in Prize Causes in British Courts of Admiralty and of the Measures proper to be taken when a Ship and Cargo are brought in as Prize within their jurisdiction," quoted extensively from the theoretical part of the report and gave their opinion that "the general Principles of Proceeding" could not "be stated more correctly or succinctly" than they were in the report in question (LS, Columbia University Libraries). Jay sent a copy of this letter to Edmund Randolph on September 13, 1794 (ALS, RG 59, Despatches from United States Ministers to Great Britain, 1791–1906, Vol. 1, April 19, 1794–June 1, 1795, National Archives).

31. *Law of Nations*, Book II, Ch. VII, Sec. 85, note a.

32. Baty, *Prize Law and Continuous Voyage*, 132. H's quotation differs slightly in wording from the published version.

This case of the Silesia debt is the only example within the present Century prior to the existing War, which I have been able to trace, violating the immunity of private debts or private property in public funds. 'Tis a precedent that can have little weight not only from its singularity but from the character of its author. FREDERICK was a consummate general, a profound Statesman, but he was far from being a severe moralist. This is not the only instance in which he tarnished his faith, and the friends of his fame must regret that he could not plead on the occasion those mighty and dazzling reasons of State which are the specious apologies for his other aberrations.

It is asserted that the present war of Europe affords examples of the practice which I reprobate and that Great Britain herself has given one.[33]

The present War of Europe is of so extraordinary a complexion and has been conducted in all respects upon such extraordinary principles, that it may truly be regarded as an exception to all general rules as a precedent for nothing. Tis rather a beacon warning mankind to shun the pernicious examples which it sets, than a model inviting to imitation. The human passions on all sides appear to have been wrought up to a pitch of phrenzy, which has set Reason justice and humanity at defiance.

Those who have nevertheless thought fit to appeal to the examples of this very anomalous War have not detailed to us the precise na-

33. See the third essay by "Decius," in which Brockholst Livingston wrote: "Mr. Jefferson . . . when speaking of the rightful acts of war, says, 'It cannot be denied that the state of war strictly permits a nation to seize the property of its enemies found within its own limits, or taken in war, and in whatever form it exists, whether in *action or possession*.' I shall not conceal that, although this practice is strictly permitted by the laws of nations, yet those sovereigns of Europe who act with good faith, have generally departed from this right, so far that public funds are generally exempted from confiscation, and seizure. Great Britain, however, regardless of the conduct of other nations, has, if we are rightly informed, confiscated or sequestered during the present war, debts of both these descriptions; although Vattel says, that a state ought never to touch the sums which it owes to the enemy. From what has been said, it results that the United States in case of a war with Great Britain, have an undoubted right to confiscate any debts due by her citizens to the subjects of Great Britain, and that if she choose to adopt the conduct of that nation, she might confiscate or sequester the property which they hold in our funds" (*The* [New York] *Argus, or Greenleaf's New Daily Advertiser*, July 13, 1795). For the authorship of the "Decius" essays, see the introductory note to "The Defence No. I," July 22, 1795.

ture or course of the transactions to which they refer, nor do I know that sufficient documents have appeared in this Country to guide us in the inquiry.

The imperfect evidence which has fallen under my observation respects France and Great Britain, and seems to exhibit these facts.

France past a decree sequestering the property of the powers at War with her,[34] and in the same or another decree obliged all those of her Citizens who had monies owing to them in foreign Countries to draw bills upon their Debtors and to furnish those bills to the Government by way of loan or upon certain terms of payment.[35]

The Government of Great Britain in consequence of this proceeding passed two different acts,[36] the objects of which were to prevent

34. The newspaper reads: ". . . the property of the subjects of the powers at War with her."
This is a reference to "Décret relatif au séquestre des biens possédés sur le territoire français par les princes ou puissances avec lesquels la France est en guerre," May 9–11, 1793, which reads: "Art. 1er. Dans les départemens ou il existe des biens possédés par les princes ou puissances avec lesquels la République est en guerre, ces biens seront séquestrés, si ce n'est fait, par les corps administratifs de ces départmens, dans la forme prescrite pour le séquestre des biens des émigrés, et ce, immédiatement après la réception du present décret.
"2. Aussitôt après le séquestre, il en sera donné avis aux administrateurs de la régie des domaines nationaux, qui les feront régir par des préposés, en prenant sous leur responsabilité tous les moyens pour assurer la sûreté de cette administration.
"3. Les sommes provenant des revenus de ces biens, seront versées dans les caisses des receveurs des districts respectifs, et par ceux-ci à la Trésorerie nationale. Ces différens comptables tiendront de ces revenus une comptabilité particulière et distincte des autres revenus nationaux, en observant un ordre de subdivision de ce qui proviendra de chaque différent possesseur et de chacun des différens objets de revenu.
"4. L'administrateur des domaines nationaux exercera sur les séquestres et la régie des biens mentionnés en la présente loi, la surveillance qui lui est attribuée sur les biens des émigrés par le décret du 12 mars dernier, et conformément audit décret." (J. B. Duvergier, *Collection Complète des Lois, Décrets, Ordonnances, Réglemens, et Avis du Conseil-d'Etat, Publiée sur les Editions Officielles du Louvre; de L'Imprimerie Nationale, Par Baudouin, et Du Bulletin des Lois* [Paris, 1824], V, 344.)
35. This is a reference to a decree issued on January 2, 1794, by a commission created by the committees of Finance, Public Safety, and General Welfare. An English translation of the decree and also of a series of resolutions, adopted on December 27, 1793, on which the decree is based is printed in *The Parliamentary Register; or History of the Proceedings and Debates of the House of Commons* . . . (London, 1794), XXXVII, 249–50.
36. The first act, entitled "An Act for preventing Money or Effects, in the Hands of his Majesty's Subjects, belonging to or disposable by Persons resident in *France*, being applied to the Use of the Persons exercising the

the payment of those bills and to secure the sums due for the benefit of the original Creditors. These acts appoint certain Commissioners to whom reports are to be made of all French property in
the hands of British subjects, and who are empowered to receive
and sell goods and other effects, to collect debts, and to deposit
the proceeds in the Bank of London, or in other safekeeping, if
preferred & requested by parties interested. The monies deposited
are to be invested in the purchase of public stock, together with the
interest or dividends arising from time to time, to be eventually
accounted for to the proprietors. The Commissioners have likewise
a discretion upon demand to deliver over their effects and monies
to such of the proprietors as do not reside within the French
Dominions.

I shall not enter into a discussion of the propriety of these acts
of Great Britain. It is sufficient to observe that they are attended
with circumstances which very essentially discriminate them from
the thing for which they are quoted. The act of the French Government was in substance, a compulsory assumption of all the
property of its citizens in foreign countries. This extraordinary
measure presented two options to the Government of these countries—one to consider the transfer as virtually effected and to confiscate the property as being no longer that of the individuals but
that of the Government of France—the other to defeat the effect
of her plan by tying up the property for the benefit of the Original
Creditors in exclusion of the drafts which they were compelled to
draw. Great Britain appears to have elected the latter course. If we
suppose her sincere in the motive and there is fairness and fidelity
in the execution, the issue will be favourable rather than detrimental
to the rights of private property.

I have said that there was an option to confiscate. A government
may rightfully confiscate the property of an adversary Government.
No principle of justice or policy occurs to forbid reprisals upon the

---

Powers of Government in *France;* and for preserving the property thereof
for the benefit of the Individual Owners thereof," was passed on March 1,
1794 (34 Geo. III, C. 9). The second, "An Act for more effectually preserving Money or Effects, in the Hands of his Majesty's Subjects, belonging
to, or disposable by, Persons resident in *France,* for the Benefit of the Individual Owners thereof," was passed on July 7, 1794, and provided for the
appointment of commissioners to carry out the provisions of the first act (34
Geo. III, C. 79).

public or national property of an enemy. That case is foreign in every view to the principles which protect private property. The exemption stipulated by the 10th article of the Treaty is accordingly restricted to the latter.

It appears that the Government of France convinced by the effect of the experiment that the sequestration of the property of the subjects of her enemies was impolitic thought fit to rescind it. Hence on the 29th of December 1794 the Convention decreed as follows—

"The decrees concerning the sequestration of the property of the subjects of the powers at War with the Republic are annulled. Such sums as have been paid by French Citizens into the Treasury in consequence of those Decrees will be reimbursed." [37]

In the course of the debates upon this decree, it was declared that the decrees which it was to repeal *had prepared the ruin of Commerce* and had severed, *against the right of Nations,* the *obligations* of Merchants in different states.[38] This is a direct admission that the sequestration was contrary to the law of Nations.

As far as respects France, then, the precedent upon the whole is a strong condemnation of the pretended right to confiscate or sequester. This formal renunciation of the ground which was at first taken is a very emphatical protest against the principle of the measure. It ought to serve us too as an instructive warning against the employment of so mischievous and disgraceful an expedient.[39]

Thus we perceive that *opinion* and *usage,* far from supporting the right to confiscate or sequester private property on account of National Wars, when referred to the *modern* standard, turn against that right and coincide with the principle of the article of the Treaty under examination.

What remains to be offered will further illustrate its propriety and reconcile to it all reflecting men.   CAMILLUS

37. Debrett, *A Collection of State Papers,* II, 242.
38. Dominique-Vincent Ramel Nogaret made this statement. For the text of the debate, see *Réimpression de L'Ancien Moniteur. Seule Histoire Authentique et Inaltérée de la Révolution Française . . .* (Paris, 1847), XXIII, 89–91.
39. In the newspaper the following sentence was added to this paragraph: "And as to England, as has been shewn, the precedent is foreign to the question."

Certificate for Ephraim Brasher [1]

[New York, October 26, 1795]

I certify as will appear by letters on file in the Office [2] that I did while Secretary of the Treasury on behalf of the Government empower Mr Seton [3] to procure the within mentioned assays to be made and that compensation was due for the same from the U States.

New York October 26. 1795
A Hamilton

Twas at the time a Report on the Mint was preparing. [4]

ADS, RG 217, Miscellaneous Treasury Accounts, 1790–1894, Account No. 7363, National Archives.

1. Ephraim Brasher, a goldsmith, was also an assistant justice of the peace of New York City in 1795.

H's certificate accompanied Brasher's account on October 24, 1795, submitted to the Treasury Department for payment for assays made in 1791 (ADS, RG 217, Miscellaneous Treasury Accounts, 1790–1894, Account No. 7363, National Archives).

2. See H to William Seton, November 16, December 2, 7, 1790, June 17, 1791; Seton to H, December 28, 1790, January 10, August 15, 1791.

Seton, who had been cashier of the Bank of New York, had resigned that position in June, 1794. See Seton to H, June 16, 1794.

3. Brasher's account was accompanied by the following note, dated October 24, 1795, from Seton: "I Do Certify, That at the request of Alexr. Hamilton Esq. the then Secretary of the Treasury I did employ Mr. Ephraim Brasher to make the Assays above mentioned & believe his Charge for the same to be just" (ADS, RG 217, Miscellaneous Treasury Accounts, 1790–1894, Account No. 7363, National Archives).

4. "Report on the Establishment of a Mint," January 28, 1791.

On November 27, 1795, Warrant No. 5502 was issued to Brasher for twenty-seven dollars (D, RG 217, Miscellaneous Treasury Accounts, 1790–1894, Account No. 7363, National Archives).

To John Stevens [1]

New York, October 26, 1795. "Lady Sterling [2] has consulted me on the subject of the enclosed letter but without more facts than she is possessed of, I cannot judge with certainty in whom the right to the certificates is. *Prima facie* it is not in Mr. Dayton. [3] But

I shall write to that Gentleman to know precisely the grounds of his claim. This information obtained I shall be able to form a final opinion on the right. It will be adviseable for you in the mean time to defer a compliance with Mr. Dayton's demand. . . ." [4]

ALS, Stevens Institute of Technology, Hoboken, New Jersey.

1. Stevens, a successful businessman who lived in Hoboken, was a pioneer in the development of steamboats.

This letter concerns a complicated and protracted dispute between Lady Stirling and her late husband's creditors over certain unspecified certificates. Stevens's interest in this dispute arose because his mother was the sister of Lord Stirling; because his father, who had died in 1792, had at one time controlled some of the certificates in question; and because he was the executor of his father's estate.

2. Lady Stirling, Sarah Livingston Alexander, was the daughter of Philip Livingston, second lord of the manor, and widow of William Alexander, self-styled Lord Stirling, a major general in the American Revolution who had died in 1783.

3. Jonathan Dayton, a veteran of the American Revolution, had served in the New Jersey Assembly in 1786, 1787, and 1790 and was a Federalist member of the House of Representatives from 1791 to 1799. Dayton was Speaker of the House from March 4, 1795, to March 3, 1799.

For an explanation of Dayton's claim to the certificates in question, see Dayton to H, January 15, 1796.

4. H had been involved earlier in the disposal of Stirling's estate, as is shown in the following item, dated, December 28, 1791, from *The* [New York] *Daily Advertiser*, January 4, 1792:

"TO BE SOLD,

"At the Merchants coffee-house, in the city of New-York, on Tuesday the seventh day of February, one thousand seven hundred and ninety two, at public auction (unless sold at private sale before)

"That elegant country seat, formerly belonging to the earl of Sterling, and well known by the name of Baskingridge. It lies on the Pasaick river in the county of Morris, state of New-Jersey, near the great road which leads from Morristown to Philadelphia, and is about thirty miles from New-York. This place when in the possession of Lord Sterling, was considered as one of the best farms in the country, and is still accounted, by those who are judges of soil and situation, to be an excellent tract of land, and capable of high and productive cultivation. There is a large orchard and several meadows upon it, of good quality, and more may be easily made. The mansion house and numerous out houses, will require some repairs. The farm contains between ten and eleven hundred acres, but will be sold in smaller parcels, if convenient to the purchaser; a good title will be given for the premises; any person wishing to view the place may apply to Daniel M'Call, who lives upon a part of the land. . . ." The advertisement was signed by H, Thomas Jones, J. H. Livingston, and Brockholst Livingston.

To George Washington

New York October 26
1795

Sir

I have noticed a piece in the Aurora under the signature of the *Calm Observer* which I think requires explanation and I mean to give one with my name.[1] I have written to Mr. Wolcott for materials from the Books of the Treasury.[2]

Should you think it proper to meet the vile insinuation in the close of it by furnishing for one year the account of expenditure of the salary, I will with pleasure add what may be proper on that point. If there be any such account signed by Mr. Lear[3] it may be useful.

I wrote to you some days since directed to you at Philadelphia chiefly on the subject of Young La Fayette.[4] I mention it merely that you may have knowlege that there is such a letter in case it has not yet come to hand.

I touched in it upon a certain *intercepted Letter.*[5] The more I have reflected, the more I am of opinion that it is inadviseable the whole should speedily appear. With affection & respect

I have the honor to be Sir   Yr. Obed serv   A Hamilton

The President of The U States

ALS, George Washington Papers, Library of Congress; copy, Hamilton Papers, Library of Congress.

1. On October 23, 1795, an article by "A Calm Observer" appeared in the [Philadelphia] *Aurora. General Advertiser.* Addressed to Oliver Wolcott, Jr., the article accused Washington of having overdrawn his annual salary of twenty-five thousand dollars. The article reads in part: "By an annual act of Congress, provision is made for the President's compensation by a specific appropriation of the sum of 25,000 dollars and no more.

"Between the 30th of April 1789, the day on which the President qualified into office and the 30th of April 1790, which completed the first year of his Presidency he drew by warrants from the late Secretary of the Treasury countersigned by the Comptroller the sum of 25,000 and no more.

"Between the 30th of April 1790 and the 30th of April 1791 being the second year of his service the President drew by like warrants the sum of 30,150 dollars, being an excess beyond annual compensation made by law and the appropriation thereof by Congress of 5,150 dollars.

"Between the 30th of April 1791 and the 30th of April 1792, being the third year of his service the President drew by like warrants the sum of 24,000 dollars which being 1000 dollars less than his annual compensation reduced the excess that he received the year before to 4.150 dollars.

"Between the 30th of April 1792 and the 30th of April 1793 being the fourth year of his service the President drew by like warrants the sum of 26,000 which again made up the excess of his second year's compensation to 5,150 dollars more than the law allows.

"On the 4th of March 1793 when the first term of four years for which the President was elected into office expired, he had drawn from the public Treasury by warrants from the late Secretary of the Treasury, countersigned by the Comptroller the sum of 1037 dollars beyond the compensation allowed him by law estimating from the day he qualified into office.

"The evidence of the sums drawn and of the truth of the facts here stated, will be seen in the official reports made to Congress of the annual receipts and expenditures of the public monies, signed by you as Comptroler of the Treasury, and which have been published for the information of the people.

"But, Sir, as if it had been determined by the late Secretary of the Treasury, and yourself as Comptroler, to set at defiance all law and authority, and to exhibit the completest evidence of service submission and compliance with the lawless will and pleasure of the President, attend to the following facts. . . .

"On the 18th of February 1793 Congress passed an act providing that 'from and after the 3d day of March in the present year (1793) the compensation of the President of the United States shall be *at the rate of 25,000 dollars per annum in full for his services, to be paid* QUARTER YEARLY *at the Treasury.*'

"Between the 4th day of March 1793, and the 4th day of June following, being the first quarter after the passing of the last mentioned act, there was paid to the President out of the public treasury by warrants from the late Secretary of the Treasury, countersigned by you as Comptroller, the sum of eleven thousand dollars, being an excess of 4750 dollars in one quarter beyond the compensation allowed by law, and making at the same rate a compensation of 44,000 dollars per annum instead of the 25,000 dollars, fixed by Congress."

On October 24, 1795, Wolcott answered the charges in a letter addressed to Benjamin Franklin Bache, editor of the [Philadelphia] *Aurora. General Advertiser.* Wolcott's letter reads: "I have read in your paper of the 23d inst. an indecent invective addressed to me, under the signature of 'A Calm Observer,' the object of which, is to impress an opinion on the public mind, that the President has received from the Treasury greater sums than were authorized by law. As connected with the main design of calumniating the Executive, the writer has, however, adduced against my predecessor and myself, the serious charges—of having violated the Constitution of the United States, by issuing monies for which there was no appropriation—of having violated the law establishing the Treasury Department, which directs that no warrants on the Treasurer, shall be signed by the Secretary, or countersigned by the Comptroller, unless pursuant to some appropriation—of having violated the oath prescribed for the officers of the treasury.

"In respect to the President, it is proper to say, that it has been well understood at the treasury, that the monies appropriated for his compensation, were applied *solely* to defray the expences of his household, of which a regular account has been kept by his private secretary. The advances from the Treasury have heretofore been uniformly made on the *application* & in the *name* of some one of the private secretaries, except in a single instance, lately, when the present secretary was absent. The *special order* of the President for monies to defray the current expences of his household, has never been deemed necessary.

"If, therefore, there has been an error in advancing monies, the President is not responsible for it; he is merely accountable in a pecuniary view for the act of his agent; as a matter affecting personal character, he is in no manner concerned.

"The responsibility for whatever is complained of by the 'Calm Observer,' therefore rests entirely upon the Treasury Department, and I readily assume it to myself. At the same time I affirm, notwithstanding what is asserted to the contrary, that not one dollar has been advanced at any time for which there was not an existing appropriation by law; & it is my belief, that nothing in the least degree contrary to law, has been practiced in respect to the time and manner of making the advances.

"Candid men will believe this to be a sincere declaration when they are told that the course of conduct which is now censured, has prevailed ever since the Treasury Department was established, and that the accounts which exhibit the evidence of this conduct, have been regularly laid before Congress, and have been printed and disseminated throughout the United States. It is not credible that the officers of the Treasury have knowingly violated the law, and at the same time have published the evidence of their guilt.

"Mr. Bache, such has been the virulence of the attacks in your paper against public measures, and the characters of men, who, until they held public appointments were thought to deserve the confidence of their fellow citizens, that I believe a common opinion prevails, that some decisive explanation is necessary: that it is time it was known whether the public officers deserve all, or any part of the abuse which you publish; or, whether there exists a confederacy whose nefarious object it is, by calumny and misrepresentations, to induce the people to believe, that those who manage their public concerns, are utterly destitute of integrity. I accede to this opinion—I invite the explanation as it respects myself—I wish that it may embrace the accusers of government—I await the consequences of the charges which you have published, that I have violated the constitution and laws of my country; and the oath of office which I have taken. I shall not avoid an investigation of my public conduct—and I hope not long to regret that slander can be published in your paper with impunity." ([Philadelphia] *Aurora. General Advertiser,* October 26, 1795.)

2. H to Wolcott, October 26, 1795.

3. Tobias Lear had served as Washington's secretary from 1786 to June, 1793.

4. H to Washington, October 16, 1795.

5. This is a reference to Fauchet's Dispatch No. 10, which had been intercepted by the British and turned over to the Washington Administration. For the way in which the contents of this dispatch led to Edmund Randolph's resignation as Secretary of State, see Wolcott to H, July 30, 1795, note 1.

To Oliver Wolcott, Junior

New York [October] 26. 1795

Dr. Sir

I have observed in the "Aurora" a piece under the signature of

"A calm Observer" which I think merits attention.[1] It is my design to reply to it with my name but for this I wish to be furnished *as soon as possible* with the account of the President and of the appropriations for him as it stands in the Secretary's office the Comptroller's and the account rendered to Congress, & also the account of appropriations for this object. Of one point I am sure that we never exceeded the *appropriations* though we may have anticipated the *service*. Add any remarks you may judge useful. The sooner the better.

Yrs. truly   A Hamilton

Oliver Wolcott Esq

ALS, Connecticut Historical Society, Hartford; copy, Hamilton Papers, Library of Congress.
1. See H to George Washington, October 26, 1795, note 1.

To Oliver Wolcott, Junior

New York October 27
1795

Dr. Sir

I wish the statements requested in my letter of yesterday may contain each particular payment not aggregates for periods. It runs in my mind that once there being no appropriation I procured an informal advance for The President from the bank—if this is so let me know the time & particulars. If the Account has been wound up to an exact adjustment since the period noticed by the calm observer,[1] it may be useful to carry it down to that period.

I should like to have a note of other instances of advances on account of salaries.

Yrs.   A Hamilton

Oliver Wolcott Esq

ALS, Connecticut Historical Society, Hartford; copy, Hamilton Papers, Library of Congress.
1. See H to George Washington, October 26, 1795, note 1.

To Oliver Wolcott, Junior [1]

New York Oct. 28. 1795

Dr. Sir.

I have seen with pleasure your reply to the calm observer.[2] I believe it is as far as you ought to go but more particular explanation will be useful & from me now a private man intirely proper. I therefore hope to receive as soon as may be the statements I requested.[3]

Yrs.   A Hamilton

Oliver Wolcott Esq

ALS, Dartmouth College Library.
   1. For background to this letter, see H to George Washington, October 26, 1795, note 1.
   2. For Wolcott's reply to "A Calm Observer," see H to Washington, October 26, 1795, note 1.
   3. H to Wolcott, October 26, 27, 1795.

From George Washington

Philadelphia 29th. Oct 1795.

My dear Sir,   (Private)

Two or three days ago I wrote you a few lines in haste,[1] and promised one more lengthy when I was more at leisure. For this purpose I am now seated.

The letters from young Fayette and Mr. Frestal;[2] my letter to Mr. Cabot; and his answer[3] (all of which are herewith enclosed for your perusal—mine in the rough state it was first drawn and to be returned when read) will give you a full view of what I have already done in this affair, up to the present moment. I have, unavailingly, owing to accidents, been endeavouring through indirect means, to learn Mr. Adets[4] sentiments relative to the coming over of this young gentleman. But if you, after the information now given; and the reiterated assurance of what I have expressed in my letter to Mr. Cabot, and which I authorise you to repeat to him again, in the very strongest terms you can conceive, should be of opinion that I ought to go further at this time, I will do so at all events: for to be in the place of a father and friend to him I am resolved, under any circumstances. If therefore, as I have just said, you should think that good would come from it; or even consolation flow therefrom to young Fayette and his Tutor; I pray you to send them hither incog, without delay, that some plan may be fixed upon: in settling of which, I pray you to give me your ideas of that which shall appear most eligable either by them, or previous to their arrival here.

Other matters which I have to communicate, shall become the subject of another letter.[5]

I am ever and Affectionately   Yours   Go: Washington

Colo. Hamilton.

ALS, Hamilton Papers, Library of Congress.
   1. Letter not found.
   2. For the letters of George Washington Motier Lafayette and Felix Frestel to Washington, see H to Washington, October 16, 1795, note 1.
   3. For Washington's correspondence with George Cabot, Federalist Senator from Massachusetts, see H to Washington, October 16, 1795, note 1.
   4. Pierre Auguste Adet, French Minister to the United States.
   5. Washington to H, October 29, 1795.

From George Washington

Philadelphia 29th. Oct. 1795.

My dear Sir,   (Private & confidential)

A voluminous publication is daily expected from Mr. R——. The paper alluded to in the extract of his letter to me, of the 8th. instt. and inserted in all the Gazettes, is a letter of my own, to him;[1] from which he intends (as far as I can collect from a combination of circumstances) to prove an inconsistency in my conduct, in ratifying the Treaty with G. Britain, without making a rescinding

ALS, Hamilton Papers, Library of Congress.
   1. For information on this exchange of letters between Edmund Randolph and Washington, see H to Washington, October 16, 1795, note 5.

(by the British government) of what is commonly called the Provision order,[2] equally with the exception of the 12th. article, by the
Senate,[3] a condition of that ratification. Intending thereby to
shew, that my *final* decision thereon, was the result of party-advice;
and that that party was under British influence. It being a letter of
my own which he asked for, I did not hesitate a moment to furnish
him therewith; and to authorise him to publish every private letter
I ever wrote, and every word I ever uttered to him, if *he* thought
they wd. contribute to his vindication: But the paper he asked for,
is but a mite of the volume that is to appear; for without any previous knowledge of mine, he had compiled every official paper (before this was asked) for publication; the knowledge of which can
subserve the purposes he has in view; and why they have not made
their appearance before this, I know not, as it was intimated in the
published extract of his letter to me, that nothing retarded it but
the want of the paper then applied for, which was furnished the
day after my arrival in this city—where (on the 20th. instt) I
found his letter, after it had gone to Alexandria & had returned.

I shall now touch upon another subject, as unpleasant as the one
I have just quitted. What am I to do for a Secretary of State?[4] I
ask frankly, & with solicitude; and shall receive kindly, any sentiments you may express on the occasion. That there may be no
concealment; & that the non-occupancy of the office until this time
may be accounted for (I tell you in confidence that) Mr. Paterson
of New-Jersey; Mr. Thos. Johnson of Maryland; Genl Pinckney
of So. Carolina; and Mr Patrick Henry of Virginia; in the order
they are mentioned, have all been applied to and refused.[5] Would

2. See Washington to H, July 7, 1795, note 3, and Oliver Wolcott, Jr., to
H, July 30, 1795, note 2.
3. On June 24, 1795, the Senate agreed to a conditional ratification of the
Jay Treaty with the stipulation that Article 12 be partially suspended and a
supplementary article added to the treaty. See H to Rufus King, June 11,
1795, notes 2 and 3, and Washington to H, July 13, 1795, note 5.
4. After the resignation of Randolph as Secretary of State on August 19,
1795, Washington appointed Secretary of War Timothy Pickering as Acting
Secretary of State. For the events leading to Randolph's resignation, see
Wolcott to H, July 30, 1795, note 1.
5. Ashworth and Carroll state that Washington's offer to William Paterson,
associate justice of the Supreme Court, was oral, but they furnish no evidence
to substantiate this statement (Freeman, *Washington*, VII, 300). For Washington's offers to the other individuals mentioned in this sentence, see Washington to Thomas Johnson, August 24, 1795 (ADfS, George Washington

Mr King accept it? [6] You know the objections I have had to the nomination, to office, any person from either branch of the Legislature; and you will be at no loss to perceive, that at the present crisis, another reason might be adduced against this appointment.[7] But maugre all objections, if Mr. King wd. accept, I would look no further. Can you sound, and let me know soon, his sentiments on this occasion. If he should seem disposed to listen to the proposition—tell him *candidly*, all that I have done in this matter; that neither he, nor I, may be made uneasy thereafter from the discovery of it; he will, I am confident perceive the ground upon which I have acted in making these essays; and will, I am persuaded, appreciate my motives. If he should decline also, pray learn with precision from him, what the qualifications of Mr. Potts. the Senator [8] are—and be as diffusive as you can with respect to others, and I will decide on nothing until I hear from you—pressing as the case is.

To enable you to judge of this matter with more lights still; I add, that Mr Marshall [9] of Virginia has declined the Office of Attorney General, and I am pretty certain would accept of no other: And I know that Colo. Carrington [10] would not come into the War

Papers, Library of Congress); Washington to Charles Cotesworth Pinckney, August 24, 1795 (ADfS, George Washington Papers, Library of Congress); and Washington to Patrick Henry, October 9, 1795 (ADfS, George Washington Papers, Library of Congress). Johnson's letter declining the position is dated August 29, 1795 (ALS, George Washington Papers, Library of Congress); Pinckney's letter is dated September 16, 1795 (ALS, George Washington Papers, Library of Congress); and Henry's letter is dated October 16, 1795 (ALS, photostat, George Washington Papers, Library of Congress).

6. Senator Rufus King of New York.

7. Washington is presumably referring to King's public defense of the Jay Treaty and his close personal association with Jay.

8. Richard Potts was a member of the Maryland House of Delegates from 1779 to 1780 and from 1787 to 1788. He was a member of the Continental Congress in 1781 and 1782, and in 1788 served as a delegate to the Maryland Ratifying Convention. From 1789 to 1791 he was the United States attorney for the District of Maryland, and from 1791 to 1793 chief judge of the fifth judicial circuit of Maryland. He was elected to the United States Senate on January 10, 1793, upon the resignation of Charles Carroll of Carrollton.

9. Washington offered the position of Attorney General to John Marshall on August 26, 1795 (ALS, George Washington Papers, Library of Congress). Marshall declined the offer on August 31, 1795 (ALS, RG 59, Miscellaneous Letters, 1790–1799, National Archives).

10. Edward Carrington. On October 9, 1795, Washington asked Carrington whether he would accept the position of Secretary of War, if Pickering were

department (if a vacancy should happen therein). Mr. Dexter,[11] it is said, would accept the Office of Attorney General. No person is yet absolutely fixed on for that office. Mr. Smith [12] of So. Carolina would, sometime ago, have had no objection to filling a respectable office under the Genl. government; but what his views might lead to, or his abilities particularly fit him for, I am an incompetent judge: and besides, on the ground of popularity, his pretensions would, I fear, be small. Mr. Chase [13] of Maryland is, unquestionably, a man of abilities; and it is supposed by some, that he wd. accept the appointment of Attorney General. Though opposed to the adoption of the Constitution, it is said he has been a steady friend to the general government since it has been in operation. But he is violently opposed in his own State by a party, and is besides, or to speak more correctly has been; accused of some impurity in his conduct.[14] I might add to this catalogue, that Colo Innis [15] is among the number of those who have passed in review; but his extreme indolence renders his abilities (great as they are said to be) of little use. In short, what with the non-acceptances of some; the known deriliction of those who are most fit; the exceptionable draw backs from others; and a wish (if it were practicable) to make a geographical distribution of the *great* officers of the Administration, I find the selection of proper characters an arduous duty.

---

moved to the State Department (ALS, George Washington Papers, Library of Congress; LC, George Washington Papers, Library of Congress). Carrington refused the appointment on October 13, 1795 (ALS, George Washington Papers, Library of Congress).

11. Timothy Pickering had recommended Samuel Dexter, a Massachusetts lawyer, for the position of Attorney General in a letter to Washington on September 21, 1795 (ALS, George Washington Papers, Library of Congress). Dexter had been a member of the House of Representatives from March 4, 1793, to March 3, 1795. On September 27, 1795, Washington rejected this proposal because Dexter had been defeated recently for re-election to the House of Representatives (Washington to Pickering [ALS, George Washington Papers, Library of Congress]).

12. William Loughton Smith of South Carolina was a member of the House of Representatives.

13. Samuel Chase, chief justice of Maryland.

14. This is apparently a reference to the fact that in 1778 Chase had used information obtained as a member of the Continental Congress to join with others in an attempt to effect a corner on flour. See "Publius Letter, I," October 16, 1778; "Publius Letter, II," October 26, 1778; "Publius Letter, III," November 16, 1778.

15. James Innes of Virginia, a veteran of the American Revolution, was a member of the Virginia Assembly from 1780 to 1782 and from 1785 to 1787. He was elected attorney general of Virginia in 1786.

The period is approaching, indeed is already come, for selecting the proper subjects for my communications to Congress at the opening of the next Session [16]—and the manner of treating them merits more than the consideration of a moment. The crisis, and the incomplete state in which most of the important affairs of this country are, at present, make the first more difficult and the latter more delicate than usual.

The Treaty with G. Britain is not yet concluded. After every consideration, however, I could bestow on it (and after entertaining very serious doubts of the propriety of doing it, on account of the Provision order) [17] it has been ratified by me: what has been, or will be done by the governmt. of G. Britain relative to it, is not now and probably will not be known by the meeting of Congress: Yet, such perhaps is the state of that business, as to make a communication thereof to the Legislature necessary: whether in the conciser form, or to accompany it with some expression of my sense of the thing itself, & the manner in which it has been treated, merits deep reflection. If good would flow from the latter, by a just & temperate communication of my ideas to the community at large, through this medium; guarded so as not to add fuel to passions prepared to blaze—and at the same time so expressed as not to excite the criticisms, or animadversions of European Powers, I would readily embrace it. But I would, decidedly, avoid every expression which could be construed a deriliction of the powers of the President with the advice and consent of the Senate to make Treaties; or into a shrinking from any act of mine relative to it. In a word, if a conciliatory plan can be assimilated with a firm, manly & dignified conduct in this business, it would be desirable; but the latter I will never yield. On this head it may not be amiss to add, that no official (nor indeed other) account have been received from France of the reception of the Treaty with G. Britain, by the National Convention. Perhaps it is too soon to expect any.

Our negociations with Spain, as far as accts. have been recd. from Mr Pinckney [18] (soon after his arrival there, but after a conference

16. Congress was scheduled to convene on December 7, 1795.

17. See Washington to H, July 7, 1796, note 3, and Wolcott to H, July 30, 1795, note 2.

18. Washington nominated Thomas Pinckney Envoy Extraordinary to Spain on November 21, 1794, and the Senate agreed to his appointment on November 24, 1794 (*Executive Journal*, I, 163, 164).

with the Duke de la Alcudia [19] on the subject, before, however, the Peace between France & that Country was publicly known) [20] stands upon the same procrastinating—trifling—undignified (as it respects that government)—and insulting as it relates to this country ground as they did at the commencement of them. Under circumstances like these, I shall be at a loss (if nothing more decisive shall arrive between this and the Assemblying of Congress) what to say on this subject, especially as this procrastination & trifling, has been accompanied by encroachments on our territorial rights. There is no doubt of this fact, but persons have, nevertheless, been sent both by Govr. Blount & Genl. Wayne, to know by what authority it is done.[21] The conduct of Spain (after having herself, invited this

---

Washington is referring to Pinckney's letter to Edmund Randolph, dated July 21, 1795, a copy of which was enclosed in Pickering to Washington, October 5, 1795 (ALS, RG 59, Miscellaneous Letters, 1790–1799, National Archives). Pinckney's letter is printed in *ASP, Foreign Relations*, I, 534–35. See also Pickering to Pinckney, October 9, 1795 (LC, RG 59, Diplomatic and Consular Instructions of the Department of State, 1791–1801, Vol. 3, June 5, 1795–January 21, 1797, National Archives).

19. Manuel de Godoy, Duque de Alcudia, a member of the Consijo de Estado.

20. This is a reference to the Treaty of Basel, July 22, 1795. See H to Wolcott, October 3, 1795, note 6.

21. William Blount, governor of the Southwest Territory, and Major General Anthony Wayne.

On September 3, 1795, Wayne wrote to Pickering: "I have this moment received the enclosed information by express from Post Vincennes, which comes so well Authenticated as not to leave a doubt of the Spaniards being in possession of the Chickasaw bluffs. . . .

"I have therefore thought it expedient to reinforce the Garrison of Massac & to endow it with Six Months supplies of Provision & Ammunition, in addition to what is now on hand;

"If my information is right, (& I have no reason to doubt it,) the place that the Spaniards have now taken possession of, is the same spot on which Lieut Wm Clark landed & deliver'd the supplies sent from Fort Washington in the year 1793 for the use of the Chickasaw Nation & called the Chickasaw Cliffs . . . near the River Margot, as marked in Hutchin's Map & within the South Western Territory. . . .

"This being an Aggression of a very high & serious nature, I esteem it my duty to dispatch a flag immediately to the Spanish Commandant to demand by what authority & by whose Orders he has thus invaded the Territory of the United States of America." (Richard C. Knopf, ed., *Anthony Wayne: A Name in Arms; Soldier, Diplomat, Defender of Expansion Westward of a Nation; the Wayne-Knox-Pickering-McHenry Correspondence* [Pittsburgh, 1960], 453–54.)

On November 12, 1795, Wayne wrote to Pickering: "I have the honor to transmit a copy of a letter from His Excellency Manuel Gayose de Lemos, Governor of Upper Louisiana, in answer to my letter of the 10th. of

negociation, and throughout the whole of its progress) has been such that I have, at times, thought it best to express this sentiment at once in the Speech, and refer to the proceedings. At other times, to say only, that matters are in the same inconclusive state they have been; and that if no alteration for the better, or a conclusion of it should take place before the Session is drawing to a close, that the proceedings will be laid fully before Congress.

From Algiers no late accts. have been received; and little favorable, it is to be feared, is to be expected from that quarter.[22]

September last, addressed to the General or Officer Commanding the Spanish troops & Armament at the Chickasaw bluffs, a copy of which I had the honor to enclose you on the 19th of the same month. . . .

"The enclosed Copy of Lieut Wm Clarks report (who was the bearer of my *flag*) together with the affadavits taken by His Excellency Govr [Arthur] St Clair upon the same subject will best demonstrate the Views & intention of the Spaniards by this aggression—which probably by this period is extended further." (Knopf, *Wayne*, 471.)

Although Arthur Preston Whitaker states in *The Spanish-American Frontier, 1783–1795* (Lincoln, Nebraska, 1927), 215, that both Blount and Wayne made "vigorous protests" against the Spanish occupation of Chickasaw Bluffs, no evidence of Blount's protest has been found.

22. James Monroe described the Algerine situation as follows: "About the last of June or beginning of July 1795, Colonel [David] Humphreys, then resident minister of the United States at Lisbon, arrived at Paris with a view to obtain of the French government its aid, in support of our negociations with the Barbary powers. . . . After some delays . . . arrangements were taken for pursuing those negociations under the care of Joel Barlow, and with the full aid of France. At the moment however when Mr. Barlow was upon the point of embarking with our presents, &c. intelligence was received that a Mr. [Joseph] Donaldson, whom Col Humphreys had left at Alicante with a conditional power, but in the expectation that he would not proceed in the business till he heard further from him, had passed over to Algiers and concluded a treaty with that regency, and of course without the aid of France . . ." (*A View of the Conduct of the Executive*, xxxi–xxxii).

Barlow, a Connecticut poet and statesman, arrived in Europe in 1788 as European agent for the Scioto Company. In 1795 Humphreys named him consul to Algiers.

Joseph Donaldson, Jr., was nominated, on June 12, 1795, by George Washington "Consul of the United States for the ports of Tripoli and Tunis, and for other places as shall be nearer to the said ports than to the residence of any other Consul or Vice-Consul of the United States within the same allegiances." The Senate confirmed the appointment on June 13, 1795 (*Executive Journal*, I, 179–81).

Humphreys rose to the rank of lieutenant colonel during the American Revolution, and he served as an aide-de-camp to Washington from 1780 to 1783. From 1784 to 1786 he was Secretary of the "Commission for Negotiating Treaties of Commerce with Foreign Powers" (*JCC*, XXVII, 375). In 1791 he was named "Minister resident from the United States to her most faithful Majesty the Queen of Portugal" (*Executive Journal*, I, 75).

From Morocco, the first communications, after our Agent arrived there, none were pleasing, but the final result, if any has taken place is yet unknown and are more clouded.[23]

Our concerns with the Indians will tell well. I hope, & believe, the Peace with the Western Indians will be permanent;[24] unless renewd difficulties with G. Britain shd. produce (as it very likely would do) a change in their conduct. But whether this matter can be mentioned in the Speech with propriety before it is advised & consented to by the Senate,[25] is questionable.—and nothing, I am sure, that is so, & is susceptible of caval or criticism, will escape the annonymous writers (if it should go unnoticed elsewhere). It will be denominated by these gentry a bolster. All the hostile Indians to the Southward have renewed the treaties of Amity & friendship with the United States; & have given the best proof, in their power of their sincerity—to wit—a return of Prisoners & property; and Peace prevails from one end of our frontier to the other. Peace also had been produced between the Creeks & Chickasaws by the intervention of this government,[26] but something untoward & unknown

23. On March 30, 1795, Washington wrote to the Emperor of Morocco: "Being desirous of establishing and cultivating peace and harmony between our nation and his Imperial Majesty the Emperor of Morocco, I have appointed David Humphreys, one of our distinguished citizens, a commissioner plenipotentiary, giving him full power to negotiate and conclude a treaty of amity and commerce with you. And I pray you to give full credit to whatever shall be delivered to you on the part of the United States by him, and particularly when he shall assure you of our sincere desire to be in peace and friendship with you and your people" (*ASP, Foreign Relations*, I, 525). Humphreys, on May 21, 1795, empowered James Simpson, American consul at Gibraltar, to conduct the negotiations (*ASP, Foreign Relations*, I, 525-26). The negotiations were concluded on September 14, 1795, and the Emperor wrote to Washington in part: "Your care to preserve our friendship is very agreeable to us, and you will experience the like from us, or more, because you were faithful to our father, who is in glory" (*ASP, Foreign Relations*, I, 526-27).

24. Washington is referring to the treaty signed with the northwestern Indians at Greenville in the Northwest Territory on August 3, 1795. For the text of the treaty, see Clarence E. Carter, ed., *The Territorial Papers of the United States* (Washington, 1934–), II, 525-35.

25. Washington submitted the treaty to the Senate on December 9, 1795, and the Senate agreed to its terms on December 22 (*Executive Journal*, I, 193, 197). Washington announced the ratification of the treaty on December 22 (Carter, *Territorial Papers*, II, 534).

26. On September 20, 1795, James Seagrove, United States Indian agent, wrote to Timothy Pickering: "I am happy in being able to inform you that by letters which I received last evening from Georgia, I am advised that a treaty of peace is actually concluded between the Creek and Chicasaw

here, has occasioned a renewal of hostilities on the part of the Creeks.[27]

The Military establishment is of sufficient importance to claim a place in the general communication, at the opening of the Session; and my opinion is, that circumstanced as things are at present, & the uncertainty of what they may be next year, it would be impolitic to reduce it, but whether to express any opinion thereupon, or leave it entirely to their own decision may be considered.

Whether a report from the Secretary of the Treasury relative to Fiscal matters, particularly on the loans of money—and another from the Secretary of War respecting the Frigates—Arsenals—Military Stores directed to be provided; and the train, in wch. the Trade with the Indians is, agreeably to the several Acts of Legislature may not be proper—and to be referred to in the Speech.

Having desired the late Secretary of State to note down every matter as it occurred, proper either for the speech at the opening of the Session or for messages afterwards—the enclosed paper contains every thing I could extract from that Office. Aid me I pray you with your sentiments on these points & such others as may have occurred to you relative to my communications to Congress.

With affectionate regard   I am always Yours   Go: Washington

Colo. A. Hamilton

Indians comformable to my desire and injunctions on the Creek Chiefs at our late meeting. My Deputies had this desirable business concluded at a full meeting in the Creek nation since the Chiefs returned home after our conference in Georgia. My letters inform that a Copy of the Treaty was forwarded to me by a vessel from Savannah to this place which may be hourly expected—as soon as it arrives I shall have the honor of presenting it to you.

"I think it cannot fail to be pleasing to the President of the United States to see his wish of not only establishing peace between his own Citizens and the numerous savage tribes in the Southern department is happily concluded, but that also, through his mediation, . . . war hath ceased between the Creeks and Chickasaws and which threatened the destruction of thousands of unfortunate people. . . ." (Copy, George Washington Papers, Library of Congress.)

27. This is a reference to murders committed by citizens of Georgia on hunting parties of the Creeks.

From Oliver Wolcott, Junior

Phila. Oct. 29. 1795

Dr. Sir

I send you abstracts of all the payments to the President to the present time.[1] It is a fact that more money has been *at times* advanced than *was due for service,* but never a Dollar for which there was no *Appropriation.*

The villany of the suggestion against the President has induced me to reply to the Calm Observer on the 26th. & 28th.[2] You will see what I have said & the inclosed papers will enable you to add anything which you think proper. I have not time *to day* to ascertain whether any advance by the Bank was ever granted.[3] You know that the Compensation to both Houses of Congress has been paid in advance frequently.

Yrs truly   Oliv. Wolcott Jr.

A. Hamilton Esqr

ALS, Hamilton Papers, Library of Congress; copy, Connecticut Historical Society, Hartford.
    1. See H to George Washington, October 26, 1795; H to Wolcott, October 26, 27, 28, 1795.
    2. For Wolcott's reply to "A Calm Observer," see H to Washington, October 26, 1795, note 1. Wolcott's reply was answered by "A Calm Observer" on October 27, 1795, in the [Philadelphia] *Aurora. General Advertiser.* Wolcott wrote a brief reply on October 28, 1795, in which he argued that the President had never received more compensation than that allowed by Congress ([Philadelphia] *Aurora. General Advertiser,* October 28, 1795). Another reply, which was signed by "A Calm Observer," appeared in the [Philadelphia] *Aurora. General Advertiser* on October 29, 1795.
    3. See H to Wolcott, October 27, 1795.

To Oliver Wolcott, Junior

[*New York, October 29, 1795.* On October 30, 1795, Hamilton wrote to Wolcott: "I wrote you yesterday." *Letter not found.*]

The Defence No. XXI[1]

[New York, October 30, 1795]

Since the closing of my last number, I have accidentally turned to a passage of VATEL,[2] which is so pertinent to the immediate subject of that paper, that I cannot refrain from interrupting the progress of the discussion to quote it. It is in these words (B 3 C 4 § 63) "The Sovereign declaring War can neither detain those *subjects* of the enemy, who are within his dominions at the time of the Declaration, *nor their effects*. They came into his country *on the public faith. By permitting them to enter his territories and continue there, he tacitly promised them liberty and security for their return.*" This passage contains explicitly the principle which is the general basis of my argument; namely that The permission to a foreigner to come with his effects into and acquire others within our Country in time of peace virtually pledges the public faith for the security of his person and property in the event of War. How can this be reconciled with the *natural* right (controuled only by the *customary* law of Nations) which this writer admits, to confiscate the debts due by the subjects of a State to its enemies? I ask once more, can there be a natural right to do that which includes a breach of the public faith?

Tis plain, to a demonstration, that the rule laid down in this passage, which is so just and perspicuous as to speak conviction to the heart & understanding, unites the natural with the customary law of Nations in a condemnation of the pretension to confiscate or sequester the private property of our enemy found in our Country at the breaking out of a War.

Let us now proceed to examine the policy and expediency of such a pretension.[3]

ADf, Hamilton Papers, Library of Congress; *The* [New York] *Argus, or Greenleaf's New Daily Advertiser*, October 30, 1795.
1. In this essay, as in "The Defence Nos. XVIII, XIX, and XX," October 6, 14, 23 and 24, 1795, H discusses Article 10 of the Jay Treaty. For further background to this essay, see "The Defence No. I," July 22, 1795.
2. Vattel, *Law of Nations*.
3. At this point in the draft H wrote and then crossed out the following paragraph: "The rage for paradox that distinguishes the tenets of certain

In this investigation, I shall assume as a basis of argument the following position—That it is advantageous to Nations to have Commerce with each other.

Commerce, it is manifest, like any other object of enterprize or industry will prosper in proportion as it is secure. Its security consequently promoting its prosperity will extend its advantages. It is indeed essential to its having a due & regular course.

The pretension of a right to confiscate or sequester the effects of foreign merchants in the case in question is in its principle fatal to that necessary security. Its free exercise would destroy external Commerce; or which is nearly the same thing reduce it within the contracted limits of a game of hazard, where the chance of large profits accompanied with great risks would tempt alone the adventurous and the desperate. Those enterprises which, from circuitous or long voyages, slowness of sales incident to the nature of certain commodities, the necessity of credit or from other causes, demand considerable time for their completion must be renounced. Credit indeed must be banished from all the operations of foreign Commerce; an engine the importance of which to its vigorous and successful prosecution will be doubted by none who will be guided by experience or observation.

It cannot need amplification to elucidate the truth of these positions. The storms of war occur so suddenly and so often as to forbid the supposition that the Merchants of one Country would trust their property to any extent or for any duration in another Country, which was in the practice of confiscating or sequestering the effects of its enemies found within its territories at the commencement of a War. That practice therefore would necessarily paralize and wither the Commerce of the Country in which it obtained. Accordingly Nations attentive to the cultivation of commerce, which formerly were betrayed by temporary considerations into particular instances

---

politicians, renders it difficult to reason upon any public subject by calling in question those established truths which may be denominated the elements or data of political reasoning. Thus one scarcely dares assume, as an admitted point, the utility of *Commerce Credit* or any other acknowleged source of national prosperity. But as discussions would never end, if we were obliged upon every occasion to retrace the first principles of public œconomy and to travel into tedious deductions of facts which the experience of ages furnishes to explain their operation it is of necessity to take a shorter course and to presume assents to truths of the description abovementioned."

of that atrocious practice have been lead by the experience of its mischiefs to abstain from it in later times. They saw that to have persisted in it would have been to abandon a competition on equal terms in the lucrative and beneficial field of Commerce.

It is no answer to this to say—that the exercise of the right might be ordinarily suspended, though the right itself might be maintained for extraordinary and great emergencies.

In the first place, as the ordinary forbearance of its exercise would be taken by foreigners as evidence of an intention never to exercise it, by which they would be enticed into extensive deposits that would not otherwise have taken place, a departure from the general course would always involve an act of treachery and cruelty.

In the second place, the *possibility* of the occasional exercise of such a right, if conceived to exist, would be at least a slow poison conducing to a sickly habit of Commerce; and in a series of time would be productive of much more evil than could be counterbalanced by any good that could possibly be obtained in the contemplated emergency—by the use of the expedient.

Let experience decide. Examples of confiscation and sequestration have been given.[4] When did the dread of them prevent a War? When did it cripple an enemy so as to disable him from exertion or force him into peace or into a submission to the views of his adversary? When did it even sensibly conspire to either of these ends? If it has ever had any such effect, the evidence of it has not come within my knowlege.

It is true, that as between Great Britain and the U States the expectation of such effects is better warranted than perhaps in any other cases that have existed; because we commonly owe a larger debt to that Country than is usual between nations and there is a relative state of things which tends to a continuance of this situation.

But how has the matter operated hitherto? In the late war between the two Countries, certain states confiscated the debts due from their citizens to British Creditors;[5] and these Creditors had actually suffered great losses. The British Cabinet must have known that it was

4. See "The Defence No. XX," October 23 and 24, 1795.
5. See "Remarks on the Treaty . . . between the United States and Great Britain," July 9–11, 1795, notes 17, 35, 36, 37.

possible the same thing might happen in another War on a more general scale. And yet the appearances were extremely strong at a particular juncture that it was their plan, either from ill will, from the belief that popular opinion would ultimately drag our Government into the war, from the union of these two or from other causes, to force us into hostilities with them. Hence it appears that the apprehension of acts of confiscation or sequestration, was not sufficient to deter from hostile views or to ensure pacific dispositions.

It may be pretended that the menace of this measure had a restraining influence on the subsequent conduct of Great Britain. But if we ascribe nothing to the measures which our government actually pursued, under the pressure of the provocations received; we at least find in the course of European events a better solution of a change of policy in the Cabinet of Great Britain than from the dread of a legislative piracy on the debts due to their Merchants.

The truth unfortunately is that the passions of men stifle calculation that Nations the most attentive to pecuniary consideration easily surrender them to ambition to jealousy to anger or to revenge.

For the same reason, the actual experiment of an exercise of the pretended Right to confiscate or sequester, by way of reprisal for an injury complained of, would commonly be as inefficacious as the menace of it, to arrest general hostilities. Pride is roused, resentment kindled, and where there is ever no previous disposition to those hostilities, the probability is that they follow. Nations like individuals ill brook the idea of receding from their pretensions under the Rod or of admitting the justice of an act of retaliation or reprisal by submitting to it. Thus we learn from the King of Prussia himself, that the sequestering of the Silesia Debt,[6] instead of procuring the reparation for which it was designed, was on the point of occasioning an open rupture between him & Great Britain, when the supervention of a quarrel with France diverted the storm by rendering him necessary as an ally.

Perhaps it may be imagined that the practice of confiscation or sequestration would be more efficacious to wound and disable Great Britain in case of War than to prevent it. But this also is a vain chimera. A nation that can at pleasure raise by loan twenty Millions

6. See "The Defence No. XX," October 23 and 24, 1795, note 30.

Sterling would be in little danger of being disconcerted or enfeebled in her Military enterprizes by the taking away or arresting three or four Millions due to her Merchants. Did it produce distress and disorder among those whom it affected and their connections? If that disorder was sufficient to threaten a general derangemt of mercantile credit and with it of the public finances, the pending War affords us an example that the public purse or credit could be brought successfully into action for the support of the sufferers. Three or four Millions of Exchequer Bills applied in loans would suffice to prevent the partial evil from growing into a national calamity.

But we forget that as far as the interruption of the payment of the debts due to her Merchants could be supposed to operate upon Great Britain, war itself would essentially answer the purposes of confiscation or sequestration. By interrupting trade and intercourse, it is in fact a virtual sequestration. Remittances to any extent become impracticable. There would be few ways, in which on account of the state of War, it would be lawful to make them, and debtors are for the most part enough disposed to embrace pretexts of procrastination.

The inconvenience of deferred payment would therefore be felt by Great Britain, with little mitigation from the bare existence of War, without the necessity of our Government incurring the discredit & responsibility of a special intereference.

Indeed, as far as dread of eventual loss can operate, it ought in a great degree to have its effect exclusive of the idea of confiscation. Great Britain must want reflection not to be sensible that in making war upon us, she makes war upon her own merchants; by the depredations upon our Trade, destroying those resources from which they are to be paid. If she be indifferent to this consideration, 'twill be because she is governed by some motive or passion powerful enough to dispose her to run the risk of the entire loss—in the reliance of obtaining indemnification in the acquisitions of War or in the terms of Peace.

Will it be said that the seizure of the debts would put in the hands of our Government a valuable resource for carrying on the War? This upon trial would prove as fallacious as all the rest. Various inducements would prevent Debtors from paying into the Treasury. Some would decline it from conscientious scruples, from a doubt of the rectitude of the thing—others with intent to make a merit with their Creditors of the concealment and to favour their own future credit and advantage—others from a desire to retain the money in their own employment—and a great number from the apprehension that the Treaty of peace might revive their responsibility to the Creditors with the embarrassment to them of getting back as well as they could the monies which they had paid into the Treasury. Of this our last Treaty of peace,[7] in the opinion of able judges, gave an example. These causes and others which do not as readily occur would oppose great obstacles to the execution of the measure.

But severe laws inflicting heavy penalties might compel it. Experience does not warrant a sanguine reliance upon this expedient, in a case in which great opportunity of concealment is united with strong motives of inclination or interest. It would require an inquisition justly intolerable to a free people—penalties which would confound the due proportion between crime and punishment; to detect or to deter from concealment and evasion and to execute the law. Probably no means less efficacious than a revolutionary tribunal and a guillotine would go near to answer the end. There are but few, I trust, to whom these would be welcome means.

We may conclude therefore, that the law would be evaded to an extent which would disappoint the expectations from it as a resource. Some monies would no doubt be collected, but the probability is that the amount would be insignificant even in the scale of a single campaign. But Should the collection prove as complete as it ordinarily is between creditor and debtor, it would little if [at] all exceed the expence of one Campaign.

Hence we perceive that regarding the measure either as a mean of disabling our enemy or as a resource to ourselves—its consequence dwindles upon a close survey. It cannot pretend to a magnitude which would apologise either for a sacrifice of national honor or candour, or for a deviation from the true principles of Commerce and Credit.

Let us now take a closer view of its disadvantages.

A nation, in case of war, is under no responsibility for the de-

7. The definitive treaty of peace between the United States and Great Britain, September 3, 1783.

linquencies or frauds of its citizens who are debtors to those of its enemy, if it does not specially interfere with the payment of the debts which they owe. But if it interposes its authority to prevent the payment it gives a claim of indemnification to its adversary for the intervening losses which those delinquencies or frauds may occasion. Whether on the making of peace this would be insisted upon or waved might depend much on the good or ill success of the War; but every thing which adds to the catalogue of our enemy's just pretensions, especially when the fortune of War has been pretty equal, is an evil, either as an additional obstacle to speedy peace or as an ingredient to render the terms of it less advantageous to us. And it is therefore unwise in a government to increase the list of such pretensions by a measure which without utility to itself administers to the indolence of negligent, and to the avidity of fraudulent Individuals.

Further. Every species of reprisal or annoyance which a power at War employs, contrary to liberality or justice, of doubtful propriety in the estimation of the law of Nations, departing from that moderation which in latter times serves to mitigate the serverities of War, by furnishing a pretext and a provocation to the other side to resort to extremities, serves to embitter the spirit of hostility and to extend its ravages. War is then apt to become more sanguinary, more wasting and every way more destructive. This is a ground of serious reflection to every nation, both as it regards humanity and policy —to this country it presents itself accompanied with considerations of peculiar force. A vastly extended sea coast overspread with defenceless towns would offer an abundant prey to an incensed and malignant enemy having the power to command the sea. The usages of modern war forbid hostilities of this kind and though they are not always respected, they are never violated, unless by way of retaliation for breaches of those usages on the other side, without exciting the reprobation of the impartial part of mankind sullying the glory and blasting the reputation of the party which has recourse to them.[8] But the confiscation or sequestration of private debts or private property in public funds, now generaly regarded as an odious

8. In the newspaper this sentence ends: "sullying the glory, and blasting the reputation of the party which disregards them, this consideration has in general force sufficient to induce an observance of them."

and unwarrantable measure, would as between us and Great Britain contain a poignant sting. Its effect to exasperate in an extreme degree both the nation and government of that Country cannot be doubted. A disposition to retaliate is a natural consequence, and it would not be difficult for us to be made to suffer beyond any possible degree of advantage to be derived from the occasion of the retaliation. It were much wiser to leave the property of British subjects an untouched pledge for the moderation of its government in the mode of prosecuting the war.[9]

Besides, (as if requisite might be proved from the records of history) in national controversies, it is of real importance to conciliate the good opinion of mankind, and it is even useful to preserve or gain that of our enemy. The latter facilitates accommodation and peace—the former attracts good offices, friendly interventions, sometimes direct support from others. The exemplary conduct, in general, of our country in our contest for independence was probably not a little serviceable to us in this way. It secured to the intrinsic goodness of our cause every collateral advantage, and gave it a popularity among nations unalloyed and unimpaired, which even stole into the Cabinets of Princes. A contrary policy tends to contrary consequences. Though nations in the main are governed by what they suppose their interest, he must be imperfectly versed in human nature who thinks it indifferent whether the maxims of a State tend to excite in others kind or unkind dispositions, or that these dispositions may not insensibly affect the views of self-Interest. This were to suppose that Rulers only reason do not feel, in other words are not men.

Moreover, the measures of War ought ever to look forward to peace. The confiscation, or sequestration of the private property of an enemy must always be a point of serious discussion when interest or necessity leads to negotiations for peace. Unless when absolutely prostrate by the war, restitution is likely to constitute an ultimatum of the suffering party. It must be agreed to, or the war

9. In the margin opposite this paragraph H wrote and crossed out the following notes: "Peace will bring restitution with damages.
        "Credit premium
        "Our peculiar invites the extremities of war
        "doubtful if validity would be recognized.
        "excites prejudices against our cause in other Nations."

protracted, and at last it is probable it must still be agreed to. Should a refusal of restitution prolong the war for only one year, the chance is that more will be lost than was gained by the confiscation. Should it be necessary finally to make it, after prolonging the war, the disadvantage will preponderate in a ratio to the prolongation. Should it be in the first instance assented to, what will have been gained? the temporary use of a fund of inconsiderable moment in the general issue of the War, at the expence of justice character credit and perhaps of having sharpened the evils of war. How infinitely preferable to have drawn an equal fund from our own resources, which with good management is always practicable! If the restitution includes damages on account of the interference, for the failures of individuals, the loan will have been the most costly that could have been made. Our Treaty of Peace with Great Britain is an example of restitution. The late one between France & Prussia is another.[10] This must become every day more and more a matter of course because the immunity of mercantile Debts becomes every day more important to commerce, better understood to be so and more clearly considered as enjoined by the principles of the law of Nations.

Thus we see that in reference to the simple question of war and peace the measure of confiscation or sequestration is marked with every feature of impolicy.

We have before seen that the pretension of a right to do the one or the other has a most inimical aspect towards Commerce and Credit.

Let us resume this view of the subject. The credit which our Merchants have been able to obtain abroad, essentially in Great Britain, has from the first settlement of our Country to this day been the animating principle of our foreign Commerce. This every Merchant knows and feels—and every intelligent merchant is sensible that for many years to come the case must continue to be the same.

10. The eighth article of the Treaty of Basel, signed between France and Prussia on April 5, 1795, reads: "Il sera accordé respectivement aux individus des deux Nations, la main-levée des effects, revenus, ou biens, de quelque genre qu'ils soient, détenus, saisis ou confisqués à cause de la guerre qui a eu lieu entre la Prusse et la France, de même qu'une prompte justice, à l'égard des créances quelconques que ces individus pourroient avoir dans les États des deux Puissances contractantes" (Martens, Recûeil, VI, 45-51).

This in our situation is a peculiar reason of the utmost force for renouncing the pretension in question.

The exercise of it or the serious apprehension of its exercise would necessarily have one of two effects. It would deprive our merchants of the credit so important to them, or it would oblige them to pay a premium for it proportioned to the opinion of the risk. Or to speak more truly, it would combine the two effects; it would cramp credit and subject what was given to a high premium. The most obvious and familiar principles of human action establish that the consideration for money or property lent or creditted is moderate or otherwise according to the opinion of security or hazard; and that the quantity of either to be obtained on loan or credit is in a great degree controuled or enlarged by the same rule.

Thus should we in the operations of our Trade pay severely and exorbitantly for a pretension which is of little value, or rather which is pernicious even in the relations pretended to constitute its utility. What folly to contend for it? How much greater the folly ever to think of exercising it? It never can be exercised hereafter in our Country without great & lasting mischiefs.

Instead of cherishing so odious a pretension as our "best our only weapon of defence" wisdom admonishes us to be eager to cast it from us as a weapon most dangerous to the wearer proscribed by the laws of Nations by the laws of honor and by every principle of true policy.

Every Merchant ought to desire that the most perfect tranquillity on this point in foreign Countries should facilitate to him on the best & cheapest terms the credit for which he has occasion. And every other Citizen ought to desire that he may be thus freed from a continual contribution, in the enhanced price of every imported commodity he consumes, towards defraying the premium which the want of that tranquilty is calculated to generate.[11]   *Camillus*

11. H addressed the cover of the draft to "Mr. Sands Junr at Mr. [James] Kents." This may be a reference to Henry Sands, second son of Comfort Sands, who graduated from Columbia College in 1795 and subsequently became a lawyer.

To Oliver Wolcott, Junior

New York October 30. [–November 12] 1795

Dr Sir

I wrote you yesterday for a statement of the advances & appropriations for the Department of State.[1]

I am very anxious that *Fauchet's* whole letter should appear just as it is [2]—strange whispers are in circulation of a nature foreign to Truth & implicating honest men with Rascals. Is it to come out? Can't you send me a copy? I will observe any conditions you annex.

The secret Journals & other files of the Department of State will disclose the following facts—that during the War a Commission to negotiate a Treaty of Commerce with G Britain was given to Mr Adams and afterwards revoked [3]—that our Commissioners for making peace were instructed to take no step whatever without a previous consultation with the French Ministry; [4] though there was at the time reason to believe that France wished us to make peace or truce with GBritain without an acknowlegement of our independence—that she favoured a sacrifice to Spain of our pretensions to the navigation of the Missisippi & the relinquishment of a participation in the fisheries.

It will appear that instructions were actually given to Mr. Jay to yield the navigation of the Mississippi to Spain, in consideration of an acknowlegement of our Independence [5]—that Mr. Jay made a proposal accordingly but clogged with some condition or qualification to bring it back to Congress before a final conclusion & expostulated with Congress against the measure.[6]

It will appear that this was effected by a Southern party [7] who would also have excluded the fisheries from being ultimatum [8] in which they were opposed by the north who equally contended for Mississippi & Fisheries.

It will appear that Chancellor Livingston as Secy of State reported a censure on our Commissioners for breaking their instructions in the negotiations for peace.[9]

It will appear that shortly after the arrival in this Country of the preliminary articles I made a motion in Congress to renew the

Commission to negotiate a Treaty of Commerce [10] with G Britain [11] —that a Committee was appointed to prepare one with instructions of which Mr Madison was one & that the Committee never reported.[12] Thus stand the facts in my memory. It is very desirable, now that a free access to the files of the Department can give the evidence, to examine them accurately, noting times places circumstances actors &c. I want this very much for a public use in my opinion essential.

It would also be useful to have a copy of Mr. Jefferson's letter to Congress concerning the transfer of the French Debt to private money lenders on which the Report of the Board of Treasury is founded.[13]

Yrs. truly   A. Hamilton

O Wolcott Esq

Nov 12

This letter by accident has lain on my desk since it was written. I send it still.

Beaches paper of the 11 has a VALERIUS [14] wh⟨ich⟩ I think gives an opportunity of oversetti⟨ng⟩ him. The leading ideas may be—

1 He discloses the object of the party to place Mr Jefferson in contrast with the President.

2 He discloses the further object—an intimate & close alliance with France subject[ing] us to the vortex European politics & attributes it to Mr. Jefferson.

3 He misrepresents totally Mr. Jeffersons returning from France. A solid answer to this paper with facts would do great good.[15]

ALS, Connecticut Historical Society, Hartford; copy, Hamilton Papers, Library of Congress.

1. Letter not found.

2. This is a reference to Fauchet's Dispatch No. 10, which was intercepted by the British and turned over to the Washington Administration. For the way in which this dispatch led to Edmund Randolph's resignation as Secretary of State, see Wolcott to H, July 30, 1795, note 1. See also H to George Washington, October 16, 1795, note 3.

3. On September 28, 1779, the Continental Congress approved instructions "for the minister plenipotentiary to negotiate a treaty of amity and commerce with Great Britain" (JCC, XV, 1117). On October 4, 1779, John Adams was appointed Minister Plenipotentiary "for negotiating a treaty of commerce with Great Britain" (JCC, XV, 1143). On July 12, 1781, the Con-

tinental Congress adopted a motion "That the commission and instructions for negotiating a treaty of commerce between these United States and Great Britain, given to the honorable John Adams . . . be and they are hereby revoked" (*JCC*, XX, 746).

4. The Continental Congress approved these instructions to the commissioners on June 15, 1781 (*JCC*, XX, 651–52).

5. The instructions to John Jay are dated February 15, 1781, and are printed in *JCC*, XIX, 152–53.

6. For Jay's objections to the instructions of February 15, 1781, see Jay to the President of Congress, October 3, 1781 (Wharton, *Revolutionary Diplomatic Correspondence*, IV, 738–47).

7. An obstacle to any change in Jay's instructions concerning the free navigation of the Mississippi River was the insistence of the Virginia members of Congress that the right not be surrendered. The Virginia members, however, somewhat modified their earlier stand, and this in turn made it possible to alter Jay's instructions. See *JCC*, XIX, 151. For a full account by someone with a firsthand knowledge of these developments, see James Madison to Hezekiah Niles, the editor of [Baltimore] *Niles' Weekly Register*, January 8, 1822 (Burnett, *Letters*, V, 578–79).

8. On February 23, 1779, a committee of Congress reported on various conditions or stipulations which had to be met before a peace could be concluded with Great Britain (*JCC*, XIII, 239–44). One such condition was "That a right of fishing and curing fish on the banks and coasts of the island of Newfoundland, equally with the subjects of France and Great Britain, be reserved, acknowledged, and ratified to the subjects of the United States" (*JCC*, XIII, 241). For an example of the southern opposition mentioned by H, see the North Carolina Delegates to the South Carolina Delegates, April 2 (?), 1779 (Burnett, *Letters*, IV, 129–30).

9. The proposed resolutions which Chancellor Robert R. Livingston submitted are contained in his letter to the President of Congress, Elias Boudinot, on March 18, 1783 (LC, Papers of the Continental Congress, National Archives; printed in Wharton, *Revolutionary Diplomatic Correspondence*, VI, 316). The resolutions propose only that the commissioners be informed of the disclosure of the secret article in the provisional treaty to the French minister together with "the reasons which influenced Congress to make it." Livingston's remarks on his dissatisfaction with the proposed resolutions suggest a stronger censure of the commissioners. In a letter which Livingston wrote to the commissioners on March 25, 1783, he made clear his disapproval of the article kept secret from France as well as the signing of the treaty without consultation with Versailles (Wharton, *Revolutionary Diplomatic Correspondence*, VI, 338–40).

10. In MS, "Congress."

11. On May 1, 1783, a committee of the Continental Congress, of which H was a member, submitted a resolution "authorising . . . [the peace commissioners] to enter into a treaty of Commerce between the United States and Great Britain, subject to the revisal of the contracting parties previous to its final conclusion; and in the mean time to enter into a commercial convention to continue in force One—year. . . ." H was the author of this resolution; for its full text, see "Continental Congress. Report of a Treaty of Commerce between the United States and Great Britain," May 1, 1783. See also *JCC*, XXIV, 321.

12. In addition to James Madison, the committee consisted of Thomas FitzSimons, Stephen Higginson, William Hemsley, and John Rutledge. H was, however, mistaken, for the committee on June 19, 1783, submitted to Congress a report favoring a commercial treaty with Great Britain (*JCC*, XXIV, 404).

13. This is a reference to Thomas Jefferson to John Jay, September 26, 1786 (Boyd, *Papers of Thomas Jefferson*, X, 405–06). For an earlier discussion by H of Jefferson's letter, see "An American No. I," August 4, 1792. See also note 10 to that document for the report of the Board of Treasury of February 19, 1787.

14. Eleven articles opposing the Jay Treaty and signed "Valerius" were published in Benjamin Franklin Bache's [Philadelphia] *Aurora. General Advertiser*. These articles were published on August 22, September 1, 9, 17, 25, October 8, 21, 29, November 11, 19, December 1, 1795.

15. Wolcott endorsed this letter: "Oct. 30 & Nov. 12 ansd. 13th. Nov. & sent on Copy of Fr—— Letters by Mr. Kuhl translated." Wolcott was probably mistaken, for it seems more likely that he answered H's letter on November 14, 1795. See Wolcott to H, November 16, 1795. For the various translations of Fauchet's Dispatch No. 10 and the copy which Wolcott sent to H, see Wolcott to H, July 30, 1795, note 1, and November 16, 1795. Henry Kuhl, formerly a clerk in the Treasury Department, in 1795 became assistant cashier of the Bank of the United States. See H to Thomas Willing, April 5, 1795.

From Oliver Wolcott, Junior [1]

Phila: Nov 2d. 1795

My Dear Sir

I enclose a statement of the Presidents account quarterly, which shews that he has not been in advance a *quarters salary* at any time.

You will see that the Aurora denies that the members of Congress have ever recd. monies which were *not earned* & refers to a Letter of mine to prove the fact.[2] I never wrote a Letter on the subject except to the Speakers Muhlenbergh [3] & Trumbull [4] in answer to an application from them on this point *Whether any advances that had been made to Members of the House of Representatives beyond their real pay had been afterwards accounted for in their subsequent accounts in a succeeding session?"*

To this I answered to the following effect

"It is certain that the Speakers of the House have in no instance advanced monies beyond the compensation claimed by the Members as actually due, of course it does not appear to have been designed in any case that monies advanced in one session, should be accounted for by services to be rendered in another."

"In the accounts of the second Session, of the first Congress two errors were discovered of six Dollars each and one other of Eighty four Dollars, which sums were overpaid in consequence of miscalculations these sums were credited by the members who recd. the monies, in the succeeding session, in consequence of Notes which were placed in the Pay Books, by the Clerks who made the examination."

"A few other errors of a trivial nature have at different times been noted as errors by the Clerks, but whether they have been explained by the members, or accounted for, does not appear from the pay Books. The foregoing three cases are all that I can find, which fall within the enquiry contained in your Letter."

The plain meaning of my Letter is that it was not the practice to advance *during a session* more than was earned in *that session*—further I never meant or examined the books to ascertain. I shall do it now.

The reference to this Letter proves either that Muhlenbergh is party to this business or what is more likely that my Letter was lodged in the Clerks Office, & that *Beckley* [5] & *Randolph* [6] are the authors of this attack.

Nothing to the purpose can be gained from the accounts of the Secy of State, but you will find them enclosed.[7] It is not best to use them in my opinion.

Yrs. truly.   Oliv. Wolcott Jr.

N.B. What I say of my own Letter to M & T. is for *your* information. I shall use the affair here.

The Clerks have disappointed me & I cannot send the Statement for the Dept. of State Salaries till tomorrow.[8]

ALS, Hamilton Papers, Library of Congress; copy, Connecticut Historical Society, Hartford.

1. For background to this letter, see H to George Washington, October 26, 1795; H to Wolcott, October 26, 27, 28, 1795; and Wolcott to H, October 29, 1795.

2. Wolcott is referring to the "Remarks" made by an anonymous writer on an excerpt from the [New York] *American Minerva; an Evening Advertiser.* The excerpt and the "Remarks" appeared in the [Philadelphia] *Aurora. General Advertiser,* on November 2, 1795. The "Remarks" read in part: "It is *not true,* that the Members of Congress are paid *any part* of their compensation before it has *strictly* become due. For the convenience of the Treasury Department, it has been the practice at the beginning of each session to give the Speaker of the House and President of the Senate a credit at the Bank; out of which, during the course of the session, the members receive part of their compensation *as they earn it, but never one cent in advance,* and at the close of the session their balance is paid them, for which their

receipt is preserved in the Treasury. Thus the practice of the legislature
cannot be cited as an excuse for the President's mal-conduct.

"The records can shew a letter from Mr. O. Wolcott, expressly certifying,
that it was not the practice of the Members of the Legislature to draw their
compensation *in advance;* but that the contrary practices *invariably* prevailed.
Will the New-York paragraphist dispute the authority? If he does other testimony may be produced."

3. Frederick A. C. Muhlenberg was Speaker of the House of Representatives during the First (March 4, 1789, to March 3, 1791) and Third (March
4, 1793, to March 3, 1795) Congresses.

4. Jonathan Trumbull was Speaker of the House of Representatives in the
Second Congress (March 4, 1791, to March 3, 1793).

5. John Beckley, clerk of the House of Representatives.

6. Edmund Randolph.

7. See H to Wolcott, October 30, 1795.

8. H had requested this material in a letter to Wolcott on October 29,
1795, which as not been found. See Wolcott to H, October 30–November
12, 1795, note 1.

The Defence No. XXII [1]

[New York, November 5–11, 1795]

The analogy of the stipulation in the 10th article with stipulations
in our other treaties and in the treaties between other Nations is the
remaining topic of discussion.[2] After this, attention will be paid to
such observations by way of objection to the article as may not
have been before expressly or virtually answered.

The 20th. article of our treaty of Amity and Commerce with
France [3] is in these words "For the better promoting of commerce
on both sides it is agreed, that if a war shall break out between the
said two Nations, *six months* after the proclamation of War shall be
allowed to the Merchants in the cities and towns where they live for
selling and *transporting* their goods and merchandizes, and *if any
thing* be taken from *them or any injury be done them within that*

ADf, Hamilton Papers, Library of Congress; *The* [New York] *Herald; A
Gazette for the Country,* November 11, 1795. Approximately the first half
of this essay was printed in *The* [New York] *Argus, or Greenleaf's New
Daily Advertiser,* November 5, 1795.

1. For background to this document, see the introductory note to "The
Defence No. I," July 22, 1795.

2. H had discussed Article 10 of the Jay Treaty in "The Defence Nos.
XVIII, XIX, XX, XXI," October 6, 14, 23 and 24, 30, 1795.

3. This is a reference to the Treaty of Amity and Commerce between the
United States and France, signed at Paris on February 6, 1778 (Miller,
Treaties, II, 3–29).

term by either party or the people or subjects of either full satisfaction shall be made for the same."

The 18th article of our Treaty of Amity and Commerce with the Netherlands [4] is in these words "For the better promoting of Commerce on both sides, it is agreed, that if a war should break out between their High Mightinesses the States General of the United Netherlands and the United States of America, there shall always be granted to the subjects on each side the term of *Nine Months* after the date of the rupture, or the proclamation of War, *to the end that they may retire with their effects and transport them where they please, which it shall be lawful for them to do, as well as to sell or transport their effects and goods, in all freedom and without any hindrance, and without being able to proceed, during the said term of Nine Months to any arrest of their effects much less of their persons;* on the contrary there shall be given them for their vessels and their effects which they would carry away passports and safe conducts for the nearest ports of their respective countries and for the time necessary for the voyage."

The 22d article of our Treaty of Amity and Commerce with Sweden [5] is in these words "In order to favour Commerce on both sides as much as possible, it is agreed that in case War should break out between the two nations, the term of *nine months* after the declaration of War shall be allowed to the *Merchants* and *subjects* respectively on one side and the other, *in order that they may withdraw with their effects and moveables, which they shall be at liberty to carry off or to sell where they please without the least obstacle; nor shall any seize their effects and much less their persons during the said nine months;* but on the contrary passports which shall be valid for a time necessary for their return shall be given them for their vessels and the effects which they shall be willing to carry with them. And if *any thing* is taken from them or any *injury* is done to them by one of the parties their people & subjects, during the term above prescribed, *full and entire satisfaction shall be made to them on that account."*

4. The Treaty of Amity and Commerce between the United States and the Netherlands was signed at The Hague on October 8, 1782 (Miller, *Treaties,* II, 59–88).
5. The treaty with Sweden was signed at Paris on April 3, 1783, and proclaimed on September 25, 1783 (Miller, *Treaties,* II, 123–49).

The 23 article of our Treaty of Amity and Commerce with Prussia [6] contains this provision "If war should arise between the two contracting parties, the merchants of either country then residing in the other shall be allowed *to remain nine months to collect their* DEBTS *and settle their affairs, and may depart freely carrying off all their effects without molestation or hindrance*."

These articles of four and the only commercial Treaties we had with foreign powers, prior to the pending Treaty with Great Britain, though differing in terms agree in substance; except as to time which varies from six to nine months. And they clearly amount to this, that upon the breaking out of a War between the contracting parties in each case, there shall be for a term of six or nine months full protection and security to the persons and property of the subjects of one which are then in the territories of the other; with liberty to collect their debts * to sell their goods and merchandizes and to remove with their effects to their own country.[7] For this term of six or nine months, there is a complete suspension of the pretended right to confiscate or sequester, giving and being designed to give an opportunity to withdraw the whole property which the subjects or citizens of the one party have in the country of the other.

The differences between these stipulations and that in the article under examination are chiefly these. The latter is confined to *debts property in the public funds,* and in public & private banks, without any limitation of the duration of the protection. The former comprehend, besides, goods and merchandizes, with a limitation of the protection to a term of six or nine months, but with the intent and supposition that the term allowed may and will be adequate to intire security. The principle therefore of all the stipulations is the same. Each aims at putting the persons and property of the subjects of one enemy, especially Merchants, being within the country of the other

---

* The term "debts" is only expressed in the Prussian Treaty but there are in the other treaties terms which include debts and this is the manifest spirit & intent of all.

6. The treaty with Prussia was negotiated in 1785. It was signed for the United States by Benjamin Franklin, Thomas Jefferson, and John Adams at different times in July and August, 1785, and by Prussia on September 10, 1785 (Miller, *Treaties,* II, 162–83).

7. In the newspaper this sentence reads: ". . . with their effects wheresoever they please."

enemy at the commencement of a war, out of the reach of confiscation or sequestration.[8]

The persons, whose names are to our other treaties, on the part of the UStates, are *Benjamin Franklin*, Silas Deane, *Arthur Lee, John Adams* and *Thomas Jefferson*. The three first are to the Treaty with France. Mr. Adams is singly to that with the United Netherlands, Doctor Franklin singly to that with Sweden, and these two with Mr. Jefferson are jointly to that with Prussia. The treaty with Sweden was concluded in April 1783 that with Prussia in August 1785. These dates repel the idea that considerations of policy relative to the war might have operated in the case.

We have consequently the sanction of all these characters to the principle, which governed the stipulation entered into by Mr. Jay, and not only from the ratification of the former treaties at different periods distant from each other by different descriptions of men in our public councils, but also from there never having been heard in the community, a lisp of murmurs against the stipulations, through a period of seventeen years counting from the date of the Treaty with France there is just ground to infer a coincidence of the public opinion of the Country.

I verily believe that if in the year 1783 a Treaty had been made with England containing an article similar to the 10th in the present Treaty, it would have met with general acquiescence. The spirit of party had not then predisposed mens minds to estimate the propriety of a measure, according to the agent, rather than according to its real fitness and quality. What would then have been applauded as wise liberal equitable and expedient is now in more instances than one, under the pestilential [9] influence of that baleful spirit condemned as improvident impolitic and dangerous.

Our Treaty with Prussia, the 23 article of which has been cited, is indeed a model of liberality, which for the principles it contains does honor to the parties, and has been in this country a subject of deserved and unqualified admiration. It contradicts, as if studiously, those principles of restriction and exclusion, which are the foundations of the mercantile and navigating system of Europe. It grants

8. In the margin opposite the end of this paragraph H wrote: "Gillimore."
9. In MS this word is "pestinential."

perfect freedom of conscience and worship to the respective subjects and citizens, with no other restraint than that they shall not insult the religion of others. Adopting the rule that free ships shall make free goods, it extends the protection to the persons as well as the goods of enemies. Enumerating as contraband only "arms amunition and military stores" it even provides that contraband articles shall not be confiscated but may be taken on the condition of paying for them. It provides against embargoes of vessels and effects. It expressly exempts women children scholars of every faculty, cultivators of the earth, artizans manufacture[r]s and fishermen unarmed and inhabiting unfortified towns villages and places, and in general all others whose occupations are for the common subsistence and benefit of mankind—their houses fields and goods, from molestation in their persons and employments and from burning wasting and destruction, in time of war; and stipulates payment at a reasonable price for what may be necessarily taken from them for military use. It likewise protects from seizure and confiscation in time of war vessels employed in trade, and inhibits the granting commissions to private armed vessels empowering them to take or destroy such trading vessels or to interrupt their commerce. And it makes a variety of excellent provisions to secure to prisoners of War a humane treatment.

These particulars are stated as evidence of the temper of the day, and of a policy which then prevailed to bottom our system with regard to foreign nations upon those grounds of moderation and equity, by which reason religion and philosophy had tempered the harsh maxims of more early times. It is painful to observe an effort to make the public opinion in the respect retrograde, and to infect our Councils with a spirit contrary to these salutary advances towards improvement in true civilization and humanity.

If we pass from our own Treaties to those between other Nations, we find that the provisions which have been extracted from ours have very nearly become formulas in the Conventions of Europe. As samples of this may be consulted the following articles of Treaties between Great Britain & other powers (to wit) the XVIII article of a Treaty of Peace & Commerce with Portugal in 1642 [10] the XXXVI article of a Treaty of Peace Commerce and Alliance

10. See *A General Collection of Treatys,* II, 322–30.

with Spain in 1667 [11] the XIX article of a Treaty of Peace and the II of a Treaty of Commerce with France both in 1713 [12] and the XII article of a Treaty of Commerce and Navigation with Russia in 1766.[13]

The article with Portugal provides that if difficulties and doubts shall arise between the two Nations, which give reason to *apprehend* the interruption of Commerce *public notice* shall be given of it to the subjects of both sides, and after that notice, *two years* shall be allowed to carry away their merchandizes and goods, and in the mean time there shall be no injury or prejudice done to any persons or goods on either side.

The articles with France, in addition to the provisions common in other cases, particularly stipulate that during the term of the protection (six months) "the subjects on each side shall enjoy good and *speedy* justice, so that during the said space of six months, they may be able *to recover* their *goods* and *effects, entrusted* as well to the *public* as to private persons."

The article with Russia, besides stipulating an exemption from confiscation for *one year* with the privilege to remove and carry away in safety, provides additionally that the subjects of each party "shall be further permitted either at or before their departure to consign the effects, which they shall not as yet have disposed of, as well as the *debts* that shall be due to them to such persons as they shall think proper, in order to dispose of them *according to their desire & for their benefit—which debts, the Debtors shall be obliged to pay in the same manner as if no such rupture had happened.*"

All these articles are with those in our treaties analogous in principle, as heretofore particularly explained, to the tenth article of the Treaty under discussion. That of the British Treaty with France designates expressly debts due from the PUBLIC as well as those due from private persons—that with Russia goes the full length of our tenth article; empowering the creditors on each side to assign the debts which they are not able to collect within the term of their residence to whomsoever they think fit for their own benefit, and

11. Chalmers, *Collection of Treaties*, II, 5–24.
12. The Treaties of Utrecht (Chalmers, *Collection of Treaties*, I, 340–90, 390–424).
13. Chalmers, *Collection of Treaties*, I, 2–13.

declaring that these debts shall be paid to the Assignees in the same manner as if no rupture had happened.

There is a document extant which may fairly be supposed to express the sense of the Government of France at the period to which [it] relates of the foundation of these stipulations. It is a memorial of Mr. *Bussy* Minister from the Court of France to that of London for negotiating peace dated in the year 1761 [14] and contains these passages "As it is impracticable for two princes who make war with each other to agree between them *which is the aggressor in regard to the other*,* Equity and Humanity have dictated these precautions, that where an unforeseen rupture happens suddenly and without any previous declaration, foreign vessels, which navigating *under the security of peace* and of treaties happen, at the time of the rupture, to be in either of the respective ports shall have time and full liberty to withdraw themselves."

"This wise provision, so agreeable to the rules of good faith, *constitutes a part of the law of Nations;* and the article of the Treaty which sanctifies these precautions, ought to be faithfully executed notwithstanding the breach of the other articles of the Treaty, which is the natural consequence of the War."

"The Courts of France & Great Britain used this salutary precaution in the Treaties of Utrecht [15] and Aix la Chapelle." [16]

Note   * Thus we find it the sentiment of this Minister that it is *impossible* for two princes who make war with each other, to agree which is the aggressor *with regard to the other*—and yet Mr. Jay was to extort from Great Britain an acknowlegement, that *she was the aggressor with regard to us*, and was guilty of pusyllanimity in waving that question.

14. On July 15, 1761, François de Bussy, the French Minister to the Court of London, presented the British Court with a "Memorial of Propositions" for a peace between France and England. Article XII of this memorial stated that "The captures made at sea by England before the declaration of the war, are objects of legal restitution, and which the king will willingly submit to the justice of the king of England and the English tribunals. . . ." On July 29, 1761, the British rejected this demand, "such a claim not being founded on any particular convention, and by no means resulting from the law of nations. . . ." In a reply to the British answer on August 5, 1761, Bussy presented the British with an ultimatum, accompanied by a separate "Memorial concerning the Vessels taken before the War" (*Parliamentary History of England* [London, 1813], XV, 1030–44, 1047–50, 1050–54, 1057–59). It is from this memorial that H is quoting.

15. See note 12.

16. This treaty was concluded in 1748 (Chalmers, *Collection of Treaties*, I, 424–67).

These passages place the security stipulated in the Treaties for the persons and property of the subjects of one party found in the Country of another at the beginning of a War upon the footing of *its constituting a part of the law of Nations;* which may be considered as a formal diplomatic recognition of the principle for which I contend. As this position was not itself in dispute between the two Governments, but merely a collateral inference from it, applicable to vessels *taken at sea* prior to a declaration of War, it may be regarded as a respectable testimony of the law of Nations on the principal point.

If the law of Nations confers this exemption from seizure upon vessels, which at the time of the rupture happen to be in the respective ports of the belligerent parties, it is evident that it must equally extend its protection to debts contracted in a course of lawful Trade. Vessels are particularly mentioned because the discussion turned upon vessels seized at sea. But the reference to the Treaties of Utrecht and Aix la Chapelle shews that the Minister in his observation had in view the whole subject matter of the articles of those treaties, which provide for the security of Merchants and their effects in the event of War.

This conformity, in principle, of the article, under examination with the provisions in so many Treaties of our own and of other Nations, taken in connection with the comment of Mr. *Bussy,* brings a very powerful support to the article. It is additional and full evidence that our Envoy in agreeing to it did not go upon new and untrodden ground, that on the contrary he was in a beaten tract, that in pursuing the dictate of reason and the better opinion of Writers as to the rule of the law of Nations respecting the point, he was at the same time pursuing the examples of all the other Treaties we had ourselves made and of many of those of other Countries.

It is now incumbent upon me to perform my promise of replying to such objections to the Article as may remain unanswered by the preceding remarks. It is with pleasure, I note, that the field is very narrow—that indeed there scarcely remains any thing which is not so frivolous and impotent as almost to forbid a serious replication. It will therefore be my aim to be brief.

It is said there is only an apparent reciprocity in the article, millions being due on our side and little or nothing on the other.[17]

The answer to this is, that no right being relinguished on either side—no privilege granted—the stipulation amounting only to a recognition of a rule of the law of Nations—to a promise to abstain from injustice & breach of faith—there is no room for an argument about reciprocity—further than to require that the promise should be mutual, as is the case. This is the only equivalent which the nature of the subject demands or permits. It would be dishonorable to expect a boon merely for an engagement to fulfil a moral obligation.[18]

But it has been shewn, that the stipulation will be beneficial to us by the confidence which it will give on the other side;[19] obviating and avoiding the obstructions to trade, the injuries to and incumbrances upon Credit naturally incident to the distrust and apprehension, which after the question had been once moved, were to be expected. Here if a compensation were required there is one. Let me add as a truth which perhaps has no exception[20] that in the wise order of Providence Nations in a temporal sense may safely trust the maxim that the observance of Justice carries with it its own and a full reward.

It is also said that having bound ourselves by Treaty we shall hereafter lose the credit of moderation which would attend a forbearance to exercise the right. But it having been demonstrated that no such right exists, we only renounce a claim to the negative merit

17. See the essay on Article 10 of the Jay Treaty by "Decius," which begins: "This article like many others, has the appearance of reciprocity, but when the situation of the two countries is attended to, this apparent equality vanishes, and Great-Britain alone derives advantage from it. . . . Millions are due to the subjects of Great-Britain from the government and from individuals of the United States while, comparatively speaking, our citizens hold nothing in the British funds or banks, and have few if any demands upon the subjects of that nation" (*The* [New York] *Argus, or Greenleaf's New Daily Advertiser*, July 13, 1795). For the authorship of the "Decius" articles, see "The Defence No. I," July 22, 1795, note 1.

18. In the newspaper the following sentence was added to this paragraph: "Indeed, as heretofore intimated, the true rule of reciprocity in stipulations of treaties is equal right, not equal advantage from each several stipulation."

In the margin opposite this paragraph H wrote and crossed out: "note right to confiscate vessels &c."

19. See "The Defence No. XXI," October 30, 1795.

20. In the newspaper the following phrase was inserted at this point: "however incongenial with the fashionable patriotic creed."

of not committing injustice, and we acquire the positive praise of being willing to renounce explicitly a pretension which might be the instrument of oppression and fraud. It is always honorable to give proof of upright intention.

It is further said, that under the protection of this stipulation, The King of Great Britain, *who has already speculated in our funds* * may engross the whole Capital of the Bank of the U States and thereby secure the *uncontrouled direction* of it—that he may hold the Stock in the name of his *ambassador* or of some citizen of the U States, perhaps a Senator, who if of the virtuous twenty,† might be proud of the honor—that thus our citizens in time of peace might experience the mortification of being beholden to *British Directors* for the accommodations they might want, that in time of War our operations might be cramped at the pleasure of his Majesty and according as he should see fit or not to accommodate our Government with loans & that both in peace and war we may be reduced to the abject condition of having the whole Capital of our national Bank administered by his Britannick Majesty.[21]

Shall I treat this Rhapsody with seriousness or ridicule?

The Capital of the Bank of the U States is ten millions of dollars; little short at the present Market Price of [three millions of] [22] pounds Sterling; but from the natural operation of such a demand in raising price 'tis not probable that much less than four Millions Stereling would suffice to complete the monopoly. I have never understood that the private purse of his Britannic Majesty, if it be true as asserted that he has already witnessed a disposition to speculate in our funds (a fact however from which it was natural to infer a more pacific disposition towards us) was so very ample as conveniently to spare an item of such size for a speculation across the Atlantic. But perhaps the national purse will be brought to his aid. As this supposes a parliamentary grant, new taxes and new loans it does not seem to be a very manageable thing, without disclosure of the object; and if disclosed so very unexampled an at-

---

* The Assertors would be puzzled to bring proof of the fact.

† Those who advised to a Ratification of the Treaty.

21. The arguments cited in the preceding paragraph have been taken from the third essay by "Decius" in *The* [New York] *Argus, or Greenleaf's New Daily Advertiser,* July 13, 1795.

22. Space left blank in MS. The words within brackets have been taken from the newspaper.

tempt of a foreign Government would present a case completely out of the reach of all ordinary rules, justifying by the manifest danger to us even war and the confiscation of all that had been purchased. For let it be remembered, that the article does not protect the public property of a foreign Government Prince or State; independent of the observation just made that such a case would be out of the reach of all ordinary rules. It may be added that an attempt of this kind from the force of the pecuniary Capital of G Britain would, as a precedent, threaten and alarm all Nations. Would consequences like these be incurred?

But let it be supposed that the inclination shall exist and that all difficulties about funds have been surmounted, still to effect the plan there must be in *all* the stockholders a willingness to sell to the British King or his Agents as well as the will and means on his part to purchase. Here too some impediment might be experienced. There are persons who might choose to keep their property in the shape of Bank Stock, and live upon the income of it, whom price would not readily tempt to part with it. Besides there is an additional obstacle to complete success. The U States are themselves the proprietors of two Millions of the Bank Stock.[23]

Of two things one—Either the monopoly by his Britannic Majesty would be known (and it would be a pretty arduous task to keep it a secret especially if the Stock was to stand as suggested in the name of his *ambassador*) or it would be unknown and concealed under unsuspected names. In the former supposition, the observations already made recur—there would be no protection to it from the article—and the extraordinary nature of the case would warrant any thing. Would his Majesty or the Parliament choose to trust so large a property in so perilous a situation?

If to avoid this the plan should be to keep the operation unknown the most effectual method would be to place the Stock in the names of our own citizens. This it seems would be attended with no diffi-

---

23. Section 11 of "An Act to incorporate the subscribers to the Bank of the United States" (1 *Stat.* 191–96 [February 25, 1791]) reads in part: "*And be it further enacted*, That it shall be lawful for the President of the United States, at any time or times, within eighteen months after the first day of April next, to cause a subscription to be made to the stock of the said corporation, as part of the aforesaid capital stock of ten millions of dollars, on behalf of the United States, to an amount not exceeding two millions of dollars. . . ."

culty; since even our senators would be ambitious of the honor; and if they should have qualms or fears, others could no doubt be found amongst the numerous sec[re]taries or adherents of Great Britain in our Country—probably some of the patriots would not be inexorable if properly solicited, or in the last resort persons might be sent from Great Britain to acquire naturalization for the express purpose.

In this supposition too the article would be at least innocent. For its provisions are intirely foreign to the case of stock standing in the names of our own citizens. It neither enlarges nor abriges the power of the Government in this respect.

Further. How will the article, work the miracle of placing the Bank under the management of *British directors?* It gives no new rights, no new qualifications.

The constitution of the Bank (Sections the 5th. and 7th of the Act of Incorporation) [24] has provided with solicitude these important guards against foreign or other sinister influence. I   That none but a *citizen of the U States* shall be *eligible* as a *Director*. II   That none but a stockholder *actually resident within the U States* shall vote in elections *by proxy*. III   That one fourth of the *Directors*, who are to be elected annually, must every year go out of the direction. IV   That a *Director* may at any time be removed & replaced by the Stockholders at a general Meeting. V   That a *single* share shall give *one* vote for directors, while any number of shares, in the same person copartnership or body politic, will not give more than *thirty* votes.

Hence it is impossible that the Bank can be in the management of *British Directors*. A British subject is *incapable* of being a *director*. It is also next to impossible that an undue British Influence could operate in the choice of Directors out of the number of our own Citizens. The British King, or British subjects out of the U States, could not even have a vote by Attorney in the choice. Schemes of secret monopoly could not be executed because they would be betrayed unless the secret was confined to a small number. A small number, no one of whom could have more than thirty votes, would be easily overruled by the more numerous proprietors of single

24. "An Act to incorporate the subscribers to the Bank of the United States" (1 *Stat.* 191–96).

or small number of shares with the addition of the votes of the U States.

But here again it is to be remembered that as to combinations with our own citizens, in which they were to be ostensible for any pernicious foreign project, the article under consideration is perfectly nugatory. It can do neither good nor harm, since it merely relates, as to the exemption from confiscation and seizure on our part to the known property of British subjects.

It follows therefore that the dangers pourtrayed to us from the speculating enterprizes of His Britannic Majesty are the vagaries of an overheated imagination or the contrivances of a spirit of Deception, and that so far as they could be supposed to have the least colour, it turns on circumstances upon which the Treaty can have no influence whatever. In taking pains to expose their futility I have been led principally by the desire of making my fellow Citizens sensible in this instance, as in others, of the extravagances of the opposers of the Treaty.

One artifice to render the article unacceptable has been to put cases of extreme misconduct on the other side, of flagrant violations of the laws of nations of war of justice and of humanity and to ask whether under such circumstances the confiscation or sequestration of debts would not be justifiable. To this the answer is, that if circumstances so extraordinary should arise as without the Treaty would warrant so extraordinary an act, they will equally warrant it under the Treaty. For cases of this kind are exceptions to all general rules. They would excuse the violation of an express or positive as well as of a tacit or virtual pledge of the public faith which describes the whole difference between the existence & non existence of the Article in question. They resemble those cases of extreme necessity (through excessive hunger for instance) which in the eye of the law of nature will excuse the taking of the property of another, or those cases of extreme abuse of authority in rulers, which amounting unequivocally to tyranny, are admitted to justify forcible resistance to the established authorities. Constitutions of Government laws, Treaties, all give way to extremities of such a description. The point of obligation is to distinguish them with sincerity and not to indulge our passions and our interests in substituting pretended for real cases.

A writer who disgraces by adopting the name of CICERO makes a curious remark by way of objection.[25] He affirms that the article is nugatory because a Treaty is dissolved by the state of War, in which the provision is designed to operate.[26] If this be true, the article is at least harmless, and the trouble of painting it in such terrific colours might have been spared. But it is not true. Reason, writers, the practice of nations all accord in this position that those stipulations which contemplate the state of War—in other words which are designed to operate in case of War preserve their force and obligation when war takes place.[27] To what end else all the stipulations which have been cited from so many Treaties? ᴬ

ᴬ Note This Writer is as profligate as he is absurd. Besides imputing to Camillus in general terms a number of things of which he never dreamt, he has the effrontery to forge as a *literal quotation* from him calling it his *own language*, & designating by *inverted commas*, a passage respecting the impressing of seamen which certainly not in terms, nor even in substance upon fair construction, are to be found in any thing he has written.[28]

25. Five articles signed by "Cicero" and addressed to H were printed in *The* [New York] *Argus, or Greenleaf's New Daily Advertiser,* October 2, 10, 19, 28, November 18, 1795.

26. In his third essay "Cicero" wrote: "I now ask you, Sir, or even Camillus, the great master of logic, whether, in times of war, all treaties are not void? Whether, in such a case, nations have not access to every means of revenue and defence? and whether in case of war between this country and England, our present treaty would not be nullified?" (*The* [New York] *Argus, or Greenleaf's New Daily Advertiser,* October 19, 1795).

27. In the newspaper the following footnote is inserted at this point: "Vattel B. iii ch. x." Vattel wrote: "The conventions, the treaties made with a nation, are broken or annulled, by a war arising between the contracting parties. . . . Yet here we must except those treaties where certain things are stipulated in case of a rupture. . . . Since by treaties of this nature, intended to provide for what shall be observed in case of a rupture, all right of annulling them by a declaration of war is renounced" (*Law of Nations,* Book III, Ch. X, Sec. 175).

28. In the newspaper the following sentence has been added to this footnote: "Not having all the numbers of CICERO at hand, I may mistake, in attributing to him the principal sentiment, which is from memory, but I have under my eye the number which witnesses his forgery." In this footnote H is referring to the following comment on "The Defence No. VI," August 8, 1795, in "Cicero's" first essay: ". . . If, then, what he [Camillus] asserts be really true, sooner than enter into an alliance with Britain, I would, if possible, push the atlantic States three thousand miles further from her! Let us listen to his own language—'The similitude between the two countries is so great, that it is impossible to discriminate the citizens of one nation from the subjects of the other; therefore the British are justified in impressing seamen from on board American vessels, because the sole existence of the British government depends upon the strength of her navy; consequently the validity of a certificate, nor the oath of a seaman, can be no preventative against the British mode of manning her fleets!' Such is the defence set up by Camillus"

Previous to a conclusion, I shall observe barely with a view to accuracy, that the article leaves unprotected all Vessels goods and merchandize, every species of property indeed, except debts between individuals and the property of individuals in the public funds and in public and private banks. With this exception whatever may have been before liable to confiscation or sequestration, still remains so, notwithstanding anything contained in this article.

To overrate the value or force of our own arguments is a natural foible of self love—to be convinced without convincing others is no uncommon fate of a writer or speaker but I am more than ordinarily mistaken if every mind open to Conviction will not have been satisfied by what has been offered that the tenth article of the Treaty lately negotiated with Great Britain does nothing but confirm by a positive agreement a rule of the law of Nations indicated by reason supported by the better opinion of Writers ratified by modern usage—dictated by justice and good faith recognised by formal acts and declarations of different nations—witnessed by diplomatic testimony—sanctioned by our treaties with other countries and by treaties between other countries—and conformable with sound policy and the true interest of the U States.

The discussion has been drawn out to so great length, because the objections to this article are among those which have been urged with most warmth and emphasis against the Treaty, and its vindication from them if satisfactory must go far towards securing to it the public suffrage. Citizens of America! tis for you to perform your part of the task; tis for you to weigh with candor the arguments which have been submitted to your judgments; to consult without byass the integrity of your hearts; to exile prejudice, and to immolate on the altar of Truth the artifices of Cabal and Falshood.[B] There can then be no danger that Patriotism will have to lament, or National Honor to blush at the sentence you shall pronounce.

The articles, which adjust the matters of controversy between

---

(*The* [New York] *Argus, or Greenleaf's New Daily Advertiser,* October 2, 1795).

[B] In applying the character of dishonesty & turpitude to the principle of confiscation or sequestration, I am far from intending to brand as dishonest men all those whose opinions favor it. I know there are some ardent spirits chargeable with the error of whose integrity I think well.

the two Countries, all those which are permanent, have now been reviewed. Let me appeal to the consciences of those who have accompanied me in the Review. If these articles were all that composed the Treaty, would it be better that they should exist, or that all the sources of rupture and War with Great Britain should have survived the negotiation to extinguish them and should still subsist in full vigour? If every enlightened and honest man must prefer the former, then let me make another observation & put another question. The remaining articles of the Treaty which constitute its commercial part expire by their own limitation at the end of *twelve* years. It is in the power of either party consistently with the instrument to terminate them at the expiration of *two* years after the present war between France & Great Britain. Is it at all probable that they can contain any thing so injurious, considering the short duration which may be assigned to them, as to counterballance the important consideration of preserving peace to this young Country, as to warrant the excessive clamours which have been raised, as to authorise the horrid calumnies which are vented and to justify the systematic efforts which are in operation to convulse our country and to hazard even CIVIL WAR. CAMILLUS

To George Washington

New York November 5th
1795

Sir

I received on the second instant your two letters of the 29th. of October with the inclosures. An answer has been delayed to ascertain the disposition of Mr. King,[1] who through the summer has resided in the country and is only occasionally in Town. I am now able to inform you—*he would not accept*. Circumstances of the moment conspire with the disgust which a virtuous and independent mind feels at placing itself *in but* to the foul and venomous shafts of calumny which are continually shot by an odious confederacy against Virtue—to give Mr. King a decided disinclination to the office.

I wish Sir I could present to you any useful ideas as a substitute. But the embarrassment is extreme as to Secretary of State. An Attorney General I believe may easily be fixed upon by a satisfactory choice. Either Mr. *Dexter*[2] or Mr. *Gore*[3] would answer. They are both men of undoubted probity. Mr. Dexter has most *natural* talent & is strong in his particular profession. Mr. Gore is I believe equally considered in his profession & has more various information. No good man doubts Mr. Gores purity but he has made money by agencies for British Houses in the recovery of debts &c. and by operations in the funds which a certain party object to him. I believe Mr. Dexter is free from every thing of this kind. Mr. King thinks *Gore* on the whole preferable. I hesitate between them. Either will I think be a good appointment.

But for a Secretary of State I know not what to say. *Smith*[4] though not of full size is very respectable for talent & has pretty various information. I think he has more real talent than the last incumbent of the Office. But there are strong objections to his appointment. I fear he is of an uncomfortable temper. He is popular with no description of men from a certain *hardness* of character and he more than most other men is considered as tinctured with prejudices towards the British. In this particular his ground is somewhat peculiar. It may suit party views to say much of other men but more in this respect is *believed* with regard to Smith. I speak merely as to *byass* and *prejudice*. There are things, & important things for which I would recommend Smith; thinking well of his abilities information & industry & integrity—but at the present juncture I believe his appointment to the office in question would be unadviseable.

Besides it is very important that he should not now be removed from the house of Representatives.

I have conferred with Mr. King with respect to Mr. Potts.[5] We both think well of his principles & consider him a man of good sense. But he is of a cast of character ill suited to such an appointment and is not *extensive* either as to talents or information. It is also a serious question whether the Senate at this time ought to be weakened.

Mr. Innis,[6] I fear is too absolutely lazy for Secy of State. The objection would weigh less as to Atty General.

The following characters in the narrowness of the probable circle as to willingness have occured to me. Judge Pendleton of Georgia [7]—Mr. Desaussure [8] (late Director of the Mint) of South Carolina—Governor Lee [9] or Mr. Lee late collector of Alexandria, of Virginia [10]—Mc.Henry of Maryland [11]—I mean the Doctor.

Judge Pendleton writes well is of respectable abilities and a Gentlemanlike smooth man. If I were sure of his political views I should be much disposed to advise his appointment under the circumstances. But I fear he has been somewhat tainted with the prejudices of Mr. Jefferson & Mr. Madison & I have afflicting suspicions concerning these men. Desaussure, I believe, has considerable talents, is of gentlemanlike manners goods views and only wants sufficient standing to put him upon a footing with any attainable man.

Governor Lee has several things for him & several against him— he ought to have a good secretary under him. His brother I only know enough of to think him worth considering.

Mc.Henry you know he would give no strength to the administration but he would not disgrace the Office—his views are good —perhaps his health &c. would prevent his accepting.

I do not know Judge Bee.[12] I have barely thought of him.

In fact a first rate charcter is not attainable. A second rate must be taken with good dispositions & barely decent qualifications. I wish I could throw more light. Tis a sad omen for the Government.

By the fifteenth I will carefully attend to other parts of your letters. I regret that bad health & a pressure of avocations will permit nothing earlier.

With the most respectful & affect attachment I have the honor to remain   Sir   Your Obedt serv   A Hamilton

The President of the U States.

ALS, George Washington Papers, Library of Congress; copy, Hamilton Papers, Library of Congress.
    1. Rufus King. See Washington to H, October 29, 1795, note 6.
    2. Samuel Dexter. See Washington to H, October 29, 1795, note 11.
    3. Christopher Gore, United States attorney for the District of Massachusetts.
    4. William Loughton Smith. See Washington to H, October 29, 1795, note 12.
    5. Richard Potts. See Washington to H, October 29, 1795, note 8.
    6. James Innes. See Washington to H, October 29, 1795, note 15.

7. Nathaniel Pendleton was United States judge for the District of Georgia.

8. Henry W. De Saussure. See Samuel Ogden to H, October 5, 1795, note 2.

9. Former Governor Henry Lee of Virginia.

10. Charles Lee. For Lee's appointment as Attorney General, see H to Oliver Wolcott, Jr., October 3, 1795, note 3.

11. James McHenry. On January 20, 1796, Washington offered McHenry the position of Secretary of War, which was available as a result of Pickering's appointment as Secretary of State (LC, George Washington Papers, Library of Congress). McHenry accepted the President's nomination on January 24, 1796 (ALS, George Washington Papers, Library of Congress). McHenry's name was sent to the Senate on January 26, 1796, and his appointment was confirmed the following day (*Executive Journal*, I, 198).

12. Thomas Bee, United States judge for the District of South Carolina.

To the Editor of The Argus [1]

[New York, November 6, 1795]

For the MINERVA. [2]

The Defence No. 22, if I recollect aright was sent you on Sunday last, accompanied with an intimation that the subsequent numbers would be transmitted with greater frequency, and requesting that their publication might be accelerated. You could be at no loss to conjecture the motive. Since that time, to facilitate dispatch, two other numbers have been sent you.

Instead of acceleration, your paper of the 5th inst. announces that you had resolved to delay the publication of No. 22 'till Saturday—and to diminish in future by one half the place you had before allowed to these papers in your Gazette; the effect of which would be extremely to retard their progress.

This circumstance obliges me to change the channel of the publication and to recall the papers now in your hands, which you will accordingly deliver to the bearer.

You are at the same time requested to insert in your paper this explanation of the reason for the change. It will remain with the Public to judge, whether considering the general uniform complexion of your paper, and the numerous columns constantly devoted to views opposite to those of *Camillus*, it would really have been truly an "imposition," to allow to that writer the full proportion of place which his performance requires and to have continued so far to give to your paper a little diversity of tint. And it will remain with you, by transcribing from other papers or not, to the extent of the six columns you mention to have destined for CAMIL-LUS, to manifest whether this resolution was designed only to check his progress or to banish him entirely from your paper.[3]   CAMILLUS

November, 6th, 1795.

The [New York] *Herald; A Gazette for the Country,* November 11, 1795.

1. Thomas Greenleaf was the editor of *The* [New York] *Argus, or Greenleaf's New Daily Advertiser.*

For background to this letter, see the introductory note to "The Defence No. I," July 22, 1795.

On November 3, 1795, the following note appeared in *The* [New York] *Argus, or Greenleaf's New Daily Advertiser:* "THE DEFENCE, No. XXII, is received, but must give way to more LOCAL matter—as several other communications have done, and must to morrow. A number of our subscribers having complained of the 'imposition' of so many lengthy columns from Camillus, the Editor conceives himself obliged to restrict him to only SIX COLUMNS PER WEEK in future, instead of from 8 to 12, as heretofore." On November 5, 1795, the *Argus* printed approximately the first half of "The Defence No. XXII" and stated that it would be continued. On November 11, the entire essay appeared in *The Herald.* It was preceded by the letter which is printed above.

2. The full title of this paper was the [New York] *American Minerva; an Evening Advertiser.* A semi-weekly edition of this paper was also published under the title of *The Herald; A Gazette for the Country.* As indicated in note 1, it was in the *Herald,* or the semi-weekly edition of the *Minerva,* in which "The Defence No. XXII" was printed.

3. The editor of the *Argus* replied to H's letter as follows: "In last Wednesday's paper the Editor declared his intention in future of publishing only six columns of the writings of CAMILLUS per week, i e. 3 columns in each of his Country papers, on account of complaints that they had occupied too much of the Register, to the exclusion of more important matter—and, as he has received a Note from that writer, informing him, that in consequence thereof the channel of publishing SHOULD BE CHANGED, he thinks proper to communicate it to the public. It being his full determination to evince an impartial line of conduct in the management of his paper with respect to parties, it cannot be expected that he would apply a different rule to the writings of Camillus, whose voluminous lucubrations would, if not restricted as to their publication, almost completely occupy the two Registers per week, which have an extensive circulation in the country, and which it was the Editor's desire to variegate by a certain proportion of all descriptions of politics. Several Communications remain to be noticed" (*The* [New York] *Argus, or Greenleaf's New Daily Advertiser,* November 7, 1795).

From George Washington

Philadelphia 10th. Nov. 1795.

My dear Sir,   (Private)

Your favor of the 5th. has been duly received, but nothing was said in it of young Fayette.[1] I am willing, as I said in my last, to receive him under any circumstances, or in any manner you may conceive best; & wish to know what that is.

Having, since I wrote to you on the 29th. ult received more agreeable—tho' not conclusive—accounts from abroad, I pray you to suspend your superstructure [2] until you receive a ground plan from me, which shall be in a few days with better, or at least with more ample materials.

Yours always—and very affectionately   Go: Washington

Colo. Hamilton

ALS, Hamilton Papers, Library of Congress.
   1. For information on George Washington Motier Lafayette, see H to Washington, October 16, 1795, note 1, and Washington to H, October 29, 1795.
   2. This is a reference to Washington's request that H assist him in the preparation of his annual message to Congress. See Washington to H, October 29, 1795.

Explanation [1]

[New York, November 11, 1795]

A very virulent attack has recently been made upon the President of the U States, the present Secretary of the Treasury, and myself

ADfS, Hamilton Papers, Library of Congress; [New York] *Daily Advertiser*, Supplement, November 20, 1795.
   1. In the *Daily Advertiser* H's article was introduced as follows: "Explanation. By Mr. Hamilton on the subject of a late attack upon the President of the United States, and the former and present Secretary of the Treasury, in relation to the compensation of the President."
   H wrote this article in reply to charges made by "A Calm Observer," who in a letter to the [Philadelphia] *Aurora. General Advertiser* on October 23,

as his predecessor [2] in office, on the ground of extra payments to The President on account of his salary. The charges against all the three are no less heinous than those of *intentional* violation of the constitution, of the laws, and of their oaths of office. I annex the epithet *intentional*, because though not expressly used in the terms of the attack, it is implied in every line of it; since an involuntary error of construction, if that could even be made out, would not warrant the imputations "of *contemning* and *despising every principle* which the people have established for the security of their rights, *of setting at defiance* all *law* and *authority*, and of *servile submission* and compliance with the *lawless will* and *pleasure* of a President."

Were considerations personal to myself alone to be consulted the present attempt would be treated with no greater attention than has been shewn to all the anonymous slanders by which I have been so long and so implacably persecuted. But convinced by a course of observation for more than four years that there exists in this country an unprincipled and daring combination,[3] to obstruct by any means, *which shall be necessary and can be commanded, not short even of force*, the due and efficient administration of the present government, to make our most important national interests subservient to those of a foreign power—and as means to these ends to destroy by calumny and misrepresentation the confidence of the people in the truly virtuous men of our country and to transfer it with the power of the State to ambitious hypochrites, and intriguing demagogues perhaps corrupted partisans perceiving likewise that this infatuated combination in the belief that the well earned esteem and attachment of his fellow Citizens towards the actual chief Magistrate of the UStates is the principal remaining obstacle to the execution of their plan are making the most systematic efforts to extinguish those sentiments in the breasts of the people—I think it a duty to depart from my general rule of Conduct and to submit to the public with my

1795, had accused the President of having repeatedly overdrawn his salary. See H to George Washington, October 26, 1795; H to Oliver Wolcott, Jr., October 26, 27, 28, 1795; Wolcott to H, October 29, November 2, 1795.

Minor word variations between H's draft and the newspaper version have been ignored; only substantive differences have been noted.

2. In MS, "precedecessor."

3. In the newspaper version the phrase "under the influence of sinister aims" is inserted at this point.

name an explanation of the principles which have governed the Treasury Department on the point in question.

I shall state in the first place, that the rule with regard to expenditures and appropriations, which has *uniformly* regulated the practice of the Department is this (viz) *to issue no money from the Treasury but for an object, for which there was a law previously passed, making an appropriation and designating the fund from which the money was to arise. But there being such a law and an adequate fund to support the expenditure, it was deemed justifiable as well before as after the service was performed or the supply obtained, for which the appropriation was designed, to make disbursements from the Treasury for the object, if it appeared safe and expedient so to do.* If made *before,* it was an *advance* or *anticipation* for which the party was charged and held accountable till exonerated by the performance of the service or the furnishing of the supply. If *afterwards,* it was a *payment* and went to some general head of Account as such.

Thus, if a sum was appropriated for provisions for the army for a particular year it was common to make *advances* on account to the contractors long before the supplies were furnished.[4] If the law was passed in one year for the next, there would be no hesitation to make the advance immediately after the passing of the law and before the year to which the appropriation was applicable had commenced. So also sums would be furnished to the Department of War in anticipation of the monthly pay of the officers and soldiers, and advances on account of pay in particular circumstances and for good reasons would be actually made by that Department to the officers and soldiers. And so likewise advances have been made for the use of the President and of the members [of] both houses of Congress in anticipation of their respective compensations.[5]

4. For the informal advances to Army contractors, see "Report on Rules and Modes of Proceeding with Regard to the Collection, Keeping, and Disbursement of Public Moneys, and Accounting for the Same," March 4, 1794, note 20.

5. At this point in the draft H wrote and crossed out the following paragraph: "It results that if the construction of the Treasury has been an erroneous one, the other heads of Departments and both houses of congress are, as much at least as the President, implicated in it by participation and acquiescence. If it be said that the whole responsibility was with the Treasury Department, why does not this exculpate the President equally with any other person except the officers of that Department. But in fact is not a rule of the

It will without difficulty be comprehended that the practice of the Treasury has in some cases been essential to the due course of the public service.

Every good judge will be sensible that from the insufficiency of individual capitals to such large advances as the supplies of an army require, it was indispensable to the obtaining of them that anticipations from the Treasury should enable the contractors to do what otherwise they would have been unable to do—and that these anticipations must also have had the effect of procuring the supplies on cheaper terms to the U States.

When it is considered too that the army has operated for several years past at [five or six] [6] hundred miles distance from the seat of Government and a considerable part of the year from the rudeness of the country & obstructions of the Waters, it is impracticable to transmit monies to the scenes of payment—it will be perceived that without advances from the Treasury in anticipation of their pay, not only a compliance with the engagements of the Government would have been impossible—but the troops must have been always left most unreasonably in arrear. In June 1794 Congress passed a law declaring that the army should in future be paid in such manner as that the arrears should not exceed two months.[7] Compliance with this regulation renders *anticipations* at certain seasons a matter of physical necessity; yet that law gave no special authority for the purpose.

A particular case, by way of example in which, distinct from general rules, advances or anticipations in the war department are necessary respects the recruiting service. The officers who are for a long time distant from their corps require the accommodation of an advance of pay to be able to discharge their duty. Towards the possibility of enlisting men, it is indispensable they should carry with them the bounty money and this upon conjecture of what

---

constitution (which is also alleged to have been violated) obligatory on every part of the Government? and does not any department or person which within its sp[h]ere partakes of a violation of it by another department or person become an accomplice in that violation?"

6. Space left blank in MS. The material within brackets has been taken from the *Daily Advertiser.*

7. "An Act in addition to the 'Act for making further and more effectual provision for the protection of the frontiers of the United States'" (1 *Stat.* 390 [June 7, 1794]).

may be done and with the possibility that from not being able to obtain the men the ultimate expenditure may not take place. This instance will suggest to reflection an infinite number of cases in the course of the public service in which a disbursement from the Treasury *must* precede *the execution of the object* and *may exceed* the sum finally requisite for it.[8]

These cases indicate the expediency, and even necessity of the construction which has regulated the practice of the Treasury. And it might be shewn if necessary that it is analogous to the practice under the former Government of the UStates and under other governments; and this too where the theory of expenditure equally is, as *expressed* in our Constitution, that no money shall be expended but *in consequence* of an appropriation by law.

It remains to see whether this rule of conduct so indispensable in the practice of the department be permitted by a fair interpretation of the constitution and the laws.

The general injunction of the Constitution (Article I § IX) is that "no money shall be drawn from the Treasury but *in consequence* of appropriations made by law." [9]

That clause appears to me to be exactly equivalent to this other clause—"No money shall be drawn from the Treasury but for which there is an appropriation made by law." In other words before money can legally issue from the Treasury for any purpose, there must be a law authorising an expenditure and designating the object and the fund. This being done the disbursement may be made consistently with the constitution either by way of *advance* or *anticipation* or by *way* of *payment*. It may precede or follow the service supply or other object of expenditure. Either will equally satisfy the words "in consequence of" which are not words of strict import, but may be taken in several senses—In one sense, *that* is *"in consequence of"* a thing, which, being bottomed upon it, follows

8. At this point in the draft H wrote and crossed out the following paragraph: "In the case of the salaries to foreign Ministers placed as they were beyond the Atlantic, a pecuniary provision by anticipation was essential to their seasonable support."

9. In the newspaper version the following paragraph is inserted at this point: "The question upon the clause is whether when an appropriation has been made for a particular service or supply, the actual disbursement from the treasury must follow the service or supply in the nature of *payment*, or may precede it in the nature of an *advance?* I hold the last construction which is that adopted by the treasury to be the true one."

it *in order of time*. A disbu[r]sement must be either an *advance* or *anticipation* or a *payment*. Tis not presumeable that the constitution meant to distinguish between these two modes of disbursement. It must have intended to leave this matter wholly to convenience.

The design of the constitution in this provision was as I conceive to secure these important ends—that the *purpose* the *limit* and the *fund* of every expenditure should be ascertained by a previous law. The public security is complete in this particular if no money can be expended but for *an object,* to an *extent,* and *out of a fund,* which the laws have prescribed.

Even in cases which affect only individual interests, if the terms of a law will bear several meanings that is to be preferred which will best accord with convenience. In cases that concern the public this rule is applicable with still greater latitude. Public convenience is to be promoted, public inconvenience to be avoided. The business of administration requires accommodation to so great a variety of circumstances, that a rigid construction would in countless instances arrest the wheels of Government. It has been shewn that the construction which has been adopted at the Treasury is in many cases essential in practice. This inclines the scale in favour of it— the words "in consequence of" admitting of various significations.

The practice of the legislature as to appropriation laws favours this construction.

These laws are generally distinct from those which create the cause of expenditure. Thus the act which declares that the President shall be allowed twenty five thousand dollars ⅌ annum, that which declares that each senator and representative shall be intitled to so much per day, that which determines that each officer and soldier shall have so much per Month &c. neither of these acts is an act of appropriation. The Treasury has not conceived itself authorised to expend a single cent upon the basis of any such act; regarding it merely as constituting a claim upon the Government for a certain compensation, but requiring prior to an actual disbu[r]sement for such claim, that a law be passed authorising the disbursement out of a specified fund. This is what is considered as the law by which the appropriation is made; from which results to the Public a double security.

Hence every year a particular act (sometimes more than one) is passed appropriating certain sums for the various branches of the public service, and indicating the funds from which the monies are to be drawn. The *object*, the *sum* and the *fund* are *all* that are to be found in these acts. They are commonly, if not universally, silent as to any thing further.

This I regard as constructive of the clause in the constitution. The appropriation laws are in execution of that provision and fulfil all its purposes. And they are silent as to the distinction between *anticipation* & *payment*, in other words, as to the manner of disbursement.

Hence I conclude that if there exist a law *appropriating* a certain sum for the salary of the President, an advance upon that sum in *anticipation* of the service, is as constitutional as a *payment* after the service has been performed; in other words, that the advance of a quarters salary at the beginning of a quarter is as much warranted by the constitution as the payment of it at the end of a quarter.

It is in the sense, that the present Secretary of the Treasury has affirmed that "not one Dollar has at any time been advanced for the use of The President for which there was not an existing appropriation." [10] He did not mean to say, that no money had been advanced in anticipation of the service; for the fact is otherwise, but nothing is more true than that the sums disbursed were within the limits of the sums appropriated. If there was an excess at the end of one year, there had been a previous appropriation for a succeeding year, upon which that excess was an advance.

It is objected to this practice, that the death of the party between the advance to him and the expiration of an equivalent term of service, by superseding the object of the advance, would render it a misexpenditure of so much money and therefore a violation of the constitution.

I answer that the same casualty might have the same effect in other cases, in which it would be against common sense to suppose that an advance might not be made with legality and propriety. [11]

Suppose for example a law was to be passed directing a given quantity of powder to be purchased for public use, and appropriating a definite sum for the purchase, and suppose intelligence brought to the secretary of the Treasury that the quantity required could be

10. See H to Washington, October 26, 1795, note 1.

11. In the margin opposite this paragraph H wrote: "Note advance to Clerk sent to N Carolina."

procured for prompt payment at Boston. It cannot in such case be doubted that the sum appropriated might legally be advanced to an Agent to proceed to Boston to make the purchase. Yet that Agent might die, and the money never be applied according to its destination, or the desired quantity might be procured for a *less* sum, and a *ballance* remain in his hands. In either case, there would be money disbursed which was not actually applied to the object of the law— in the last case there is *no final object* for the disbursement because the ballance is a surplus. This proves that the possibility of a failure or falling short of the object for which an advance is made is not an objection to its legality. Indeed the consequence is a possible one in every case of an *anticipation*, whether to contractors or to other public agents, for a determinate or an indeterminate purpose.

The only consequence is that the sum unapplied must be accounted for and refunded. The distinction here again is between an *advance* and a *payment*. More cannot certainly be finally *paid* than is equal to the object of an appropriation, though the sum appropriated exceed the sum necessary. But more may be *advanced*, to the full extent of the appropriation, than may be ultimately exhausted by the object of the expenditure, on the condition which always attends an advance of accounting for the application & refunding an excess. This is a direct answer to the question whether more can be *paid* than is necessary to satisfy the object of an appropriation. More cannot be *paid*, but more may be *advanced*, on the accountability of the person to whom it is advanced.[12]

But risk of loss to the public may attend this principle? This is true, but it [is] as true in all the cases of advances to Contractors &c. as in those of advances upon salaries and compensations—nor does this point of risk affect the question of legality—it to touches merely that of a prudent exercise of discretion. When large sums are advanced it is usual to obtain security for their due application or for indemnification. This security is greater or less according to the circumstances of the parties to whom the advances are made. When small sums are advanced, especially if for purposes quickly fulfilled, and to persons who are themselves adequate sureties, no collateral security is demanded. The head of the department is re-

12. In the newspaper version the following paragraph appears at this point: "The case stated by way of example is also conclusive to the point that money may be drawn from the Treasury in anticipation of the object of expenditure."

sponsible to the Government for observing proper measure and taking proper precautions. If he acts so as to incur justly the charge of improvidence or profusion he may be dismissed or punished according to the nature of his misconduct.

But the principle which is set up would, it is said, be productive of confusion distress and bankruptcy at the Treasury, since the appropriation for the support of Government is made payable out of the accruing duties of each year, and an *established right* in the officers of Government to claim their compensations, which amount to several hundred thousand dollars per annum, either on the first day of the year, or on the first day of a quarter before the services were rendered, would create a demand at a time when there might not and possibly would not be a single shilling in the Treasury arising out of that appropriation to satisfy it.*

It is not pretended, that there is an *established right* in the Officers to claim their salaries, *by anticipation,* at the beginning of a year or at the beginning of a quarter—no such right exists. The performance of the service must precede the right to demand payment. But it does not follow that because there is no right in the officer to demand payment, it may not be allowable for the Treasury to advance upon account for good reasons. A discretion of this sort in the head of the department can at least involve no embarrassment to the Treasury, of the formidable evils indicated; for the officer who makes the advance being himself the judge whether there is a competent fund and whether it can be made with convenience to the Treasury he will only make it when he perceives that no evil will ensue.

Let me recur to the example of advances to contractors for supplying the army. Suppose that in the terms of contract certain advances were stipulated and made; but it turned out nevertheless that the contractor disappointed in the funds on which he had relied could not execute his contract without further advances. Here there would be no right on his part to demand such further advances; but there would be a discretion in the Treasury to make them. This is an example of a discretion to do what there is not a right to demand. The existence of this discretion can do no harm, because the head

---

* These ideas with regard to the administration of the fund appropriated are very crude & incorrect—but it would complicate the subject to go into the developpemts.

of the Treasury will judge whether the state of it permits the required advances. But It is essential that the discretion should exist, because otherwise there might be a failure of supplies which no plan that could be substituted might be able to avert.

Yet the discretion is in neither case an arbitrary one. It is one which the head of the department is responsible to exercise with a careful eye to the public interest and safety. The abuse of it, in other words, the careless or wanton exercise of it, would be a cause of dismission for incapacity or of punishment for malconduct.

Thus advances on account of salaries or to Contractors for procuring public supplies might be carried so far and so improvidently managed as to be highly culpable and justly punishable; but this is a distinct question from the violation of constitution or law.

In all the cases, it is a complete answer to the objection of embarrassment to the Treasury, that not the will of the parties but the judgment of the head of the department is the rule and measure of the advances which he may make within the bounds of the sums appropriated by law.

I consider the law which has been cited with regard to the pay of the army as a legislative recognition of the rule of practice at the Treasury. The legislature could not have been ignorant that it was impracticable at certain seasons of the year to convey the money to the army to fulfil their injunction, without an advance from the Treasury before the pay became due. They presuppose a right to make this advance and enjoin that the Troops shall not be left more than two months in the year. The origin of this law enforces the observation. It is known that it passed in consequence of representations that the pay of the army was left too long in arrear, and it was intended to quicken the measures of payment. No person in either house of the legislature, I believe, doubted that there was power to precede the service by advances so as to render the payment even more punctual than was enjoined.

Indeed such advances when the army operated at a distance were necessary to fulfil the contract with the army. Its pay became due monthly, and in strictness of contract was to be made at the end of each month; a thing impossible unless advanced from the Treasury before it became due. No special authority was ever given for this purpose to the Treasury, but it appears to have been left to take

its course on the principle, that the disbursement might take place
as soon as there was an appropriation, though in anticipation of the
term of service.

The foregoing observations vindicate, I trust, the construction
of the Treasury as to the power of making disbursements in anticipation of services and supplies, if there has been a previous appropriation by law for the object, and if the advances never exceed the
amount appropriated; and at the same time evince that this practice
involves no violation of the constit[ut]ional provision with respect
to appropriations.

I proceed to examine that clause which respects the pay of the
President. It is in these words—"The President shall at stated times
receive for his services a compensation, which shall neither be increased nor diminished, during the period for which he shall have
been elected, and he shall not receive within that period any other
emolument from the UStates or any of them."

I understand this clause as equivalent to the following—"There
shall be established by law for the services of the President a
periodical compensation, which shall not be increased nor dim[in]-
ished during the term for which he shall have been elected, and
neither the U States nor any state shall allow him any emolument
in addition to his periodical compensation."

This will I think, at first sight, appear foreign to the question of
a provisional advance by the Treasury on account of the compensation periodically established by Law for his services.

The manifest object of the provision is to guard the independence
of the President from the legislative controul of the UStates or of
any state, by the ability to withold lessen or increase his compensation.

It requires that the law shall assign him a definite compensation
for a definite time. It prohibits the legislature from increasing or
dim[in]ishing this compensation during any term of his election,
and it prohibits every state from granting him an additional emolument. This is all that the clause imports.

It is therefore satisfied, as to the U States, when the legislature
has provided that the President shall be allowed a certain sum for a
certain term of time and so long as it refrains from making an alteration in the provision. All beyond this is foreign to the subject.

The Legislature having done this, an advance by the Treasury in anticipation of the service cannot be a breach of the provision. Tis in no sense an additional allowance by the UStates. Tis a mere advance or loan upon account of the established periodical compensation. Will legal ideas or common parlance warrant the giving the denomination of *additional* compensation to the mere anticipation of the term of an established allowance? If they will not, tis plain such an advance is no breach of this part of the constitution.

If the clause is to be understood literally it leads to an absurdity. The terms are "The President shall *at stated times receive* &c" and again "he *shall not receive* within that period &c."

His allowance is at the rate of 25000 Dollars per annum, 6250 Dollars quarter yearly. Suppose at the end of a year, an arrear of 5000 Dollars was due to him, which he omits to receive till some time in the succeeding year, and in the succeeding year actually receives that ballance with his full salary for the last year. Tis plain that he would not have received in the whole more than he was allowed by law, and yet in the *stated* period of one year he would have received 30,000 Dollars, five thousand more than his salary for the year. In a literal sense then constitutional provision as to *actual* payment would not have been complied with; for within the first of the *stated periods* he would *not have received* the compensation allotted and within the second of them, he *would have received* more. In a *literal* sense, it would be necessary to make the payment at the precise day, to the precise amount, neither more nor less; which as a general rule the indispensable forms of the Treasury render impossible. It follows that actual receipt or payment are not the criterion but the absolute definitive allowance by law. An advance beforehand or a payment afterwards are equally consistent with the true spirit & meaning of this part of the constitution.

Let us now see, if the construction of the Treasury violates the law which establishes the Presidents compensation.

The act of the 24th Septr. 1789 [13] allows to the President at the rate of 25000 dollars per annum, to commence from the time of his

13. In MS, H first wrote "30th of September 1790." Above this he wrote "(24th Septr 1789)." H is referring to "An Act for allowing a Compensation to the President and Vice President of the United States" (1 *Stat.* 72 [September 24, 1789]). The correct date appears in the newspaper version of this article.

entering on the duties of his office, and *to be paid quarterly out of the Treasury of the U States.*"

The question is what is to be understood by these words, *to be paid quarterly out of the Treasury of the UStates?*

The conception of the Treasury has been that these words, as used in this and in the analogous cases, were meant to define the time, when *the right* of an individual *to the compensation earned* became *absolute;* not as a command to the Treasury *to issue the money at the precise day and* no other.

As mentioned above, the indispensable forms of the Treasury, in compliance with the law establishing the department and to secure a due accountability, make it impracticable to pay at the day; and if expressions of the kind in question are to be construed literally and as a positive injection to the Treasury to issue the money at the period defined, it will be as much a breach of the law to pay afterwards as to advance beforehand.

The position that an after payment would be a breach of the law will hardly be contended for, and if not—the alternative seems to be the construction adopted by the Treasury. Such expressions denote simply that at certain periods individuals acquire a perfect right to particular sums of money for their services which it becomes a matter of course to pay; but they are not obliged to receive it at the day, nor is the Treasury restrained from paying it afterwards or from anticipating by way of loan, if there are adequate reasons for such anticipation.

It is not true as alleged that the invariable practice of the Treasury, as to *compensations for services* differs in principle from what was done in the case of the President.

Instances to the contrary have been stated. As to what regards the army, there has been sufficient explanation.

But it will be useful to be more particular as to the course which has been pursued with reference to the two houses of Congress.

The law that regulates their compensation (passed the 22d of Sep. 1789) [14] allows to each member a compensation of six dollars

14. In MS, H first wrote "29 Sept 1789." Above this he wrote "(22d)." He is referring to "An Act for allowing Compensation to the Members of the Senate and House of Representatives of the United States, and to the Officers of both Houses" (1 *Stat.* 70–72 [September 22, 1789]). In the newspaper version the date is mistakenly given as September 29, 1789.

for every day he shall attend the House, to which he belongs, together with six Dollars for every 20 Miles of distance to & from his place of residence, and directs that the compensation which shall be due shall be certified by the President of the Senate or Speaker of the House of Representatives and shall be passed as public accounts and paid out of the Treasury.

By an arrangement between each house and the Treasury Department the course actually pursued has been as follows.

Certain gross sums usually of   [15] at the commencement of each session & from time to time afterwards have been advanced from the Treasury, at request to the President of the Senate for the members of the Senate, to the Speaker of the House of Representatives, for the members of that house; on account and frequently in anticipation of their accruing compensations. The President of the Senate in the Senate & the Speaker of the House of Representatives in that house disbursed the monies to the individuals, & afterwards upon the close of each session settled an account at the Treasury, accompanied with the certificates required by the law and the receipts of the members which were examined adjusted & passed as other public accounts.[16]

Whether there were any advances actually made to the members, in anticipation of their compensations, was a point never discussed between the Treasury & the presiding officers of the two houses, with whom the money was deposited, but I understand that examples of such advances did exist in relation to the House of Representatives. The fact is however immaterial to the point in issue. That must be tested by the *times* of the *advances from the Treasury*, and it is certain that these were usually made in *anticipation of compensations to grow due;* and it is also certain that the course was well understood by both houses of Congress, & is exhibited by the Accounts of the Treasurer laid before them in each session.

15. Space left blank in MS. In the newspaper version after the words "Certain gross sums usually" there is a footnote which reads: "The advances for the Senate have usually been about 5,000 dollars—and for the House of Representatives from 12 to 20,000 dollars."

16. In the newspaper version the following sentence was added to this paragraph: "They also refunded to the Treasury the monies which remained in their hands respectively beyond the compensations due to the members of the Senate and house of Representatives as will appear by referring to the printed statements annually laid before Congress."

If therefore the advances for the President were unconstitutional and illegal; those for both houses of Congress were equally so; and if the President be chargeable with a violation of the constitution of the laws and of his oath of office on account of extra-advances to his secretaries, whether with or without his privity, the members of both houses of Congress, without exception, have been guilty of the same crimes, in consequence of the extra advances with their privity to the presiding officers of their respective houses.

A distinction may possibly be attempted to be taken in the two cases from this circumstance—that the law which allots the compensation of the members of the two houses does not use the words *"to be paid every day* out of the Treasury" while that which establishes the Presidents compensation does use the terms "to be paid quarterly out of the Treasury." But this distinction would be evidently a cavil. When a law fixes the term of a compensation; whether per day ⅌ month per quarter or per annum, if it says nothing more, it is implied that it is payable at each epoch out of the Treasury, in the same sense as if this was expressly said. This observation applies as well to the monthly pay of the Army as to the dayly pay of Congress. The motive to the arrangement which was made for the payment of the members of Congress was two fold. It was to obviate embarrassment to them by facilitating and accelerating the receipt of their compensations and to avoid an inconvenient multiplication of adjustments entries warrants & payments. The theory of the provision admitted of as many Treasury settlements entries warrants & payments each day as there were members in both houses.

Having examined the question as it stands upon the constitution & the laws, I proceed to examine the course of the fact.

But previous to this, I shall take notice of one point, about which there has been doubt [17] and which it is not within my present recollection whether definitively settled or not by the accounting officers of the Department. It respects the time of the commencement of the Presidents compensation. The law establishing it refers to the time of his entering upon the duties of his office, but without defining that time.

17. In the newspaper version the remainder of this sentence reads: "and which was not definitively settled by the accounting office of the department until after the President's first term of four years was completed."

When in a constitutional & legal sense did the President enter upon the duties of his Office?

The constitution enjoins that before he enters upon the execution of his office, he shall take a certain oath, which is prescribed. This oath was not taken till the 30th. of April 1789. If we date the entrance upon the duties of his office at the time of taking this oath, it determines the epoch to be the 30th. of April 1789.

But there is room for another construction. The 3 of March 1789 [18] is the day, when the term, for which the President Vice President & the members of Congress were first elected, was deemed to commence. The constitution declares that the President shall hold his office for four years; and it is presumeable that the clause respecting his compensation contemplates its being for the whole term for which he is to hold his office. Its object may otherwise be evaded.

It is also (I believe) certain that the President may execute his office and do valid acts as President without previously taking the oath prescribed; though in so doing if voluntary he would be guilty of a breach of the constitution & would be liable to punishment. The taking of the oath is not therefore necessarily the criterion of entering upon the duties of office.

It is a fact too if I remember right that at New York the place assigned for the first meeting of the Government on the 3d. of March 1789—which might be considered as an entrance upon the duties of his office; though from the delays which attended the meeting of Congress the oath was deferred till the 30th of April following.[19]

On the strength of these facts, it may be argued that by force of the constitution, dating the commencement of the Presidents term of service on the 3d.[20] of March 1789, the law respecting his compensation ought to be considered as referring to that period for a virtual entrance upon the duties of his Office.

In stating this construction, I must not be understood to adopt it. I acknowlege that the other as most agreeable to the more familiar sense of the terms of the law has appeared to me preferable; though I had reason to believe that an important officer of the Government

18. In the newspaper this date has been changed to "the 4th of March 1789."
19.. This paragraph has been omitted in the newspaper version.
20. In the newspaper the date has been changed to the "4th of March 1789."

(I do not mean the President) once thought otherwise. The result in point of fact will vary as the one or the other is deemed the true construction.[21]

I return to an examination of the course of the transaction.

Authentic statements which have been published with some supplementary ones received from the Treasury upon the occasion exhibit the following results.

1 RESULT. The sums advanced for the use of the President from the Treasury have never exceeded the sums previously appropriated by law; though they have sometimes exceeded sometimes fallen short of the sums actually due for services. This is thus explained—

An Act of the 24th of September 1789 [22] Appropriated for paying the compensation of the President   Dollars 25000

The sums advanced to the 8th. of April 1790 & charged to this appropriation are   25000

An Act of the 26 of March 1790 [23] appropriates for the same purpose   25000

The sums advanced from May 4th. 1790 to the 28 Feby. 1791 & charged to this appropriation   25000

An Act of the 11th. of Feby. 1791 [24] appropriates for the same purpose   25000

The sums advanced from the 28th. February 1791 to 27 [25] of December in the same year & charged to this appropriation are 22150

Excess of appropriation beyond the Advances   Dr.   2850

21. In the newspaper version of this article this paragraph reads: "In stating this construction, however equitable it may be deemed, I must not be understood to adopt it. I acknowledge that the other as most agreeable to the more familiar sense of the terms of the law has appeared to me preferable, and it was accordingly established, tho' not till after all the advances, for the first four years had been made. The result in point of fact would however have varied as the one or the other had been deemed the true construction."
22. "An Act making Appropriations for the Service of the present year" (1 Stat. 95).
23. "An Act making appropriations for the support of government for the year one thousand seven hundred and ninety" (1 Stat. 104–06).
24. "An Act making appropriations for the support of Government during the year one thousand seven hundred and ninety-one, and for other purposes" (1 Stat. 190).
25. In the newspaper this date is "28th of December."

An Act the 23 of December 1791 [26] appropriates for the
same purpose   25000

The sums advanced from the 3d. of Jany. 1792 to the 15
of January 1793 & charged to this appropriation are   25000

An Act of the 28 of February 1793 [27] appropriates for the
same purpose   25000

The sums advanced from the 9th. of March 1793 to the 27
of December in the same year & charged to this appropriation are   25000

An Act of the 14th of March 1794 [28] appropriates for the
same purpose   Dollars 25000

The sums advanced from the 17 of March 1794 to the first
of January 1795 & charged to the same appropriation are   25000

An Act of the 2d. of January 1795 [29] appropriates for the
same purpose   25000

The sums advanced from the 12 of January 1795 and prior
to the 1st of October in the same year and charged to this appropriation are   12500

Excess of appropriation beyond advances on the first of
August [30] 1795   12500

Excess of Appropriation on the Act of the 11 of February
1791 [31]   2850

Total Excess of appropriations beyond advances to the 1st of
October 1795.[32]   Dr. 15350

The residue of the proposition is illustrated by the quarterly statement of salary and advances at foot.

26. "An Act making Appropriations for the Support of Government for the
year one thousand seven hundred and ninety-two" (1 *Stat.* 226–29).
27. "An Act making appropriations for the support of Government for the
year one thousand seven hundred and ninety-three" (1 *Stat.* 325–29).
28. "An Act making Appropriations for the support of Government, for the
year one thousand seven hundred and ninety-four" (1 *Stat.* 342–45).
29. "An Act making appropriations for the support of Government for the
year one thousand seven hundred and ninety-five" (1 *Stat.* 405–08).
30. In the newspaper this reads "October."
31. See note 24.
32. At this point in the newspaper the following paragraph appears: "Thus
it appears not only that the disbursements have never exceeded the appropriations; but, on the contrary, that the appropriations have exceeded the disbursements. An accurate attention to dates shews particularly that there was always

II RESULT The Treasury never has been in advance for the President beyond the sums actually accrued and due to him for services to the amount of one quarter's salary. The largest advance at any one time is 6154 dollars. A quarter's salary is 6250 Dollars. Deducting the sums at certain times in arrear from those at other times in advance, the average of the advances for the whole term of his service is about   .[33] The particulars of this result appear in the statement at foot. This statement is digested by quarters of the Calendar year which is the established course of the Treasury & a course essential to the order of its affairs; that is to say it is essential there should be certain fixed periods to which the ordinary stated disbursements are referred & in conforming with which the Accounts of the Treasury are kept.

III Result On the first of October 1795, there were *actually due* to the President for his compensation over and above all advances for his use the sum of 846 Dollars. This likewise appears from the statement at foot and intirely refutes the malevolent suggestion which has appeared of an accumulation of advances to twelve or fifteen [thousand] [34] Dollars.

IV Result The sums advanced for the President prior to the commencement of the term of his second election the 3d. of March 1793 [35] fall short of the sums appropriated for his compensation 2850 Dollars: thus

The aggregate of the sums appropriated for four years from the 29 of September 1789 to the 23 of December 1791 inclusively is   Ds.   100 000

The amount of all the sums advanced prior to the 3d.[36] of March 1793 is   97 150

Excess of appropriations beyond advances.   = 2 850

It is nevertheless true that not only there have been frequent anticipations of the Presidents salary (as appears more particularly in the statement at foot) but counting from the 30th of April 1789

---

a pre-existing appropriation which was never exceeded by the disbursements, having regard to order of time."

33. Space left blank in MS. The entire sentence was omitted in the newspaper.

34. The bracketed word has been taken from the newspaper.

35. In the newspaper this reads "4th of March 1793."

36. See note 35.

as the commencement of his compensation the sums advanced for his use prior to the 3d. of March 1793 the expiration of his first term of election exceed those actually due to that period by 1108 Dollars & 34 Cents.[37]

If on the contrary, the construction were adopted which dates his compensation on the 4th of March 1789 there would have been a ballance due to him on the 4 of March 1795 [38] of 2850 Dollars.

But proceeding on the first supposition the whole question still turns upon the legality of advances. If it was legal to make him an advance in anticipation of his salary within any period of his election—within one quarter on account of a succeeding quarter, it was equally legal to do it within one year on account [of] a succeeding year and within one term of an election on account of a succeeding term. The only inquiry would be in either case—will the sum advanced be within the bounds of the sums before that time appropriated? It has been seen, that the sums appropriated for the first four years of service exceeded those advanced prior to the commencement of the second period of election by 2850 Dollars. Besides this on the 28 of February 1793 there was a further appropriation of 25000 Dollars so that at the beginning of the second term, the total appropriation exceeded the total disbursements by 27850 Dollars.

Thus has it been shewn, that the advances for the use of the President have been governed by a rule of construction, which has obtained in analogous cases, or more truly which has regulated the general course of disbursements from the Treasury—a rule which I trust has been demonstrated to be consonant with the Constitution and the laws.

It is requisite to inquire a little further whether there has been any improper use or rather abuse of the discretion which is contended for, for here there is likewise an unquestionable responsibility. It is seen that the advances have at no time equalled one quarters salary.

I ask was it [39] unreasonable or unfit, if constitutional and legal, to afford the President of the U States an accommodation of this extent?

37. In the margin opposite the end of this paragraph H wrote "Qr." In the newspaper the figures read "1042 dollars and 69 cents."
38. In the newspaper, "1793."
39. In MS, "is."

I pledge my veracity, that I have always understood and to this moment I have good reason to be satisfied, that the expences of the President, those of his household and others incident to his official situation, have fully equalled if not on some occasions exceeded the allowance made to him by the U States. Under this conviction, especially, how could the head of a department hesitate by so *small an accommodation* as the advance of *less than* a quarters salary to enable the President of the U States to meet his expences as they accrued, without being obliged to intrench upon his own private resources, or to resort to the expedient of borrowing to defray expences imposed upon him by public situation? I knew that no possible risk could attend the advance, little considerable as it was. The estate of the President was answerable in case of death or other premature vacancy, and abundant for the indemnification of the Government.

Reasons of a peculiar kind forbade hesitation. The scale of expence was unavoidably such as to render the income even of what is deemed a large landed property in this country a slender auxiliary. Without an advance from the Treasury it was not improbable borrowing might be necessary. Was it just to compel the President to resort to that expedient for a purpose in fact public, at his private expence? Was it for the dignity of the Nation that he should have been exposed to a necessity, an embarrassment of this sort?

My judgment and feelings answered both these questions in the negative. I entertained no doubt of the constitutionality or legality of the advance, and I thought the making of it due to the situation—due to propriety—due to every public consideration connected with the subject. I can never regret it.[40]

How far the President was privy to the course of advances, I cannot say. But it is certain they have been all made to his private secretaries upon a general arrangement and not by special directions from him. And I think it proper to add that very early in the day,

40. In the newspaper version there is a footnote at this point which reads: "Those who are acquainted with the great expence for several years past of living in New-York and Philadelphia will not be surprised that the expences of the President should have equalled or exceeded his salary, upon a scale which no friend to the reasonable respectability of the Chief Magistrate and to national dignity would wish to see diminished, But the removal of the seat of Government, was an occasion, in different ways, of a large extraordinary expense."

and probably before any was made, on an application by Mr. Lear,[41] for a sum which would constitute an advance he qualified it by this observation—"if in your opinion it can be done with legality & perfect propriety." I answered that I had no doubt of either.

I shall not attempt to assume any greater responsibility in this transaction than belongs to me but [42] I have been accustomed to think that the responsibility for the due and regular disbursement of monies from the Treasury lies exclusively with the Officers of the Department. And that except in a very palpable and glaring case, the charge of blameable participation could not fall on any other person.

As between the officers of the Treasy, I take the responsibility to stand thus. The Secretary and Comptroller in granting warrants upon the Treasurer are both answerable for their *legality*. In this respect the Comptroller is a check upon the Secretary. With regard to the *expediency* of an advance, in my opinion the right of judging is exclusively with the head of the Department. The Comptroller has no voice in this matter. So far therefore as concerns legality, in the issues of money, while I was in the Department, the Comptroller must answer with me. So far as a question of expediency, or the due exercise of discretion may be involved, I am solely answerable. And so uniformly was the matter understood between successive Comptrollers & myself—So also it is essential to the due administration of the department, that it should be understood.

I have stated my reasons for considering the advances made for the use of the President as constitutional legal and proper. But I pretend not to infallibi[li]ty. 'Tis possible I may have erred. But to convert error into guilt it must be supposed to have been wilful. To suppose it wilful it is necessary to trace it to some interested or sinister motive. If any appears let it be pointed out. It is not common for men to commit crimes of a deep die without some adequate inducement.

What criminal inducement could have probably influenced the rule of construction as to advances which has been stated to have been adopted & acted upon at the Treasury? What criminal inducement particularly could have led to the application of this rule to

41. Tobias Lear was Washington's secretary from 1786 to 1793.
42. In the newspaper this sentence begins at this point.

the Presidents compensation in so restricted a form as never once to equal one quarter's salary? Who in his senses will believe that the President would consciously have hazarded the imputation of violating the constitution the laws and his oath of office, by imposing on the officers of the Treasury the necessity of making him so paltry an advance? falsely and ridiculously called a donation? Who will believe that those officers would have consented to expose themselves to the same imputation by a compliance, when they knew that the evidence of their guilt must regularly be communicated in each succeeding session to both houses of Congress and to the public at large? To believe either is to believe all the parties concerned foolish in the extreme, as well as profligate in the extreme, destitute equally of intellect as of principle.

To an observation made by Mr. Wolcott on the communications from the Treasury,[43] it has been answered that there was no merit in the disclosure, because the number of Agents and the forms of the Treasury rendered it unavoidable.[44] The fact is so. But the force of the observation turns upon the egregious folly of intentionally committing the crimes imputed, when it was certain beforehand that the means of detection must be furnished and without delay by the Treasury itself.

It is certain that there never has been the least attempt at mystery or concealment. The documents reported by the Treasury to both houses of Congress carried in their face the prominent evidence of what was done. Frequent and indiscriminate personal suggestions revealed the principle of action. It is evident, that it must have been understood and acquiesced in by all the members of the two houses of congress.

Hard would be the condition of public officers, if even a misconstruction of constitutional & legal provisions, attended with no symptom of criminal motive, carrying the proof of innocence in the openness and publicity of conduct, could justly expose them to the odious charges which on this occasion are preferred. Harder still would be their condition if in the management of the great and complicated business of a Nation the fact of misconstruction which

43. Wolcott's statement was made in his letter of October 24, 1795, to the editor of the [Philadelphia] *Aurora. General Advertiser.* See H to Washington, October 26, 1795, note 1.
44. In MS, "unavoivable."

is to constitute their guilt is to be decided by the narrow and rigid rules of a criticism—no less pedantic than malevolent! Preeminently Hard in such circumstances, was the lot of the man who called to the head of the most arduous department in the public administration, in a new Government, without the guides of antecedent practice & precedent, had to trace out his own path and to adjust for himself the import and bearings of delicate and important provisions in the constitution & in the laws!

Reposing myself on a consciousness which in no possible situation can fail to prove an invulnerable shield to my tranquillity I leave to a candid Public to pronounce the sentence which is due to an attempt, on such a foundation, to erect against The President of the U States, my successor in Office and myself, the heinous charges of violation of the constitution, violation of the laws, exertion of arbitrary will on the one side, abject submission on the other misapplication of the public money and to complete the newspaper groupe—intentional PERJURY! [45]   A H

Quarterly statements of the account for compensation of the President of the United States from his taking the oath of office on the 30th April, 1789, to the 30th September, 1795.[46]

1789		Dollars.
Sept. 30 Compensation from 30 April to 30th June, 1789.		4,246
Compensation one quarter ending 30th September, 1789,		6,250
	10,496	
Warrants drawn 26th sept. 1789,	1,000	
due to the President 30th sept.		9,496
Dec. 31. Compensation due,		6,250
	15 746	
Warrants drawn this quarter,	13,500	

45. In the newspaper version the following postscript was added to this article: "P. S. An imperfect state of health and much occupation have delayed the explanation longer than was wished."

46. The quarterly statements of Washington's salary are not in the MS and have been taken from the [New York] *Daily Advertiser.*

1790. due the President 31st December,		2,246
March 31 compensation due		6,250
	8,496	
Warrants drawn,	8,246 66	
Due the President 31st March,		249 34
June 30 compensation due,		6,250
	6,499 34	
Warrants drawn,	8,253 34	
Due the United states 30th June,		1,754
Sept. 30 Warrants drawn,		9,000
	10,754	
Compensation due,	6,250	
Due the United states 30th sept.		4,504
Dec. 31 Warrants drawn,		6,000
	10,504	
Compensation due,	6,250	
1791, Due the United states, 31st Dec.		4,254
March 31, warrants drawn,		8,150
	12,404	
compensation due,	6,250	
Due the United states 31st March,		6,154
June 30, warrants drawn,		4,500
	10,654	
compensation due,	6,250	
Due the United states 30th June,		4,404
Sept. 30, warrants drawn,		8,050
	12,404	
compensation due,	6,250	
due the United states 30th sept.		6,154
Dec. 31, warrants drawn,		5,500
	11,654	
compensation due,	6,250	
1792. due the United states, 31st Dec,		5,404
March 31, warrants drawn,		6,000
	11,404	
compensation due	6,250	
due United States 31st March,		5,154

June 30, warrants drawn,   6,000

            11,154
    compensation due,   6,250
    due the U states, June 30,   4,904
Sept. 30, warrants drawn,   2,500

            7,404
    compensation due,   6,250
    due the United states 30th sept   1,154
Dec. 31, warrants drawn,   8,000

            9,154
    compensation due,   6,250
1793 Due the United states 31st Dec.   2,904
March 31, Warrants drawn,   8,500

            11,404
    compensation due,   6,250
    due the United states 31st March,   5,154
June 30, warrants drawn,   6,000

            11,154
    compensation due,   6,250
    due the United states 30th June,   4,904
Sept. 30, warrants drawn,   6,000

            10,904
    compensation due,   6,250
    due the United states 30th sept   4,654
Dec. 31 warrants drawn   7,000

            11,654
    compensation due   6,250
1794. Due the United states 31st Dec.   5,404
March 31. warrants drawn,   5,000

            10,404
    compensation due,   6,250
    due the United states 31st March,   4,154
June 30 warrants drawn,   6,000

            10,154
    compensation due,   6,250
    due the United states 30th June,   3,904
Sept. 30. warrants drawn   7,000

	10,904	
compensation due,	6,250	
due the United states 30th sept.		4,654
Dec 31 warrants drawn,		6,000
	10,654	
compensation due,	6,250	
1795. Due the United states 31st Dec.		4,404
March 31 warrants drawn,		7,000
	11,404	
compensation due,	6,250	
due the United states 31st March,		5,154
June 30. warrants drawn,		4,000
	9,154	
compensation due,	6,250	
due the United states 30th June,		2,904
Sept. 30. warrants drawn,		2,500
	5,404	
compensation due,	6,250	
Due the President, 30th Sept. 1795,		846

PROOF.

Compensation from April 30, to June 30, 1789, 62 days,	4,246
Compensation from July 1, 1789, to Sept. 30, 1795, 6 years 3 months,	156,250
Total due dollars,	160,496
Advanced till the end of 1791, pr. printed statement,	72,150
Ditto in 1792,	22,500
Ditto in 1793,	27,500
Ditto in 1794,	24,000
Ditto in 1795, to Sept. 30,	13,500
	159,650
Balance due the President,	846
Dols.	160,496

Treasury Department,
Register's Office, Nov. 13, 1795.
Extract from the books of the Treasury.

Joseph Nourse, Register.

To Oliver Wolcott, Junior

[New York, November 11, 1795]

Dr. Sir

At length I am able to send you the explanation I mentioned to you.[1] The papers upon which it is founded are returned that you may compare & if necessary correct. You may by altering the body or by a note rectify any *inaccuracy*.

You will observe marks in the margin which will require particular attention.[2] A   Let the distance if not so now be rightly stated.

B   insert the most usual sum or sums. I think twas 10000 to Senate 20000 to House of Representatives.

C   If you think it best you may leave out here & afterwards all that concerns the construction referring the commencement of the compensation to the 4th of March 1789. I think in this respect something will depend on question whether the Treasury has finally taken its ground. And even then a *note* at foot as after closing the letter may be considered instead of striking out. Do as you please on this point.

F   examine the calculation that gives this ballance.

I will thank you to have a proof Sheet brought you. You observe the quarterly statement is to be subjoined? Will it not be best that the Register [3] should sign it.

Yrs.   A Hamilton

Novr. 11. 1795
O Wolcott Esq

ALS, Connecticut Historical Society, Hartford.
  1. See "Explanation," November 11, 1795.
  2. The marginal notes to which H is referring do not appear in the draft of H's "Explanation" in the Hamilton Papers, Library of Congress. They were presumably written on the copy which H sent to Wolcott.
  3. Joseph Nourse.

[*The Defence No. XXIII*] [1]

[New York, November 14, 1795]

ADf, in the handwriting of Rufus King, Hamilton Papers, Library of Congress; *The* [New York] *Herald; A Gazette for the Country*, November 14, 1795.
1. For background to this document, see the introductory note to "The Defence No. I," July 22, 1795. Except for several words and phrases inserted by H, the draft of "The Defence No. XXIII" is in the handwriting of Rufus King.

[*The Defence No. XXIV*] [1]

[New York, November 14, 1795]

ADf, in the handwriting of Rufus King, Hamilton Papers, Library of Congress; *The* [New York] *Herald; A Gazette for the Country*, November 14, 1795.
1. For background to this document, see the introductory note to "The Defence No. I," July 22, 1795.
Except for several words and phrases and one paragraph inserted by H, the draft of this essay is in the handwriting of Rufus King. The paragraph added by H reads: "It has not appeared that this was ever done [the renewal of the powers given to Edmond Charles Genet to negotiate a commercial treaty between France and the United States]. His immediate successor Mr. [Jean Antoine Joseph] Fauchet, it is believed, gave no evidence of his having any powers relative to a Commercial Treaty; and if reports which arrived with the present Minister, having greater marks of authenticity, may be creditted—he has power only to *digest* the articles of such a treaty not to *conclude* one." See H to Oliver Wolcott, Jr., October 3, 1795, note 4; Wolcott to H, October 6, 1795.

From Oliver Wolcott, Junior

[*Philadelphia, November 14, 1795.* On November 16, 1795, Wolcott wrote to Hamilton: "I sent you on Saturday [1] an imperfect translation of Fauchet's letter." *Letter not found.*]

1. Saturday was November 14, but Wolcott endorsed H to Wolcott, October 30–November 12, 1795: "ansd. 13th. Nov. & sent on Copy of Fr—— Letters. . . ."

From Jean Marie de Bordes [1]

Philadelphia, November 15, 1795. ". . . On the end of 1776 being recommended to you by General Washington, I was received and Served as a volunteer in your company of Artillery. . . . Few days after, from your company I was promoted to the duty of an aid-de-camp and temporaly acted as a Brigade-major . . . to the end of this memorable Campain. Called afterwards by peculiar reasons to the South of America, I . . . made the tedious and fruitless expedition of Florida. About this very time war was declared between france and England. . . . I repaired to the french west-indies, there got a commission in their Colonial troops, and soon coming over again to this Continent had an active part . . . in the unsuccessful Siege of Savannah. Thus was constantly addicted my military life and abilities to the Service of these both countries, to the proclamation of the peace, in 1783. Confined from that time to the retired line of a farmer in st. Domingo, I am now one of those recent and wretched victims whose properties are cruelly became the alternative prey of either consuming flames or of Successive ennemies who mutually contended for and snatched them out of their own bloody hands. . . . But . . . being now destitute of every way of living, I am under the unfortunate necessity of petitioning to the Congress the military emoluments which from the month of November 1776 to the end of 1778 are owed to me for my Services in America.[2] In this you may and make no doubt but you'll be particularly Serviceable to me. . . ."

ALS, Hamilton Papers, Library of Congress.
1. Jean Marie de Bordes was an officer in the Georgia line during the American Revolution.

This letter was enclosed in John Habersham to H, December 7, 1795. De Bordes wrote a similar letter to George Washington on November 13, 1795 (ALS, RG 59, Miscellaneous Letters, 1790–1799, National Archives).

2. On January 4, 1796, the House of Representatives referred to the Committee of Claims "A Petition of Jean Marie de Bordes, a Lieutenant in the late Continental Army . . . praying compensation for military services rendered the United States, during the late war" (*Journal of the House*, II, 396).

From Robert Morris

Alexander Hamilton Esqr   Phila Novr 16. 1795

Dear Sir

I have a Negotiation in hand which will probably enable me to transfer to Mr Church the Deferred Debt which my Son agreed to. pay him.[1] Before I can speak positively a Correspondence which is opened with Boston must ripen, and I expect that the intercourse of a few Posts will reduce the matter to a certainty one way or other. I have $140,000 Deferred Debt deposited with the Treasurer of Massachusetts and my present Object is to redeem it by a payment in Money or other Paper.[2]

I am Yrs   RM

LC, Robert Morris Papers, Library of Congress.

1. This is a reference to a debt which Morris owed to John B. Church and which Morris's son, Robert Morris, Jr., had agreed to pay with the deferred debt. For an explanation of this debt and the various plans of Morris and his son to pay it, see the introductory note to Morris to H, June 7, 1795. See also Morris to H, July 20, 1795.

2. James Swan was Morris's representative in the negotiations which Morris mentions in the preceding two sentences. On December 3, 1795, Morris wrote to Swan: "My Bond to the state of massachusetts for $50,000 is payable on the 11 May 1796 & my Bond for $33,333 33/100 is paya[ble] on 11 May 1797 both with Int from 29 Decr 1792 at 6 p. Ct. until paid—$140,000 deferred Debt is deposited & must be liberated if the Land is sold" (LC, Robert Morris Papers, Library of Congress). On January 5, 1796, Morris again wrote to Swan: "The want of money is one of the worst wants a Man can be plagued with & rather than Submit to it much longer I will consent to sell the five thousand Acres of Land under your management for one third of a Dollar p acre payable in the following manner if sold at Boston or in New England. I have 140,000 Dollars of Deferred Debt of the US pledged with the Treasurer of the state of Massachusetts to secure the payment of my Bonds to the said Treasurer or state, One for £15000 lawful Money and Interest from Novemr 1791 or 1792 (I do not just now recollect which) which Bond falls due on the 11th of May 1796, the other for £10,000 Lawful Money & Interest as above falls due 11 May 1797. If the Purchaser of the Land will assume these Payments & deliver up my Bonds and deferred Debt immediately, the remainder of the Purchase Money may be divided into two equal Payments, one to be made in May 1798 & the other in May 1799 with Interest, to be secured by approved Negotiable Notes in which the Interest must be included. If a better price & shorter Periods of Payment can be obtained I expect it will be done" (LC, Robert Morris Papers, Library of Congress).

From George Washington

Philadelphia 16th. Novr. 1795.

My dear Sir, (Private & confidential)

The papers herewith enclosed are so full, on the subject of my former request, that nothing more remains than to refer to them for every information I can give, as the ground work of the Superstructure you are to build.[1] When you are done with them be so good as to return the whole to me again, with those sent before; together with the letter respecting young Fayette,[2] and the result, relative to him.

I would beg the favor of you to run your eye over the letter from Madam de Segur [3] & let one of your young men make some enquiry into the truth of her narrative and if found just, to seal & forward my letter to her, safely. The reason why I give you this trouble, is, that applications of ye kind have been, and still are very frequent; and in more instances than one, impositions have been practiced on me. If this lady's tale be true, her case is pitiable; and I have only to regret that the frequent calls upon my private purse, render it inconvenient for me to do more for her than the pittance I enclose to her.

With sincere, and affectionate esteem and regard   I am ever yours
Go: Washington

PS. Be so good as to drop me a single [line] [4] merely to say that this letter & its enclosures have got safely into your hands.

Colo. Hamilton

ALS, Hamilton Papers, Library of Congress; ADfS, George Washington Papers, Library of Congress.

1. On October 29, 1795, Washington asked H for suggestions on subjects to be covered in the President's annual message to Congress. On November 10, 1795, Washington again wrote to H asking him "to suspend your superstructure until you receive a ground plan from me."

2. For information on George Washington Motier Lafayette, see H to Washington, October 16, 1795, note 1, and Washington to H, October 29, 1795.

3. On November 7, 1795, Mrs. R. V. de Segur wrote to Washington from

New York City asking him for assistance. In the course of this letter she stated: "mother of Seven children i had formerly the certitude to put them in an happy situation—Six of them are with me and that is the only fortune that is left to me. all the rest was lost for me in St Domingo where i had my estates. . . . i am now out of the power to furnish any more bread to my children and to some old Servants who followed me here. . . . all of us are reduced to suffer the nudity and famine" (ALS, George Washington Papers, Library of Congress).

4. This word has been taken from the draft.

From Oliver Wolcott, Junior

Philadelphia Novr. 16. 1795.

My Dear Sir   Private

I sent you on Saturday [1] an imperfect translation of Fauchets Letter [2] I now send you a Copy of the original; you may at your discretion use the Letter, except causing copies to be taken, or suffering it to be printed.

Mr. Randolph has intensively circulated a Letter in which he attributes his disgrace to the artifices of a "British Faction" [3]—his Letter is accompanied with an explanatory Certificate from Fauchet written at New port,[4] which I have not seen. I am told however by persons who have seen it, that it is a weak evasive performance & only makes bad, worse. When the affair was opened to Randolph, he denied having recd. money or having made any proposition relative to money except on one occasion—which was this.[5] He said that in the summer of 1794 *Fauchet told him, that there was a meeting of persons in New York consisting among others of Mr. Hammond & Mr. Jaudenes,*[6] *who were conspiring to destroy him* (R) *& Govr. Clinton.* Being asked what he meant by *destroying him & Govr. Clinton,* Randolph answered, to destroy his character as Secretary of State, & Governr. Clintons as Govr. of New York. Randolph said, that he then enquired, whether proof could be got of this conspiracy, and that after some conversation he suggested to Mr. Fauchet, that as he (F) had *the resources of the French Govt. at command he could obtain the proof.* This foolish story could make no impression, & though Mr. Randolph promised to reduce it to writing, he omitted to do so.

There are reports in circulation I find which change the complection of this first declaration of Randolph & represent the *conspiracy* as one to *ruin France*. I also *suspect* that attempts will be made to represent you as concerned in it. But of this I am not certain—at any rate the whole is idle nonsense & Fauchets attempt by a posterior act, to invalidate the evidence of a confidential Letter will not succed. What must have been the footing of these men when they could familiarly talk about the subversion of the Govt. & inviting the French to aid the insurrection with money.

Yrs truly   Oliv. Wolcott Jr

Pray let me [know] [7] if the Letters are *recd.*

ALS, Hamilton Papers, Library of Congress; copy, Connecticut Historical Society, Hartford.

1. Wolcott's letter of Saturday, November 14, 1795, has not been found.
2. This is a response to Fauchet's Dispatch No. 10. This dispatch, dated October 31, 1794, was intercepted by the British on March 28, 1795, and in the last week of July, 1795, George Hammond, the British Minister to the United States, made its contents available to Wolcott. For the way in which Dispatch No. 10 led to Edmund Randolph's resignation as Secretary of State, see Wolcott to H, July 30, 1795, note 1. The translation which Wolcott sent to H is in the Hamilton Papers, Library of Congress, and is in the handwriting of Henry Kuhl, a former clerk in the Treasury Department. Wolcott endorsed H to Wolcott, October 30–November 12, 1795, as follows: "Oct. 30 & Nov. 12 ansd. 13th. Nov. & sent on Copy of Fr—— Letters by Mr. Kuhl translated." For a list and brief description of the extant translations made in 1795 of Fauchet's Dispatch No. 10, see Wolcott to H, July 30, 1795, note 1.
3. Randolph's letter concerning a "British Faction" has not been found, but it is a term which Randolph used on more than one occasion. In the *Vindication*, which was not published until December 18, 1795, Randolph refers in passing to a "British Faction" (Randolph, *Vindication*, 86), and on page 89 of the same pamphlet he wrote: "I will here inquire from Mr. Hammond, and the British faction, which through him have been put in motion; from those who for the sake of party, interest, or personality, have propagated falsehoods in every town; or who persevere in the hatred of a connection between the United States and France;—what is become of their base assertions, that tens and hundreds of thousand dollars have been received from the French minister? . . ."
4. Immediately after submitting his resignation to the President on August 19, 1795, Randolph set out for Newport, Rhode Island, to interview Jean Antoine Joseph Fauchet, former French Minister to the United States, who was about to sail for France. Following a conference with Fauchet, Randolph secured the certificate which he desired. Fauchet's certificate is printed in Randolph, *Vindication*, 13–17.
5. This sentence refers to the events on August 19, 1795, when Washington in the presence of Timothy Pickering and Wolcott confronted Randolph with Pickering's translation of Fauchet's Dispatch No. 10, parts of which could be interpreted to mean that Randolph had asked Fauchet for money in return for influencing United States policy. See Wolcott to H, July 30, 1795, note 1.
In the remainder of the paragraph Wolcott gives a somewhat confusing and

confused account of Randolph's reaction on August 19 to one of the charges made against him. In Dispatch No. 10, Fauchet wrote: ". . . Mr. Randolph vint me voir avec un air fort empressé, & me fit les ouvertures dont je t'ai rendu compte dans mon No. 6. Ainsi avec quelques milliers de Dollars las République aurait décidé ici sur la Guerre Civile ou Sur la paix!" (Turner, "Correspondence of French Ministers," 451). Not having seen Fauchet's Dispatch No. 6 (dated September 5, 1794, and printed in Turner, "Correspondence of French Ministers," 411–18), Randolph was understandably at a loss to reply to this charge. In explaining his reactions, Randolph wrote: ". . . My observations therefore were but short. However, I had some recollection of Mr. Fauchet having told me of machinations against the French Republic, Governor [George] Clinton and myself; and thinking it not improbable, that the overture, which was spoken of in No. 6, might be, in some manner, connected with that business, and might relate to the obtaining of intelligence, I mentioned my impression; observing at the same time, that I would throw my ideas on paper. The President desired Messrs. Wolcott and Pickering to put questions to me. . . . But Mr. Pickering put no question; and Mr. Wolcott only asked an explanation of what I had said, as to Governor Clinton and myself. This I did not object to repeat, nearly as I had spoken it. Had I not been deprived of No. 6, the terms used in it, 'of sheltering from British persecution,' would probably have reminded me fully of the supposed machinations of Mr. Hammond and others" (Randolph, *Vindication*, 6–7). Randolph's reference to "of sheltering from British persecution" is taken from the following passage in Fauchet's Dispatch No. 6: "A Peine l'explosion connüe le Sécrétaire d'Etat s'est rendu chez moi; toute sa physionomie étoit douleur; il me demande un entretien particulier; c'en est fait, me dit-il, la guerre civile va ravager notre malheureuse Patrie. Quatre hommes par leur talent, leur influence et leur énergie peuvent la Sauver mais debiteurs de negocians et au moindre pas qu'ils feront ils seront privés de leur liberté. Pourriez-vous leur prêter momentanement des fonds suffisans pour les mettre à l'abri de la persecution Anglaise?" (Turner, "Correspondence of French Ministers," 414).

Subsequently Randolph recalled: "The day, on which I visited Mr. Fauchet, was about the 5th of August, 1794 . . ." (Randolph, *Vindication*, 84). For an extended defense and explanation by Randolph of his visit with Fauchet, see Randolph, *Vindication*, 84–92. Several years after Randolph's resignation, Wolcott described as follows Randolph's reaction on August 19, 1795, to the charge concerning his meeting with Fauchet: ". . . After a short hesitation, he [Randolph] proceeded to look over the letter [Fauchet's Dispatch No. 10] with great attention. . . . When he arrived at the passage in which Fauchet refers to the overtures mentioned in No. 6, and the 'tariff' which regulated the consciences of certain 'pretended patriots,' his conduct was very remarkable. He expressed no strong emotion, no resentment against Fauchet. He declared that he could not certainly tell what was intended by such remarks. He said that he indeed recollected having been informed that Mr. Hammond and other persons in New York, were contriving measures to destroy Governor Clinton, the French Minister, and himself, and that he had inquired of Mr. Fauchet whether he could not by his flour contractors provide the means of defeating their machinations. He asserted, however, that he had never received or proposed to receive money for his own use or that of any other person, and had never made any improper communications of the measures of government.

"One question only was put to Mr. Randolph, namely, how he intended to be understood when he represented Mr. Hammond as contriving to destroy Governor Clinton, Mr. Fauchet, and himself? His answer was, that their influence and popularity were to be destroyed." (Wolcott to John Marshall,

June 9, 1806 [George Gibbs, *Memoirs of the Administrations of Washington and John Adams, Edited from the Papers of Oliver Wolcott, Secretary of the Treasury* (New York, 1846), I, 245].)

6. Josef de Jaudenes was Spanish commissioner to the United States. Wolcott's reference to Jaudenes is, to say the least, obscure, for the others present at the meeting of August 19, 1795, do not state that Jaudenes's name was even mentioned by Randolph on that occasion. Nor does Wolcott in his other accounts of what happened on August 19 state that Jaudenes was in any way involved.

7. The word in brackets has been taken from the copy.

From Timothy Pickering

(Private)

Philadelphia Nov. 17. 1795.

Dear Sir,

The interest you take in all public measures of importance, and the peculiar solicitude you must feel at this time of general agitation, when so many are busy apparently to undermine the government which you so effectually laboured to establish, and have so eminently contributed to maintain—induce me, with that sincerity which I trust has ever marked my character, and that frankness which an entire confidence in your judgement & candour inspires, to exhibit to your view the present situation of the great public offices.

Near three months have elapsed since the office of Secretary of State became vacant.[1] At that moment matters of magnitude respecting the treaty with Great Britain demanded attention; & the general business of the office could not be suspended. With the President's approbation I undertook the conduct of whatever required the uninterrupted agency of that officer: hoping however to have been relieved long ere this time from the burthen. The President, I know, took immediate measures to fill the office.[2] He first tendered it to Judge Patterson, then to Governor Johnson of Maryland, to Gen-

ALS, Hamilton Papers, Library of Congress; ALS, letterpress copy, Massachusetts Historical Society, Boston.

1. Edmund Randolph had resigned as Secretary of State on August 19, 1795. See Oliver Wolcott, Jr., to H, July 30, 1795, note 1.

2. See George Washington to H, October 29, 1795; H to Washington, November 5, 1795.

eral Pinckney [3] & to Mr. King,[4] in succession: and by all it has been refused. The three former nominations the President early communicated to me: but the last he did not mention till about six days ago; nor indeed till then had he spoken of the subject since his last return from Mount Vernon. He recited these attempts to fill the office of Secretary of State; and that finally he had, thro' Colo. Carrington, made a tender of it to Patrick Henry, who also declined it.[5] In the event of this repulse, he proposed to Colo. Carrington's acceptance the department of war, under the idea of removing me to the department of state. Colo. Carrington chose to remain where he is.[6] The President having given this detail, made me the tender. I declined it, as not possessing the talents so much to be desired in a secretary of state, in the propriety and ability of whose conduct the dignity as well as the interests of the nation were so materially involved. On various grounds the President urged my acceptance: and after the many fruitless endeavours he had used to fill the office, I felt reluctant to give him a denial. I promised to consider of it.

The same day Mr. Wolcott called upon me: I found he had been consulted: I related what had passed: and he pressed me to accept the office: but I remained undecided. We repeatedly conversed about it afterwards: I still wished the office in abler hands. Last friday evening, going to see Mrs. Washington, I found the President & Mr. Wolcott in the antichamber: the President's countenance manifestly uneasy. As soon as an opportunity offered, I spoke to Mr. Wolcott: the president was anxious for my determination; and again Mr. Wolcott urged me to take the office. I reflected a few minutes: the company retired: and I then made to the president the following declaration.

That I wished to keep him no longer in suspense; & that I would accept the office of secretary of state: but as I had no ambitious views; and fresh embarrassments might arise in his attempts to fill

3. For Washington's offers to William Paterson, Thomas Johnson, and Charles Cotesworth Pinckney, see Washington to H, October 29, 1795, note 5.
4. Senator Rufus King of New York. Washington had asked H to ascertain if King wished the position. See Washington to H, October 29, 1795; H to Washington, November 5, 1795.
5. For Washington's offer to Patrick Henry, see Washington to H, October 29, 1795, note 5. For Washington's letter to Edward Carrington concerning Henry, see Washington to Carrington, October 9, 1795 (ALS, George Washington Papers, Library of Congress).
6. See Washington to H, October 29, 1795, note 10.

the department of war; I would propose, with submission to his opinion, that things should for the present remain as they were; I would continue my attention to both departments; if that of war could be filled to his satisfaction, I would go to the department of state; if a character well adapted to the latter should present, I would remain where I was: in one word, to free him from all embarrassment, I would serve in one office or the other as the *public good* should require. The president answered "That is very liberal;" and desired me to call the next morning to consider of a successor in the department of war.

The President had examined his list of offices in the late war; and selected the most prominent characters, whose names you will find in the inclosed list. Of these you will see but few to be recommended for the office, especially to the southward of Pennsylvania, where, of choice, the President would name one. With ample military talents, General Lee [7] is conceived to want others essential to a secretary of war. Embracing some great objects, the department comprehends a multitude of details, and demands economy in its numerous expenditures. This appointment would doubtless be extremely unpopular: it would be disapproved by the enemies of the government, without acquiring the confidence of its friends. These ideas I have already suggested to the President. Expressing his earnest desire to find a gentleman southward of Pennsylvania, the President remarked, that it would be much less difficult to choose one from the other side of this state. But even there the object may perhaps be found not very easy to accomplish.

The state of New-York has not now one officer *on the general staff of government.* Colonel William North [8] you will see is on the President's list: I have thought favourably of his character & abilities: but am not sufficiently acquainted to form any decisive opinion: you must know him well. Will you have the goodness to express your mind? Will you consider the whole list? Will you indulge me with your sentiments on all the subjects of this letter? One other idea ought perhaps to be taken into view: the President, be-

7. Henry Lee, who had served with distinction during the American Revolution, had been governor of Virginia from 1791 to November 30, 1794.
8. North, who had served during the American Revolution with both Henry Knox and Henry Lee as an aide-de-camp to Baron von Steuben, was inspector of the Army from 1784 to 1785.

yond all doubt, will, at the close of his present term, retire forever from public life: we do not know who will succeed him. Our internal politics and our exterior relations may be deeply affected by the character and principles of the President and the Secretary of State.

The tenor of this letter shows that it is *perfectly confidential*. The President has no knowledge of it. He will be impatient to decide to whom the department of war shall be tendered. I shall therefore be anxious to receive your answer. I earnestly hope your health & business will allow you to put it into the mail of friday, that it may reach me on saturday.

With the truest respect,   I am, dear sir,   your obedient servant,

Timothy Pickering.

P.S. Mr. Wolcott informed me of your wish to see Mr. Fauchet's letter.[9] I furnished him with a French copy of it, and with my translation to be copied and forwarded for your revision and correction.[10] I was sorry to propose this labour for you: but the letter is of no small importance; it must soon be published; and you are implicated in every page: I therefore wish the translation may be exact.

Alexander Hamilton Esq.

Captain Dayton [11]	N Jersey
Genl. Hand [12]	Pennsylvania
Genl. Huntington [13]	Connecticut

9. This is a reference to Fauchet's Dispatch No. 10. See Wolcott to H, July 30, 1795, note 1.

10. For information concerning the various translations of this document, see Wolcott to H, July 30, 1795, note 1. Wolcott had sent both a translation of this dispatch and a copy of the original to H on November 14, 1795. See Wolcott to H, November 16, 1795.

11. Jonathan Dayton served throughout the American Revolution, and when the war ended he was a captain in the Third New Jersey Regiment. During the seventeen-eighties he was a member of the New Jersey Assembly, the Continental Congress, and the Constitutional Convention. He was a Federalist member of the House of Representatives from 1791 to 1799 and Speaker of the House during the Fourth and Fifth Congresses.

12. Edward Hand, a native of Ireland, served throughout the American Revolution. He was adjutant general of the Army from 1781 to 1783, and at the end of the war he was brevetted a major general. He was a member of the Continental Congress in 1784 and 1785.

13. This is a reference to either Ebenezer Huntington or Jedediah Huntington, both of whom were from Connecticut. Both men served throughout

Genl. Irvine [14]	Pennsylvania
Colo. Phil. B. Bradley [15]	Connecticut
Colo. David Forman [16]	N. Jersey
Colo. Howard [17]	Baltimore
Colo. Wm. Heth [18]	Virginia
Colo. Nathl. Ramsay [19]	Maryland
Genl. James Wood [20]	Virginia
Colo. John Brooks [21]	Masstts.
Colo. David Cobb [22]	do.

the American Revolution, and both were brevetted major general in 1783. Jedediah Huntington, in addition, served in the Washington Administration as collector of customs at New Haven, Connecticut.

14. William Irvine, a native of Ireland, served throughout the American Revolution, and at the end of the war he was a brigadier general. He was a member of the Continental Congress from 1786 to 1788 and of the House of Representatives from 1793 to 1795.

15. During the American Revolution Bradley was a colonel of the Connecticut State Regiment and then the Fifth Connecticut Regiment until he retired on January 1, 1781. During the Washington Administration he was the United States marshal for Connecticut.

16. Forman served throughout the American Revolution, and at the end of the war he was a brigadier general of the New Jersey militia. After the war he was a judge of the Court of Common Pleas in Monmouth County, New Jersey.

17. John Eager Howard served during the American Revolution, and at the end of the war he was a lieutenant colonel. He was a member of the Continental Congress from 1784 to 1788, governor of Maryland from 1789 to 1791, and a member of the Maryland Senate from 1791 to 1795.

18. William Heth served during the American Revolution and was a colonel of the Third Virginia Regiment when he was taken prisoner at Charleston in 1780. During the Washington Administration he was collector of customs at Bermuda Hundred, Virginia.

19. Nathaniel Ramsay, a signer of the Declaration of Independence, was a lieutenant colonel in the Continental Army during the American Revolution. He was a member of the Continental Congress from 1785 to 1787, United States marshal for Maryland from 1790 to 1794, and naval officer of the port of Baltimore from 1794 until his death in 1817.

20. During the American Revolution Wood served as a colonel of the Eighth Virginia Regiment. In 1784 he was elected a member of the Executive Council of Virginia and through seniority in that body rose to the position of lieutenant governor, a post which he held when this letter was written. He subsequently (1796–1799) became governor of Virginia.

21. Brooks served throughout the American Revolution and at the end of the war was a lieutenant colonel. From 1792 to 1796 he was a brigadier general in the United States Army. He was United States marshal for Massachusetts during most of Washington's administration.

22. Cobb served throughout the American Revolution, and from 1781 to 1783 he was an aide-de-camp to Washington. At the end of the war he was brevetted brigadier general. He was a member of the Massachusetts General Court from 1789 to 1793 and a Federalist member of the House of Representatives from 1793 to 1795.

Colo. Henry Lee [23]	Virga.
Colo. Jereh. Olney [24]	Rhode Island
Colo. Wm. Davis [25]	Virginia
Colo. U. Forrest [26]	Maryland
Colo. Wm. Hull [27]	Masstts.
Colo. D. Humphreys [28]	Connecticut
Colo. Wm. North [29]	N. York
Colo. Robt. Troup [30]	do
Wm. Winder [31]	Maryland
Lt. Colo. John Armstrong [32]	N. York

23. See note 7.

24. Olney served throughout the American Revolution and at the end of the war was a lieutenant colonel. During Washington's administration he was collector of customs at Providence, Rhode Island.

25. This is a reference to William Davies, who served throughout the American Revolution and at the end of the war was a lieutenant colonel of the First Virginia Regiment. After the Revolution he was engaged in settling the accounts between the United States and Virginia.

26. Uriah Forrest, who lost a leg at Germantown, served in the American Revolution until 1781, when he resigned as a lieutenant colonel. He was a member of the Continental Congress in 1786 and 1787, and he was a Federalist member of the House of Representatives from March 4, 1793, to November 8, 1794, when he resigned.

27. Hull served throughout the American Revolution, and at the end of the war he was a lieutenant colonel. After the war he took a prominent part in suppressing Shays's Rebellion, and he served as judge of the Massachusetts Court of Common Pleas and as a state senator. He is remembered today, insofar as he is remembered, as the commanding general in the War of 1812 who surrendered his forces and fortifications at Detroit to General Isaac Brock.

28. See Washington to H, October 29, 1795, note 22.

29. See note 8.

30. Troup and H had first become friends when both were students at King's College. During the war Troup reached the rank of lieutenant colonel and served as aide-de-camp to General Horatio Gates and as secretary to the Board of Treasury. After the war he practiced law, speculated in land, and remained a close friend of H.

31. During the American Revolution Winder was a member of the Continental Navy Board at Philadelphia. After the war he was appointed to settle the accounts between Delaware and the United States, and between Virginia and North Carolina and the United States. He was a resident of Somerset, Maryland, and a state senator from 1793 to 1795. In 1798 President John Adams named Winder to the position of Accountant of the Navy (*Executive Journal,* I, 292–93).

32. During the American Revolution Armstrong served as an aide-de-camp to General Hugh Mercer and General Horatio Gates. In March, 1783, he was (at the time the unknown) author of the famous—or infamous—"Newburgh Letters" proposing that the Army act on its own if Congress refused to meet its demands. He was secretary of the Commonwealth of Pennsylvania from 1783 to 1787, and in 1784 he was in command of the Pennsylvania militia sent to restore order in the Wyoming Valley. In 1789, after marrying a sister of Chancellor Robert R. Livingston, he moved to Dutchess County, New York, where he became a farmer.

added by T.P. Matthew Clarkson [33]   New-York

(Perhaps some suitable character not in the list, may occur.   T.P.)

33. During the American Revolution Clarkson was an aide-de-camp to General Benedict Arnold and General Benjamin Lincoln. He was taken prisoner at Charleston in 1780 and brevetted a lieutenant colonel in 1783. After the war he served as a brigadier general and major general in the New York militia. He was a member of the New York Assembly in 1789 and 1790, United States marshal for New York from 1791 to 1792, and a member of the New York Senate in 1794 and 1795.

The Defence No. XXV [1]

[New York, November 18, 1795]

It will be useful, as it will simplify the Examination of the commercial articles of the Treaty, to bear in mind and preserve the Division that we find established by the 12.[2] 13.[3] & the 14.[4] & 15.[5] articles. Each respects a particular Branch or portion of the trade between the two Countries, the regulations whereof, differ from, and are severally independent of each other. Thus one is relative to the west Indies, another to the east Indies, and the third distinct from both the former respects our Trade with the british Dominions in Europe.

That Great Britain will consent to place our Trade with her west India Colonies, upon an equally advantageous footing with her own, is improbable. This would be doing what none of the great coloniz-

Df, Hamilton Papers, Library of Congress; *The* [New York] *Herald; A Gazette for the Country*, November 18, 1795.

1. Although most of the draft was written by Rufus King, substantial portions of the MS are in H's handwriting. The material by H is enclosed in brackets.

For background to this document, see the introductory note to "The Defence No. I," July 22, 1795.

2. For the text of Article 12 of the Jay Treaty, see H to Rufus King, June 11, 1795, note 2. See also H to William Bradford, June 13, 1795; Bradford to H, July 2, 1795; George Washington to H, July 13, 1795; Thomas FitzSimons to H, July 14, 1795; and "Horatius No. II," July, 1795. See also "Remarks on the Treaty . . . between the United States and Great Britain," July 9–11, 1795.

3. For the text of Article 13 of the Jay Treaty, see "Remarks on the Treaty . . . between the United States and Great Britain," July 9–11, 1795, note 54. See also "Horatius No. II," July, 1795.

4. For the text of Article 14 of the Jay Treaty, see "Remarks on the Treaty . . . between the United States and Great Britain," July 9–11, 1795, note 56.

5. For the text of Article 15 of the Jay Treaty, see "Remarks on the Treaty . . . between the United States and Great Britain," July 9–11, 1795, note 57.

ing Nations has done, or is likely to do. It would be to relinquish the principal ends of the Establishment, and Defence, of her Colonies—it would be equivalent to making her Islands in the west Indies, the common Property of Great Britain & america for all commercial, & profitable, purposes; and exclusively her own, in the Burthen of Support & Defence.

The Senate have however, & I think wisely, considered the Terms and Conditions on which it is agreed by the XII article that we should participate in the Trade to the British west Indies as less liberal than we may with reason expect.[6] The exclusion of all vessels above the Burthen of Seventy Tons, would diminish the Benifits, and value, of this Trade; and tho we cannot calculate upon obtaining, by future negotiation, a total removal of a Limitation on this Subject, it is altogether improbable that a Tonnage something larger may be procured.

Those who are conversant with our present intercourse with the west Indies can best determine, whether many Vessels under Seventy Tons Burthen are not at this Time profitably employed in that Trade: It is believed to be true, that previous to our Independence, Vessels of this Burthen were much engaged in this Employ, as well in the southern, as in the eastern, States.

This Limitation tho' disadvantageous, is not the strongest Objection to the XII Article; the Restraining, or regulating of a Portion of our Trade, which does not proceed from, and is independent of the Treaty, forms a more decisive Reason against the article, than any thing else that it contains.

The cause of this Restraint is found in that commercial Jealousy, and Spirit of monopoly, which have so long reigned over the Trade of the Colonies. Under [our Treaty with France &] the french colonial Laws, it has been shewn, that we could not procure from the french Islands, Sugar, Coffee, Cocoa, Cotton, or any of their other Productions, Melasses and Rum excepted [7]—Great Britain has seen

6. See H to King, June 11, 1795, note 2.
7. See Article 30 (originally 32) of the Treaty of Amity and Commerce between the United States and France, February 6, 1778, which states that subjects of the United States might use ". . . the free Ports which have been and are open in the french Islands of America . . . , agreable to the Regulations which relate to them" (Miller, *Treaties*, II, 27). See also the "Arrêt du conseil concernant le commerce étranger dans les îles françaises de l'Amérique," August 30, 1784, which established seven entrepôt ports for the islands of St.

it, to be compatible with her Interests, to admit us to share more extensively in the Productions of her Islands; but she has desired to place limitations on this Intercourse—to have left it entirely open & free, would have been [to have enabled us not only to supply ourselves by means of our own navigation, but to have made it an instrument of the supply of other Nations with her West Indian productions.]

When we reflect upon the established maxims of the colony System, and moreover when we consider that an entire Freedom of Trade with the British west Indies, might at Times materially raise the Price of west India productions on the British consumers, the supply of whom is essentially a monopoly in the Hands of the British Planters; we shall be the less inclined to believe, that Great Britain will yield an unrestrained commerce with her West India possessions to any nation whatever.

But if this was the Object of *the Restraint*, it may be asked why it was not confined to such enumerated articles as were of the Growth or Production of her own Islands; instead of being so extended, as to comprehend, all molasses, Sugar, Coffee, Cocoa, & Cotton, including even the Cotton of the growth of our own Country. It is very possible that the Circumstance of our native Cotton's becoming an article of Export to foreign Markets might not have occured to our negotiator. This would be the less extraordinary, as heretofore it has not been cultivated except in a [very] limited degree, and as an article of export rather, in the manner of Experiment than otherwise, and as moreover, from the Expence and Difficulty of separating the Seeds from the Cotton,[8] we have been [hardly] able hitherto, to class Cotton among our Exports. It's cultivation is said latterly to have become an object of attention in Georgia, & South Carolina—still however it cannot yet be considered as a staple

Lucia, Martinique, Guadeloupe, Tobago, and St. Domingo, and declared: "Il sera permis aux navires étrangers qui iront dons les ports d'entrepôt, soit pour y porter les marchandises permises par l'art. 2, soit à vide, d'y charger pour l'étranger, uniquement des sirops et taffias, et des marchandises venues de France" (Isambert, *Recueil Général des Anciennes Lois Françaises*, XXVII, 460).

8. In the draft at this point an asterisk has been crossed out. At the bottom of the page H wrote and crossed out the following: "Note * Some recent inventions of machinery promise to obviate this disadvantage—but their effects have hitherto been ⟨negligi⟩ble."

commodity. But from the recent Invention of an ingenious, & simple, Machine, for ginning Cotton, It is hoped that the cultivation may be extended, so that not only our own Domestic manufactures may be relieved from a Dependence on foreign Supply, but the catalogue of our valuable Exports inriched by the addition of this inestimable production.

In answer to the Question that has been stated, it may be further observed, that these enumerated articles, though the production of different Territories [being] so much alike, as not easily to be distinguished, It is probable that the Difficulty in discriminating the productions of the British Islands, from those of a different Growth, was supposed to be so great, that an apprehension was entertained that the prohibition to reexport the former would be easily evaded, and illusory, while the latter remained free.

This apprehension however, it is believed, [was carried too far,] as on a minute examination of the subject it will be found, that our Laws relative to Drawbacks [with a few analogous provisions in addition] can be made sufficiently to discriminate, and identify [on reexportation,] all such articles of the Growth of the British Islands as may be within our Country, and that they will afford the same security, for a faithful, and exact, execution of the prohibition to reexport such articles, as that on which our own Government relies against Frauds upon the Revenue. [The application of these laws with the requisite additions and sanctions may be secured by a precise stipulation for that purpose in the Treaty in such manner as would afford an adequate guard against material evasions.] [9]

But though the conduct of the Senate in with-holding their assent to this article, is conceived to have been upon the whole well judged and wise, yet there were not wanting reasons of real weight to induce our negotiator to agree to it as it stands.

The inviolability of the principles of the navigation act [10] had become a kind of axiom incorporated in the habits of thinking of the British government and nation. Precedent, it is known, has great influence as well upon the councils as upon the popular opinions of

9. At this point in the MS, H wrote: "Take in A seperate." As the material marked "A" has not been found, the next three paragraphs have been taken from the newspaper.

10. See "Remarks on the Treaty . . . between the United States and Great Britain," July 9–11, 1795, note 80.

nations!—and there is perhaps no country in which it has greater force than that of Great Britain. The precedent of a serious and unequivocal innovation upon the system of the navigation act dissolved as it were the spell, by which the Public prejudices had been chained to it. It took away a mighty argument derived from the past inflexibility of the system, and laid the foundation for greater inroads upon opinion for further and greater innovations in practice. It served to strip the question of every thing that was artificial and to bring it to the simple test of real national interest, to be decided by that best of all arbiters, experience.

It may upon this ground be strongly argued that the precedent of the privilege gained was of more importance than its immediate extent—an argument certainly of real weight and which is sufficient to incline candid men to view the motives that governed our negotiator in this particular, with favor, and the opinion to which he yielded with respect. It is perhaps not unimportant, by way of precedent that the article, tho' not established, is found in the treaty.

Though the XII. article so far as respects the Terms and conditions of the Trade to the British Islands forms no part of the Treaty, having been excepted, and made the Subject of further negotiation, it may nevertheless be useful to take notice of some of the many ill founded Objections that have been made against it. Of this character is that which asserts that the Catalogue of articles permitted to be carried by us to the British Islands, may be abridged, at the pleasure of Great Britain, and so the trade may be annihilated.

The article stipulates that we may carry to any of his majesty's Islands and Ports in the west Indies from the United States in american vessels not exceeding Seventy Tons, any Goods or merchandizes, "being of the Growth manufacture or Production of the said States, *which it is,* or *may be,* lawful to carry to the said Islands from the said States in british Vessels"—not all such articles *as it is,* & MAY *be,* lawful to carry; but in the disjunctive, all such as it is, *or may be* lawful to carry; in other words, all such articles as it is now lawful to carry, together with such others, as hereafter it may be lawful to carry: the Catalogue may be enlarged, but cannot be diminished. [It may also be remarked incidentally that this objection sounds ill in the mouths of those who maintain the essentiality of the supplies of this Country under all possible circumstances to the British West

Indies; for if this position be true there never can be reasonable ground of apprehension of too little latitude in the exportation in British vessels, which is to be the standard for the exportation in ours.]

The article has been further criticised, on account of the adjustment of the impost and tonnage Duties payable in this Trade, and it has been attempted to be shewn that the Footing, on which we were to share in the same, would on this account be disadvantageous and the competition unequal. What is this adjustment? The Article proposed that British vessels employed in this Trade shall pay on entering our Ports the alien Tonnage Duty payable by all foreign Vessels, which is now Fifty Cents per Ton; [11] further, the Cargoes imported in british Bottoms from the british west Indies shall pay in our Ports the same impost, or Duties, that shall be payable on the like articles imported in american Bottoms; and on the other Side, that Cargoes imported into the British Islands in american Bottoms shall pay the same impost or Duties that shall be payable on the like articles imported in British Bottoms—that is to say the Cargoes of Each, shall pay in the Ports of the other, only native Duties, it being understood that those imposed in the british west Indies on our Productions are small and unimportant, while those imposed in our Ports on the productions of the west Indies are high, and important to our Revenue. The vessels of each shall pay in the ports of the other, an equal alien Tonnage Duty and our Standard is adopted as the common Rule.

Is not this equal? Can we expect, or ask, that british vessels should pay an alien Tonnage Duty in our ports, and that american vessels should enter their ports freely, or on payment only of native Tonnage Duties? can we in equity require them to pay on the importation of their Cargoes in British Vessels, an addition of ten per Cent on the Duties payable on the importation of the like articles in american Vessels, and at the same Time, demand to pay no higher or other Duties on the Cargoes carried in our Vessels to the British Islands, than those payable by them on the like articles imported in British Vessels? The very stating of the Question suggests to a candid mind, an answer that demonstrates the injustice of the Objection. [To expect more were to expect that in a Trade in which

11. This is a reference to Section 1 of "An Act imposing duties on the tonnage of ships or vessels" (1 *Stat.* 135 [July 20, 1790]).

the opinions and practices of Europe contemplate every privilege granted to a foreign nation as a *favour*—we were by Treaty to secure a greater advantage to ourselves, than would be enjoyed by the Nation which granted the privilege.] But it is added that our Laws impose a Tonnage Duty of six Cents per Ton on the entry of american vessels engaged in foreign Trade,[12] and it is not known that british Vessels pay any Tonnage Duty on their Entry in their Ports in the West-Indies, and so uniting the two entries, that is the entry in the west Indies and the entry on a return to our Ports, an american vessel will pay Fifty Six Cents per Ton, when the British vessel will pay only Fifty Cents per Ton. If the British Government impose no tonnage Duty on their own Vessels, and we do impose a Tonnage Duty on ours, this certainly cannot form an Objection against them. They are as free to abstain from the imposition of a Tonnage Duty on their own Ships, as we are to impose one on ours. If their policy is wiser than ours in this respect, we are at liberty to adopt it by repealing the Tonnage Duty levied on american navigation [which if we please may be confined to the particular case;] the effect of such a measure [as far as it should extend] tho the Duty is small, would be to add a proportional advantage to our Shipping in foreign competition. But the object of the Article in this particular, is to equalize not the Duties that each may choose to impose on their own Vessels, but those that they shall impose on the Vessels of each other; and in this Respect the Article is perfectly equal. [It is perhaps the first time that the question of inequality was founded on a circumstance depending on the laws of the party affected by it and removeable at his own option.]

This view of the Subject authorises a Belief that in the revision of the article, a modification of it may be agreed [to], that will prove satisfactory. Indeed from the short duration of the article taken in connexion with the Expressions made use of towards the close of it, relative to the renewal of the Negotiation for the purpose of such further Arrangements as shall conduce to the mutual advantage, and *Extension,* of this Branch of commerce, we may infer that Great Britain contemplates a more enlarged, and equal adjustment on this Point.

The Relaxations which now exist in the colonial Systems, in con-

12. This is a reference to Section 1 of "An Act imposing duties on the tonnage of ships or vessels" (1 *Stat.* 135).

sequence of the necessities of the War, and which will change to our Disadvantage, with the return of Peace, have been considered by some as the permanent State of things. And this Error has had its influence in misleading the public in respect to the Terms & Conditions in which we may reasonably expect to participate in the Trade to the British west Indies. But let it be remembered that the Restoration of Peace will bring with it a Restoration of the Laws of limitation, & Exclusion, which constitute the colonial System. Our Efforts therefore should be directed to such an adjustment with Great Britain on this Point, as will secure to us, a Right, after the return of Peace, to the greatest attainable Portion of the Trade to her Islands in the west Indies.

It has been alledged should the expected modification of this article retain its present stipulation on the subject of Impost & Tonnage Duty, that as France by Treaty may claim to enjoy the Rights & privileges of the most favoured nation, she would demand an exemption from the ten per Cent on the Duties [upon] the productions of the west Indies imported in foreign Bottoms, and would moreover be free to impose an alien Tonnage on our Vessels entering their Ports in the West Indies, equal to that imposed on her Vessels in our Ports. This is true, but in order to make this Demand, France must agree *by Treaty* to open all her Ports in the west Indies, to give us a Right to import into them Flour, Bread, Tobacco, and such other articles as Great Britain shall permit, and which France prohibits; she must also concede to us a Right to purchase in her Islands, and bring away Sugar, Coffee, & Pimento, which by her permanent System [13] she prohibits. [She must do all this because by our Treaty with her she can only intitle herself to a special privilege granted to another Nation by granting on her part to us, the equivalent of what was the consideration of our Grant.] [14] Should France be inclined, so to arrange the Trade between us and her Islands, we certainly shall not object; because, [besides the right,] such an arrangement would be more advantageous to us, than that, which now regulates our intercourse with her west Indies.

So much of the twelfth article as respects its duration, and the

13. See note 7.
14. See Article 2 of the Treaty of Amity and Commerce between the United States and France, February 6, 1778 (Miller, *Treaties*, II, 5).

renewal of the negotiation, previous to the expiration of two years after the conclusion of the war, in order to agree in a new arrangement on the subject of the west Indies Trade, as well as for the Purpose of endeavouring to agree whether in any, and in what Cases, neutral Vessels shall protect Enemy Property, and in what cases Provisions and other articles not generally contraband may become such, form a part of the Treaty as ratified by the President. These Clauses sufficiently explain themselves, and require no comment in this Place. They however prove one point, which is, that after every Effort on the Part of our Negotiator the Parties were not able to agree in the Doctrine that free Bottoms should make free Goods, nor in the Cases in which alone Provisions and other Articles not generally contraband should be deemed such—*leaving therefore both these Points, precisely as they found them* (except in respect to provisions, the payment for which, when by the law of Nations liable to capture & used as contraband [15] is secured) to be regulated by the existing Law of Nations, it is stipulated to renew the Negotiation on these Points, at the Epoch assigned for the future adjustment of the west India Trade, in order then to endeavour to agree in a conventional Rule, which, instead of the Law of Nations, should thereafter regulate the conduct of the Parties in these Respects.

[The 11th Article [16] has been passed over in silence as being merely introductory & formal.   CAMILLUS]

15. See "Remarks on the Treaty . . . between the United States and Great Britain," July 9–11, 1795, note 65.
16. For the text of Article 11 of the Jay Treaty, see "Remarks on the Treaty . . . between the United States and Great Britain," July 9–11, 1795, note 51.

From George Washington

Philadelphia 18th. Novr. 1795

My dear Sir,

Having *no* doubt that the petition contained in the enclosed Gazette, will make its appearance in the Virginia Assembly; [1] and *nearly* as little of its favourable reception in that body, I resolved to give you the perusal of it, at this moment.

But my principal view in writing to you now, is, to request that you would desire young Fayette and his Tutor [2] to proceed to this place without delay; having resolved, unless some powerful reasons can be suggested to the contrary, to take them at once into my family.

The young gentleman must have experienced some unpleasant feelings already from being kept at a distance from me, and I feel as unpleasantly as he can do, from the same cause.

Very sincerely & affectionately   I am Yours   Go: Washington

Colo. Hamilton.

ALS, Hamilton Papers, Library of Congress.

1. Washington is referring to the following proceedings in the Virginia House of Delegates on November 17, 1795: "A motion was made that the House do come to the following resolution:

"*Resolved*, That this House do approve of the conduct of Henry Tazewell and Stephens Thompson Mason, Esquires, Senators from this state in the Congress of the United States in voting against the ratification of the treaty lately negociated between the United States and Great-Britain.

"And the said resolution being read, a motion was made to amend the same, in the following words, to wit:

" 'Whereas the powers granted by the people to the continental government, and to the state governments, are and should remain separate and distinct, so that neither exercise what is granted to the other; and this General Assembly have full confidence in the public servants in each branch of the general government.

" '*Resolved*, That the discussion of the late treaty between the United States and Great-Britain, as ratified by the President and Senate, is unnecessary in the House of Delegates, and ought to be avoided, and that without a full discussion and investigation thereof, this House cannot be prepared to express any mature opinion upon the conduct of the Senators from Virginia touching that subject.' " (*Journal of the House of Delegates of the Commonwealth of Virginia* [Richmond, 1795], 21.)

For the actions of Tazewell and Mason, see H to Oliver Wolcott, Jr., June 26, 1795, note 2; William Bradford to H, July 2, 1795.

On November 20, 1795, the House of Delegates again debated the motions. The Committee of the Whole House reported: "*Resolved*, That this House do approve of the conduct of Henry Tazewell and Stephens Thompson Mason, Senators from this state in the Congress of the United States, in voting against the ratification of the treaty, lately negociated, between the United States and Great-Britain.

"And the said resolution being again read, and the question being put to amend the same by substituting in lieu thereof the following resolution:

" 'Whereas the General Assembly have full confidence in the Senators of this state, and in the other public servants in each branch of the central government;

" '*Resolved*, That the discussion of the late treaty between the United States, and Great-Britain, as ratified by the President and Senate, which they have a right to make, is unnecessary in the House of Delegates, except as to its constitutionality, and that without a full investigation thereof, this House cannot be prepared to express any mature opinion upon the conduct of the Senators from Virginia, touching on that subject.'

"It passed in the negative: Ayes 52—Noes 98. . . .

"And then the question being put, that the House do agree to the Resolution as reported from the committee of the whole House?

"It was resolved in the affirmative: Ayes 100—Noes 50." (*Journal of the House of Delegates of the Commonwealth of Virginia*, 27.)

On November 21 the Virginia House of Delegates "*Resolved,* That the motives which influenced the President of the United States, to ratify the treaty lately negociated with Great-Britain, meet the entire approbation of this House; and that the President of the United States for his great abilities, wisdom, and integrity, merits and possesses the undiminished confidence of his country.

"And the said resolution being again read, and a motion made to amend the same by striking out from the word 'resolved' to the end, and inserting in lieu thereof, the following words:

"'That the House do entertain the highest sence of the integrity and patriotism of the President of the United States; and that while they approve the vote of the Senators of this State in the Congress of the United States, relative to the treaty with Great-Britain, they in no wise mean to censure the motives which influenced him in his conduct thereupon.'

"It passed in the affirmative. Ayes 89—Noes 56. . . .

"A motion was then made to amend the said amendment, in the words following:

"'*Resolved,* That the President of the United States, for his great abilities, wisdom, and integrity, merits and possesses the undiminished confidence of this House. . . .'

"It passed in the negative: Ayes 59—Noes 79. . . .

"And then the question being put that the House do agree to the first resolution as amended.

"It passed in the affirmative." (*Journal of the House of Delegates of the Commonwealth of Virginia*, 28–29.)

In a letter to James Madison on November 26, 1795 (AL, letterpress copy, Thomas Jefferson Papers, Library of Congress), Thomas Jefferson enclosed the following extract of a letter written to him from Richmond on November 22: "Mann Page's motion for a resolution appr⟨oving⟩ the conduct of the minority in the national senate was warmly agit⟨ated⟩ three whole days . . . . it was much less ⟨ably⟩ defended than opposed. John Marshall it was once apprehended would make a great number of converts by an argument which cannot be considered in any other light than an uncandid artif⟨ice⟩. . . . It is clear that it was brought forward for the purpose of gaining over the unwary & the wavering. . . . It's author was disappointed however—upon a division the vote stood 100 to 50. After the question Charles Lee brought forward a motion of compliment to the P. . . . A resolution so worded as to acquit the P. of all evil intention, but at the same time silently censuring his error, was passed by a majority of 33. 89 to 56" (D, in the handwriting of Jefferson, Thomas Jefferson Papers, Library of Congress).

For evidence that the above extract was written by Thomas Mann Randolph, Jefferson's son-in-law, see Jefferson to Randolph, November 25, 1795 (ALS, Thomas Jefferson Papers, Library of Congress).

2. For information on George Washington Motier Lafayette and Felix Frestel, his tutor, see H to Washington, October 16, 26, 1795; Washington to H, October 29, November 10, 1795.

To George Washington

New York November 19. 1795

Sir

Your letters of the 16 and 18 instant with their inclosures are received.

An extraordinary pressure of professional business has delayed my reply on the subject of Young La Fayette;[1] in which another cause cooperated. I wished without unvieling the motives incidentally to sound the impressions of other persons of Judgment who I knew had been apprised of his being in the Country.

The byass of my in[c]lination has been that you should proceed as your letter of yesterday proposes and I cannot say it is changed, though it is weakened. For I find, that in other minds and judicious ones, a doubt is entertained whether at the actual crisis it would be prudent to give *publicity* to your protection of him. It seems to be feared, that the factious might use it as a weapon to represent you as a favourer of the Anti Revolutionists of France; and it is inferred that it would be inexpedient to furnish at this moment any aliment to their slanders.

These ideas have enough of foundation & importance to make me question my own impressions, which, from natural disposition, are in similar cases much to be distrusted.

I shall therefore do nothing more at present than write to La fayette & his Preceptor to come to New York & I shall forbear any definitive communication to them till I hear further from you, after you have reflected on the information I now give.

Should you on reconsideration conclude on yielding to the doubt as a matter of greater caution, perhaps it will be then best for you to write Young La Fayette a Letter; affectionate as your feelings will naturally lead you to make it, announcing your resolution to be to him a parent & friend but mentioning that very peculiar circumstances of the moment impose on you the necessity of deferring the gratification of your wishes for a personal interview; desiring him at the same [time] to concert with me a plan for disposing of himself satisfactorily & advantageously, in the mean time. I shall with pleasure execute any commands you may give me on the subject. The papers respecting this matter are herewith returned. I shall without delay attend to all the others.

Very respectfully & Affecty I have the honor to be Sir Your obedt serv.   A Hamilton

The President of The UStates

ALS, George Washington Papers, Library of Congress; copy, Hamilton Papers, Library of Congress.
    1. For information on George Washington Motier Lafayette, see H to Washington, October 16, 26, 1795; Washington to H, October 29, November 10, 18, 1795.

To Timothy Pickering

New York November 20. 1795

My Dear Sir

I duly received your letter of the 17th. which needed no apology as it will always give me pleasure to comply with any wish of yours connected with the public service, or your personal satisfaction.

Good men, in the idea of your appointment to the office of Secretary of State, will find many consolations for your removal from one in which your usefulness was well understood.

I wish it was easy to replace you in the department you will leave. But this is a most difficult point.

I consider it as absolutely necessary that the person shall come from some State South of Pensylvania. All the great offices in the hands of men from Pensylvania Northward would do *the lord knows what mischief*. I speak as to public opinion. Hence I forbear any remarks on Characters from that quarter.

Of those South, notwithstanding there are real and weighty objections, I incline on the whole to LEE.[1]

Of the others whom you present (and none others have occured to me) whose qualifications are known to me, I believe I should prefer *Howard*.[2]

Yet I speak with hesitation, for I am afraid he is not enough a man of sense or business. But he is of perfect worth is respectable in the community and has reputation as a soldier.

There are others who would stand better as to Talents, but temper or fairness of character is wanting. I do not known enough of Winder.[3]

Since writing the above Judge Pendleton of Georgia[4] has occurred to me. He was a military man—Aide to General Greene[5] & esteemed by him. He is certainly a man of handsome abilities. I have however within a few days heared that he had some agency in the purchase of the Georgia lands.[6] If he has had any interested concern in this transaction it would be an immense objection. Otherwise, if he would accept, all things considered I should prefer him. He is tinctured with Jeffersonian Politics but I should be mistaken, if among good men & better informed, he did not go right.

I have received the French copy of a certain paper & thank you for it.[7] The translation you mention has not yet come to hand. I will with pleasure revise & if requisite correct it. I even wish for the opportunity; for as you say, it much concerns me, & it is also very important to the public & there are many nice turns of expression, which to be rendered perfectly demand a very critical knowledge of the language.

Yrs. with true esteem & regard   A Hamilton

Timothy Pickering Esq

ALS, Massachusetts Historical Society, Boston.
1. Henry Lee. See Pickering to H, November 17, 1795, note 7.
2. John Eager Howard. See Pickering to H, November 17, 1795, note 17.
3. William Winder. See Pickering to H, November 17, 1795, note 31.
4. Nathaniel Pendleton, United States judge for the District of Georgia.
5. During the American Revolution Pendleton rose to the rank of captain. He was taken prisoner in 1776, exchanged in 1780, and served as aide-de-camp to General Nathanael Greene from November, 1780, to the close of the war.
6. For a description of the Yazoo land companies, see H to James Greenleaf, October 9, 1795, note 3.
7. This is a reference to Fauchet's Dispatch No. 10. See Oliver Wolcott, Jr., to H, July 30, 1795, note 1; Wolcott to H, November 16, 1795; and Pickering to H, November 17, 1795.

From George Washington[1]

Philadelphia 23d Novr 1795.

My dear Sir,

Enclosed are letters for Mr. de la Fayette, and his Tutor.[2] I leave them open for your perusal; and notwithstanding the request in my letter of the 18th. I shall cheerfully acquiesce in any measures respecting them which you (and others with whom you may be disposed to consult) may deem most eligible.

As there can be no doubt, that the feelings of both are alive to every thing which may have the semblance of neglect or slight, and indeed, expectant as they must have been (without adverting perhaps to the impediments) of an invitation to fly to me without delay—and distressing & forlorn as the situation of one of them is—It is necessary that every assurance & consolation should be administered to them. For these reasons I pray you to send my letters to them by Express, the expence of which I will repay with thankfulness.

The doubt which you have expressed of the propriety of an open and avowed conduct in me towards the son of Mr. de la Fayette, and the subject it might afford to malignancy to misinterpret the cause, has so much weight that I am distrustful of my own judgment in deciding on this business lest my feelings should carry me further [than][3] prudence (while I am a public character) will warrant. It has, however, like many other things in which I have been involved—two edges, neither of which can be avoided without falling on the other. On one side, I may be charged with countenancing those who have been denounced the enemies of France; on the other with *not* countenancing the Son of a man who is dear to America.

When I wrote to you last[4] I had resolved to take both the Pupil & Tutor into my own family, supposing it would be most agreeable to the young gentleman, & congenial with friendship—at the same-time that it would have given me more command over him—been more convenient & less expensive to myself than to board them out. But now, as I have intimated before, I confide the matter entirely to your decision, after seeing, & conversing with them.

Mr. Adet[5] has been indirectly sounded on the coming over of the family of Fayette *generally*, but not as to the *exact* point—his answer was, that as France did not make war upon women & children he did not suppose that their emigration could excite any notice. The case however, might be different, if one of them (with his Tutor, whose character, conduct & principles may, for ought I know to the contrary, be very obnoxious) was brought into my family, & of course, into the company that visited it. But as all these things will be taken into consideration by you I shall not dwell upon them, and only add that

With esteem, regard & sincere Affn.   I am ever yours

Go: Washington

PS. I have no doubt but that young Fayette and his Tutor might be boarded at German Town or in the vicinity of this City, and would be at hand to receive assistance & advice as occasion might require although he might not be a resident under my roof.

Colo. Hamilton.

ALS, Hamilton Papers, Library of Congress; ADfS, George Washington Papers, Library of Congress.

1. For background to this letter, see H to Washington, October 16, 26, November 19, 1795; Washington to H, October 29, November 10, 18, 1795.
2. Washington's letter to George Washington Motier Lafayette, dated November 22, 1795, reads: "It was with sincere pleasure I received your letter from Boston, and with the heart of affection I welcome you to this City.

"Considerations of a political nature added to those which were assigned by yourself, or Mr. Frestal of a sort more private, but not less interesting to your friends left no doubt in my mind of the propriety of your remaining incog until some plan advantageous to *yourself* and eligable for *all* parties could be devised for bringing you forwd. under more favorable auspices.

"These considerations, and a journey which I was in the act of commencing when I received your letter (and from which I have not long since been returned to this city) restrained me from writing to you at that time, but I imposed upon Mr Cabot a gentleman of character & one in whose discretion I could place entire confidence, the agreeable office of assuring you, in my name, of my warmest affection and support—of my determination to stand in the place of a father and friend to you—requesting him at the same time to make arragemts. with Mr. Frestal for supplying your immediate wants—and moreover that he would add thereto every thing consolatory on my part. All of which I now renew to you in the most unequivocal terms; for you may be assured, that the sincere, & affectionate attachment which I had to your unfortunate father, my friend & compatriot in arms will extend with not less warmth to you, his son; do not therefore ascribe my silence from the period of your interview with Mr Cabot to a wrong cause.

"The causes, which have imposed this conduct on us both, not being entirely removed, it is my desire that you, & Mr Frestal would repair to Colo Hamilton, in the City of New York, who is authorised by me to fix with you on the most eligable plan for your present accomodation. This gentleman was always in habits of great intimacy with, & is warmly attached to Mr. de la Fayette; you may rely therefore on his friendship and the efficacy of his advice.

"How long the causes wch. have withheld you from me may continue, I am not able, at this moment to decide but be assured of my wishes to embrace you so soon as they shall have ceased and that whenever the period arrives I shall do it with fervency. In the meantime let me begin with fatherly advice to you to apply closely to your studies that the season of your youth may be improved to the utmost; that you may be found the deserving Son of a meritorious father." (ADfS, George Washington Papers, Library of Congress.)

Washington's letter to Frestel, also dated November 22, 1795, reads: "The enclosed letter for Mr. Fayette is left open, and put under cover to you, for your perusal. Indeed it is intended as much for your information as his, as it will render a second letter in detail unnecessary, at a time when I am under a pressure of public business, occasioned by the approaching Session of Congress.

"To the above, I shall just add, that as the Preceptor, & friend of Mr. de la Fayette, I pray you to count upon my attentions & friendship; and learn that it is my expectation, that you wd. accompany him into whatever situation he may be placed; & moreover that you will let me know, at all times, what he has occasion for." (ADfS, George Washington Papers, Library of Congress.)

3. The word in brackets has been taken from the draft.
4. Washington to H, November 18, 1795.
5. Pierre Auguste Adet, French Minister to the United States.

[*The Defence No. XXVI*] [1]

[New York, November 25, 1795]

ADf, in the handwriting of Rufus King, Hamilton Papers, Library of Congress; *The* [New York] *Herald; A Gazette for the Country*, November 25, 1795.

1. For background to this document, see the introductory note to "The Defence No. I," July 22, 1795. Except for several words, phrases, and footnotes inserted by H, the draft of this essay is in the handwriting of Rufus King.

To George Washington

New York November 26
1795

Sir

Since my last,[1] La Fayette & his tutor have been here.[2] I conversed with them concerning a future destination, as by way of

consultation, without proposing any thing, and in a way best calculated to sooth. But I found that the idea of not being permitted
to see you is very painful to them—though they both profess submission to whatever may be your decision & behave modestly. The
declaration, however, was not unaccompanied by remarks that witnessed the chagrin produced.

Yesterday they were to dine with me at a Friends house. They
came in, while I was out, & left word that they had just received
some interesting letters, among them one for a friend in the Country, which they must carry him and would be absent till early in
the ensuing week. I was sorry for this, but I presume it means nothing more than is declared.

Seeing the impression made on them, I took occasion to converse
with General Knox,[3] now here, on the subject, who is very firm in
a similar opinion with the other Gentlemen I mentioned to you.
This coincidence of so many judicious opinions cannot but increase
a distrust of contrary impressions. And yet there are possible consequences of a very unpleasant sort on the other side.

The wish of the two Young Men appears to go only to one interview with you & then to any destination you may prescribe—but
even this is thought by other Gentlemen consulted inexpedient.

They both seem averse to any connection with a public seminary.
In this idea I see no place where they would be more comfortable or
better than Hartford under the good offices & attentions of Wadsworth.[4]

Very respectfully & Affecty I have the honor to be Sir   Your
obed serv   A Hamilton

The President of The U States

ALS, George Washington Papers, Library of Congress.
    1. H to Washington, November 19, 1795.
    2. George Washington Motier Lafayette and Lafayette's tutor, Felix Frestel.
See H to Washington, October 16, 26, November 19, 1795; Washington to H,
October 29, November 10, 18, 23, 1795.
    3. Henry Knox.
    4. Jeremiah Wadsworth.

[*The Defence No. XXVII*] [1]

[New York, November 28, 1795]

ADf, in the handwriting of Rufus King, Hamilton Papers, Library of Congress; *The* [New York] *Herald; A Gazette for the Country,* November 28, 1795.

1. For background to this document, see the introductory note to "The Defence No. I," July 22, 1795. Except for a few phrases and sentences inserted by H, the draft of "The Defence No. XXVII" is in the handwriting of Rufus King.

From George Washington

Philadelphia 28th. Nov. 1795

My dear Sir,

If indisposition, or business of a pressing nature, should have prevented your looking into, and making a digest of the papers I sent you on the 16th. Inst I pray you to return them to me by the *first* Post after this letter is received.

The meeting of Congress is near at hand [1] and there is good reason to expect a punctual attendance of the members. I should be extremely unwilling therefore to be unprepared for this event; and shall endeavor to work the materials (no copy of which I have by me) into the best form I am able so soon as I get them, if it is yet to do.

You omitted in your last, to enclose the letters of Mr. Fayette, his tutor and Mr. Cabot, to me, and the copy of mine to the latter.[2] I beg they may accompany the other papers.

I am always & Affectionately Yours   Go: Washington

Colo. Hamilton

PS. I had written the foregoing letter, to go by young Mr. Jay,[3] this morning, but he having postponed his journey, I now add, that your letter of the 26th. came to me by the Mail of to day, without the papers, or any mention thereof; which (as I requested, if you could possibly make it convenient, to let me have them by the 24th.) has given me a good deal of alarm, lest they should have been entrusted to a private hand who may be dilatory or may have met with some other mischance on the way.

Did my letter to young Fayette (under cover to you) get to hand in time to be presented to him, at the interview you had with him? [4] My desire of seeing, and assuring him from my own mouth, of my fixed determination to be his friend & supporter, is such, that I hardly know how to reconcile to my feeling, the denial of permitting him to come hither for a few moments to receive it. But supposing that whatsoever you decide on will be for the best, I shall acquiesce therein.

Yrs.   G:W

ALS, Hamilton Papers, Library of Congress.
    1. Congress was scheduled to convene on December 7, 1795.
    2. See Washington to H, October 29, 1795; H to Washington, November 19, 1795.
    3. Peter Augustus Jay, son of John Jay.
    4. See Washington to H, November 23, 1795; H to Washington, November 26, 1795.

From George Washington

[*Philadelphia, November 28, 1795. Second letter of November 28* [1] *not found.*]

    1. In the "List of Letters from G—— Washington to General Hamilton," Columbia University Libraries, two letters to H from Washington for November 28, 1795, are listed.

Draft of George Washington's Seventh Annual Address to Congress [1]

[New York, November 28–December 7, 1795]

I trust, I do not deceive myself, while I indulge the persuasion, that I have never met you at any period, when more than at the

ADf, Hamilton Papers, Library of Congress.
    1. On October 29, 1795, Washington wrote to H and asked him for suggestions on subjects to be covered in the President's annual message to Congress.

present, the situa⟨tion⟩ of our public affairs has afforded just cause for mutual congratulation and for inviting you to join with me in profound gratitude to the Author of all Good for the numerous and signal [2] blessings we enjoy.

The Termination of the long expensive and distressing war, in which we have been engaged with certain Indians N W of the Ohio is placed in the option of the U States by a Treaty which the Com of our army has provisionally conclu⟨ded⟩ with twelve of the most powerful of the hostile tribes in that Region.[3] In the adjustment of t⟨he⟩ terms, the satisfaction of the Indians was deemed an object worthy no less of the policy than of the liberality of the U States, as the necessary basis of permanent tranquillity. This object it is believed has been fully attained. The articles agreed upon will be immediately laid before the Senate for their advice and consent.[4]

The Creek & Cherokee Indians who alone of the Southern Tribes had annoyed our frontier have lately confirmed their preexisting Treaties with us, and were giving unequivocal evidence of a sincere disposition to carry them into effect; by the surrender of the prisoners and property they had taken. But we have to lament that the fair prospect in this quarter has been momentarily clouded by wanton murders which some citizens of Georgia have perpetrated on hunting parties of the Creeks, which have again involved that frontier in disquietude and danger which ⟨w⟩ill be productive of ⟨f⟩urther expence & is ⟨l⟩ikely to occasion ⟨so⟩me ⟨ef⟩fusion of blood.[5] ⟨M⟩easures are in ⟨tr⟩ain to obviate or ⟨m⟩itigate the conse⟨qu⟩ences, and with ⟨th⟩e reliance of being ⟨ab⟩le at least to ⟨pr⟩event general hostility.

A letter from The Emperor of Morrocco announces to me the renewal of our Treaty and consequently the restoration of peace with

---

On November 10, Washington again wrote to H asking him "to suspend your superstructure until you receive a ground plan from me." On November 16, the President sent H papers to be used in preparation for the message, and on November 28 he urged H to finish it as soon as possible. Congress convened on December 7, 1795, and the President's seventh annual message was delivered on December 8, 1795.

The letter in which H enclosed this draft to Washington has not been found.

2. H wrote the word "distinguished" over the word "signal."
3. See Washington to H, second letter of October 29, 1795, note 24.
4. See Washington to H, second letter of October 29, 1795, note 25.
5. See Washington to H, second letter of October 29, 1795, note 26.

that Power.[6] But the instrument for this purpose, which was to pass through the hands of our Minister Resident at Lisbon,[7] who was temporarily absent on business of importance, is not yet received. It is with peculiar satisfaction I can add to this intelligence that an Agent [8] deputed on our part to Algiers communicating that the preliminaries of a Treaty with the Regency of that Country had been settled, and that he had no doubt of completing the business of his mission; comprehending the Redemption of our unfortunate fellow Citizens from a grievous captivity.[9]

The last advices from Our Envoy to the Court of Madrid [10] give moreover the pleasing information, that he had received positive assurances of a speedy and satisfactory conclusion of his negotiation. While the Event, depending on unadjusted particulars, cannot be regarded as ascertained, it is agreeable to cherish the expectation of an issue, which securing amicably very important [11] interests of the U States, will at the same time establish the foundation of durable harmony with a power whose friendship we have so uniformly and so sincerely [12] endeavoured to cultivate.[13]

Though not before officially disclosed to the House of Representatives, You are all apprised, that a Treaty of Amity Commerce and Navigation has been negotiated with Great Britain, and that the Senate by the voice of two thirds have advised and consented to its ratification, upon a condition which excepts part of one Article.[14]

6. For United States relations with Morocco, see Washington to H, second letter of October 29, 1795, note 23.

7. David Humphreys.

8. Joseph Donaldson, Jr.

9. For the treaty with Algiers, see Washington to H, second letter of October 29, 1795, note 22.

10. Thomas Pinckney. See Washington to H, July 7, 1795, note 2, and second letter of October 29, 1795, note 18. The "last advices" Pinckney sent to Pickering are dated August 11 and 27, 1795 (Pickering to Pinckney, November 6, 1795 [LC, RG 59, Diplomatic and Consular Instructions of the Department of State, 1791–1801, Vol. 3, June 5, 1795–January 21, 1797, National Archives]). Pinckney's letter of August 11 is printed in *ASP, Foreign Relations*, I, 535–36.

11. H wrote the word "essential" over the word "important."

12. Above the words "so uniformly and so sincerely" H wrote "highly prized & sincerely cultivated." Under the word "prized" H wrote "value."

13. On October 27, 1795, Pinckney and Manuel de Godoy signed a treaty at San Lorenzo. For the text of the treaty, see Miller, *Treaties*, II, 318–38.

14. On June 24, 1795, the Senate agreed to the Jay Treaty with the exception of Article 12. For the Senate's opposition to Article 12, see H to Rufus King, June 11, 1795, notes 2 and 3.

Agreeably to this advice and consent and to the best judgment I was able to form of the public interest, after full and mature deliberation—I have added my sanction.[15] The result on the part of His Britannic Majesty is unknown. When received, the subject will without delay be placed before Congress.

This interesting summary of affairs with regard to the foreign Powers between whom & the U S controversies have subsisted and with regard also to those of our Indian Neighbours with whom we have been in a state of enmity or misunderstanding opens a wide field for consoling and gratifying reflections. If by prudence and moderation on every side, the extinguishment of all the causes of external discord which have heretofore menaced our tranquillity, on terms consistent with our national rights and honor, Shall be the happy result—how firm and how precious a foundation will have been laid for establishing accelerating and maturing the prosperity of our Country!

Contemplating the situation of the UStates in their internal as well as external relations, we find equal cause for contentment and satisfaction. While the greater part of the nations of Europe with their American dependencies have been and several of them continue to be involved in a contest unusually bloody exhausting and calamitous —in which the ordinary evils of foreign war are aggravated by domestic convulsion riot and insurrection—in which many of the arts most useful to society are exposed to decay or exile, and in which scarcity of subsistence embitters other suffering while even the anticipations of the blessings of peace and repose are alloyed by the sense of heavy and accumulating burthens which press upon all the departments of Industry and threaten to clog the future springs of Governt—Our favoured country happy in a striking contrast enjoys universal peace a peace the more satisfactory because preserved at the expence of no duty. Fait[h]ful to ourselves, we have *not been unmindful ⟨of⟩* [16] *any obligation* to others. Our agriculture our commerce and our manufactures prosper beyond former example (the occasional depredations upon our Trade however detrimental to in-

---

15. For insertion after the word "sanction," H wrote in the margin: "a sanction which the constitution ⟨gran⟩ts to The President." Washington did not use this insertion.

16. Above the words "not been unmindful of" H wrote "violated no."

dividuals being greatly overballanced by the aggregate benefits derived to it from a neutral position). Our population advances with a celerity which exceeds the most sanguine calculations augmenting fast our strength and resources and guaranteeing more and more our national security. Every part of the Union display indications of rapid and various Improvement. With burthens so light as scarcely to be perceived with resources more than adequate to our present exigencies—with a mild constitution and wholesome laws—is it too much to say that our Country affords a spectacle of national happiness never surpassed if ever before equalled in the annals of human affairs? [17]

Placed by a Providence in a situation so auspicious motives the most sacred & commanding admonish us with sincere gratitude to heaven and pure love of our country to unite our efforts to preserve prolong and improve the immense advantages of our condition. To cooperate with you in this most interesting work as may depend on me, is the dearest wish of my heart.[18]

Fellow Citizens—Amongst the objects which will claim your attention in the course of the session a review of our military establishment will not be the least important. It is called for by the events which have changed and are likely still further to change the relative situation of our Interior frontier. In this review you will no doubt allow due weight to the consideration that the questions between us and certain foreign powers are not yet finally adjusted—that the War in Europe is not yet terminated and that the evacua-

17. In the margin opposite the end of this paragraph, H wrote: "⟨—⟩ American River Cap Clark."

18. At this point Washington inserted a paragraph which closely follows a paragraph drafted by John Jay. The paragraph which Jay wrote and which includes several changes by H is in the Hamilton Papers, Library of Congress. The paragraph, with H's changes indicated by brackets, reads: "[It is an encouraging circumstance in the general view of our prosperity] that the Country which was [lately] the Scene of the disorder & Insurrection now enjoys the Blessings of Tranquility and order. The misled have abandoned their Errors and pay [the] respect to our [constitution &] Laws which is due from good Citizens to the [established Public] authorities. These Circumstances [have] induced me to extend clemency and pardon to the few who were adjudged to capital Punishmt for Altho I shall always think it my duty to exercise the constitutional [powers] with which I am vested, with Energy and Firmness, yet it appears to me to be no less consistent with the public good, than [it is] with my own feelings, to [accompany] the operatives of [governmt. with] every degree of mildness moderation and Tenderness which the national Justice Safety and [dignity] may permit."

tion of our Western posts when it shall happen will demand a provision for garrisoning and securing them. You will consider the subject with a comprehensiveness equal to the extent & variety of its relations. The Secretary at War will be directed to lay before Congress The present state of the ⟨m⟩ilitary force, ⟨inc⟩luding the terms of service, to⟨ge⟩ther with that ⟨of⟩ the fortification ⟨of⟩ our harbours.[19]

With the review of our army is naturally connected that of our Militia establishment. It will merit inquiry what imperfections in the existing plan experience may have unfolded, what improvements will comport with the progress of public opinion. The subject is of so much magnitude in my estimation as to beg a constant solicitude that the consideration of it may be renewed till the greatest attainable degree of perfection is accomplished. Time, while it may furnish others is wearing away some advantages for forwarding the object. None better deserves the presevering attention of our public councils.

In contemplating the actual condition of our Western borders, the pleasure, which it is calculated to afford ought not to cause us to lose sight of a truth to the confirmation of which every days experience contributes (viz)—that the provisions heretofore made are inadequate to protect the Indians from the violences of the irregular and lawless part of the frontier inhabitants—and that without some more effectual plan, for restraining the murthers of those people by bringing the murderers to condign punishment, all the exertions of the government to prevent or repress the outrages of the Indians and to preserve peace with them must prove fruitless—all our present agreeable prospects fugitive and illusory. The frequent distruction of innocent women and children, chiefly the victims of retaliation, must continue to shock humanity; while an expence truly enormous will drain the treasure of the Union.

19. On December 14, 1795, "The Speaker laid before the House a letter from the Secretary of War, accompanying sundry statements and reports relative to the present military force of the United States; to the measures which have been pursued to obtain proper sites for arsenals; to the measures which have been taken to replenish the magazines and military stores; to the measures which have been taken for opening a trade with the Indians; and to the progress made in providing materials for the frigates, and in building them; which were read, and ordered to be committed to the Committee of the Whole House on the state of the Union" (*Journal of the House*, II, 378).

To enforce the observance of Justice upon the Indians, tis indispensable there should be competent means of rendering justice to them. If to these means could be added a provision to facilitate the supply of the articles they want on reasonable terms (a measure the mention of which I the more readily repeat as in all the conferences with them they urge it with solicitude) I should not hesitate to entertain a strong hope of permanent good understanding with them. It is agreeable to add that even the probability of their civilization by perseverance in a proper plan has not been diminished by the experiments thus far made. G of the H of Representatives:

The state of the Revenue in its several relations with the sums which [have] been borrowed and reimbursed pursuant to different acts of Congress will be submitted by the proper Officer: together with an estimate of the appropriations necessary to be made for the current service of the ensuing year.[20] Reports from the late & present Director of the Mint [21] (which I shall also cause to be laid before you) will shew the situation & progress of that institution and the necessity of some further legislative provisions for carrying the business of it more completely into execution and for checking abuses which appear to be arising in particular quarters.

Whether measures may not be adviseable to reinforce the provision for the Redemption of the public Debt will not fail, I am sure, to engage your attention. In this examination the question will natu-

20. On December 14, 1795, the House received "a letter from the Secretary of the Treasury, accompanied with estimates of the sums necessary to be appropriated for the service of the year one thousand seven hundred and ninety-six; also, statements of the application of certain sums of money granted by law; which were read, and ordered to lie on the table" (*Journal of the House*, II, 378).

21. On December 14, 1795, the House received "a letter from the Secretary of State, enclosing the reports of the late and present Director of the Mint, exhibiting the state of that establishment, and shewing the necessity of some further legislative provisions to render it more efficient and secure; which were read, and ordered to be committed to a Committee of the Whole House on the state of the Union" (*Journal of the House*, II, 378).

The reports of Henry William De Saussure, October 27, 1795, and of Elias Boudinot, December 3, 1795, together with Timothy Pickering's letter of December 14, 1795, are printed in *ASP, Finance*, I, 356–58. Boudinot's report may also be found in RG 59, Miscellaneous Letters, 1790–1799, National Archives, and in the George Washington Papers, Library of Congress. A letter book copy of Pickering's letter may be found in RG 59, Domestic Letters of the Department of State, Vol. 9, October 12, 1795–February 28, 1797, National Archives.

rally occur whether the present be not a favourable juncture for the disposal of the vacant lands of the UStates N W of the Ohio. Congress have demonstrated their sense to be and it were superfluous to repeat mine—that whatever will tend to accelerate the honorable extinguishment of our public Debt will accord as much with the true interest of our country as with [22] the general sense of our Constituents.

Gentlemen &c

The progress in providing materials for the frigates, & in building them; the state of the fortification of our harbours—the measures which have been pursued for obtaining proper sites for Arsenals and for furnishing our Magazines with military stores—and the steps which have been taken in execution of the law for opening a Trade with the Indians [23] will also be presented for the information of Congress.[24]

22. In MS, "will."
23. This is a reference to "An Act to regulate Trade and Intercourse with the Indian Tribes" (1 *Stat.* 329-32 [March 1, 1793]).
24. See note 19.
On the back of this draft H wrote: "Remonstrance against provision order." For information on the British order in council of April 25, 1795, see Washington to H, July 7, 1795, note 3; second letter of October 29, 1795, note 17; Oliver Wolcott, Jr., to H, July 30, 1795, note 2.

From James Butler [1]

Alexandria [Virginia] 1st. Xbr. 1795

Sir,

(Tho' I have not the honour of your acquaintance) I shall take the liberty of addressing you, to inform you of the real pleasure & satisfaction it gives me to read your Explanation in favour of the Ilustrious President.[2] And to inform you of Some of his Charitable donations—I mean What came Within my knowledge, which I am Sure are but trifling if compar'd With the imense Charities he bestows, that none besides himself, & the many Objects that receive them, know's.

He pays £50 ꝑ annum for the Tuition of twenty Orphans at the Accademy in Alexandria,[3] if any of his Overseers die he will give the Widows A house & garden & grass for their Cows &c—if any of his Domestics or Slaves get Sick he Will Visit 'em, & Send for a doter if requisite; his house is always open for travellers & strangers & Will give them money to support them to their journey's End. I livd with him as Overseer for two years; three months of which I was confin'd to my bed, & room, With a Violent feavr Not able to render him the Smallest Service. (Notwithstanding) he paid my Salary in full; & paid for my board for three months, & 'till I was able to teach in the Accademy. (In Short Sir) there is not A better mind'd or more humane Man on Earth. (thank god) his Charactr. is too Well known To be hurt by any Spurious, envenom'd Reptile that Wrote again him; their malice now falls in their own dirt.

Pardon this liberty I take With you, which flows, from the real regard, & good Wishes I have for him, Of My Esteem for you, on Acct. of your just & candid explanation Which I duly read With real joy & Satisfaction. I have the honor Sir of being   your most obt hble. Servt.   Jams. Butler

ALS, Hamilton Papers, Library of Congress.

1. Butler had been Washington's overseer at Mount Vernon in 1793 and 1794. As early as May, 1793, Washington was dissatisfied with Butler's services, and on May 19, 1793, the President wrote to Anthony Whiting, his plantation manager: "If Mr. Butler is the kind of man you describe him to be, he certainly can be of no use to me—and sure I am, there is no obligation for me to retain him from charitable motives; when he ought rather to be punished as an imposter: for he well knew the Services he had to perform, & which he promised to fulfil with zeal, activity & intelligence" (ALS, George Washington Papers, Library of Congress).

Although William Pearce, Washington's new plantation manager, hired Butler for 1794, the President had decided by August, 1794, to release Butler at the end of his current term (Washington to Pearce, August 3, 1794 [ALS, George Washington Papers, Library of Congress]).

2. See H's "Explanation," November 11, 1795.

3. On June 14, 1795, Washington wrote to Pearce: "By the last Post, I received the enclosed letter from James Butler. I wish you to let him know (& as soon as you conveniently can, that he may be under no mistake in the case) that he must look to those who placed him where he is—(if they think him qualified for the Office—) for his money; not a copper will he receive from me. I allow £50 pr. Annum to the Academy in Alexandria for the purpose of instructing the children of poor persons who are unable to be at that expence themselves, but I have nothing to do with providing, or paying the Master who is employed for this purpose. This is left to the Trustees of the School . . ." (ALS, letterpress copy, George Washington Papers, Library of Congress; see also GW, XXXIV, 214).

From Oliver Wolcott, Junior

Phila. Decr. 1. 1795

Dr. Sir

I have not been able to ascertain all the points upon which you requested me to write to you.[1]

In February 1780 a Comtee. reported a conference with the Minister of France, the substance of which was[2]—That the King of Spain wished for an alliance with the United States, but that it was necessary that the United States should explain their claims precisely.

That the Cabinet of Madrid, construed the western rights of the U.S. to extend no further westward, than the line of settlement permitted by the British proclamation of 1763.

That the United States had no Right to navigate the Missippi.

That the King of Spain would conquer Florida for himself.

And that the lands westward of the line of 1763, were proper subjects of conquest by Spain, from G. Britain.

The French Minister said, that his most Christian Majesty, was united by ties of blood to the King of Spain, & to the United States by Treaty & Freindship & that he would endeavour to conciliate the differences of opinion with liberality &c. There are many intimations in the French conferences, exhorting the United States to *moderation* in their claims—it was stated that France might not be able to obtain an *explicit* acknowledgement of independence, in which case the U.S. ought to consider whether a *tacit* acknowledgement ought not to be accepted.

There are intimations at several times that Mr. Adams required *positive instructions* to prevent him from acting too inflexibly &c &c (this is the idea—not the expression).

June 17th. 1781 Mr. Adams was instructed, thus—"to make the most candid & confidential communications upon all subjects to the Ministers of our generous ally the King of France, to undertake nothing in the negociations for peace or truce without the knowledge & concurrence & *ultimately to govern your self by their advice & opinion endeavouring* in your whole conduct to make them sensible how much we rely upon his Majestys influence for effectual support in every thing that may be necessary to the present security or future prosperity of the US of America." [3]

It is worthy of remark that the draft of instruction was communicated to the French Minister, & the words scored with a line underneath, inserted afterwards by way of amendment.

I send Chancellor Livingstons draft of a Treaty with England.[4] It furnishes good matter for testing the opinions of Cato,[5] by a rule of authority for himself.

You will judge of the manner of using these hints—but perhaps under present circumstances, they ought only to be considered as information, from which to state facts & reason.

You will hear from me on other points when I can get time.

Yrs truly   Oliv. Wolcott Jr.

I lately requested a corrected translation of a document which I sent to you.[6] I hope it reached you.

ALS, Hamilton Papers, Library of Congress.

1. See H to Wolcott, October 30–November 12, 1795.
2. This is a reference to a report dated January 31, 1780, which is printed in *JCC*, XVI, 114-16, and in Wharton, *Revolutionary Diplomatic Correspondence*, III, 485.
3. The instructions, which are dated June 15, 1781, are addressed to ". . . John Adams, Benjamin Franklin, John Jay, Henry Laurens, and Thomas Jefferson, Ministers Plenipotentiary on Behalf of the United States of America to Negotiate a Treaty of Peace" (*JCC*, XX, 651-52, and Wharton, *Revolutionary Diplomatic Correspondence*, IV, 504-05).
4. Wolcott is presumably referring to the letter which Robert R. Livingston, Secretary for Foreign Affairs, wrote to Benjamin Franklin, one of the American peace commissioners, on February 7, 1782. In this letter Livingston outlined the terms on which the United States should insist in the treaty of peace. The letter is printed in Wharton, *Revolutionary Diplomatic Correspondence*, V, 87-94.
5. The essays signed "Cato," a sustained attack on the provisions of the Jay Treaty, were written by Robert R. Livingston. These essays appeared in *The* [New York] *Argus, or Greenleaf's New Daily Advertiser* in July, August, and September, 1795. For the authorship and dates of publication of the "Cato" essays, see the introductory note to "The Defence No. I," July 22, 1795.
6. See Wolcott to H, November 16, 1795.

[*The Defence No. XXVIII*] [1]

[New York, December 2, 1795]

ADf, in the handwriting of Rufus King, Hamilton Papers, Library of Congress; *The* [New York] *Herald; A Gazette for the Country,* December 2, 1795.
  1. For background to this document, see the introductory note to "The Defence No. I," July 22, 1795. Except for a few phrases and sentences inserted by H, the draft of this essay is in the handwriting of Rufus King.

From James Hardie [1]

Princeton [*New Jersey*] *December 2, 1795.* ". . . During the time of the yellow fever in New York,[2] some business called me to that city. A person to whom I had rendered very considerable service served a writ upon me even in his own house & as it happened at a late hour I was sent to jail, where I continued for three days. . . . The trial will come on, during the Christmas week, when I shall endeavour to be in New York. Should you Sir, condescend, to be my attorney, I am certain that I should obtain justice & this is all I require. . . ."

ALS, Hamilton Papers, Library of Congress.
  1. Hardie attended Marischal College, University of Aberdeen, Scotland, from 1779 to 1781, but he did not receive a degree. He was a teacher of languages in New York from 1786 to 1791. In April, 1796, he announced the opening of his academy at No. 90, Fair Street (*The* [New York] *Argus, or Greenleaf's New Daily Advertiser,* April 23, 1796).
  2. Late summer and fall, 1795.

[*The Defence No. XXIX*] [1]

[New York, December 5, 1795]

ADf, in the handwriting of Rufus King, Hamilton Papers, Library of Congress; *The* [New York] *Herald; A Gazette for the Country,* December 5, 1795.
  1. For background to this document, see the introductory note to "The Defence No. I," July 22, 1795. Except for minor changes in wording made by H,

the draft of "The Defence No. XXIX" is in the handwriting of Rufus King. On a page attached to the draft, H wrote: "Mr. Moreton is requested to do Mr. H the favour of copying the within as soon as conveniently may be."

From John Habersham [1]

Philadelphia, December 7, 1795. Encloses a letter from "Monsr. De Bordes, a French Gentleman, who was formerly an Officer in the Georgia Line." [2] Describes De Bordes's service during the American Revolution.

ALS, Hamilton Papers, Library of Congress.
1. Habersham served in the American Revolution in the First Georgia Continental Regiment. He was a member of the Continental Congress in 1785 and 1786. From 1789 until his death on December 17, 1799, he was collector of customs at Savannah. In addition he was United States agent for Indian affairs.
2. Jean Marie de Bordes to H, November 15, 1795.

To James Hardie

New York, December 7, 1795. "I have received your Letter of the 2d. instant. As I do not practice in the Mayor's Court I cannot act for you as Attorney in the Cause you mention. But if you think my assistance at the Trial necessary—I shall be ready to give—if on knowing the Circumstances there appears a ground of Defence."

Copy, Hamilton Papers, Library of Congress.

[The Defence No. XXX] [1]

[New York, December 9, 1795]

ADf, in the handwriting of Rufus King, Hamilton Papers, Library of Congress; *The* [New York] *Herald; A Gazette for the Country,* December 9, 1795.
1. For background to this document, see the introductory note to "The Defence No. I," July 22, 1795. Except for a few words inserted by H, the draft of "The Defence No. XXX" is in the handwriting of Rufus King.

The Defence No. XXXI[1]

[New York, December 12, 1795]

I resume the subject of the two last papers for the sake of a few supplementary observations.[2]

The objections to the Treaty for not adhering to the rule "that free ships make free goods and enemy ships enemy goods" as being the relinquishment of an advantage which the modern law of Nations gives to Neutrals have been fully examined and I flatter myself completely refuted.[3]

I shall however add one or two reflections by way of further illustration. A preestablished rule of the law of Nations can only be changed by their COMMON CONSENT. This consent may either be express, by treaties declarations &c. adopting and promising the observance of a different rule or it may be implied by a course of practice or usage. The consent in either case must embrace the great community of civilized nations. If to be inferred from Treaties, it must be shewn that they are uniform and universall. It can at least never be inferred, while the treaties of different nations follow different rules, or the treaties between the same nation and others vary from each other. So also as to usage; it must be uniform and universal, & let it be added it must be *continued*. A usage adopted by some nations and resisted by others or adopted by all temporarily and then discontinued is insufficient to abolish an old or substitute a new rule of the law of Nations. It has been demonstrated, that no consent of either description has been given to the rule which is contended for in opposition to the Treaty.

The armed neutrality[4] so much quoted is intirely deficient in the

ADf, Hamilton Papers, Library of Congress; *The* [New York] *Herald; A Gazette for the Country*, December 12, 1795.

1. For background to this document, see the introductory note to "The Defence No. I," July 22, 1795.

2. In "the last two papers" ("The Defence Nos. XXIX and XXX," December 5, 9, 1795), Rufus King discussed Article 17 of the Jay Treaty. For the text of Article 17, see "Remarks on the Treaty . . . between the United States and Great Britain," July 9–11, 1795, note 59.

3. See "The Defence Nos. XXIX and XXX," December 5, 9, 1795.

4. See "Remarks on the Treaty . . . between the United States and Great Britain," July 9–11, 1795, note 60.

requisite characters. Its name imports that it was an *armed combination* of particular powers. It grew up in the midst of a War and is understood to have been particularly levelled against one of the belligerent parties. It was resisted by that power. There were other powers which did not accede to it. It is a recent transaction and has never acquired the confirmation of continued usage. What is more it has been virtually abandonned by some of the parties to it, and among these by the principal promoter of it, the politic and enterprising CATHARINE.[5] Tis therefore a perversion of all just ideas to ascribe to such a combination the effect of altering a rule of the law of the Nations.

In most important questions it is remarkable that the opposers of the Truth are as much at variance with each other as they are with the Truth they oppose. This was strikingly exemplified when the present constitution of the UStates was under deliberation. The opposition to it was composed of the most incongruous materials. The same thing is observable in relation to the Treaty. And one instance of the contrariety applies to the rule cited above.

While some of the adversaries of the Treaty complain of the admission of a contrary principle by that instrument as the abandonment of a rule of the present law of Nations; others, conceding that there is no such rule yet established, censure that admission as a *check* to its *complete* and *formal* establishment, and as a retrograde step from this desireable point.

The objection in this form is more plausible than in the other but it is not less destitute of substance. If there has been any retrograde step, it was taken by the Government prior to the Treaty. Authentic documents which have been communicated by the Executive to Congress contain the evidence of this fact.

5. On March 25, 1793, soon after the outbreak of war between France and Great Britain, Catharine II of Russia signed an agreement with George III that both sovereigns would undertake ". . . to shut all their ports against French ships, not to permit the exportation in any case from their said ports for France, of any military or naval stores, or corn, grain, salt, meat or other provisions; and to take all other measures in their power for injuring the commerce of France, and for bringing her, by such means, to just conditions of peace" and ". . . to unite all their efforts to prevent other Powers, not implicated in this war, from giving, on this occasion of common concern to every civilized State, any protection whatever, directly or indirectly, in consequence to their neutrality, to the commerce or property of the French on the sea, or in the ports of France" (*ASP, Foreign Relations,* I, 243).

Early in the year 1793 some British cruisers having stopped vessels of the U States and taken out of them articles which were the property of French Citizens, Mr. Genet, the then Minister of France in a letter of the 9 of July of that year made a lively representation upon the subject to our Governt; [6] insisting in a subsequent letter of the 25 of that month [7] in which he recurs to the same point that the principles of neutrality establish that friendly vessels make friendly goods, and, in effect, that the violation of this rule by GBritain was a violation of our neutral rights which we were bound to resent.

The reply of our Government is seen in a letter from our Secretary of State to that Minister of the 24 of July.[8] It is in these terms. "I believe (says Mr. Jefferson) it *cannot be doubted*, but that by the general law of Nations, the goods of a friend found in the vessel of an enemy are free and the goods of an enemy found in the vessel of a friend are lawful prize. Upon this principle, I presume, the British armed vessels have taken the property of French Citizens found in our vessels in the cases abovementioned, and, I confess, *I should be at a loss on what principle to reclaim them.* It is true that sundry nations desirous of avoiding the inconveniences of having their vessels stopped at sea, ransacked, carried into port and detained, under pretence of having enemy goods on board have in many instances introduced, by *their special treaties,* another principle *between them,* that enemy bottoms shall make enemy goods and friendly bottoms friendly goods; a principle much less embarrassing to Congress [9] and equal to all parties in point of gain and loss; but *this is altogether the effect of particular Treaty, controuling in special cases the general principles of the law of Nations and therefore taking effect between such nations only as have so agreed to controul it.*"

Nothing can be a more explicit or unequivocal abandonment of the rule that free ships make free goods and *vice versa* than is contained in this communication. But this is not all. In the letter from Mr. Jefferson to our Minister in France of the 26 of Augt. 1793 in-

6. Edmond Charles Genet's letter to Thomas Jefferson is printed in *ASP, Foreign Relations,* I, 164.

7. This letter is printed in *ASP, Foreign Relations,* I, 165.

8. For Jefferson's letter to Genet, see "Remarks on the Treaty . . . between the United States and Great Britain," July 9–11, 1795, note 61. The letter is printed in *ASP, Foreign Relations,* I, 166–67.

9. In the newspaper this word is "commerce."

structing him to urge the recall of Mr. Genet,[10] the subject is resumed—the position asserted in answer to Mr Genet insisted upon
anew and enforced by additional considerations. Among other suggestions, we find these. "We suppose it to have been *long an established principle of the law of Nations,* that the goods of a friend
are free in an enemy's vessel and an enemy's goods lawful prize in
the vessel of a friend. The inconvenience of this principle has induced several nations latterly to stipulate against it by Treaty and
to substitute another in its stead, that free bottoms shall make free
goods and enemy bottoms enemy goods. We have introduced it into
our Treaties with France Holland and Prussia [11] and French goods
found by the two latter nations in American bottoms are not made
prize of.[12] It is *our wish* to establish it with other nations. But this
requires their consent also, is a *work of time,* and in the mean while
*they have a right to act on the general principle without giving to
us or to France cause of complaint.* Nor do I see that France can
lose by it on the whole. For though she loses *her* goods, when found
in our vessels, by the nations with whom we have no treaties, yet
she gains *our* goods, when found in the vessels of the same and all
other nations; and we believe the latter mass to be greater than the
former."

Thus then stood the business antecedent to the Treaty. Great
Britain adhering to the principle of the general and long established
law of Nations captures French property in our vessels and leaves
free our property in French vessels. We acquiesce in the practice
without even a remonstrance or murmur. The French Minister complains of it as contrary to the principles of neutrality. We reply that
in our opinion it is not contrary to those principles, that it is fully
warranted by the general law of nations, that treaties which establish a different rule are merely exceptions to that law binding only
on the contracting parties, that having no Treaty of the sort with

10. The date which H gives is incorrect, for he is referring to Jefferson to
Gouverneur Morris, August 16, 1793 (ALS, Thomas Jefferson Papers, Library
of Congress; *ASP, Foreign Relations,* I, 167–72).

11. In the margin opposite this sentence H wrote and crossed out *"Sweden."*

12. See Article 23 (originally 25) of the Treaty of Amity and Commerce
with France, February 6, 1778 (Miller, *Treaties,* II, 20–21); Articles 11 and 22
of the Treaty of Amity and Commerce with the Netherlands, October 8, 1782
(Miller, *Treaties,* II, 68–70, 78); Articles 12 and 19 of the Treaty of Amity
and Commerce with Prussia, September 10, 1785 (Miller, *Treaties,* II, 170, 175).

Great Britain we should be at a loss on what ground to dispute the legitimacy of her practice. We do not simply forbear to oppose it. We do not offer to France as an excuse for our forbearance that it is inconvenient to us at the moment to assert a questionable right at the hazard of War. But we tell her peremptorily that in our opinion no such right exists & that the conduct of Great Britain in the particular case is justified by the law of Nations. Neither do we wrap the motive of our forbearance in silence nor content ourselves with revealing it confidentially to France alone. But we publish it without reserve to the world, and thus in the presence of Great Britain and of every other Nation make a formal renunciation of the pretension that "free ships shall make free goods and enemy ships enemy goods." No counter declaration is heared from either house of Congress.

It was impossible to give a more full sanction to the opposite principle than was given by this conduct and these public and positive declarations of our Government. It was impossible more completely to abandon the favourite ground. It is puerile to attempt to discriminate between the force of this species of renumeration and that of an admission of its propriety by Treaty. The conduct of a Government avowed and explained as to motives by authentic public declarations may assert or renounce a pretension as effectually as its compacts. Every nation with whom we had no contrary stipulation could say to us as well before as since the Treaty with G B—"Your Government has explicitly admitted that free ships do not make free goods and you have no right to complain of our not observing that rule towards you." Candour therefore would oblige us to say that the Treaty has left this point where it found it, that it has only not obtained from Great Britain a concession in favour of an innovation upon the law of nations which it is desireable to establish but which cannot be claimed as matter of right. Though therefore it may not have the merit of strengthening, it has not the demerit of weakening the ground.

The difference in our position in this respect before & since the Treaty amounts to this that before the Treaty the Government had abandonned the ground, through one organ, *Mr. Jefferson;* by the Treaty it continued the abandonment, through another organ, *Mr. Jay*. If we consider the organ as the voluntary cause in each case, (the presumption of which is equally fair in both cases), and if there be any blame it falls more heavily on Mr. Jefferson than on Mr. Jay; for the former sounded and made the retreat and the latter only did not advance from the disadvantageous post to which he had retreated. In other words Mr. Jay did only not recover the ground which Mr. Jefferson had lost. And we know that in general 'tis a far more difficult task to regain than to keep.[13]

But in truth no blame can justly be imputed in either case. The law of Nations was against the rule which it is desired to introduce. The U States could not have insisted upon it as matter of right— and in point of policy it would have been in them madness to go to war to support an innovation upon the preestablished law. It was not honorable to claim a right and suffer it to be infracted without resistance. It is not for young and weak nations to attempt to enforce novelties or pretensions of equivocal validity. It is still less proper for them to contend at the hazard of their peace against the clear right of others. The object was truly not of moment enough to risk much upon it. To use a French proverb—"The *play was not worth the candle.*" In every view therefore it was wise to desert the pretension.

So also, in the midst of a War, like that in which Great Britain was engaged, it were preposterous to have expected that she would have acceded to a new rule, which under the circumstances of her great maritime superiority would have operated so much more conveniently to her enemy than to herself. And it would have been no less absurd to have made her accession to that rule the *sine qua non* of an arrangement, otherwise expedient. *Here again the play would not have been worth the candle.*[14]

The importance of the rule has artfully been very much magnified to depreciate proportionably the treaty for not establishing it. It is to be remembered that if something is gained by it something *is also given up.* It depends on incalculable circumstances whether in a particular war most will be lost or gained. Yet the rule is upon the whole a convenient one to neutral powers. But it cannot rea-

13. In the newspaper this sentence ends as follows: ". . . 'tis a far more difficult task to regain than to keep an advantageous position."

14. In the margin opposite this paragraph H wrote and crossed out: "Note these war provisions will probably be superseded by the expiration of the Treaty before another war."

sonably be pretended that it is of so great value as that the U States ought to adopt it as a maxim never to make a Treaty of Commerce in which it was not recognised. They might by this maxim forego the advantages of regulating their commercial intercourse in time of peace with several foreign Powers with whom they have extensive relations of Trade by fixed and useful conventional rules and still remain subject in time of war to the inconveniences of not having established with those powers the principle to which they make that sacrifice.

Though therefore it be a merit to a certain extent in a Treaty to contain this principle it is not a positive fault or blemish that it does not contain it. The want of it is not a good cause of objection to a Treaty otherwise eligible.

Let me add too in the spirit of Mr. Jefferson's letter—that however it may be our wish to establish the rule with other nations than those with whom we have already done it—this requires their consent also, of course their conviction that it is their interest to consent and that considering the obstacles which lie in the way the attainment of the object must be *"a work of time."* It presupposes in some of the principal maritime powers a great change of Ideas, which are not to be looked for very suddenly. It was not therefore to have been expected of our Envoy, that he was to have accomplished the point at so premature and so unfavourable a conjuncture.

The assertion, that he has abandonned it, is made in too unqualified a manner. For while he admits the operation for the present of the general rule of the law of Nations, he has by the 12th article engaged G Britain in a stipulation that the parties will at the expiration of two years after the existing war *"renew* their *discussions* and *endeavour to agree* whether in any & what cases neutral vessels shall protect enemy's property." It is true it will be in the option of Great Britain then to agree or not, but it is no less true that the principle is retained with consent of G B in a *negotiable* state. So far perhaps some ground has been retrieved.

I confess, however, that I entertain much doubt as to the probability of a speedy general establishment of the rule that friendly ships shall make friendly goods & enemy ships enemy goods. It is a rule against which it is to be feared the preponderant maritime power, to whatever nation this character may belong, will be apt to struggle with perseverance and effect; since it would tend to contract materially the means of that power to annoy and distress her enemies, whose inferiority on the sea would naturally cause their commerce during war to be carried on in neutral bottoms. This consideration will account for the resistance of Great Britain to the principle and for the endeavours of some other powers to promote it. And it deserves notice that her last Treaty with France was severely assailed by some of the Chiefs of the opposition for containing a stipulation in favour of that principle.[15] The motive for consenting to it in this instance probably was that the stipulation was likely to be rendered in a great degree nugatory by the relative situation of the two nations which in almost any war in which one of the two was engaged on one side would probably render the other a party on the opposite side.

If these conjectures be right it is a reflection which lessens much the value of stipulations in favour of the rule, that so long as one or more of the principal maritime powers disavow it, there will be

15. The Treaty of Navigation and Commerce between his Britannic Majesty and the Most Christian King, signed at Versailles, September 26, 1786. Article XX of this treaty reads: "It shall be lawful for all the subjects of the King of Great Britain, and of the most Christian King, to sail with their ships, with perfect security and liberty, no distinction being made who are the proprietors of the merchandizes laden thereon, from any port whatever, to the countries which are now or shall be hereafter at war with the King of Great Britain, or the most Christian King. It shall likewise be lawful for the aforesaid subjects to sail and traffic with their ships and merchandizes, with the same liberty and security, from the countries, ports, and places of those who are enemies of both, or of either party, without any opposition or disturbance whatsoever, and to pass directly not only from the places of the enemy aforementioned to neutral places, but also from one place belonging to an enemy to another place belonging to an enemy, whether they be under the jurisdiction of the same or of several Princes. And as it has been stipulated concerning ships and goods, that every thing shall be deemed to be free which shall be found on board the ships belonging to the subjects of the respective kingdoms, although the whole lading, or part thereof, should belong to the enemies of their Majesties, contraband goods being always excepted, on the stopping of which, such proceedings shall be had as are conformable to the spirit of the following articles; it is likewise agreed, that the same liberty be extended to persons who are on board a free ship, to the end that, although they be enemies to both or to either party, they may not be taken out of such free ship, unless they are soldiers actually in the service of the enemies, and on their voyage for the purpose of being employed in a military capacity in their fleets or armies" (Chalmers, *Collection of Treaties*, I, 530–31). The treaty was debated in the House of Commons from February 12 to 21, 1787, and in the House of Lords from March 1 to 6, 1787 (*Parliamentary History of England* [London, 1816], XXVI, 381–514, 534–94).

a strong temptation to depart from a scrupulous observance of such stipulations; as we, on the part of France, have experienced in the present War.

In the course of the arguments against the 17th article for virtually admitting the right of search in time of War—the objectors have had the temerity to cite the opinion of VATEL [16] as in opposition to that right, and a mutilated quotation has given an appearance of truth to the assertion. It has been heretofore shewn by passages extracted from his work that his opinion so far from denying explicitly supports the right to search.[17] But it may be useful to examine the part of it, which has been tortured into a contrary inference.

After affirming the right to search (B 3 C 7 § 114) he proceeds thus, "But to avoid inconveniences violence and every other irregularity, the manner of the search is settled in the Treaties of Navigation and Commerce. According to the present CUSTOM credit is to be given to certificates and bills of lading produced by the Master of the Ship." Hence it is alleged the right to search is turned into the right of inspecting the Ships papers which being intitled to credit are to preclude further scrutiny.

But what immediately follows destroys this conclusion; the words *"unless any fraud appear in them or there be very good reason for suspecting their validity"* are subjoined to the clause just quoted. This admits clearly that the Ships papers are not to be conclusive, but that upon just cause of suspicion the papers may be disregarded and the right of search may be exercised.

Who is to be the Judge of the credit due to the paper & of the just cause of suspicion? Manifestly The Officer of the belligerent

16. This is a reference to "Cato No. 9" (*The* [New York] *Argus, or Greenleaf's New Daily Advertiser*, August 22, 1795), which is in fact a discussion of Article 18 of the Jay Treaty. "Cato" attributes the following words to Vattel, *Law of Nations:* "That it is now received, that full faith and credit should be given to certificates and sea letters, &c. that the master of the ship presents, unless a fraud appears, or there be good reason of suspicion." H's version of Vattel is the correct one.

For the authorship of the "Cato" articles, see the introductory note to "The Defence No. I," July 22, 1795. For the text of Article 18 of the Jay Treaty, see "Remarks on the Treaty . . . between the United States and Great Britain," July 9–11, 1795, note 63.

17. H is referring to "The Defence No. XXIX," December 5, 1795, which was written by Rufus King.

party who visits the neutral vessel. Then what does the whole amount to? Merely this—That Ships papers are intitled to a certain degree of respect and credit, how much is left to the discretion of the officer of the belligerent party, who if he be not satisfied of the fairness and validity of the papers may proceed to their verification by a more strict and particular search, and then if he still sees or supposes he sees just cause of suspicion he may carry the vessel into a port of his own Country for judicial investigation. In doing this he acts at his peril and for an abuse of his discretion exposes himself to damages and other punishment.

This is the true and evident sense of Vatel and it agrees with the doctrine which advocated in these papers, and I will add with the Treaty under examination.

The 17 article admits that the vessels of each party for *just cause* of suspicion of having on board enemy's property or of carrying to the enemy contraband articles may be captured or detained and carried to the nearest or most convenient port of the belligerent party to the end that enemy's property and contraband articles on board may become lawful prize. But so far from countenancing any proceeding without just cause of suspicion or from exonerating the Officer of the belligerent party from a responsibility for such proceeding it leaves the law of nations, in this particular in full force [18] and contemplating that such Officer shall be liable for damages when he proceeds without just cause of suspicion, provides that all proper measures shall be taken to prevent delay in deciding the cases of Ships or cargoes brought in for adjudication, *or in the payment or recovery of any indemnification adjudged or agreed to be paid to the Masters or Owners of such Ships*. Besides which, the 19th article [19] stipulates "in order that more abundant care may be taken for the security of the respective subjects and citizens of the contracting parties and to prevent their suffering injuries by the men of War and privateers of either party that the Commanders of Ships of War and Privateers shall forbear doing any damage to those of

18. See, for instance, Articles 12 (originally 14) and 13 (originally 15) of the Treaty of Amity and Commerce with France, February 6, 1778 (Miller, *Treaties*, II, 12–14), and Articles 10 and 11 of the Treaty of Amity and Commerce with the Netherlands, October 8, 1882 (Miller, *Treaties*, II, 68–70).

19. For Article 19 of the Jay Treaty, see "Remarks on the Treaty . . . between the United States and Great Britain," July 9–11, 1795, note 67.

the other party or committing any outrage against them, and that if they act to the contrary *they shall be punished* and shall also be bound in their persons and estates *to make satisfaction and reparation for all damages and the interest thereof of whatever nature the said damages may be.*" And further, after establishing that the Commanders of privateers shall before they are commissioned give security to satisfy all damages and injuries, it adds that in all cases of aggressions their commissions shall be revoked and annulled.

These provisions not only conform to, & corroborate the injunctions of the laws of Nations, but they refute the assertion that the Treaty is altogether deficient in precaution for guarding neutral rights—since those above mentioned are among the most efficacious. It is not presumeable that any stipulations have been or can be made which will take away all discretion from the marine Officers of the belligerent parties for this would be a total surrender of the rights of belligerent to neutral nations; and so long as any discretion is left its right or wrong exercise will depend on the personal character of each officer, and abuses can only be restrained by the penalties that await them. Those stipulations of treaties then which reinforce the laws of nations as to the infliction of penalties are the most effectual of the precautions which treaties can adopt for the security of neutral rights; and in this particular the Treaty with Great Britain is to the full as provident as our other Treaties. In one particular it is, I believe, more so; for it expressly stipulates a revocation of the commissions of Commanders of privateers for the aggressions they may commit.

Is not the passage last cited from VATEL a true commentary on those stipulations for regulating and mitigating the right of search which are found in our own and other Treaties? Do they not all intend to reserve to the belligerent party the right of judging of the validity & fidelity of the papers to be exhibited and of extending the search or not according to the circumstances of just suspicion which do or do not appear? And if this be their true construction, as it certainly is their construction in practice, which our own experience testifies—to what after all do they amount—more than without them the laws of nations, as universally recognized, of themselves pronounce? What real security do they afford more than the Treaty with Great Britain affords?

It is much to be suspected that there [20] will always be found advantages essentially criminal operating or not according to the strength or weakness of the neutral party, which if strong will find abundant foundation in the acknowleged laws of Nations on which to rest the protection of its rights.

It is said to be just matter of surprise that these precautions should have no place in a Treaty with Great Britain, whose conduct on the seas so particularly suggested & enforced every guard to our rights that could be reasonably insisted on. Observations of this kind assume constantly the supposition that we had it in our power to fashion every provision of the Treaty exactly to our own palate and that the ideas of the other contracting party were to have no influence even upon the minor features of the contract. But this supposition is absurd; and a Treaty may still be intitled to our approbation which adjusts acceptably the great points of interest though in some of its details it fall[s] short of our desires. Nor can any informed man sincerely deny that it was to have been expected that an adjustment of the particulars in question would fall short of our ideas. It may be answered that we were then at liberty not to make the Treaty; so we were—but does it follow that it would have been wise to split on such points? On a just estimate, their intrinsic value is very moderate.[21]   CAMILLUS

20. In MS, "they."
21. H endorsed this document: "Mr. Hamilton requests the favour of Mr. Sands to copy this as early as convenient." See "The Defence No. XXI," October 30, 1795, note 11.

To Rufus King

[New York] Decr. 14. 1795

My Dear Sir
An extraordinary press of occupation has delayed an answer to your letter [1] on the subject of Mr R.[2] Though it may come too late, I comply with your request as soon as I can.

The subject is truly a perplexing one; my mind has several times fluctuated. If there was nothing in the case but his imprudent sally upon a certain occasion [3] I should think the reasons for letting him pass would outweigh those for opposing his passage. But if it be really true—that he is sottish or that his mind is otherwise deranged, or that he has exposed himself by improper conduct in pecuniary transactions, the byass of my judgment would be to negative. And as to the fact I would satisfy myself by careful inquiry of persons of character who may have had an opportunity of knowing.

It is now, and in certain probable events will still more be, of infinite consequence that our Judiciary should be well composed. Reflection upon this in its various aspects weighs heavily in my mind against Mr R, upon the accounts I have received of him, and balances very weighty consideration the other way.

Yrs
A Hamilton

From what a Mr. Wadsworth [4] lately in Philadelphia tells me of a conversation between Burr [5] Baldwin [6] & Gallatin [7] it would seem *that the two last* Gentlemen have made up their minds to consider the Treaty, if ratified by G Britain, as *conclusive upon the H of Representatives*. I thought it well this should be known to you, if not before understood from any other quarter.

ALS, New-York Historical Society, New York City.
  1. Letter not found.
  2. John Rutledge. See Oliver Wolcott, Jr., to H, first letter of July 28, 1795, note 3.
  3. This is a reference to a speech which Rutledge had made on July 17, 1795, denouncing the Jay Treaty. For the text of Rutledge's speech, see Wolcott to H, first letter of July 28, 1795, note 3.
  4. Probably Peleg Wadsworth, a member of the House of Representatives from Massachusetts.
  5. Aaron Burr, United States Senator from New York.
  6. Abraham Baldwin, a member of the House of Representatives from Georgia.
  7. Albert Gallatin, United States Senator from Pennsylvania.

To Robert Morris

[*New York, December 14, 1795.* On December 18, 1795, Morris wrote to Hamilton and referred to "Your friendly letter of the 14th." *Letter not found.*]

From Timothy Pickering[1]

Philadelphia Decr. 14. 95.

Dear Sir,

The printer of Mr. Randolph's vindication advertises that it will be published next Friday.[2] The translation of Fauchet's letter will be in it.[3] This translation was made by Mr. Taylor[4] at Randolph's request; but Mr. Taylor, who desired the use of mine, told me that he had made but few variations. Now if I have mistaken the sense in any material passages, it is highly probable that they will be transferred to Mr. Taylor's translation: or Mr. Taylor may mistake the meaning of some passages; to which he will always be liable from the want of a *comprehensive* view of his subject. I have met with such instances in his other translations, altho' he is more familiar with the French than I am.

Now it seems to me important that the first translation of Fauchet's letter that shall be published, should convey its true meaning: and therefore I wish earnestly that yours, or the one you are correcting,[5] may be returned by to-morrow's post (if not already on its way) that it may be printed in Fenno's paper[6] before the vindication appears.

I am very sincerely & respectfully yours   T. Pickering

Colo. Hamilton

ALS, Hamilton Papers, Library of Congress; ALS, letterpress copy, Massachusetts Historical Society, Boston.
1. For background to this letter, see Oliver Wolcott, Jr., to H, July 30, 1795, note 1.
2. This is a reference to Edmund Randolph, *A Vindication of Mr. Randolph's Resignation* (Philadelphia: Printed by Samuel H. Smith, No. 118, Chesnut Street, 1795). This pamphlet was published on December 18, 1795.
3. This is a reference to Fauchet's Dispatch No. 10. The translation to which Pickering is referring may be found in Randolph, *Vindication*, 41–48.
4. George Taylor, Jr., chief clerk of the State Department. In a note on page 61 of Randolph, *Vindication*, Randolph wrote: "The translation [of Dispatch No. 10] has been made by a gentleman at my request, and delivered to the Printer, after I left Philadelphia. . . ."
5. See Pickering to H, November 17, 1795.
6. John Fenno was editor of the [Philadelphia] *Gazette of the United States*.

A translation of Dispatch No. 10 was published in the *Gazette* on December 21, 1795. This translation was taken from Randolph, *Vindication*, 41–48. On December 22, 1795, "Features of Fauchet's Letter, as published in Mr. Randolph's Vindication," appeared in the same paper.

The Defence No. XXXII [1]

[New York, December 16, 1795]

The 18th Article of the Treaty,[2] which regulates the subject of contraband, has been grievously misrepresented. The objections urged against it with most acrimony are disingenuous and unfounded; yet while I make this assertion which I flatter myself I shall be able to prove, I shall not pretend to maintain that it is an article completely satisfactory. I even admit that it has one unpleasant ingredient in it. And I am convinced that our envoy must have consented to it with reluctance.

But while Candour demands this concession it equally admonishes us that under the circumstances of the moment the points in this respect to be adjusted were peculiarly unmanageable—that the position of the other party rendered an arrangement intirely agreeable to us impracticable—that without compromise nothing could have been regulated—that the article made no change for the worse in our prior situation but in some particulars made our ground better, and that estimating truly the relative circumstances of the parties there is no probability that any thing more acceptable could have been established.

I will add that the degree of imperfection which may fairly be attributed to this article is far from being of such importance as on solid calculations ought to defeat the Treaty. No clear right is abandonned—no material interest of the nation injured. It is one thing whether every part of a Treaty be satisfactory—another and a very different thing whether in the aggregate it be eligible or not and

ADf, Hamilton Papers, Library of Congress; *The* [New York] *Herald; A Gazette for the Country*, December 16, 1795.

1. For background to this document, see the introductory note to "The Defence No. I," July 22, 1795. The material within brackets in this essay has been taken from the newspaper.

2. For the text of Article 18 of the Jay Treaty, see "Remarks on the Treaty . . . between the United States and Great Britain," July 9–11, 1795, note 63.

ought to be accepted or rejected. Nations could never make contract with one another if each were to require that every part of it should be adjusted by its own standard of right and expediency. The true question always is upon the collective merits of the instrument; whether upon the whole it reasonably accommodates the opinions and interests of both parties. Tried by this test, the Treaty negotiated with Great Britain fully justifies the acceptance of it by the constituted authorities of our country, and claims the acquiescence of every good Citizen.

The most laboured and at the same time the most false of the charges against the 18th article is that it allows provisions to be contraband in cases not heretofore warranted by the laws of Nations [3] and refers to the discretion of the belligerent party the decision of what those cases are. This is the general form of the charge. The draft of a Petition to the Legislature of Virginia [4] reduces it to this shape. The Treaty "*expressly* admits that provisions are to be held contraband in cases other than when bound to an invested place, and *impliedly* admits that such cases exist at present." The first is a palpable untruth which may be detected by a bare perusal of the article. The last is an untrue inference impregnated with the malignant insinuation that there was a design to sanction the unwarrantable pretension of a right to inflect Famine on a whole Nation.

Before we proceed to an analysis of the article let us review the prior situation of the parties.

Great Britain it is known had taken and acted upon the ground that she had a right to stop and detain, on payment for them, provisions belonging to neutrals going to the dominions of France.[5] For this violent and impolitic measure, which the final opinion of mankind will certainly condemn, she found colour in the saying, of

3. See "Remarks on the Treaty . . . between the United States and Great Britain," July 9–11, 1795, note 65.
4. The petition "To the General Assembly of the Commonwealth of Virginia" was presented in a letter addressed "To the Independent Citizens of Virginia," dated October 11, 1795 (*The* [Richmond] *Virginia Gazette, and General Advertiser,* November 11, 1795). The petition was also reprinted in *The* [New York] *Argus, or Greenleaf's New Daily Advertiser,* November 11, 1795, from the *Petersburg* [Virginia] *Intelligencier.* The quotation is from Article II of the petition.
5. This is a reference to the British order in council of June 8, 1793. See "Remarks on the Treaty . . . between the United States and Great Britain," July 9–11, 1795, note 66.

some Writers of Reputation on public Law. A Passage of this kind from Vatel has been more than once quoted in these terms "Commodities particularly used in war and the importation of which to an enemy is prohibitted are called *contraband* goods. Such are arms military and naval stores, timber horses, and *even provisions in certain junctures when there are hopes* of reducing the enemy by famine." [6] [HEINECEIUS * countenances the same opinion and even Groties seems to lean towards it.†]

The U States with reason disputed this construction of the law of nations; restraining the general propositions which seemed to favour it to those cases in which the chance of reducing by famine was *manifest* and *palpable,* such as the cases of *particular places bona fide* besieged blockaded or invested. The Government accordingly remonstrated against the proceeding of Great Britain [9] and made every effort against it which prudence in the then posture of affairs would permit. The order for seizing provisions was after a time revoked.[10]

In this state our Envoy found the business. Pending the very war in which Great Britain had exercised the pretension, with the same administration which had done it, was it to have been expected that she would in a Treaty with us even virtually or impliedly have acknowleged the injustice or impropriety of the conduct? Here was no escape as in the instance of the order of [the 6th of Nov. 1793] [11]

[* *Law of Nature & Nations B 2 C 9 S 201 Navibus ob vect.*] [7]
[† *Book III Chpt I & V 3 Cap I & X*] [8]
6. *Law of Nations,* Book III, Ch. VII, Sec. 112.
7. Johann Gottlieb Heineccius, *A Methodical System of Universal Law; or The Laws of Nature and Nations Deduced From Certain Principles, and applied to Proper Cases. Written in Latin . . . Translated and illustrated with Notes and Supplements, By George Turnbull* (London, 1741).
8. Grotius, *On the Law of War of Peace.* This reference should read: "Book III, Ch. I, Sec. V, Paragraphs 1-5."
9. See Thomas Pinckney to Lord Grenville, December 2, 1794 (PRO:F.O., 15/3), a copy of which Pinckney sent to Secretary of State Edmund Randolph on January 28, 1794 (ALS, RG 59, Despatches from United States Ministers to Great Britain, 1791–1906, Vol. 3, November 29, 1791–May 4, 1797, National Archives). See also "Conversation with George Hammond," April 15–16, 1794; H to Randolph, April 27, 1794.
10. This is a reference to the British order in council of August 6, 1794 (*ASP, Foreign Relations,* I, 482). See also Mayo, *Instructions to British Ministers,* 66, note 54.
11. Space left blank in MS. The British order in council to which H is referring was addressed "to the commanders of our ships of war and privateers that have, or may have, letters of marque against France" and instructed them

in the misconceptions of her officers—the question was to condemn a deliberate and unambiguous act of the administration itself. The pride the reputation the interest of that administration forbade it.

On our side to admit the pretension of Great Britain was still more impossible. We had every inducement of character right and interest against it.

What was the natural and only issue out of this embarrassment? Plainly to leave the point *unsettled*—to get rid of it—to let it remain substantially where it was before the Treaty.

This I have good ground to believe was the real understanding of the two negotiators; and the article has fulfilled their view.

After enumerating specifically what articles shall be deemed contraband it proceeds thus—"And whereas the difficulty of *agreeing on* the *precise cases*, in which alone *provisions* and *other articles* not generally contraband may be regarded as such, renders it expedient to provide against the inconveniences and misunderstandings which might thence arise: It is further agreed that whenever any such articles, so becoming contraband *according to the existing laws of Nations*, shall for that reason be seized, the same shall *not be confiscated*, but the owners thereof shall be *speedily* and *completely indemnified*; and the Captors or in their default the Government under whose authority they act shall pay to the Masters or Owners of such vessels the full value of all articles with a reasonable mercantile profit thereon, together with the freight and also the demurrage incident to such detention."

The difficulty of agreeing on the precise cases in which articles not generally contraband become so from particular circumstances is expressly assigned as the motive to the Stipulation which follows. This excludes the supposition that any cases whatever were intended to be admitted or agreed. But this difficulty renders it expedient to provide against the inconveniences and misunderstandings which might thence arise. A provision with this view is therefore made, which is that of liberal compensation for the articles taken. The

---

as follows: "That they shall stop and detain all ships laden with goods the produce of any colony belonging to France, or carrying provisions or other supplies for the use of any such colony, and shall bring the same, with their cargoes, to legal adjudication in our courts of admiralty" (*ASP, Foreign Relations*, I, 430). See the introductory note to H to George Washington, March 8, 1794.

evident intent of this provision is that in *doubtful* cases the inconvenience to the neutral party being obviated or lessened by compensation, there may be the less cause for or temptation to controversy and rupture—the affair may be the more susceptible of negotiation and accommodation.

More than this cannot be pretended because it is further "agreed that whenever any such articles so becoming contraband *according to the existing laws of nations* shall for that reason be seized, the same shall not be confiscated but the owners thereof shall be speedily and completely *indemnified* &c."

Thus the CRITERION of the cases in which articles not generally contraband may from particular circumstances become so is expressly the *existing laws of nations*, in other words the laws of nations at the time the transaction happens. When these laws pronounce them contraband they may for that reason be seized; when otherwise they may not be seized. Each party is as free as the other to decide whether the laws of nations do in the given case pronounce them contraband or not, and neither is obliged to be governed by the opinion of the other. If one party on a false pretext of being authorised by the laws of nations makes a seizure, the other is at full liberty to contest it—to appeal to those laws and if it thinks fit, to oppose even to reprisals and war. This is the express tenor of the provision—there is nothing to the contrary—nothing that narrows the ground—nothing that warrants either party in making a seizure, which the laws of nations independent of the Treaty do not permit—nothing which obliges either to submit to one, where it is of opinion the law of nations has been violated by it.

But as liberal compensation is to be made in every case of seizure where a difference of opinion happens, it will become a question of prudence and expediency whether to be satisfied with the compensation or to seek further redress. The provision will in doubtful cases render an accommodation of differences of opinion the more easy, and as a circumstance conducing to the preservation of peace is a valuable ingredient in the Treaty.[12]

12. In the newspaper the following sentences have been added to this paragraph: "A very different phraseology was to have been expected if the intention had been to leave each party at liberty to seize agreeably to its own opinion of the law of nations upon the condition of making compensation. The stipulation would thus have been 'It is agreed that whenever either of

A cavil has arisen on the term *"existing"* as if it had the effect of enabling one of the parties to make a law of nations for the occasion. But this is a mere cavil. No one nation can make a law of nations; no positive regulation of one state or of a partial combination of states can pretend to this character. A law of nations is a law which nature agreement or usage has established between nations. As this may vary from one period to another by agreement or usage the article very properly uses the term "existing" to denote that law which at the time the transaction may happen shall be the then law of Nations. This is a plain and obvious use of the term, when nothing but a spirit of misrepresentation could have perverted to a different meaning.

The argument against the foregoing construction is in substance this (viz) It is now a settled doctrine of the law of nations that provisions and other articles not generally contraband can only become so when going to a place beseiged blockaded or invested— Cases of this kind are fully provided for in a subsequent part of the article. The implication therefore is that something more was intended to be embraced in the antecedent part.

Let us first examine the fact whether all the cases of that kind are comprehended in the subsequent part of the article. I say they are not. The remaining clause of the article divides itself into two parts. The first describes the case of a vessel sailing for a port or place belonging to an enemy *without knowing* that the same is either besieged, blockaded or invested, and provides that in such case the vessel may be turned away but *not detained nor* her cargo, if not contraband, *confiscated* unless *after notice* she shall *again* attempt to enter: The second describes the case of a vessel or goods which *had entered* into such port or place *before* it was besieged blockaded or invested and declares that the one or the other shall not be liable to confiscation but shall be *restored* to the Owners thereof. These are the only cases described or provided for. A third which occurs on the sligh[t]est reflection is not mentioned—the case of a vessel going to a port or place which is beseiged blockaded

the contracting parties shall seize any such articles as contraband &c.'—and not 'It is agreed that whenever any such articles to *becoming* contraband and shall for that reason be seized.' This makes not the opinion of either party, but the *fact* of the articles having *become* contraband by the laws of nations the condition of the seizure."

or invested, *with notice* of its being in that state *when she commences her voyage or previous* to her receiving notice from the beseiging blockading or investing party. This is left to the operation of the general law of Nations except so far as it may be affected by the antecedent clause. Thus the fact which is the foundation of the argument fails and with it of course the argument itself.[13]

But had this been otherwise the conclusion would still have been erroneous. The two clauses are intirely independent of each other, and though they might both contemplate the same cases in whole or in part they do it with an eye to very different purposes.

The object of the first is to lessen the danger of misunderstanding, by establishing this general rule that where ever articles not commonly contraband become so from particular circumstances, according to the laws of nations, they shall still not be confiscated but when seized the Owners of them shall be indemnified.

The object of the last is to regulate some special consequences with regard to vessels and goods going to or which had previously gone to places besieged blockaded or invested; and in respect to which the dispositions of the laws of nations may have been deemed doubtful or too rigorous. Thus it is held that the laws of nations permit the confiscation of ships & goods going to places besieged blockaded or invested; but this clause decides that if going without notice, so far from being confiscated, they shall not even be detained but shall be permitted to go whithersoever they please. If they persist after notice then the contumacy shall be punished with confiscation. In both instances the consequence is intirely different from every thing in the antecedent clause. There, there is *seizure* with *compensation*. Here in one instance seizure is forbidden and permission to go elsewhere is enjoined—in the other instance the offending things are *confiscated* which excludes the idea of compensation. Again the last part of the last clause stipulates in the case which it supposes the *restoration* of the property to its Owners, and so excludes both *seizure* and *compensation*. Hence it is apparent the objects of the two clauses are intirely foreign to each other, and that no argument nor inference whatever can be drawn from the one to the other.[14]

13. In the margin opposite this paragraph H wrote: "These provisions do not occur in other Treaties."

14. In the margin opposite this paragraph H wrote "Qr."

If it be asked what other cases there can be, except those of places besieged blockaded or invested, and if none other what difficulty in defining them—why leave the point so vague and indeterminate? One answer, which indeed has already been given in substance, is that the situation of one of the parties prevented an agreement at the time—that not being able to agree they could not define and that the alternative was to avoid definition. The want of definition only argues want of agreement. It is strange logic to assert that this or that is admitted because nothing is defined.

Another answer is that even if the parties had been agreed that there were no other cases than those of besieged blockaded or invested places—still there would have remained much room for dispute about the *precise cases*, owing to the impracticability of defining what is a besieged blockaded or invested place. About this, there has been frequent controversy; and the fact is so complicated a one, puts on such a variety of shapes that no definition can well be devised which will suit all. Hence nations in their compacts with each other have not attempted one. At least, I recollect no instance of the attempt.[15]

Moreover is it impossible to conceive *other* cases in which provisions and other articles not generally contraband might on rational grounds be deemed so? What if they were going expressly and *with notice* to a *besieging* army, whereby it might obtain a supply essential to the success of its operations? Is there no doubt that it would be justifiable in such case to seize them? Can the liberty of trade be said to apply to any instance of direct & immediate aid to a military expedition? It would be at least a singular effect of the rule, if provisions could be carried without interruption for the supply [of] a Spanish Army besieging Gibraltar when, if destined for the supply of the garrison in that place, the[y] might of right be seized by a Spanish fleet?

The Calu[m]niators of the article have not had the candour to notice that it is not confined to provisions but speaks of provisions and *other articles*. Even this is an ingredient which combats the

15. In the newspaper the last two sentences of this paragraph have been changed to read: "Thence nations in their compacts with each other frequently do not attempt one: and where the attempt has been made it has left almost as much room for dispute about the definition as there was about the thing."

supposition that countenance was intended to be given to the pretension of Great Britain with regard to *provisions,* which depending on a reason peculiar to itself cannot be deemed to be supported by a clause including other articles, to which that reason is intirely inapplicable.

There is one more observation against this part of the article which may deserve a moment's attention. It is this, that though the true meaning of the clause be such as I contend for still the existence of it affords to Great Britain a pretext for abuse which she may improve to our disadvantage. I answer, it is difficult to guard against all the perversions of a contract which ill faith may suggest. But we have the same securities against abuses of this sort which we have against those of other kinds namely the right of judging for ourselves and the power of causing our rights to be respected. We have this plain and decisive reply to make to any uncandid construction which Great Britain may at any Time endeavour to raise. "The article pointedly and explicitly makes the existing law of Nations the standard of the cases in which you may rightfully seize provisions and other articles not generally contraband. This law does not authorise the seizure in the instance in question. You have consequently no warrant under the Treaty for what you do."

The same disingenuous spirit which tinctures all the conduct of the adversaries of the Treaty has been hardy enough to impute to it the last order of Great Britain to seize provisions going to the dominions of France.[16] Strange that an order issued before the Treaty had even been considered in this Country and embracing the other neutral powers besides the UStates should be represented as the fruit of that instrument! [17]

The appearances are that a motive no less imperious than that of impending scarcity had great share in dictating the measure, and Time, I am persuaded will prove, that it will not even be pretended to justify it by any thing in the Treaty.   CAMILLUS [18]

16. H is referring to the British order in council of April 25, 1795. See Washington to H, July 7, 1795, note 3.

17. In the newspaper there is an asterisk at the end of this sentence indicating a footnote which reads: "As reasonable would it be to place to its account the similar order which was issued before the mission of an envoy was thought of." This is presumably a reference to the British order in council of November 6, 1793. See note 11.

18. On the cover of this essay H requested "Mr. Moreton to copy this as early as convenient."

From Rufus King

[Philadelphia] Wednesday 16 Decr. [1795]

I send you Dunlap[1] of this Morning, in it you have the foreign intelligence. Fenno[2] Dunlap & others have erroneously stated that Mr Warder brought the Ratification of Great Britain—no official Dispatch has been received.[3] Rutledge was negatived yesterday by the Senate.[4] From present appearances the address to the President by the House will pass without a Debate. The Draft[5] has been by agreement in the Committee[6] who reported it, shaped so as to reserve all points intended to be discussed relative to the Treaty; the words underscored in the inclosed Draft,[7] were offered in the Committee by Mr. Madison, who agreed to concur in the paragraph if they were added—you perceive the object.[8]

Adieu I am &c   R King

A. Hamilton

ALS, Hamilton Papers, Library of Congress.

1. *Dunlap and Claypoole's* [Philadelphia] *American Daily Advertiser* printed the following item on December 16, 1795: "Mr. John Warder, merchant of this city, who comes passenger in the Richmond, from Bristol, has brought the Ratification of the Treaty between the United States and Great Britain, on the part of his Britannic Majesty." John Dunlap and David C. Claypoole were the publishers of this newspaper.

2. John Fenno, publisher of the [Philadelphia] *Gazette of the United States.*

3. On October 28, 1795, William Allen Deas informed Acting Secretary of State Timothy Pickering that Great Britain had ratified the treaty that day. Deas also enclosed a copy of the British instrument of ratification (ALS, RG 59, Despatches from United States Ministers to Great Britain, 1791–1906, Vol. 3, November 29, 1791–May 4, 1797, National Archives). Deas's dispatch is endorsed as received on December 28, 1795. The original British instrument of ratification, sent by Thomas Pinckney, arrived on April 22, 1796 (Pickering to Pinckney, April 23, 1796 [LC, RG 59, Diplomatic and Consular Instructions of the Department of State, 1791–1801, Vol. 3, June 5, 1795–January 21, 1797, National Archives]).

4. See Oliver Wolcott, Jr., to H, July 28, 1795, note 3.

5. This is a reference to the draft of the reply of the House of Representatives to George Washington's seventh annual message. See H's "Draft of George Washington's Seventh Annual Address to Congress," November 28–December 7, 1795.

6. The House committee to prepare the reply was composed of James Madison, Theodore Sedgwick, and Samuel Sitgreaves.

7. The "inclosed Draft" reads: "Made the 14th of December, 1795.

"REPORT

"From the Committee appointed to prepare and report an address to the PRESIDENT of the United States, in answer to his speech to both Houses of Congress."

The report reads: "As the Representatives of the people of the United States, we cannot but par[t]icipate in the strongest sensibility to every blessing which they enjoy, and cheerfully join with you in profound gratitude to the author of all good for the numerous and extraordinary blessings which he has conferred on our favored country.

"A final and formal termination of the distressing war which has ravaged our North Western Frontier, will be an event which must afford a satisfaction proportioned to the anxiety with which it has long been sought; and in the adjustment of the terms, we perceive the true policy of making them satisfactory to the Indians as well as to the United States, as the best basis of a durable tranquility. The disposition of such of the southern tribes as had also heretofore annoyed our frontier, is another prospect in our situation so important to the interest and happiness of the United States, that it is much to be lamented that any clouds should be thrown over it, more especially be excesses on the part of our own citizens.

"While our population is advancing with a celerity which exceeds the most sanguine calculations—while every part of the United States displays indications of rapid and various improvement—while we are in the enjoyment of protection and security, by mild and wholesale laws, administered by governments founded on the genuine principles of rational liberty, a secure foundation will be laid for accelerating, maturing and establishing the prosperity of our country, if by treaty and amicable negotiation, all those causes of external discord which heretofore menaced our tranquility shall be extinguished on terms compatible with our national rights and honor, *and with our constitution, and great commercial interests.*

"Contemplating that, probably, unequalled spectacle of national happiness, which our country exhibits, to the interesting summary which you, Sir, have been pleased to make, in justice to our own feelings, permit us to add the benefits which are derived from your presiding in our councils, resulting as well from the undiminished confidence of your fellow citizens, as from your zealous and successful labors in their service.

"Among the various circumstances in our internal situation, none can be viewed with more satisfaction and exultation, than that the late scene of disorder and insurrection, has been completely restored to the enjoyment of order and repose. Such a triumph of reason and of law, is worthy of the free government under which it happened, and was justly to be hoped from the enlightened and patriotic spirit which pervades and actuates the people of the United States.

"The several interesting subjects which you recommend to our consideration will receive every degree of it, which is due to them: And whilst we feel the obligation of temperance and mutual indulgence in all our discussions, we trust and pray that the result of the happiness and welfare of our country may correspond with the pure affection we bear to it." (Copy, Hamilton Papers, Library of Congress.)

8. In the final version of the House's reply to Washington's annual address, which was agreed to on December 16, 1795, the fourth paragraph of the draft became the fifth paragraph and was amended to read: "In contemplating the spectacle of national happiness which our country exhibits, and of which you, Sir, have been pleased to make an interesting summary, permit us to acknowledge and declare the very great share which your zealous and faithful services have contributed to it, and to express the affectionate attachment which we feel for your character" (*Journal of the House*, II, 379–80).

From Thomas FitzSimons [1]

Philadelphia, December 17, 1795. "Inclosed is the state of the Case depending between Mr. Church & Hollker,[2] taken from the information given to me & submitted to Hollkers attorney here. . . . I have stated the facts as they Appear & in a Way that requires no evidence. If you approve them, after you have Named a Professional Man I will Name some other & let them chuse a third so that their decision may be final. . . ." [3]

ALS, Hamilton Papers, Library of Congress.
  1. For background to this letter, see FitzSimons to H, March 21, July 14, 1795. FitzSimons, a native of Ireland, was a Philadelphia merchant. From 1789 to 1795 he was a Federalist member of the House of Representatives.
  2. For information on the case between John B. Church and John Holker, see H to John Chaloner, June 11, 1793; FitzSimons to H, March 21, July 14, 1795.
  3. H endorsed this letter: "Ansr. Feby. 4, 179[6] agreeing & naming Mr. Lewis—Referees to decide as Judges in Chancellory Law & Fact." H's letter has not been found. Presumably H is referring to William Lewis, a Philadelphia attorney and Federalist, who had been judge of the Federal District Court for the Eastern District of Pennsylvania from July 20, 1791, to April 11, 1792.

From Robert Morris [1]

Alexander Hamilton Esqre New York   Philada December 18. 1795

Dear Sir

Your friendly letter of the 14th [2] came to hand on the 16th. It should have been answered yesterday, but my engagements did not permit. I wrote to you on the 16th of Novemr last mentioning a Negotiation opened with Boston in consequence of which I expected to redeem $140,000 Deferred Debt which I have pledged there. This Negotiation was opened under the auspices of Mr Swan,[3] but I begin to think now that like many other things which look promising in the Outsett, it will go off in Air. I shall therefore gladly acquiesce with the proposition contained in your letter of the 14 Inst. My Estate called Morrisville [4] formerly the Delaware Works, is worth upwards of Three hundred thousand Dollars. A person proposing to buy it two years ago proposed two hundred and fifty thousand as the price, and I have since then added Several Improvements and valuable buildings and shall continue doing so, because I persevere in my desire of having a Manufactoring Town there. I have already borrowed upon the Security of this Estate the Amot of about One hundred thousand Dollars for which it is mortgaged. I propose to give to you or to Mr Church as you please a Mortgage upon the same Estate for the Amot of his Claim with my Bond payable as you mention with Interest annually—if the Deferred Debt is changed into Money, or for the stock say one hundred thousand Dollars deferred Debt if that is to remain the Claim. If it is to be changed to a Money Debt the price must be fixed I suppose according to the price of the day, & then the Bond will carry Interest from the date. I am ready to fix it either way and agreeably to what you shall think right. The Security now proposed I consider as ample, even for a much larger sum than will be charged upon it after Mr Churchs is added to the other. Besides that it is ample it is also a Saleable property. There are not less than 17 Farms and the Land (about 3000 acres) has lately risen from £ 10 & £ 12. to above £ 15 p Acre through that neighborhood. I have in all about sixty Houses Three ferries, two Fisheries, Grist Mill, Brewery, Bake House, slitting & Rolling Mill, Fulling Mill, snuff Mill saw Mill, Quarry &ca. It is one of those lively Estates that brings in a Regular annual Income which is constantly increasing. My son Robert lives there and I think it the first Estate and the best for a Gentlemans Residence of any in America. In short I expect to double its present value in the Course of a few years. I observe you seem to think it may be necessary for me to justify my Conduct if I give you Security. I have no such Idea, I want time and nothing but time to pay every farthing that I owe in the World, and I have Property that will do that and leave to myself and family enough to Satisfy Ambition, if they should be ambitious, or Avarice should they be avaricious. I did not know that you had become uneasy on this Subject but I suppose the Stories that are propagated have made you so, and I am not surprized at it. I want Ready Money sadly, but it is not want of property—property however will not command Ready Money at this time without great sacrifices. I do not like to sacrifice if I can help it, because I have worked hard to get what I have, and I will fight a good Battle to keep it. Another year will probably produce the Change in my situation which I wish & altho' you give me five Years to pay Mr Church I will do it sooner if sooner it shall be convenient.

I am Dr Sir   Yours &ca   RM

P.S. If you agree I will have a Mortgage drafted & send it for your Inspection.   RM

LC, Robert Morris Papers, Library of Congress.
    1. This letter concerns Morris's proposal to mortgage lands which he owned to secure a debt which he owed to John B. Church. For this debt and Morris's efforts to pay it, see the introductory note to Morris to H, June 7, 1795. See also Morris to H, July 20, November 16, 1795.
    2. Letter not found.
    3. For Morris's correspondence with James Swan concerning this "Negotiation," see Morris to H, November 16, 1795, note 2.
    4. Morrisville, one of two settlements by that name in Pennsylvania (see Morris to H, July 20, 1795, note 4), was and is located in Bucks County directly across the Delaware River from Trenton, New Jersey.

The Defence No. XXXIII [1]

[New York, December 19, 1795]

The course thus far pursued in the discussion of the 18th article [2] has inverted the order of it as it stands in the Treaty. It is composed of three clauses the two last of which have been first examined. I thought it adviseable in the outset to dispose of an objection which has been the principal source of clamour.

The first clause, or that which remains to be examined, enumerates the articles which it is agreed shall be deemed contraband of war. These are "all arms and implements serving for the purpose of war such as cannon, muskets, mortars, petards, bombs, grenadoers, carcasses, saucisses, carriages for cannon, musket rests, bandoliers, gun powder, match, salt petre, ball, pike, swords head pieces,

ADf, Hamilton Papers, Library of Congress; *The* [New York] *Herald; A Gazette for the Country*, December 19, 1795.
    1. For background to this document, see the introductory note to "The Defence No. I," July 22, 1795.
    2. See "The Defence No. XXXII," December 16, 1795. For the text of Article 18 of the Jay Treaty, see "Remarks on the Treaty . . . between the United States and Great Britain," July 9–11, 1795, note 63.

cuirasses, halberts, lances, javelins, horse furniture, ho[l]sters, belts and generally all other implements of War; as also timber for ship building, tar or rosin, copper in sheets, sails, hemp and cordage, and generally whatever may serve directly to the equipment of Vessels, unwrought iron & fir planks only excepted." All which articles are declared to be just objects of confiscation, when attempted to be carried to an enemy of either party.

It is well understood that War abridges the liberty of Trade of neutral nations; and that it is not lawful for them to supply either of two belligerent parties with any article deemed contraband of war nor may they supply any article whatever to a place besieged blockaded or invested. The former case includes a special catalogue of articles which have an immediate reference to war. The latter extends to all kinds of goods and merchandizes. The penalty in both cases is confiscation.

These positions have not been disputed. The only question which has been or can be raised must respect the enumeration of the articles which are to be considered as contraband.

In comparing the enumeration in the present Treaty with that of our former Treaties we find the differences to be these. Our former treaties include *"horses"* [3] and one of them "soldiers" [4] which our present does not; but our present includes "timber for ship building tar or resin copper in sheets sails hemp and cordage and generally whatever may serve directly to the equipment of vessels unwrought iron and fir planks only excepted" which are not to be found in our former treaties.

It is alleged that the including of these articles is an extension of the list of contraband beyond the limit of the *modern* law of nations; in support of which allegation it is affirmed that they have been excluded by the uniform tenor of the Treaties which have been formed for more than a Century past.

Though this position will not upon careful examination appear correct; yet it is so far founded as to claim an acknowlegement,

3. See Article 24 (originally 26) of the Treaty of Amity and Commerce with France, February 6, 1778 (Miller, *Treaties*, II, 21–23); Article 24 of the Treaty of Amity and Commerce with the Netherlands, October 8, 1782 (Miller, *Treaties*, II, 79); Article 9 of the Treaty of Amity and Commerce with Sweden, April 3, 1783 (Miller, *Treaties*, II, 130).

4. See Article 24 of the Treaty of Amity and Commerce with the Netherlands, October 8, 1782 (Miller, *Treaties*, II, 79).

that the article under consideration has in this instance pursued the *rigor* of the law of nations. 'Twas to this I alluded, when I observed that it contained one unpleasant ingredient.[5]

Though it be true, that far the greater proportion of modern Treaties exclude naval stores or articles for Ship building; yet this is not universally the fact.

By the third article of the Treaty of alliance and commerce between GB & Denmark in 1670 [6] the parties agree "not to furnish the enemies of each other with any provisions of War, as soldiers arms engines guns ships or other necessaries for the use of War nor to suffer the same to be furnished by their subjects." An explanation of this article was made by a Convention dated the 4 of July 1780 [7] which after enumerating as contraband the usual catalogue of military implements adds in the precise terms of our article "as also timber for shipbuilding, tar rosin, copper in sheets sails hemp and cordage and generally whatever may serve directly to the equipment of vessels, unwrought iron and fir planks only excepted."

In a series of Treaties between GBritain and Portugal down to the year 1703 [8] I do not discover that there has ever been a regulation of the articles, which are to be treated as contraband between those powers.

An⟨d⟩ between Sweden and Great Britain the 11th article of a Treaty entered into in 1661 (and still in force unaltered, though a subsequent Commercial Treaty was made between those powers

5. See "The Defence No. XXXII," December 16, 1795.
6. For this treaty, see Chalmers, *Collection of Treaties*, I, 78–87.
7. See Chalmers, *Collection of Treaties*, I, 97–98.
8. The treaties to which H is referring are the Articles of Peace and Commerce between Charles I of England and John IV of Portugal, January 29, 1672; the Treaty of Peace and Alliance between Oliver Cromwell and John IV of Portugal, signed at Westminster, July 10, 1654; the Marriage Treaty of Charles II of England and the Infanta of Portugal, August 18/28, 1661; the Treaty of Alliance Offensive and Defensive between Peter II of Portugal on the one hand and the emperor Leopold of Austria, Queen Anne of England, and the States General of the Netherlands on the other, "for asserting the Liberty of Spain, for averting the common Danger of all Europe, and for defending the Right of the most august House of Austria, to the Spanish Monarchy," to which was added a defensive treaty between Great Britain and Portugal, May 16, 1703; and the Treaty of Commerce between Queen Anne and Peter II of Portugal, December 27, 1703. The first and second treaties are printed in *A General Collection of Treatys*, II, 322–30; IIII, 97–111. The Anglo-Portuguese Marriage Treaty of 1661 is printed in Chalmers, *Collection of Treaties*, II, 286–96. See also Clive Parry, ed., *List of English Treaties, 1101–1968* (H.M. Stationery Office, 1969). The fourth, fifth, and sixth treaties are printed in Jenkinson, *Collection of Treaties*, I, 335–47, 347–53, 353–54.

as late as 1766) [9] subjects to confiscation generally all articles called *contraband,* and *especially money provisions* &c. The specification not being complete, naval stores are left upon the open ground of the law of nations, but money and provisions are superadded. This latitude would leave little doubt as to the intention to include naval stores.*

* Note. An opinion has been propagated [10] that Sweden armed in concert with Denmark in order to maintain the neutral right of carrying corn and Flour to France,[11] in opposition to the Convention of March 1793, between Great Britain and Russia, to prevent the same; [12] and that in consequence of this proceeding, the Remonstrances of these Powers have proved more successfull than we have been, in obtaining satisfaction from Great Britain.[13]

This opinion is throughout an error, made use of by those whose persevering aim has been by silencing truth, reason, and moderation, and inflaming the angry passions of the community to involve the Country in anarchy and war. The authors of this imposture, as well as the exalted Patriots who have seen in the memorial of our Envoy [14] the humiliation of our Country are referred to "a Collection of State papers relative to the War against France" published by *Debret,* in 1794.[15] The perusal of the Swedish State papers, as well as the memorials of the able and prudent Bernstorff [16] may teach these gentlemen a little of what is deemed good manners on these occasions.

So far from even remonstrating, much less arming on account of the British instruction of June 1793,[17] when that order was notified at Stockholm by the British Resident there, the Government of Sweden by their Resident at London acknowledge in terms too respectful to be repeated in the hearing of our exclusive Patriots, that Sweden was perfectly satisfied with the instruction [18]—since instead of payment which the order insured, all provisions, in virtue of an existing treaty between the two nations were liable to confiscation, when seized on their way to an enemy.

This Note is added for the purpose of refuting a popular error, and not to vindicate the instruction alluded to which I consider as an injury to the rights of neutral nations that has not been justified by the answers that have been given by Great Britain to the American and Danish memorials.[19]

9. The Treaty of Alliance between Charles II of England and Charles XI of Sweden was signed at Whitehall on October 21, 1661 (*A General Collection of Treatys,* III, 240–53). The commercial treaty is dated February 5, 1766 (Martens, *Recûeil,* I, 314–16. Chalmers, *Collection of Treaties,* I, 60–62).

10. The remainder of this note is not in H's handwriting.

In his first essay, "Cato" (Robert R. Livingston) wrote: ". . . Sweden and Denmark, who had received insults from Britain, were ready to make a common cause with her [the United States]; and as the marine of England and France were nearly ballanced, the weight of America had she been forced into the war, would have turned the scale, and have compleated the ruin of the British commerce, without any other effort than that of granting letters of marque. Independent of which without a violation of their neutrality by those acts of sovereignty which no one would dispute their right to exercise, they could involve the British trade in the utmost distress, by an additional duty on British tonnage, by granting advantages to rival manufactures, by retaining debts due to her merchants, till the injuries ours had sustained were compensated" (*The* [New York] *Argus, or Greenleaf's New Daily Advertiser,* July 15, 1795). See also "The Defence No. II," July 25, 1795, note 4.

For the authorship of the "Cato" articles, see the introductory note to "The Defence No. I," July 22, 1795.

It appears from these specimens, that there is not a perfect uniformity in the Conventions between Nations, and that no purely positive law of nations can be deduced from that source.

If we call to our aid the principles of reason and natural justice which are the great foundations of the law of nations, we shall not discover in this instance *data* as certain as could be wished for a satisfactory conclusion, and the soundest determination which we can adopt will be that beyond a certain point, the question is in a great degree arbitrary, and must depend materially upon conventional regulation between nation and nation. Hence it is that there is so great diversity in the stipulations of different Treaties, on this point, indicating that there is no absolute rule. Hence also it is that several nations at different times being at war have thought themselves au-

---

11. H is referring to the convention of armed neutrality between Sweden and Denmark, March 27, 1794 (James Brown Scott, ed., *The Armed Neutralities of 1780 and 1800* [New York, 1918], 440).

12. The convention was signed on March 25, 1793 (Debrett, *A Collection of State Papers*, I, 3–5).

13. See note 16.

14. See Thomas Pinckney to Lord Grenville, December 2, 1793 (PRO: F.O., 15/3). See also "The Defence No. XXXII," December 16, 1795, note 9.

15. Debrett, *A Collection of State Papers*, I.

16. On July 17, 1793, the British Minister at Copenhagen, Daniel Hailes, presented the Danish cabinet with a copy of the British instructions of June 8, 1793, together with a note justifying the direction of British policy against neutral trade with France (PRO: F.O., 115/3; Debrett, *A Collection of State Papers*, I, 326–29 [incomplete]; Martens, *Recûeil*, V, 569–73). For the British instructions, see "Remarks on the Treaty . . . between the United States and Great Britain," July 9–11, 1795, note 66. Count Andreas Peter von Bernstorff, the Danish Foreign Minister, replied in an official note, dated July 28, 1793, enclosing a memorial in which he defended the rights of neutral nations to trade with belligerent powers (Debrett, *A Collection of State Papers*, I, 329–34; Hailes to Lord Grenville, July 30, 1793 [PRO: F.O. (Great Britain), 22/17]).

17. See note 16.

18. The note to the Swedish government, dated July 26, 1793, of Charles Keene, British chargé d'affaires, accompanying a copy of the British instructions of June 8, 1793, and the reply of the Swedish chargé d'affaires at London, Erik Bergstedt, of August, 1793, are printed in Debrett, *A Collection of State Papers*, I, 344–46; Martens, *Recûeil*, V, 582–84.

19. No evidence of a written British reply to Bernstorff's memorial has been found. For accounts of conversations between Hailes and Bernstorff on matters in Bernstorff's memorial, see Hailes to Grenville, July 22, August 3, 17, 1793, March 22, 1794 (PRO: F.O. [Great Britain], 22/17, 22/18). For the United States memorial on the instructions, see note 14. For the British reply to this, see George Hammond to Edmund Randolph, April 11, 1794 (*ASP, Foreign Relations*, I, 449–50).

thorised to regulate by public declaration the articles which they would consider and treat as contraband.

The opinions of Writers will be found to support the article as it stands in the particular, which is now the subject of discussion.

VATEL we have before seen (B III C VII § 112) expressly ranks *naval stores* and *timber* under the denomination of contraband goods.[20]

HEINECIUS (*de navibus* &c Chap I § X. XI & XIV)[21] accords in the same proposition to the extent of whatsoever appertains to the eqipment of Vessels.*

Bynkershoeck[22] is less explicit. After laying it down as the general rule that naval stores or the materials of Ships are not contraband, he proceeds thus: "Yet it sometimes happens that the materials of ships may be prohibitted, if an enemy is in great want of them and without them cannot conveniently carry on the War" † and he afterwards cites with approbation several edicts or proclamations which the States General in different Wars with different nations have published, declaring those articles contraband—thus referring it to the belligerent party to judge of and pronounce the cases when they may rightfully be deemed so. And the same idea seems to have been adopted by GROTIUS ‡ and some other writers on public law. I have not met with one whose opinion excludes naval stores from the list of contraband.

Grotius in discussing this question divides goods into three classes

---

* *Vela, Restes et si quæ alia ad apparatum nauticum pertinent.*

† Quandoque tamen accidit ut & navium materia prohibeatur, si hostis ea quam maxime indigeat et absque ea commode bellum gerere haud possit. Quæstionum Juris Publici L I Cap X Page 80.

‡ B III C I § V[23]

20. See "The Defence No. XXXII," December 16, 1795, note 6.

In the Hamilton Papers, Library of Congress, are some notes written by Rufus King which read: "Bynkershoek has also classed naval stores in ye Cat. of contraband. Puff. & Heinecius as well as Vattel & Marten, have also placed them under this Denomination. The Opinion of the Writers on the Law of Nations is believed to agree in this point."

21. J. G. Heineccius, *De Navibus Ob Vecturam Vetitarum Mercium Comissis*, in *Io. Gottlieb Heineccii, potent. Prussorum Regis quondam a Consil. sanctior. Iur. ac Philosoph. in ill. Frideric. Professoris publ. ord. Operum ad Universam Iuris Prudentiam, Philosophiam, et Litteras Humaniores Pertinentium Tomus Secundus* (Geneva: Cramer and Philibert, 1746), II, 321–22, 322–24, 328–29.

22. Bynkershoek, *Quæstionum.*

23. Grotius, *On the Law of War and Peace.*

1   those which are of use only in war as arms &c   2   those which
serve only for pleasure   3   those useful for peaceable as well as
warlike purposes "as money *provisions* ships and *naval stores*" concerning which he argues in substance that the first class are clearly
contraband, that the second class are clearly not contraband and
that the third class may or may not be so according to the state &
circumstances of the war; alleging that if necessary to our defence
they may be intercepted but upon condition of restitution unless
there be just cause to the contrary; which just cause is explained
by the example of sending them to a besieged or blockaded place.

The reasoning about this third class has a very inconvenient latitude. It subjects the Trade of neutral nations too extensively to the
discretion of belligerent powers and yet there is a serious embarrassment about drawing the true line; one which will duely conciliate
the safety of the belligerent with that of the neutral party.

What definition of contraband, consulting reason alone, shall we
adopt? Shall we say that none but articles peculiar to war ought to
receive this denomination? But is even powder exclusively *applicable*
to War? Are nitre and surphur its chief ingredients *peculiar* to
War? Are they not all useful for other purposes; some of them, in
medicine & other important arts? Shall we say that none but articles
prepared or organised for war as their primary object ought to have
that character? But what substantial difference can reason know between the supply to our enemy of powder, and that of sulphur and
salt petre, the easily convertible materials of this mischievous compound?

How would either of these definitions or any other comport with
what those of our treaties, which are thought unexceptionable in
this particular, have regulated or with what is common in the Treaties between other nations? Under which of them shall we bring
horses and their furniture?

If we say that in wars by land these are instruments little less
important, than men and for that reason ought to be comprehended
it may be asked in return what can be more necessary in Wars by
sea than the materials of Ships, and why should they not for the
like reason be equally comprehended?

In wars between maritime nations, who transfer its calamities
from the land to the Ocean and wage their most furious conflicts

on that element, whose dominions cannot be attacked or defended without a superiority in naval strength, who moreover possess distant territories, the protection & commercial advantages of which depend upon the existence & support of navies, it is difficult to maintain that it is against reason or against those principles which regulate the description of contraband, to consider as such the materials which appertain to the construction and equipment of Ships.

It is not a sufficient objection that these articles are useful for other purposes & especially for those of maritime commerce. Horses are of primary utility in Agriculture; and it has been seen that there are other articles indisputably on the list of contraband which are intirely within the principle of that objection.

RUTHERFORD, a sensible modern Writer,* after truly observing "that the notion of contraband goods is of some latitude, so that it is not easy precisely to determine what are and what are not of this sort—that all *warlike stores* are certainly contraband but that still the question returns what are to be reckoned *warlike* stores"— after noticing the division of articles by Grotius and the difficulties with regard to the third class—draws this conclusion that "Where a war *is carried on by sea* as well as by land not only ships of war which are already built but the materials for building or repairing of Ships will come under the notion of *warlike stores.*" This is a precise idea and it must be confessed, on principle, not an irrational one.

If we resort to the opinions which have been entertained & evidenced in our country they will be found to have given great extent to the idea of contraband. Congress by an act of May 8th 1777 [25] establishing the form of Commissions for Commanders of Privateers authorise them "to attack subdue and take all ships and other vessels whatsoever carrying soldiers arms gunpowder ammunition *provisions* or any other contraband goods to any of the British armies or ships of War employed against the U States." And in their act of the 27 of November 1780 acceding in part to the rule of the armed neutrality [26] they declare that contraband shall be thereafter

* Institutes of Natural Law Book II Chap IX § XIX [24]
24. Thomas Rutherforth, *Institutes of Natural Law: Being the substance of a Course of Lectures on Grotius de Jure Belli et Pacis* (Cambridge, 1754-1756).
25. *JCC*, VII, 339-40.
26. This is a reference to "Additional instructions to the captains and commanders of all ships of war and private armed vessels, who shall have commis-

confined to the articles contained under this character in our Treaty with France, indicating, by this, their opinion that the list of those articles is abriged by that Treaty. If the first mentioned act was well founded (and there are strong reasons for it) it establishes that even *provisions* may be contraband, if going directly to *invading* fleets & armies; which affords an instance of their being so,[27] in addition to the cases of places besieged blockaded or invested. And as to naval stores I do not fear to be mistaken when I assert a belief that the common opinion of those persons in this country whose contemplation had embraced the subject included them in the catalogue of contraband.

Nevertheless from the number of modern Treaties which exclude from that list naval stores, and moreover from the manifest interest of Nations truly considered to narrow the rights of war in favour of those of peace, this clause of the treaty, which takes a different route, is to be regretted as pursuing the Rigor of the law of Nations. Still however it cannot be objected to as a departure from that law; and agreeing with the course observed by Great Britain antecedent to the Treaty, it does not place our trade in these articles upon a worse footing than it was independently of the Treaty.

The period of the negotiation was more unpropitious to a change for the better. In the midst of any maritime war a belligerent nation enjoying a naval superiority was likely to have been tenacious of a right which she supposed herself to possess to intercept naval

---

sions or letters of marque and reprisal" (*JCC*, XVIII, 1097–98). The first two points of these instructions were similar to those of the declaration of armed neutrality of 1780 (see "Remarks on the Treaty . . . between the United States and Great Britain," July 9–11, 1795, note 60), with the addition of a clause which allowed the obstruction of neutral vessels "employed in carrying contraband goods or soldiers to the enemies of these United States." The third section reads: "The term contraband shall be confined to those articles which are expressly declared to be such in the treaty of amity and commerce, of the 6th of February, 1778, between these United States and his Most Christian Majesty, namely, arms, great guns, bombs with their fuses and other things belonging to them, cannon ball, gun powder, match, pikes, swords, lances, spears, halberts, mortars, petards, grenadoes, saltpetre, muskets, musket ball, bucklers, helmets, breastplates, coats of mail, and the like kind of arms proper for arming soldiers, musket rests, belts, horses with their furniture, and all other warlike instruments whatever." The list is similar to that given by Catharine II of Russia in the third section of the declaration of armed neutrality. See Scott, *The Armed Neutralities of 1780 and 1800*, 274, 329.

27. At this point in the newspaper the following words were added: "(analogous to the case heretofore put of a besieging army)."

supplies to her enemy. But in a war in which it was more than ordinarily possible that the independent existence of a Nation might depend on the retaining that naval superiority, it was to have been foreseen that she would not consent to relinquish such a right. The alternative was to insert the article as it stands or to omit it wholly.

Had it been omitted the condition of naval stores would have been the same as with it. But our Merchants would then have continued to be exposed to uncertain risks, which is always a great inconvenience. It is desireable in similar cases to have a fixed rule. Merchants can then accommodate their speculations to the rule; and causes of national contention are avoided. It is in this view to be regretted that the cases when provisions may be treated as contraband could not have been agreed upon; but as this was impracticable, the next best thing has been done, by establishing the certainty of compensation in all such cases. This gives one important species of security, obviates one source of contention. And if really there may be other cases than the admitted ones, in which provisions can fairly be deemed contraband, (as the one designated by the act of Congress of May 1777) [28] the securing of compensation was truly a *point gained* by the article.

But while I confess that the including of naval stores among contraband articles is an ineligible feature of the Treaty, I ought to declare that its consequences to the interests of the U States, as it regards the Trade in those articles in time of War, do not appear to me important. War between other nations, when we are at peace, will always increase the demand for our bottoms so as to require much additional building of Vessels and probably to produce a more beneficial species of employment of the naval stores our country affords, than that of their exportation for sale.

The adversaries of the Treaty are eagle-eyed to spy out instances in which it omits any favourable minutiae which are found in our other Treaties but they forget to ballance the account by particulars which distinguish it favourably from those Treaties. Of this nature

28. The act of May 8, 1777, established a new form of commission for commanders of private ships of war, authorizing them "to attack, subdue, and take all ships and other vessels whatsoever, carrying soldiers, arms, gun-powder, ammunition, provisions or any other contraband goods to any of the British armies or ships of war employed against . . . [the] United States" (*JCC*, VII, 339).

is the omission of horses from the list of contraband, and still more the salutary regulations with regard to vessels & their cargoes going to places besieged blockaded or invested. I do not discover that these useful provisions, or their equivalents, are in either of our Treaties with France Holland or Sweden.

It has been said in reference to this article that "whenever the law of Nations has been a topic for consideration, the result of the Treaty accommodates Great Britain in relation to one or both of the republics at War with her as well as in the abandonment of the rights and interests of the U States." And the following examples are given to each of which will be annexed a reply.[29]

I   "American Vessels bound to Great Britain are protected by sea papers against French and Dutch searches: but when bound to France or Holland are left exposed to British searchers without regard to Ships papers." The truth of this proposition depends on another, which is, that the sea papers are to be absolutely conclusive; but reasons have been given for doubting this construction, which it has been remarked does not obtain in practice. And it is certainly a violent one, in as much as it puts it in the power of the neutral to defeat the rights of the belligerent party in points of great consequence to its safety.

II   "American provisions in American vessels bound to the enemies of Great Britain are left by the treaty to the seizure and use of Great Britain; but provisions whether American or not in American vessels cannot be touched by the enemies of Great Britain." The construction of the Treaty upon which this difference is supposed has been demonstrated to be erroneous. The difference therefore does not exist.

III   "British property in American vessels is not subject to French or Dutch confiscation. French or Dutch property in American Vessels is subject to British confiscation." This was the case before the Treaty, which makes no alteration in the matter. Moreover it is counterballanced by this circumstance—that American property in British vessels is subject to confiscation by France or Holland, but American property in French or Dutch vessels is not subject to confiscation by Great Britain.

29. H took the quotations which follow from Article III of the petition "To the General Assembly of the Commonwealth of Virginia" (*The* [Richmond] *Virginia Gazette, and General Advertiser,* November 11, 1795). See "The Defence No. XXXII," December 16, 1795, note 4.

IV "Articles of Ship building bound to the enemies of Great Britain for the equipment of vessels of Trade only are contraband— bound to Great Britain for the equipment of vessels of War are not contraband." This also was the case before the Treaty, which consequently has not in this particular more than in the former produced any benefit to one party to the prejudice of the other. I forbear to dwell upon the article of horses as falling under a contrary discrimination; nor shall I insist on the additional circumstance that all American goods not generally contraband, if going to a place besieged blockaded or invested by French or Dutch forces are liable to confiscation by France or Holland; if going to a place besieged blockaded or invested by British forces are not liable to confiscation by Great Britain.

Differences of these several kinds are the accidental results of the varying views of different contracting powers; and from slender grounds of blame or praise of the respective contracts made with them.

The form of the criticism last stated leaves little doubt that it was designed to insinuate an intention in this article to favour the MONARCHY of G Britain at the expence of the REPUBLICS of France & Holland. The candour of it may be judged of by the two facts, first that it makes no alteration in this view in the antecedent state of things, and 2dly That the relative situation of Holland as the enemy of Great Britain [30] is subsequent to the adjustment of the article.   CAMILLUS [31]

30. Late in 1794, French armies had overrun the Netherlands. On May 16, 1795, at The Hague, the government of the United Provinces signed a Treaty of Peace and Alliance with the French Republic agreeing to fight in the European war on the side of France (Martens, *Recueil*, VI, 88–91).

31. On the back of this document H wrote: "Mr. Sands is requested to be so obliging as to copy this by Monday Morning." See "The Defence No. XXI," October 30, 1795, note 11.

From John Lowell, Junior [1]

Boston, December 19, 1795. "I . . . enclose to you two notes of hand against two Gentlemen in New York for 750 dollars each.[2] The money you perceive ought to have been long since paid and I am informed that the nonpayment has not been occasioned by inability. The notes were put into my hands to collect under the ex-

pectation that ye parties would have been in this place some time
since. Having no acquaintance with any profissional Gentlemen in
your City, I have taken ye liberty to forward them to you. . . ."³

ALS, Hamilton Papers, Library of Congress.
   1. Lowell, a Boston attorney, was the son of John Lowell, the United States
judge for the District of Massachusetts.
   2. Lowell's letter concerns the collection of two notes signed by Edward
and Elias Parker. An entry in H's Law Register, 1795–1804, on this case reads:
"Sup. Court ⎤
Isaac Parker ⎟
& Oliver Mann ⎥   No Retainer
      v   ⎟   £800 upon Promise
Edward Parker ⎟
& Elias Parker ⎦
June 14th [1796]   Capias
June 20

              requested Sheriff not to serve writ at request of
              Plaintiff Isaac Parker
              See Letter Lowel June 15 P. Hole
              returned papers ended"
(D, partially in H's handwriting, New York Law Institute, New York City;
also in forthcoming Goebel, *Law Practice*, III). Isaac Parker, a lawyer in
Castine, District of Maine, was a member of the House of Representatives
from 1797 to 1799. Oliver Mann was a Boston physician. Edward Parker is
listed in the New York City directories from 1791 to 1796 as a merchant.
Elias Parker is probably the same Elias Parker who during the American Revolution was first a cadet in the Third Continental Artillery and then a lieutenant in the First Massachusetts Regiment. After the war, he served as a captain in the Virginia militia. See Benjamin Goodhue to H, December 8, 1798.
The capias, dated May 7, 1796, is in the Hamilton Papers, Library of Congress. Lowell's letter to H, dated June 15, 1796, has not been found.
   3. H endorsed this letter: "John Lowel Jun with two Notes of hand. See
Rect for Notes within."

From George Washington

Phila. 22d. Decr. 1795.

My dear Sir,

   Have you seen or heard more of young Fayette since you last
wrote to me on that subject? ¹ Where did he go to? Did you deliver him the letter I sent under cover to you for him? His case
gives me pain, and I do not know how to get relieved from it. His
sensibility I fear is hurt, by his not acknowledging the receipt of
my letter to him; and yet, if considerations of a higher nature are

opposed to a more uncovert countenance, it must be submitted to. If he wants money, I am ready to furnish it.

'Ere this, I presume you have seen the long promised vindication, or rather accusation.[2] What do you think of it and what notice should be taken of it? You are fully acquainted with my Sentiments relative to the rival & warring powers of F. & E; and have heard as strong sentiments from me with respect to both, as ever he did. His declaration, that he was always opposed to the Commercial part of the Negociation is as impudent and insolent an assertion, as it is false, if he means more than that it was contingent (as the Instructions to Mr. Jay declare) and to apply the knowledge of it to me. But if you have seen his performance, I shall leave you to judge of it, without any comments of mine.

With much sincerity & truth   I am always & Affectly. Yours

Go: Washington

Alexr. Hamilton Esqr.

ALS, Hamilton Papers, Library of Congress; ADfS, George Washington Papers, Library of Congress.

1. H to Washington, November 26, 1795. For information on George Washington Motier Lafayette, see H to Washington, October 16, 26, November 19, 26, 1795; Washington to H, October 29, November 10, 18, 23, 28, 1795.

2. Edmund Randolph's *A Vindication of Mr. Randolph's Resignation* (Philadelphia: Printed by Samuel H. Smith, No. 118, Chesnut Street, 1795) was published on December 18, 1795. See Timothy Pickering to H, December 14, 1795, note 2.

[*The Defence No. XXXIV*] [1]

[New York, December 23, 1795]

ADf, in the handwriting of Rufus King, Hamilton Papers, Library of Congress; *The* [New York] *Herald, A Gazette for the Country*, December 23, 1795.

1. For background to this document, see the introductory note to "The Defence No. I," July 22, 1795. Except for some words and phrases and one full paragraph inserted by H, the draft of "The Defence No. XXXIV" is in the handwriting of Rufus King.

To George Washington

N York December 24. 1795

Sir

I have received your letter of the   .[1]

Young La Fayette [2] is now with me. I had before made an offer of money in your name & have repeated it—but the answer is that they are not yet in want and will have recourse when needed

Young La Fayette appears melancholy and has grown thin. A letter lately received from his mother which speaks of something which she wishes him to mention to you (as I learn from his preceptor) [3] has quickened his sensibility and increased his regret. If I am satisfied that the present state of things is likely to occasion a durable gloom, endangering the health & in some sort the mind of the young man, I shall conclude, on the strength of former permission, to send him to you for a short visit—the rather as upon repeated reflection I am not able to convince myself that there is any real inconvenience in the step and as there are certainly delicate opposite sides. But it will be my endeavour to make him content to remain away.

I have read with care Mr. Randolph's pamphlet.[4] It does not surprise me. I consider it as amounting to a confession of guilt and I am persuaded this will be the universal opinion. His attempts against you are viewed by all whom I have seen as base. They will certainly fail of their aim, and will do good, rather than harm to the public cause and to yourself. It appears to me that by You no notice can be or ought to be taken of the publication. It contains its own antidote.

I perceive that Mr. Fauchet & with him Mr. Randolph have imputed to me the having asked to *accompany you* on the Western expedition.[5]

The true course of the fact was as follows: You had mentioned and that early in the affair *as a question for consideration*—the propriety and expediency of your going out with the Militia. But no opinion had been given to you and you had not announced *any determination* on the point when my letter to you of the 19th of

September was written. That letter does not ask to *accompany you*, but to be permitted to go on the expedition. A short time after it was sent, you mentioned to me that you had concluded to go as far as Carlisle in the first instance, and to take your ulterior determination according to circumstances and proposed to me to accompany you.

My request was independent of your going or not going. Its objects were 1. that mentioned in my letter 2dly an anxious desire that by being present, I might have it in my power, in a case *very interesting to my department*, as well as the Government generally, to promote, in the event of your not going on the expedition, a course of conduct the best calculated to obviate impediments & secure its object. I had serious fears of treachery in Governor Mifflin,[6] and I thought that even Lee [7] might miss the policy of the case in some particulars &c &c. These were the considerations that determined me & not the little cunning policy by which Mr. Fauchet supposes me to have been governed.

I greatly miscalculate if a strong and general current does not now set in favor of the Government on the question of the Treaty.

With true respect & attachment   I have the honor to be Sir Your obed ser   A Hamilton

The President of the U States

ALS, George Washington Papers, Library of Congress.
    1. Space left blank in MS. See Washington to H, December 22, 1795.
    2. George Washington Motier Lafayette. For background information on Lafayette, see H to Washington, October 16, 26, November 19, 26, 1795; Washington to H, October 29, November 10, 18, 23, 28, December 22, 1795.
    On December 21, 1795, the following entry appears in H's Cash Book, 1795–1804: "George Washington President   Dr. for this sum paid for an express to Messrs. Frestel & Motier   16" (AD, Hamilton Papers, Library of Congress; also in forthcoming Goebel, *Law Practice*, III).
    3. Felix Frestel, Lafayette's tutor.
    4. For "Mr. Randolph's pamphlet," see Timothy Pickering to H, December 14, 1795, note 2; Washington to H, December 22, 1795, note 2.
    5. This is a reference to the military expedition against the insurgents of western Pennsylvania in October, 1794.
    6. Thomas Mifflin was governor of Pennsylvania during the Whiskey Insurrection and commander in chief of the Pennsylvania militia which marched against the insurgents.
    7. Henry Lee was governor of Virginia during the Whiskey Insurrection. Washington appointed Lee commander in chief of the militia army which marched against the insurgents. See H to Lee, second letter of August 25, 1794; Lee to H, September 2, 1794.

[*The Defence No. XXXV*] [1]

[New York, December 26, 1795]

ADf, in the handwriting of Rufus King, Hamilton Papers, Library of Congress; *The* [New York] *Herald; A Gazette for the Country*, December 26, 1795.
 1. For background to this document, see the introductory note to "The Defence No. I," July 22, 1795. Except for some phrases, sentences, and two paragraphs inserted by H, the draft of "The Defence No. XXXV" is in the handwriting of Rufus King.
 On the back of this document H wrote: "Mr. Moreton will oblige me by copying the within. It will be the last with which he will be troubled." Below H's note is written: " 'But the Master whom I serve quickens what's dear and makes my Labours pleasure.' JM."

To Timothy Pickering

New York, Dec. 26th, 1795.

Dear Sir:

Mr. Cutting has given to me a perusal of his papers, respecting his agency in revealing our seamen from British impress.[1] He wished my opinion *professionally* respecting the validity of his claim, which I declined to give, because it would contradict certain maxims I have prescribed to myself with regard to public questions pending while I was part of the administration.

But there are reasons which induce me to convey to you privately my view of the subject.

It appears to me clearly established that Mr. Cutting rendered a very meritorious and an important service to the United States. Its value is not to be estimated merely by the number of persons relieved, but by the influence of the exertion upon other cases—indeed upon our trade generally with the English ports at the juncture. It is also a service very interesting to the feelings of all our citizens—and there was certainly much good zeal and address displayed upon the occasion. It sufficiently appears, too, that the nature of the case must have involved considerable expense, and in ways which frequently would not admit of after authentication.

Under these circumstances I feel a strong impression that it is of the policy as well as of the justice of the government to go lengths in giving satisfaction to Mr. Cutting. 'Tis a case which calls for liberality, not scrupulous or prying investigation. Mr. Cutting's own testimony from necessity ought to be received as to expenditures. This observation, to be sure, has reasonable limits. But still the case demands that the testimony should be received with influential effect.

Mr. Dorhman [2] is an example of similar compensation in circumstances not unlike. Our own citizen has not an inferior claim.

What has been hitherto done for Mr. Cutting appears to be manifestly inadequate. If it could be supposed that there was risk of doing too much, it is of the reputation of the government that the error should be on that side. Care ought to be taken that a zealous citizen, who has rendered real service, should not be out of pocket, and out of reputation, too, by his bargain. I include a reasonable compensation for service as well as reimbursement of expenses.

These ideas will, I am sure, be received as they are intended.

Copy, Massachusetts Historical Society, Boston; copy, George Washington Papers, Library of Congress.

1. During the American Revolution John Browne Cutting was Apothecary General of Hospitals in the Eastern Department from 1777 to 1779 and in the Middle Department from 1779 to 1780.

Cutting's "agency" is explained in the following letter which Thomas Jefferson wrote to George Washington on February 7, 1792: "An account presented to me by Mr. John B. Cutting, for expenditures incurred by him in liberating the seamen of the United States in British ports during the impressments which took place under that Government in the year 1790, obliges me to recall some former transaction to your mind.

"You will be pleased to recollect the numerous instances of complaint or information to us, about that time, of the violences committed on our seafaring citizens in British ports by their press gangs and officers; and that not having even a Consul there at that time, it was thought fortunate that a private citizen, who happened to be on the spot, step forward for their protection; that it was obvious that these exertions on his part must be attended with expense, and that a particular demand of £50 sterling for this purpose coming incidentally to my knowledge, it was immediately remitted to Mr. Cutting, with a request to account for it in convenient time. He now presents an account of all his expenditures in his business, which I have the honor to communicate therewith." (LC, RG 59, Domestic Letters of the Department of State, Vol. 5, February 4, 1792–December 31, 1793, National Archives.) See also Jefferson to H, January 26, 1792, note 1.

Cutting petitioned Congress for compensation for his expenses in 1792, and on May 4, 1792, the House resolved: "That, in consideration of certain expenditures on behalf of the United States, made by John Brown Cutting, in the year one thousand seven hundred and ninety, there be advanced and paid to the said John Brown Cutting, the sum of two thousand dollars, out of any money not otherwise appropriated: and that the Secretary of State be authorized to inquire into the entire claim of the said John Brown Cutting against the United States; and upon receipt of the proofs and exhibits in support thereof, to ascertain what sum shall thereupon appear to be due to or from him . . ." (*Journal of the House*, I, 597). In accordance with this resolution, on May 8, 1792, Congress enacted "An Act concerning the Claim of John Brown Cutting against the United States" (6 *Stat.* 10). On February 27, 1799, the report of Secretary of State Timothy Pickering on Cutting's claim was ordered to lie on the table (*Journal of the House*, III, 497).

2. On June 21, 1780, the Continental Congress appointed "Arnold Henry Dohrman, of the city of Lisbon, merchant, . . . agent for the United States, in the kingdom of Portugal, for the transaction of such affairs of the said States as may be committed to his direction" (*JCC*, XVII, 541). In subsequent years his principal task was to aid American seaman who had been brought to Lisbon as prisoners. For Dohrman's compensation, see *JCC*, XXXIII, 586–88.

To George Washington

[New York, December 27–30, 1795] [1]

Sir

I have the pleasure to send you enclosed two letters one from Young La Fayette the other from his Preceptor.[2] They appear reconciled to some further delay.

I take the liberty to inclose copy of a letter to the Secy of State respecting Mr. Cutting.[3] I do not know upon the whole what sort of a man Mr. Cutting is, and I have heared unfavourable whispers. But as to the particular subject of his ⟨claim⟩ [4] I really think it deserves an indulgent consideration, and that it is expedient & right to favour it to a liberal extent. Some reflections have made me think it adviseable to place the matter under your eye. Neither the Secy of State nor Mr. Cutting will be informed of this.

I wrote you a few lines two or three days ago [5] in answer to your letter concerning Mr. Randolph's pamphlet.[6]

Yr. very respectful & Affect servt   A Hamilton

The President of the US

ALS, George Washington Papers, Library of Congress.
    1. On the cover of this letter, Washington wrote: "Colo. Alexr Hamilton recd. 31st. Decr. 1796." This is a mistake, for the year should read "1795."
    In *JCHW*, VI, 82, and *HCLW*, X, 140, this letter is dated "Dec 95."
    2. George Washington Motier Lafayette to Washington, December 25, 1795

(ALS, George Washington Papers, Library of Congress); Felix Frestel to Washington, December 25, 1795 (ALS, George Washington Papers, Library of Congress). For information on Lafayette and Frestel, see H to Washington, October 16, 26, November 19, 26, December 24, 1795; Washington to H, October 29, November 10, 18, 23, 28, December 26, 1795.

3. H to Timothy Pickering, December 26, 1795.
4. The word within broken brackets has been taken from *JCHW*, VI, 82.
5. H to Washington, December 24, 1795.
6. Washington to H, December 22, 1795.

American Jacobins

[1795–1796] [1]

For the Minerva [2]

It is remarkable how uniform our Jacobins have been in blaming and vilifying our own Government and in excusing and justifying the conduct of the French towards us. Before there was ever the pretence of any subject of complaint against this Country France violated that article of her Treaty with us which stipulates that *free* ships shall make *free* goods.[3]—This breach of Treaty was apologised for by the necessity of putting herself upon an equal footing with her enemies. Genet came to this Country with the affectation of not desiring to embark us in the war—and yet he did all in his power by indirect means to drag us into it—He insulted our Government and set it at defiance. He endeavoured without the national sanction to carry on expeditions against the possessions of neighbouring nations with whom we were at peace.[4] He did not claim our participation in the war on the score of any obligation we were under to take part in it; but he endeavoured to seduce the passions of the people, to create a scism between them and their government, to disorganise and thus to extort from the passions of our Citizens what never could have been expected from the rational policy of our public Councils—Yet our Jacobins vindicated *Genet* and calumniatd our Government—In pursuance of an earnest desire to preserve peace Our Government has made a Treaty with Great Britain, which while it promotes important interests of our own is so perfectly consistent with our engagements with France that it excepts them from controul by an express and positive clause; [5] so that the moment it can be shewn that our Treaties with France require *a thing* of us, any clause in the Treaty with Britain which may be in term contrary to it, becomes *ipso facto* inoperative as to that thing. Yet our Jacobins have represented this Treaty, this ⟨–⟩ measure of peace, as the effort of a deep laid design to form an intimate connection with Great Britain and dissolve all connection with France; and indefatigable in their endeavour to transfer their discontents to the Rulers of France, to deprive the Government of the cre⟨dit⟩ of preserving peace, they seem at length to have succeeded.

ADf, Hamilton Papers, Library of Congress.
    1. This document is undated. On the first page of the MS John Church Hamilton wrote: "[1796?]."
    2. [New York] *American Minerva: an Evening Advertiser.* This article has not been found in this newspaper.
    3. This provision was stipulated in Article 23 (originally 25) of the Franco-American Treaty of Amity and Commerce of February 6, 1778 (Miller, *Treaties*, II, 20).
    4. For Edmond Charles Genet's conduct in recruiting forces in the United States to be used against Spanish and British colonies in North America, see "Proposed Presidential Message to Congress Concerning Revocation of Edmond Charles Genet's Diplomatic Status," January 6–13, 1794, note 1.
    5. A sentence in Article 25 of the Jay Treaty reads: "Nothing in this treaty contained shall however be construed or operate contrary to former and existing Public Treaties with other Sovereigns or States" (Miller, *Treaties*, II, 262).

Relations with France [1]

[1795–1796] [2]

There are circumstances, which render it too probable that a very delicate state of things is approaching between the United States and France. When threatened with foreign danger, from whatever quarter, it is highly necessary that we should be united at home; and considering our partiality hitherto for France, it is necessary towards this Union, that we should understand what has really been

ADf, Hamilton Papers, Library of Congress.
    1. A note, which accompanies this article and which is in H's handwriting, reads: "The following paper was written some time since. It was laid by from a reluctance in the writer to do any thing that might seem like widening the breach. But the events foreseen ripen so fast that it becomes indispensable to give a free course to the truth. A B."
    2. This document is undated. On the first page of the MS John Church Hamilton wrote: "[1796]." In *JCHW*, VII, 594, and *HCLW*, VI, 206, this document is dated "1796."

the conduct of that Country towards us. It is time for plain truth; which can only be unacceptable to the hirelings or dupes of that Nation.

France in our Revolution–War took part with us. At first she afforded us secret and rather scanty succours, which were more the complection of a disposition to nourish a temporary disturbance in the dominions of a rival power, than of an intention to second a Revolution. The capture of Burgoyne and his army decided the 'till then hesitating councils of France—produced the ackowlegement of our independence and Treaties of Commerce and defensive alliance. These again produced the War which ensued between France and Great Britain.

The cooperation and succour of France after this period were efficient and liberal. They were extremely useful to our cause and no doubt contributed materially to its success.

The primary motives of France for the assistance which she gave us was obviously to enfeeble a hated and powerful Rival, by breaking in pieces the British Empire. A secondary motive was to extend her relations of commerce in the new world, and to acquire additional security for her possessions there, by forming a connection with this country when detached from Great Britain. To ascribe to her any other motives—to suppose that she was actuated by Friendship towards us, or by a regard for our particular advantage, is to be ignorant of the springs of action which invariably regulate the Cabinets of Princes. He must be a fool, who can be credulous enough to believe that a despotic Court aided a popular revolution from regard to Liberty, or friendship to the principles of such a Revolution.

In forming the conditions upon which France lent her aid, she was too politic to attempt to take any unworthy advantage of our situation. But they are much mistaken, who imagine that she did not take care to make a good bargain for herself. Without granting to us any material privilege in any of her external possessions, she secured in perpetuity a right to participate in our trade on the foot of the most favoured nation. But what is far more important, she in return for the guarantee of our sovereignty and Independence obtained our guarantee of her West India possessions in every future *defensive* ⟨war.⟩ [3] This may appear at first sight a mutual & equal

3. Bracketed material has been taken from *JCHW*, VII, 594–600.

advantage, but in the permanent operation it is not so. The Guarantee of our sovereignty and Independence, which is never likely to be again drawn into question, must hereafter be essentially nominal: While our guarantee of the West India possessions must grow into a solid advantage, increasing in importance as we advance in strength and exposing us often to the chances of being engaged in wars, in which we may have no direct interest. However this guarantee may be regarded as nominal on our part in this very early stage of our national career, it cannot be so in time to come. We shall be able to afford it with effect and our faith will oblige us to do so.

But whatever were the motives of France and though the conditions of alliance may be in their permanent tend⟨ency⟩ more beneficial to her than to us—it was our duty to be faithful to the engagements which we contracted with her—and it even became us without scanning too rigidly those motives to yield ourselves to the impulses of kind and cordial se⟨nt⟩iments toward a Power by which we were succoured in so perilous a crisis.

Nor should we ever lightly depart from the line of conduct which these principles dictate. But they ought not to be carried so far as to occasion us to shut our eyes against the just causes of complaint which France has given or may hereafter give us. They ought not to blind us to the real nature of any instances of an unfair or unfriendly policy which we have experienced or may hereafter experience from that Country. Let us Cherish faith justice and as far as possible good will but let us not be dupes.

It is certain that in the progress and towards the close of our Revolution–War the views of France, in several important particulars, did not accord with our interest. She manifestly favoured and intrigued to effect the sacrifice of our pretension on the Mississippi to Spain. She looked coldly upon our claim to the privileges we enjoy in the cod fisheries—and she patronised our negotiating with Great Britain, *without* the previous *acknowlegement of our Independence:* a conduct which whatever colour of moderation may be attempted to be given to it can only be rationally explained into *the desire of leaving us in such a state of half-peace half-hostility with Great Britain as would necessarily render us dependent upon France.*

Since the peace every careful observer has been convinced that the policy of the French Government has been adverse to our acquiring internally the *consistency of which we were capable*,[4] in other words, a well constituted and efficient Government. Her Agents every where supported with too little reserve that feeble and anarchial system—the old confederation; which had brought us almost to the last stage of national *nothingness*, and which remained the theme of their eulogies, when every enlightened and virtuous man of this country perceived and acknowleged its radical defects and the necessity of essential alterations.

The truth of all this, of which no vigilant and unbiassed friend to his Country had before the least doubt, has been fully confirmed to us by the p⟨res⟩ent Government of France, which has formally proclaimed to us and to the World, the *Machieavellian* conduct of the old Government towards this Country.[5] Nor can we suspect the promulgation to have been the effect of the enmity of the *new* against the *old* Government—for our own records and our own observations assure us that there is no misrepresentation.

This disclosure, which has not sufficiently attracted the attention of the American People, is very serious and instructive. Surely it ought to put us upon our guard—to convince us that it is at least possible the succeeding Rulers of France may have been on some

4. See, for example, a letter from Pierre Henri Hélène Lebrun-Tondu, French Minister of Foreign Affairs, to the president of the National Assembly, dated December 20, 1792. In this letter Lebrun, in commenting on the relationship between the monarchy and the United States, wrote that "dans le temps même où ce bon peuple nous exprimait de la manière la plus touchante son amitié et sa reconnaissance, Vergennes et Montmorin pensaient 'qu'il ne convenait pas à la France de lui donner tout la consistance dont il était susceptible, parce qu'il acquerrait une force dont il serait probablement tenté d'abuser' " (*Archives Parlementaires de 1787 à 1860* [Paris, 1868–], LV, 349).

5. On January 13, 1795, James Monroe, United States Minister Plenipotentiary to France, wrote to Edmund Randolph: "The operations of this government continue to progress in the same course that they have done for some time past. During the time of Robespierre, a period of the administration which is emphatically called the reign of terror, much havoc was made, not only on the rights of humanity, but great confusion was likewise introduced, in other respects, in the affairs of government. It has been the systematic effort of the administration to repair this waste, and heal the bleeding wounds of the country, and in this, great progress has been made. By the same report which proposed the execution of the violated articles of the treaty of amity and commerce with the United States, it was likewise proposed to open wide the door of commerce to every citizen (excluding them from navigation only) and which was adopted . . ." (Monroe, *A View of the Conduct of the Executive*, 99).

occasions tinctured with a similar spirit. They ought to remember
that the magnanimity and kindness of France under the former
governt. were as much trumpeted by its partisans among us as are
now the magnanimity & kindness of the present Governt. What say
facts?

Genet was the first minister sent by the new Government to this
Country. Are there no marks of a *Machiavellian* policy in his *be-
haviour* or in his *instructions?* Did he say to us, or was he instructed
to say to us with frankness and fair dealing—Americans! France
wishes your cooperation. She thinks you bound by your Treaty—
or by gratitude—or by affinity of principles to afford it? Not a
word of all this. The language was—France does not require your
assistance. She wishes you to pursue what you think your interest.

What was the conduct? Genet came out with his pocket full of
commissioners to arm Privateers. Arrived at Charlestown, before he
had had any opportunity of sounding our Government, he begins
to issue them and to fit out privateers from our ports; certain that
this was a practice never to be tolerated by the enemies of France
and that it would infallibly implicate us in the War. Our Government mildly signifies to him its disapprobation of the measure.[6] He
affects to acquiesce, but still goes on in the same way—very soon
in open defiance of the Government: between which and our own

6. On June 5, 1793, Thomas Jefferson wrote to Genet: ". . . it is the *right*
of every nation to prohibit acts of sovereignty from being exercised by any
other within its limits, & the *duty* of a neutral nation to prohibit such as
would injure one of the warring powers: that the granting military commissions within the US. by any other authority than their own, is an infringe-
ment on their sovereignty & particularly so when granted to their own citizens
to lead them to committing acts contrary to the duties they owe their own
country: that the departure of vessels thus illegally equipped from the ports
of the US. will be but an acknowlegement of respect analogous to the breach
of it, while it is necessary on their part as an evidence of their faithful neutrality. On these considerations, Sir, the President thinks that the US. owe it
to themselves, & to the nations in their friendship, to expect this act of reparation on the part of vessels marked in their very equipment with offence to
the laws of the land, of which the laws of nations makes an integral part. The
expressions of very friendly sentiment, which we have already had the satisfaction of receiving from you, leave no room to doubt that the conclusions of
the President being thus made known to you, these vessels will be permitted
to give no further umbrage by their presence in the ports of the US" (ADf,
Thomas Jefferson Papers, Library of Congress; LC, RG 59, Domestic Letters
of the Department of State, Vol. 5, February 4, 1792–December 31, 1793, National Archives).

citizens he presently endeavours to introduce jealousy and scism. He sets on foot intrigues with our Southern and Western extremes and attempts to organise without our territory and to carry on from it military expeditions against the terrtiories of Spain in our neighbourhood [7]—a nation with which we were at peace.

It is impossible to doubt that the end of all this was to drag us into the war, with ⟨the⟩ humiliation of being plunged into it without even ⟨being⟩ consulted and without any volition of our own.

No Government or People could have been more horridly treated than we were by this foreign Agent. Our Executive nevertheless from the strong desire of maintaining good understanding with France forebore to impute to the French Government the conduct of its Agent made the controversy personal with him and requested his recall.[8] The French Government could not refuse our request without a rupture with us, which at that time would have been extremely inconvenient for many plain reasons. The application for the recall accordingly had full success; and the more readily as it arrived shortly after the overthrow of the *Brissotine* Party [9] (to which *Genet* belonged) and thus afforded another opportunity of exercising vengeance on that devoted Party.

But it were to be very credulous to be persuaded that *Genet* acted in this extraordinary manner, from the very beginning, without the authority of the Government by which he was sent and did not the nature of his conduct contain an internal evidence of the

7. See "Proposed Presidential Message to Congress Concerning Revocation of Edmond Charles Genet's Diplomatic Status," January 6–13, 1794, note 1.

8. On August 16, 1793, Jefferson wrote to Gouverneur Morris, United States Minister Plenipotentiary to France, requesting Genet's recall (ALS, Thomas Jefferson Papers, Library of Congress). See also "Cabinet Meetings. Proposals Concerning the Conduct of the French Minister," August 1–23, 1793; "Cabinet Meeting. Notes Concerning the Conduct of the French Minister," August 2, 1793; "Conversation with George Hammond," August 2–10, 1793; "Notes for a Letter to Gouverneur Morris," August 2–16, 1793; "Proposed Presidential Message to Congress Concerning Revocation of Edmond Charles Genet's Diplomatic Status," January 6–13, 1794; "Cabinet Meeting. Opinion on a Presidential Message to Congress on the Recall of Edmond Charles Genet," January 19, 1794.

9. During the French Revolution, Jacques Pierre Brissot de Warville was one of the leaders of the Girondists, who were also known as Brissotins. The Girondists were succeeded by the party known as the Maintain, led by Robespierre. On June 2, 1793, the arrest of Brissot and other leading Girondists was ordered; they were executed on October 31, 1793.

source it could be easily traced in the instructions which he published.[10] These instructions demonstrate three things though the last is couched in very covert terms 1 That *France* did not consider us as bound to aid her in the War 2 That she desired to engage us in it and the principal bribe was to be large privileges in her West India Trade 3 That if direct negotiation did not succeed indirect means were to be taken to entangle us in it whether so disposed or not. It is not matter of complaint, that France should endeavour to engage by fair means our assistance in the War if she thought it would be useful to her, but it is just matter of bitter complaint, that she should attempt against our will to ensnare or drive us into it.

Fauchet succeeded *Genet*. Twas a *Meteor* following a *Comet*. No very marked phoenomena distinguished his course. But the little twinkling appearances which are here and there discerned indicate the same general spirit in him which governed his predecessor. The Executive of our Country, in consequence of an Insurrection to which one of them had materially contri⟨buted⟩, had publicly arraigned political Clubs.[11] *Fauchet* in opposition openly patronises them. At the festivals of these clubs he is always a guest swallowing toasts full of sedition and hostility to the Government. Without examining what is the real tendency of these clubs, without examining even the policy of what is called the Presidents denunciation of them, it was enough for a foreign Minister that the Chief Magistrate of our Country had declared them to be occasions of calamity to it. It was neither friendly nor decent in a foreign Minister, after this, to countenance these institutions. This conduct discovered towards us not only unkindness but contempt. There is the more point in it as this countenance continued after similar societies had been proscribed in France.[12] What were destructive poisons there were in this Country salutary medicines. But the hostility of the

10. *The Correspondence between Citizen Genet, minister of the French Republic, to the United States of North America, and the officers of the Federal government; to which are prefixed the Instructions from the constituted authorities of France to the said minister. All from authentic documents* (Philadelphia: Printed and sold by Benjamin Franklin Bache, 1793).

11. For Washington's condemnation of the Democratic societies, see his sixth annual address to Congress, November 19, 1794 (*GW*, XXXIV, 28–37).

12. The French Jacobin Club, ineffective after July 27, 1794, was finally closed on November 11, 1794.

views of this Minister is palpable in that intercepted letter of his which unviels the treachery of *Randolph*.[13] We there learn, that he pretended to think it was a duty of patriotism to second the Western Insurrection; that he knew and approved of a conspiracy which was destined to overthrow the administration of our Government even by the most irregular means.

Another Revolution of party in *France* placed Mr. *Adet* in the room of Mr. *Fauchet*.[14] Mr. *Adet* has been more circumspect than either of his predecessors—and perhaps we ought scarcely to impute it to him as matter of reproach, that he openly seconded the opposition in Congress to the Treaty concluded with *Great Britain*.[15] This was a measure of a nature to call forth the manœvres of diplomatic tactics. But if we are wise, we shall endeavour to estimate rightly the probable motives of whatever displeasure France or her Agents may have shewn at this measure. Can it be any thing else than a part of the same plan which induced the Minister of *Louis the 16* to advise us to treat with Great Britain without the previous acknowlegement of our Independence? [16] Can it be any thing else

13. For information on Edmund Randolph and the interception of Fauchet's Dispatch No. 10, see Oliver Wolcott, Jr., to H, July 30, 1795, note 1.

14. Pierre Auguste Adet was appointed by the Directory to replace Jean Antoine Joseph Fauchet. Adet arrived in Philadelphia on June 13, 1795.

15. When Adet arrived in the United States on June 13, 1795, the Senate was debating the ratification of the Jay Treaty, which President Washington had submitted to a special session of that body on June 8, 1795. According to a letter from Edmund Randolph to Adet on July 6, 1795, Adet in a letter to Randolph dated June 30, 1795, had expressed his opposition to the Jay Treaty (LC, RG 59, Domestic Letters of the Department of State, Vol. 8, December 6, 1794–October 12, 1795, National Archives). Randolph described Adet's position in the following letter to Rufus King on July 6, 1795: "I have since [July 1, 1795] received his [Adet's] objections, feeble in themselves, and more feebly urged. They are these three simple things. 1. that we have *granted* to G.B., the liberty of seizing contraband beyond what was agreed between us and France. 2. that we have annulled the 17th Article of the French treaty; and 3 that we have incapacitated ourselves from forming a new commercial treaty with France by the last clause of the 25th article in that with England . . ." (Charles R. King, *The Life and Correspondence of Rufus King* [New York, 1895], II, 15). Adet also maintained that he had supplied Benjamin Franklin Bache, editor of the [Philadelphia] *Aurora. General Advertiser,* with an abstract of the treaty (Turner, "Correspondence of French Ministers," 742). See also H to Oliver Wolcott, Jr., June 26, 1795, note 3.

16. George III's first commission to Richard Oswald, the British negotiator with the Americans, authorized Oswald "to treat, consult, and conclude with any *commissioner or commissioners, named or to be named by the said colonies or plantations, and anybody or bodies, corporate or politic, assembly or assemblies, or descriptions of men, or person or persons whatsoever, a peace or*

than a part of that policy which deems it useful to France, that there should perpetually exist between us and Great Britain ⟨germs⟩ of discord and quarrel! Is it not ⟨manifest⟩ that in the eyes of France the unpardonable sin of that Treaty is that it roots up for the present those germs of discord and quarrel.

To pretend that the Treaty interferes with our engagement with France is a ridiculous absurdity—for it *expressly excepts* them.[17] To say that it establishes a course of things hurtful to France in her present struggle is belied by the very course of things since the Treaty. All goes on exactly as it did before.

Those who can justify displeasure in France on this account are not *Americans* but *Frenchmen*. They are not fit for being members of an independent Nation but prepared for the abject state of colonists. If our Government could not without the permission of France terminate its controversies with another foreign power & settle with it a Treaty of Commerce to endure three or four years, our boasted independence is a name. We have only transferred our allegiances! we are slaves!

---

truce with the said colonies or plantations, or any of them, or any part or parts thereof" and thus refused to acknowledge the independence of the United States (Wharton, *Revolutionary Diplomatic Correspondence*, V, 613–14). Oswald's commission, dated July 25, 1782, was not signed by the King until August 7. Charles Gravier, Comte de Vergennes, France's Minister of Foreign Affairs, advised John Jay and Benjamin Franklin, the American commissioners, to disregard the form of the commission and exchange full powers with Oswald. Franklin accepted Vergennes's formula, but Jay informed the French Minister that this solution did not satisfy him. For additional information on this phase of the peace negotiations, see Richard B. Morris, *The Peacemakers: The Great Powers & American Independence* (New York, 1965), 282–311.

17. H is referring to Article 25 of the Jay Treaty. For the text of this article, see "Remarks on the Treaty . . . between the United States and Great Britain," July 9–11, 1795, note 74.

INDEX

COMPILED BY JEAN G. COOKE

"An Act concerning the Claim of John Brown Cutting against the United States" (May 8, 1792), 518

"An Act for allowing a Compensation to the President and Vice President of the United States" (September 24, 1789), 411, 416

"An Act for allowing Compensation to the Members of the Senate and House of Representatives of the United States, and to the Officers of both Houses" (September 22, 1789), 412-13

"An Act for the relief of Stephen Sayre" (March 3, 1807), 296

"An Act imposing duties on the tonnage of ships or vessels" (July 20, 1790), 446, 447

"An Act in addition to the 'Act for making further and more effectual provision for the protection of the frontiers of the United States'" (June 7, 1794), 403, 409

"An Act in addition to the act for the punishment of certain crimes against the United States" (June 5, 1794), 274

"An Act making Appropriations for the Service of the present year" (September 29, 1789), 416

"An Act making appropriations for the support of Government during the year one thousand seven hundred and ninety-one, and for other purposes" (February 11, 1791), 416

"An Act making appropriations for the support of government for the year one thousand seven hundred and ninety" (March 26, 1790), 416

"An Act making Appropriations for the Support of Government for the year one thousand seven hundred and ninety-two" (December 23, 1791), 417

"An Act making appropriations for the support of Government during the year one thousand seven hundred and ninety-three" (February 28, 1793), 417

"An Act making Appropriations for the support of Government, for the year one thousand seven hundred and ninety-four" (March 14, 1794), 417

"An Act making appropriations for the support of Government for the year one thousand seven hundred and ninety-five" (January 2, 1795), 417

"An Act making provision for the (payment of the) Debt of the United States" (August 4, 1790), 34-35, 39

"An Act supplementary to the act, intituled 'An act to provide more effectually for the collection of the Duties on goods, wares and merchandise imported into the United States, and on the tonnage of ships or vessels'" (February 26, 1795), 179, 190

"An Act to extend the time limited for settling the Accounts of the United States with the individual States" (January 23, 1792), 38

"An Act to incorporate the subscribers to the Bank of the United States" (February 25, 1791), 390, 391

"An Act to provide more effectually for the collection of the duties imposed by law on goods, wares and merchandise imported into the United States, and on the tonnage of ships or vessels" (August 4, 1790), 174-75, 178-79

"An Act to provide more effectually for the settlement of the Accounts between the United States and the individual States" (August 5, 1790), 37-38

"An Act to regulate trade and intercourse with the Indian Tribes" (July 22, 1790), 14-15

"An Act to regulate Trade and Intercourse with the Indian Tribes" (March 1, 1793), 467

Adams, John, 241, 291, 375, 376-77, 383, 440, 469-70

Adams, John Quincy, 112-13, 205, 207

Adet, Pierre Auguste, 205, 206, 207, 297, 298, 308, 354-55, 428, 456, 527

Africa, 145, 206

Aix la Chapelle, Treaty of, 386, 387

Albany, N.Y., 178, 179

Albany County, N.Y., 202, 278

Alburg, Vt., 142, 167, 174

Alexander, Sarah Livingston (Mrs. William), 348-49

Alexander, William, 349

Alexander the Great, 331, 337

Alexandria, Va., 297, 468

Algiers: U.S. treaty with, 361, 462

Alibamon Indians, 173

Aliens: property rights of, 64, 279-94; under Jay Treaty, 164-65, 169-70, 188, 229, 282-85, 292-94

Altahama River, 15

American Iron Co., 200-1, 202

"American Jacobins," 519-20

American Revolution, 98, 144; expenses of, 8-22, 24, 27-28, 44, 47-48, 49, 50-51, 58; French aid in, 521, 522; and proscribed persons, 108-9; and "Trespass Act," 127-29

Amity, declaration of: in Jay Treaty, 108-11

Amsterdam: U.S. consul at, 310

Anne (queen of England), 172, 502

Argou, Gabriel: *Institution au droit françois . . .* , 279-81, 287

Argus, see *The* [New York] *Argus, or Greenleaf's New Daily Advertiser*

Armed Neutrality, League of: (1780), 473-74, 507-8; (1794), 503-4

Armstrong, John, 440

Arnold, Benedict, 441

Articles of Confederation, 18, 79, 248

Assumption of state debts, 30-35, 42, 43, 46-70

"Atticus," 278-79

Attorney General: candidates for office of, 396-98; vacancy of office of, 357-58, 396-98. *See also* Bradford, William, *and* Lee, Charles

Aurora, see [Philadelphia] *Aurora. General Advertiser*

Austria, 55-56, 121, 122

Bache, Benjamin Franklin, 295, 376, 378, 527; *letter from* Oliver Wolcott, Jr., 351-52

Baldwin, Abraham, 485

Ball, Blackall William, 88

Baltimore, Md., 439

Bank of New York, 348

Bank of the U.S., 15, 378, 389-92

Barbary Powers: negotiations with, 361

Barlow, Joel, 361

Basel, Treaty of, 298, 373

Batavian Republic, 42

Baty, Thomas: *Prize Law and Continuous Voyage*, 342, 343

Bayard, Samuel, 306-8, 317

Beckley, John, 295, 379-80

Bee, Thomas, 398

Belgium, 335

"Belisarius," 278-79

Bellegarde, Marquis de, 280-81, 290-91

Belligerents: right to search, 481-83

Bergstedt, Erik, 504

Berlin, 296

Bermuda Hundred, Va., 179, 439

Bernstorff, Andreas Peter, count von, 503-4

Betsey, 306

Big Stone Lake, 239

Black River, 232

Blackstone, Sir William: *Commentaries on the Laws of England*, 281, 283, 336

Bleecker, Barent, 200, 202

Blockade of ports, 307-8, 501, 510, 511

Blount, William, 311, 360, 361

Board of Treasury, 376, 378

Bombay: trade with, 234

Bond, Phineas, 201, 202, 205-6; *letter from*, 217; *letter to*, 216
Boon, Gerrit, 313, 329
Bordes, Jean Marie de, 472; *letter from*, 429
Boston, Mass., 263
Boudinot, Elias, 299, 377, 466
Brabant, 208
Bradford, William, 97; death of, 297; *letter from*, 86-87
Bradley, Joel, 147
Bradley, Philip B., 439
Brasher, Ephraim, 348
Breslau, Treaty of, 342
Brissot de Warville, Jacques Pierre, 525
Bristoll, Eli, 146
British debts: commissioners for recovery of, in Jay Treaty, 251-53, 255-56, 257, 279-81, 307, compensation for, 139, 140, 249-54, 258; confiscation or sequestration of, by states, 81-84, 133-34, 136-37, 153-58, 246-47, 367-74; discussed, 245-56; Thomas Jefferson on, 255-56; and retention of western posts, 119, 137, 144; and Treaty of 1783, 245, 246, 249, 254-55
British East India Co., 234
British East Indies: U.S. trade with, in Jay Treaty, 74, 177, 188-89, 193, 228, 234, 441
"British Rule of 1756," 307
British West Indies: Courts of Admiralty, 250-60, 262, 263, 267; U.S. trade with, in Jay Treaty, 74, 177, 233-34, 441-49
Brock, Isaac, 440
Brooks, John, 439
Burgoyne, John, 521
Burr, Aaron, 203, 318, 485
Bussy, François de, 386, 387
Butler, James: *letter from*, 467-68
Bynkershoek, Cornelius van: *Quæstionum*, 274, 304, 332, 334-35, 336, 337, 505

Cabot, George, 354-55, 456, 459-60; *letter from* George Washington, 325; *letter to* George Washington, 325-26
"Caius," 238
Caldwell's Manor, 142, 167
Caligula, 103

"A Calm Observer," 350-51, 352, 353, 354, 364, 400
Cambridge University, 325-26
"Camillus," 298, 398-99; defense of, see "Philo Camillus." *See also* "The Defence"
"Camillus refuted by A. Hamilton," 131
Canada, 117; boundary of, 219-20; and France, 172; and fur trade, 143, 146, 219, 221, 222, 224-26; and Indians, 138, trade with, 136, 143, 146, 189, 219, 221-26; protection of, 139; and U.S. trade, in Jay Treaty, 75, 172-78, 184, 187-96, 211, 218, 220, 221, 225-27, 230, 231
"Candid Remarks on the Treaty of Amity and Commerce between Great Britain and the United States," 285
Canton: U.S. trade with, 234
Carey, Mathew: *The American Remembrancer*, 238
Carleton, Sir Guy, see Dorchester, Lord
Carnes, Thomas P., 311
Carriage tax case, 86-87, 88, 97, 149
Carrington, Edward, 1, 16, 357-58, 436
Carroll, Charles, of Carrollton, 357
Castine, District of Maine, 9
Castorland project, 232
Cataraquy River, 193
Catharine II, 474, 508
"Cato," 135, 142, 186, 187-92, 194, 197, 198, 207-15, 217-18, 221-22, 224, 260, 265, 470, 481, 503
Catskill, N.Y., 179
Charles I, 502
Charles II, 502, 503
Charles XI, 503
Charleston, S.C.: opposition to Jay Treaty in, 87, 108-9, 164-65, 211, 218, 253; and outfitting of privateers, 271, 524
Chase, Samuel, 358
Cherokee Indians, 9, 14, 461
Chickamauga Indians, 9
Chickasaw Bluffs, 360, 361
Chickasaw Indians, 14, 173, 360, 362-63
China: U.S. trade with, 234
Choctaw Indians, 14, 173
Church, Angelica Schuyler (Mrs. John B.), 311-12
Church, John B., 88, 312-13; Robert Morris's debt to, 309, 430, 498-500

Cicero, M. Tullius, 332-34
"Cicero," 393
"Cinna," 98-105, 124-34, 154-55
Citizenship: in Jay Treaty, 115, 164, 168-69, 207, 210, 211
Clark, Erastus, 146-47
Clark, William, 360, 361
Clarke, Henri Guillaume, 147-48
Clarkson, Matthew, 441
Claypoole, David C., 496
Clinton, George, 432-34
Cobb, David, 439
Cocoa, 442, 443
Codfisheries: U.S. claim to, 75, 375, 377, 522
Coffee, 442, 443, 448
Coke, Sir Edward: *Institutes of the Laws of England*, 199, 283, 301-2
Collier, George, 9
Cologne, 335
Columbia County, N.Y., 278
Commerce: advantages of, 174, 336; and British Courts of Admiralty, 259-60, 262, 263, 267; dangers to, 366-67, 374; with French West Indies, 442-43, 448; spoliations of, 92, 93, 94, 165, 295, 306-8, 463-64 (*see also* Great Britain: orders in council). *See also* Fur trade; Jay Treaty: and commerce
Commissioners for settling the accounts between the U.S. and the individual states, 37-38
Commissioners of loans, 35
Confederation, 28, 244, 523
Congress of the U.S.: acts of, *see under* Act; and appropriations, 405-6; and assumption, 39; and compensation, of Army, 403, 405, 409-10, 412, of members of Congress, 364, 378-80, 402, 405, 412-14, of George Washington, 350, 351, 353, 410-11, 416-19; convening of, 359, 459-60; and economic situation, 297; and Georgia land claims, 14; and Jay Treaty, 359; and public debt, 29, 39, 72-73; and George Washington's message to, 205, 359-63, 400, 431, 459-60, 460-67, 496, 526. *See also* House of Representatives; Senate
Connecticut: and American Revolution, 17; debts of, 2, 13, 15-16, 17-19, 20, 26-27, 31, 36; land claims, 18; U.S. marshal for the District of, 439

Connecticut Land Co., 18
Constitution (U.S.), 249, 302, 358, 415, 474; Article I, Section 9, 404, Section 10, 32; and expenditure of money, 404-6, 410, 411, 414, 419, 420, 421; and public debt, 5, 7; and taxation, 22, 23, 25, 28; treaties under, 157
Constitutional Convention: and taxation, 23
Continental Congress, 13, 18, 21, 50-51, 82-83, 155, 201, 241, 255, 341, 375-77, 518; and contraband, 507-8, 509; and Treaty of 1783, 79, 131, 132, 160, 161, 162, 248
Contraband, 384, 449; horses as, 501, 507, 508, 510, 511; in Jay Treaty, 235, 487-95, 500-11, 527; listing of, 500-1, naval stores as, 304, 501-2, 503, 505-9, 511; provisions as, 503, 507, 508, 509, 510 (*see also* Great Britain: orders in council [April 25, 1795]); soldiers as, 501
Contracts: under Constitution (U.S.), 302; and public debt, 70-73
Copenhagen, 296
Corpus Juris Civilis, 332
Cosby Manor, 200-1, 202, 203, 216
Cotton, Daniel, 232
Cotton, 442, 443-44
Cotton gin, 444
Coxe, Tench: and Jay Treaty, 97; *letter from*, 88
Cozine, John, 318
Credit: public and private, Hamilton on importance of, 47, 57, 58, 60, 299-300
Creditors: in Jay Treaty, American, 256-58, 260-69, British, 256-58, 263, 269-77; and public debt, 4-5, 7, 30-35, 44, 60, 61, 70, 71-73
Creek Indians, 15, 173, 362-63, 461
Croft, Sir James, 199
Cromwell, Oliver, 502
Cumberland Head, N.Y., 174
Cutting, John Browne: claim of, 516-18

Dallas, Alexander J.: and Jay Treaty, 229, 258, 292, 294-95, 299
Davies, William, 440
Dayton, Jonathan, 349, 438
Dean, James, 146
Deane, Silas, 383
Deas, William Allen, 112-13, 496

Debrett, John: *A Collection of State Papers*, 503-4

"Decius," 164, 186-87, 190, 191, 194, 197, 207-12, 218, 247, 254, 255, 269-70, 282, 285, 292, 299, 344, 388, 389

Declaration of Independence, 439

Deerfield, N.Y., 200

"The Defence": change of place of publication, 398-99; No. II, 135, 259, 503; No. III, 93, 98, 128, 131, 135, 162, 248; No. IV, 77-75, 124, 127, 130, 135, 153, 248; No. V, 89-97, 135, 248; No. VI, 105-11, 211, 393; No. VII, 92, 115-24, 163, 172; No. VIII, 92, 134-46, 163, 167, 168, 172, 207, 211, 267; No. IX, 92, 163-71, 172, 207, 210, 211; No. X, 116, 172-86, 190, 191, 195, 196, 226; No. XI, 116, 177, 186-99, 207, 213, 217, 218, 226; No. XII, 116, 177, 207, 214, 217-31; No. XIII, 237-44, 253; No. XIV, 245-46, 257; No. XV, 92, 256-69; No. XVI, 269-77; No. XVII, 279-94; No. XVIII, 248, 299-305, 334, 335; No. XIX, 248, 305, 318-24; No. XX, 248, 305, 329-47, 367, 368; No. XXI, 248, 365-74, 388; No. XXII, 248, 380-95, 398-99; No. XXIII, 428; No. XXIV, 298, 428; No. XXV, 441-49; No. XXVI, 457; No. XXVII, 459, 471; No. XXVIII, 471; No. XXIX, 471-72, 473, 481; No. XXX, 472, 473; No. XXXI, 473-84; No. XXXII, 487-95, 500, 502, 505, 510; No. XXXIII, 500-11; No. XXXIV, 513; No. XXXV, 516; No. XXXVI, 281; No. XXXVII, 243, 281; No. XXXVIII, 281

Delaware, 201

Delaware River, 187

Democratic societies, 526

Denisort, J. B.: *Collections de Décisions Nouvelles et de Notions Relatives à la Jurisprudence Actuelle*, 286, 288

Denmark, 335; relations with Great Britain, 210, 211, 259, 335, 502, 503-4

De Saussure, Henry William, 298, 397-98, 466

Detroit, 142, 165, 167, 168, 207, 223, 440

Dexter, Samuel, 358, 396-97

Dohrman, Arnold Henry, 517-18

Domat, Jean: *Les Loix Civiles . . .*, 286

Dominica, 171

Donaldson, Joseph, Jr., 361, 462

Dorchester, Lord, 90-91, 165, 208, 209, 210

Drake, Sir Francis, 184

Dundas, Henry, 208

Dunlap, John, 496

Dunlap and Claypoole's [Philadelphia] *American Daily Advertiser*, 496

Dutchman's Point, 142, 167, 168, 207

Duties, 23, 25, 27, 29; in Jay Treaty, 182-85, 187, 191-92, 193-94, 211-12, 214-15, 218, 225, 226, 234-35, 446, 447, 448

Elizabeth I, 199

Elliot, Robert, 244

Ellison, Thomas, 312-13

Esopus, N.Y., 178

Euclid, 103, 130

"An Examination of the pending Treaty with Great Britain," 97

Excise taxes, 2, 25, 26, 27

Exiles: claims of, 292, 294

"Explanation," 400-26, 427, 467-68

Faden, William: map of, 238

Faneuil Hall, 263

Fauchet, Jean Antoine Joseph, 206, 297; Dispatch No. 10, 296, 327, 352, 375-76, 378, 428, 432-34, 454, 470, 486-87, 526-27; and proposed French commercial treaty, 298, 308, 428; and Whiskey Insurrection, 514-15

"Features of Jay's Treaty," 229, 258, 292, 294-95, 299

Federal City: land speculation in, 310

Fenner, Arthur, 205-7

Fenno, John, 486-87, 496

FitzSimons, Thomas, 377; *letter from*, 498

Flanders, 123-24

Fletcher v Peck, 311

Fleurus, Battle of, 123

Florida, 429, 469

Foot, Moses, 146

Ford, David, 298-99

Forman, David, 439

Forrest, Richard, 298

Forrest, Uriah, 440

Fort Massac, 360

Fort Miami, 165, 168

Fort Stanwix, Treaty of, 135

Fort Washington, 360

France: and Algerine negotiations, 361; and alien rights, 279-81, 285-91, 293; and American independence, 375; and American Revolution, 521, 522; and Austria, 122; and Canada, 172; economy of, 55-56, 58; and Great Britain, 208-10, 211, 240-41, 261, 345-46, orders in council of, 112, 150, 151, 204, 264-65, treaties with, 171, 220, 222-23, 238, 385, 386, 387, 480, war with, 95, 120-22, 123, 124, 342, 343, 368, 395, 429, 474, 521; Hamilton on, 75-77, 520-28; and Indian trade, 172; Jacobin club, 526; and Jay Treaty, 96-97, 359, 519-20; Minister to U.S., see Adet, Pierre Auguste, and Fauchet, Jean Antoine Joseph, and Genet, Edmond Charles; and Mississippi River, 75, 222-23, 375, 522; and Newfoundland fisheries, 377, 522; North American possessions, 238, 240-41; "Ordonnance de la Marine," 308-9; privateers of, 271, 275-76; prizes of, 96; proposed commercial treaty with, 297-98, 308, 428, 527; and Prussia, 373; and the Ranger, 297-98; revolutionary parties in, 525; sequestration of debts by, 335, 339, 345, 347; and Spain, 298, 360; Treaty of 1783, 75, 375, 377, 469, 522; and United Netherlands, 42, 511; and U.S., 98-99, 209; U.S. debt to, 13; U.S. Minister to, see Jefferson, Thomas, and Morris, Gouverneur; U.S. relations with, 75-77, 520-28; U.S. trade with, 175, 442-43, 448; U.S. treaty with (1778), 100, 227, 235, 272, 275, 279-81, 285, 287-92, 294, 380-81, 383, 442-48, 476, 482, 501, 508, 510, 519-20, 521, 523, 524, 527, 528; and war in Europe, 121-24; George Washington on, 513; western posts, 163-64, 211

Frankfort, N.Y., 200
Franklin, Benjamin, 100, 383, 470, 528
Frederick II, 342, 343, 344
Frederick William (of Prussia), 123-24
"Free ships, free goods," 235, 304, 384, 449, 473, 475, 476, 477, 478, 479-80, 481, 519
Frelinghuysen, Theodore, 299
French West Indies, 316, 521-22, 526
Frestel, Felix, 324-26, 354-55, 451, 455-

57, 457-58, 459-60, 514-15, 518-19; letter from George Washington, 457
Funding system: Hamilton's defense of, 1-73; notes and queries concerning, 1-2; opposition and objections to, 46, 48-49, 50-51, 53, 54-55, 56, 57, 58, 59, 61; and public credit, 53-55, 56 57, 58, 60, 61; and speculation, 34
Fundy, Bay of, 240
Furlong, William, 306
Fur trade: in Canada, 146, 219, 221, 222, 224; and Great Britain, 210, 213-15, 218, 221, 222, 224, 225-26, 229; with Indians, 143; and Jay Treaty, 75, 185, 187-89, 193, 194, 210, 212-13; in U.S., 192, 193, 194, 218, 221, 222, 224, 225-26, 229, 230

Gallatin, Albert, 485
Leonard Gansevoort v Gerrit Boon, 313, 329
Gates, Horatio, 440
Gayoso de Lemos, Manuel, 360-61
Genet, Edmond Charles, 77, 297, 428, 476, 519; Hamilton on, 524-26; letters from Thomas Jefferson, 475, 524
Genoa, 210, 211
George II, 261, 474, 527, 528
Georgia, 443; acts of, 14, 310, 311; and alien ownership of land, 280-81, 290, 291; and American Revolution, 13-14; and British debts, 247; debt of, 13-15, 31; and Indians, 14, 363, 461; land speculation in, 309-11, 454; and public land, 14, 15, 18; U.S. judge for the District of, see Pendleton, Nathaniel; U.S. Representatives from, see Baldwin, Abraham, and Carnes, Thomas P., and Jackson, James; U.S. Senator from, see Gunn, James
Georgia Co., 309-11
Georgia Mississippi Co., 310
Georgia Yazoo Co., 310-11
Gibraltar, 362
Gilbert, Ezekiel: letter from, 277-78
Giles, William B., 156, 158
Gilman, John Taylor, 38
"Glorious First of June," 123
Godoy, Manuel de, 360, 462
Goelet, Peter, 201, 202, 203
Gold, Thomas R., 146-47
Good Peter, 147

Goold, Edward, 200, 202
Gore, Christopher, 396-97
Gorham, Nathaniel, 18
Gouverneur, Isaac, 318
Great Britain, 100, 121, 124, 125, 127, 201, 339; acts of, 345-46, Navigation Act, 188, 198, 199, 213, 214, 444-45, Quebec Act, 219; Admiralty Courts, 306-8, 316, 343; and Austria, 55-56, 121; boundaries with U.S., 117, 237-44; and Brabant, 208; common law of, 335-36, 341, 342; and Denmark, 210, 211, 259, 335, 502, 503-4; economy of, 55, 57, 69, 121; and France, 208-10, 211, 240-41, 261, 345-46, treaties with, 171, 220, 222-23, 238, 385, 386, 387, 480, war with, 95, 120-21, 122, 123, 124, 342, 343, 345, 368, 395, 429, 474, 521; and fur trade, 210, 213-15, 218, 221, 222, 224, 225-26, 229; and Genoa, 210, 211; and impressment of seamen, 106-8, 152, 206, 235; and Indians, 94, 117, 119, 135, 136, 138, 144, 172, 189, 192, 194-99, 208, 209, 212-15, 362; King of, 103, 261, 342; Magna Charta, 301, 335; Minister to U.S., see Hammond, George; and Mississippi River, 181-82, 212, 217-18, 222-23, 224-25; and Negro slaves, 82, 83, 84, 92-94, 98, 99-105, 131, 132, 152, 155, 159, 160, 161, 162, 236, 247, 277; and Newfoundland fisheries, 377; and Nootka Sound, 184, 264; North American possessions, 172, 283, 240-41 (see also Canada); orders in council, (June 8, 1793) 264-65, 307, 488, 504, (November 6, 1793) 262, 264, 316, 489-90, 495, (August 6, 1794) 259, 260, 262, 489, (April 25, 1795) 111-12, 149-53, 204, 206, 356, 359, 467, 495; and Portugal, 384, 385, 502; privateers, 152, 306-8; Proclamation of 1763, 469; and Prussia, 368; and Russia, 385-86, 474, 503, 504; and Spain, 117, 212, 264, 335, 342, 384-85; and Sweden, 210, 211, 259, 502-3; Treaty of 1783, 77-85, 136-37, 153, 158, 160, 161, 162, 247, 248, 249, 375-77, 522; and United Netherlands, 42, 208; and U.S., 9, 98, 139-40, 145, 375, 376-77; and U.S. commerce, 174-75, 177-85, 187-99, 207-15, 233-36, 441, spoliations of, 92, 93, 94, 111-12, 149, 165,

256-57, 260-77, 306-8, 475-77; and U.S. creditors, 256-58, 260-66; U.S. Minister to, see Pinckney, Thomas; and George Washington, 513; western posts, 81-82, 83, 84, 90-91, 92, 93, 94, 115-24, 131, 134-46, 153, 155, 159, 161, 163-71, 207-10, 247, 249, 250. See also British debts; Jay Treaty
Great Lakes, 173-74, 188, 189, 194
Greene, Nathanael, 454
Greene, William, 200, 202, 203
Greenleaf, James: letter to, 309-11
Greenleaf, Thomas, 98, 399
Greenville, Treaty of, 362
Grenada, 171
Grenadines, 171
Grenville, Lord, 489; and Jay Treaty, 90-91, 135, 188, 189, 205, 209, 316; letter to George Hammond, 117
Grotius, Hugo: On the Law of War and Peace, 10, 118, 246, 274, 287, 331, 333-34, 489, 505-6, 507
Guadaloupe, 306, 443
Gunn, James, 105, 309-11

Habersham, John: letter from, 472
The Hague: Minister Resident at, see Adams, John Quincy
Hailes, Daniel, 504
Haldiman, Sir Frederick, 189
Halifax, 237
Hamilton, Alexander: on Pierre Auguste Adet, 527; on candidates for office, of Attorney General, 396-98, of Secretary of State, 396-98, of Secretary of War, 453-54; and carriage tax case, 86-87, 149; and John B. Church, 88, 313, 498-500; duel with Aaron Burr, 203; on Jean Antoine Joseph Fauchet, 526-27; on France, 75-77, 519, 520-28; on French party, 519-20; on funding system, 1-73; on Edmond Charles Genet, 519, 524-26; and Hamilton-Oneida Academy, 146-47; on John Jay, 95-96; Jay Treaty, defense of, see "Camillus" and "The Defence" and "Horatius"; and George W. M. Lafayette, 452-53, 457-58, 514-15; on James McHenry, 397-98; and Robert Morris, 309; on Negro slaves, 101-2; and New York–Massachusetts land controversy, 18; on peace, 90; Timothy Pickering requests ad-

Hamilton, Alexander (*Continued*) vice of, 435-41; on poll taxes, 25; on Edmond Randolph, 296, 327; and Edmond Randolph's *Vindication*, 514; resignation of, 1; and *Rutgers* v *Waddington*, 78; on John Rutledge, 484-85; and Philip Schuyler, 200-4; on U.S. economy, 296; and George Washington, compensation of, 350, 351, 353, 354, 400-26, 467-68, message to Congress by, 205, 400, 431, 459-67, 496 (*see also* "Explanation"), request of advice from 205, 356-63; and Whiskey Insurrection, 514-15; and Yazoo land cases, 311

Hamilton, Elizabeth, 204, 297, 308, 312

Hamilton, John Church, 520

Hamilton College, 147

Hamilton-Oneida Academy, 146-47

Hammond, George, 83, 205-6, 209, 241, 269, 277, 432-34; and Jay Treaty, 150; *letter from* Lord Grenville, 117; *letters from* Thomas Jefferson, 77, 104, 270, 271, 272; *letters from* Edmund Randolph, 145, 206; *letter to* Thomas Jefferson, 77

Hampton Roads, Va., 179

"Hancock," 278-79

Hand, Edward, 438

Hardie, James: *letter from*, 471; *letter to*, 472

Harison, Richard, 201, 216, 318; *letter to* Thomas Jefferson, 133

Harper, Robert Goodloe, 311

Harrowby, Baron, 342

Hasenclever, Peter, 200-1

Heineccius, Johann Gottlieb: . . . *The Laws of Nature and Nations . . .* , 489; *De Navibus Ob Vecturam Vetitarum Mercium Commissis . . .* , 505

Hemsley, William, 377

Henry, Patrick, 356-57, 436

Herkimer County, N.Y., 200

Heth, William, 439

Higginson, Stephen, 377

Holker, John, 498

Holland Land Co., 313

Home, Rodham, 145, 204-6, 233

Hopewell, Treaty of, 14

Hopkins, Sewall, 146

"Horatius No. II," 74-77

Horses: as contraband, 501, 507, 508, 510, 511

House of Representatives, 295, 427, 429, 496-97, 517

Howard, John Eager, 439, 453-54

Howe, Lord, 123

Hudson, N.Y., 178, 179, 190, 192, 193

Hudson River, 179, 187

Hudson's Bay Co., 176, 213, 217, 218-22

Hull, William, 440

Hume, David: *Political Discourses*, 67

Humphreys, David, 361, 362, 440, 462

Huntington, Ebenezer, 438-39

Huntington, Jedediah, 438-39

Hylton v *United States*, 87, 88, 97

Iberville River, 222

Impressment of seamen: 105-8, 152, 206, 235-36, 393, 516-18

Indians, 18; buffer state, 117; commissioners, 135; and Georgia, 14, 363, 461; and Great Britain, 94, 117, 119, 135, 136, 138, 144, 172, 189, 192, 194-99, 208, 209, 212-15, 362; trade with, 14-15, 173, 209, 211, 212, 213-15, 221, 222, 223, 231, 363, 465-66, 467, and Jay Treaty, 135-36, 142-43, 172, 176, 185, 187-89, 191, 192, 194-99; treaties, 14, 15, 143, 362, 461; U.S. relations with, 362-63, 463, 465-66; wars, 36, 94, 116, 119, 138, 141-44, 145, 189, 197-98, 208, 209, 210-11, 214, 461, 497, compensation for, 208, 209, 210, 211; and western posts, 116, 135, 136, 138, 143. *See also* Alibamon Indians; Cherokee Indians; Chickasaw Indians; Choctaw Indians; Creek Indians; Six Nations; Talapoosas Indians

Innes, James, 358, 396-97

Irvine, William, 38, 439

Italy, 121

Izard, Ralph, 312-13

Jackson, James, 72-73

Jane of Dublin, 270, 271

Jaudenes, Josef de, 432, 435; *letter to* Thomas Jefferson, 224

Jay, John, 108, 149, 278, 343, 357, 460, 464, 528; and Jay Treaty, 85, 90-91, 93, 94-96, 107, 113, 115, 119, 123, 124, 127, 134-36, 142, 163-64, 165-66, 175, 188, 189, 205, 208, 209, 213, 214, 221, 239, 240, 241, 250, 276, 383, 386, 444, 445, 470, 477-78, 479, 487, 489,

490, 495, 513; *letter from* Thomas
Jefferson, 291; *letter from* Timothy
Pickering, 315-16; *letter from* Edmund Randolph, 150-53; *letters to*
Edmund Randolph, 113-14, 150; and
Treaty of 1783, 375, 377
Jay, Peter Augustus, 459-60
Jay Treaty, 515; and alien ownership
of property, 164-65, 169-70, 188,
229, 282-85, 292-94, right of conveyance of, 282-85, 292-94; amity,
declaration of, in, 108-11; Article 1,
108-11; Article 2, 92, 115-24, 134-46,
163-71, 172, 207-10, 211; Article 3,
75, 116, 172-99, 211-15, 217-31; Article 4, 237-44; Article 5, 237-44;
Article 6, 139, 245-46, 257, 258, 307;
Article 7, 92, 256-77, 306-8, 314-17;
Article 8, 279-81; Article 9, 281-
94; Article 10, 248, 299-305, 318-24,
329-47, 365-74, 380-95; Article 11,
177, 449; Article 12, 74, 214, 233,
356, 441-49, 462, 479; Article 13, 74,
228, 234, 441; Article 14, 188, 213,
214, 441; Article 15, 183, 214, 234,
441; Article 17, 262, 473-84; Article
18, 112, 235, 487-95, 500-11; Article
19, 482; Article 24, 96; Article 25,
520, 527, 528; Article 26, 189; Article 28, 74; and British creditors,
256-58, 263, 269-77; and British
debts, 139, 140, 245-58, 307, commission for, 251-53, 255-56, 257, 279-
81, 307, compensation for, 249-54,
258; citizenship, choice of, in, 115,
164, 168-69, 207, 210, 211; constitutionality of, 243, 281; and contraband, 235, 487-95, 500-11, 527; defense of, 357 (*see also* "Camillus";
"The Defence"; "Horatius"; "Philo
Camillus"); duration of, 74, 395;
and duties, 182-85, 187-88, 191-92,
193-94, 211-12, 214-15, 218, 225, 226,
234-35, 446, 447, 448; and France,
96-97, 359, 519-20; and fur trade,
185, 187-89, 193, 194, 210, 212-13;
and Hudson's Bay Co., 176, 213,
217, 220; and Indian trade, 135-36,
143-44, 172, 176, 185, 187-89, 191,
192, 194-99; and Mississippi River,
commerce on, 177, 181-82, 185-86,
190, 212-13, 217-18, 222, 224-25, survey of, 223, 237, 238-40; "Notes of
Objections to," 207-15; opposition
and objections to, 74-75, 90-91, 95-

97, 105-11, 115, 118, 119-20, 134-35,
136, 138, 140-41, 142, 148-49, 164-65,
171, 175-76, 177-78, 180, 186-91, 194,
195-99, 217-18, 221-22, 224, 225-27,
229, 238, 239, 240, 242, 253, 254, 257-
60, 263, 265, 269-70, 277, 278-79, 281,
282, 285, 292, 294-95, 299-300, 337,
342, 376, 378, 387-88, 389, 392, 393,
445, 446, 448, 474, 481, 485, 487, 488,
494, 495, 503, 509-10, 519-20, 527,
in Boston, Mass., 263, in Charleston,
S.C., 87, 108-9, 164-65, 218, in Philadelphia, Pa., 165, 229, in Virginia,
450-51, 488, 510 (*see also* "Atticus";
"Belisarius"; "Caius"; "Camillus refuted by A. Hamilton"; "Cato";
"Cicero"; "Cinna"; "Hancock";
"Juricola"; "Valerius"); and private property, 318-24; and privateers, 257, 269-77, 482-83; and
prizes, 96; and proscribed persons,
108-10, 164-65, 169; ratification of,
111-12, 148-53, 355-56, 359, 449, 450,
462, 485, 496; and St. Croix River,
237-38, 240-44, 253; and Senate, 74,
111, 152, 205, 207, 236, 356, 442, 444,
450, 452, 527; and sequestration of
debts, 299-305, 318-24, 329-47, 365-
74, 380-95; and tonnage of ships,
233, 442, 445, 447; traders, rights of
in, 115, 188, 198-99, 211; and treaties, 520, 527; and U.S., boundaries,
164, 166-67, 208, 223, 237-44, 253,
279-81, creditors, 256-58, 260-69, objectives in, 92; and George Washington, 90-91, 112, 113, 148-49, 150,
151, 152, 205, 355-56, 359, 449, 450-
51, 527; and western posts, 90-91,
92, 93, 94, 115-24, 134-46, 163-71,
207-10
—— and commerce: with British
East Indies, 74, 177, 188-89, 193, 228,
234, 441; with British West Indies,
74, 177, 233-34, 441-49; with Canada,
75, 172-78, 184, 187-96, 211, 218, 220,
221, 225-27, 230, 231; internal, 172,
175-86, 187-99, 210-15, 218-31; spoliations of, 92, 93, 94, 256, 257, 258,
260-69, 307-8, 314-17, compensation
for, 257-58, 260-77, 314-17; spoliations commissioners, 257-58, 260-69,
271, 279-81, 307-8, 314-17
Jefferson, Thomas, 78, 80, 83, 241, 276,
295, 344, 376, 378, 383, 470, 475, 477-
78, 479; and alien ownership of

Jefferson, Thomas (*Continued*)
land, 280-81, 290-91; and British debts, 156, 158, 255-56; Hamilton on, 397; *letter from* George Hammond, 77; *letter from* Richard Harison, 133; *letter from* Josef de Jaudenes, 224; *letter from* James Monroe, 156-58; *letter from* Josef de Viar, 224; *letters to* Edmond Charles Genet, 475, 524; *letters to* George Hammond, 77, 104, 270, 271, 272; *letter to* John Jay, 291; *letter to* James Madison, 451; *letters to* Gouverneur Morris, 475-76, 525; *letter to* George Washington, 517; and Negro slaves, 103-4, 160; and Treaty of 1783, 129, 131, 156, 159, 160, 209
John IV, 502
Johnson, Thomas, 356-57, 435-36
Jones, Thomas, 349
"Juricola," 97
Justinian I: *Institutes*, 286, 331, 332

Kean, John, 15, 38
Keene, Charles, 504
Kemble, Peter, 318
Kent, James, 374
Kinderhook, N.Y., 178
King, Rufus, 153, 357, 395, 397, 436; and "The Defence," 279-81, 287, 291, 298, 428, 441, 457, 459, 471-72, 505, 513, 516; *letter to*, 484-85; *letter from*, 496-97; *letter from* Edmund Randolph, 527
Kirkland, Samuel, 147
Knox, Henry, 437, 458; *letter to* George Washington, 325
Kuhl, Henry, 378, 433

Labrador, 189
Lac Qui Parle, 239
Lafayette, George Washington Motier, 350, 354-55, 400, 431, 450-51, 452-53, 455-57, 457-58, 459-60, 512-13, 514-15, 518-19; *letter from* George Washington, 456-57; *letter to* George Washington, 324-25
Lafayette, Marie Joseph du Motier, marquis de, 324-27, 455, 456, 457
Lahontan, Louis-Armand de Lom de l'Arce, baron de, 239
Lake Champlain, 142, 168, 174, 227
Lake Huron, 166
Lake Maurepas, 222, 223

Lake Michigan, 166
Lake of the Woods, 165, 166, 219, 220, 223, 237, 239
Lake Ontario, 193
Lake Pontchartrain, 222, 223
Lake Superior, 166
Land, 69; alien ownership of, 64, 279-94, in Jay Treaty, 164-65, 169-70, 188, 282-85, 292-94; public, 14, 15, 18, 467; right of conveyance of, 282-85, 292-94
Langdon, Woodbury, 38
Laurens, Henry, 470
Law of nations, 92, 105-6, 118, 185, 246, 257, 261-62, 265-66, 268, 273, 274, 314-16, 329-47, 365, 371, 373, 374, 386, 387, 388, 392, 394, 449, 473, 474, 475, 476, 477, 478, 479, 482, 483, 484, 488, 489, 490, 491, 492, 493, 495, 501, 502, 503, 504, 505, 508, 510, 524
Law of nature, 329, 337, 338, 392
Lear, Tobias, 350, 352, 421
Lebrun-Tondu, Pierre Henri Hélène, 523
Lee, Arthur, 296, 363
Lee, Charles, 297, 397-98, 451
Lee, Sir George, 342
Lee, Henry, 150, 397-98, 437, 440, 453-54, 515
Lee, Richard: *letter from*, 147
Lee, Richard, and Son, 147
Lee, Thomas: *letter from*, 147
Lee, Thomas, and Richard, and Son: *letter from*, 147
Lee, Sir William, 342
Le Guen, Louis, 318
Le Guen v *Gouverneur and Kemble*, 318
Leib, Michael, 295
Leopold I (Austria), 502
Lewis, William, 315-16, 498
Lincoln, Benjamin, 441
Livingston, Alice (Mrs. Robert C.), 312-13
Livingston, Brockholst, 318, 349; and Jay Treaty, 98, 105, 124, 154, 164, 186, 207, 247, 269-70, 282, 299, 344. *See also* "Cinna" *and* "Decius"
Livingston, John Henry, 349
Livingston, Philip, 349
Livingston, Robert R., 375, 377, 440; and Jay Treaty, 135, 186, 207, 260, 470, 503. *See also* "Cato"
Loans, 1, 8, 13, 33-34, 35, 54, 55

Logan, George, 294-95
Long River, 239
Louis XIV, 172, 308
Louis XVI, 75, 527
Louisville, District of, 174
Lovell, Solomon, 9
Lovely Lass, 270, 271
Low, Nicholas, 203, 312-13
Lowell, John, 512
Lowell, John, Jr.: *letter from*, 511-12
"A Loyalist of '75," 145
Lynch, Dominick, 312-13

McCall, Daniel, 349
McHenry, James: Hamilton on, 397-98
Mackenzie, Alexander, 219
Maclay, William, 73
Macomb, Alexander, 232, 312-13
McRea, James M., 85-86
Madison, James, 72, 73, 376, 377, 496; Hamilton on, 397; *letter from* Thomas Jefferson, 451
Mann, Oliver, 512
Mansfield, Earl of, 342
Marcus Aurelius, 103
Marcy, N.Y., 200
Margot River, 360
Marshall, Hetty Morris (Mrs. James), 309
Marshall, James, 309
Marshall, John, 357, 451
Marshy (Marsh) Lake, 238-39
Martens, G. F. von: *Law of Nations*, 505
Martinique, 443
Maryland, 18, 201, 439; U.S. attorney for the District of, *see* Potts, Richard; U.S. marshal for the District of, *see* Ramsay, Nathaniel; U.S. Representatives from, *see* Carroll, Charles, *and* Forrest, Uriah, *and* Potts, Richard, *and* Smith, William
Mason, Stephens T., 450, 451
Massachusetts, 9, 430; boundary of, 241, 243-44; debt of, 2, 13, 15, 17-19, 20, 26-27, 31, 36; Shays's Rebellion in, 18, 36; U.S. attorney for the District of, *see* Gore, Christopher; U.S. judge for the District of, *see* Lowell, John; U.S. marshal for the District of, *see* Brooks, John; U.S. Representatives from, *see* Cobb, David, *and* Dexter, Samuel, *and* Parker, Isaac, *and* Wadsworth,

Peleg; U.S. Senator from, *see* Cabot, George
Massachusetts Bay Colony, 240-41
Maumee River, 165
Medusa, 206, 296
Mercer, Hugh, 440
Mézières, Chevalier de, 280-81, 290, 291
Michilimackinac (Mackinac) Island, 166, 168, 207, 223
Mifflin, Thomas, 515
Miller, Joseph I., 88
Minerva, see [New York] *American Minerva; an Evening Advertiser*
Minneapolis, Minn., 166, 239
Minnesota River, 239
Mint: director of, 298-99, 466
Miranda, Francisco de, 296
Mississippi River, 14, 166, 229; commerce on, 174, and Jay Treaty, 177, 181-82, 185-86, 190, 212-13, 217-18, 222, 224-25; and France, 75, 222-23, 375, 522; and Great Britain, 181-82, 212, 217-18, 222-23, 224-25; navigation of, 116, 212, 213, 224, 225, 375, 377, 469; and Spain, 75, 222, 224, 225, 375, 469, 522; survey of, and Jay Treaty, 223, 237, 238-40; and Treaty of Paris (1763), 212, 222-23; and Treaty of 1783, 75, 237
Mitchel, John: map of, 238
Mitchell, —— (Mr.), 156-57
Mobile, 173, 223
Mohawk River, 200, 202
Molasses, 442, 443
Monroe, James, 145, 361; *letter to* Thomas Jefferson, 156-58; *letter to* Edmund Randolph, 523
Montesquieu, Charles Louis de Secondat, baron de La Brède et de: *De l'esprit des loix*, 302
Montmorin Saint-Herem, Armand Marc, comte de, 523
Montreal, 178, 180, 187, 193
Montserrat, 171
Moore, Andrew, 72
Moore, Thomas William, 206
Moreton, J., 472, 495, 516
Morocco, 362; treaty with, 461-62
Morris, Gouverneur, 298; *letters from* Thomas Jefferson, 475-76, 525
Morris, Robert (N.J.), 201, 202; *letter to*, 216-17
Morris, Robert (Pa.), 13, 18, 310, 311; debt to John B. Church, 309, 430,

Morris, Robert (Pa.) (*Continued*) 498-500; debt to Hamilton, 309; *letters from*, 309, 430, 498-500; *letters to*, 305, 485; *letter to* James Swan, 430

Morris, Robert, Jr., 430, 499

Morton, Jacob, 312-13

Most favored nation clause: and France, 521

Motier, *see* Lafayette, George Washington Motier

Mount Vernon, 468

Muhlenberg, Frederick A. C., 378, 379, 380

Murray, William, 342

Myers, Michael, 146

Naval stores: as contraband, 235, 304, 501-2, 503, 505-9, 511; in Jay Treaty, 501-2, 508-9, 511

Navigation: in Jay Treaty, external, 177, internal, 172, 175-86, 187-99, 210-11, 212, 213-15, 218-34

Negro slaves: carried off by Great Britain, 82, 83, 84, 98, 99-105, 131, 132, 155, 159, 160, 161, 162, 247, compensation for, sought, 92-94, 102-3, 105, 152, 164, 165, 236, 277; as property, 101-2; and Treaty of 1783, 128-29

Neutrality: advantages of, 463-64; rules of, 273

Neutrality, Proclamation of (1793), 341-42

Neutral rights, 319, 324, 473-84, 501, 504

Neutral ships, 449, 475, 479, 480, 481-83

Nevis, 171

New Albion, 184

Newburgh, N.Y., 178

"Newburgh Letters," 440

New England Mississippi Co., 311

Newfoundland: fisheries, 75, 375, 377, 522

New Hampshire: treasurer of, 38

New Hartford, N.Y., 200

New Haven, Conn., 439

New Jersey, 189, 247; U.S. judge for the District of, *see* Morris, Robert; U.S. Representative from, *see* Dayton, Jonathan

New Orleans, 173, 222, 223

Newport, R.I., 16, 206, 296

New Windsor, N.Y., 178

New York, Treaty of, 15

[New York] *American Minerva; an Evening Advertiser*, 399; *letter to* editor of, 113-14

The [New York] *Argus, or Greenleaf's New Daily Advertiser*, 98, 113-14; *letter to* editor of, 398-99

New York City, 192, 201; and foreign commerce, 178, 179, 187, 190, 211; yellow fever in, 279, 311-13, 471

The [New York] *Herald; A Gazette for the Country*, 399

New York State, 13, 277-78, 284; acts of, 81, 133-34, 159, 329, "Trespass Act," 77-81, 84, 127-33, 153, 160; debt of, 19, 20, 36; ports of, 178-79; public land of, 18, 19; and Treaty of 1783, breaches of, 77-81, 84, 127-33, 153, 159, 160; U.S. attorney for District of, *see* Harison, Richard; U.S. marshal for the District of, *see* Clarkson, Matthew; U.S. Senators from, *see* Burr, Aaron, *and* King, Rufus

Niagara, 145, 168, 207, 208

Nicholl, Sir John, 317, 343

Nicholson, John, 310

Nogaret, Dominique-Vincent Ramel, 347

Nootka Sound, 184, 264

Norfolk, Va., 179

North, William, 437, 440

North America: map of, 238

North American Land Co., 309

North Carolina, 13, 18, 35, 247

North Hero Island, 142

North West Co., 219, 221

Norton, Asahel S., 147

Nourse, Joseph, 45, 423-26, 427

Nova Scotia, 178, 184, 190, 229, 240-41

Ogden, Samuel: *letter from*, 298-99

Ogdensburg, N.Y., 298

Oglethorpe, James, 280-81, 290, 291

Ohio River, 117, 223, 461

Olive, Nicholas: *letter from*, 232; *letter to*, 232

Olney, Jeremiah, 440

Oneida County, N.Y., 200

Orleans, Duke of, 147, 148

Oswald, Richard, 527-28

Oswegatchie, 207

Oswego, 168, 207, 208

Page, John, 72

Page, Mann, 451
Paris, N.Y., 147
Paris, Treaty of (1763), 212, 222-23
Parker, Edward, 512
Parker, Elias, 512
Parker, Isaac, 512
Paterson, William, 356, 435-36
Patterson, George, 306
Patterson, William, 306
Paul, George, 342
Pearce, William: *letter from* George Washington, 468
Peggy, 206
Pendleton, Nathaniel, 311, 454; *letter from*, 397-98
Pennsylvania, 117, 201, 295, 515; U.S. attorney for the District of, *see* Rawle, William; U.S. Representatives from, *see* FitzSimons, Thomas, *and* Irvine, William; U.S. Senators from, *see* Gallatin, Albert *and* Maclay, William
Penobscot Bay, 9
Pensacola, 173
Peter II, 502
Phelps, Oliver, 18
Phelps-Gorham Purchase, 18
Philadelphia, 117, 165, 190, 206, 211
[Philadelphia] *Aurora. General Advertiser*, 295, 351-53, 378
Philadelphia Democratic Society, 295
[Philadelphia] *Gazette of the United States*, 486-87
"Philo Camillus": No. II, 98-105; No. III, 124-34; No. IV, 153-62
"Philo Cinna," 131, 159-61
Pickering, Timothy, 433-34; as acting Secretary of State, 113, 206, 299, 318, 327-28, 356-58, 496; asks Hamilton's advice, 435-41; *letters from*, 435-41, 486-87; *letter from* James Seagrove, 362-63; *letters from* Anthony Wayne, 360-61; *letters to*, 453-54, 516-18; *letter to* John Jay, 315-16; *letter to* Oliver Wolcott, Jr., 308; and Oliver Wolcott, Jr., opinion of, 308
Pinckney, Charles Cotesworth, 356-57, 435-36
Pinckney, Thomas, 107-8, 489, 503-4; envoy to Spain, 111-12, 359-60, 462; and Jay Treaty, 113-14, 496; *letter to* Edmund Randolph, 108
Platt, Jonas, 146-47
Point-au-Fer, 142, 168, 207

Poland, 124
Pomona, 145
Pope, Alexander: *Essay on Criticism*, 292
Popham, William, 201, 202
Portsmouth, Va., 179
Portugal, 384, 385, 502; U.S. Minister Resident at, *see* Humphreys, David
Potts, Richard, 357, 396-97
Poughkeepsie, N.Y., 178
President (U.S.): and boundary commissioners, 237; and debt commissioners, 251. *See also* Adams, John, *and* Washington, George
Prime, Nathaniel, 310-11
Prince William Henry, 270, 271
Privateers, 152, 524; and Jay Treaty, 257, 269-77, 482-83
Prize cases, 259-60, 262, 267, 343
Prize ships, 270-71, 272, 273, 274, 275, 276, 277; and Jay Treaty, 96
Property, 5, 32; alien right of ownership of, 64, 279-94, in Jay Treaty, 164-65, 169-70, 188, 229, 282-85, 292-94; as booty, 100; confiscated by states, 9-10, 15, 16, 69, 81, 153, 154; Negro slaves as, 101-2; private, and Jay Treaty, 318-24; in war, 10, 299-305, 319-24, 331-47, 365
Providence, R.I., 440
"Provision order," *see* Great Britain: orders in council (April 25, 1795)
Provisions: as contraband, 111-12, 149, 152, 204, 235, 264-65, 306-8, 448, 449, 488-95, 503, 507-10
Prussia, 55-56, 121, 123, 373; and Silesia loan, 336, 342, 343, 368; U.S. Treaty of 1785 with, 227, 272, 382, 383-84, 476
Public credit: and assumption, 30-35, 42; and funding system, 53-58, 60, 61, importance of, 47, 57, 58, 60, 229-300; and party spirit, 51; and payment of debts, 47, 58; and property, 32; and public opinion, 33; and war, 53-58
Public debt, 322-23; and assumption, 2-3, 8-46; and bankruptcy, 35; and commissioners of loans, 35; and Constitution of U.S., 5; and contracts, 2, 7, 70-73; deferred, 430, 498; domestic, 2, 7, 8, 24, 35, 71, 72, plan to fund, 46-70; foreign, 2, 7, 24, 70, plan to fund, 46-70; to France, 13; and funding system, 1-

Public debt (*Continued*)
73; and impost duties, 29; and loans, 8, 33-34, 35, 54, 55; as money, 66-70; and North Carolina, 35; plan for payment of, 8, 34-35, 466-67, importance of, 46-50, 58-59, methods for, 47, 50, 71-73; plan to fund, 2, 7, 8, 34-35, 46-70; and property, 2, 5; and public creditors, 4-5, 7, 30-35, 44, 60, 61, 70, 71-73; and public land, 467; and public opinion, 2-6, 31, 32, 43; and speculation, 33-34, 61-65; and state debts, 1, 2, 7, 8-46; and taxation, 31
Public land, 14, 15, 18, 467
"Publius," 358
Pufendorf, Samuel: *Of the Law of Nature and Nations*, 274, 287, 505

Quebec, 178, 180, 187, 219

Ramsay, Nathaniel, 439
Randolph, Edmund, 308, 343, 360, 379-80, 489, 527; Hamilton on, 296, 327; and Jay Treaty, 135, 149, 150-53; *letter from*, 149-53; *letters from* John Jay, 113-14, 150; *letter from* James Monroe, 523; *letter from* Thomas Pinckney, 108; *letter from* George Washington, 328; *letters to* George Hammond, 145, 206; *letter to* John Jay, 150-53; *letter to* Rufus King, 527; *letters to* George Washington, 296, 327-28; resignation of, 113, 205, 207, 294-96, 327-28, 350-52, 376, 432-35; *A Vindication of Mr. Randolph's Resignation*, 355-56, 433, 486-87, 513, 514-15, 518
Randolph, Thomas Mann, 451
Ranger, 297-98
Rawle, William, 86-87, 315-16
Rayneval, Joseph-Matthias Gerard de, 291
Real estate: taxes on, 25, 27
Red Lake, 239
Red Lake River, 239
Red River, 239
"Relations with France," 520-28
"Remarks," 379-80
"Report on a Plan for the Further Support of Public Credit" (January 16, 1795), 322
"Report on Manufactures" (December 5, 1791), 68, 70

"Report on Rules and Modes of Proceeding with Regard to the Collection, Keeping, and Disbursement of Public Moneys, and Accounting for the Same" (March 4, 1794), 402
"Report on the Establishment of a Mint" (January 28, 1791), 348
"Report Relative to a Provision for the Support of Public Credit" (January 9, 1790), 2, 8, 39, 54, 68, 70, 72
Revenue, 25, 26, 27-28, 466
Rhode Island, 2, 50-51, 206; in American Revolution, 15-17; and British debts, 247; debt of, 13, 15-17, 31
Rideau Lake, 193
Ringwood Co., 200, 203, 216-17
Rittenhouse, David: resignation of, 298
Robespierre, Maximilien François Marie Isidore de, 52, 523
Roman law, 331-36, 337
Rouvray, Gaston, vicomte de, 147-48
Rouvray, Laurent-François Le Noir, marquis de: *letter from*, 147-48
"Rule of the War of 1756," 307
Russia, 55-56, 121, 122, 385-86, 474, 503-4
Rutgers, Elizabeth, 80
Rutgers v *Waddington*, 78, 80-81, 132
Rutherforth, Thomas: *Institutes of Natural Law*, 113, 507
Rutledge, John, 377, 496; Hamilton on, 484-85; and Jay Treaty, 87, 90-91
Ryder, Sir Dudley, 342

Sag Harbor, N.Y., 178
St. Anthony, Falls of, 166, 237, 238, 239, 240
St. Christopher, 171
St. Clair, Arthur, 361
St. Croix River (eastern Maine and southwest New Brunswick), 166, 231; in Jay Treaty, 237-38, 240-44, 253
St. Croix River (in present states of Minnesota and Wisconsin), 239
St. Lawrence River, 187, 188, 190, 192, 193, 194, 211, 213
St. Lucia, 171, 442-43
St. Mary's River, 231
St. Vincent, 171
Saltonstall, Dudley, 9
Sands, Comfort, 374
Sands, Henry, 374, 484, 511

San Francisco, 184
Sanger, Jedediah, 147
San Lorenzo, Treaty of, 462
Santo Domingo, 148, 429, 443
Sardinia, 121
Savannah, Ga., 429, 472
Sayre, Stephen, 294, 296
Schuyler, Catharine Van Rensselaer, (Mrs. Philip), 204, 312
Schuyler, Philip, 216-17; *letters from,* 200-4, 311-13; *letter to,* 186
Schuyler, N.Y., 200
Scioto Co., 361
Scott, Sir William, 317, 343
Seagrove, James: *letter to* Timothy Pickering, 362-63
Secretary of State, 363, 379-80, 466; acting, see Pickering, Timothy; individuals considered for office of, 356-57, 395-98. *See also* Pickering, Timothy, *and* Randolph, Edmund
Secretary of Treasury, 363, 466. *See also* Hamilton, Alexander, *and* Wolcott, Oliver, Jr.
Secretary of War, 363, 465; individuals considered for office of, 357-58, 436, 437-41, 453-54. *See also* McHenry, James, *and* Pickering, Timothy
Sedgwick, Theodore, 496
Segur, R. V. de (Mrs.), 431
Seixas, Benjamin, 312-13
Senate: appointments by, 38, 297, 299, 361, 398; and boundary commissioners, 237; and British debt commissioners, 251; compensation of, 427; and Indian treaties, 362, 461; and Jay Treaty, 74, 111, 152, 205, 207, 236, 356, 442, 444, 450, 462, 527; and Negro slaves, 104-5; and John Rutledge, 496; "virtuous twenty" in, 389
Sequestration of debts: and Jay Treaty, 299-305, 318-24, 329-47, 365-74, 380-95; by states, 81-84, 133-34, 136-37, 153-58, 246-47, 367-74
Sergeant, John, 147
Seton, William, 348
Seven Years' War, 307
Sewell's Point, Va., 179
Shays's Rebellion, 18, 36, 440
Shelby, Evan, 9
Shippen, Thomas Lee, 295
Ships: arming of, 270, 274, 275-76, 277; seizure of, 111-12, 149, 204, 256-57, 260-69, 475-77; tonnage of, and Jay Treaty, 233, 442, 445, 447; of war and Jay Treaty, 482-83
Silesia, 336, 342, 343, 344, 368
Simcoe, John Graves, 165
Simpson, James, 362
Sitgreaves, Samuel, 496
Six Nations, 189
Smith, Francis Joseph, 88
Smith, Peter: *letter to,* 313
Smith, William (Md.), 73
Smith, William Loughton, 358; Hamilton on, 396-97
Smuggling, 212, 218, 226-27
Society for Establishing Useful Manufactures, 203
Soldiers: as contraband, 501
South Carolina, 18, 443; acts of, 153, 154, 159, 247; in American Revolution, 9-10, 13-14; and British debts, 81-82, 84, 153, 154, 247; debt of, 13-15, 26-27, 31; and Treaty of 1783, 81-82, 84, 153, 154, 159; U.S. judge for the District of, *see* Bee, Thomas; U.S. Representatives from, *see* Harper, Robert Goodloe, *and* Smith, William Loughton
South Carolina Yazoo Co., 14
Southwest Territory, 360
Spain: colonies of, 360-61, 520; and Florida, 469; and France, 298, 360; and fur trade, 224; and Great Britain, 55-56, 117, 121, 212, 264, 335, 342, 384-85; and Indians, 173, 222, 223; and Mississippi River, 75, 222, 224, 225, 375, 469, 522; and Nootka Sound, 184, 264; and U.S., commissioners to, 224, negotiations with, 112, 359-61, 462, relations with, 14, 224, 525, Treaty of 1783, 469, Treaty of San Lorenzo (1795), 462
Speculation: and public debt, 33-34, 61-65; in public funds by King of England, 389-92
Spoliations: of commerce, 111-12, 149, 256-57, 475-77, compensation sought for, 92-94; and Jay Treaty, commissioners to settle claims for, 165, 257-58, 260-69, 271, 279-81, 307-8, 314-17
Stamp taxes, 25, 26
State Department, 375, 486
States, 302; accounts with U.S., 8, 11, 19, 21, 22, 37-38, 43; and alien ownership of land, 284-85, 292, 293; and

States (*Continued*)
American Revolution, 2, expenses of, 8-22, 24, 27-28, 44, 47-48, 49, 50-51; and British debts, 81-84, 133-34, 136-37, 153-58, 246-47, 367-74; and confiscation of property, 9-10, 15, 16, 19, 69, 81, 153, 154; debts, 1, 7, assumption of, 5-70; and taxes, 22-23, 25, 26-28, 30, 36; and treaties, 79, 104, 130-34, 154, 157, 159, 244, 254, 281, 290-91; and Treaty of 1783, 136-37, 153, 154-60
Stedman, Philip, 145
Steuben, Frederick William Augustus Henry Ferdinand, baron von, 437
Stevens, Edward, 278-79
Stevens, John: *letter to*, 348-49
Stirling, Lady, *see* Alexander, Sarah Livingston (Mrs. William)
Stirling, Lord, *see* Alexander, William
Stith, William, 311
Stockholm, 296
Stonington, Conn., 206
Sugar, 442, 448
Superintendent of Finance, 13
Supreme Court of the U.S.: associate justice, *see* Wilson, James; and carriage tax case, 86-87, 149; Chief Justice, *see* Jay, John; and restoration of prizes, 274-75; and Yazoo land cases, 311
Swan, James, 498-50; *letter from* Robert Morris, 430
Sweden, 503-4; and Great Britain, 210, 211, 259, 502-3; U.S. Treaty of 1783 with, 227, 272, 381, 383, 501, 510

Talapoosas Indians, 173
Talbot v *Jansen*, 274
Taxes: under Constitution of U.S., 22, 28; direct, 25, 28; and national government, 22-23, 26-28, 29, 30, 31, 54; poll, 25; and public debt, 31; and states, 25, 26-28, 30, 36; and war, 24-25, 26, 28
Taylor, George, Jr., 308, 486
Taylor, John, of Caroline, 86-87
Tazewell, Henry, 450, 451
Ten Broeck, Peter B., 278
Tennessee, 311
Tennessee Co., 310
Tennessee River, 9-10, 14
Tennessee Yazoo Co., 14
Thebes, 331, 337
Thessaly, 331, 337

Tobacco, 448
Tobago, 171, 443
Tombigbee River, 14
Tonnage: and Jay Treaty, 233, 442, 445, 447
Tordesillas, Treaty of, 184
Tories: and Jay Treaty, 126
Traders; rights of, and Jay Treaty, 115, 188, 198-99, 211
Treasury Department, 378; and advance payments, 402-26; and compensation of George Washington, 402-26
Treaties, 274; under Articles of Confederation, 79, 244, 248; with Indians, 143; and state laws, 104, 130-34, 154, 157, 159, 244, 254, 290-91; as supreme law, 78-79, 83, 104, 133, 154, 157, 254, 281, 290-91
Treaty of 1783, 11, 189, 375-77, 429, 469-70; breaches of, 77-85, 89-94, 104, 127-33, 136-37, 141, 142, 153-62, 209, 247-49; and British debts, 370, 373; and creditors, 82, 245, 246, 249, 254-55; declaration of amity in, 109; and Mississippi River, 75, 166, 181, 223, 225, 237; and Negro slaves, 125-29; pardons under, 169; and property rights, 129, 159, 170-71, 283-84; ratification of, 84, 129, 131, 137, 159; and St. Croix River, 237, 240; and U.S. boundaries, 187, 193, 207, 208, 223, 243; and western posts, 115, 118-19, 135, 208, 210, 248
"Trespass Act," 127-33, 153, 160
Trevett, John, 16
Trevett v *Weeden*, 16
Tripoli: U.S. consul to, 361
Troup, Robert, 201, 216, 440
Trumbull, Jonathan, 378, 380
Tryphonius, 331
Tunis: U.S. consul to, 361
Turcoing, Battle of, 123
Tuttle, Timothy, 147

United Netherlands, 42, 121, 122, 123-24, 208, 335, 336, 502, 511; U.S. Treaty of 1782 with, 227, 272, 381, 383, 476, 501, 510
United States: accounts with states, 8, 11, 19, 21, 22, 37-38, 43; Army, 1, 363, 403, 405, 409-10, 412, 414, 464-65, contractors, 402-3, 407, 408; boundaries, 94, 117, 164, 166-67, 171, 187, 193, 207, 208, 223, 237-44, 253,

279-81; claims against, 429; economy, 295-96; frigates, 363, 465, 467; harbors, 467; objectives in Jay Treaty, 92; and privateers, arming of, 274, 275-76, 277; western territory, 117
United States attorney for the District: of Maryland, see Potts, Richard; of Massachusetts, see Gore, Christopher; of New York, see Harison, Richard; of Pennsylvania, see Rawle, William
United States judge for the District: of Georgia, see Pendleton, Nathaniel; of Massachusetts, see Lowell, John; of New Jersey, see Morris, Robert; of South Carolina, see Bee, Thomas
United States marshal for the District: of Connecticut, see Bradley, Philip B.; of Maryland, see Ramsay, Nathaniel; of Massachusetts, see Brooks, John; of New York, see Clarkson, Matthew
Upper Mississippi Co., 310
Utica, N.Y., 200
Utrecht, Treaty of, 172, 219-20, 238, 385, 386, 387

"Valerius," 278-79, 376, 378
Vancouver Island, 184
Vanderwater, ——— (Mrs.), 80
Van Rensselaer, Robert, 204
Van Rensselaer, Stephen, 204
Van Vechten, Abraham: letter to, 329
Vattel, Emeric de: Law of Nations, 106, 118, 265, 274, 287, 337-41, 343-44, 365, 393, 481, 482, 483, 489, 505
Vergennes, Charles Gravier, comte de, 280-81, 290, 291, 523, 528
Vermont, 167
Viar, Josef de: letter to Thomas Jefferson, 224
Villaret-Joyeuse, Louis-Thomas, comte, 123
Virginia, 18, 297; acts of, 153-58, 247; in American Revolution, 9-10; and British debts, 82-84, 153-58, 246-47; and carriage tax, 86; debt of, 1, 2, 16, 17, 35; governor of, 437, 439, 515; and Jay Treaty, 450-51, 488, 510; and navigation of Mississippi River, 375, 377; and Negro slaves, 82, 83, 155; and Treaty of 1783, 82-84, 104, 153-58; U.S. Representatives

from, see Giles, William B., and Madison, James, and Moore, Andrew, and Page, John, and White, Alexander; U.S. Senator from, see Monroe, James; and western posts, 155
Virginia Yazoo Co., 14

Waddington, Joshua, 80
Wadsworth, Jeremiah, 326, 458
Wadsworth, Peleg, 485
Wallis, ——— (Mr.), 156-57
War: expense of, 24; Hamilton on, 56-57; and property, 10, 229-305, 319-24, 331-47, 365; and public credit, 53, 54, 55, 56, 299-305; rightful acts of, 331-47; and taxes, 24-25, 26, 28
Ward, Samuel, 310-11
War Department, 17, 402-4
Warder, John, 496
War of 1812, 440
Washington, George, 42, 43, 105, 429; aides-de-camp, 361, 439; and British "provision order," 149-52; charity of, 431, 467-68; compensation of, 350-52, 353, 354, 364, 378-80, 400-426, 427, 467-68; on Democratic societies, 526; and French privateers, 524; Hamilton's advice requested by, 205, 356-63; and illegal seizure of British ships, 269, 270, 272, 273, 275, 276; and Indians, 14, 15, 189, 197-98, 362; and Jay Treaty, 90-91, 112, 113, 148-49, 150, 151, 152, 205, 355-56, 359, 449, 450-51, 527; and George W. M. Lafayette, 324-27, 450-51, 452-53, 455-57, 457-58, 459, 512-13, 518-19; letters from, 85-86, 204-7, 354-55, 355-63, 400, 431-32, 449-51, 455-57, 459-60, 460, 512-13; letter from George Cabot, 325-26; letter from Thomas Jefferson, 517; letter from Henry Knox, 325; letter from George W. M. Lafayette, 324-25; letters from Edmund Randolph, 296, 327-28; letters to, 232-36, 324-28, 350-52, 395-98, 452-53, 457-58, 514-15, 518-19; letter to George Cabot, 325; letter to Felix Frestel, 457; letter to George W. M. Lafayette, 456-57; letter to William Pearce, 468; letter to Edmund Randolph, 328; letter to Anthony Whiting, 468; message to Congress, 205, 400, 431, 459-60, 460-67, 496, 526; and Mint,

Washington, George (*Continued*) 298-99; nominations by, 38, 87, 297, 299, 398; and office of Secretary of State, 435-37; and office of Secretary of War, 436-41; proclamation of, 15, 341-42; and Edmund Randolph, 296, 355-56, 433-34, 513; secretary of, 421; and western posts, 90-91; and Whiskey Insurrection, 514-15

Watson, James, 310, 312-13

Watson and Greenleaf, 310

Watts, —— (Mrs. Robert), 312

Watts, John, 312-13

Wayne, Anthony, 165; *letters to* Timothy Pickering, 360-61

Webster, Noah, Jr., 113-14

Weeden, John, 16

Wells, Samuel, 147

Western posts: and British debts, 119, 137, 144, 155; detention of, by Great Britain, 81-82, 83, 84, 90-94, 115-24, 131, 132, 134-46, 153, 159, 161, 163-71, 207-10, 247, 249, 250, 277, compensation for, sought, 141-43, 144, 145, 163-64, 165, 207, 209, 210, 211, 277; enumeration of, sought, 164, 165-68, 207; evacuation of, 92, 94, 155, 172, 208, 210, 465; and extension of trade, 116; and Indians, 116, 135, 136, 138, 143; and Jay Treaty, 90-91, 92-94, 115-24, 134-46, 163-71, 207-10; and Treaty of 1783, 115, 118-19, 135, 138, 208, 210, 248; and U.S. boundary line, 164-67

Western Reserve, 18

Whelen, Israel, 88

Whiskey Insurrection, 2, 24, 117, 244, 464, 497, 514-15, 527-28

White, Alexander, 72

White Bear Lake, 239

Whiting, Anthony: *letter from* George Washington, 468

Wickham, John, 87

Wilkins, Martin S., 318

William V, 42

Williams, Elie: *letter from*, 244

Wilson, James, 311

Winder, William, 440, 454

Witbeck, Thomas L., 204

Wolcott, Elizabeth (Mrs. Oliver, Jr.), 297

Wolcott, Oliver, Jr., 21, 244, 328, 438; and Jay Treaty, 148, 294, 306-8, 469-70; *letters from*, 86, 148-49, 294-96, 306-9, 364, 378-80, 428, 432-35, 469-70; *letter from* Timothy Pickering, 308; *letters to*, 97, 111-13, 278-79, 296-98, 314-15, 327, 352-53, 353, 354, 364, 375-78, 427; *letter to* Benjamin Franklin Bache, 351-52; and office of Secretary of State, 436; on Timothy Pickering, 308; and Edmund Randolph, 294-95, 432-35; on U.S. economic situation, 295; and George Washington's salary, 350, 351, 353, 354, 364, 378-80, 400, 406, 422, 423

Wood, James, 439

Yazoo land: cases, 311; companies, 454

York, Duke of, 123

"Z," 14